SEC
ACCOUNTING

SEC ACCOUNTING

JOHN W. BUCKLEY
University of California, Los Angeles

MARLENE H. BUCKLEY
Loyola Marymount University

TOM M. PLANK
Consultant, SEC Accounting Rules and Regulations

John Wiley & Sons
New York   Chichester   Brisbane   Toronto

193302

Library of Congress Cataloging in Publication Data:

Buckley, John W
  SEC accounting.

  Bibliography: p.
  Includes index.
  1. Financial statements—United States. 2. Corpo-
rations—United States—Accounting. 3. Disclosure of
information (Securities law)—United States. 4. United
States. Securities and Exchange Commission. I. Buck-
ley, Marlene H., 1938–   joint author. II. Plank,
Tom M., 1919–   joint author. III. Title.
KF 1446.B8   346′.73′0664   79-23146
ISBN 0-471-01861-9

Printed in the United States of America

10 9 8 7 6 5 4 3 2 1

Preface

This book on SEC accounting is directed at two audiences: (1) students who study accounting in colleges and universities in preparation for careers in public accounting or corporate financial accounting; and (2) managers and accountants in practice who wish to improve their knowledge of SEC regulations, releases, and administrative procedures.

Accounting curricula generally are deficient in giving students an SEC orientation, even though knowledge of SEC regulations and procedures is an important element of practice for the certified public accountant in auditing SEC registrants or for the executive who directs the financial affairs of a publicly held company.

Under the Securities Exchange Act of 1934 Congress established the Securities and Exchange Commission and gave it the authorization to establish principles of accounting to be used in preparing the financial reports of publicly held companies.

These principles are enunciated through Regulation S-X and its attendant Accounting Series Releases. These regulations constitute authoritative accounting pronouncements and therefore are part of the body of "generally accepted accounting principles," as that term is applied to the preparation and interpretation of financial statements.

Every student of accounting should be familiar with these SEC pronouncements, but especially those who expect to manage or audit publicly held companies. In addition to the pragmatic reasons for understanding the SEC pronouncements, many of the Accounting Series Releases examine important theoretical and empirical questions, such as, how to value assets or measure income.

Furthermore, SEC regulations and pronouncements make extensive contributions to the modern business vocabulary. Terms such as registration statements, Form 10-K, and Form 8-K, are used daily in business conversations. The literate student of business must be familiar with these terms, and with the workings of the SEC.

ORGANIZATION OF THE BOOK

The book is divided into two parts. Chapters 1 to 4 provide an introduction to the SEC and the securities laws and portray the environment in which the accountant practices. Chapter 1 describes the securities laws in their historical setting. Prior to enactment of the securities laws, small investors lacked the information and financial influence necessary to protect their interests. Chapter 1 shows why laws were needed in the context of documented abuses pervasive in the securities markets of the 1920s and 1930s. Of these laws the Securities Act of 1933 and the Securities Exchange Act of 1934 have had the greatest impact on accountants' responsibilities and, therefore, are discussed in detail in the chapters that follow.

Chapter 2 is a study of the Securities and Exchange Commission which was created to administer and enforce the securities acts. Its organization is uniquely adapted to the many functions that it performs.

Chapter 3 discusses the processes that are affected by the Securities Act of 1933, that is, the issuance of securities for public sale, and the circumstances under which an issue is exempt from registration. A discussion of legal liabilities imposed by the act is included.

Chapter 4 discusses the processes that are affected by the Securities Exchange Act of 1934: (1) filing for listed status on an exchange; (2) periodic reporting (the annual, quarterly and current reports); and (3) proxy solicitations. Exemptions granted under the 1934 Act and by administrative proclamation are discussed, as are the legal liabilities imposed by this act. The material in these chapters provides the background needed to understand the specific topics of regulation that are presented in the second part of the book, Chapters 5 to 8 and the Epilogue.

Fortified by an introduction to the securities laws and the SEC, in these later chapters we then take a closer look at the ways in which federal regulations have affected accounting and auditing standards. As the SEC has gained experience in administering the securities acts the Commission has encouraged a division of labor between itself and the accounting profession. It has assumed primary responsibility for establishing standards of disclosure in financial reporting and has, for the most part, delegated to the profession the responsibility for setting auditing and accounting standards. The major exception to this allocation of responsibility is auditors' independence. The SEC polices the independence of accountants when abusive practices come to its attention. Rightly so, because the requirement for independent audits arises directly from the securities laws themselves.

Over the years, too, the SEC has improved the organization of its disclosure requirements to promote greater uniformity among the multifarious reports prepared under its aegis. We hope, in our presentation, to show how this has been accomplished; how Forms S-1, 10-K, 10-Q, and the quarterly and annual reports to stockholders share similar disclosure standards.

Chapters 5 and 6 present SEC standards of disclosure for financial information with which the independent accountant is directly involved—their source: Regulation S-X. Chapter 5 focuses on the basic financial statements; Chapter 6 on detailed financial disclosure presented in the form of *footnotes* to the financial statements and *schedules* filed with the SEC. Chapter 7 examines the disclosure of financial data in which the accountant is indirectly involved. It underscores our contention that SEC standards of disclosure are uniform by showing how the information in one report can be *incorporated by reference* into another. Alternatively, it is possible to *integrate* two complete reports into one multipurpose report, a practice that is encouraged by the SEC. Chapter 7 surveys the general purpose forms, S-1, 10-K, and 10-Q, and the related reports to stockholders.

Chapter 8 reviews the implications and additional responsibilities of auditing an SEC registrant. Our Epilogue began its life as a chapter, but chapters imply a certain degree of finality. Our topic does not lend itself to the constraints of a "chapter." Instead, the purpose of our Epilogue is to collect many current developments and to organize them in such a way as to suggest to the reader the possible events to come.

A separate Instructor's Manual is available to adopters from the publisher.

John W. Buckley
Marlene H. Buckley
Tom M. Plank

Acknowledgments

Many individuals contributed to the preparation of this book. John T. Crain, Editor with John Wiley & Sons, now deceased, motivated the project and tried to keep us on schedule, which is a difficult and thankless task. Professor Jeremy Wiesen at New York University and Gerald Finnell SEC Partner of Peat, Marwick, Mitchell & Co. (Los Angeles) reviewed two drafts of the manuscript and offered many helpful suggestions and corrections of fact. Professor Donald Kieso at Northern Illinois University reviewed the first draft of the book and encouraged us to continue our project. Larry Rowland critiqued our final draft. His efforts have greatly improved the readability of the text. We thank them for their efforts while exonerating them from any responsibility for the final product.

Bryan Plank contributed valuable editorial suggestions and typed preliminary drafts of the manuscript. We have benefited from the publications supplied to us over the years by Donald Owens of Ernst & Whinney, whose company's SEC accounting materials have helped us to keep up to date with the rapidly moving developments that characterize the accounting topics covered in this book. Rita Korney of Bowne of Los Angeles, Inc., furnished valuable technical materials pertinent to the preparation of corporate documents for SEC filings. Gloria Moore typed the finished copy for the publisher and made helpful editorial corrections of the illegible insertions and difficult copy with which she was inundated. We recognize the exceptional contribution of Sandra Brodie who coped with the various versions of each draft, making useful observations with respect to the book's pedagogical soundness. She also assisted with the essential tasks necessary to prepare the final manuscript for publication.

Without the help of all of these individuals, and others, this book would not have been written. We gratefully acknowledge those many contributions.

J. W. B.
M. H. B.
T. M. P.

Contents

List of Exhibits   xvii

1 The Securities Laws and Why They Came About   1
THE SECURITIES ACTS—AN OVERVIEW   3
SECURITIES ACT OF 1933   6
   Provisions of the Securities Act of 1933   8
   Accountant's Responsibility   8
GLASS-STEAGALL ACT (THE BANKING ACT OF 1933)   8
   Provisions of the Glass-Steagall Act of 1933   9
SECURITIES EXCHANGE ACT OF 1934 (THE EXCHANGE ACT)   10
   Provisions of the Securities Exchange Act of 1934 (as amended)   11
   Accountant's Responsibility   14
PUBLIC UTILITY HOLDING COMPANY ACT OF 1935 (THE HOLDING
   COMPANY ACT)   14
   Provisions of the Public Utility Holding Company Act of 1935   15
   Accountant's Responsibility   17
TRUST INDENTURE ACT OF 1939   18
   Provisions of the Trust Indenture Act of 1939   19
   Accountant's Responsibility   19
INVESTMENT COMPANY ACT OF 1940   19
   Accountant's Responsibility   20
INVESTMENT ADVISERS ACT OF 1940   20
   Accountant's Responsibility   21
SECURITIES INVESTOR PROTECTION ACT OF 1970   21
STATE BLUE SKY LAWS   22
SUMMARY   23
FOOTNOTES FOR CHAPTER 1   24
GLOSSARY   24
QUESTIONS   26

2 Organization and Operations of the SEC 27

WHAT IS THE SEC? 27
ORGANIZATION OF THE AGENCY 31
  The Commission, the Executive Director, and the Secretary 32
  Operating Divisions 32
  Staff Service Offices 38
  Regional Offices 40
  Administrative Offices 42
POWERS TO ENFORCE THE LAWS 44
SERVICES PROVIDED TO THE PUBLIC 44
SUMMARY 44
FOOTNOTES 45
GLOSSARY 46
QUESTIONS 46

  Appendix **A** Authoritative Literature and References (How to
  Find What You Want) 48

3 Issuing Securities Under the Securities Act 57

THE PROCESS OF OFFERING SECURITIES 57
  A Closer Look at the Registration Process 62
LIABILITY UNDER THE SECURITIES ACT 66
  Privity 66
  Civil Liability 68
  Criminal Liability 70
  Section 17(a) 70
EXEMPTIONS 71
  Exempted Securities 72
  Exempted Transactions 72
  "No Sale" Rule 73
  Miscellaneous Exemptions 73
  Exemptions by Regulation 73
REGULATION A 73
  Special Rules 74
SUMMARY 75
FOOTNOTES 76
GLOSSARY 78
QUESTIONS 79

  Appendix **B** Legal Liability Under Common Law and the Securities
  Act of 1933 80

4 Trading Securities Under the Securities Exchange Act of 1934 83

OBTAINING LISTED STATUS (SECTION 12) 83
  The Process of Obtaining Listed Status 83
  Over-the-Counter Securities 87
FILING PERIODIC REPORTS (SECTION 13) 87
  Annual Reports 88
  Quarterly Report 88

Current Report—Form 8-K 88
Amendments 89
Requests for Extension of Time 89
ANNUAL REPORT TO STOCKHOLDERS—PROXIES (SECTION 14) 90
The Process of Soliciting Proxies 90
Filing the Proxy Material 90
The Proxy Material 91
Relationship with the Independent Public Accountant 94
The Information Statement 95
LIABILITY UNDER THE SECURITIES EXCHANGE ACT 96
Civil Liability (Rule 10(b)-5) 97
Criminal Liability 102
EXEMPTIONS 104
SUMMARY 104
FOOTNOTES 105
GLOSSARY 107
QUESTIONS 108

Appendix **C**   Legal Liability Under The Securities Exchange Act of
1934 and Administrative Sanctions Under Rule 2(e) 109

5   Regulation S-X and the Basic Financial Statements 111
CONCEPTS UNDERLYING THE FINANCIAL STATEMENTS 113
Financial Statements—the Representations of Management 113
Substantial Authoritative Support 113
Fair Disclosure 114
FINANCIAL STATEMENTS IN GENERAL 115
Materiality 116
Succinctness 117
Completeness 118
BALANCE SHEETS 119
CURRENT ASSETS 119
CURRENT LIABILITIES 125
INCOME STATEMENT 130
CONTENT OF STATEMENTS OF OTHER STOCKHOLDERS EQUITY (ARTICLE 11) 133
STATEMENT OF SOURCE AND APPLICATION OF FUNDS (ARTICLE 11A) 134
CONSOLIDATED AND COMBINED FINANCIAL STATEMENTS (ARTICLE 4) 135
SUMMARY 136
FOOTNOTES 136
GLOSSARY 137
QUESTIONS 137

6   Regulation S-X Footnotes and Schedules 139
FOOTNOTES 139
Summary of Accounting Principles and Practices 141
Disclosure of Unusual Risks and Uncertainties in Financial Reporting
Accounting Series Release No. 166 158
Oil and Gas Reserves 160
Segments of a Business Enterprise, International Operations 160

SCHEDULES 161
SUMMARY 161
FOOTNOTES 163
QUESTIONS 164
GLOSSARY 164

Appendix **D** Regulation S-X Schedules 167

7 Reporting to Shareholders and the SEC 185
INCORPORATION AND INTEGRATION 186
  Incorporation 186
  Integration 187
SUMMARY OF OPERATIONS AND MANAGEMENT'S DISCUSSION
    AND ANALYSIS 187
DESCRIPTION OF BUSINESS—INDUSTRY SEGMENTS 191
  Developments Leading to Regulation S-K 191
  Regulation S-K 193
THE ANNUAL REPORT TO STOCKHOLDERS 195
FORM 10-K 198
  Financial Statements 200
FORM 10-Q AND THE QUARTERLY REPORT TO STOCKHOLDERS 201
  10-Q Additional Disclosures 203
THE REGISTRATION STATEMENT FORM S-1 205
  Financial Statements 207
SUMMARY 210
FOOTNOTES 212
QUESTIONS 213

8 The Auditor's Professional Standards 215
RULES OF PRACTICE—ADMINISTRATIVE ACTIONS 215
PROFESSIONAL STANDARDS 217
INDEPENDENCE—AICPA 217
INDEPENDENCE—SEC 219
  Timing of the Independent State 221
  Relationships of Interested Parties 221
  Financial Dependence 222
  Operational Dependence 223
  Audit Committee 223
  Litigation and Unpaid Professional Fees 225
AUDITOR'S REPRESENTATION—THE OPINION 225
  Scope Limitation 227
  First-Time Audits 228
  Material Uncertainties 228
  Going Concern Problems 228
  Consistency 229
  Other Opinions 230
  Examination of Financial Statements by More Than One Accountant 233

AUDITOR'S REPRESENTATIONS—LETTERS 233
  Assurances 233
  SEC Correspondence 237
  Form-Related Letters 237
SUMMARY 240
QUESTIONS 241
FOOTNOTES 241

Appendix **E** Disciplinary Actions Taken Against Accountants 242

Epilogue 253

INVESTIGATIONS 253
FEDERAL LAWS 254
COMMISSION ON AUDITORS' RESPONSIBILITIES 256
THE METCALF COMMITTEE 257
THE SEC PRACTICE DIVISION 258
SEC ADVISORY COMMITTEE ON CORPORATE DISCLOSURE 260
WHAT PORTENDS FOR THE FUTURE? 262
FOOTNOTES 263
QUESTIONS 266

Appendix **F** Bibliography of Articles, Books, Publications, and Case References by Accounting Topic 267

Index 477

List of Exhibits

Number	Title	Page
1-1	Economic Indicators—Dow-Jones Averages and GNP, 1925–1935	2
1-2	Economic Indicators—Unemployment, Bank Suspensions, Non Farm Foreclosures, 1925–1935	3
1-3	Summary of the Securities Laws	4
1-4	The Insull Utility System	16
1-5	Corporate Security Issues (Volume in Dollars) 1920–1970	18
2-1	Appropriated Funds Versus Fees Collected	28
2-2	Number of SEC Employees	29
2-3	SEC Budget	29
2-4	Effective Registrations	30
2-5	Registered Stock Market Participants	31
2-6	Organization Chart—Securities and Exchange Commission	33
2-7	Operating Division Functions	34
2-8	Division of Corporation Finance Organization	36
2-9	Regional Office Organization	41
2-10	SEC Enforcement Powers	42
2-11	Facilities & Records	45
A-1	Summary of Authoritative Literature	50
3-1	Effective Securities Act Registrations	58
3-2	Functions of Team Members in a Public Offering	60
3-3	"Tombstone Ad"	61
3-4	Flowchart of Registration Process	62
3-5	Conditions Barring Acceleration	65
3-6	Sales Activities Regulated by the Securities Act	66
3-7	The Issuer's Undertakings	67

Number	Title	Page
3-8	Calculation of Damages	70
3-9	Offerings Under Regulation A	74
3-10	Regulation A Sales Activities	75
4-1	Volume of Securities Transactions	84
4-2	The Process of Obtaining Listed Status	86
4-3	Announcement of Stockholders' Meeting	91
4-4	The Proxy	92
4-5	The Proxy Statement	93
4-6	Comparison of Accountants' Civil Liability	103
5-1	Contents of Regulation	112
6-1	Rule 3-16 and 3-17 Footnote Disclosure	140
6-2	Decision Diagram—Exemptions Under Rule 3-16(t) of Regulation S-X	157
6-3	Schedules to Be Filed by Commercial & Industrial Registrants	162
7-1	Description of Business—Comparison of Forms S-1 and 10-K	192
7-2	Schedule of Amendments—Regulation or Form to Which Amended Disclosure Provisions Apply	194
7-3	The Organization of Documents Affecting the Annual Report to Stockholders	195
7-4	Regulation 14A Requirements for Financial Information—A Decision Diagram	196
7-5	Reference—Rule 14a-3 to the Annual Report	197
7-6	The Organization of Documents Affecting Forms 10-K and 10-Q	198
7-7	Form 10-K Table of Contents	199
7-8	Decision Diagram–Short Period Financial Statements	201
7-9	Form 10-Q Table of Contents	202
7-10	10-Q Financial Statement Condensation Criteria	203
7-11	Organization of Documents Affecting Form S-1	205
7-12	Comparison of Forms S-1 and 10	206
7-13	Form S-1 Balance Sheet(s)—Decision Diagram	209
7-14	Form S-1 Income Statements—Decision Diagram	210
7-15	Summary of Statements Requiring the Auditor's Opinion	211
8-1	Letter to Succeeded Firm	234
8-2	Comfort Letter to the Underwriters	235
8-3	Accountant's Consent	236
8-4	Response to Notification of Limited SEC Review	237

1 The Securities Laws and Why They Came About

More than 45 years have passed since Congress enacted the first federal legislation regulating *securities* transactions. The intention of the securities laws was to proscribe activities that were viewed as being detrimental to the public interest, to prescribe practices that allow investors to make informed decisions, and to create a means for enforcing the laws.

Securities legislation was conceived during the worst financial and social crisis in our history. It was part of a much broader program of social reform that promised to give a New Deal[1] to Mr. Everyman[2] at a time when the economy was prostrate. Twenty-five percent of the labor force was unemployed in 1933. Four thousand banks failed that year, and 252,400 nonfarm properties were foreclosed. The GNP in 1933 declined to 53 percent of its 1929 level. (Refer to Exhibits 1-1 and 1-2 for changes in the economic indicators during the period 1925 to 1935.)

To understand better the significance of the securities laws, we must ask the following questions. Were the securities laws a political strategem trading on the public's frustration, pandering to its feelings of impotence? (If so, the benefits of the government's intervention into the affairs of the financial community might be expected to have been short-lived.) Would we be exposed today to the same hazards faced by the investors of 1929 if the laws did not now exist? Or were conditions unique to that particular time in history?

Ferdinand Pecora was counsel to the Senate Committee on Banking and Currency during the period 1933 to 1934 while it investigated the causes of the Crash. Having personally elicited much of the damaging evidence from the "Street's mightiest and best-informed men," he cautioned, in 1939:

The public, however, is sometimes forgetful. As its memory of the unhappy market collapse of 1929 becomes blurred, it may lend at least one ear to the persuasive voices of the Street, subtly pleading for a return to the "good old times." Forgotten, perhaps, by some are the shattering revelations of the Sen-

ate committee's investigation; forgotten the practices and ethics that the Street followed and defended when its own sway was undisputed in those good old days . . . we may now need to be reminded what Wall Street was like before Uncle Sam stationed a policeman at its corner, lest, in time to come, some attempt be made to abolish that post. . . .[3]

Yes, memories do fade. In the day-to-day business of being in business, perspective often is lost.

The laws that regulate the securities industry today respond to the conditions, to the events that preceded and precipitated the Great Depression. The practices in the stock market, by and large, were not the machinations of fly-by-night promoters. The laws were designed to counteract the typical practices that respected members of the financial community employed. Fraud and corruption did not cause the collapse; rather, legitimate practices were instrumental in bringing it about.

Exhibit 1-1 Economic Indicators—Dow-Jones Averages and GNP, 1925–1935

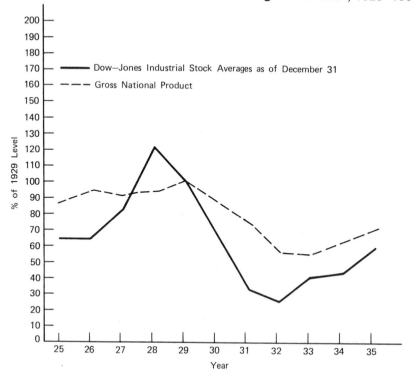

SOURCES. U.S. Department of Commerce, *Historical Statistics of the United States, Colonial Times to 1956*, pp. 73, 398, 636. *The Dow-Jones Averages, 1865–1970*, (New York: Dow-Jones Books, Inc., 1972).

Exhibit 1-2 Economic Indicators—Unemployment, Bank Suspensions, Nonfarm Foreclosures, 1925–1935

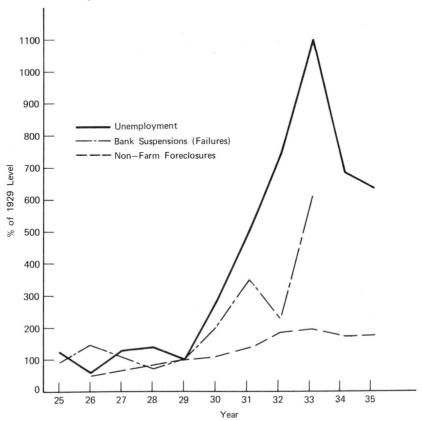

SOURCES. U.S. Department of Commerce, *Historical Statistics of the United States, Colonial Times to 1956*, pp. 73, 398, 636. *The Dow-Jones Averages, 1885–1970*, (New York: Dow-Jones Books, Inc., 1972).

THE SECURITIES ACTS—AN OVERVIEW

Starting from a point of virtually no federal authority over securities transactions, Congress enacted a number of laws. Each law arose from an investigation of specific abuses in the financial community. Some laws, such as the Securities Act of 1933 and the Securities Exchange Act of 1934, were the result of congressional investigations; others, such as the Public Utility Holding Company Act and the Trust Indenture Act, were the result of studies performed by enforcement agencies at the direction of Congress. Congress addressed the major categories of abuse by means of this building block approach so that today a comprehensive system of federal regulations governs the practices of the financial community.

Exhibit 1-3 Summary of the Securities Laws

Title	Year Enacted	Abuses	Major Provisions
Securities Act	1933	• Inadequate financial disclosure for newly issued securities. • Exhorbitant organization costs and underwriting fees. • Fraudulent practices in issuing securities.	• Requires disclosure of financial data for issues not exempted from registration. • Prohibits certain fraudulent acts and misrepresentations and omission of material facts.
Glass–Steagall Act	1933	• Banks simultaneously engaged in investment, underwriting and commercial banking activities.	• Prohibits banks from engaging in both investment and commercial banking activities.
Securities Exchange Act	1934	• Inadequate financial disclosure for publicly traded securities. • Price manipulation of securities. • Use of highly speculative margins.	• Requires disclosure of financial data for all securities listed on a national exchange—both initially and on a continuing basis. • Prohibits price manipulation practices and regulates activities of certain securities market participants. • Empowers the Federal Reserve Board to set margin requirements. • Creates the Securities and Exchange Commission.
Amendments: Maloney Act	1938	• Abusive practices similar to those observed with listed securities continued in the over-the-counter market.	• Gives over-the-counter broker/dealers the ability to regulate themselves.
	1964	• Inadequate financial disclosure for widely traded securities.	• Places over-the-counter securities dealers under the requirements of the securities acts.
	1968	• Fraudulent practices in the growing merger movement.	• Requires registration of most over-the-counter traded securities. • Regulates disclosure of tender offers.

Act	Year		
Public Utility Holding Company Act	1935	• Use of the holding company device to leverage control of operating utility companies.	• Regulation of public utility holding companies. • Restructure of companies into economically viable units. • Redistribution of voting power to common stockholders.
Trust Indenture Act	1939	• Incompetence, lack of independence, and fraudulent practices by bond trustees.	• Requires a trust agreement for each bond issue with certain provisions for safeguarding the financial interest of investors to be filed with the SEC. • Sets minimum qualifications for the trustee, including independence.
Investment Company Act	1940	• Excessive power over the securities markets, brokers, and underwriters by large investment companies.	• Disclosure through registration of mutual funds. • Sets minimum qualifications of management including competence, and independence. • Provides for shareholder participation in management decisions.
Investment Advisers Act	1940	• Conflict of interest of parties advising investors in financial matters.	• Registration of individuals who provide securities advice for compensation, including disclosure of control relationships.
Securities Investor Protection Act	1970	• Mismanagement, financial instability and misuse of customer assets held by brokerage houses.	• Creates the Securities Investors Protection Corporation to insure securities and cash held in a customer's account by a bankrupt broker to a $50,000 maximum.

The following laws are discussed in this chapter:

Securities Act of 1933 (Securities Act).
Banking Act of 1933 (Glass–Steagall Act).
Securities Exchange Act of 1934 (Exchange Act).
Public Utilities Holding Company Act of 1935.
Trust Indenture Act of 1939.
Investment Company Act of 1940.
Investment Advisers Act of 1940.
Securities Investor Protection Act of 1970.

Exhibit 1-3 summarizes these statutes.

SECURITIES ACT OF 1933

The objectives of the Securities Act are to: (1) require full disclosure of all material facts concerning securities offered for sale to the public, and (2) prohibit fraudulent acts and practices by those issuers of securities.

President Franklin D. Roosevelt defined the purpose of the first securities law in his speech recommending legislation for the federal supervision of traffic in investment securities. He said:[1]

> . . . *the federal Government cannot and should not take any action which might be construed as approving or guaranteeing that newly-issued securities are sound in the sense that their value will be maintained or that the properties which they represent will earn profit.*
>
> *There is, however, an obligation upon us to insist that every issue of new securities to be sold in interstate commerce shall be accompanied by full publicity and information, and that no essentially important element attending the issue shall be concealed from the buying public.*
>
> *This proposal adds to the ancient rule of* caveat emptor, *the further doctrine "let the seller also beware." It puts the burden of telling the whole truth on the seller. It should give impetus to honest dealing in securities and thereby bring back public confidence.*
>
> *The purpose of the legislation I suggest is to protect the public with the least possible interference to honest business.*
>
> *This is but one step in our broad purpose of protecting investors and depositors. It should be followed by legislation relating to the better supervision of the purchase and sale of all property dealt in on exchanges, practices on the part of officers and directors of banks and corporations.*
>
> *What we seek is a return to a clearer understanding of the ancient truth that those who manage banks, corporations, and other agencies handling or using other people's money are trustees acting for others. . . .*

The legislation was long overdue. As the Honorable Huston Thompson reported to the Banking Committee of the House of Representatives:[5]

> . . . the United States is farther behind than any other civilized nation that I know of with respect to preserving the rights of the purchasers of securities. In 1908, England put through what was known as the Companies Act . . . Belgium has perhaps the best law . . . Germany has a very strict law. France has a law. All of the dominions of Great Britain have laws. And so I might go through the list and tell you that practically all civilized nations except ourselves have laws protecting the public by informing the investor. . . .

Accustomed as we are to enunciated accounting standards and stringent disclosure requirements, we can imagine only with difficulty the conditions that existed in the absence of federal laws. Private investigations exposed a few examples:

1. It was frequently the practice to disclose average earnings over a period of years without showing the year-to-year fluctuations that made up the average.
2. Voting rights of stockholders seldom were disclosed.
3. Balance sheets usually were obsolete at publication date.
4. Fifty-seven percent of the corporations listed on the exchanges failed to report gross income or gross sales.
5. Depreciation policies were not stated.
6. The nature of the corporation's business often was not described.
7. "Earned surplus" (retained earnings) and "capital surplus" (additional paid-in capital) usually were combined.
8. In the case of utility offerings, a balance sheet rarely was included in the *prospectus*.

It was not until 1929 that the *New York Stock Exchange* finally established more rigid requirements for new listings, such as the following:

1. Treating stock dividends as earned income was forbidden.
2. Disclosing indirect and direct holdings in subsidiaries was required.

And, the exchange informally encouraged listed companies to:

1. Stop the constant revision of depreciation charges.
2. Stop writing off unamortized bond discounts and expenses directly against capital surplus.

Against this background, we can understand why half of the $50 billion in new securities that were issued in the United States during the 1920s became worthless in the aftermath of Tuesday, October 24, 1929. On that Black Tuesday alone more than $9 billion in the paper value of stocks and bonds was wiped out. The ensuing congressional investigations disclosed that the existence of meaningless, inadequate, and misleading financial information produced investor behavior that lead, ultimately, to the collapse of the securities market.

Provisions of the Securities Act of 1933

The Securities Act is a "disclosure"[6] statute concerned primarily with the initial distribution of a security rather than with trading subsequent to its issue. Its scope covers all initial offerings and initial sales of securities, except when the issue is sold only through intrastate transactions or when other statutory exemptions apply. Exemptions from the *registration* requirements are discussed in Chapter 3.

The Securities Act sets the ground rules by which an *issuer* lawfully can distribute securities to the public. It requires that: (1) a *registration statement* be in effect before an issuer may sell, transport for sale, or deliver its securities after sale using the mail or interstate commerce; and (2) a prospectus be distributed to each and every purchaser of a new securities offering.

The registration statement, a formal public record of financial representations regarding the issuer, is filed with the Securities and Exchange Commission (SEC) office in Washington, D.C. The registration statement applies to all shares of an "offering."[7] The prospectus is the first half of the registration statement. It contains the information considered by the Securities and Exchange Commission to be necessary for the average investor to make an informed decision. The prospectus is also distributed as a separate document to members of the investing public. Information contained in Part II of the registration statement is intended for regulatory personnel and for technically sophisticated users, such as institutional investors. Although the registration statement and prospectus have not completely eliminated biased promotional advertising, they have reduced its frequency and have moderated its enthusiasm.

Accountant's Responsibility

The Securities Act requires a public accountant or certified public accountant to express an opinion regarding the financial statements that accompany the registration statement. The auditor also is expected to have reviewed the registration statement for inconsistencies between it and the financial statements, and to review any other disclosures that might affect the financial statements or his opinion. Although the Securities Act and SEC pronouncements refer to a "certification" of financial statements, in this book we use the term "auditor's opinion" or "opinion letter," as these terms are preferred by the accounting profession.

GLASS–STEAGALL ACT (THE BANKING ACT OF 1933)

Although lending and deposit operations are the primary business of thousands of commercial banks, the investment banking function is performed by a relatively few highly capitalized organizations. Few corporations possess the expertise required to market their own securities; therefore, most corporations issue securities through an *investment banker*. Investment bankers "underwrite" new issues of corporate securities; that is, they provide corporations with the service of developing a marketable product (the security) and selling it to the public. The investment banker's remuneration is commensurate with his expertise and with the risk of underwriting.

Prior to 1933, investment banking was the business of private bankers (e.g., J. P. Morgan and Company, Dillon Read and Company) or of corporations closely affiliated with commercial banks (e.g., National City Company controlled by National City Bank). Underwriting, by its nature, is an activity characterized by a great deal of financial risk. For this reason, among others, underwriting has been considered inappropriate for commercial banks whose duty it is to safeguard the assets of depositors. Commercial bank activities properly were limited to certain conservative financial practices. The National Banking Act, enacted in the early 1900s, prohibited commercial banks from engaging in underwriting activities but was ineffective in stopping the practice.

Private bankers did not fall within the provisions of the National Banking Act because they limited their dealings to a small, select clientele who presumably had access to the necessary financial information and enjoyed a relatively strong bargaining position. Private banks were closely held corporations, whereas commercial banks were publicly owned, primarily in the business of offering banking services to the public, and subject to the restrictions of the National Banking Act. Commercial banks organized separate affiliate corporations to circumvent the law.

For example, National City "Bank" created the National City "Company" in 1911 in order to enter the highly lucrative investment banking business. The company's $10 million capital came from the proceeds of a 40 percent "dividend" declared on the bank. Before the dividends were declared, however, the shareholders had "unanimously" agreed to: (1) invest the entire dividend in Company stock, and (2) relinquish to a group of trustees legal title to and voting power in their stock. The trustees were chosen from bank officers and directors—the chairman, the president, and one director of the bank's board were ex officio trustees of the company. Successors were chosen from bank officers and directors, a provision that assured future control. Officers of the bank were able to use the retained earnings of the bank to begin operations in a potentially high-risk business that otherwise would have been prohibited by law.

It is this conflict between conservative practices required of commercial bank management and the speculative nature of underwriting which led to the Glass–Steagall Act.

Provisions of the Glass–Steagall Act of 1933

Having determined, during the months of congressional hearings, that combining the activities of commercial banking and investment banking created a conflict of interest that severely threatened the overall health of the securities market, Congress enacted the Banking Act of 1933. On March 6, 1933, two days after Roosevelt's inauguration, every bank in the United States was closed for four days by presidential Executive Order. Those that reopened did so in conformance with the provisions of the Banking Act. To weaken the connection between commercial banking and speculation, institutions that previously had engaged in both commercial and investment banking activities were required to elect which one of the two activities they intended to pursue. By June 16, 1934, the banks had divested themselves, by means of dissolution and liquidation, of affiliates engaged in conflicting businesses.

The act also created the Federal Deposit Insurance Corporation (FDIC) (open to all commercial banks) to insure individual deposits (to a maximum of $40,000 under current law).

SECURITIES EXCHANGE ACT OF 1934 (THE EXCHANGE ACT)

Although the Securities Act of 1933 imposed new standards of disclosure on securities issuers, it did not go far enough. Investors required reliable information regarding all securities in which they wished to trade. It was the purpose of the 1934 Act to come to grips with the more complicated problems involved in regulating stock market activities and the public trading of securities.

The Exchange Act deals with three aspects of regulation:

1. Disclosure of significant financial data.
2. Regulation of securities market practices and operations.
3. Control of credit extended for the purchase and short sales of securities.

Since the need for disclosure has been discussed, let us go on to the practices of securities market participants.

It is a truism that, while public outcry occurs when the price of a stock drops, the actual damage occurs when the price appreciates unrealistically.[8] It was the purpose of most manipulative practices to increase the price of a stock. "Pooling" is an example. Simply stated, a pool is created when several operators obtain a sizeable stock interest in a corporation. By buying and selling among themselves at ever-increasing prices they attract investors' attention. When enough unwary fish have taken the bait and purchased the stock, inflating the price further, the participants sell out. The stock price usually drops like a lead sinker. A variant of this technique is a "bear raid" in which participants drive the price down by *short-selling,* purchase the underpriced stock, and obtain a controlling interest in a corporation at bargain rates.

The Senate investigating committee learned that the stocks of 107 corporations traded on the New York Stock Exchange in 1929 were the subjects of pool manipulation, including American Telephone and Telegraph, American Tobacco, B.F. Goodrich, Radio Corporation of America, and Safeway Stores. The committee determined that between January 1, 1929, and August 31, 1933, 175 members of the New York Stock Exchange participated in pools, syndicates, or joint accounts (that are different names for the same procedure.) Joseph P. Kennedy participated in the Libbey Owens Ford Glass Company pool in June,

1933, one year before he was appointed by President Roosevelt to chair the SEC! These practices and many others made fortunes for insiders at great cost to the American public.

Credit was freely available to the speculator. Not only did credit serve to destabilize a market where as little as $100 invested could purchase $1,000 in securities, it also misallocated the supply of investment capital in the economy. Investment capital was lured away from operating businesses because credit used for stock market speculation drew higher interest rates than industry could afford to pay. There was geographical disallocation also as money that was deposited throughout the United States drained from the smaller communities into New York.

These were but a few of the ills that the Securities Exchange Act was intended to cure.

Provisions of the Securities Exchange Act of 1934 (as amended)

The Exchange Act regulates disclosure, market practices, and credit.

DISCLOSURE. All corporations whose securities are listed on a national securities exchange or are traded nationally over-the-counter must disclose financial information meeting acceptable standards.

LISTING. A corporation applying to list its security on an exchange must also file a registration statement and a copy of the application for listing with the SEC.

LISTED STATUS. As long as a corporation remains listed on an exchange, it must file periodic reports to its stockholders.

UNLISTED STATUS. Certain securities may be traded on an exchange without being listed on it, but provisions for registration are so encompassing that almost all securities that have unlisted status are required to be registered for other reasons.

DELISTING. The corporation whose securities are listed may delist only under narrowly defined conditions that prevent harm to existing stockholders. The exchange or the SEC may suspend trading temporarily for investigative purposes or delist a security for punitive reasons. Restricting the ability to delist assures that investors will continue to receive financial information and that there will continue to be a market for the securities.

PROXY SOLICITATIONS. A *proxy,* the legal power to vote the stock of another person, must be solicited under standards of disclosure prescribed by the SEC.

TENDER OFFERS. The offer to purchase a stockholder's shares in an effort to gain control of a corporation must be disclosed to the SEC and others when a significant change in ownership occurs.

OVER-THE-COUNTER SECURITIES. When these securities are sold in the over-the-counter market they are subject to disclosure requirements similar to those for securities sold on the exchanges.

Regulation of securities market practices is achieved by requiring the registration of several categories of market participants, by control over their activities and the activities of corporation "insiders," and by specific prohibition of fraud. All securities exchanges, the *National Association of Securities Dealers, Inc. (NASD), brokers dealers,* and specialists must register and file periodic reports with the SEC. Because each category of participant enjoys special advantages over the public, the activities of each are governed by law and closely scrutinized by the SEC. Fraudulent dealings in securities, specified and unspecified, by all participants are prohibited.

The control of credit is delegated to the Federal Reserve Board[9] (through Regulations T and U), whose responsibility it is to set margin requirements for the purchase of securities on credit.

Finally, to administer the various securities laws, the Exchange Act provides for the creation of a government agency with quasi-judicial powers—the Securities and Exchange Commission.

Disclosure of Financial Information A security listed on a national exchange also must be registered with the SEC under the 1934 Act. Disclosure of financial information is achieved in a way similar to that of a Securities Act registration; filing with the SEC makes the reported financial data public information. It is important to note that the class of the corporation's security, not the corporation itself, is the subject of the listing. Once a class of security (Class A Common Stock, Class A Preferred, etc.) is registered, all subsequent issues of the same class also are considered to be registered. This means that if 1 million shares of Class A Preferred Stock are registered and listed by an exchange, the corporation subsequently can issue 250,000 additional shares of Class A Preferred that also can be traded on the exchange without a second registration; but it cannot issue Class B Preferred without filing a separate registration statement. (This contrasts with registration under the 1933 Act that requires a separate filing for each issue.)

Securities Markets The most far-reaching provisions of the 1934 Act regulate trading practice of the securities markets. However, since the accountant does not have significant direct responsibility in these matters, our discussion will be brief.

Each national securities exchange must be registered with the SEC. The SEC bases its approval, to a great extent, upon the ability of the exchange to exert adequate control over the actions of its members. Not only must the rules and regulations of an exchange provide a means for control, control must be "exercised" as well. Each exchange files with the SEC annual reports that are accompanied by a CPA's opinion.

The Maloney Act amendment passed by Congress in June, 1938 extended to *over-the-counter securities* broker/dealers the same power to organize, the same right of self-regulation, and the same obligation to register that apply to members of a national securities exchange. Only one such organization has been formed under the act, the National Association of Securities Dealers, Inc. (NASD), incorporated in 1939. Although membership is not required in the NASD, the inducement to join is strong because the Maloney Act requires members to deal with nonmembers on the same terms as with the public. This denies nonmember broker/dealers access to wholesale prices for securities.

Brokers and dealers are subject to SEC supervision. They must, with few exceptions, register, maintain specified records, observe prescribed debt restrictions, and file annual reports. The SEC conducts surprise examinations of brokerage houses. In addition, brokerage houses must be audited annually and the securities that they hold must be counted on a surprise basis by an independent accountant.

"Insiders" (defined to be officers, directors, and owners with an interest exceeding 10%) are subject to especially stringent rules. They are prohibited from selling "short," and must deliver any securities that they sell within 20 days of the sale (or mail them for delivery within 5 days of sale). Profits must be turned over to the corporation if they are realized on the sale and purchase (or purchase and sale) of any security within a period of less than 6 months between the date of purchase and of sale. An insider must disclose to the other party to a sale or purchase any information he has as a result of his inside relationship with the company. He must report to the SEC and to any exchange on which the security is traded: (1) any beneficial interest in any nonexempted equity security at the time the security is registered, and (2) any change in that interest within 10 days after the close of the calendar month of the change.

Market stabilization activities by underwriters are permitted only under rigidly controlled conditions. Where manipulative practices are used to support the price of a new issue (to "make a market"), the prospectus must disclose this fact and reports must be made to the SEC. In short, the activities, documented in congressional hearings, that created vast profits for the perpetrators to the detriment of the individual investor are punishable by fine, imprisonment, or both.

Credit   The Exchange Act directs the Board of Governors of the Federal Reserve System to administer the extension of margin credit in the securities market. The ability to control margin is both the means by which credit is made available to the securities market and a tool of Federal Reserve monetary policy.

Credit used in trading securities is collateralized by the securities themselves and can be obtained either by means of a bank loan or from the securities broker/dealer directly.

Two regulations have been imposed by the Federal Reserve Board: (1) Regulation T controls loans by broker/dealers, and (2) Regulation U governs bank loans whose purpose it is to permit the purchase or carrying (owning) of securities. It should be noted that these regulations pertain only to the amount of money lent on the original purchase price of the stock, called the *initial margin percentage*. Should the market value of the securities held as collateral subsequently decline below the minimum maintenance requirement of the stock exchange, the regulations do not require partial payoff of the debtor deposit with additional collateral. (The rules of the exchanges, however, do require a *margin call* when the market value of the collateral falls below the minimum maintenance requirement.) For example, supposing an investor purchased stock with a market value of $10,000, at the maximum initial margin percentage set by the Federal Reserve of 50 percent when the minimum maintenance requirement set by the Exchange was also 50 percent. The investor would pay $5000 and borrow $5000 leaving the securities with the broker as collateral. Should the market value of the stock drop to $4000 the minimum maintenance requirement of the exchange would force the investor to either pay down the loan to $8000 or to deposit an additional $1000 in collateral to cover the account.

Accountant's Responsibility

Unlike the Securities Act, the Exchange Act requires the auditor's involvement by an administrative ruling of the SEC, not by provision of the law itself. The independent accountant is included in the 1934 Act registration in much the same way as he is under the 1933 Act, and under both gives his opinion of the financial statements. The accountant reviews the complete application for listing and the registration statement filed with the SEC, and assumes various degrees of responsibility with respect to periodic reports. The principal objective of this review is to locate any new information and any inconsistencies between the financial statements and the remainder of the registration statement. Periodic reports filed under the 1934 Act are more important to most registrants than the registration. They represent a continuing obligation to prepare and publicize financial information for as long as the corporation is publicly traded. The corporation's management and counsel have primary responsibility for all filings. This position is consistent with that of the accounting profession—the financial statements are the responsibility of management.

The accountant's legal liability under the Exchange Act differs from that under the Securities Act, as will be shown in later chapters.

PUBLIC UTILITY HOLDING COMPANY ACT OF 1935 (THE HOLDING COMPANY ACT)

Of all industries the power utilities seemed to invite practices most detrimental to the small investor's interests. Utilities began as small local enterprises, but burgeoning technological changes in power generating and transmission facilities soon demanded expansion. Most often this was achieved by merging a number of small companies. An alternative method was to form mutual or cooperative service companies to provide economical services to member utilities. Danger to the public interest was not attributable to the need for large-scale regional utility operations, but rather to the means by which this was accomplished. It is to be expected that the means would be chosen that offered the greatest ancillary benefits and, as we shall see, such benefits could be sizeable.

In 1905 General Electric (GE), at that time primarily a manufacturer of electrical production and of transmission equipment, pioneered a new form of utility organization, the holding company. Electric Bond and Share, a holding company totally owned by GE, was chartered to help customers (small utility companies) finance equipment purchases. The financing was accomplished by trading equipment manufactured by GE for voting stock in the utility company. It was the function of Electric Bond and Share to hold the utility securities for General Electric. Because ownership in most utilities was widely held, ownership of a minority percentage of shares quite often yielded a controlling interest in the utility. Soon GE was providing financial, sales, engineering, and construction services for its subsidiaries. GE eventually controlled 13 percent of total U.S. generating capacity, $3 billion in assets, and received a proportionate share of revenues from its utility system, the largest in the United States.

It is easy to see how such a relationship could be used. For example, fixed management fees, exorbitant interest rates, and distribution of dividends to the holding company were some of the devices that were used to skim profits from the operating utilities to the holding company.

The holding company took on forms beyond comprehension in the hands of financiers less temperate than GE. Nine years after General Electric began to expand into operations by means of the holding company (1914) 85 "systems" of holding companies controlled 67 percent of private electrical output in the United States. Sixteen holding companies controlled 92 percent by 1929. Familiar names participated in the public utility holding company bonanza, including J. P. Morgan and Company's United Corporation, second-largest power producing system in the United States.

Without a doubt, however, the man who brought the holding company to its ultimate development was Samuel Insull. It was contended that the very complexity of the Insull empire created an uncontrollable situation which doomed it to collapse. Before it collapsed, however, it was providing over one-eighth of total U.S. power and serving over 4 and a half million customers. It was the third largest power and light system in the United States in 1930, only slightly smaller than either Electric Bond and Share or United Corporation.

The Insull family, with an initial investment of $8 to 9 million, originally purchased minority interests in five utility holding companies. The sole purpose of the holding companies was to control operating companies engaged in marketing gas and electricity (Refer to Exhibit 1-4). Because the securities of the holding companies were traded on the national exchanges and were widely held, a small investment was sufficient to control the operating affiliates that held combined assets of $2.4 billion.

The Insull's domain was vulnerable because a well-financed competitor could simply buy up sufficient shares on the open market and secure the power to vote down the family. Clearly, something had to be done. Samuel Insull and several prominent financiers formed another holding company in 1928, the Insull Utility Investments (Incorporated). Insull obtained a 19.2 percent interest in the company that was capitalized at $150 million by donating his stock in the five original holding companies. Part of the remaining 80.8 percent contributed by the public was used to purchase more shares of the five holding companies. Insull was a bit more secure in his control . . . temporarily.

Exhibit 1-4   The Insull Utility System

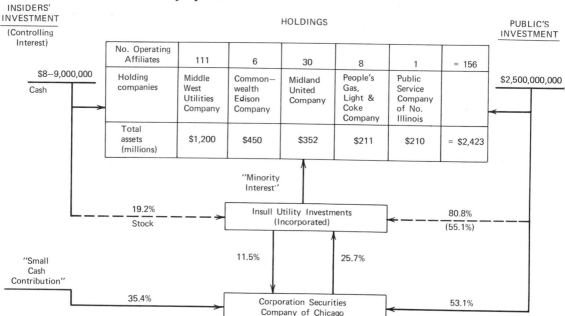

Soon Insull's 19.2 percent interest was vulnerable to a takeover, so he formed the Corporation Securities Company of Chicago. This time he obtained a 46.9 percent interest in a holding company with a market value of $150.7 million by investing a small amount of cash. His investment created an interlocking ownership which secured his interest, but which created an uncontrollable financial labyrinth. By January 31, 1932, the Insull pyramid consisted of 95 holding companies and 255 operating companies.

The economic climate of the early 1930s attacked the weaker elements of the system. Healthy companies were drained to save the weak. The impossibility of conceptualizing (much less controlling) financial relationships eventually brought the system to bankruptcy. The collapse of the Insull pyramid was the single most compelling argument for the Holding Company Act.

Provisions of the Public Utility Holding Company Act of 1935

Because of such conditions in the electric power and gas industry and the exposure of other similar abuses by a far-reaching Federal Trade Commission investigation, the Public Utility Holding Company Act was signed into law by President Roosevelt in 1935. Four of its provisions immediately placed a heavy burden on the newly formed Securities and Exchange Commission:

1. Public utility holding companies in the electric, light, power, and gas indus-

tries had to register with the SEC in order to do business after December 1, 1935. A company or individual was considered to be a holding company if it held 10 percent or more of the voting stock of a public utility or of a public utility holding company that fell within the law.

2. The SEC had the power to evaluate the financial structure of each holding company and to determine whether the structure served any useful economic purpose. If the SEC determined that it was possible to simplify the corporate structure, reorganization was mandated.

3. Companies were recombined under SEC direction into "integrated utility systems" capable of economic operation as a single coordinated system within a state, region, or group of contiguous states.

4. Voting power was redistributed to those to whom it belonged.

Finally, all companies were required to maintain the status quo in order to give the SEC time to implement the law. No new securities could be issued, no change of preferences, priorities or voting power could be made until adequate regulations were in force.

The provisions fell short of the President's desire to see holding companies eliminated, but they were fought bitterly by the interests that stood to lose the most. Despite the opposition, the SEC acquitted itself of its initial task and supervised extensive mergers, reorganizations, and exchanges of property and securities. Today most utility companies no longer fall within the scope of the Holding Companies Act.

For the remaining active registered companies, the following provisions of the act apply:

1. Except for short-term obligations, a declaration must be filed with the Commission in order to: (a) issue or sell securities; (b) exercise any privilege or right, or to alter voting or any other stockholder right; and (c) acquire securities, assets, or other business interests. The businesses in which utility companies can engage are limited.

2. Intercompany loans, dividends, security transactions, sales of assets, proxies, services, sales, and construction contracts are prohibited.

3. Holding companies are required by federal law to observe the state laws governing them.

Accountant's Responsibility

Financial statements that are part of the registration statement and the annual reports are accompanied by an independent auditor's opinion. The SEC has established the Uniform System of Accounts for Mutual Service Companies and Subsidiary Service Companies to apply to the few enterprises that are regulated under the provisions of this law.

TRUST INDENTURE ACT OF 1939

It was necessary, in the aftermath of the Crash, to reorganize and restructure great numbers of corporations; but the public's taste for speculation had been replaced by a cautious preference for steady income. Bonds, again, became the predominant means of financing business operations (Refer to Exhibit 1-5).

The terms of the contractual debt relationship in a bond issue are stated in the *trust indenture,* also called the "trust agreement," and a trustee usually is appointed by the debtor corporation under the terms of the indenture to administer and to protect the interest of bondholders. The indenture is "qualified" under the Securities Act of 1933, but that act imposes no restrictions on the trustee relationship. An early SEC investigation of "the work, activities, personnel, and functions of protective and reorganization committees" revealed abuses stemming from conflicts between trustees' loyalty to the debtor corporation and fiduciary duty to the bondholders.

The Trust Indenture Act of 1939 developed from this investigation based on the premise that " . . . the national public interest and the interest of investors in notes, bonds, debentures, evidence of indebtedness, and certificates of interest or a participation therein, which are offered to the public are adversely affected

Exhibit 1-5   **Corporate Security Issues (Volume in Dollars) 1920–1970**

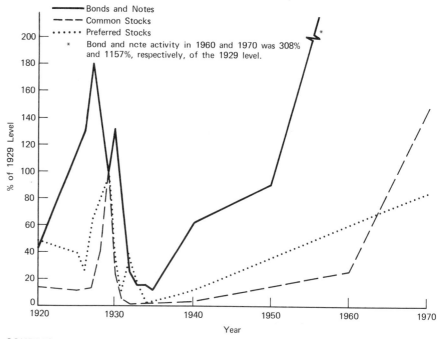

SOURCES.   1920–1955—U.S. Department of Commerce, *Historical Statistics of the United States, Colonial Times to 1956,* p. 658. 1960–1974—Board of Governors of the Federal Reserve System, various *Federal Reserve Bulletins.*

. . ." if the trustee lacks sufficient powers and responsibilities, or has mutual interests with the debtor or his underwriter that involve a material conflict with bondholders, whose rights and interests the trustee is primarily responsible to serve.

Provisions of the Trust Indenture Act of 1939

The Trust Indenture Act insures financial responsibility of the trustee and independence from the issuing corporation and its underwriters in public debt (bond) offerings. It provides that, in addition to complying with provisions of the Securities Act, the issuing corporation must:

1. Enter into a trust agreement with a qualifiable trustee and grant the trustee at least the minimum powers required by law.
2. Assume responsibility for the trustee to file with the SEC and to set forth his qualifications.
3. Prepare a trust indenture that contains all required provisions and an analysis of those provisions.
4. File a copy of the indenture with the SEC.

Except where the company's total offerings are less than a minimum size over a given period of time, all debt security issues must conform to this law.

Accountant's Responsibility

The CPA does not participate in the preparation of the registration statement or of the annual reports filed under the Trust Indenture Act. He should, however, be familiar with the terms of any trust indenture that affect his audit of a corporation whose ownership securities are registered under the Securities and Exchange Acts.

INVESTMENT COMPANY ACT OF 1940

Authorized by the Public Utility Holding Company Act, the SEC embarked on a four-year investigation into the practices of investment trusts during the 1920s. The SEC concluded in its report that special regulatory legislation was necessary to augment provisions of prior securities laws. Investment companies, controlling enormous amounts of capital, had significant influence over corporations, brokers, investment bankers, and over virtually every other aspect of business finance. Congress enacted the Investment Company Act of 1940, the most complex of all federal securities laws, in response to the SEC report. The body of the law sets forth requirements regulating activities of investment companies and leaves little discretionary power to the SEC, aside from the power to exempt companies in the case of hardship.

Investment companies are those primarily in the business of investing, reinvesting, and trading in securities. *Open-end* (mutual funds) and *closed-end investment companies* are the principal forms of organization currently supervised under this law. Holding companies that otherwise would fall under its provisions are exempted if they are engaged primarily in another business through subsidiaries. As with the Securities Act, registration of the investment company by the SEC does not imply a guarantee of management quality or investment safety.

Although registration under the act is not required, the operations of nonregistered, nonregulated investment companies are severely restricted. (They cannot use the mails, for example.) They also lose significant tax advantages. Regulation of the registered investment companies includes requirements designed to ensure: (1) independent management, (2) sound financial management, (3) shareholder participation in company policy, (4) disclosure of corporate finances, and (5) bookkeeping and accounting procedures conforming to detailed regulations.

Accountant's Responsibility

The opinion of an independent accountant must accompany the financial statements and schedules contained in the registration statement and in the periodic reports of regulated companies. If securities are held in the custody of a member of a national stock exchange or the company itself, periodic examinations of the securities by the independent accountant are required, some on a surprise basis.

INVESTMENT ADVISERS ACT OF 1940

The Investment Advisers Act regulates the activities of persons who are compensated for providing securities advice to the public. It requires registration via a "filing statement" with the SEC by all but specifically exempted advisers. Approximately 3,600 persons were registered under the act in 1976.

Very little information is required on the filing statements other than the following:

1. Name and address of registrant.
2. Form of business organization.
3. Identity of persons controlling the registrant.
4. Any record of convictions in the securities field (anyone so convicted is automatically disqualified).
5. Other businesses in which the applicant engages.
6. Methods of rendering services and compensation.

The act does not provide for the disclosure of education and/or experience qualifications. Perhaps the youngest, although not necessarily the least qualified, registered investment adviser was featured in the *Wall Street Journal*. He is the editor of the *Stock Market Trader*, Robert D. LaMater, age 16.[10]

The Investment Advisers Act also prohibits investment advisers from sharing the capital gains or appreciation on a client's funds. Contracts may not be assigned without the consent of the client. Investment advisers are required to disclose to clients the nature of their interest in transactions executed on the client's behalf, and they are enjoined from engaging in fraudulent activities. The SEC now requires that all registered investment advisers prepare periodic financial reports and maintain records.

Accountant's Responsibility

Registration under this act does not require the involvement of an accountant. However, clients' funds and securities that are held by an investment counselor must be examined annually by an independent accountant on a surprise basis.

SECURITIES INVESTOR PROTECTION ACT OF 1970

As we have seen in Exhibit 1-5, the dollar volume of securities transactions increased at a phenomenal rate after 1935. The inability of the stock market, particularly brokerage house management, to process and control the influx of business was a principal factor leading to the failure of so many brokerage houses in the late 1960s. Some filed bankruptcy; some merged with stronger, better managed houses. The SEC conducted an extensive investigation into operations of the securities market seeking long-term solutions for modernizing the trading mechanism. This investigation, concluded in 1974, resulted in an amendment to the Exchange Act and in recommendations for far-reaching modernization.

In the meantime, it was necessary to protect present investors. The Securities Investor Protection Act created the Securities Investor Protection Corporation (SPIC) to insure cash and securities held in the customer accounts of broker/dealers to a maximum of $100,000 per customer. Generally speaking, insiders (partners, directors, and officers) of the brokerage houses and brokers, dealers, or banks are not covered by the SPIC. Membership in the SPIC, with limited exceptions, includes all registered broker/dealers and exchange members. Although the SPIC is funded primarily by means of assessments on its members, it has access to up to $1 billion in additional emergency funding from the U.S. Treasury.

The assessment rate amounts to one-half of one percent of gross revenues from the securities business of each member, adjusted depending upon the total balance of the fund. If emergency funds are necessary to meet the purpose of the act, the SPIC must apply to the SEC for funds and submit a proposed plan for repayment. If the SEC determines that the needs and plan for repayment are proper, it issues notes to the Secretary of the Treasury in exchange for the required funds. In order to permit repayment of Treasury funding, the SEC has the power to impose a transaction fee of up to one-fiftieth of one percent on all purchases of equity securities over $5,000 that are handled by an exchange or over-the-counter.

STATE BLUE SKY LAWS

The state securities laws are known as "Blue Sky Laws," the derivation of the name being a matter of disagreement. The earliest documented use of the term occurred in a 1917 court decision in which the judge described certain speculative schemes as having " . . . no more basis than so many feet of blue sky."

Before federal laws regulating securities transactions were enacted, a great tide of public opinion had taken its effect on many state legislatures. Every state but Delaware had some form of regulation governing the sale and distribution of securities within its borders by 1933.

Kansas enacted the earliest state law in 1911 in response to numerous land, mining, and insurance company frauds. Typical of securities laws in general, its purpose was to protect the financially naive. Records of the legislative hearings preceding enactment of the law contain references to "innocent widows," "school teachers," and "helpless females." Unfortunately, parliamentary records do not disclose how many of all the investors who actually were defrauded by these schemes were women and how many were not. Approximately 1,500 applications to sell securities were filed in the first year following enactment of the Kansas Blue Sky Law. Seventy-five percent were rejected as being fraudulent and about 11 percent were rejected as being highly speculative.

Blue-sky laws can be classified into three types:

1. *Registration Laws.* Designed to prevent securities transactions that are detrimental to the public interest. Most state registration laws are patterned after the federal laws. Unlike the federal law, however, certain states impose minimum risk standards. In evaluating unseasoned companies for registration, authorities in some states are required to assess the speculative qualities of an offering and prohibit distribution where minimum standards do not exist. For example, the Kansas commissioner is empowered to grant a license to sell securities, if the firm(s) "provide(s) for fair transaction of business and in his judgment promise(s) a fair return on investment." Other states require that only highly speculative and unseasoned companies qualify their securities. Some states have "reasonable" standards with respect to underwriters' fees, sellers' discounts, commissions, promoters' profits, stock options, and the like.
2. *Licensing Laws.* Place the emphasis on the activities of dealers rather than on the securities sold. They require licensing of all securities dealers doing business in the state, but do not require that securities be qualified.
3. *Fraud Laws.* Provide for prosecution after an illegal act has been committed. Fraud laws are remedial, not preventive, in purpose. Only New York, New Jersey, Delaware, and Maryland have true fraud laws.

Enacting federal statutes did not make state laws obsolete. Federal law covers only securities that are sold by means of the mails or through interstate commerce. Securities that are subject to federal law also are subject to state regulation, but the states alone enjoy jurisdiction over securities sold by means of intra-state transactions.

SUMMARY The federal securities laws are designed to prevent documented abuses of the public interest by members of the securities market community:

The *Securities Act of 1933* was enacted to prevent inadequate financial disclosure for newly-issued securities, exorbitant organization costs and underwriting fees, and fraudulent practices in issuing securities. It requires the disclosure of financial data for issues not exempted from registration and prohibits certain fraudulent acts and misrepresentations and omission of material facts in the issue of securities.

The *Glass—Steagall Act of 1933* was enacted to prevent banks from simultaneously engaging in investment/underwriting and commercial banking activities.

The *Securities Exchange Act of 1934* was enacted to prevent inadequate financial disclosure for publicly traded securities, price manipulation of securities, and use of highly speculative margins. It requires disclosure of financial data for all securities listed on a national exchange, prohibits all price manipulation practices and regulates activities of certain securities market participants, empowers the Federal Reserve Board to set margin requirements, and creates the Securities and Exchange Commission. The Maloney Act in 1938 extended provisions of the act to securities traded in the over-the-counter market by giving the over-the-counter broker/dealers the ability to regulate themselves and by placing them under the requirements of the act. In 1964 and 1968 further amendments required the registration of most over-the-counter traded securities and regulated the disclosure of tender offers in an attempt to end fraudulent practices in corporate mergers.

The *Public Utility Holding Company Act of 1935* was enacted to prevent the use of the holding company device to leverage control of operating utility companies. It regulated public utility holding companies, restructured companies into economically viable units, and redistributed voting power to common stockholders.

The *Trust Indenture Act of 1939* was enacted to eliminate incompetence, lack of independence, and fraudulent practices of bond trustees. It required a trust agreement for each bond issue with certain provisions for safeguarding the financial interest of investors to be filed with the SEC, and set minimum qualification standards for the trustee, one of which was independence.

The *Investment Company Act of 1940* was enacted to limit the power that large investment companies wield over the securities markets, brokers, and underwriters. It required the disclosure of financial information and registration by mutual funds, set minimum qualifications for management of funds, including competence and independence, and provided for shareholder participation in management decisions.

The *Investment Advisers Act of 1940* was enacted to prevent a conflict of interest in persons whose business it is to advise investors in financial matters. It provided for the registration of persons who provide securities advice for compensation, including disclosure of control relationships.

The *Securities Investor Protection Act of 1970* was enacted to reduce mismanagement and financial instability and the misuse of customer assets held by brokerage houses. It created the Securities Investors Protection Corporation to insure securities and cash held in a customer's account by a bankrupt broker to a maximum of $100,000 per account.

FOOTNOTES FOR CHAPTER 1

[1]The term "New Deal" was coined by Raymond Moley, adviser, collaborator, and chief of Franklin D. Roosevelt's "brain trust." It was first used by FDR in his acceptance speech at the Chicago Democratic Convention on July 2, 1932, was immediately adopted by the press, and became the Roosevelt campaign slogan. The term, New Deal, describes executive actions taken by FDR during his first term in office and the legislation produced by the "100-Day Congress," which convened in January, 1933. The Securities Act of 1933, the abandonment of the gold standard, the closing of all banks by presidential order, and their reopening under provisions of the Banking Act are numbered among the reforms of that period.

[2]In this book the word "he" and other masculine references are used only in the generic sense and are in no way intentionally sexist.

[3]For the spellbinding highlights of the investigation by the Senate Committee on Banking and Currency (the Fletcher Committee) see Ferdinand Pecora, *Wall Street Under Oath,* (New York: Simon and Schuster, 1939).

[4]Special message to the 73rd Congress, March 24, 1933.

[5]The House Banking Committee conducted an independent investigation. See U.S. House of Representatives, Rayburn Committee, *Hearings,* 73rd Congress, 1933. Mr. Thompson became Chairman of the Federal Trade Commission, the federal agency that administered the Securities Act until organization of the SEC in 1934.

[6]Disclosure is a technical concept which will be discussed throughout the book.

[7]These matters will be elaborated upon in later chapters.

[8]This observation was made in an excellent discussion of the methods and consequences of securities market speculation authored by John T. Flynn, *Securities Speculation: Its Economic Effects,* (New York: Harcourt, Brace and Company, 1934).

[9]Because of the effect that credit transactions have on the supply of money, Congress gave the Federal Reserve Board authority over margin requirements as part of its general power to set monetary policy.

[10]*The Wall Street Journal,* February 19, 1976, p. 32.

GLOSSARY

Broker. A person in the business of buying and selling securities, for a commission, on behalf of other parties.

Closed-End Investment Company. A corporation in the business of investing its funds in securities of other corporations for income and profit. Investors wishing to "cash out" of the investment company do so by selling their shares on the open market, as with any other stock.

Dealer. A person in the business of buying and selling securities for his own account.

Exchange. An organized association providing a market place for bringing together (through their brokers) buyers and sellers of securities.

Initial Margin Percentage. The percentage of the purchase price (or the proceeds of a short sale) that an investor must deposit with his broker in compliance with Federal Reserve Board requirements.

Investment Banker/Underwriter. A person in the business of financing (underwriting) and selling new issues of corporate securities. The underwriter purchases from the issuing corporation the entire issue of securities for resale to the public.

Issuer. Any corporation that sells a security interest in itself.

Listed Status. Condition under which a security has been accepted by an exchange for full trading privileges.

Margin Call. The demand by a broker that an investor deposit additional cash (or acceptable collateral) for securities purchased on credit when the price of the securities declines to a value below the minimum equity required by the stock exchange.

National Association of Securities Dealers, Inc. (NASD). An association of brokers/dealers who are in the business of trading over-the-counter securities.

New York Stock Exchange (and Regional Exchanges). An association organized to provide physical and mechanical facilities for the purchase and sale of securities by the investor through brokers and dealers.

Open-End Investment Company (Mutual Fund). A corporation in the business of investing its funds in securities of other corporations for income and profit. (See closed-end investment companies). An open-end company continuously offers new shares for sale and "redeems" shares previously issued to investors who wish to "cash out."

Over-the-Counter Securities. Corporate and government securities that are not listed for trading on an exchange. Refer to National Association of Securities Dealers, Inc.

Prospectus. Document consisting of Part I of the registration statement filed with the SEC by the issuing corporation that must be delivered to all purchasers of newly issued securities.

Proxy. A power of attorney whereby a stockholder authorizes another person or group of persons to act (vote) for him at a stockholders' meeting.

Registration. Act of filing with the SEC required information concerning the issuing corporation and the security to be issued.

Registration Statement. The document filed with the SEC containing legal, commercial, technical, and financial information concerning a new security issue.

Security. Any instrument representing a debt obligation or an equity interest in a corporation, or any instrument "commonly known as a 'security' as defined in Section 2(1) of the Securities Act of 1933."

Short-Selling. Selling a security that is not owned with the expectation of buying that specific security later at a lower market price.

Tender Offer. An offer by any party to buy the voting stock of a corporation from its shareholders.

Trust Indenture. A legal document that contains the provisions of the agreement between the three parties to a corporate bond contract.

QUESTIONS

1. Discuss the accounting practices that prevailed prior to the enactment of the Securities Acts.
2. What is the underlying philosophy of the Securities Act of 1933?
3. What general types of information can be found in a prospectus?
4. For whom is Part II of the registration statement intended?
5. What is the main distinction between the 1933 and 1934 Acts?
6. What are some of the reasons for Congress' legislating SEC regulation of:
   (a) The stock exchanges?
   (b) The activities of stock brokers?
   (c) The trading in a corporation's stock by a corporate officer (called an "insider")?
   (d) The disclosure to the public of information about publicly held securities?
7. What are the objectives of the NASD?
8. What is the over-the-counter market? How does this market differ from a national securities exchange?
9. What are the regulatory concerns of the SEC in administering the Public Utility Holding Company Act since the dissolution of holding companies?
10. Why was the Trust Indenture Act of 1939 necessary? What are its important provisions?
11. What is the objective of the Investment Company Act of 1940?
12. What are the significant provisions of the Investment Company Act of 1940?
13. Would you agree that the SEC's regulatory powers have gradually expanded over the years? If so, how have they expanded?

2

Organization and Operations of the SEC

For most of us the SEC is a "black box" into which a corporation feeds forms and from which are issued *deficiency letters, stop orders,* and the like. The lack of precision with which we refer to the SEC is indicative of the confusion which prevails. For example, journalists report that "the SEC warns . . ." when they mean "the Chief Accountant of the SEC in a speech made today said. . . ." We refer to "the Commission's" bringing criminal action against so-and-so when it is the Department of Justice that has the power to prosecute and that acts at its own discretion only at the request of the SEC. This confusion of terms is counter- productive to dealing professionally with an organization that plays a pivotal role in the development of accounting principles and auditing standards, as well as in the regulation of securities transactions. In this book we will use the term "Commission" to refer to the committee of commissioners that directs the Securities and Exchange Commission. The term "SEC" will refer to the agency as a whole. Federal legislation and the official pronouncements of the SEC do not make this distinction, but refer instead to "the Commission."

Let us examine the organization of the SEC. How are its many functions allocated among its complex arrangement of parts? What are the SEC's powers of enforcement? What services does it provide?

WHAT IS THE SEC?

The SEC is an independent agency of the United States government. Neither Congress nor the executive branch directs or controls its operations.

Both parties, however, play a role in funding the agency. The SEC prepares its preliminary budget each year and submits it to the executive Office of Management and Budget. After reviewing, and perhaps revising, the agency's budget, the Bureau incorporates it into the national budget presented to Congress. The final budget is approved by Congress, usually after sizeable modifications.

Exhibit 2-1 Appropriated Funds Versus Fees Collected

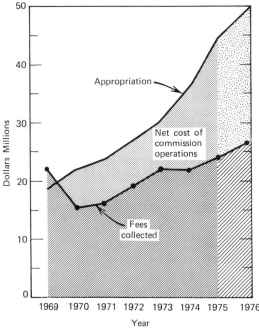

SOURCE. *1976 Annual Report of the SEC* (Washington, D.C., 1976), p. 214.

The SEC has been approximately 60 percent self-supporting in recent years; the remainder of its budget comes from general funds appropriated for the needs of the agency (Refer to Exhibit 2-1).

SEC operations are overseen by both the executive and legislative branches. Briefs and petitions for *certiorari* filed by the SEC with the Supreme Court are first reviewed by the U.S. Solicitor General. Supervision of the agency's general operations is the responsibility of the House Interstate and Foreign Commerce Committee and the Senate Banking and Currency Committee. Congress can make inquiries into aspects of SEC operations[1] and requires that reports be made by the agency. One such report is the *Annual Report of the SEC,* covering each federal fiscal year. Although it is prepared for the purpose of reporting to Congress, it is available to the public and is an excellent review of the SEC activities during the year.

As provided in the Securities Exchange Act of 1934, the responsibilities of the SEC are quasi-legislative in nature in that the agency has far-reaching authority to impose rules and regulations in order to administer the securities acts. They are quasi-judicial in that the agency also has the power to enforce the laws it administers and to interpret its own rules and regulations.

The SEC also undertakes specific assignments at the request of Congress from time to time. It:

Exhibit 2-2 **Number of SEC Employees**

Year	Number of Employees
1935	1077
1940	1670
1945	1131
1950	998
1955	666
1960	980
1965	1420
1970	1464
1975	1951
1976	1922

SOURCE: Various *Annual Reports*, Securities and Exchange Commission.

1. *Advises* Congress on proposed and existing securities legislation.
2. *Investigates* conditions in the securities markets. For example, in 1961, Congress appropriated $750,000 for a full-scale investigation of the stock market. The study, concluded in 1963, provided the basis for the 1964 and 1968 amendments to the Exchange Act establishing new standards for proxy solicitation and for tender offers.
3. *Analyzes* data regarding the financial community obtained from filings made with the agency.

From its inception in 1934, the SEC grew rapidly to a strength of approximately 1,700 employees by the beginning of World War II. This increase was necessary for the agency to meet its responsibilities legislated by the Public Utilities Holding Company Act and to conduct the several investigations ordered at

Exhibit 2-3 **SEC Budget**

Year	Appropriation
1935	$3,029,494
1940	5,470,000
1945	4,696,704
1950	5,878,250
1955	4,813,180
1960	8,100,000
1965	15,422,000
1970	21,904,977
1975	44,427,000
1976	49,291,000

SOURCE: Various *Annual Reports*, Securities and Exchange Commission.

Exhibit 2-4　Effective Registrations (Dollars in millions)

Fiscal Year Ended June 30	Total Number	Total Value	Cash Sale for Account of Issuers Common Stock	Cash Sale for Account of Issuers Bonds Debentures, and Notes	Cash Sale for Account of Issuers Preferred Stock	Cash Sale for Account of Issuers Total
1935[a]	284	$ 913	$ 168	$ 490	$ 28	$ 686
1936	689	4,835	531	3,153	252	3,936
1937	840	4,851	802	2,426	406	3,635
1938	412	2,101	474	666	209	1,349
1939	344	2,579	318	1,593	109	2,020
1940	306	1,787	210	1,112	110	1,433
1941	313	2,611	196	1,721	164	2,081
1942	193	2,003	263	1,041	162	1,465
1943	123	659	137	316	32	486
1944	221	1,760	272	732	343	1,347
1945	340	3,225	456	1,851	407	2,715
1946	661	7,073	1,331	3,102	991	5,424
1947	493	6,732	1,150	2,937	787	4,874
1948	435	6,405	1,678	2,817	537	5,032
1949	429	5,333	1,083	2,795	326	4,204
1950	487	5,307	1,786	2,127	468	4,381
1951	487	6,459	1,904	2,838	427	5,169
1952	635	9,500	3,332	3,346	851	7,529
1953	593	7,507	2,808	3,093	424	6,326
1954	631	9,174	2,610	4,240	531	7,381
1955	779	10,960	3,864	3,951	462	8,277
1956	906	13,096	4,544	4,123	539	9,206
1957	876	14,624	5,858	5,689	472	12,019
1958	813	16,490	5,998	6,857	427	13,281
1959	1,070	15,657	6,387	5,265	443	12,095
1960	1,426	14,367	7,260	4,224	253	11,738
1961	1,550	19,070	9,850	6,162	248	16,260
1962	1,844	19,547	11,521	4,512	253	16,286
1963	1,157	14,790	7,227	4,372	270	11,869
1964	1,121	16,860	10,006	4,554	224	14,784
1965	1,266	19,437	10,638	3,710	307	14,656
1966	1,523	30,109	18,218	7,061	444	25,723
1967	1,649	34,218	15,083	12,309	558	27,950
1968	[b]2,417	[b]54,076	22,092	14,036	1,140	37,269
1969	[b]3,645	[b]86,810	39,614	11,674	751	52,039
1970	[b]3,389	[b]59,137	28,939	18,436	823	48,198
1971	[b]2,989	[b]69,562	27,455	27,637	3,360	58,452
1972	3,712	62,487	26,518	20,127	3,237	49,882
1973	3,285	59,310	26,615	14,841	2,578	44,034
1974	2,890	56,924	19,811	20,997	2,274	43,082
1975	2,780	77,457	30,502	37,557	2,201	70,260
1976	2,813	87,733	37,115	29,373	3,013	69,502
Cumulative Total	52,816	943,535	396,624	309,863	31,841	738,335

[a]For 10 months ended June 30, 1935.
[b]Includes registered lease obligations related to industrial revenue bonds.
SOURCE: 1976 Annual Report of the SEC (Washington, D.C. 1976), p. 199.

that time by Congress. Despite constantly increasing work loads since then its staff has fluctuated between 600 to 2,000 employees (Refer to Exhibit 2-2). Its budget, on the other hand, has increased steadily (Refer to Exhibit 2-3). The work load, as measured by the number of corporate registrants (Refer to Exhibit 2-4) and the number of stock market participants registered with the SEC (Refer to Exhibit 2-5), requires an efficient operation.

The SEC provides an excellent training ground for accountants and attorneys wishing to make securities regulation their field of specialization either in public or private practice.

ORGANIZATION OF THE AGENCY

The essential concept underlying the organizational structure of the Commission is functional. Assignment of responsibilities to its various divisions and offices arising under the statutes it administers is determined by the nature of the problem, and not by the particular statute involved.[2]

Exhibit 2-5   Registered Stock Market Participants

	Fiscal year-end				
	1971	1972	1973	1974	1975
Exchange member primarily engaged in floor activities	16	15	17	17	21
Exchange member primarily engaged in exchange commission business	37	33	28	20	19
Broker or dealer in general securities business	79	69	66	65	67
Mutual fund underwriter and distributor	27	27	24	18	19
Broker or dealer selling variable annuities	22	21	18	18	15
Solicitor of savings and loan accounts	15	10	9	7	7
Real estate syndicator and mortgage broker and banker	16	18	21	33	43
Broker or dealer selling oil and gas interests	4	3	3	6	4
Put and call broker or dealer or option writer	23	22	20	15	7
Broker or dealer selling securities of only one issuer or associated issuers (other than mutual funds)	15	17	18	19	20
Broker or dealer selling church securities	21	15	16	17	16
Government bond dealer	4	3	3	7	8
Broker or dealer in other securities business	19	30	26	31	42
Broker or dealer in interests in condominiums	a	a	a	14	6
Inactive	3	11	7	13	8
Total	301	294	276	300	302

[a]Not separately tabulated in prior years.
SOURCE: 1975 Annual Report of the SEC (Washington, D.C., 1975).

The Washington, D.C. headquarters of the SEC houses the Commission, five operating divisions, five staff service offices, and seven administrative offices. Nine regional offices support the operating and staff service functions; and most regional offices are represented by branch offices in other cities (Refer to Exhibit 2-6).

The Commission, the Executive Director, and the Secretary

The SEC is headed by a "Commission" whose function is much like that of the board of directors of a corporation. It develops agency policy and assumes overall responsibility for the agency's performance of its duties. Its five members are appointed by the President for five-year terms. The terms are staggered, one beginning each June. The political make-up of the Commission is restricted so that no more than three members may be of the same political party. These provisions are intended to encourage a bipartisan body. Customarily the Chairman is of the same political party as the President who appoints him. Although only one commissioner is designated by the President to be "Chairman of the SEC," that individual is coequal in terms of voting power and leads as much by the status of his position and public image as through administrative powers. He tenders his resignation to the incoming President as a courtesy. When the President is of the opposing political party, the resignation usually is accepted. Any action taken by the Commission must be based on a majority decision. Therefore, the administrative policies of the SEC are determined to a large extent by the composition of the Commission.

The Executive Director, who reports directly to the Commission, coordinates the operations of all divisions and offices and is responsible for the agency's operating performance. The Secretary represents the SEC to the public. Press announcements, various releases, new and amended rules and regulations are all prepared and issued from this office. The Secretary also maintains minutes of Commission proceedings and is responsible for issuing the *Annual Report of the SEC*, which has been prepared by the Office of Opinions and Review.

Operating Divisions

The five operating divisions are responsible for the regulatory functions of the agency. They are:

The Division of Corporation Finance.
The Division of Corporate Regulation.
The Division of Market Regulation.
The Division of Enforcement.
The Division of Investment Management.

Accountants deal primarily with the Division of Corporation Finance. (Refer to Exhibit 2-7 for a summary of functions performed by the operating divisions.)

Exhibit 2-6   Securities and Exchange Commission

SECURITIES AND EXCHANGE COMMISSION

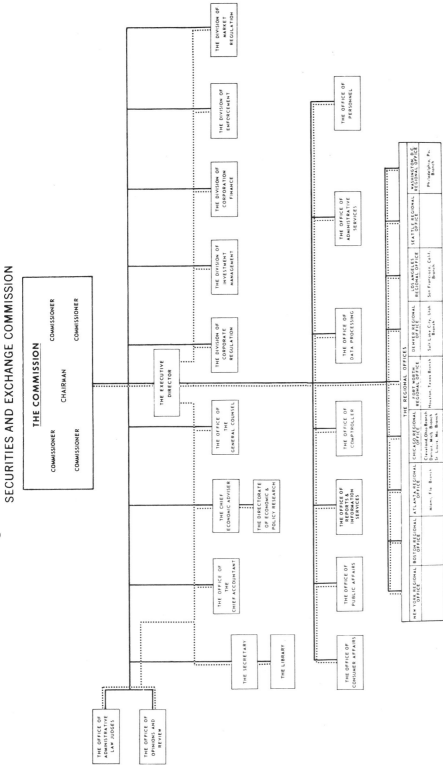

SOURCE. Securities and Exchange Commission, Annual Report, 1975, p. iv.

Exhibit 2-7 Operating Division Functions

	Corporation Finance	Corporate Regulation	Market Regulation	Enforcement	Investment Management
Securities Act	Examines and processes filings.			Investigates and enforces all provisions of the act.	
Securities Exchange Act	Examines and processes applications for listing, registration statements, periodic reports, proxy statements, insider reports, tender offer filings. Enforces involuntary delisting under Section 19(a) (2).		Regulates exchanges broker/dealers, and NASD, and examines their filings.	Investigates and enforces all provisions of the act.	
Public Utility Holding Company Act	Examines and processes applications and filings of companies also filing under the Securities Exchange Act.	Administers the provisions of the act in all other matters.			
Trust Indenture Act	Examines and processes filings.			Investigates and enforces all provisions of the act.	

Act / Activity			
Investment Companies Act Examines and processes filings	Administers the provisions of the act.	Enforces all provisions of the act.	Administers and investigates matters having to do with investment companies, their economy, distribution methods and services.
Investment Advisers Act	Examines and processes filings. Administers and investigates matters pertaining to investment advisers and enforces all provisions.		Administers certain matters having to do with investment advisers.
Chandler Act – Chapter X	Advises the court and represents investors' interests in corporate reorganizations.		
Miscellaneous Drafts forms, rules, regulations, and amendments for the Office of the Chief Accountant.	Collaborates with the Office of the General Counsel in recommending criminal prosecution by the Justice Department.		

Division of Corporation Finance The Division of Corporation Finance examines and processes all filings under the Securities Act, the Trust Indenture Act, and the Investment Companies Act. It also has responsibility under the Securities Exchange Act for examining listing applications, the accompanying registration statement, and the required periodic reports of corporate registrants; and it handles proxy statements, insider reports and tender offer filings. It reviews filings for companies jointly registered under the Securities Exchange and the Public Utility Holding Company Acts. The division guides registrants attempting to comply with the requirements of the SEC by means of: (1) prefiling conferences with the registrant's management, attorneys, and/or accountants, (2) *no-action letters,* and (3) letters of comment (deficiency letters). Because of its practical experience, it prepares the first drafts of forms, rules, regulations, and all subsequent amendments for review by the Office of the Chief Accountant. The Division solicits the advice of the business community in its policy-making role.

The organization of the Division of Corporation Finance is shown in Exhibit 2-8. A "team" consisting of a financial analyst, an accountant, and an attorney examines the filing. Each team specializes in an industry or group of industries. Several teams are supervised by a "branch chief." There are eighteen branches, three of which are supervised by each "assistant director" and his staff. Overall supervisory responsibility for the division belongs to the "director." The division staff includes a chief accountant, counsel, and engineering specialists who provide the day-to-day advisory services required by teams as they process filings.

A filing received by the Division Director's Office is assigned to a branch. That branch handles all matters relating to the registrant from then on. Registrations

Exhibit 2-8   Division of Corporation Finance Organization

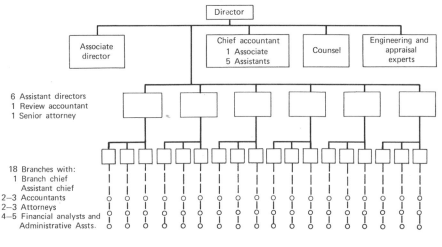

under the Securities Act and proxy regulations receive highest priority because timing in these matters is critical. Applications and registration statements under the Securities Exchange Act are scheduled next. Periodic filings under the Securities Exchange Act and other filings have the lowest priority.

Each member of the team examines the filing for compliance in his area of expertise and makes recommendations to the branch chief for necessary deficiency comments. The branch chief drafts a comment letter incorporating the inputs of each team member and submits it to the chief accountant of the division for review. In difficult or untested areas the letter may go to the Office of the Chief Accountant of the SEC and even to the Commission itself before it is dispatched to the *registrant*. The registrant may take a problem through the same channels if he feels his case is justified.

Division of Corporate Regulation The major responsibility of the Division of Corporate Regulation is to administer the regulatory provisions of the Public Utility Holding Company and Investment Companies Acts. The division also processes filings made solely under the Public Utility Holding Company Act.

The division's responsibilities under *Chapter X* of the Chandler *(Bankruptcy) Act,* are to provide expert advisory services in corporate reorganization proceedings. It represents security holders who otherwise would be unrepresented in such proceedings. Bankruptcy proceedings are heard in the federal district courts. Chapter X requires that the SEC submit a plan of reorganization to the court in proceedings where the liabilities of a bankrupt corporation exceed $3 million. However, the judge may request the SEC to submit a plan if aggregate liabilities are less than that amount. The SEC's report is based on its research which might include an investigation into matters such as the organization's prospects for future earnings and its competitive position in the industry. The report evaluates the plan of reorganization, the qualifications and independence of the trustee or counsel, the fee structure, the terms of property sale, the propriety of interim distributions to security holders, and other information pertinent to the reorganization plan. Ordinarily the report takes the form of a letter or oral presentation; however, the SEC prepares formal reports in cases involving substantial investor interest.

The regional office of the geographical area in which the bankrupt corporation resides usually does the actual investigating and reporting under the supervision of headquarters. Regional offices also review *Chapter XI* proceedings in their respective areas to determine whether the facts of the case support proceedings under Chapter XI or whether the case should be processed under Chapter X. The headquarters reviews the report prepared by the regional office and brings action, when necessary, requesting that the court dismiss the Chapter XI petition in favor of Chapter X proceedings.

Division of Market Regulation The Division of Market Regulation directs the activities of the securities markets under provisions of the Securities Exchange Act and has complete responsibility for administering and enforcing provisions of the Investment Advisers Act. It examines and processes all filings not handled by the Division of Corporation Finance: that is, it examines filings of exchanges, broker/dealers, and investment advisers. It investigates the practices of investment advisers and takes disciplinary action when necessary.

Its duties under the Securities Exchange Act are far-reaching:

1. It monitors trading activities for indications of fraud, manipulation, or other prohibited practices.
2. It investigates stock market operations. For example, it might initiate an investigation of a broker in response to consumer complaints.
3. It tracks the trading prices of certain securities for signs of erratic behavior that may be symptomatic of financial difficulties.
4. It reviews disciplinary and policy-making actions taken by the exchanges and the NASD.
5. It supervises the broker dealer inspection program that includes surprise examinations of brokerage houses by the regional offices.

Division of Enforcement   The Division of Enforcement is responsible for supervising enforcement procedures for all securities laws except the Public Utility Holding Company Act. It supervises all investigations whether conducted by itself or by another division. It determines whether the evidence indicates that enforcement proceedings are necessary. It initiates administrative and *injunctive* actions. It collaborates with the Office of the General Counsel to review recommendations for criminal prosecution by the Justice Department.

Division of Investment Management   This division administers the Investment Companies and the Investment Advisers Act. It conducts investigations into the economics, distribution methods, and the services of investment companies.

Staff Service Offices

The staff offices are technical advisers to the Commission and to the divisions. They are the:

Office of the Chief Accountant.
Office of the General Counsel.
Directorate of Economic and Policy Research.
Office of Opinions and Review.
Office of Administrative Law Judges.

Office of the Chief Accountant   The Chief Accountant is the liaison between the SEC and the accounting profession. He and his staff advise the SEC and supervise the divisions in matters relating to accounting and auditing. In this role the office:

1. Conducts research for the purpose of improving standards of accounting

and auditing, and where possible it coordinates research efforts with professional organizations such as the American Accounting Association, American Institute of Certified Public Accountants, Financial Accounting Standards Board, Financial Executives Institute, and National Association of Accountants.

2. Advises the Commission on accounting and auditing issues where new policies are under consideration or existing policies are being administered.
3. Supervises the preparation of pronouncements in the areas of accounting and auditing.
4. Establishes standards of accounting for regulated parties such as exchanges, broker/dealers, and investment advisers. For example, this office developed the system of accounts required for use by regulated public utilities.
5. Establishes precedents in accounting matters based on filings referred by the Division of Corporation Finance examining teams and advises registrants on filing matters pertaining to accounting.
6. Supervises investigations where accounting or auditing practices are in question.
7. Reviews files submitted by the Division of Enforcement on criminal and administrative actions for the accounting and auditing aspects of the case.
8. Informally publicizes SEC policy regarding accounting and auditing issues by means of personal appearances and press interviews by the Chief Accountant.

Office of the General Counsel   The General Counsel is the chief legal officer of the SEC. With his staff he:

1. Provides technical and advisory services to the Commission, other divisions and offices of the agency and to Congress.
2. Supervises divisions and regional offices in the legal aspects of operations.
3. Represents the SEC in judicial proceedings.

The General Counsel is consulted by the Commission on legal policy matters. His office interprets statutes, reviews proposed forms and rules, and represents the SEC during congressional hearings and investigations. For example, when Congress considers securities market legislation, the General Counsel's office researches the specific problem and prepares comments presenting the SEC's position. Also, the SEC's counsel may recommend specific provisions for the proposed legislation and remains available to advise the lawmakers.

The office coordinates all legal activities of the SEC and reviews legal matters that cross division lines. It maintains a file of all persons who have been charged with federal or state securities law violations. The General Counsel reviews all investigative reports in which the SEC Division of Enforcement recommends criminal prosecution by the Justice Department and informs other authorities when the SEC investigation indicates that there has been a violation of a statute administered by another agency, for example, where mail fraud has occurred. It directs contested civil litigation.

The General Counsel represents the SEC as *amicus curiae* (friend of the court) in court proceedings regarding the securities market where the issue is of general importance. The office represents the SEC in other judicial proceedings. For example, a registrant who appeals a decision of the SEC by filing a suit in an appellate court is opposed by the General Counsel of the SEC.

Directorate of Economic and Policy Research—Office of the Chief Economic Adviser   The Directorate of Economic and Policy Research is headed by the Office of the Chief Economic Adviser. As the data-gathering agent of the SEC it:

1. Compiles and publishes statistical data that it has analyzed from filings made with the SEC. For example, the following information is published on a regular basis:
    a. Plant and equipment expenditures of U.S. business (prepared in cooperation with the U.S. Department of Commerce).
    b. Working capital of corporations.
    c. Quarterly financial reports (prepared in cooperation with the Federal Trade Commission).
    d. Individual savings.
    e. Corporation pension fund data.
    f. New securities offerings.
2. Prepares statistical analyses of the capital markets for use by the Commission in its policy-making activities and for public use.
3. Recommends the undertaking and modification of programs to the Commission based on its analyses.

Office of Opinions and Review   The primary function of the Office of Opinions and Review is to draft findings, opinions, and orders issued in the name of the Commission. The office helps investigating divisions to draft appropriate opinions in uncontested cases of securities law violations. It is also in charge of preparing the *Annual Report of the SEC*.

Office of Administrative Law Judges   Examiners in the Office of Administrative Law Judges hold public and private hearings on behalf of the Commission, and are empowered to administer oaths, to subpoena witnesses, and to take testimony. The examiner hears the case and prepares a preliminary decision. This decision may be reviewed by the Commission or it may be contested within a 30-day period by any party to the hearing. If the opinion is uncontested and unreviewed, the decision becomes final after the 30-day period.

Regional Offices

Regional offices are the field representatives of the SEC, assuming responsibility for stock market activities and for registrants domiciled in their respective geographical area (Refer to Exhibit 2-9). They perform limited regulatory functions

Exhibit 2-9   Regional Office Organization

SOURCE.   The Work of the Securities and Exchange Commission (Washington, D.C., April 1974).

and conduct investigations for the divisions, which have been discussed. They examine Regulation A and A-M filings, that pertain to small corporate security offerings. Reports filed by exchange members and by broker/dealers also are examined by the regional offices. The remaining regional functions, supervised directly by headquarters, include:

1. Enforcing securities laws which govern stock market practices (under the direction of the Division of Market Regulation). The offices investigate violations of securities statutes and recommend punitive action.
2. Conducting criminal investigations (under the supervision of the Office of the General Counsel).
3. Fact finding, advising, and preparing the report for the court in Chapter X corporate reorganization proceedings (under the direction of the Division of Corporate Regulation).
4. Conducting surprise audits of brokers and dealers (under the supervision of the Division of Market Regulation).
5. Prosecuting injunctive actions before the U.S. District Courts, administering proceedings before the hearing examiners, and assisting U.S. attorneys

in the prosecution of criminal charges (where the Division of Enforcement has recommended the action to the Justice Department).
6. Rendering interpretative advice and offering guidance to registrants, the public, and the press (for the Department of Corporate Finance).
7. Maintaining public reference services and libraries.

Administrative Offices

The administrative offices support the divisions and staff offices by providing general services such as accounting, payroll, purchasing, and data processing.

Exhibit 2-10   SEC Enforcement Powers

Power (Examples)	Purposes
Persuasion (Speeches, press interviews, informal relationships with the business community, *amicus cureae* court briefs)	To improve and maintain public relations, to encourage improved reporting standards and professional conduct, to represent investors and the public in court proceedings.
Policy Statements (Pre-filing conferences, "no-action" letters, interpretive letters)	To provide registrants with assistance in complying with the requirements of securities laws and SEC administrative requirements.
(Censure)	To indicate formal disapproval of standards practiced by a member of the (accounting) profession.
Specific Findings (Deficiency letter)	To inform the registrant his filing does not meet SEC standards in that it is incomplete, inaccurate, or misleading.
(Administrative proceedings and formal hearings)	To gather evidence on a specific issue in order to take administrative or policy making action.
(Investigations)	Authorized by all securities acts to determine facts related to consumer complaints, possible securities law infractions, etc., which have potential impact on the securities market.
Impeding Actions (Refusal)	To prevent a defective registration from becoming effective.

Exhibit 2-10 (Continued)

Power (Examples)	Purposes
(*Stop orders, suspension of trading*)	To suspend the effective status of a registration. Prevents trading a security. The period of an individual suspension may not exceed 10 days.
(*Delisting*)	To take disciplinary action against a registrant preventing trade in its securities in the marketplace.
(*Revocation and suspension of registration*)	To take disciplinary action against stock market participants preventing the party from engaging in its usual business.
(*Suspension* or *disbarment from practice before the SEC*)	To take disciplinary action against an accountant or attorney preventing the individual or firm from carrying out its responsibilities to its publicly traded clients. This action customarily follows an investigation in which professional standards have been found to have been violated.
(Miscellaneous *consent actions*)	To take disciplinary action against a registrant, stock market participant or professional practicing before the SEC. This action customarily follows an investigation in which violations of securities laws and/or professional standards probably have occurred. It is an alternative to the preceding three actions, taken to minimize harm to the public. Customarily the consent specifically denies the admission of guilt.
Court Proceedings (*Injunctions and civil actions*)	To enjoin continued or threatened violations of securities laws or SEC requirements.
(*Criminal actions*)	To inform the Justice Department of violations of securities laws discovered in SEC investigations, or to prosecute where an injunction has been violated.

POWERS TO ENFORCE THE LAWS

The SEC has a wide range of statutory powers to enforce the securities laws. A summary of the actions that it can take is presented in Exhibit 2-10 in order of increasing severity. These actions will be discussed in detail in subsequent chapters.

SERVICES PROVIDED TO THE PUBLIC

The services offered by the SEC are intended to promote disclosure of financial data to the investing public. The SEC offers library and document reproduction services for public use. Any document filed with the SEC and not classified as "confidential" can be obtained in xerography or microfilm form from headquarters in Washington, D.C. The regional offices maintain limited files and those facilities and records that are available at the various SEC offices are summarized in Exhibit 2-11.

A complete list of SEC publications and instructions for ordering them appear in the *Annual Report of the SEC*. Although some publications can be ordered directly from the SEC, others must be ordered through the Superintendent of Documents, U.S. Government Printing Office, Washington, D.C. (Refer to Appendix A for a list of the principal SEC publications.)

SUMMARY The SEC is an independent agency of the U.S. government. The *Annual Report of the SEC* is prepared by the agency to inform Congress of its activities. Although this report usually suffices, either house of Congress also has the power to conduct special investigations into SEC activities.

The agency is organized along functional lines much like a corporation. The Commission is the agency's board of directors setting policy and assuming responsibility for performance. An Executive Director is its president who coordinates and oversees operations. The Secretary is in charge of public relations and the distribution of information to Congress and to the public. The divisions (Corporation Finance, Corporate Regulation, Market Regulation, Enforcement, and Investment Management) perform the regulatory functions of the agency. The staff offices (Chief Accountant, General Counsel, Opinions and Review, Administrative Law Judges, and The Directorate of Economic and Policy Research) provide expert advice on technical matters to the Commission and the divisions. Regional offices do much of the regulatory and investigatory legwork for the divisions and staff offices and are supervised by them. Administrative offices support the operating functions with various services such as data processing.

The SEC has been given statutory power to administer and enforce all securities laws and has adopted a wide variety of methods for doing so. These methods range from gentle persuasion to the abilities to recommend criminal prosecution, and to prevent an expert accountant or attorney from representing corporate SEC registrants before the Commission.

Exhibit 2-11 Facilities and Records

Service	Washington Headquarters	Regional Offices		
		New York	Chicago	Other
Public reference room	X	X	X	X
Regulaton A notifications and offering circulars				
All filings	X			
Domiciled corporations only		X	X	X
Prospectus' for all effective registrations	X	X	X	X
Application for registration of securities listed on all exchanges	X	X	X	X
Applications for registration of securities listed on all exchanges other than the NYSE and AMX (The New York Regional Office does not duplicate the files of the two exchanges located in New York City.)	n/a	X		
Annual reports, supplementary reports, and amendments filed under the Exchange Act.	X	X	X	X
Application for registration and financial statements of broker-dealers and their periodic reports:				
All filings	X			
Domiciled houses only		X	X	X
Application for registration and supplementary statements of investment advisers and their periodic reports:				
All filings	X			
Domiciled advisers only		X	X	X
Library of SEC publications	X	X	X	X

The services provided by headquarters and the regional offices support the agency's objective to encourage disclosure of financial information to the investing public.

FOOTNOTES FOR CHAPTER 2

[1] The Metcalf Committee investigation and the Moss Committee report are two recent examples of Congress' supervisory role in action. These topics will be discussed later.

[2] Andrew D. Orrick, "Organization, Procedures and Practices of the Securities and Exchange Commission," *George Washington Law Review,* Vol. XXVIII, October, 1959, pp. 50–85.

GLOSSARY

Amicus curiae. "Friend of the Court." Assisting a court in the interpretation of some matter concerning a securities law or regulation.

Censure. A formal reprimand for improper professional behavior.

Certiorari, Writ of. An order issued by a superior court directing an inferior court to deliver its record for review.

Chapter X Bankruptcy. Deals with voluntary or involuntary reorganization of a corporation with publicly held securities.

Chapter XI Bankruptcy. Deals with individuals, partnerships and corporations whose securities are not publicly held. Affects only voluntary arrangements of unsecured debts.

Civil Action. Involves the private rights and remedies of the parties to a suit; that is, actions arising out of a contract.

Comment Letter. Refer to *Deficiency Letter*. Also referred to as a letter of comment.

Consent Action. Issued when a person agrees to the terms of a disciplinary nature without admitting to the allegations in the complaint.

Criminal Action. Suits initiated for the alleged commission of an act in violation of a public law.

Deficiency Letter. A letter from the SEC setting forth needed corrections and amendments to the issuing corporation's registration statement. Also called a comment letter or letter of comment.

Delisting. Permanent removal of a listed security from a national securities exchange.

Disbarment. Permanent removal of a professional's authority to represent clients before the SEC.

Domiciled Corporation. A corporation doing business in the state in which its charter was granted.

Filing. The process of completing and submitting a registration statement to the SEC.

Injunction. A court order directing a corporation to stop alleged violations of a securities law or regulation.

No-Action Letter. The SEC's written reply to a corporate issuer of securities stating its position regarding a specific filing matter.

Refusal. SEC action prohibiting a filing from becoming effective.

Registrant. A corporation that has filed a registration statement with the SEC.

Stop Order. SEC order stopping the issue or listing of securities.

Suspension. SEC order temporarily prohibiting the trading of a security.

QUESTIONS

1. What is meant by the phrase "the SEC is an independent agency"?
2. What statute created the Securities and Exchange Commission?
3. What is meant by the concept that the SEC powers are "quasi-legislative"?
4. Who heads the SEC?
5. Discuss briefly the administrative responsibilities of the five Divisions.
6. What division is responsible for examining registration statement filings?
7. When must the SEC participate in a Chapter X proceeding?
8. The SEC has received a report from a stockholder that the officers of the corporation

in which the stockholder has invested money may be in violation of the securities laws. What division will supervise an investigation?

9. List five duties of the Office of Chief Accountant?
10. Does the SEC have the power to subpoena corporate records and witnesses in investigations?
11. What does the legal term *amicus curiae* mean and how does the procedure apply to the SEC?
12. List five functions of an SEC Regional Office.

Appendix
A
Authoritative Literature and References (How to Find What You Want)

To serve the SEC registrant effectively, an accountant must possess a thorough knowledge of the authoritative literature and reference material. Requirements for reporting and professional standards come from many different sources, and the accountant must constantly update his knowledge. This appendix identifies and briefly describes the authoritative literature and lists the most popular references.

A warning is appropriate at this point. The documents described in this appendix are those that an accountant should refer to for any aspect of SEC regulations. The purpose of this text is merely to introduce the student to SEC accounting. Because of its brevity and lack of timeliness, it is not suitable for practical application. Before undertaking any aspect of an SEC engagement an accountant should acquire a library of the most recent printings of needed source materials. Exhibit A-1 summarizes the authoritative literature.

Securities Act of 1933

Provides the legal basis for federal regulation of initial sales of securities. Eleven amendments to the act were incorporated into the Securities Exchange Act in 1934 (Sections 201–211); however, subsequent amendments have been incorporated directly into the Securities Act itself.

The law establishes a very extensive scope of authority by means of the definitions that appear in Section 2. It exempts certain securities and transactions (Section 3 and 4 respectively) from the requirement to register; it defines the conditions under which a registration statement becomes effective and prohibits specific sales activities prior to the date of an effective registration; it defines fraudulent acts and provides civil and criminal penalties for persons convicted of violating the act; it establishes the authority of the "Commission" to administer and enforce the law.

Two schedules are part of the Securities Act. Schedule A states the requirements for registration of securities. For example, it describes the balance sheet required in a registration statement to be "of a date not more than 90 days prior to the date of filing. . . ." Schedule B is entitled Requirements for Registration of Securities Issued by a Foreign Government or Political Subdivision Thereof."

Securities Exchange Act of 1934.

Provides the legal basis for federal regulation of trading in securities, and establishes the Securities and Exchange Commission, giving it the "power to make such rules and regulations as may be necessary or appropriate to implement the provisions. . . ." Again, the definitions (contained in Section 3) extend the scope of the law to virtually every type of public equity transaction. It defines prohibited acts and establishes civil and criminal penalties for violations. It sets basic requirements for registration statements, periodic and other reports and proxies. Note, in Exhibit A-1, that only these two acts are organized into "sections." The reference to a section, preceded or not by the title of the act, implies the status of law.

General Rules and Regulations.

Cover matters relating to filings of an administrative or general nature.

Regulations.

Regulations pertaining to the 1933 Act are identified by a letter, whereas regulations pertaining to the 1934 Act are prefaced by a number. For example, Regulation A governs reporting under the 1933 Act. (Most readers are familiar with the term, "Reg A offering.") Regulation 14A, on the other hand, is related to Section 14 of the 1934 Act and concerns proxy solicitations. The regulations specify filing requirements.

Regulation S-X.

The principal document governing reporting for financial statements, footnotes and schedules' standards under all securities acts. No filing can be made without reference to it.

Prior to 1940 the SEC's requirements for the form and content of financial statements and the accounting rules that had been adopted up to that time were contained in various instruction books. The language of the many instructions and forms was not consistent, amendments were difficult because all forms had to be changed when any one form was amended, and many specific types of transactions were not covered by the rules during the first few years of the SEC's existence.

A program, therefore, was begun to simplify publication of accounting requirements. Instead of using many sets of instructions, the SEC developed a single pamphlet explicating the accounting rules and the requirements for form, content, and detail of financial statements and schedules filed under the Securities Act of 1933 and the Securities Exchange Act of 1934. It was adopted on February 21, 1940 and designated Regulation S-X.

S-X integrates all previous accounting requirements into a single regulation, thereby eliminating the possibility of inadvertent differences and inconsistencies between forms. The requirements contained in it are applicable to all statements filed under the Securities Act of 1933 and the Securities Exchange Act of 1934 and to all forms for application for registration and annual reports under the Securities Exchange Act of 1934, except those for railroads and foreign issuers.

Exhibit A-1 Summary of Authoritative Literature

Document	Legal Status	Function	Organization of Contents	Comments
Securities Act of 1933	Federal law	The legal basis for federal regulation of initial sales of securities	26 Sections Schedules A and B 1 Appendix	Amendments are incorporated in the body of the law except for those made in 1934.
Securities Exchange Act of 1934	Federal law	The legal basis for federal regulation of trading in securities	Title I: 35 Sections Title II: Amendments to the 1933 Act.	Amendments are incorporated in the body of the law.
General rules and regulations under the Securities Act of 1933	Effect of law	Gives general requirements for and administrative information related to filings under the law. Establishes 3 exemptions from filing.	6 articles of rules numbered with 3 digits (e.g., Rule 120 in Article 3)	Amended occasionally
1933 Act regulations	Effect of law	Defines reporting requirements for specific types of issues	Regulations A, B, C, E, F 4 Appendices	Amended periodically. Regulation C governs Form S-1 registration statements.
General rules and regulations under the Securities Exchange Act of 1934	Effect of law	Gives general rules of application for filing and practicing under the law. Establishes exemptions from reporting. Explains Section 10b prohibitions against manipulation and deceptive practices.	Rules are numbered according to the section of the law to which they refer (e.g., n10.03)	Amended occasionally
1934 Act regulations	Effect of law	Defines standards for reporting events required by statute.	Regulations 12B, 13A and D, 14A, C and D, and 15D 1 appendix	Amended periodically

Regulation S-X	Effect of law	The authoritative statement of standards for financial statement disclosure under the 1933 and 1934 acts.	12 articles of rules numbered by article (12.01)	Amended periodically
Regulation S-K	Effect of law	The authoritative statement of disclosure standards for requirements other than the financial statements, footnotes and schedules.		
Forms	Effect of law	Establish standards of disclosure in filings with the SEC	Varies	Forms must be modified for the circumstances of the individual registrant.
Guides for Preparation and Filing of Registration Statements under the Securities Act of 1933	Guidelines	General information regarding the registration process. Contains some guidelines of interest to accountants such as, Guide 22.	59 Guides numbered consecutively.	—
Guides for Preparation and Filing of Reports and Registration Statements under the 1934 Act	Guidelines	General information regarding the filing of registrations and reports. Guide 4 is of particular interest to accountants	4 Guides numbered consecutively	—
Accounting Series (Releases (ASR's))	Disputed	Update Regulation S-X between amendments. Means of communicating accounting information to the profession, and announcing the disciplinary actions taken against accountants		
Securities Releases	"Memos" to the business community	Varied		Importance is the use of SR's as exposure drafts for proposed SEC rule changes.
Staff Accounting Bulletins	SEC policy and interpretations	Clarify specific accounting problems related to ASR requirements	Items numbered consecutively	
Rules of Practice	SEC policy	Establishes standards of conduct for professionals practicing before the SEC		Coordinates with the AICPA Professional Code of Ethics
Decisions and reports	SEC policy	Communication of SEC policy regarding specific issues		Accumulated and published regularly
Annual Report of the SEC	Report to Congress	Similar to that of a corporate annual report	Soft-cover book	Published annually

While the requirements set forth in S-X are comprehensive, they do not attempt to prescribe the accounting practices to be followed in every situation or the disclosures to be made of all business transactions. Instead, the SEC requires that generally accepted accounting principles be followed in recording the many transactions not specifically covered by its rules.

Regulation S-X is amended from time to time by a revised printing; however, minor corrections and additions occur very frequently. Temporary amendments of this nature are made by means of an Accounting Series Release until such time as the entire regulation is fully amended (Refer to the discussion of Accounting Series Releases below).

Regulation S-K.

Also establishes disclosure standards under all securities acts. The regulation was created in 1977 to set standards of disclosure for financial information not presented in the financial statements, footnotes or schedules. For example, it establishes standards of disclosure for information presented in the section of various registration forms describing the registrant's line of business.

Forms.

Statements of standards with which registration statements and other filings must comply. They itemize and describe information registrants must present in order to file in their particular circumstances. The SEC discourages precise copying of the forms, but rather requires that the forms be adapted to the individual needs of the registrant to maximize useful disclosure and to avoid misleading investors. That is, SEC forms are really a set of instructions to guide the registrant in the preparation of the reports to be filed. The most common forms used to file under the 1933 Act are prefaced by a letter (Form S-1, etc.). Those used to register and report under the 1934 Act are prefaced by numbers (Forms 8-K, 10-K, 10-Q, etc.).

Guides for Preparation and Filing of Registration Statements under the 1933 Act.

Offer suggestions for the effective filing of documents and provide information such as the working hours of the SEC headquarters office.

Guides for Preparation and Filing of Reports and Registration Statements under the 1934 Act.

Provide the same function for the 1934 Act as the 1933 Guides, above.

Accounting Series Releases (ASRs).

In addition to its rules, regulations, and decisions on accounting matters, the SEC issues periodic releases, Accounting Series Releases, to serve certain specialized purposes. They afford a medium for making known to companies and to the public established SEC policy on particular accounting issues. They constitute the SEC's principal instrument (other than its formal decisions and reports) for informing the public of the policies followed by its staff. These releases have also been valuable in dealing with specialized types of accounting issues that are so unusual or complex that establishment of a general and inflexible accounting rule would be inadvisable.

The status of ASRs is not as well established as that of other publications. However, many authorities consider them to have the effect of law and it is the safest position to consider them as such. Appendix D summarizes the status of the ASRs and identifies those that amend Regulation S-X but have already been incorporated into revisions. The remaining ASRs either establish specific standards of accounting and professionalism or are announcements of disciplinary action taken by the SEC against accountants. (Refer to Appendix E).

Securities Releases (SRs).

Numbered separately for the 1933 and 1934 Acts, have been issued in the thousands. They are usually of primary interest to attorneys specializing in SEC registrations because they serve the function of "memos" from the SEC to the business community on matters of regulation. Occasionally, however, an accounting topic is the subject of a securities release. For example, exposure drafts that discuss pending SEC rule changes are introduced in the form of a release for comment by interested parties prior to being adopted as an ASR. The issuance of an ASR is announced via an SR.

Staff Accounting Bulletins.

A recent innovation of the Office of the Chief Accountant. They clarify problems of application related to Accounting Series Releases based on practical experience gained in administering them and announce SEC administrative policy in dealing with special accounting issues.

Rules of Practice.

Coordinate with the AICPA Professional Code of Ethics to define the standards of professional conduct for persons practicing before the SEC. It is an essential reference in that it extends the responsibilities of accountants beyond those generally acknowledged by the profession.

REFERENCE SOURCES

We have discussed the source documents that communicate the requirements of federal securities regulation. What are the reference materials available to the accountant that contain this information, that gather and organize it?

Probably the most popular publication is the *Federal Securities Law Reporter* published in Chicago by Commerce Clearing House, Inc. This is a five-volume loose-leaf service organized as follows:

Volume 1   Topical index, general guide, Securities Act of 1933.
Volume 2   Securities Exchange Act of 1934.
Volume 3   Public Utility Holding Company, Investment Company, Trust Indenture, Investment Advisers and related acts, Rules of Practice.

| Volume 4 | Finding lists, accounting rules, securities law articles, and release lists. |
| Current Volume | Case table, cumulative index, case table for new developments, topical index to new developments, new SEC rules, new court decisions. |

Incidentally, Commerce Clearing House, Inc. also publishes the *Blue Sky Reporter* [four-volume loose leaf service (Volumes 1, 1-A, 2, and 3)] containing:

State securities laws by alphabetically arranged states.

Topical and cumulative indices.

Case table.

New matters.

The last report letter.

Finding lists of information such as fees, addresses of state securities administrators, exemptions, etc.

Both series contain a short section that describes its organization and offers instructions for its use.

The loose-leaf services provide the most current information available. Another source of documents listed in Exhibit A-1 is financial printing firms. Pandick Press of New York, Sorg Printing Company, Jeffries & Company, Inc., Bowne of Los Angeles, Inc., to mention a few, provide most of the documents listed in Exhibit A-1 in pamphlet form as a service to their customers.

Books written for the knowledgeable practitioner help organize information from all sources and discuss SEC regulation in depth. The most widely distributed is Louis H. Rappaport's *SEC Accounting Practice and Procedure,* now in its third edition (1972), published by the Ronald Press Company in New York City. Another well-known book is Howard L. Kellogg and Morton Poloway (Partners, Touche Ross & Co.), *Accountants SEC Practice Manual,* (Chicago, Illinois: Commerce Clearing House, Inc.), 1971.

All large public accounting firms publish material for in-house use which also is available on a limited basis to fellow accountants; their newsletters announce the most recent developments in SEC practice.

PERIODIC SEC REFERENCE PUBLICATIONS

The SEC regularly publishes information pertaining to federal regulation of securities trading. A brief synopsis of the major publications and their contents follows:

Daily

SEC Digest

- Major Commission announcements, rule-making actions, and court and administrative decisions.

- The registration statements filed under the Securities Act of 1933.
- Form 8-K filings.
- Reports filed pursuant to Section 13(d) of the Securities Exchange Act of 1934.

Weekly

SEC Docket

- All Commission releases for the week (litigation releases are also filed separately in the SEC public reference rooms).

Monthly

Official Summary of Securities Transactions and Holdings

- Trading activities of insiders in publicly traded reporting companies.

Statistical Bulletin

- Trading information for securities listed on the New York and American Stock Exchanges.
- Data on registered security offerings.

Annually

Directory of Companies Filing Annual Reports with the SEC

- Lists companies alphabetically and by industry.

SEC Corporation Index for Active and Inactive Companies

- Discloses the name, address, file number, and branch in the Division of Corporation Finance to which the issuer is assigned. Also, the filing and reporting requirements of the issuer and the state in which the executive office is located.

Broker/Dealer and Investment Adviser Directory

- Lists all registered broker/dealers and investment advisers.

Annual Report of the SEC

- Summarizes its major activities.

Work of theSecurities and Exchange Commission

- Summarizes and explains its responsibilities.

Periodically

Securities Violations Bulletins

- Index of violations under the securities laws.

RESEARCHING COURT DECISIONS

If you need to research court decisions regarding litigation in SEC matters, the following sources are available:

1. Federal Securities Law Reporter (CCH).
2. Bureau of National Affairs.
3. Warren, Gorham, and Lamont.
4. United States Code Annotated.

3 Issuing Securities Under the Securities Act

Approximately 3,000 corporations offer securities each year; the average annual value of these securities is $60 billion (Refer to Exhibit 3-1). Although a large portion of these corporations are first-time registrants, only 10 to 15 percent of those filing registration statements fail to actually issue securities. The process is arduous, difficult, and complex, requiring precision timing and a fair share of luck; but, as the figures show, it can pay off.

This chapter describes the process of issuing securities which includes registration with the SEC. Keep in mind that the registration statement covers a specified *class* (or classes) of securities, all issued at the same time (or within a rather limited time period). Should the corporation seek more capital after the first group of securities is sold or should wish to issue another class of security, it must repeat the process, that is, register and issue another group of securities.

Many issues that otherwise would come under the provisions of the Securities Act are exempt from filing a registration statement. (Exemptions from filing are *not* exemptions from the legal penalties for violating other provisions of the law.) Exemptions are granted by law or by administrative action of the SEC. This chapter summarizes all the exemptions.

Finally, the chapter discusses the legal liabilities imposed by the Securities Act on *all* parties related to the sale of securities.

THE PROCESS OF OFFERING SECURITIES

A corporation seeking capital through the public offering of securities contacts an investment banker, also referred to as an underwriter. The investment banker's primary function is to distribute securities, but he is also an excellent source of marketing information, and resolves such questions as:

1. What type of securities should be offered?
2. How many shares should be offered, at what price?

3. When should the issue be made?
4. To whom should it be offered?

The investment banker also assists in preparing the registration forms filed with the SEC.

If the corporation has staff sufficiently competent to handle the technical problems associated with a securities offering, it is less dependent on the underwriter for guidance and can shop around for the lowest *spread* (underwriter's fee). Most companies do not price-shop. Indeed, some investment bankers refuse to bid for business, depending upon their reputation to attract clients.

The corporation's contract with the underwriter, the *underwriting agreement*, can take one of several forms:

1. FIRM COMMITMENT. The underwriter guarantees the success of a new issue by agreeing to purchase the entire issue at a set price, assuming the risk that he may not be able to resell the securities. Only seasoned companies can expect these terms.
2. BEST EFFORTS. The underwriter agrees to do his best to distribute all securities in the issue but makes no guarantee to purchase those he does not sell. This is the usual arrangement for the offerings of small corporations with unproven track records.
3. ALL OR NONE. If the underwriter is unable to sell the entire issue, he agrees to redeem all shares from the purchasers. This arrangement reduces the investor's risk that the company will receive insufficient funds to achieve the objectives of the issue.

Exhibit 3-1   Effective Securities Act Registrations (Dollars in Millions)

Fiscal Year Ended June 30	Total		% of First-Time Registrants
	Number	Value	
1965	1266	$19,437	33
1966	1523	30,109	25
1967	1649	34,218	24
1968	2417	54,076	34
1969	3645	86,810	50
1970	3389	59,137	48
1971	2989	69,562	29
1972	3712	62,487	33
1973	3285	59,310	28
1974	2890	56,924	25
1975	2780	77,457	18
1976	2813	87,733	19

SOURCE: Data compiled from *The Annual Report of the SEC.*

The underwriting agreement is a contract between the issuer and the "managing underwriter" who assumes responsibility for distributing the securities. Usually, the managing underwriter organizes an "underwriting syndicate," consisting of "participating underwriters," to assist in distributing the securities. The managing underwriter improves his ability to market the issue by involving other underwriters and distributes his risk (responsibility to pay off the issuer) among several parties.

The underwriting syndicate, equivalent to the wholesaler in commerce, distributes the securities to the *selling group,* brokers and/or dealers, that retails the securities to the public. The wholesaling and retailing functions in many cases are done by the same brokerage house.

The underwriter's spread usually is the largest single item of expense in a public issue and ranges from 1 percent to 10 percent of the proceeds of the issue depending upon the nature of the security (e.g., stock or bonds), the size of the issue, and the issuing company. Generally speaking, bond issues bring a smaller spread than stocks, a larger issue brings a smaller spread than a small issue, and a blue-chip company pays a lower spread than a company in the developmental stage. The underwriter also may receive (in addition to his spread) warrants, discounted shares, or the right of first refusal on subsequent offerings.

Issuing securities requires the coordinated efforts of a team consisting of:

1. The issuing corporation.
2. The managing underwriter.
3. Legal counsel.
4. The independent accountant.
5. Other experts (e.g., engineers and appraisers).

Exhibit 3-2 describes the functions of the team members.

After the corporation's management and the underwriters have met and have come to a gentlemen's agreement on the terms of the offering, the team holds a preliminary meeting (preunderwriting conference) to lay out strategy and to design the offering so that it can be presented to the board of directors for approval by the stockholders. Next, the team members turn their attention to locating potential problems, preparing the pro forma registration statement, and meeting with the SEC in a prefiling conference, if necessary. The securities are designed and printed by one of several firms specializing in such work (Jeffries & Company, Inc., Bowne of Los Angeles, Inc.). Once questionable points are resolved and the audit is nearly complete (if it is not already completed), the corporation's counsel prepares the final registration statement. The accountant reviews it, the board of directors approves it and it is filed with SEC headquarters in Washington, D.C.

During the period that the SEC is examining the registration statement, the underwriter begins his marketing effort. His first step is to organize the underwriting group. Obviously the prospective members of the group require information regarding the offering before they are willing to commit themselves. Other members of the securities market such as institutional investors also

Exhibit 3-2 Functions of Team Members in a Public Offering

Member	Functions
Issuing company represented by the president, the chief financial officer, etc.	• Primary responsibility for all aspects of the offering. The registration statement is considered by the SEC to be that of the issuer.
Managing underwriter	• Heads the underwriting group composed of participating underwriters. • Has responsibility for distribution of securities to retailers. • Provides expert advice on financial matters.
Counsel	• Provides expert advice on legal matters especially compliance with state and federal securities law • Usually serves as the "agent for service" (liason with the SEC). • Helps the issuer to prepare the registration statement.
Independent accountant	• Audits the financial statements of the company and provides the opinion required by the SEC. • Provides expert advice on accounting matters.
Other experts (engineers, appraisers)	• Provide technical services and opinions required by the SEC.

demand hard facts. The underwriter is permitted to release copies of the preliminary prospectus to meet these needs. The prospectus issued to a small number of interested parties is called a *red herring prospectus*. The outside front cover of the prospectus must bear the red ink caption "Preliminary Prospectus," the date it is issued, and a caveat that warns:

> *A registration statement relating to these securities has been filed with the Securities and Exchange Commission, but has not yet become effective. Information contained herein is subject to completion or amendment. These securities may not be sold nor may offers to buy be accepted prior to the time the registration statement becomes effective. This prospectus shall not constitute an offer to sell or the solicitation of an offer to buy in any State in which such offer or solicitation would be unlawful prior to registration or qualification under the securities laws thereof.*

Persons who receive a copy of the preliminary prospectus must receive a corrected copy if the prospectus is changed during the course of registration, which occurs frequently. For this reason, the distribution of the red herring prospectus is carefully limited.

Next, the underwriters alert the financial community and potential investors that an offering is forthcoming. This is done by means of a *tombstone ad* (Refer to Exhibit 3-3). Tombstone ads appear in periodicals as diverse as the *Wall Street Journal*, *Business Week*, the *Los Angeles Times*, and *Newsweek*. Each publica-

Exhibit 3-3   **"Tombstone Ad"**

This announcement is neither an offer to sell nor a solicitation of an offer to buy any of these securities. The offering is made only by the Prospectus.

New Issue

$25,000,000

Chris ★ Craft ®
INDUSTRIES, INC.

13% Subordinated Sinking Fund Debentures Due 1999
Interest Payable February 1 and August 1

Price 100%

These securities are redeemable prior to maturity as set forth in the Prospectus. Copies of the Prospectus may be obtained in any State in which this announcement is circulated from only such of the underwriters, including the undersigned, as may lawfully offer the securities in such State.

Bear, Stearns & Co.

Bache Halsey Stuart Shields Incorporated	**Donaldson, Lufkin & Jenrette** Securities Corporation	**Drexel Burnham Lambert** Incorporated
Goldman, Sachs & Co.	**E. F. Hutton & Company Inc.**	**Kidder, Peabody & Co.** Incorporated
Loeb Rhoades, Hornblower & Co.		**Paine, Webber, Jackson & Curtis** Incorporated
L. F. Rothschild, Unterberg, Towbin		**Warburg Paribas Becker** Incorporated
Wertheim & Co., Inc.		**Shearson Hayden Stone Inc.**
Bateman Eichler, Hill Richards Incorporated	**Boettcher & Company**	**Crowell, Weedon & Co.**
Dain, Kalman & Quail Incorporated	**Foster & Marshall Inc.**	**Piper, Jaffray & Hopwood** Incorporated
Robertson, Colman, Stephens & Woodman	**Shuman, Agnew & Co., Inc.**	**Sutro & Co.** Incorporated

Wedbush, Noble, Cooke, Inc. Morgan, Olmstead, Kennedy & Gardner Seidler, Arnett & Spillane
Incorporated   Incorporated

January 24, 1979

tion, of course, reaches a somewhat different reader. The ad is simply an announcement and must carry the statement, as the ad in Exhibit 3-3 does:

> *This announcement is neither an offer to sell nor a solicitation of an offer to buy any of these securities. The offering is made only by the Prospectus.*

Just prior to the date the registration statement becomes effective the team meets again for a *due diligence meeting.* The purpose of the meeting is to share information regarding the registration which may affect the involvement of other members of the team—to make sure that all parties (especially the underwriters) who can be held liable for violations of the securities laws or SEC requirements have all the information required to support their involvement in the offering. The underwriter's agreement is signed around this time, the counsel submits his opinion, and the independent accountant delivers his letter to the underwriter. (These matters will be explained in greater detail.)

Once the registration statement becomes effective, on the *closing date,* the corporation officers deliver the securities to the underwriter. If the terms of the underwriter's agreement are a firm commitment, the corporation receives the proceeds of the sale, less the underwriter's spread and expenses. Otherwise the proceeds depend on the results of the sale. The expenses of a public offering are not limited to those incurred by and on behalf of the underwriter. Others are incurred by the corporation directly. A brief summary of expenses follows:

1. The underwriter's spread and out-of-pocket expenses.
2. Legal fees.
3. Independent accountant's fees.
4. Printing expenses.
5. Filing fees and expenses (SEC and the states in which the securities will be sold).
6. Insurance.
7. Transfer taxes.
8. Registrar fees.

A Closer Look at the Registration Process

The purpose of registration is to make public that information regarding the issuer which will allow investors to make competent decisions. The information must be adequate and otherwise not misleading. It is the purpose of the SEC review of the registration statement to evaluate the fairness of the information provided in the statement. No guarantee of the accuracy of the facts presented in the statement and no guarantee as to the safety of the investment is implied when the SEC allows a registration statement to become effective.

The registration process (summarized in Exhibit 3-4) begins with selecting and preparing the application (registration statement). Selection of the proper form is determined either by the nature of the registrant's business or the nature of the security interest. For example, companies in specialized lines of business such as closed-end management investment companies file on prescribed forms; com-

Exhibit 3-4   Flowchart of Registration Process

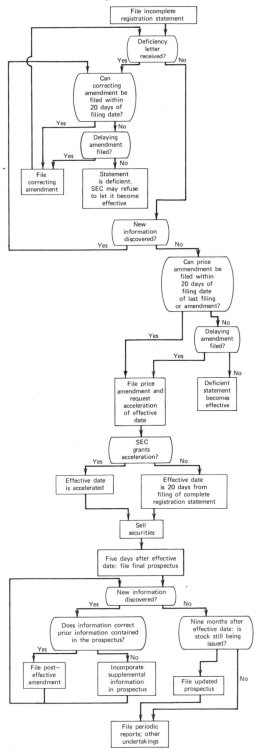

panies in nonproductive states of development may be required to report on a special form; securities offered to employees under stock option plans are also registered on a special form. The most common form, Form S-1, is a general-purpose application for all registrants for which no other form is prescribed.

The registrant files three complete copies of the registration statement and ten copies of the registration statement without exhibits (for use by the SEC staff), and pays a filing fee of one-fiftieth of one percent of the maximum aggregate offering price (or a minimum of $100). This preliminary registration statement is incomplete if it lacks the following information, which varies with fluctuations in the securities market:

1. The underwriter's commission.
2. The public offering price.
3. The expected proceeds.

Although the independent accountant's opinion letter that accompanies the preliminary prospectus is dated as of completion of the audit, the accountant has the responsibility for examining all events occurring up to the effective date of the registration statement. In order to meet this responsibility he makes a due diligence review of events occurring up to that date. (The features of the review will be discussed later).

The SEC Review   An officer of the Division of Corporate Finance reviews the application, assigns it to an examining team and recommends any one of four alternative review procedures:

1. CUSTOMARY REVIEW. The application receives a thorough examination.
2. SUMMARY REVIEW. The application receives an abbreviated review and the comment letter contains only deficiencies noted in the items examined. When this type of review is performed, the SEC informs the registrant and requires letters from the corporation's chief executive officer, the independent accountant, and the managing underwriter acknowledging the fact.
3. CURSORY REVIEW. The application receives an abbreviated review and a no-comment letter is prepared. This type of review also requires acknowledging letters from the above parties.
4. NO REVIEW AT ALL. A very poorly prepared application is not reviewed at all. With no further comment, the SEC notifies the registrant of the need to withdraw and resubmit the application.

Amendments   An application automatically becomes effective 20 days after the *filing date* unless the registrant files an amendment. Any amendment automatically begins the 20-day period anew. Although it gives S-1 applications top priority, the SEC rarely is able to issue its comment letter in the 20-day period. This makes it possible for a deficient statement to become effective and it is the responsibility of the registrant to prevent this from happening. In order to do so the registrant files a "delaying amendment" that postpones the effective date for the statutory period or longer.

Exhibit 3-5   Conditions Barring Acceleration

An indemnification provision in favor of a director, officer or controlling person exists.

An indemnification provision in favor of an underwriter exists.

The SEC is investigating any party related to the registration.

The underwriter is firmly committed to purchase securities and fails to meet the financial responsibility provisions of the 1934 Exchange Act.

Transactions in the securities of the company are occurring or have occurred which artificially affect the security price.

Preferred stock with par value substantially less than liquidating preference value (where retained earnings are not restricted) are being offered.

Part or all of the issue is being made by individual stockholders who are not paying their fair share of the expenses of issue.

If a deficiency letter is received, the issuer must file a "correcting amendment" before the statement is due to become effective or postpone the effective date with a delaying amendment if the corrections cannot be made in time. When the statement meets SEC requirements, the issuer files a "completing amendment" (the "price amendment") that contains the market information mentioned previously. Since the filing of this amendment begins the waiting period again, the issuer usually accompanies the price amendment with a request for acceleration. Barring the conditions listed in Exhibit 3-5, the SEC is likely to grant acceleration and the application takes effect. As discussed below, "post-effective amendments" are sometimes required.

Sales Activities Allowed   The Securities Act rigidly constrains sales activities by the issuer or his agents. It defines allowable sales activities in terms of three time periods: prefiling, waiting, and posteffective (Refer to Exhibit 3-6). The prefiling period is any time prior to the filing date. No sales activities are permitted during this period. The waiting period is the time between the filing and effective dates when the limited sales activities shown in Exhibit 3-6 may take place. The posteffective period begins on the effective date when the full range of legal sales activities can begin.

Completing the Registration Process.   The issuer's responsibility to update the registration statement ends on the effective date. He files 25 copies of the final prospectus, complete in all respects, five days after the effective date. In two cases posteffective amendments must be filed:

1. If the issue is unsold after nine months and sales activities continue, the prospectus must be updated.
2. If events occur that affect information contained in the prospectus, it must be updated with a posteffective amendment or with "supplemental information."

Exhibit 3-6   Sales Activities Regulated by the Securities Act

Period	Activities		
	Prohibited Sales	Permissible Sales	Others
Prefiling	• To offer or sell securities until a registration statement is filed.	• None.	• Organize underwriter group. • Notify stockholders of the company's intent to issue rights.
Waiting (Period between filing and effective dates)	• To carry or transmit a prospectus after the registration statement is filed unless the prospectus meets Section 10 requirements.	• Distribute "red herring" prospectus. • Advertise by means of a "tombstone ad." • Accept oral offers.	• Amend and complete the registration statement.
Post-effective	• To sell securities until a registration statement is effective. • To carry for purpose of sale or delivery a security unless a prospectus accompanies or has preceeded delivery.	• Distribute final prospectus. • Distribute supplemental selling material. • Accept written offers. • Confirm sales. • Issue the securities to purchasers.	• File 25 copies of the final prospectus with the SEC.

Finally, when filing the registration statement, the issuer agrees to the *undertakings* listed in Exhibit 3-7, that is, he undertakes to do them if and when necessary.

LIABILITY UNDER THE SECURITIES ACT

The Securities Act establishes civil liability under Section 11 for filing materially false or misleading information, and criminal liability under Section 17 for prohibited acts related to the issuing of securities. Criminal prosecution of accountants is relatively rare; usually SEC administrative powers are effected to discipline professionals practicing before the Commission. (This topic will be discussed in Chapter 8). On the other hand, civil provisions of the Securities Act anticipated the general trend of investor litigation by laying the responsibility for misleading financial statements on the parties involved in their preparation (as in common law actions in which damages suffered from the purchase of a defective automobile no longer are recovered from the dealer, but are recovered from the manufacturer), and by holding preparers responsible to more and more categories of users of financial statements.

Privity

To understand the impact that securities laws have had on the civil liability of accountants, it is necessary first to understand the common law concept of "priv-

Exhibit 3-7   The Issuer's Undertakings to:

- Supplement the prospectus after the subscription period stating:
  1. The results of the subscription offer (e.g. the number of shares sold).
  2. Transactions by underwriters during the subscription period.
  3. The amount of unsubscribed securities to be purchased by underwriters.
  4. The terms of any subsequent offering.
- File an amendment stating the terms of the underwriters' offer.
- Provide supplementary and periodic information,ndocuments and reports as required by the Securities Exchange Act, Section 13, for listed and registered securities if:
  1. The aggregate value of securities registered is $2,000,000 or more. And
  2. The value does not fall below $1,000,000 outstanding as determined by the offering price for the last issue.
  3. The requirement is suspended if:
     a. The company must file similar information for other reasons. Or
     b. The number of stockholders falls below 300.
- Offer to the public securities which were offered to existing stockholders but not subscribed to by them.
- File an amendment to reflect results of bidding (and terms of any reoffering unless no reoffering will be made) when securities are to be offered in competitive bidding.

ity.'' Under common law the accountant could be held liable for damages caused by his negligence only if the damages were sustained by his client. The classic case illustrating this concept is *Ultramares Corporation* v. *Touche, 1931* (refer to Appendix B for brief statements of the legal issues involved in this case and other significant court decisions). More recently the concept of privity in the contractual relationship has been extended *(Rusch Factors, Inc.,* v. *Levin, 1968)* to include parties whom the auditors could ''foresee'' would depend upon the statements. This extension of privity includes bankers and creditors.

The Securities Act abandons the common law principle of privity between contracting parties. The Ultramares opinion, written by Judge Cardozo,[1] was prophetic in anticipating the statutory change in the principle of privity. It read, in part:

The assault upon the citadel of privity is proceeding in these days apace. . . . From the foregoing analysis the conclusion is, we think, inevitable that nothing in our previous decisions commits us to a holding of liability for negligence in the circumstances of the case at hand, and that such liability, if recognized, will be an extension of the principle of those decisions to different conditions, even if more or less analogous. The question then is whether such an extension shall be made. . . . Many also are the cases that have distinguished between the willful or reckless representation essential to the maintenance at law of an action for deceit, and the misrepresentation, negligent or innocent, that will lay a sufficient basis for rescission in equity. If [the Ultramares] action is well conceived, all these principles and distinctions, so nicely wrought and formulated, have been a waste of time and effort. . . . A change so revolutionary, if expedient, must be wrought by legislation. *(Authors' emphasis)*

Civil Liability

Section 11. (a) In case any part of the registration statement, when such part became effective, contained an untrue statement of a material fact or omitted to state a material fact required to be stated therein or necessary to make the statements therein not misleading, any person acquiring such security (unless it is proved that at the time of such acquisition he knew of such untruth or omission) may, either at law or in equity, in any court of competent jurisdiction, sue. . . .

Today, the accountant's liability extends to any purchaser of securities who suffers damages that are traceable to the original issue and to a flaw in the registration statement, and who was ignorant of any untruth or omission in the effective registration statement at the time of purchase. If the statement contains a material misstatement of fact or omits a material fact required to make the statement not misleading, the injured investor may sue at law or in equity in the federal district court which has jursidiction in the matter.

The test of materiality is a subjective one in which the criterion is whether that omission or misstatement is sufficient to alter the decision of a reasonable investor in such a way that it could affect the value of the securities.

Civil action can be taken against any of the following parties involved in the preparation of the financial statements:

1. Every person who signed the registration statement.
2. Every person who was a director of or partner in the issue, or any person performing similar functions on the date that the part of the registration statement in question was filed.
3. Every consenting person who is named in the registration statement as being or about to become a director or partner or person performing similar functions.
4. Every consenting accountant, engineer, or appraiser or any person who is named as having prepared or certified a part of the registration statement or any report or valuation used in connection with the registration statement, and whose profession give authority to a statement made by him.
5. Every underwriter with respect to the security. The liability of each underwriter is limited to his participation in the offering. That is, an investor who purchased securities from one of several participating underwriters can seek recourse only from the underwriter(s) who actually participated in selling his securities.

Because *experts* such as accountants are directly responsible for statements made in the registration statement, the law holds the expert liable only for that part of the registration statement that purports to have been prepared or "certified" by him. The SEC requires that the registrant submit a *letter of consent* in order to protect the expert from unauthorized use of his name to establish the fact that he did consent to the association of his name with the portion of the statement in question, and to permit him to define the precise limits of his responsibility. (The accountant's consent letter will be discussed in detail in Chapter 8.)

Common law places the burden of proof on the plaintiff, whereas the Securities Act reverses the procedure and places the burden of proof on the accused whose defenses in proving his innocence are that:

1. Before the effective date of the registration statement he had resigned or attempted to resign from the office in which he was named as a liable party and he had informed the SEC of his action.
2. He had made reasonable public notice of the fact and had informed the SEC if the registration statement or any part thereof had become effective without his knowledge.
3. As regards any portion of the registration statement for which he had not consented to be named, he believed, based on a reasonable investigation, that the statement was true and not misleading.
4. As regards the portion of the registration statement for which he had consented to be named, at the time the registration statement became effective:
    a. He believed, based on a reasonable investigation, that the statement was true and not misleading. Or
    b. That the portion did not fairly represent his statement as an expert (it was not a fair copy of or quote from his report).

Only under the following condition must the plaintiff prove that he acquired the security by relying on an untrue statement or omission in the registration statement (although he does not have to establish proof that he read the statement):

If the issuer has made generally available to its security holders an income statement covering a period of at least twelve months beginning after the effective date of the registration statement.

The accountant is liable for damages suffered by a purchaser of securities either jointly, with other liable parties, or individually. That is, all liable parties must bear their share of compensation to the injured purchaser if they are able to do so, and if they are not, the other(s) must bear the full burden of compensation owed by all liable parties. As is often the case where the accountant's ability to pay damages is greater than the other liable parties, the liability for damages can be very great indeed.

Damages are calculated as the difference between the amount paid for the security (but not exceeding the offering price) and:

Exhibit 3-8   Calculation of Damages

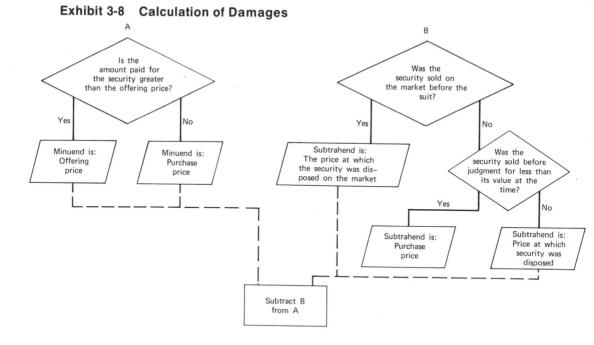

1. Its value at the time of the suit.
2. The price at which it was disposed of on the market before the suit.
3. The price at which it was disposed of on the market after the suit but before judgment (if greater than no. 1 above).

Exhibit 3-8 charts the process of calculating damages.

Criminal Liability

Section 24 establishes criminal penalties for anyone who: . . . *willfully, in a registration statement filed under [the Securities Act], makes any untrue statement of a material fact or omits to state any material fact required to . . . make the statements therein not misleading. . . .*

The same criminal penalties are in effect for violations of the antifraud provisions of Section 17.

Section 17

(a)   It shall be unlawful for any person in the offer or sale of any securities by the use of any means or instruments of transportation or communication in interstate commerce or by the use of the mails, directly or indirectly . . .

1.   to employ any device, scheme, or artifice to defraud, or

2.   to obtain money or property by means of any untrue statement of a material fact or any omission to state a material fact necessary in order to make the statements made, in the light of the circumstances under which they were made, not misleading, or

3. *to engage in any transaction, practice, or course of business which operates or would operate as a fraud or deceit upon the purchaser.*

Accountants are liable under Section 17 of the Securities Act for:

1. Making false statements,
2. Failure to give material information, and
3. Failure to comply with the provisions of the act.

The law also makes it illegal to publicize a security for a consideration without disclosing the fact of that consideration. Section 17 continues:

(b) It shall be unlawful for any person, by the use of any means or instruments of transportation or communication in interstate commerce or by the use of the mails, to publish, give publicity to, or circulate any notice, circular, advertisement, newspaper, article, letter, investment service, or communication which, though not purporting to offer a security for sale, describes such security for a consideration received or to be received, directly or indirectly, from an issuer, underwriter, or dealer, without fully disclosing the receipt, whether past or prospective, of such consideration and the amount thereof.

Section 24 establishes the penalties upon conviction for fraudulent acts:

1. A fine of up to $10,000.
2. Imprisonment of not more than five years.
3. Both.

Fraudulent activities in issuing securities also are prosecuted under provisions of the Criminal Code relating to perjury, aiding and abetting, and under provisions of the Federal Mail Fraud, and the Conspiracy and False Statements statutes.

EXEMPTIONS

There are several categories of exemptions from the requirement to register an offering. Exemptions allowed by *law* are:

Section 3. *Exempted Securities.*
Section 4. *Exempted Transactions.*

Issues of securities exempted by law may be made with no notification to the SEC. Other exemptions are granted by the SEC under its "administrative" powers and are found in *The General Rules and Regulations under the Securities Act of 1933*. They are:

The "No Sale" Rule (Rule 145).
Miscellaneous exemptions (Rules 234–237).
Exemptions by regulation (Regulations A, B, E, and F).

The SEC takes several matters into consideration in determining whether a security conforms to the exemptions criteria:

1. The "ultimate" distribution of the securities (whether a restricted issue can be expected to be sold to the public eventually).
2. The capacity of the purchaser to obtain reliable information similar to that contained in the prospectus.
3. The need to integrate, that is, whether, for purposes of observing the intent of the law, separate security offerings should be combined and treated as one offering. Security offerings issued at different times and securities which are different in nature may be integrated into one offering.

Exempted Securities

Types of securities are exempted either because they are regulated under the provisions of other acts (e.g., the Banking Act of 1933), or because they do not have a potentially significant impact on the welfare of the general public.[2]

Exempted Transactions

The Securities Act pertains only to securities sold in interstate and foreign commerce and through the mails; that is, the act excludes *intrastate* issues from the requirement to register.

The law also exempts from registration transactions that are made by:

1. Any person other than an issuer, underwriter, or dealer (Rule 144).
2. A dealer after 40 days have elapsed from the first date the security was offered to the public, or 40 days after the effective date of a registration statement, whichever is later. (The period is 90 days for first-time issues.) Securities that are part of an unsold allotment or subscription do not meet this exemption.
3. Brokers, executed upon customers' orders on any exchange or over-the-counter market, but not the solicitation of such orders.
4. An issue not involving any public offering (the "private offering"). (Rule 146 defines "private offering").
5. An offer or sale of one or more promissory notes directly secured by a first lien on a single parcel of real estate on which is a residential and commercial structure.

The most important of these transactions from the accountant's standpoint is the private placement, Number 4 on page 72.[3]

No Sale Rule

When stockholders vote to approve a merger, consolidation, reclassification of securities, or a proposal to transfer assets in exchange for securities, there is no sale of securities (Refer to Rule 145).

Miscellaneous Exemptions

The SEC periodically determines that certain transactions, while technically falling within the letter of the law, in practice do not affect the public. Therefore it has exempted: certain first lien notes (Rule 234): securities of cooperative housing corporations (Rule 235); securities sold in order to provide funds for existing shareholders in lieu of fractional shares, etc. (Rule 235); and certain securities owned for five years or more that have been *restricted* (Rule 237).[4]

Exemptions by Regulation

Issuers whose offerings are exempted by regulation file a *notification* form with the SEC.[5] We will discuss only the process of notifying the SEC of a public issue under Regulation A. The process is similar to the registration process itself. Lately, Regulation A filings have been used less frequently because the cost of offering securities in this manner does not warrant the low sales price of a small offering. A recent study by the SEC indicated that the average expenses of a small offering were $125,000 (Refer to Exhibit 3-9 for statistics regarding Regulation A filings.) The decreasing use of Form 1-A, as shown in the exhibit may change now that Congress has increased the maximum offering price for a Regulation A issue.

REGULATION A

Regulation A, the small offering exemption, applies to issues of securities whose aggregate sales price to the ultimate investor does not exceed $1½ million. Whether or not a small offering qualifies for Regulation A treatment depends on such factors as the need to integrate other issues with the current offering in order to determine whether the total sales price exceeds the maximum, that is, the sales price to the ultimate distributee, not the proceeds to the issuer. Also, the existence of certain conditions that bar the availability of the exemption are considered. For example, if the issuer, within the last five years, has been convicted of any crime or offense involving the purchase or sale of securities, the exemption is not available.

The process of notifying the SEC of the pending Regulation A offering and the

Exhibit 3-9 Offerings Under Regulation A

		Fiscal Year		
	1976	1975	1974	1973
Size				
$100,000 or less	24	28	40	69
$100,000–$200,000	36	42	79	107
$200,000–$300,000	27	39	66	96
$300,000–$400,000	39	24	39	86
$400,000–$500,000	114	132	214	459
Total	240	265	438	817
Underwriters				
Used	37	44	115	402
Not Used	203	221	323	416
Total	240	265	438	317
Offerors				
Issuing companies	222	227	394	787
Stockholders	12	7	34	18
Issuers and stockholders jointly	6	31	10	12
Total	240	265	438	817

SOURCE: *Annual Report of the SEC.* (Washington, D.C.: Superintendent of Documents, U.S. Government Printing Office), 1976, p. 203.

nature of prohibitions on sales activities are similar to that under a full registration. The three time periods—prefiling, waiting, and posteffective—are separated by two events: the filing of the notification and the expiration of a ten-day waiting period. Certain activities are prohibited during each of these periods. (Refer to Exhibit 3-10).[6] The SEC recently permitted the use of a preliminary offering circular between the date of filing a notification relating to an underwritten public offering of securities and the issue date in order to expedite the distribution of such securities.

In a Regulation A filing, the financial statements need not be audited. As a result the investor lacks the independent assurance that the financial statements are fairly presented which the auditor's opinion letter provides. As with large SEC registrations, management is responsible for seeing that the financial statements are not misleading. The notification becomes effective after the waiting period. If the SEC takes no action disallowing or suspending the exemption, the issue may take place.[7]

Special Rules

Special rules acknowledge that new and/or small issuers should not have to meet even the requirements of Regulation A. No offering circular is required to be

Exhibit 3-10   Regulation A Sales Activities

Period	Prohibited Sales	Permissible Sales	Other Required
		Activities	
Prefiling	• To offer or sell securities until the notification has been filed.	• None.	• Prepare and file Form 1-A.
Waiting (10 days)	• To distribute selling material except the preliminary offering circular	• To accept oral offers.	• File 4 copies of sales material (circular) five days prior to use.
Post-effective	• To make written offers unaccompanied by an offering circular. • To confirm a sale or accept payment before delivery of an offering circular.	• Full legal sales activities.	• File Form 2-A reporting the sales made under the issue at completion of the offer or every six months until sold. • File a revised circular if the issue is not completed after nine months.

filed or used where an offering is for less than $50,000; and the maximum issue allowed in one year is $100,000 if an offering is made by or on behalf of a person other than the issuer or a decedent's estate within two years of death. Finally, newly organized companies and those without a history of net income for at least one of the last two years may issue their own securities, but other parties dealing in the issue are not eligible for a Regulation A exemption. Offering circulars for those organizations must be used regardless of the size of the issue and certain additional securities must be included in computing the aggregate sales price.

SUMMARY   The Securities Act governs virtually all initial public transactions in debt and ownership securities. It requires registration with the SEC via a registration statement for all but certain exempt securities and types of transactions, and limits the kind of sales activities that legally may occur.

The registration statement consists of Part I, the prospectus, and Part II, technical information that is not needed by the investing public. The SEC may perform either a regular review, a cursory review, a summary review, or no review at all on the registration statement. Because it becomes effective automatically 20 days after the latest filing, the issuer usually must file sufficient amendments to delay the *effective date* and to correct and complete the application. Permissible sales activities are determined by the three time periods—prefiling, waiting, and posteffective. Only in the posteffective time period can written orders be accepted, sales be consummated and securities be delivered.

The parties who participate directly in a registration and offering are the issuing corporation and its directors, the underwriters, legal counsel, accountants, engineers, appraisers, and other experts. Any and all of the above bear civil and criminal liability for omissions and misstatements of fact in the registration statement, for fraudulent acts related to the sale of securities, and for noncompliance with reporting requirements.

In addition to exemptions granted by law, the SEC, under its administrative powers, has excused certain other categories of securities from the need to register and describes them in *The General Rules and Regulations under the Securities Act of 1933* and in Regulations A, B, E, and F.

Regulation A, the small offering exemption, is available for offerings not to exceed 1.5 million. The process of notifying the SEC under this regulation is similar to that of a full registration, except that audited financial statements are not required. Sales activities are constrained by the same three time periods as for large SEC registrations. The waiting period under Regulation A, however, is ten days instead of the 20 days required for full registration.

FOOTNOTES FOR CHAPTER 3

[1]*Ultramares Corporation* v. *Touche.* [255 N.Y. 170 (1931)].

[2]The following types of securities have been exempted by law from the requirement to register:

- Securities issued or guaranteed by the federal government and its authorized instrumentalities, by any territory or state or political subdivision or public instrumentality thereof, or any certificate of deposit for same.
- Securities issued or guaranteed by the Federal Reserve Bank.
- Securities (except any interest or participation in a collective trust fund) issued or guaranteed by any national or state bank whose business is primarily banking.
- Industrial development bonds not exceeding $5 million.
- Certain interests or participations in a single or collective trust fund managed by a bank or in a separate account managed by an insurance company issued in connection with a specified type of bonus, pension, profit sharing, or annuity plan.
- Short term paper (notes, drafts, etc.) with a maturity not exceeding nine months.
- Securities issued by nonprofit, religious, charitable, and other eleemosynary organizations.
- Certain securities issued by a building and loan or savings and loan association, cooperative bank, homestead association, or farmers' cooperative.
- Securities issued by a common or contract carrier subject to Section 20a of the Interstate Commerce Act.
- Certificates issued by a trustee or receiver in bankruptcy with the approval of the court.
- Insurance policies, endowment policies, or annuities issued by an organization subject to government supervision.
- Securities wholly exchanged with existing security holders where no commission or remuneration is paid: cash may change hands only to adjust transactions to nearest whole interests.
- Securities issued in a reorganization approved by a court or governmental authority.
- Securities that are part of an offer and sale made between parties domiciled within the same state (Rule 147).

[3]Whether an offering can be considered "private" hinges on these criteria:

1. The number of offerees and the closeness of their relationship to each other. The guideline figure of 15 individuals has generally been considered to be the maximum number.

2. The prospective purchasers' need for, and the availability of information similar to that provided in the prospectus.
3. The number of units sold. (The issue of many units of small denomination indicates the possibility of a subsequent reissue.)
4. The size of the offering. (The issue of many units of a type previously registered and traded indicate the possibility of a subsequent reissue.)
5. The manner of offering. (The use of an underwriter indicates a public offering.)
6. An "investment letter" indicating that the intention of each purchaser is to invest, not trade in the securities. (The letter supports a case for private offering, but is not proof positive.)
7. An agreement between the issuer and the purchaser(s) giving the issuer right of first refusal in the event that the securities are resold. (The agreement supports a case for a private offering, but is not *prima facie* evidence.)
8. The issue of warrants or options would prejudice the determination of a private offering because the issuer maintains an outstanding obligation over a long period of time.

[4]Sales of restricted securities (securities acquired in nonpublic offering) in any three-month period are limited to no more than 500 shares and a maximum sales price of $10,-000. This rule permits persons purchasing securities in a private offering to enjoy a measure of liquidity in securities purchased primarily for investment purposes.

[5]Offerings exempted by regulation are as follows:

* Regulation A. Small offerings (Form 1-A).
* Regulation B. Certain fractional undivided interests in oil or gas rights (Form 1-B).
* Regulation E. Securities of small business investment companies that are regulated under the Investment Companies Act of 1940 and licensed under the Small Business Investment Company Act of 1958 (Form 1-E).
* Regulation F. Assessments and assessable stock offered or sold to realize the amount of an assessment levied thereon or reoffered to the public by an underwriter or dealer, where the issue does not exceed $300,000 per annum (Form 1-F).

[6]Information supplied by the issuer in the notification includes:

1. The names of predecessor corporations, affiliates, principal security holders, directors, officers, and promoters.
2. All information that will enable the SEC to determine whether the exemption is applicable.
3. The jurisdictions in which the securities are to be offered.
4. An offering circular (similar in function to the prospectus) that includes the following information:
   a. The offering price.
   b. Specified financial statements that need not be audited and on which an auditor's report need not be made.
   c. The purposes for the proceeds.
   d. A description of the securities offered.
   e. A description of the business of the issuer.
   f. A description of the property of the issuer.
   g. Information regarding directors and officers and their remuneration.
5. Exhibits:
   a. Instruments defining holders' rights.
   b. Underwriting contracts.

    c. Written consent of experts whose names are used in connection with the offering.

    d. Consent of the underwriters to be named and their certification of the accuracy of the information contained in the notification.

[7]The SEC recently introduced a short registration form (S-18), for issues between $1.5 and $5 million in size which requires audited financial statements.

GLOSSARY

Class of Securities. A group of similar securities that give shareholders similar rights.

Closing Date. Effective date of a registration statement (Refer also to offering date).

Cooling-Off Period. The period between the filing and effective dates.

Due Diligence Meeting. A meeting of all parties to the preparation of a registration statement to assure that a high degree of care in investigation and independent verification of the company's representations has been made.

Effective Date. Twentieth day after the filing date of a registration statement or amendment there to, unless the Commission shortens or extends that time period.

Exempt Security. A security that does not have to be registered with the SEC.

Exempt Transaction. A transaction in securities that does not require registration with the SEC.

Expert. Any specialist (attorney, accountant, engineer, etc.) who participates in the preparation of a registration statement.

Filing Date. The date a registration statement is received by the SEC.

Indemnification Provision. An agreement protecting one party from liability arising from the occurrence of an unforeseeable event.

Letter of Consent. Written permission from participating experts to include their names in the registration statement.

Notification. Filing the terms (on Form 1-A) of an offering of securities that are exempt from registration with the SEC under Regulation A.

Offering Date. The date a new issue is presented for sale to the public.

Prefiling Conference. A meeting of corporate officers and experts outlining the SEC requirements for the filing of a registration statement. Occasionally a SEC staff member may attend.

Red Herring Prospectus. Preliminary prospectus with a statement, in red, on each page indicating that the security described has not become effective, that the information is subject to correction and change without notice, and is not an offer to buy or sell.

Restricted Security. "Private Offering" of an issue that cannot be resold to the public without prior registration. Also called investment letter securities for the letter that the purchaser of such securities must submit to the SEC stating that the securities are being acquired for investment purposes, not for immediate resale.

Sale. Every contract of sale, disposition, or offer of a security for value.

Selling Group. Several broker/dealers who distribute a new issue of securities at retail.

Solicitation. Any request for a proxy or other similar communication to security holders.

Spread. The difference between the price paid for a security by the underwriter and the selling price of that security.

Tombstone Ad. An announcement identifying the class, price, and underwriters of the security to be offered.

Undertaking. Agreement of registrant to furnish the SEC information required by the Commission's rules and regulations in the future.

Underwriting Agreement. Contract between the underwriting syndicate and the issuer stating the terms of a new issue.

QUESTIONS

1. Describe the relationship of the investment banker/underwriter to: the corporate issuer of securities; the purchasers of a new security issue.
2. Distinguish between a firm commitment and a best efforts contract of the underwriter.
3. Is the underwriting business risky? If so, why?
4. Assume that you are participating in a "preunderwriting" conference. What topics regarding the registration and marketing of a new issue would be discussed?
5. Are underwriters responsible to make a reasonable investigation of the accuracy of an issuer's registration statement through an independent verification of the issuer's representations?
6. For what part of a registration statement is the independent auditor responsible?
7. What is a "red herring" prospectus? What purpose does it serve?
8. Can a new security issue be registered if there is no intention to offer the issue to the public within a reasonable time following registration?
9. What is the difference between a civil and a criminal liability for securities acts violations?
10. List any three criminal violations of the statutes.
11. Can the independent auditor be held liable by the investors who buy the stock of an issuing corporation that he has audited?
12. Review and discuss the type and conditions for the exempted securities in Footnote 2.
13. Must an intra-state offering be registered with the SEC?
14. What is meant by notifying the SEC?
15. What is a due diligence meeting? Its purpose?
16. Does registration guarantee the accuracy of the facts represented in the registration statement and prospectus?
17. What is a deficiency letter?
18. Why must a prospectus be distributed to the prospective purchasers of a new securities offering?

Appendix

B

Legal Liability Under Common Law and the Securities Act of 1933

COMMON LAW

Ultramares Corporation v. Touche
New York Court of Appeals, 1931
255 N.Y. 170, 174 N.E. 441.

Action: In tort for damages suffered through the misrepresentations of accountants who were merely negligent and for misrepresentations charged to have been fraudulent.
Facts: Accountants issued an unqualified opinion on the balance sheet of their client. Plaintiff made loans to the client on the strength of the balance sheet. The company went bankrupt.
Decision: An auditor should not be held liable for simple negligence to anyone other than the party in privity—the client.

State Street Trust v. *Ernst,* 278.
Court of Appeals of New York, 1938.
278 N.Y. 104, 15 N.E. 2d 416.

Action: Auditor was charged with gross negligence.
Facts: Auditor certified a balance sheet on which the receivables were overstated. The auditor verified the receivables, but failed to detect the overstatement.
Decision: Auditor was negligent to such an extent as to amount to a reckless disregard for the accuracy necessary for a balance sheet to properly reflect the financial condition of the business.

Fischer v. Kletz (Yale Express)
United States District Court,
Southern District of New York, 1967.
266 F. Supp. 181.

Action: Plaintiffs (owners of shares of capital stock or debentures of Yale Express System, Inc.) to recover damages from the auditor and some of the former directors and officers of the corporation.

Facts: Accountant was engaged to perform special work and examine the financial statements for 3 years, 1962–1964, for purposes of a public offering of stock. The accountant's test for adequacy of the reserve for doubtful accounts included double counting of offsets and inclusion of liabilities as part of the reserve. Accountants were charged with negligence and constructive fraud in the preparation of false and misleading financial statements.

Decision: The court found no reasons to justify barring plaintiffs from the opportunity to prove a common law action of deceit against the accountant.

SECURITIES ACT OF 1933, SECTION 11—CIVIL CASES

National Surety Corp. v. *Lybrand*
Appellate Division, New York, 1939 256 App. Div.
226, 9 N.Y.S. 2d 554

Action: Defendant accountants were charged with: (1) failure to perform their audit properly; (2) negligence; (3) fraudulently misrepresenting material facts.

Facts: Accountants failed to discover and report substantial cash shortages during their audit.

Decision: Appellate court ruled that the accountants did not comply with generally accepted auditing standards for verifying cash in banks.

Rusch Factors, Inc. v. *Levin*
United States District Court, District
of Rhode Island, 1968.
284F Supp. 85

Action: Plaintiff claims injury as a result of reliance upon fraudulent or negligent misrepresentations in the financial statements certified by defendant accountant.

Facts: Plaintiff loaned a corporation money based upon certified financial statements which represented the corporation to be solvent when the corporation was in fact insolvent.

Decision: Privity of contract is no defense in a fraud action. An intentional misrepresentation by an accountant causes the accountant to be liable to all persons who could have been foreseen to be injured by his misrepresentation

Shonts v. *Hirlimans*
28 f. Supp. 478 Cal. 1939

Action: Plaintiffs alleged that they purchased stock on the basis of the registration statement and that the statement was false. They sued to recover their losses.

Facts: A lease was being negotiated at the date of the auditor's certificate, and the proposed $35,000 annual rental expense was not in the books.

Decision: Accountants were not held liable for failing to note a contingent liability which did not exist at the date of the certification. No firm contract between the lessor and lessee had been signed at the date of the accountants' certification.

Escott v. Barchris Construction Corporation
U.S. District Court, Southern District of New York, 1968
283 F. Supp. 643

Action: Plaintiffs alleged that the registration statement for an issue of debentures contained material false statements and omissions.

Facts: Capital Lanes, a bowling alley built by Bar Chris, was recorded as having been sold in a sale-lease back transaction when, in fact, it was not. This caused material errors in reported sales and computation of a contingent liability and, in addition, errors were made in the valuation of current assets. Company went bankrupt.

Decision: The accountants were held liable. The in-charge accountant was inexperienced, was too easily satisfied with glib answers to his questions and failed to conform to professional standards in performing a due diligence audit.

SECURITIES ACT OF 1933, SECTION 17—CRIMINAL CASES

United States v. White
124 F. 2d Circuit 181, 1941

Action: Accountant was charged with certifying misleading financial statements.

Facts: Inadequate allowances for doubtful receivables resulted in inflated profits.

Decision: The accountant was found liable. An experienced accountant should have been on notice as to the questionable nature of the receivables.

United States v. Benjamin
328 F. 2d Circuit 854, 1964

Action: Willfully conspired by use of the mails to defraud in the sale of unregistered securities.

Facts: Accountant prepared ''pro forma'' balance sheets: claimed he did not know the reports were to be used for purposes of stock sales.

Decisions: Defendant convicted. The accountant deliberately closed his eyes to facts he had a duty to see.

Getchell v. United States
282 F. 5th Circuit 681, 1960

Action: Against Getchell for fraud in the use of the mails.

Facts: Accountant overestimated profits in pro forma statements.

Decision: Conviction of accountant was reversed on insufficient evidence, the court ruling that the accountant was simply too optimistic about the company's future.

United States v. Bruce
U.S. Fifth Circuit Court of Appeals
488 F. 1224, 1973

Action: Against CPA where circumstantial evidence indicated the auditor knew of a fraudulent scheme of an insolvent issuer of investment securities.

Facts: Auditor certified the financial statements in two prospectuses; the information in which by intent was designed to deceive potential investors.

Decision: Accountant was convicted on two counts of fraud.

4 Trading Securities Under the Securities Exchange Act of 1934

Although the scope of the Securities Exchange Act is far-reaching, the independent accountant is involved to a significant degree in only three processes:

1. Obtaining listed status.
2. Filing periodic reports.
3. Soliciting proxies.

This chapter will discuss the ways in which the Securities Exchange Act affects each of these processes, the legal liabilities imposed by the act, and the many exemptions that have been granted by law or by the SEC.

OBTAINING LISTED STATUS (SECTION 12)

Six and four-tenths billion shares were traded on the stock exchanges in 1975 (Refer to Exhibit 4-1); the dollar value of trading aggregated more than $157 billion; 1.4 billion shares were traded in the over-the-counter market. This volume accounts for virtually all secondary trading in securities. Without the liquidity offered by this market mechanism few issuers would find purchasers for their securities. Therefore, the process of *going public* is closely related to the process of applying for listed status on one or more of the exchanges or registering for trading in the over-the-counter system.

The Process of Obtaining Listed Status

Obtaining listed status on a national securities exchange is a twofold process (Refer to Exhibit 4-2):

1. The corporation submits an *application for listing* to the exchange on which it wishes its securities traded.
2. It files duplicates of the listing application and a registration statement with the SEC.

Exhibit 4-1   Volume of Securities Transactions

Share Volume by Exchanges[a]

Year	Total Shares Volume (thousands)	NYSE	AMEX	MSE	PSE	PHLX	BSE	DSE	CSE	Other[b]
1935	681,971	73.13	12.42	1.91	2.69	1.10	0.96	0.85	0.03	6.91
1940	377,897	75.44	13.20	2.11	2.78	1.33	1.19	0.82	0.08	3.05
1945	769,018	65.87	21.31	1.77	2.98	1.06	0.66	0.79	0.05	5.51
1950	893,320	76.32	13.54	2.16	3.11	0.97	0.65	0.55	0.09	2.61
1955	1,321,401	68.85	19.19	2.09	3.08	0.85	0.48	0.39	0.05	5.02
1960	1,428,552	69.08	22.46	2.22	3.14	0.89	0.39	0.34	0.04	1.41
1961	2,121,050	65.65	25.84	2.24	3.45	0.80	0.30	0.31	0.04	1.33
1962	1,699,346	71.84	20.26	2.36	2.97	0.87	0.31	0.36	0.04	0.95
1963	1,874,718	73.17	18.89	2.33	2.83	0.83	0.29	0.47	0.04	1.10
1964	2,118,326	72.81	19.42	2.43	2.65	0.93	0.29	0.54	0.03	0.86
1965	2,663,495	70.10	22.59	2.63	2.34	0.82	0.26	0.53	0.05	0.64
1966	3,306,386	69.54	22.89	2.57	2.68	0.86	0.40	0.45	0.05	0.51
1967	4,641,215	64.48	28.45	2.36	2.46	0.87	0.43	0.33	0.02	0.57
1968	5,406,582	62.00	29.74	2.63	2.65	0.89	0.78	0.31	0.01	0.95
1969	5,133,498	63.17	27.61	2.84	3.47	1.22	0.51	0.12	0.00	1.00
1970	4,835,222	71.27	19.02	3.16	3.68	1.63	0.51	0.10	0.02	0.57
1971	6,172,668	71.34	18.42	3.52	3.72	1.91	0.43	0.15	0.03	0.44
1972	6,518,132	70.47	18.22	3.71	4.13	2.21	0.59	0.15	0.03	0.45
1973	5,899,678	74.92	13.75	4.09	3.68	2.19	0.71	0.18	0.04	0.39
1974	4,950,833	78.47	10.27	4.39	3.48	1.82	0.86	0.19	0.04	0.44
1975	6,371,545	81.05	8.97	4.06	3.10	1.54	0.85	0.11	0.13	0.15

Table Dollar Volume by Exchanges[c]

Year	Total Dollar Volume (thousands)	NYSE	AMEX	MSE	PSE	PHLX	BSE	DSE	CSE	Other[d]
1935	15,396,139	86.64	7.83	1.32	1.39	0.88	1.34	0.40	0.04	0.16
1940	8,419,772	85.17	7.68	2.07	1.52	1.11	1.91	0.36	0.09	0.09
1945	16,284,552	82.75	10.81	2.00	1.78	0.96	1.16	0.35	0.06	0.13
1950	21,808,284	85.91	6.85	2.35	2.19	1.03	1.12	0.39	0.11	0.05
1955	38,039,107	86.31	6.98	2.44	1.90	1.03	0.78	0.39	0.09	0.08
1960	45,276,616	83.86	9.35	2.72	1.95	1.04	0.60	0.34	0.07	0.03
1961	64,032,924	82.48	10.71	2.75	1.99	1.03	0.49	0.37	0.07	0.05
1962	54,823,153	86.37	6.81	2.75	2.00	1.05	0.46	0.41	0.07	0.04
1963	64,403,991	85.23	7.52	2.72	2.39	1.06	0.42	0.51	0.06	0.04
1964	72,415,297	83.54	8.46	3.15	2.48	1.14	0.42	0.66	0.06	0.04
1965	89,498,711	81.82	9.91	3.44	2.43	1.12	0.42	0.70	0.08	0.03
1966	123,643,475	79.81	11.84	3.14	2.85	1.10	0.56	0.57	0.07	0.02

Exhibit 4-1 (Continued)

Share Volume by Exchanges[a]

Year	Total Shares Volume (thousands)	In Percentage								
		NYSE	AMEX	MSE	PSE	PHLX	BSE	DSE	CSE	Other[b]
1967	162,136,387	77.31	14.48	3.08	2.79	1.13	0.67	0.43	0.03	0.03
1968	197,061,776	73.57	18.00	3.12	2.66	1.13	1.04	0.35	0.01	0.08
1969	176,343,146	73.50	17.60	3.39	3.12	1.43	0.67	0.12	0.01	0.12
1970	131,707,946	78.44	11.11	3.76	3.81	1.99	0.67	0.11	0.03	0.04
1971	186,375,130	79.07	9.98	4.00	3.79	2.29	0.58	0.18	0.05	0.03
1972	205,956,263	77.77	10.37	4.29	3.94	2.56	0.75	0.17	0.05	0.05
1973	178,863,622	82.07	6.06	4.54	3.55	2.45	1.00	0.21	0.06	0.01
1974	118,828,272	83.62	4.39	4.89	3.50	2.02	1.23	0.22	0.06	0.01
1975	157,555,360	85.04	3.65	4.82	3.25	1.72	1.18	0.12	0.17	0.00

[a]Share Volume for Exchanges includes Stocks, Rights, and Warrants.
[b]Others include Intermountain, Spokane, National, and Honolulu Stock Exchanges.
[c]Dollar Volume for Exchanges includes Stocks, Rights, and Warrants.
[d]Others include Intermountain, Spokane, National, and Honolulu Stock Exchanges.
SOURCE: 1976 Annual Report of the SEC (Washington, D.C.: Superintendent of Documents, U.S. Government Printing Office, 1976), p. 194.

Listing is a simpler process than registering a new issue of securities with the SEC under the Securities Act because underwriters need not be involved, time considerations associated with marketing usually are not as compelling, and detailed reporting requirements are absent. As we shall see in Chapter 7 the registration form for listing is a condensed version of Form S-1; the items of information that it includes are enumerated in Section 12(b) of the 1934 Act. Because the initial issue of securities is not offered on an exchange, the issuer does not have to obtain listed status in order to issue securities—only in order to provide a market for their subsequent trading.

The registration statement and listing application usually are prepared by the registrant and its counsel. Each exchange has its own requirements and application form. The staffs of the exchanges assist corporations by reviewing applications while they are in draft form and suggesting corrections. The applicant is able to incorporate these corrections before printing the application and submitting it to the formal listing committee of the exchange. The committee evaluates the application and signifies its approval by certifying its acceptance of application with the SEC.

The SEC registration may be filed prior to, concurrent with, or subsequent to applying for listing. Companies that have not registered any security under the Securities Exchange Act file a more detailed registration form than companies that have previously registered at least one class of securities. The former applicants file Form 10, the general form for securities registration, whereas the latter file Form 8A, under Section 13 or 15(d).

Exhibit 4-2 The Process of Obtaining Listed Status

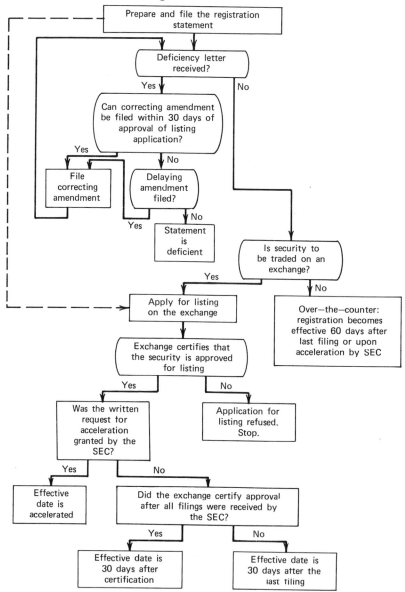

The SEC reviews the registration form and issues a comment letter if it finds that the application is deficient. Since under Section 12(d), the registration cannot become effective until 30 days after the exchange certifies its application, the danger of a defective form becoming effective through the expiration of time is not as great as it is with registration under the Securities Act. If this could happen, however, the registrant files a delaying amendment. The SEC has the power to accelerate the effective date of a registration once the exchange has approved the listing and the registrant has submitted a written request. The exchange is autonomous with respect to corporate listings. Should the exchange refuse to certify a security for listing after all steps have been taken to comply with its requirements, the Secutiries Exchange Act provides no recourse. The issuer can submit an application for listing to another exchange, however, or the securities can be traded over-the-counter.

Over-the-Counter Securities

The Securities Exchange Act was amended in 1964 to require the registration of securities traded over-the-counter if the total assets of the issuer are in excess of $1 million or 500 or more persons at any fiscal year-end hold any one class of equity security. The registration is filed with the SEC on the same forms as are used for a listed security and automatically becomes effective 60 days after the last filing. As with all filings, an amendment initiates a new 60-day waiting period.

FILING PERIODIC REPORTS (SECTION 13)

Section 13 of the Securities Exchange Act authorizes the SEC to require registrants to file annual reports and such documents as are needed to keep information in the registration statement reasonably current. It requires that duplicates of these reports also be filed with any exchange on which the securities are listed. The SEC may determine

> "... the form or forms in which the required information shall be set forth, the items or details to be shown in the balance sheet and the earnings statement, and the methods to be followed in the preparation of reports, in the appraisal or valuation of assets and liabilities, in the determination of depreciation and depletion, in the differentiation of recurring and nonrecurring income, and in the preparation, where the Commission deems it necessary or desirable, of separate and/or consolidated balance sheets or income accounts of any person directly or indirectly controlling or controlled by the issuer, or any person under direct or indirect common control with the issuer. ..."[1]

It also authorizes the SEC to require that the financial statements so filed bear the opinion of an independent accountant. Section 15(d) extends these reporting requirements to all issuers of securities registered under the Securities Act, but suspends reporting requirements for issuers whose securities are held by less than 300 persons at the beginning of the year. In addition, the SEC, under its administrative powers, requires that annual reports, quarterly reports for the first three fiscal quarters, current reports of certain events, and amendments of previously filed documents be filed by all registrants whose securities are traded on national securities exchanges or over-the-counter.

Annual Reports

The primary and most detailed of the periodic reports is the *Annual Report to the SEC*. The most common form used for annual reporting is Form 10-K (discussed in detail in Chapter 7). It is filed with the SEC no later than 90 days after the close of the fourth quarter of the fiscal year. Supporting schedules required by Regulation S-X may be filed by amendment up to 120 days following the fiscal year-end.

Form 10-K requires that the supporting schedules filed with the financial statements be audited. Some independent accountants, therefore, modify the scope paragraph of their opinion to specifically include the schedules and additional footnotes. Others simply refer to the financial statements without specifically enumerating them or mentioning the footnotes and schedules.

Quarterly Reports

Quarterly, or interim, reports are filed 45 days after the close of the first, second, and third quarters and are a recent reporting innovation, replacing the semi-annual report in 1970. Registrants also have issued stockholders' quarterly reports since 1976. Both reports are brief, but conform to the accounting standards set forth by the profession for interim reports in *APB Opinion No. 28*.

Although the independent accountant may assist with the preparation of the quarterly filing, he performs no audit and therefore assumes only limited responsibility. *Statement on Auditing Standard No. 24* defines the nature of the limited review given by the auditor in such cases. (Form 10-Q, the quarterly report to the SEC, will be discussed in Chapter 7)

Current Report—Form 8-K

Certain significant events have great potential impact on the future of a company and on the value of its securities. Therefore, the investing public has a need to be informed promptly when they occur. Form 8-K must be filed no later than 15 days after the date on which any of the following specified events occur, unless a previous report has been filed with the SEC that contains substantially the same information:

ITEM 1   Changes in control of the registrant.

ITEM 2   Acquisition or disposition of a significant amount of assets other than in the ordinary course of business.

ITEM 3   The appointment of a receiver of the registrant in a bankruptcy or similar proceeding.

ITEM 4   Changes in the registrant's certifying accountant.

A fifth item is a voluntary disclosure item. The registrant may report any event that it deems to be of material importance to security holders and that is not otherwise called for in Items 1 to 4. An Item 5 event must be reported within ten days after the end of the month during which the event occurred.

Item 4 is of particular importance to accountants. Because a change of auditors is often symptomatic of a serious disagreement between the registrant and its auditors as to disclosure in the financial statements, the SEC requires the filing of not only the Form 8-K, but also of a separate letter from the registrant disclosing any disagreements with the former auditor over accounting principles and a letter from the succeeded independent accountant that, in effect, confirms or disputes management's account of the disagreement.

These provisions considerably enhance the accountant's authority to assert his independence. The accountant's response is due within 30 days after the 8-K is filed; it will be discussed in Chapter 8.

The accountant's role in Form 8-K filings depends upon the nature of the event that is being reported. In all events the independent accountant obtains a copy of the filing and reviews it for information that affects his opinion regarding financial statements or that will affect his future involvement with the client. Items 1, 3, and 5 usually require no other auditor involvement in the filing.

Item 2 events are the exception. When a registrant corporation succeeds to or acquires an interest in a business, the financial statements of that business must be presented in the 8-K filing.[2]

Amendments

All amendments to a registration application are filed on Form 8. An amendment can either contain information that has not been filed previously, or it can correct information that has been filed already. In correcting an item, exhibit, or financial statement, the amendment deletes and completely restates it so that the filing includes a copy of the original item, Form 8, and (if the amendment pertains to the financial statements) an accountant's report that incorporates the amendment into the opinion. This report is discussed in Chapter 8.

Requests for Extension of Time

Because the value of financial statements lies in their timeliness, the SEC encourages registrants to file their reports promptly. Occasionally, however, it is impossible to comply with this standard. If so, the registrant may file an application requesting up to 30 additional days to file a periodic report. He may request an extension for the entire filing or he may file a partial statement and request an extension for the unfinished portion. The application must include statements that:

1. Identify the information, report, and the like, in question.
2. State in detail the specific reasons why the filing cannot be made without unreasonable effort or expense.
3. Request the extension for a specified period of time, not to exceed 30 days.
4. Show that the extension is in the public interest and for the protection of investors.

If the reason for the delay is due to the inability of the auditor to furnish an opinion by the deadline, a statement from the auditor also must be included in the application.

If the SEC does not deny the application within 15 days after its receipt, the application can be considered granted. A second request for an additional 30 days can be made but is considered refused unless it is specifically granted within 15 days from its receipt. These provisions should not be mistaken to imply that extensions are granted freely. On the contrary, the SEC is very reluctant to grant extensions and, as we have seen in Chapter 3, has the power to discourage unapproved delays in meeting deadlines.

ANNUAL REPORT TO STOCKHOLDERS—PROXIES (SECTION 14)

The SEC plays a dominant role in determining the form of the registrant's annual report to stockholders. It does this through the back door, so to speak, for none of the securities acts directly empowers the SEC to determine the form of these reports. The SEC does, however, regulate the solicitation of proxies and the relationship between the two becomes evident by the requirement that an annual report precede or accompany a *proxy statement*. The content of the annual report will be discussed in Chapter 7.

The Process of Soliciting Proxies

Section 14 of the Securities Exchange Act prohibits any person from soliciting proxies unless the stockholder has been furnished with a written proxy statement. The act gives the SEC the administrative power to regulate the solicitation process, and the exchanges impose restrictions on the proxy solicitation as well. For example, the New York Stock Exchange imposes certain disclosure standards which are more extensive than either generally accepted accounting principles or SEC requirements.

It is management who usually determines the proposals to be considered at the *stockholders' meeting* and who solicits proxies on its own behalf; however, any stockholder can do so. Regulation 14-A establishes the formal procedures for soliciting proxies. It also establishes formal procedures, which are beyond the scope of this book, for placing a proposal on the agenda of the stockholders' meeting and informing stockholders of the proposal's merits. Management is legally bound to:

1. Send all stockholders written notification of meetings.
2. Include on the agenda any proposals which comply with Regulation 14-A.
3. Distribute or assist others to distribute proxy solicitations; and, if it intends to oppose any proposal appearing on the proxy statement, to declare this intention to the stockholders in the proxy statement.

Filing the Proxy Material

Five copies of preliminary proxy material, accompanied by a filing fee of $125 to $1,000, are filed with the SEC at least ten days before distribution to the stock-

Exhibit 4-3   Announcement of the Stockholders' Meeting

THE GREYHOUND CORPORATION

NOTICE OF ANNUAL MEETING OF SHAREHOLDERS

April 2, 1979

To the Holders of Common Stock and
3% Second Cumulative Preference Stock of
The Greyhound Corporation:

The Annual Meeting of Shareholders of The Greyhound Corporation, an Arizona corporation, will be held in the Coronado Room of the TowneHouse, 100 West Clarendon Avenue, Phoenix, Arizona, on Tuesday, May 8, 1979, at 9:30 o'clock in the forenoon, Mountain Standard Time, for the following purposes:

1. To elect directors of the Company for the ensuing year.

2. To vote on a proposal to ratify the appointment of Touche Ross & Co. by the Board of Directors to audit the accounts of the Company for the year 1979.

3. To transact such other business as may properly come before the meeting or any adjournment or adjournments thereof.

Only shareholders of record at the close of business March 9, 1979, will be entitled to receive notice of and to vote at the meeting. The list of shareholders entitled to vote will be available for inspection by any shareholder, for any purpose germane to the meeting, during the time of the meeting.

The Annual Report for the year 1978, including financial statements, was mailed to shareholders by March 31, 1979.

To assure your representation at the meeting, please sign and mail promptly the enclosed proxy, which is being solicited on behalf of management. If your registered address is in the United States, a return envelope which requires no postage if mailed in the United States is enclosed for that purpose.

FREDERICK G. EMERSON
Secretary

---

holders. The SEC reviews the material and may issue a deficiency letter. Any deficiencies must be corrected before the proxy material is distributed to the stockholders. No later than the day on which the solicitation material is sent to stockholders, management files eight definitive copies of the proxy material and seven copies of the annual report with the SEC, and submits three copies of the same material to any exchange on which the securities of the issuer are traded.

The Proxy Material

A package of material is sent to each stockholder of record at least 20 days prior to the stockholders' meeting. The package includes the following:

1. The announcement of the stockholders' meeting (Exhibit 4-3).
2. The proxy (Exhibit 4-4).
3. The proxy statement (or the *information statement* if proxies are not being solicited) (Exhibit 4-5).

4. The annual report to stockholders (if it is an annual meeting and members of the board of directors are to be elected). (Refer to the Dart Industries report at the end of the text.)

5. Financial statements of the soliciting party (if a merger, consolidation, or acquisition or sale of assets is at issue).

6. Miscellaneous additional material.

Exhibit 4-4   Proxy

PROXY   THE GREYHOUND CORPORATION

The undersigned hereby appoints Gerald H. Trautman, Howard Boyd and Robert Minge Brown and each of them, with power of substitution, attorneys and proxies for the undersigned, to vote at the annual meeting of the shareholders of The Greyhound Corporation to be held in the Coronado Room, of the TowneHouse, 100 West Clarendon Avenue, Phoenix, Arizona, on Tuesday, May 8, 1979, and at any adjournment thereof, all shares of stock which the undersigned is entitled to vote, with all voting rights the undersigned would have if personally present:

(1) FOR ☐ the election of thirteen Directors. Authority to vote for Directors withheld ☐;

(2) FOR ☐ or AGAINST ☐ the proposal to ratify the appointment by the Board of Directors of Touche Ross & Co. as auditors;

and to vote upon any other business that may properly come before said meeting.

The undersigned hereby acknowledges receipt of Notice of Meeting, Proxy Statement and Annual Report for the calendar year 1978.

The directors recommend a vote FOR proposal (2) above.

(over)

PLEASE SIGN ON REVERSE SIDE AND RETURN PROMPTLY IN THE ENCLOSED ENVELOPE

GLOBE 903265-X9

The shares represented hereby will be voted as directed by this proxy, **BUT IF NO DIRECTION IS MADE, THIS PROXY WILL BE VOTED FOR THE ABOVE MATTERS UNLESS CONTRARY INSTRUCTIONS HAVE BEEN NOTED HEREON.**

Dated _____, 1979

_____

_____

Signature of Shareholder

(Please sign exactly as name appears hereon. Executors, Administrators, Trustees, etc., should so indicate when signing. For joint accounts, each joint owner should sign.)

(THIS PROXY IS SOLICITED ON BEHALF OF THE MANAGEMENT)

GLOBE 903264-0

Exhibit 4-5 Proxy Statement

PROXY STATEMENT
(First Mailed April 2, 1979)

GENERAL INFORMATION

This Proxy Statement is furnished in connection with the solicitation by management of proxies for the 1979 Annual Meeting of Shareholders of The Greyhound Corporation (the Company). The cost of soliciting proxies will be borne by the Company. Solicitation will be made primarily through the use of the mails, but regular employees of the Company may solicit proxies personally, by telephone or telegram. Brokers and nominees will be requested to forward soliciting material to, and obtain voting instructions from, beneficial owners of stock registered in their names. The enclosed proxy, if properly executed and returned, will be voted according to your specifications but may be revoked at any time before exercise by giving notice in writing to the Secretary of the Company or by voting in person at the meeting.

Only shareholders of record as of the close of business on the record date, March 9, 1979, will be entitled to vote at the meeting. The number of shares outstanding as of such record date was 43,918,632 shares of Common Stock and 2,508 shares of 3% Second Cumulative Preference Stock, excluding any shares of Common Stock held by the Company. For the election of directors, each outstanding share entitles the holder to as many votes as there are directors to be elected, and such votes may be cumulated and voted for one nominee or divided among as many different nominees as desired. For all other matters which may come before the meeting, each such share will be entitled to one vote.

The Board of Directors holds regular quarterly meetings, and met four times in 1978. It has established the following committees of certain of its members to deal with particular areas of responsibility:

1. The Executive Committee, which met eight times in 1978, exercises powers of the Board in the management of the business and affairs of the Company between Board meetings.

2. The Audit Committee, which met three times in 1978, recommends appointment of the independent auditors and reviews financial statements, audit fees, the scope of audit and non-audit services performed by the auditors, accounting policies and reporting practices, internal auditing and controls, and certain officers' expenses.

3. The Executive Compensation Committee, which met three times in 1978, considers and makes recommendations to the Board regarding the compensation of officers of the Company and its subsidiaries who receive annual salaries of $100,000 or more, and supervises the Stock Units Incentive Compensation Plan.

The announcement of the stockholders' meeting identifies the company, states the nature of the meeting, gives the time and location of the meeting, and states the purpose for the meeting (the general agenda).

The proxy is dated and identifies the matters to be acted upon. It provides for a yes or no vote on each matter and indicates whether the proxy is solicited on behalf of management.

The forms for proxy statements are determined by whether management or another party is soliciting the proxy. Schedule 14-A is issued by management; Schedule 14-B is used by others. The schedules define the information that must be furnished and require that the issues put to vote be presented clearly, that statements be grouped by subject matter, and that the groups be headed by a descriptive title.

Recent amendments of Regulation 14A have expanded disclosures in such areas as the reporting of executive perquisites, and further proposals announced for comment in recent Securities Exchange Act releases range from requiring

Exhibit 4-5   (Continued)

The Board does not have a Nominating Committee.

The mailing address of the principal executive office of the Company is The Greyhound Corporation, P. O. Box 21688, Phoenix, Arizona 85036.

A copy of the Company's 1978 Annual Report on Form 10-K filed with the Securities and Exchange Commission is available without charge to shareholders upon written request to J. M. Coleman, P. O. Box 21688, Phoenix, Arizona 85036.

ELECTION OF DIRECTORS

The persons named in the enclosed proxy intend to vote at the shareholders meeting to be held on May 8, 1979, or any adjournment thereof, for the election of the nominees for directors whose names appear below, or in their discretion, for the largest number of such nominees which can be elected by cumulative voting, for a term of one year or until their respective successors have qualified, or, in the event of disqualification, refusal or inability of any of them to serve, for the election of such other persons as they believe will carry on the present policies of the Company. The management has no reason to believe any of the nominees will be disqualified or unable, or will refuse, to serve if elected.

Certain information, as of March 1, 1979, regarding the nominees is set forth below:

Name	Principal Occupation, Other Directorships, and Age	Director Since	Common Shares Owned Beneficially (1)
Ralph C. Batastini*	Vice Chairman of the Company. Also director of Armour and Company, Greyhound Computer Corporation, Greyhound Leasing & Financial Corporation and Verex Corporation. Age 49.	1971	6,122 (2)
Howard Boyd*†	Chairman of the Board and director, The El Paso Company, gas and oil production and transmission and chemical manufacturer. Also director of Armour and Company, Texas Commerce Bancshares, Inc. and Texas Commerce Bank N.A. Age 69.	1967	2,800
Robert Minge Brown*†	Partner, law firm of McCutchen, Doyle, Brown & Enersen, San Francisco, California, and Chairman of the Board, California Water Service Company. Also director of Hewlett-Packard Company and San Jose Water Works. Age 67.	1971	2,000

institutional investors to disclose information about the way they vote the stock they own to the reason for a director's resignation when caused by a policy dispute.

The intention of the SEC clearly is to use the proxy statement as a primary means of communicating information to investors.

Relationship with Independent Public Accountants (Schedule 14A, Item 8)

Recently the SEC increased the amount of disclosure pertaining to the relationship between the company and its independent public accountants in the proxy statement. If a proxy solicitation is made on behalf of management of the issuer and relates to an annual meeting of security holders at which directors are to be elected, or financial statements are included, the proxy statement must contain information specified in Item 8 of Schedule 14A.[3]

Exhibit 4-5 (Continued)

Name	Principal Occupation, Other Directorships, and Age	Director Since	Common Shares Owned Beneficially (1)
Samuel A. Casey	Chairman and Chief Executive Officer and director, Great Northern Nekoosa Corporation, manufacturer of paper and paper products. Also director of The Armstrong Rubber Company, General Signal Corp., Pitney-Bowes, Inc., The Trane Company and United States Trust Company of New York. Age 64.	1977	200
Clifton B. Cox*	Vice Chairman of the Company and Chairman of the Board and Chief Executive Officer, Armour and Company. Also director of Greyhound Computer Corporation, Greyhound Leasing & Financial Corporation and Stop & Shop Companies, Inc. Age 62.	1971	5,589
Charles F. Fogarty	Chairman and Chief Executive Officer and director, Texasgulf, Inc., a producer of metals and chemicals for agriculture and industry, and oil and gas. Also director of Armco Inc. and Lehman Corporation. Age 57.	1978	2,000
Martha W. Griffiths	Partner, law firm of Griffiths & Griffiths, Romeo, Michigan, for four years and three months, and Member of Congress of the United States for 20 years prior thereto. Also director of Burroughs Corporation, Consumers Power Company, K mart Corporation, Chrysler Corporation, National Detroit Corp., National Bank of Detroit and Verex Corporation. Age 67.	1977	200
Frank R. D. Holland	Chairman, C.E. Heath & Co., Limited, an international insurance broker and managing agent for one of the underwriting syndicates at Lloyd's, London, England. Age 54.	1974	1,000
John H. Johnson*†	President and director, Johnson Publishing Company, Inc., publisher of Ebony and other magazines, and Chairman and President and director, Supreme Life Insurance Company. Also director of Bell & Howell Company, The Marina Bank, Twentieth Century-Fox Film Corporation, Verex Corporation and Zenith Radio Corporation. Age 61.	1974	500

The Information Statement

But how does the solicitation of proxies affect all annual reports? It is obvious that if proxies are not solicited for the stockholders' meeting the provisions we have discussed do not apply. It is equally important, however, for investors to be notified of the stockholders' meeting and be informed of the agenda when they intend to vote their own stock. Therefore Schedule 14-C requires that information similar to that in the proxy statement be distributed to the stockholders (in the information statement), in the event that proxies are not solicited.

The items of information required in the information statement include,

1. The fact that proxies are *not* solicited.
2. The date, time and place of the meeting.
3. The interests of certain persons in favor of or opposed to matters to be acted upon.

Exhibit 4-5 (Continued)

Name	Principal Occupation, Other Directorships, and Age	Director Since	Common Shares Owned Beneficially (1)
John M. Martin	Retired Chairman of the Board, Hercules, Inc., manufacturer of chemical products and related industrial systems. Also director of Chemical Fund, Lehman Corporation, Delaware Trust Co., Perini Corporation, and P. H. Glatfelter Co. Age 66.	1975	500
Harold C. Stuart	Partner, law firm of Doerner, Stuart, Saunders, Daniel & Anderson, Tulsa, Oklahoma, and Chairman and Chief Executive Officer and director, Southwestern Sales Corporation, investor in oil, real estate and broadcasting. Also director of Armour and Company, Getty Oil Company, Morrison-Knudsen Company, Inc. and First National Bank and Trust Company, Tulsa, Oklahoma. Age 66.	1959	8,700
Donn B. Tatum	Chairman of the Board and director, Walt Disney Productions. Also director of Armour and Company, BankAmerica Corp., Union Oil Company of California and Western Digital Corporation. Age 66.	1975	1,000
Gerald H. Trautman*	Chairman and President and Chief Executive Officer of the Company. Also director of Armour and Company, Greyhound Computer Corporation, Greyhound Leasing & Financial Corporation, Lehman Corporation, Twentieth Century-Fox Film Corporation and Verex Corporation. Age 66.	1965	11,172 (2)

* Member of Executive Committee of the Company. Messrs. Batastini and Cox serve as such on an alternating basis.

† Member of Executive Compensation Committee of the Company.

(1) Includes shares held in the names of spouses, minor children or certain relatives, as to which beneficial ownership is disclaimed.

(2) Additional holdings, including holdings in the names of spouses, minor children or certain relatives, as to which beneficial ownership is disclaimed, of other equity securities of the Company or its subsidiaries, are as follows:

4. Any proposals (including those initiated by other participants) to be considered at the meeting.
5. Any information that the annual report would have contained, if it is not furnished.

In summary, publicly owned corporations must hold at least one stockholders' meeting a year, notify all stockholders of that meeting, and distribute to each and every stockholder an annual report that conforms to SEC requirements.

LIABILITY UNDER THE SECURITIES EXCHANGE ACT

The Securities Exchange Act contains provisions establishing civil liability (Section 18) and criminal liability (Section 10) for making false or misleading statements in any document required to be filed under the act.[4] Recently, Section

Exhibit 4-5 (Continued)

Name	Equity Securities Held
Ralph C. Batastini	100 shares of Common Stock of Greyhound Lines of Canada Ltd. 3,200 shares of Common Stock of Greyhound Computer of Canada Ltd.
Gerald H. Trautman	600 shares of Common Stock of Greyhound Lines of Canada Ltd. $90,000 principal amount of 6½% Convertible Subordinated Debentures of the Company due 1990. $5,000 principal amount of 6% Convertible Subordinated Debentures of Greyhound Computer Corporation due 1986.

(3) At March 1, 1979, all directors and officers as a group beneficially owned 268,894 shares of the Company's Common Stock, which was less than 1% of such shares outstanding. Also, this group owned amounts of other equity securities of the Company and of certain subsidiaries of the Company, aggregating less than 1/10th of 1% of each such security outstanding.

REMUNERATION OF DIRECTORS AND OFFICERS

The table below sets forth all remuneration paid or payable by the Company and its subsidiaries for 1978 to each of the five most highly compensated directors or executive officers of the Company and all directors and officers as a group, in all their capacities while serving as officers or directors of the Company. The amounts shown include remuneration for 1978 services paid in 1979.

		Cash and Cash-Equivalents		
Name of Individual or Number of Persons in Group	Capacities in Which Served	Salaries, Fees, Directors' Fees, Commissions and Bonuses (1)	Securities or Property, Insurance Benefits or Reimbursement, Personal Benefits	Contingent Remuneration (2) (8)
Ralph C. Batastini	Vice Chairman and Director	$ 215,775	$ 4,591	$ 37,197
Clifton B. Cox	Vice Chairman and Director	$ 196,266	$ 2,941	$ 46,604
Leo S. McDonald, Jr.	Group Vice President-Convention Services	$ 241,004 (3)	$ 1,131	—
Donald J. Shaughnessy	Group Vice President-Armour	$ 178,833	$ 4,808	$ 10,089
Gerald H. Trautman	Chairman and President and Director	$ 275,357 (4)	$ 6,707	$ 4,068
All Directors and Officers as a group (43 persons) (5)		$3,428,012 (6)(7)	$62,866	$233,624

10(b) has been used in civil actions against accountants via the SEC's Rule 10b(5). Although many persons associated with an SEC filing are liable under these three sections, our discussion will focus primarily on the accountant's liability.

Civil Liability

Section 18 establishes liability for involvement with false and misleading statements by preparers of the statements.

Section 18 (a)   Any person who shall make or cause to be made any statement in any application, report, or document filed pursuant to this title or any rule or regulation thereunder or any undertaking contained in a registration statement as provided in subsection (d) of Section 15 of this title, which statement was at the time and in the light of the circumstances under which it was made false or

Exhibit 4-5 (Continued)

(1) Includes amounts paid under incentive bonus plans adopted annually by the Company and certain of its subsidiaries. The Executive Committee of the Board of Directors of the Company may, upon recommendation of the Chief Executive Officer of the Company, award bonuses under these plans to key executives of the Company and certain of its subsidiaries. While plans vary for individual subsidiaries, awards are related to outstanding performance by individuals and individual subsidiaries and groups, and generally a bonus is limited to 50% of an individual's salary.

(2) Deferred under the Stock Units Incentive Compensation Plan and agreements with the participants therein under which they receive stock unit credits based upon market prices of the Company's Common Stock, each stock unit being equivalent to one share. Payment is to be made in forty quarterly installments, after termination of employment. These payments may be made either in cash or stock, and the payment period may be modified, at the option of the Company. To the extent they are made in cash, the payments will be equal to the market value, at the time of payment, of the stock otherwise payable. The Company provides for anticipated liability under this Plan by adjusting its account for remuneration expense to reflect changes in the Company's Common Stock market value, and amounts shown are after credits to such account, as follows: Mr. Batastini, $2,373; Mr. Cox, $32,613; Mr. Shaughnessy, $191; Mr. Trautman, $58,116; and directors and officers as a group, $164,649.

(3) Includes payments under a 5-year employment agreement expiring May, 1983, providing for an annual salary of $85,000, subject to certain adjustments, and an incentive compensation award based on the profits of the Convention Services Group. During 1978, Mr. McDonald borrowed $56,700 from the Company for a non-business use. The indebtedness was paid in full on March 6, 1979, and did not bear interest. The largest aggregate amount outstanding since January 1, 1978 was $56,700.

(4) Includes payments under a 6-year employment agreement, as amended, expiring May, 1980, providing for an annual salary of $220,690; and excludes $134,310 paid in 1978 under the pension plan and related agreements.

(5) Includes payments to an officer under a 5-year employment agreement, as amended, expiring November, 1980, providing for an annual salary of $121,000.

misleading with respect to any material fact, shall be liable to any person (not knowing that such statement was false or misleading) who, in reliance upon such statement, shall have purchased or sold a security at a price which was affected by such statement, for damages caused by such reliance, unless the person sued shall prove that he acted in good faith and had no knowledge that such statement was false or misleading. A person seeking to enforce such liability may sue at law or in equity in any court of competent jurisdiction. In any such suit the court may, at its discretion, require an undertaking for the payment of the costs of such suit, and assess reasonable costs, including reasonable attorneys' fees, against either party litigant.

(b) Every person who becomes liable to make payment under this section may recover contribution as in cases of contract from any person who, if joined in the original suit, would have been liable to make the same payment.

Notice that Section 18 holds the accountant liable for any statement that was

Exhibit 4-5 (Continued)

(6) Does not include (a) $167,363 paid in 1978 for legal services to McCutchen, Doyle, Brown & Enersen, of which Robert Minge Brown, a director, is a partner; it is expected that payments for services will be paid to this firm in 1979; and (b) $8,296 paid in 1978 for legal services to Doerner, Stuart, Saunders, Daniel & Anderson, of which Harold C. Stuart, a director, is a partner.

(7) Directors who are not employees receive an annual retainer of $13,500 and a fee of $850 for each Board, Audit and Executive Committee meeting attended, except that a fee of $1,000 per meeting is paid for each Executive Committee meeting attended not in conjunction with a meeting of the Board.

(8) Does not include Company contributions to pension plans, the amount of which cannot be readily allocated to individual accounts. The Company contributions for pension plan participants were 12.4% for the Greyhound Employees' Retirement Income Plan and 14.5% for the Armour and Company Salaried Employees' Pension Plan, respectively, of all plan participants' salaries. The remuneration covered by the plans is base salary exclusive of bonuses and other forms of remuneration, except that the Armour plan includes commissions. Of the persons named in the table above, Messrs. Cox and Shaughnessy are participants in the Armour plan.

Estimated annual benefits payable to participants who retire at age 65, or later, are illustrated in the following table (benefits exceeding the maximum prescribed for qualified plans are not payable under the Company's pension plans, but are payable under contractual arrangements):

Annual Average Base Salary*	Estimated Range of Annual Pension Benefits Years of Service to Age 65			
	10	20	30	40
70,000	12,250 to 12,800	24,500 to 25,600	31,500 to 36,900	35,000 to 46,700
100,000	17,500 to 18,800	35,000 to 37,600	45,000 to 54,000	50,000 to 68,000
140,000	24,500 to 26,800	49,000 to 53,600	63,000 to 76,800	70,000 to 96,400
170,000	29,750 to 32,800	59,500 to 65,600	76,500 to 93,900	85,000 to 117,700
200,000	35,000 to 38,800	70,000 to 76,000	90,000 to 111,000	100,000 to 139,000

*Under the Greyhound plan—average of highest five years of salary or 63rd year if participant retires at 65, whichever is higher. Under the Armour plan—average of highest consecutive five years of salary.

false or misleading "at the time and in light of the circumstance under which it was made." Section 11 liability under the Securities Act, on the other hand, extends responsibility for false and misleading information to the effective date of the registration statement. Therefore, although the auditor must extend his audit review procedures in Securities Act filings to the effective date of the registration statement, he may terminate the audit review of 1934 filings as of the date of the opinion letter. Although an auditor is not obligated to search for subsequent information under either act, he has an obligation to report information that inadvertently comes to his attention after the date of the opinion letter if the information indicates that the statements were, at the date of the opinion letter, false or misleading. (This will be discussed more fully later.)

(Refer to Exhibit 4-6 for a comparison of civil liability under the Securities Act and the Securities Exchange Act).

Section 10 prohibits the use of manipulative and deceptive devices and is not limited to "preparers" of financial statements as is Section 18:[5]

Exhibit 4-5 (Continued)

STOCK OPTIONS AND OTHER INFORMATION

The following table shows as to certain directors and officers, and as to all directors and officers as a group, (i) the number of stock options granted between January 1, 1978, and March 1, 1979, (ii) the number of stock options exercised between January 1, 1978, and March 1, 1979, and (iii) the number of shares subject to all unexercised options held as of March 1, 1979:

	Ralph C. Batastini	Clifton B. Cox	Leo S. McDonald, Jr.	Donald J. Shaughnessy	Gerald H. Trautman	All Directors and Officers As a Group
COMMON SHARES						
Granted:						
Number of shares	6,000	6,400	2,800	5,000	11,800	81,900
Average per share option price	$13.38	$13.38	$13.38	$13.38	$13.38	$13.38
Exercised:						
Number of shares	—	—	—	—	1,000	3,800
Aggregate option price	—	—	—	—	$11,625	$44,550
Aggregate market value on date exercised	—	—	—	—	$13,000	$50,863
Unexercised:						
Number of shares	14,200	14,900	2,800	11,000	24,300	153,400
Average per share option price	$12.95	$13.16	$13.38	$12.92	$12.93	$13.13

Since January 1, 1978, subsidiaries of the Company have paid, in the ordinary course of business, C. E. Heath (Agencies) Limited, a subsidiary of a company of which Frank R. D. Holland is an officer and director, for services, Walt Disney Productions, of which Donn B. Tatum is an officer and director, for concessions, and Johnson Publishing Company, Inc., of which John H. Johnson is an officer and director, for advertising. It is expected that subsidiaries of the Company will continue to do similar business in the future with the same three companies. In no case were the amounts involved material in relation to the business of the Company, and management believes the amounts paid were reasonable and competitive for what the Company received and that the payments were not material in relation to the business of the other companies or to the individual directors concerned. In lieu of any other separation payments and in exchange for a covenant not to compete and other agreements, James L. Kerrigan, a director and officer of the Company who resigned during 1978, was paid $250,000 under an agreement with the Company.

It shall be unlawful for any person, directly or indirectly, by the use of any means or instrumentality of interstate commerce or of the mails, or of any facility of any national securities exchange—

(a) To effect a short sale, or to use or employ any stop-loss order in connection with the purchase or sale, of any security registered on a national securities exchange, in contravention of such rules and regulations as the Commission may prescribe as necessary or appropriate in the public interest or for the protection of investors.

(b) To use or employ, in connection with the purchase or sale of any security registered on a national securities exchange or any security not so registered, any manipulative or deceptive device or contrivance in contravention of such rules and regulations as the Commission may prescribe as necessary or appropriate in the public interest or for the protection of investors.

Exhibit 4-5 (Continued)

APPROVAL OF AUDITORS

The following resolution concerning the appointment of independent auditors will be offered at the meeting:

"Resolved, That the appointment by the Board of Directors of Touche Ross & Co. to audit the accounts of the Company and its subsidiaries for the fiscal year 1979 is hereby approved."

Touche Ross & Co. has audited the accounts of the Company and its subsidiaries for many years and has been selected to continue as the Company's independent auditors for 1979 by the Board of Directors upon the recommendation of the Company's Audit Committee. A representative of Touche Ross & Co. is expected to attend the meeting, will respond to appropriate questions and will be afforded the opportunity to make a statement.

The audit services provided by Touche Ross & Co. during 1978 included examinations and reviews of the financial statements of the Company and its subsidiary companies; audits of companies acquired; assistance in connection with filings with the Securities and Exchange Commission and other regulatory agencies; and consultation relating to various audit-related accounting matters.

The non-audit services provided during 1978 (fees for which aggregated approximately 17% of audit fees) included assistance in designing a new accounting reporting system (approximately 8% of audit fees) and examination of financial statements of pension trusts and other employee benefit plans (approximately 4% of audit fees). Other such services, all individually under 3% of audit fees, included consultation and assistance in preparing certain foreign subsidiaries' tax returns, tax consultation in highly specialized areas and review of accounting systems. The Audit Committee has reviewed and approved the non-audit services described above and has determined that the performance of such services should not have impaired the independence of Touche Ross & Co.

If the shareholders should not approve the appointment of Touche Ross & Co., the selection of other auditors would be considered by the Board of Directors for the year 1980.

Members of the Audit Committee of the Board of Directors who are not employees of the Company are John M. Martin, Chairman, Martha W. Griffiths and Frank R. D. Holland. Mr. Gerald H. Trautman, Chairman and President, attends the Committee meetings ex officio.

OTHER BUSINESS

The management knows of no other matters to be brought before the meeting. If any other business should properly come before the meeting, the persons named in the proxy have discretionary authority to vote in accordance with their best judgments.

By order of the Board of Directors.

FREDERICK G. EMERSON
Secretary

Section 10 has not been interpreted as strictly as Section 18 and as a result has been applied with increasing frequency in recent years in civil actions.

The SEC issued Rule 10(b)-5 to elaborate upon the intent of Section 10(b) and to provide a means of implementing the provisions of the section.

RULE 10(b)-5

It shall be unlawful for any person, directly or indirectly by the use of any means or instrumentality of interstate commerce, or of the mails, or of any facility of any national securities exchange: (1) to employ any device, scheme, or artifice to defraud, (2) to make any untrue statement of a material fact or to omit to state a material fact necessary in order to make the statements made, in the light of the circumstances under which they were made, not misleading, or (3) to engage in any act, practice or course of business which operates or would operate as a fraud *or deceit upon any person in connection with the purchase or sale of any security. (authors' emphasis)*

Notice that (1) and (3) above refer specifically to fraud, whereas (2) does not. While (1) and (3) seem to preclude negligence as a basis for civil action against accountants, the intention of (2) is not as clear. Most suits against the auditor of record, therefore, have been based on the more easily proven accusation of negligence under Rule 10b-5, Subsection (2) rather than on the basis of fraud required by Subsections (1) and (3).

The intention of Subsection (2) was examined by the Supreme Court in the Hochfelder case *(Ernst & Ernst v. Hochfelder, 1976)*. If Subsection (2) is interpreted in relationship to Subsections (1) and (3), it can be "read as proscribing, respectively, any type of material misstatement or omission, and any course of conduct, that has the effect of defrauding investors, whether the wrongdoing was intentional or not."

The court decided that Subsection (2) should be interpreted in relation to the other subsections and that an accountant's liability be limited to fraudulent acts. This decision suggests that the auditor's liability must be based on knowledge of or actual participation in the fraud and affirms the validity of the accounting profession's right to set its own standards for professional behavior. Further court decisions interpreting the Hochfelder findings are necessary to explore fully the implications in practice. It should be understood that the decision does *not* reduce an auditor's exposure for a negligence charge under common law principles of legal liability.

Criminal Liability

Section 32(a) establishes criminal liability for "willfully" and "knowingly" making false or misleading statements in reports required to be filed under the Securities Exchange Act. It also provides criminal penalties for violating the anti-fraud provisions of Section 10(b).

The element of guilty knowledge *(scienter)* can, however, be inferred from the defendant's actions as was done in *U.S.* v. *Natelli* and in the criminal trial of three auditors in the Equity Funding Corporation of America fraud (Refer to Appendix C).

Accountants rarely are prosecuted under the criminal provisions of the Securities Exchange Act. Criminal convictions have been upheld only in U.S. v. Simon, U.S. v. *Natelli* and the Equity Funding cases.

Rather than prosecute violators of securities laws under the criminal provisions of Section 32(a), the SEC usually prefers to obtain an injunction against the responsible parties, anticipating that civil suits will follow in short order. The SEC is rarely disappointed. Rappaport[6] cites the case of Occidental Petroleum Corporation in which the SEC announcement of the complaint was followed in only four days' time by *Frank* v. *Occidental Petroleum Corporation* (1971). The obvious benefits from this method of regulation are a savings in the resources of the U.S. Government, and the potential for greater penalties than are allowed by statute.

Exhibit 4-6 Comparison of Accountants' Civil Liability

Statute	Responsibility for Financial Statements	Liability		Plaintiff's Burden of Proof	Defendant's Burden of Proof	Statute of Limitations
		Parties	Acts			
Securities Act (Section 11)	Financial statements in the registration statement to effective date	Purchasers of securities	Simple negligence Gross negligence Fraud	Proof of loss	Statutory defenses of due diligence and good faith	1 year from discovery or 3 years from date of the cause of action
Securities Exchange Act (Section 18)	Financial statements in SEC "filings" to the opinion date	Purchasers of securities	Intent to defraud	Reliance on false or misleading statement as to material fact	Due diligence and good faith belief in the verity of financial statements	Same as above
Securities Exchange Act (Section 10(b))	Financial statements in SEC "filings," information distributed to the public by other means, any relevant information discovered as insider and known to be material	Purchasers of securities	Gross negligence Fraud	Reliance on false or misleading statement as to material fact	Due diligence and good faith belief in verity of financial statements	Same as above

The penalties following conviction of an accountant for criminal acts, as set forth in Section 32 are a fine of not more than $10,000, imprisonment of not more than five years, or both (except that a defendant who proves that he had no knowledge that he was violating the law cannot be imprisoned). A fine of up to $500,000 can be imposed on a stock exchange.

EXEMPTIONS

A security may be exempt from certain provisions of the Securities Exchange Act for one of four reasons:

1. It has been granted *unlisted* status by Section 12(f) (1).[7]
2. The security is *defined* as being an exempted security for all purposes of the act except fraud (Section 3(a) (12).[8]
3. The security is *exempt* from the registration requirements of the act (Section 12(g) (12).[9]
4. The security is one that the SEC has exempted (Regulation 240, Rule 3a).

In practice these categories overlap, so that some securities are exempted under more than one provision. The determination of whether or not a security is exempt from filing requirements under the Securities Exchange Act is the responsibility of an attorney.

SUMMARY

The Securities Exchange Act regulates the trading of securities and amends certain provisions of the Securities Act. The independent accountant participates to a significant degree in three processes governed by the act:

1. Obtaining listed status.
2. Filing periodic reports.
3. Soliciting proxies.

The process of registration under the Securities Exchange Act is similar to that under the Securities Act except that the SEC filing is simpler and includes applying to the exchange for listed status. The Securities Exchange Act was amended in 1964 to require registration of securities traded over-the-counter. The most common form used by companies filing under this act for the first time is Form 10. Companies that have filed previously may use an abbreviated registration form, 8A.

Section 14, governing proxy solicitations, has been extended by SEC regulation to affect the methods used by registrants to notify their investors of the annual stockholders' meeting and to inform them of proposals on the agenda. These requirements include the filings of all proxy material with the SEC, the distribution of all proxy material to the owners of record, and the distribution of an information statement containing information similar to that required in the proxy statement when proxies are *not* solicited.

The Securities Exchange Act contains provisions for criminal and civil liability. Liability under the Securities Exchange Act differs from that under the Securities Act in that the plaintiff must prove reliance on the misleading statements. Section 10(b) was originally intended to define criminal acts, but increasingly it is being used in civil actions against accountants.

Exemptions from provisions of the act apply if:

1. The security has been granted unlisted status by the act.
2. The security is defined as being exempt from all purposes of the act except fraud.
3. The security is exempt from the registration requirements of the act.
4. The security is one that the SEC has exempted in its Rule 3a of Regulation 240.

FOOTNOTES FOR CHAPTER 4

[1]Securities Exchange Act of 1934 as amended, Securities Act of 1933 as amended.

[2]The financial statements must include:

a. A balance sheet dated reasonably close to the acquisition date. If the balance sheet is unaudited, an audited balance sheet as of the close of the preceding year must be included.
b. Audited income and source and application of funds statements for each of the last three full fiscal years, plus unaudited stub period statements.
c. If the acquired company is in bankruptcy proceedings, the balance sheet need not be audited and no stub period statements are required.

[3]Item 8 requires the following information:

a. The name of the principal accountant selected or being recommended to shareholders for election, approval or ratification for the current year. If no accountant has been selected or recommended, the fact should be stated and the reasons therefor given.
b. The name of the principal accountant for the fiscal year most recently completed if different from the accountant named in (a) above.
c. If a change or changes in accountants have taken place since the date of the proxy statement for the most recent annual meeting of shareholders, and if in connection with such change(s) a disagreement between the accountant and issuer has been reported on Form 8-K or in the accountant's letter filed as an exhibit thereto, the disagreement shall be described. The issuer must furnish the description of the disagreement to the accountant involved and if that accountant believes that the description of the disagreement is incorrect or incomplete, he may include a brief statement of approximately 200 words (or less). The accountant's statement should be submitted to the issuer within ten business days of the date the accountant receives the issuer's description for its inclusion in the proxy statement.
d. The proxy statement shall indicate whether or not representatives of the principal accountants for the current year and for the most recently completed fiscal year are expected to be present at the stockholders' meeting with the opportunity to make a

statement if they desire to do so and whether or not such representatives are expected to be available to respond to appropriate questions.

e. If the issuer has an audit or similar committee of the board of directors, state the names of the members of the committee. If the board of directors has no audit or similar committee, so state.

f. If any change in accountants has taken place since the date of the proxy statement for the most recent annual meeting of shareholders, state whether such change was recommended or approved by: (1) any audit or similar committee of the board of directors, if the issuer has such a committee; or (2) the board of directors, if the issuer has no such committee.

g. For the fiscal year most recently completed, describe each professional service provided by the principal accountant and state the percentage relationship that the aggregate of the fees for all non-audit services bear to the audit fees, and, except as provided below, state the percentage relationship that the fee for each non-audit service bears to the audit fees. Indicate whether, before each professional service provided by the principal accountant was rendered, it was approved by, and the possible effect on the independence of the accountant was considered by: (1) any audit or similar committee of the board of directors and (2) for any service not approved by an audit or similar committee, the board of directors. (Refer also to *Staff Accounting Bulletin No. 33.*)

[4] Because annual reports to stockholders are required by proxy rules but are not filed under the provisions of the Securities Exchange Act, legal recourse for false statements contained in annual reports can be obtained under the Federal False Statements Statute.

[5] It is interesting to note that originally only buyers were protected under Section 10(b) but in 1942 Rule 10(b)-5 was adopted extending the same protection to sellers of securities induced to sell by fraudulent means.

[6] Louis H. Rappaport, *SEC Accounting Practices and Procedures,* 3rd Edition, (New York: The Ronald Press Company, 1972), pp. 27.12–14.

[7] Unlisted securities are:

Securities admitted for trading on an exchange prior to March 1, 1934, could continue to be traded as an unlisted security.

A security already listed on an exchange and registered previously with the SEC enjoys unlisted trading privileges on other exchanges. The corporation files a notification with the SEC and applies to the second exchange for unlisted status.

A security issued by a corporation that has agreed to file periodic reports with the SEC under the Securities Act also can be traded on the exchange. The corporation follows the procedure in (2) above.

[8] Securities defined as exempt are:

Direct obligations of or obligations guaranteed by the United States.

Securities issued or guaranteed by corporations in which the United States has a direct or indirect interest if designated as exempt by the Secretary of the Treasury.

Municipal securities.

Interests or participations in any common trust fund or similar fund maintained by a bank exclusively for the purpose of collective investment and reinvestment of assets contributed by the bank in a fiduciary capacity.

Interests or participations in a collective trust fund maintained by a bank or in a separate account maintained by an insurance company for designated purposes.

Securities that the Commission may exempt from time to time.

[9]Securities exempted from registration are:

Any security already listed and registered on a national securities exchange.

Any security issued by an investment company that is registered pursuant to provisions of the Investment Company Act.

Certain securities issued by savings and loan associations, building and loan associations, cooperative banks, homestead associations, etc. that are supervised by state or federal authorities.

Securities issued by mutual or cooperative non-profit organizations engaged in supplying services or commodities to the securities holders.

Securities of non-profit religious, education, benevolent, fraternal, charitable or reformatory organizations.

Securities of cooperative associations as defined in the Agricultural Marketing Act of 1929, or federations of cooperative associations.

Securities of insurance companies where restrictive conditions are met.

Interests or participations in a collective trust fund maintained by a bank or in a separate account maintained by an insurance company where the interest is designated for the purpose of tax-qualified stock-bonus, pension or profit sharing, or annuity plans.

[10]Securities exempted by SEC Regulation 240, to varying degrees, are:

Mortgages sold by the Federal Home Loan Mortgage Corporation.

Securities whose income is guaranteed by states or by political subdivisions thereof.

Securities of certain foreign issuers.

Certain whole mortgages.

Certain investment contract securities.

GLOSSARY   **Application for Listing.** A detailed questionnaire filed with a national securities exchange providing information concerning the corporation's history and current status.

Information Statement. A statement on any pending corporate matters furnished by the registrant to every shareholder who is entitled to vote when a proxy is not solicited.

Proxy Statement. Information furnished in conjunction with a formal solicitation for the power to vote stockholder's shares (proxy).

Scienter. Intent to deceive, manipulate, or defraud. Requires proof that defendant knew of material misstatements or omissions, or that he acted willfully and knowingly.

Stockholders Meeting (Regular). Annual meetings for the election of directors and for action on other corporate matters.

Stockholders Meeting (Special). Meeting in which only specified agenda items can be considered.

Unlisted Trading Privileges. A security issue authorized by the SEC for trading on an exchange without requiring the corporation to complete a formal listing application.

QUESTIONS

1. What are the three areas of responsibility for accountants under the 1934 Act?
2. If a corporation applies for listing on a national securities exchange, must its securities be registered with the SEC?
3. What is the difference between registration with the SEC and listing with a national securities exchange?
4. What is the difference between Form 10 and Form 8A?
5. Identify the most common form used for annual reports to the SEC.
6. What periodic reports must corporations file with the SEC? Distribute to its shareholders?
7. When and in what report should a corporation disclose any unusual event that may have a significant effect upon the future of the company?
8. Discuss the nature of a few events that should be disclosed promptly to the SEC and to the public.
9. How do the requirements of Form 8-K enhance the independent auditor's independence?
10. Is the SEC concerned with annual reports to shareholders, or only with reports filed with the agency?
11. What does Section 14 of the Securities Exchange Act say about the solicitation of proxies?
12. What regulation governs the solicitation of proxies?
13. Are willful, false and misleading statements in reports filed with the SEC a civil or a criminal liability?
14. Would a purchaser of a security have to prove that he relied only on a misleading statement at the time he was deciding to purchase the security if the suit is based on the grounds that the statement was misleading?
15. Does exemption from provisions of the Act extend to acts of fraud?

Appendix

C

Legal Liability Under the Securities Exchange Act of 1934

SECTION 18 and RULE 10b-5

H. L. Green v. Childree
185 F. Supp. 95 (S.D.N.Y. 1960)

Action: Plaintiff sued defendant accountants alleging conspiracy to defraud by inducing the plaintiff to agree to a merger.

Facts: Accountants knowingly certified false financial statements in connection with a merger transaction. Defendants claimed a merger is not a purchase or sale.

Decision: Court ruled a merger is a "purchase or sale" and the false financial statements involved accountant as a participant in the sale. The fact the accountants' activities were confined to the preparation of false and misleading financial statements does not immunize the defendants from civil suit for their alleged participation. Court denied accountants' motion to dismiss the Rule 10b-5 action.

Decision: Motion by defendants to dismiss was denied. The action should not fail because of a lack of privity.

Heit v. Weitzen
402 F. 2d 909 (2d Cir., 1968)

Action: Plaintiffs alleged various insiders and the company auditors' failure to disclose overcharges on government contracts.

Facts: Plaintiffs purchased the company's securities at inflated prices in reliance on various materially false, misleading, and untrue statements about net assets and past and prospective income contained in the annual report and in press releases.

Decision: Plaintiff had a valid claim under Rule 10b-5 and Section 18.

1136 Tenants v. Max Rothenberg & Co.
Appellate Division, New York, 1971,
36 A.D. 2d 804, 319 N.Y.S. 2d 1007

Action: Alleged that accountants were negligent.

Facts: Accountants failed to report missing material invoices that covered up an embezzlement.

Decision: Accountant was retained to audit, not merely to "write-up" the books and records. Procedures of the accountant were incomplete and inadequate.

Herzfeld v. Laventhol, Krekstein,
Horvath & Horvath
540 F. 2d 27 (2d Cir. 1976)

Action: Plaintiff alleges inadequate disclosure of material facts surrounding a real estate transaction to which the auditor had rendered a "subject to" qualification.

Facts: Land was sold to produce a $2,030,000 "profit" with only a nominal down payment by the buyer. The buyer was a company in such a weak financial condition to make payments of the balance of the purchase price uncertain. The auditor issued a qualified opinion subject to collection of the balance of the money owed. Buyer underwent a Chapter XI reorganization.

Decision: The court ruled that a "subject to realization" qualification does not necessarily provide investors with all the facts necessary to make intelligent decisions. The financial statements did not fairly present the financial condition of the buyer "to the untutored eye of an ordinary investor." Compliance with GAAP is no assurance of satisfying the statutory requirement for fair presentation.

Rhode Island Hospital Trust National Bank
v.
Swartz, Biesenoff, Yavner & Jacobs
455 F. 2d 847
(4th Cir., 1972)

Action: In tort for damages. Action brought by clients who, although not in privity with the accountant, were known by the accountant to be relying upon auditor's report at the time the engagement was undertaken (or prior to accountant's report).

Facts: Plaintiff alleged auditors to be liable for negligence by failing to explain the reason for a qualified opinion with respect to client's fixed assets and the effect upon the company's financial statements.

Decision: Auditor held liable for not complying with AICPA standards for the profession. Neither qualified opinions nor disclaimers can be relied upon by auditors to avoid liability.

Section 32

United States v. Simon
(2d Cir., 1969)

Action: Indictment charged defendants with drawing up and certifying a false financial statement for Continental Vending Corporation.

Facts: Statement failed to disclose that the President of Continental borrowed money from an affiliate in which he owned about 25% of the stock. The statement inaccurately reported the status of the affiliate's receivables.

Decision: Motion for acquittal was denied and defendants fined by the judge.

United States v. Natelli
F. 2d (2d Cir., 1975)

Action: Indictments charged the auditor willfully made false and misleading statements in a proxy statement filed with the SEC.

Facts: Footnotes concerning net sales and earnings were materially misleading.

Decision: Conviction affirmed.

5 Regulation S–X and the Basic Financial Statements

Accounting standards that are applicable to the financial statements of publicly owned corporations come from three basic sources. First and foremost, the accounting profession establishes generally accepted accounting principles (GAAP) through its standard-setting organizations. Second, the Securities Act of 1933 enumerates the statements required to be filed by registrants. (The Securities Exchange Act does not have a similar provision.) Finally, Section 19 of the Securities Act gives the SEC the power to:

> . . . prescribe . . . the items or details to be shown in the balance sheet and the earnings statement, and the methods to be followed in the preparation of accounts, in the appraisal or valuation of assets and liabilities, in the determination of depreciation and depletion, in the differentiation of recurring and nonrecurring income, in the differentiation of investment and operation income, and in the preparation, where the Commission deems it necessary or desirable, of consolidated balance sheets or income accounts of any person directly or indirectly controlling or controlled by the issuer, or any person under direct or indirect common control with the issuer. . . .

Section 13(b) of the Securities Exchange Act makes similar provisions giving the SEC the power to establish accounting standards. The SEC, acting under that authority, has issued Regulation S-X. The regulation, supported by the Accounting Series Releases (ASRs), is the authoritative source of SEC requirements regarding the form and content of all financial statements, their notes and schedules, filed as part of registration statements meeting the requirements of:

1. The Securities Act of 1933.
2. Section 12, annual or other reports under Sections 13 and 15(d), and proxy

and information statements under Section 14 of the Securities Exchange Act of 1934.

3. Public Utility Holding Company Act of 1935, and annual reports filed thereunder.

4. Investment Company Act of 1940, and annual reports filed thereunder.

Regulation S-X is organized into articles by subject matter. Exhibit 5-1 summarizes the matters addressed in the regulation.

Before we study the provisions of Regulation S-X and the ASRs let us first examine some important concepts underlying the financial statements. Financial statements are the representations of management. The statements must reflect accounting practices and principles which have *substantial authoritative support*. Their use must result in the financial statements' presenting fairly the financial condition of the registrant.

Exhibit 5-1 Contents of Regulation S-X

Article	Subject
1	*Application of Regulation S-X*
	Regulation S-X applies to filings (1) through (4) above. Article 1 also defines terms used throughout the regulation.
2	*Qualifications and Reports of Accountants*
	Article 2 will be discussed in Chapter 8.
3	*Rules of General Application*
4	*Consolidated and Combined Financial Statements*
5	*Commercial and Industrial Companies*
	Specific accounting requirements for all companies which do not fall under one of the special categories in Articles 5A-10.
5A	*Companies in the Development Stage*
	Specific accounting requirements for.
6	*Management Investment Companies*
6A	*Unit Investment Trusts*
6B	*Face-Amount Certificate Investment Companies*
6C	*Employee Stock Purchase, Savings and Similar Plans*
7	*Insurance Companies Other Than Life Insurance Companies*
7A	*Life Insurance Companies*
8	*Committees Issuing Certificates of Deposit*
9	*Bank Holding Companies and Banks*
10	*Natural Persons*
11 and 11A	*Statement of Other Stockholders Equity and Statement of Source and Application of Funds*
12	*Form and Content of Schedules*

CONCEPTS UNDERLYING THE FINANCIAL STATEMENTS

Financial Statements—the Representations of Management

The accounting profession has long held the position that financial statements are the representations of management. This premise was reaffirmed in *Statement on Auditing Standard No. 1* (Section 110.02). *Accounting Series Release No. 62,* issued in 1947, states the SEC's concurrence that: "Financial statements filed for the registrant and its subsidiaries have been recognized by this Commission and by public accountants generally as representations of management upon whom rests the primary responsibility for their propriety and accuracy."

The function of the independent accountant is to verify the statements, and his opinion letter does not relieve management of its primary responsibility.

Substantial Authoritative Support

It is the nature of the accounting discipline to accommodate many ways of doing the same thing, and this characteristic makes identifying the most appropriate GAAP in a specific circumstance troublesome. The profession uses the standard *substantial authoritative support,* a term that itself is not definitive, to define what are and are not generally accepted accounting principles. Until 1964, when the Council of the American Institute of Certified Public Accountants resolved that future Opinions of the Accounting Principles Board would have the status of substantial authoritative support, the respect accorded professional pronouncements depended upon their considerably varied powers to persuade.

In 1973 the SEC recognized the newly formed body responsible for establishing accounting principles, the Financial Accounting Standards Board (FASB) ASR No. 150 announced the SEC's intention to accept FASB pronouncements as having substantial authoritative support.

The SEC, in its report to Congress entitled *The Accounting Profession and the Commission's Oversight Role,* in June 1978, added the Statements of Position (SOP) published by the Accounting Standards Executive Committee (AcSec) on industry accounting standards to its body of authoritative sources until such time as the FASB can deal with the problem.

Today the hierarchy of authority that is generally accepted is:

Highest Authority[1]	Accounting Research Bulletins
	Accounting Principles Board Opinions
	Financial Accounting Standards Board Statements and Interpretations
Secondary Authority	SEC and other regulatory agency requirements
	AICPA Accounting Interpretations
	AICPA Industry Accounting Guides
	Industry accounting practices (e.g., those shown to

Varied Power of Influence

prevail in the AICPA publication *Accounting Trends and Techniques*)

Accounting Principles Board Statements

AICPA Statements of Position (SOPs)

Statements of other professional associations

Accounting Research Studies

Accounting textbooks and articles

The hierarchy recognized by the SEC in *ASR No. 4* (1938) is somewhat different (and its position is supported by federal law):

> *In cases where there is a difference of opinion between the Commission and the registrant as to the proper principles of accounting to be followed, disclosure will be accepted in lieu of correction of the financial statements themselves only if the points involved are such that there is substantial authoritative support for the practices followed by the registrant and the position of the Commission has not previously been expressed in rules, regulations or other official releases of the Commission, including the published opinions of its Chief Accountant. (Authors' underscore)*

The SEC claims the authority to substitute its principles for those of the accounting profession by means of rules, regulations, and the Accounting Series Releases and to require a registrant to make whatever disclosures it deems necessary.

Fair Disclosure

The underlying purpose of SEC accounting requirements is to provide the investing public with fair disclosure of financial information regarding publicly traded companies. The SEC Advisory Committee on Corporate Disclosure[2] has concluded that the primary function of disclosure is to assure public availability of informed investment information. A secondary objective is to regulate corporate conduct. To those ends the committee recommended that "the commission ought to provide information for reasonably sophisticated investors and not attempt to simplify complex disclosure so that every investor can understand it."

Where alternative generally accepted accounting principles with substantial authoritative support exist or where the use of generally accepted accounting principles would result in misleading financial statements, it is necessary to determine on a case by case basis what disclosure is fair.

As Appeals Judge Henry J. Friendly wrote in his 1969 decision regarding the Continental Vending Corp. case:

> *The first law for accountants [is] not compliance with generally accepted accounting principles but, rather, full and fair disclosure, fair presentation*

and, if principles [do] not produce this brand of disclosure, accountants [can] not hide behind the principles but . . . [should] go behind them and make whatever disclosures [are] necessary for full disclosure . . . 'present fairly' [is] a concept separate from 'generally accepted accounting principles,' and the latter [does] not necessarily result in the former.

The American Institute of Certified Public Accountants reaffirms this position in the Code of Professional Ethics, Section 203:

There is a strong presumption that adherence to officially established accounting principles would in nearly all instances result in financial statements that are not misleading . . . upon occasion there may be unusual circumstances where the literal application of pronouncements on accounting principles would have the effect of rendering financial statements misleading. In such cases, the proper accounting treatment is that which will render the financial statements not misleading. . . .

Fair disclosure, then, is information that is qualitatively and quantitatively sufficient to make the financial statements not misleading. Perhaps more than any other, the criterion used by the SEC in evaluating financial statements is: Is the form and content of the whole and any part such that it will tend to mislead the reader? For example, in the 1930s it was a common practice, when management and the independent accountants could not agree on appropriate GAAP, for the accountant to accept financial statements that did not conform to GAAP and to footnote or qualify the opinion "subject to" the nonconforming principle. The SEC considered this double negative approach to have the effect of misleading the reader and issued *ASR No. 4* that states, in part:

In cases where financial statements filed with this Commission pursuant to its rules and regulations under the Securities Act of 1933 or the Securities Exchange Act of 1934 are prepared in accordance with accounting principles for which there is no substantial authoritative support, such financial statements will be presumed to be misleading or inaccurate despite disclosures contained in the certificate of the accountant or in footnotes to the statements provided the matters involved are material.

The SEC continues to consider this practice to be contrary to fair disclosure except in limited cases (for example, when the requirements of a regulating agency conflict with generally accepted accounting principles).

FINANCIAL STATEMENTS IN GENERAL

Because the SEC has delegated the responsibility of establishing generally accepted accounting principles to the accounting profession, Regulation S-X is primarily directed toward establishing ground rules for the presentation of investment information. That is, the major focus of Regulation S-X is to delineate standards of financial statement *disclosure*.

These standards reflect the assumption that financial statements that communicate investment information fairly share similar characteristics. Their form, content, and terminology are determined by the nature of the registrant's business; no one statement is appropriate for all entities. They are succinct and report only material items. They mislead neither by omission nor by commission. And the accounting principles used in their preparation are both explicit and applied consistently from one period to the next.[3]

FORM, ORDER, AND TERMINOLOGY (RULE 3-01)

(a) Financial statements may be filed in such form and order, and may use such generally accepted terminology, as will best indicate their significance and character in the light of the provisions applicable thereto.

(b) All money amounts required to be shown in financial statements may be expressed in whole dollars, in thousands of dollars or in hundred thousands of dollars, as appropriate; provided that, when stated in other than whole dollars, an indication to that effect is inserted immediately beneath the caption of the statement or schedule, or at the top of the money columns, or at an appropriate point in narrative material. The individual amounts shown need not be adjusted to the nearest dollar, or thousand or hundred thousands if in a note it is stated that the failure of the items to add to the totals shown is due to the dropping of amounts less than $1.00, $1,000 or $100,000, as appropriate.

(c) Negative amounts (red figures) shall be shown in brackets or parentheses and so described in the related caption, columnar heading or a note to the statement or schedule, as appropriate.

Dart Industries' financial statements (beginning on page 283) reflect the requirements of this rule. The amounts are reported rounded to the nearest thousand dollars; negative amounts are indicated in parentheses. The form and order of the statements are as described in accounting textbooks, and the only deviation from terminology we are familiar with is where specialized terms are needed to describe adequately the nature of the item.

Materiality

ITEMS NOT MATERIAL (3-02)

If the amount which would otherwise be required to be shown with respect to any item is not material, it need not be separately set forth.

Items that are *material* contain information of significance to the reader. If a reasonable decision-maker would consider the information important, it is material. Materiality, however, does not necessarily depend upon the amount of the item. The SEC concept of materiality is derived from statutory provisions and court decisions, and its intention is that no significant items be permitted to be omitted.

The SEC concept of materiality includes some matters that are material by right of their nature, if not necessarily significant in amount. *ASR No. 41* places the following items in this category:

> *. . . amounts due to and from officers and directors, because of their special nature and origin, ought generally to be set forth separately even though the dollar amounts involved are relatively small. Likewise, disclosure of the various types of surplus, the important reserve accounts, and, under present conditions, the accrued liability for taxes is of importance. In the same way, in the corporate income statement of a company having large investments in subsidiaries or in the securities of unaffiliated companies, the disclosure of income from dividends and interest is necessary irrespective of the amount, since the absence or smallness of dividend and interest income is of as great importance as the exact amount thereof. In the income statement generally, it is important that the major elements such as sales and cost of sales, substantial items of other income and income deductions, and the provision for income and excess profits taxes be separately disclosed, unless to do so would violate the provisions of the Code of Wartime Practices. Finally, care should be taken that the necessary descriptive and explanatory footnotes applicable to the particular statements are set forth.*

The SEC provides concrete materiality criteria in very limited cases. *ASR No. 41* limits the permissible amount of compensation in disclosing balance sheet items. Generally, an item amounting to more than 10 percent of its immediate category (such as deferred charges), or more than 5 percent of total assets must be disclosed separately. Further, where the immediate category is 5 percent or more, components of that category cannot be combined under a single caption.

Another SEC definition of materiality regards Management's Discussion and Analysis of the Summary of Operations filed as an item in Forms S-1 and 10-K. (To be discussed in Chapter 7).

Succinctness

INAPPLICABLE CAPTIONS AND OMISSION OF UNREQUIRED OR INAPPLICABLE FINANCIAL STATEMENTS (RULE 3-03)

> *(a) No caption need be shown in any financial statement as to which the items and conditions are not present.*
>
> *(b) Financial statements not required or inapplicable because the required matter is not present need not be filed.*
>
> *(c) Financial statements omitted and the reasons for their omission shall be indicated in the list of financial statements required by the applicable form.*

OMISSION OF SUBSTANTIALLY IDENTICAL NOTES (RULE 3-04)

If a note covering substantially the same subject matter is required with respect to two or more financial statements relating to the same or affiliated persons, for which separate sets of notes are presented, the required information may be shown in a note to only one of such statements, provided that a clear and specific reference thereto is made in each of the other statements with respect to which the note is required.

OMISSION OF NAMES OF CERTAIN SUBSIDIARIES (RULE 3-05)

Notwithstanding the requirements as to particular statements, subsidiaries, the names of which are permitted to be omitted from the list of affiliates required by the applicable form, need not be named in any financial statement. Reasonable grouping of such subsidiaries may be made, with an explanatory group caption which shall state the number of subsidiaries included in the group.

Dart Industries' financial statements contain no captions for which there is a zero balance. The note to the financial statements entitled "Segment Operating Data" (page 308) pertain to the balance sheet and to the statement of earnings and retained earnings, as do many of the others. None of the financial statements names any of the subsidiaries individually.

Completeness

Presenting information that meets specified requirements still is insufficient if its probable effect would be to mislead the reader.

ADDITIONAL INFORMATION (RULE 3-06)

The information required with respect to any statement shall be furnished as a minimum requirement to which shall be added such further material information as is necessary to make the required statements in the light of the circumstances under which they are made not misleading. This rule shall be applicable to all statements required to be filed, including copies of statements required to be filed in the first instance with other governmental agencies.

Dart Industries discloses its resort development assets separately from its investments and other assets on its balance sheet, page 303. Because the resort development segment of the corporation is unrelated to the other segments and because of the operating considerations specific to resort development, it is necessary to disclose the amount of assets invested in that activity. *ASR No. 41* anticipates this type of situation in imposing its materiality criteria. Resort developments are only 4 percent of total assets, but are 38 percent of the investments and other assets category. Therefore, under the criteria of *ASR No. 41*, resort development assets are disclosed as a separate line item.

BALANCE SHEETS (RULE 5-02)

Standards of disclosure for balance sheets, income statements, the statement of stockholders' equity, and the statement of source and application of funds are found in Articles 3, 11, and 11A of Regulation S-X and standards specific to commercial and industrial companies are the topic of Article 5, Rule 5-02 dealing with the balance sheet.[4]

CURRENT ASSETS

The total amount of current assets should be presented.

CURRENT ASSETS (RULE 3-11)

Assets and other resources classed with cash and its equivalent as current assets shall be reasonably expected to be realized in cash or sold or consumed within one year. However, if the normal operating cycle of the company is longer than one year, generally recognized trade practices may be followed with respect to the inclusion of items such as installment receivables or inventories long in process, provided an appropriate explanation of the circumstances is made and, if practicable, an estimate is given of the amount not realizable within one year. The captions specified under Rules 3-11 and 3-12 are not required for persons which do not normally distinguish current assets and liabilities from noncurrent.

1. **Cash and cash items** *State separately (a) cash on hand and unrestricted demand deposits; (b) legally restricted deposits held as compensating balances against short-term borrowing arrangements; (c) time deposits and certificates of deposit (excluding amounts included in (b) above or Rule 5-02-18(c) below); (d) funds subject to repayment on call or immediately after the date of the balance sheet required to be filed; and (e) other funds, the amounts of which are known to be subject to withdrawal or usage restrictions, e.g., special purpose funds. The general terms and nature of such repayment provisions in (d) and withdrawal or usage restrictions in (b) or (e) shall be described in a note referred to herein. In cases where compensating balance arrangements exist but are not shown on the balance sheet, describe in the notes to the financial statements these arrangements and the amounts involved, if determinable, for the most recent audited balance sheet required and for any subsequent unaudited balance sheet required in the notes to the financial statements. Compensating balances that are maintained under an agreement to assure future credit availability shall* *be disclosed in the notes to the financial statements along with the amount and terms of such agreement.*

Accounting Series Release No. 148 and *Staff Accounting Bulletin No. 1* interpret the requirement for *compensating balances* and offer guidelines for disclosure. For example, undisclosed comingling of compensating balances with other funds that have different liquidity characteristics and that bear no determinable relationship to borrowing arrangements is prohibited. *ASR No. 148* also covers time deposits and certificates of deposit for special purpose funds. We can see from Dart's balance sheet (page 303) and notes to its statements that Dart Industries has no compensating balances but discloses time deposit balances, as required.

2. **Marketable securities.** *Include only securities having a ready market and which represents the investment of cash available for current operations; securities which are intended to be used for nonworking capital purposes shall be excluded. Securities of affiliates and of other persons the investments in which are accounted for by the equity method shall not be included here. State, parenthetically, or otherwise, the basis of determining the aggregate amounts shown in the balance sheets for the portfolio of equity securities and for all other securities and for each category state the alternative of the aggregate cost or the aggregate market value at the balance sheet date. When the original cost of securities purchased on a yield basis has been properly adjusted to reflect amortization of premium or accumulation of discount since acquisition, the basis of determining their amount may be described "at cost."*

ASR No. 188 requires that marketable securities and long-term investment holdings in New York City notes that are in moratorium, other securities issued by the City of New York that will mature within three years, securities of the Municipal Assistance Corporation that were issued in exchange for New York City notes in moratorium, or securities of the Municipal Assistance Corporation that were made subject to an agreement modifying terms that amount to more than 10 percent of stockholders' equity require disclosure in the notes of pertinent information specified in the release.

As a general rule, valuation and qualifying accounts for marketable securities or other accounts must be shown separately in the financial statements as deductions from the specific assets to which they apply (Rule 3-09).

Dart Industries' marketable securities are presented at cost that approximates market.

3. **Accounts and notes receivable.** *(a) State separately amounts receivable from (1) customers (trade); (2) parents and subsidiaries; (3) other affiliates and other persons the investments in which are accounted for by the equity method; (4) underwriters, promoters, directors, officers, employees, and principal holders (other than affiliates) of equity securities of the person and its affiliates; and (5)* *others. Exclude from (4) amounts for purchases by such persons subject to usual trade terms, for ordinary travel and expense advances and for other such items arising in the ordinary course of business. With respect to (2) and (3), state separately in the registrant's balance sheet the amounts which in the related consolidated balance sheet are (i) eliminated and (ii) not eliminated.*

(b) If receivables maturing after one year are included here under a longer current operating cycle (see Rule 3-11), state in a note to the financial statements the amount thereof and, if practicable, the amounts maturing in each year. Interest rates on major receivable items maturing after one year, or classes of receivables so maturing, shall be set forth, or an indication of the average interest rate, or the range of rates, on all receivables shall be given.

(c) Receivables from a parent, a subsidiary, an affiliate or other person designated under (a) (2) and (a) (3) above shall not be considered as current unless the net current asset position of such person justifies such treatment.

(d) If the aggregate amount of notes receivable exceeds 10 percent of the aggregate amount of receivables, the above information shall be set forth separately for accounts receivable and notes receivable.[5]

(e) If receivables include amounts representing balances billed but not paid by customers under retainage provisions in contracts, state the amount thereof either in the balance sheet or in a note to the financial statements. In addition, state the amounts, if any expected to be collected after one year. If practicable, state by years when the amounts are expected to be collected.

(f) If receivables include amounts (other than amounts reportable under paragraph (g) below) representing the recognized sales value of performance under long-term contract (see Rule 5-02.6(d)) and such amounts had not been billed and were not billable to customers at the date of the balance sheet, state separately in the balance sheet or in a note to the financial statements, the amount thereof and include a general description of the prerequisites for billing. In addition, state the amount, if any, expected to be collected after one year.

(g) If receivables include amounts under long-term contracts (see Rule 5-02.6(d)), whether billed or unbilled, representing claims or other similar items subject to uncertainty concerning their determination or ultimate realization, state separately in the balance sheet or in a note to the financial statements, the amount thereof and include a description of the nature and status of the principal items comprising such amount. In addition, state the amount, if any expected to be collected after one year.

4.   **Allowances for doubtful accounts and notes receivable.** *Accounts and notes receivable known to be uncollectible shall be excluded from the assets as well as from the allowance accounts.*

5.   **Unearned income.** *Unearned discounts, finance charges and interest included in receivables shall be shown separately and deducted from the applicable receivable caption.*

Installment sales receivables maturing within one year from the balance sheet date are current assets and any deferred income tax liability relating thereto is a separate current liability. Such receivables maturing in later periods are classified as noncurrent *(ASR No. 102).*

Dart Industries presents only current receivables. We can infer from its presentation that the company has no material notes receivable, nor receivables from affiliated corporations, underwriters, promoters, directors, officers, employees, and principal holders of equity securities of the corporation. This is confirmed by the note to the financial statements entitled "Details of Balance Sheet." Receivables other than trade account for only 7 percent of the total category. The statement meets Rule 3-09 in that the balance in the valuation account, Allowance for Doubtful Accounts, is disclosed.

*6. **Inventories.** (a)State separately here, or in a note referred to herein, if practicable, the major classes of inventory such as (1) finished goods; (2) inventoried costs relating to long-term contracts or programs (see (d) below and Rule 3-11); (3) work in process (see Rule 3-11); (4) raw materials; and (5) supplies.*

(b) The basis of determining the amounts shall be stated.

If "cost" is used to determine any portion of the inventory amounts, describe the method of determining cost. This description shall include the nature of the cost elements included in inventory.

If "market" is used to determine any portion of the inventory amounts, describe the method of determining "market" if other than current replacement cost.

The method by which amounts are removed from inventory (e.g., "average cost," "first-in, first-out," "last-in, first-out," "estimated average cost per unit") shall be described. If the estimated average cost per unit is used as a basis to determine amounts removed from inventory under a total program or similar basis of accounting, the principal assumptions (including, where meaningful, the aggregate number of units expected to be delivered under the program, the number of units delivered to date and the number of units on order) shall be disclosed.

If any general and administrative costs are charged to inventory, state in a note to the financial statements the aggregate amount of general and administrative costs incurred in each period and the actual or estimated amount remaining in inventory at the date of each balance sheet.

(c) If the LIFO inventory method is used, the excess of replacement or current cost over stated LIFO value shall, if material, be stated parenthetically or in a note to the financial statements.

(d) For purposes of Rules 5-02.3 and 5-02.6, long-term contracts or programs include (1) all contracts or programs for which gross profits are recognized on a percentage-of-completion method of accounting or any variant thereof (e.g., delivered unit, cost to cost, physical completion) and (2) any contracts or programs accounted for on a completed contract basis of accounting where, in either case, the contracts or programs have associated with them material amounts of inventories or unbilled receivables and where such contracts or programs have been or are expected to be performed over a period of more than

twelve months. Contracts or programs of shorter duration may also be included, if deemed appropriate.

For all long-term contracts or programs, the following information, if applicable, shall be stated in a note to the financial statements:

(i)   The aggregate amount of manufacturing or production costs and any related deferred costs (e.g., initial tooling costs) which exceeds the aggregate estimated cost of all in-process and delivered units on the basis of the estimated average cost of all units expected to be produced under long-term contracts and programs not yet complete, as well as that portion of such amount which would not be absorbed in cost of sales based on existing firm orders at the latest balance sheet date. In addition, if practicable, disclose the amount of deferred costs by type of cost (e.g., initial tooling, deferred production, etc.).

(ii)   The aggregate amount representing claims or other similar items subject to uncertainty concerning their determination or ultimate realization, and include a description of the nature and status of the principal items comprising such aggregate amount.

(iii)   The amount of progress payments netted against inventory at the date of the balance sheet.

Dart has complied with the requirements of Rule 5-02 in footnotes entitled "Details of Balance Sheet" and "Unaudited General Description of the Impact of Inflation." The condensed figure for inventories is supported in the footnote by detailed information concerning raw material and supplies, work in process, and finished goods. The bases for accounting for inventories are stated in the "Summary of Accounting Policies" (page 302) that precedes the financial statements. They are the lower of cost or market, cost being manufacturing or purchase cost, with appropriate reduction in value for obsolete and damaged merchandise.

7.   **Other current assets.**   *Any amounts in excess of 5 percent of total current assets must be separately stated, and any others remaining may be classified under a heading, "other current assets."*

Dart presents prepaid expenses and deferred future income tax benefits separately although at 2 and 4 percent, respectively, neither is required to be segregated.

10.   **Securities of affiliates and other persons.**   *Include under this caption amounts representing investments in affiliates and investments in other persons which are accounted for by the equity method, and state the basis of determining these amounts. State separately in the registrant's balance sheet the amounts which in the related consolidated balance sheet are (a) eliminated and (b) not eliminated.*

11. **Indebtedness of affiliates and other persons—not current.** *Include unde this caption indebtedness of affiliates and indebtedness of other persons th investments in which are accounted for by the equity method. State separatel in the registrant's balance sheet the indebtedness which in the related consol dated balance sheet is (a) eliminated and (b) not eliminated.*

12. **Other security investments.** *State, parenthetically or otherwise, the basi of determining the aggregate amounts shown in the balance sheet for the port folio of equity securities and for all other securities, and for each category stat the alternate of the aggregate cost or the aggregate market value at the balanc sheet date.*

13. **Other investments.** *State separately, by class of investments, any items i excess of five percent of total assets.*

Dart presents its holdings in 3M common stock in conformance with thes requirements, at the lower of cost or market, disclosing current market valu parenthetically. Its other security holdings amount to five percent or less of tota assets and are not disclosed separately.

14. **Property, plant and equipment.** *(a) State separately here, or in a note referred to herein, if practicable, each major class, such as land, buildings machinery and equipment, leaseholds, or functional grouping such as revenu producing equipment or industry categories and the basis of determining the amounts; i.e., cost, cost plus manufacturing profit, etc.*

(b) Tangible and intangible utility plant of a public utility company shall be seg regated so as to show separately the original cost, plant acquisition adjustments and plant adjustments, as required by the system of accounts prescribed by th applicable regulatory authorities. This rule shall not be applicable in respect o companies which are not otherwise required to make such a classification o have not completed the necessary original cost studies. If such classification i not otherwise required or if such original cost studies have not been completed an appropriate explanation of the circumstances shall be set forth in a note which shall include a specific statement as to the status of the original cost stud ies and, to the extent practicable, the results indicated thereby.

A separate disclosure of accumulated depreciation, depletion and amortizatio of property, plant and equipment is necessary. Some of Dart Industries' plan and equipment is reported as a capitalized financial lease. The footnote disclo sure requirements for leases will be discussed separately. Again Dart meets the requirements for disclosure of major classes of properties in the note, "Details of Balance Sheet." The properties, owned and leased, consist of land, buildings and improvements, machinery and equipment, and construction in progress.

16. **Intangible assets.** *State separately each major class, such as goodwill franchises, patents or trade-marks, and the basis of determining their respectiv amounts.*

Dart Industries reports its intangibles net of amortization accumulated to date

17. **Other assets.** *State separately (a) non-current receivables from persons specified in captions 3(a) (1) and (4) above; (b) each pension or other special fund; (c) legally restricted deposits held as compensating balances against long-term borrowing arrangements; and (d) any other item not properly classed in one of the preceding asset captions which is in excess of five percent of total assets.*

18. **Prepaid expenses and deferred charges.** *State separately any material items. Items properly classed as current may, however, be included under caption 8.*

19. **Preoperating expenses and similar deferrals.** *State separately each major class and, in a note referred to herein, the policy for deferral and amortization. Where the amounts deferred or amortized are material, such amounts as shown by Rule 12-08 shall be stated in the note for each period reported on.*

20. **Deferred organization expense.** *State, in a note referred to herein, the policy for deferral and amortization.*

21. **Deferred debt expense.** *State, in a note referred to herein, the policy for deferral and amortization.*

22. **Deferred commissions and expense on capital shares.** *State, in a note referred to herein, the policy for deferral and amortization. These items may be shown as deductions from other stockholders' equity.*

Dart Industries' resort development assets represent, in part, long-term installment sales receivables. The requirement for disclosure of their nature is met in the "Summary of Accounting Policies," under "Resort Development," page 302.

CURRENT LIABILITIES

The total amount of current liabilities should be disclosed.

CURRENT LIABILITIES (RULE 3-12)

Obligations which are payable within one year or whose liquidation is reasonably expected to require the use of existing current assets (see Rule 3-11) or the creation of other current liabilities shall be classed as current liabilities. However, if the normal operating cycle of the company is longer than one year, generally recognized trade practices may be followed with respect to the exclusion of items such as customers' deposits and deferred income, provided an appropriate explanation of the circumstances is made.

Rule 3-13 requires reacquired evidences of indebtedness to be deducted from the liability caption except for those held for pension and other special purposes that may be shown as assets of the fund if parenthetical disclosure is made of the amount of the indebtedness, the cost thereof, and the amount at which it is stated.

23. **Accounts and notes payable.** *(a) State separately amounts payable to (1) banks for borrowings; (2) factors or other financial institutions for borrowings; (3) holders of commercial paper; (4) trade creditors; (5) parents and subsidiaries; (6) other affiliates and other persons the investments in which are accounted for by the equity method; (7) underwriters, promoters, directors, officers, employees and principal holders (other than affiliates) of equity securities of the person and its affiliates; and (8) others. Exclude from (7) amounts for purchases from such person subject to usual trade terms, for ordinary travel expenses and for other such items arising in the ordinary course of business. With respect to (5) and (6) state separately in the registrant's balance sheet the amounts which in the related consolidated balance sheet are (i) eliminated and (ii) not eliminated.*

(b) The weighted average interest rate and general terms (as well as formal provisions for the extension of the maturity) of each category of aggregate short term borrowings (the sum of items (a) (1), (a) (2) and (a) (3) above) reflected on each balance sheet required shall be disclosed along with the maximum amount of aggregate short-term borrowings outstanding at any month end (or similar time period) during each period for which an end-of-period balance sheet is required. In addition, the approximate average aggregate short-term borrowing outstanding during the period and the approximate weighted average interest rate (and a brief description of the means used to compute such averages) for such aggregate short-term borrowings shall be disclosed in the notes to the financial statements.

(c) The amount and terms (including commitment fees and the conditions under which lines may be withdrawn) of unused lines of credit for short-term financing shall be disclosed, if significant, in the notes to the financial statements. The amount of these lines of credit which support a commercial paper borrowing arrangement of similar arrangements shall be separately identified.

24. **Accrued liabilities.** *State separately (a) payrolls; (b) taxes, indicating the current portion of deferred income taxes; (c) interest; and (d) any other material items, indicating any liabilities to affiliates.*

25. **Other current liabilities.** *State separately (a) dividends declared; (b) current portion of bonds, mortgages and similar debt; and (c) any other item in excess of five percent of total current liabilities, indicating any liabilities to affiliates. The remaining items may be shown in one amount.*

Dart Industries discloses financial information pertaining to current liabilities in conformance with these requirements. (Trade) accounts payable are presented separately from payables on foreign short-term notes. The notes are held either by banks or by other holders of commercial paper, we cannot tell which. Their general terms and weighted average interest rates at year-end and during the period, maximum amount of borrowings at any month end, average short-term borrowings outstanding during the period, and the method of calculating the interest rate are disclosed in the note to the financial statements entitled "Short-Term Loans and Borrowing Arrangements" (page 312). The current installments of long-term debt are unsecured notes. The footnote, "Details of Balance Sheet,

Long-Term Debt Less Current Installments,'' discloses the interest rates for unsecured notes and the fact that they mature in part in 1978. The part maturing in 1978 is classified as current. Notice that because long-term debt balances are less volatile than short-term borrowings, less detail regarding the former is required.

We will discuss the requirements for obligations under capital leases later. This topic affects both the current installments of obligations under capital leases, and the long-term liability classification, resort development liabilities.

Dart presents separate accrued liabilities balances for (income) taxes, payroll, and accrued expenses other than for payrolls, taxes and interest. The disclosure required for the deferred income taxes related to installment sales receivables will be covered later under income tax footnote disclosure.

Dart's unused lines of short-term credit and the immateriality of compensating balance requirements complete the disclosure required for current liabilities.

29. **Bonds, mortgages and similar debt.** *(a) State separately here, or in a note referred to herein, each issue or type of obligation and such information as will indicate (see Rule 3-13) (1) the general character of each type of debt including the rate of interest; (2) the date of maturity, or if maturing serially, a brief indication of the serial maturities, such as 'maturing serially from 1980 to 1990'; (3) if the payment of principal or interest is contingent, an appropriate indication of such contingency; (4) a brief indication of priority; (5) if convertible, the basis; and (6) the combined aggregate amount of maturities and sinking fund requirements for all issues, each year for the five years following the date of the balance sheet. For amounts owed to affiliates, state separately in the registrant's balance sheet the amounts which in the related consolidated balance sheet are (i) eliminated and (ii) not eliminated.*

(b) The amount and terms (including commitment fees and the conditions under which commitments may be withdrawn) of unused commitments for long-term financing arrangements that would be disclosed under this rule if used shall be disclosed in the notes to the financial statements if significant.

30. **Unamortized debt discount and premium.** *The amounts applicable to debt issues under captions 5-02-29, 31, 32 or 33 shall be deducted from or added to the face amounts of the issues under the particular caption either individually or in the aggregate, but if the aggregate method is used the face amounts of the individual issues and the applicable unamortized discount or premium shall be shown parenthetically or otherwise.*

31. **Indebtedness to affiliates and other persons—not current.** *Include under this caption indebtedness to* affiliates *and indebtedness to other persons the investments in which are accounted for by the equity method. State separately in the registrant's balance sheet the indebtedness which in the related consolidated balance sheet is* (a) *eliminated and* (b) *not eliminated.*

32. **Other long-term debt.** *(a) Include under this caption all amounts of long-term debt not provided for under captions 29(a) and 31 above. State separately amounts payable to (1) persons specified in captions 25(a) (1), (2), (3) and (6);*

and (2) others, specifying any material item. Indicate the extent that the debt i collateralized. Show here, or in a note referred to herein, the information required under caption 29.

(b) The amount and terms (including commitment fees and the condition. under which commitments may be withdrawn) of unused commitments for long term financing arrangements not provided for under caption 29 (b) above shal be disclosed in the notes to the financial statements if significant.

33. **Other liabilities.** *State separately any item not properly classed in one o the preceding liability captions which is in excess of five percent of tota liabilities.*

34. **Commitments and contingent liabilities.** [*See Rule 3-16(i).*]

35. **Deferred credits.** *State separately amounts for (a) deferred income taxes (b) deferred tax credits, and (c) material items of deferred income. The curren portion of deferred income taxes shall be included under caption 26 (see ASF No. 102). [See also Rule 3-16(o).]*

Each of Dart Industries' three bond issues and two unsecured notes are dis closed in the footnote, "Details of Balance Sheet." The general character o each obligation (its interest rate; maturity date(s), and the convertible provision where applicable) is disclosed. We can assume that no payment of principal o interest is contingent, and that no unconsolidated indebtedness to affiliates, no priority of claim exists. From the information given we can determine the amoun of maturities for the next five years and the amount of unamortized discount fo the 7½ percent sinking fund debentures.

Notice that total liabilities need not be shown and our example does not do so

37. **Minority interests in consolidated subsidiaries.** *State separately in a note referred to herein amounts represented by preferred stock and the applicable dividend requirements if the preferred stock is material in relation to the consol idated stockholders' equity.*

Dart apparently has no minority interest represented by preferred stock.

38. **Capital shares** *State for each class of shares the title of issue, the number of shares authorized, the number of shares issued or outstanding, as appropriate (see Rules 3-14 and 3-15), and the dollar amount thereof, and, if convertible, the basis of conversion (see also Rule 3-16 (f) (3)). Show also the dollar amount, i any, of capital shares subscribed but unissued, and show the deduction of sub scriptions receivable therefrom. Show here, or in a note or statement referred to herein, the changes in each class of capital shares for each period for which an income statement is required to be filed.*

39. **Other stockholders' equity.** *(a) Separate captions shall be shown for (1 paid-in additional capital, (2) other additional capital and (3) retained earnings (i) appropriated and (ii) unappropriated.*

(b)   If undistributed earnings of unconsolidated subsidiaries and 50-percent-or-less-owned persons *are included, state the amount in each category parenthetically or in a note referred to herein.*

(c)   For a period of at least 10 years subsequent to the effective date of a quasi-reorganization, any description of retained earnings shall indicate the point in time from which the new retained earnings dates and for a period of at least three years shall indicate the total amount of the deficit eliminated.

(d)   A summary of each account under this caption setting forth the information prescribed in Rule 11-02 shall be given for each period for which an income statement is required to be filed.

REACQUIRED SHARES (RULE 3-14)

Reacquired shares not retired shall be shown separately as a deduction from capital shares, or from the total of capital shares and other stockholders' equity, or from other stockholders' equity, at either par or stated value, or cost, as circumstances require.

DISCOUNT ON CAPITAL SHARES (RULE 3-15)

Discount on capital shares, or any unamortized balance thereof, shall be shown separately as a deduction from capital shares or from other stockholders' equity as circumstances require.

Dart Industries has authorized two classes of stock, Preferred Series A, and Common. The number of shares authorized and the number and dollar amount of shares issued are shown. No subscriptions are outstanding, but the preferred stock is convertible, and, therefore, the basis of conversion is disclosed. [We will discuss Rule 3-16 (f) (3), Preferred Stocks, footnote disclosure requirements in Chapter 6.] The description of stock changes during the period is disclosed in the statements required by Rule 11-02 and will be discussed under that caption. Dart also discloses the balance of its paid-in capital and retained earnings accounts. No retained earnings are restricted, no reorganization of the corporation has occurred to require the dating of the retained earnings account. Dart's holdings in treasury shares are deducted, at cost, from stockholders' equity.

Two Accounting Series Releases pertain to special stock valuation problems: *ASR No. 113* deals with the evaluation of restricted securities; *ASR No. 124* deals with accounting for stock distributions. Securities issued by private and/or small corporations under Rule 237 (discussed in Chapter 3) are restricted as to their transferability. That is, they may not be sold for a period of five years after issue. This restriction adversely affects the value of the securities to an indeterminate degree. Because there are no market quotations for securities that are not saleable, it is necessary to establish a value for the securities by other means. *ASR No. 118* requires the board of directors of the issuing corporation, acting in good faith, to determine the fair value of the securities if market quotations are not readily available. Factors that determine fair value might include the discount from market of a similar, freely traded security and the use of a multiple of earnings. Transactions such as these usually require a "subject to" opinion and the release contains suggested wording in such a case. *ASR No. 113* also pertains to restricted securities.

ASR No. 124 defines distributions of less than 25 percent of the shares of the same outstanding class to be a stock dividend. A distribution of less than 25 percent of the shares of the same outstanding class must be accounted for by a transfer from retained earnings to other capital accounts at the fair value of the shares issued. This provision supports the position taken by the accounting profession in *Accounting Research Bulletin No. 43* and prevents the transfer to permanent capital of an amount exceeding the balance in retained earnings. It, therefore, subjects stock dividends to the same limitations as for cash dividends.

Dividend income on the registrant's own stock held in a sinking fund cannot be reported as income of the registrant *(ASR No. 5)*.

BASIS OF DETERMINING AMOUNTS —BOOK VALUE (RULE 3-10)

If an instruction requires a statement as to "the basis of determining the amount," the basis shall be stated specifically. The term "book value" will not be sufficiently explanatory unless, in a particular instruction, it is stated to be acceptable with respect to a particular item.

Dart avoids the term "book value" as required.

INCOME STATEMENT

(a) All items of profit and loss given recognition in the accounts during each period covered by the income statements, except retroactive adjustments, shall be included in the income statement for each such period (see Rule 3-07).

(b) Only items entering into the determination of net income or loss may be included.

(c) If income is derived from sales of tangible products (caption 1A below) and/or operating revenues of public utilities (caption 1B below) and/or other revenues (caption 1C below), each class which is not more than 10 percent of the sum of the items may be combined with another class. If these items are combined, the cost of tangible goods sold (caption 2A below), operating expenses of public utilities (caption 2B below), and costs and expenses applicable to other revenues (caption 2C below) may be combined in the same manner.

1A. **Net sales of tangible products (gross sales less discounts, returns and allowances).** *State separately, if practicable, (a) sales to unconsolidated affiliates, including 50-percent-owned persons, and (b) sales to others. If the total of sales and revenues under captions 1A, 1B and 1C includes excise taxes in an amount equal to 10 percent or more of such total, the amount of such excise taxes shall be shown parenthetically or otherwise.*

2A. **Cost of tangible goods sold.** *(a) State the amount of cost of tangible goods sold as regularly computed under the system of accounting followed. State separately here or in a note referred to herein, if practicable, (a) purchases from unconsolidated affiliates, including 50-percent-owned persons and (b) purchases from others. Indicate the amount of beginning and ending inventories and state the basis of determining such amounts.*

(b) Merchandising organizations, both wholesale and retail, may include occupancy and buying costs under this caption. However, publicity costs shall be included under caption 4 below or shown separately.

3A. **Research and development expenses.** *State here or in a note referred to herein the amount of the total research and development costs charged to expense.*

1C. **Other revenues (such as royalties, rents and the sales of services and intangible products, e.g., engineering and research and development).** *State separately, if practicable, revenues from and sales to (a) unconsolidated affiliates, including 50-percent-owned persons, and (b) others.*

2C. **Costs and expenses applicable to other revenues (caption 1C).** *State the amount of costs and expenses applicable to other revenues as regularly computed under the system of accounting followed. State separately here or in a note referred to herein, if practicable, purchases from and services rendered by (a) unconsolidated affiliates, including 50-percent-owned persons, and (b) others.*

3. **Other operating costs and expenses.** *State separately any material amounts not included in caption 2A, 2B or 2C above.*

4. **Selling, general and administrative expenses.** *Any unusual material items shall be disclosed parenthetically or otherwise.*

5. **Provision for doubtful accounts and notes.**

6. **Other general expenses.** *Include items not normally included in caption 4 above. State separately any material amount.*

7. **Dividends.** *State separately, if practicable, the amount of dividends from (a) securities of affiliates, (b) marketable securities, and (c) other securities. Exclude from this caption dividends from both subsidiaries and investments which are accounted for by the equity method.*

8. **Interest on securities.** *State separately, if practicable, the amount of interest from (a) securities of affiliates, (b) marketable securities, and (c) other securities. Disclose, parenthetically or in a note referred to herein, interest from securities of companies the investments in which are accounted for by the equity method.*

9. **Profits on securities.** *Profits shall be stated net of losses. No profits on the person's own equity securities, or profits of its affiliates on their own equity securities, shall be included under this caption. State, here or in a note referred to herein, the method followed in determining the cost of securities sold, e.g., "average cost," "first-in, first-out," or "identified certificate." Consideration should be given to reporting such transactions under caption 19, when appropriate.*

10. **Miscellaneous other income.** *State separately any material amounts, indicating clearly the nature of the transactions out of which the items arose. Miscellaneous other income may be stated net of miscellaneous income deductions, provided that any material amounts are set forth separately.*

Income Deductions

11. **Interest and amorization of debt discount and expense.** *State separately (a) interest on bonds, mortgages and similar debt; (b) amortization of debt discount and expense (or premium); and (c) other interest.*

12. **Losses on securities.** *Losses shall be stated net of profits. No losses on the person's own equity securities, or losses of its affiliates on their own equity securities, shall be included under this caption. State, here or in a note referred to herein, the method followed in determining the cost of securities sold, e.g., "average cost," "first-in, first-out," or "identified certificate." Consideration should be given to reporting such transactions under caption 19, when appropriate.*

13. **Miscellaneous income deductions.** *State separately any material amounts, indicating clearly the nature of the transactions out of which the items arose. Miscellaneous income deductions may be stated net of miscellaneous other income, provided that any material amounts are set forth separately.*

14. *Income or loss before income tax expense and appropriate items below.*

15. **Income tax expense.** *Include under this caption only taxes based on income. [See Rule 3-16(o).]*

16. **Minority interest in income of consolidated subsidiaries.**

17. **Equity in earnings of unconsolidated subsidiaries and 50 percent or less owned persons.** *The amount reported under this caption shall be stated net of any applicable tax provisions. State, parenthetically or in a note referred to herein, the amount of dividends received from such persons. If justified by circumstances, this item may be presented in a different position and a different manner. [See Rule 3-01 (a).]*

19. **Extraordinary items, less applicable tax.** *State separately any material items and disclose, parenthetically or otherwise, the tax applicable to each.*

20. **Cumulative effects of changes in accounting principles.** *State separately any material items and disclose, parenthetically or otherwise, the tax applicable to each.*

21. **Net income or loss.** *See Rule 5-02 [caption 39(d)].*

22. **Earnings per share data.** *Refer to the pertinent requirements in the appropriate filing form.*

Dart Industries, in its "Statement of Earnings and Retained Earnings" (page 305), discloses net sales and there were no material sales to unconsolidated affiliates or excise taxes collected in excess of 9 percent of sales. Dart's other income is 1 percent of total revenues and, therefore, is too immaterial for disclosure of interest and dividends from securities.

The "Cost of Goods Sold" combined with "Operating Expenses" relating to the other income are reported separately from "Selling," Distribution, and Administrative Expenses." No material research and development expenses were incurred. "Interest Expense" and the "Provision for Income Taxes" are presented in conformance with Rule 5-03. "Depreciation and Amortization Expense" is disclosed as a material amount although, at 4 percent of costs and expenses, it does not meet the 5 percent rule. It is, however, in conformance with the Rule 3-16(m) footnote requirement for disclosure of the depreciation/amortization provisions.

Three Accounting Series Releases have been issued concerning ratios calculated from income statement data. Although data on earnings per share are required, *ASR No. 142* prohibits the use of cash flow per share information in the financial statements. *ASR Nos. 119* and *122* require that where a computation of the ratio of earnings to fixed charges is made, the fixed charges denominator may not be reduced by such items as investment interest income or certain gains, nor may the numerator be adjusted to exclude subsidiaries' operations otherwise reported in the consolidated income statement.

CONTENT OF STATEMENTS OF OTHER STOCKHOLDERS' EQUITY (ARTICLE 11)

1. Balance at beginning of period. *State separately the adjustments to the balance at the beginning of the first period of the report for items which were retroactively applied to periods prior to that period. (See Rule 5-03 (a))*

2. Net income or loss from income statement.

3. Other additions. *State separately any material amounts, indicating clearly the nature of the transactions out of which the items arose.*

4. Dividends. *For each class of shares state the amount per share and in the aggregate. (a) Cash, and (b) Other. (Specify)*

5. Other deductions. *State separately any material amounts, indicating clearly the nature of the transactions out of which the items arose.*

6. Balance at end of period. *The balance at the end of the most recent period shall agree with the related balance sheet caption.*

By combining the "Income Statement" and "Statement of Changes in Retained Earnings," Dart meets Article 11's requirements for disclosure of retained earnings balances and transactions during the period, specifically those transactions pertaining to dividend distribution, in aggregate and per share, for each class of stock outstanding. The value and nature of the stock dividend, therefore, was presented as a separate item from cash dividends.

The remaining requirements of Article 11 are met through the use of two statements (page 306), the "Statement of Capital Stock" and the "Statement of Capital in Excess of Par Value." Other additions to the capital stock accounts were stock dividends, exercise of options, and conversion of preferred stock. Each of these transaction categories produced concurrent capital in excess of par value.

STATEMENT OF SOURCE AND APPLICATION OF FUNDS (ARTICLE 11A)

As a minimum, the following shall be reported:

(a) Sources of funds:

(1) Current operations (showing separately net income or loss and the addition and deduction of specific items which did not require the expenditure or receipt of funds; e.g., depreciation and amortization, deferred income taxes, undistributed earnings or losses of unconsolidated persons, etc.)

(2) Sale of noncurrent assets (identifying separately such items as investments, fixed assets, intangibles, etc.)

(3) Issuance of debt securities or other long-term debt

(4) Issuance or sale of capital stock

(b) Disposition of funds:

(1) Purchase of noncurrent assets (identifying separately such items as investments, fixed assets, intangibles, etc.)

(2) Redemption or repayment of debt securities or other long-term debt

(3) Redemption or purchase of capital stock

(4) Dividends

(c) Increase (decrease) in net funds or working capital.

Dart Industries' "Statement of Changes in Financial Position" (page 307) reports the above categories of items. No working capital was provided from the increases in capital stock and capital in excess of par accounts, but working capital was provided by operations, sale of noncurrent assets and the issuance of long-term debt. Working capital was used to purchase noncurrent assets, to redeem long-term debt and to pay dividends.

CONSOLIDATED AND COMBINED FINANCIAL STATEMENTS (ARTICLE 4)

The overriding goal of Article 4 is to help establish principles of consolidation "which . . . clearly exhibit the financial position and results of operations of the registrant and its *subsidiaries.*" Of subsidiaries which are majority owned only the following situations may prevent consolidation with the *parent:*

1. Subsidiaries whose financial statements are as of a date or for periods different from those of the registrant may not be consolidated unless the difference is 93 days or less.[6]
2. Where foreign subsidiaries are operated under political, economic or currency restrictions, consolidated reporting may not be permitted.[7]

The retroactive combination of financial statements following a pooling of interests, is an exception to the 93-day rule. However, when the fiscal years of the entities do not end within 93 days of each other, the financial statements for the most recent fiscal year usually must be recast to dates which do not differ by more than 93 days and disclosures are then made of: (1) the periods combined; and (2) the sales or revenues and net income (before and after extraordinary items) exluded or included more than once in the results of operations as recast.

The 93-day rule also does not apply to the results of operations of 50-percent-or-less-owned-persons accounted for by the equity method. In accounting for these affiliates, the registrant should eliminate intercompany items and transactions, and if this is not done, a statement of the reasons why not and the accounting methods used must be made. Finally, where there is a difference between the book value of the 50-percent-or-less-owned-person and the parent's investment account reported on the equity method, a statement must be made in a note to the latest balance sheet of the amount and accounting treatment of that difference.

In addition to consolidated financial statements, separate financial statements are necessary for significant consolidated subsidiaries engaged in the business of: (1) life insurance; (2) fire and casualty insurance; (3) securities broker/dealer; (4) finance (including factoring, mortgage banking and leasing, but excluding subsidiaries with only nonfinancing leases); and (5) savings and loan or banking (including all subsidiaries of banks). Separate financial statements are also necessary for all nonsignificant consolidated subsidiaries in businesses other than those itemized above where the registrant's investment in those subsidiaries exceeds 10 percent of the registrant's total assets.

The requirement for separate financial statements is not without its exceptions, however. Separate financial statements may be omitted when the consolidated subsidiary or group of consolidated subsidiaries are in the same business as the registrant and if either: (1) more than 90 percent of their sales and revenues are derived from the registrant and its other subsidiaries; or (2) the registrant and its other subsidiaries' proportionate share of total assets, total sales and revenues, and income before income taxes and extraordinary items of the subsidiary (or group of subsidiaries) each exceeds 90 percent of those amounts on the consolidated financial statements. Separate financial statements must be filed, however, if the amounts of net income before income taxes and extraordinary items are not both income or both loss. If the consolidated average income (or loss) is less than the most recent consolidated income (or loss), the average over five years can be used in lieu of the most recent figure.

Dart Industries' foreign subsidiaries are apparently not operated under political, economic or currency restrictions, and are, therefore, consolidated. According to the "Summary of Accounting Policies" Dart's insurance subsidiary is wholly owned but not significant, and, therefore, the parent does not present separate financial statements for the subsidiary. Dart also participates with a third party in a joint operating agreement and the ownership of a corporation. Therefore its 50 percent interest in all the related assets, liabilities, revenue, and expense accounts is reflected in the consolidated accounts. We will discuss footnote disclosure requirements for consolidated entities further in Chapter 6.

SUMMARY   The objective of SEC requirements for financial statements is to provide the public with reliable investment information. The reliability of financial statements is epitomized by the concept fair disclosure that comes about by preparing financial statements that: (1) conform to generally accepted accounting principles with substantial authoritative support; (2) report material matters; and (3) report in a way which does not mislead the reader.

Regulation S-X, entitled "Form and Content of Financial Statements," is the authoritative source for SEC accounting requirements. It is augmented by certain of the Accounting Series Releases. In Chapter 5 we have examined: (1) the general requirements for financial statements (Article 3); (2) the specific requirements for the balance sheet and income statement of commercial and industrial corporations (Article 5); (3) the statement of other stockholders' equity (Article 11); (4) the statement of source and application of funds (Article 11A); and (5) the standards for consolidating financial statements (Article 4).

The consolidated financial statements of Dart Industries illustrate the application of the SEC's standards. The standards of disclosure are primarily applicable to the financial statements themselves, but because each registrant's situation is unique, the required disclosures can be made in a variety of ways, provided the means chosen enhances the fairness of the presentation. For this reason, Dart has elected to disclose the more detailed data in footnotes to the financial statements and to condense the financial statements to the extent permissible under Regulation S-X. Further requirements for footnote disclosure follow in Chapter 6.

FOOTNOTES FOR CHAPTER 5

1. As defined in the Code of Professional Ethics, Rule 203-2, (New York: American Institute of Certified Public Accountants, p. 4582).
2. The Report of the Advisory Committee on Corporate Disclosure appears in *The Journal of Accountancy,* (January, 1977), p. 3.

3. The excerpts below are quoted from Regulation S-X, December, 1977.
4. Regulation S-X caption numbers have been retained in this text for ease of reference. Missing caption numbers contain only titles and in the interest of clarity have been excluded.
5. This provision specifically applies the materiality criterion originally published in *ASR No. 41*.
6. If such a subsidiary is consolidated, the registrant must also report the closing date of the subsidiary and briefly explain the need for the difference.
7. If the foreign subsidiary is consolidated, disclosure must be made, where reasonably determinable, of the effect of foreign exchange restrictions upon the consolidated financial position and operating results of the consolidated entity.

GLOSSARY   **Affiliate**   An affiliate of or with a person is one that directly or indirectly, through one or more intermediaries, controls or is controlled by or is under common control with, the person specified.

Amount   When used to reference securities means:
   a. The *principal* amount of a debt obligation if "amount" relates to evidence of indebtedness.
   b. The number of *shares* if "amount" relates to shares.
   c. The number of *units* if "amount" relates to any other kind of securities.

Compensating Balance   Restricted deposits required by a bank to be held against short-term borrowings.

Disclosure   The identification of accounting policies and principles that materially affect the determination of financial position, changes in financial position, or results of operations.

Fifty-Percent-Owned-Person   A person whose outstanding voting shares are approximately 50 percent owned by another specified person directly, or indirectly through one or more intermediaries.

Material   Pertains to information regarding any subject, limits the information required to those matters about which an average prudent investor ought reasonably to be informed.

Parent   An affiliate that controls another specified person directly, or indirectly through one or more intermediaries.

Person   An individual, a corporation, a partnership, an association, a joint-stock company, a business trust, or unincorporated organization.

Subsidiary   An affiliate controlled by a specified person directly, or indirectly through one or more intermediaries.

Substantial Authoritative Support   FASB principles, standards, and practices (found in the Statements and Interpretations), and AICPA Accounting Research Bulletins and AICPA Opinions (except to the extent altered, amended, supplemented, revoked, or superseded by an FASB Statement).

QUESTIONS   1. What is Regulation S-X?
   2. Do the rules of Regulation S-X absolutely insure a careful, competent, and accurate audit of a publicly held corporation for public information?

3. Do the securities acts expect an investor to possess a depth of accounting and analytical knowledge in order to obtain a reasonable picture of the registrant's financial reports?

4. Is the primary responsibility for the accuracy of financial statements that of the management of the corporation or of the independent auditor?

5. What is meant by "substantial authoritative support?"

6. If there is a conflict between "substantial authoritative support" for an accounting procedure and an SEC accounting rule, which in your opinion will prevail, insofar as the SEC is concerned?

7. Does following generally accepted accounting principles assure that all material information has been "fairly disclosed?"

8. What does the phrase "not misleading" mean?

9. What is meant by the "form and content" of financial statements governed by S-X? For example, does S-X specify what statements are to be included in a registration statement?

10. Does S-X include all of the accounting principles and procedures promulgated by the SEC?

11. What is a "note" to a financial statement? Is an auditor responsible for the accuracy of a note?

12. Must a registrant disclose any unusual circumstances which may affect significantly the business outlook for the company?

6 Regulation S–X: Footnotes and Schedules

We discussed disclosure requirements for the four basic financial statements for commercial and industrial corporations in Chapter 5. We learned that in many cases Dart Industries has employed footnotes to the financial statements to present financial information that as a practical matter could not be disclosed in the statements themselves. Chapter 6 discusses financial disclosure that, by reason of its scope, detail, and complexity is intended to be presented in *footnotes* to the financial statements or in *schedules* filed with the SEC. The distinction between footnotes and schedules is an important one.

Footnotes append the financial statements that are both distributed in reports to stockholders and filed with the SEC. The nature of information required to be disclosed is set forth in Regulation S-X, but the precise form in which the information appears is left to the discretion of the registrant. Schedules, on the other hand, are required only in filings with the SEC, for example, on Form S-1 or 10-K, not in the annual report to stockholders. Regulation S-X prescribes what schedules are required and the form those schedules must take. Schedule information is the more detailed and specific, so is not considered to be of interest to the general reader. For example, the schedule required by Rule 12-02 requires that the registrant provide detailed information concerning its material holdings of marketable securities, by issuer. For registrants with sizeable holdings in equity securities, this schedule is longer than all the financial statements taken together.

FOOTNOTES

The nature of footnote disclosure for all categories of registrants is detailed in Rules 3-07, 3-16 and 3-18 of Regulation S-X. Certain accounting series releases also impose disclosure requirements that usually pertain to registrants who face special reporting problems due to the nature of their industry. Exhibit 6-1 sum-

Exhibit 6-1 Rule 3-16 and 3-18 Footnote Disclosure

Rule 3-16	Item	Disclosure
(a)	Principles of consolidation or combination	A
(b)	Principles of translation of items in foreign currencies	A
(c)	Assets subject to lien	B
(d)	Intercompany profits and losses	A
(e)	Defaults	B
(f)	Preferred shares	B
(g)	Pension and retirement plans	
	Subheadings: (1), (2), (4), (5)	A
	Subheading: (3)	B
(h)	Restrictions that limit the availability of retained earnings for dividend purposes	B
(i)	Commitments and contingent liabilities	B
(j)	Bonus, profit sharing, and other similar plans	A
(k)	Significant changes in bonds, mortgages, and similar debt	B
(l)	Bases of revenue recognition	A
(m)	Depreciation, depletion, obsolescence and amortization	A
(n)	Capital stock optioned, sold or offered for sale to directors, officers and key employees	A
(o)	Income tax expense	A
(p)	Warrants or rights outstanding	B
(q)	Leased assets and lease commitments	C
(r)	Interest capitalized	A
(s)	Disagreements on accounting and financial disclosure matters	A
(t)	Disclosure of selected quarterly financial data in notes to financial statements	A
3-17*		D
3-18	Oil and gas reserves	B

KEY

A For all statements required to be filed.

B As of the most recent audited balance sheet and any subsequent unaudited balance sheet being filed.

C As specified therein.

D As of the end of each fiscal year for which a balance sheet is to be filed.

*The requirement to disclose replacement cost information was deleted effective for fiscal years ending after December 25, 1979.

marizes the time period or date(s) when this information must be presented. We discuss these topics shortly, but first, a few words about the summary of accounting principles and practices.

Summary of Accounting Principles and Practices

The summary of accounting principles and practices is usually the first footnote in corporate annual reports. When using financial statements, the decision-maker must know what accounting principles and practices have been followed in their preparation. Regulation S-X establishes the specific requirements for disclosure of accounting principles and practices. For commercial and industrial registrants they are found in: (1) Rules 3-16, and 3-18; (2) Rule 4-04; and (3) Rules 5-02 and 5-03. We have already identified in Dart's "Summary of Accounting Policies" disclosures that are required by Rules 5-02 and 5-03. They concerned inventories and resort development principles. As the discussion of Rules 3-16 and 3-18 proceeds, we will return to the summary of accounting principles and practices.

Rule 3-08 encourages registrants to summarize these disclosures under one footnote.

SUMMARY OF ACCOUNTING PRINCIPLES AND PRACTICES (RULE 3-08)

Information required in notes as to accounting principles and practices reflected in the financial statements may be presented in the form of a single statement. In such case, specific references shall be made in the appropriate financial statements to the applicable portion of such single statement.

Dart Industries' presentation, "Summary of Accounting Policies" (page 302), is typical of most registrants' disclosure in that it does summarize these accounting matters into one footnote subheaded by item.

PRINCIPLES OF CONSOLIDATION OR COMBINATION [RULE 3-16 (a)]

With regard to consolidated or combined financial statements, refer to Article 4 for requirements for supplemental information in notes to the financial statements.

Rule 3-16(a) requires the registrant to present a statement of the principles used in *consolidating* or combining *financial statements,* which statement must include the information specified in Rule 4-04.

STATEMENT AS TO PRINCIPLES OF CONSOLIDATION OR COMBINATION FOLLOWED (RULE 4-04)

(a) A brief description of the principles followed in consolidating or combining the separate financial statements, including the principles followed in determining the inclusion or exclusion of (1) subsidiaries in consolidated or com-

bined financial statements and (2) companies in consolidated or combined financial statements, shall be stated in the notes to the respective financial statements.

(b) As to each consolidated financial statement and as to each combined financial statement, if there has been a change in the persons included or excluded in the corresponding statement for the preceding fiscal period filed with the Commission which has a material effect on the financial statements, the persons included and the persons excluded shall be disclosed. If there have been any changes in the respective fiscal periods of the persons included made during the periods of the report which have a material effect on the financial statements, indicate clearly such changes and the manner of treatment.

Accounting Series Release No. 3 prohibits the elimination from the parent's investment account of an amount equal only to the par or stated value of a subsidiary's stocks held by the parent. Only that part of the parent's investment account remaining after the elimination of a proportionate share of par value, paid-in capital in excess of par, and retained earnings (that is, the amount representing the excess cost of the subsidiary's stock over the equities in the net assets represented thereby) is properly a component of the consolidated assets.

Because this position reflects current generally accepted accounting principles, *ASR No. 3* is primarily of interest today for its statement that "(T)he purpose of a consolidated balance sheet is to reflect the financial condition of a parent company and its subsidiaries as if they were a single organization." It is by this criterion that bases of consolidation continue to be evaluated.

Dart discloses, in its note, "Basis of Consolidation (Summary of Accounting Policies)," the bases of inclusion and exclusion of entities in the consolidated financial statements; it also states that significant intercompany items have been eliminated and that any subsidiaries not consolidated are accounted for by the equity method.

Rule 4-04(b) information appears separately in the footnote, "Business Combinations and Dispositions" (page 310). The fiscal periods of the consolidated entities have not changed, but during the current fiscal year United States Rexall Drug Company was sold. This subsidiary's net sales of $45 million were material, hence it is mentioned by name. The effect of other disposals and discontinued operations on the financial statements was immaterial and, therefore, it is unnecessary to identify the items specifically. The same holds true for the purchases made during 1977.

PRINCIPLES OF TRANSLATION OF ITEMS IN FOREIGN CURRENCIES [RULE 3-16(b)]

When items in foreign currencies *are included in the financial statements being presented, there shall be stated (1) a brief description of the principles followed in translating the foreign currencies into United States currency and (2) the amount and disposition of the unrealized gain or loss.*

Dart Industries' note "Translation of Foreign Currencies (Summary of Accounting Policies)" complies with the disclosure requirements of Rule 3-16(b) and with *FASB Statement No. 8, Accounting for the Translations of Foreign Currency Transactions and Foreign Currency Financial Statements.* Nonmonetary balance sheet items, cost of goods sold, depreciation and amortization are translated at their historical rates, monetary items at the current exchange rate. Income statement items other than cost of goods sold, depreciation and amortization are translated at the average rate of exchange in effect during the year. Exchange gains and losses are an element of the current year's net income. The note, "International Operations" (page 311) tells us that exchange losses in 1976 and 1977 were immaterial.

Dart's footnote, "International Operations," discloses the undistributed earnings of foreign subsidiaries included in consolidation and the dividends received from them.

ASSETS SUBJECT TO LIEN [RULE 3-16(c)]

Assets mortgaged, pledged, or otherwise subject to lien, and the approximate amounts thereof, shall be stated. If impracticable of accurate determination without unreasonable effort or expense, give an estimate or explain. Dart Disclose: None

DEFAULTS [RULE 3-16(e)]

The facts and amounts concerning any default in principal, interest, sinking fund, or redemption provisions with respect to any issue of securities or credit agreements, or any breach of covenant of a related indenture or agreement, which default or breach existed at the date of the most recent balance sheet being filed and which has not been subsequently cured, shall be stated. Notation of such default or breach of covenant shall be made in the financial statements and the entire amount of obligations to which the default or breach relates shall be classified as a current liability if said default or breach accelerates the maturity of the obligations and makes it current under the terms of the related indenture or agreement. Classification as a current obligation is not required if the lender has waived the accelerated due date or otherwise agreed to a due date more than one year from the balance sheet date. If a default or breach exists, but acceleration of the obligation has been waived for a stated period of time beyond the date of the most recent balance sheet being filed, state the amount of the obligation and the period of the waiver.

Without this provision serious liquidity problems could go undisclosed. Not only unremedied defaults and breaches of covenants must be reported, but also situations wherein the lender has waived acceleration of the defaulted debt. Of interest is not the disposition of the default as much as the occurrence of the default in the first place. Dart has reported neither default nor breach of covenant and we can therefore assume that none has occurred.

PREFERRED SHARES [RULE 3-16(f)]

(1) If callable, the date or dates and the amount per share at which such shares are callable shall be stated. If convertible, the terms of conversion shall be stated briefly.

(2) Arrears in cumulative dividends per share and in total for each class of shares shall be stated.

(3) Aggregate preferences on involuntary liquidation, if other than the par or stated value, shall be shown parenthetically in the equity section of the balance sheet. When the excess involved is material there shall be shown (i) *the difference between the aggregate preference on involuntary liquidation and the aggregate par or stated value;* (ii) *a statement that this difference, plus any arrears in dividends, exceeds the sum of the par or stated value of the junior capital shares and other stockholders' equity applicable to junior shares, if such is the case; and* (iii) *a statement as to the existence of any restrictions upon retained earnings growing out of the fact that upon involuntary liquidation the preference of the preferred shares exceeds its par or stated value.*

Dart Industries' footnote, "Preferred Stock" (page 313), indicates that the preferred shares are callable at any time at $55 per share, and are convertible on an adjusted share for share basis. No dividends in arrears are reported and the "Statement of Changes in Financial Position" (page 307) supports the conclusion that preferred dividends are up to date; the $5,902,000 paid in dividends to preferred stockholders is approximately the amount required, at $2 per share, to pay the annual dividends on all outstanding preferred shares.

The equity section of the balance sheet (page 304) discloses an aggregate preference on liquidation of $149,050,000, that is equal to the preferred stock par value account. If this were not the case, the additional disclosures would serve to emphasize the adverse effect that the difference between liquidating preferences, including dividends in arrears, and the related par capital stock account has on the remaining capital accounts.

PENSION AND RETIREMENT PLANS [RULE 3-16(g)]

(1) A brief description of the essential provisions of any employee pension or retirement plan and of the accounting and funding policies related thereto shall be given.

(2) The estimated cost of the plan for each period for which an income statement is presented shall be stated.

(3) The excess, if any, of the actuarially computed value of vested benefits over the total of the pension fund and any balance sheet pension accruals, less any pension prepayments or deferred charges, shall be given as of the most recent practicable date.

(4) If a plan has not been fully funded or otherwise provided for, the estimated amount that would be necessary to fund or otherwise provide for the past service cost of the plan shall be disclosed as of the date most recently determined.

(5) A statement shall be given of the nature and effect of significant matters affecting comparability of pension costs for any periods for which income statements are presented.

(1) The first paragraph of Dart's footnote, "Retirement Plans" (page 313), briefly describes the basic provisions of the company's pension and retirement plans such as: (a) inception date of each of the two plans; (b) whether the plan is contributory (profit sharing retirement) or noncontributory (pension); and (c) type of employees eligible for participation.

(2) The annual cost (on both a cash and accrual basis) of the pension plan is given in the second paragraph of the footnote. The total pension expense includes the amortization of prior service costs over a 30-year period. The basis of calculating Dart's cash contribution obligation is the subject of the next paragraph.

(3) Vested benefits exceeded total pension fund assets and accruals by approximately $26.8 million at December 31, 1977 (last paragraph of the footnote).

(4) Total estimated unfunded prior service cost was approximately $55.7 million at December 31, 1977.

(5) Dart discloses no changes affecting comparability of the above figures between 1976 and 1977. Because the calculations are extremely sensitive to changes in actuarial assumptions, the requirement to disclose such changes limits the ability of registrants to smooth reported income by this means.

RESTRICTIONS WHICH LIMIT THE AVAILABILITY OF RETAINED EARNINGS FOR DIVIDEND PURPOSES [RULE 3-16(h)]

Describe the most restrictive of any such restrictions, other than as reported in (f) above, indicating briefly its source, its pertinent provisions, and, where appropriate and determinable, the amount of retained earnings (i) so restricted or (ii) free of such restrictions.

Dart discloses, in its footnote "Long Term Debt" (page 313), a restriction on the payment of cash dividends out of retained earnings from loan agreements with insurance companies.

COMMITMENTS AND CONTINGENT LIABILITIES [RULE 3-16(i)]

(1) If material in amount, there shall be disclosed the pertinent facts relative to firm commitments for the acquisition of permanent or long-term investments and property, plant and equipment and for the purchase, repurchase, construction, or rental of assets under material leases.

(2) A brief statement as to contingent liabilities not reflected in the balance sheet shall be made. In the case of guarantees of securities of other issuers, periodic reports shall include a reference to Schedule XI and reports or pros-

*pectuses which do not include that schedule shall briefly describe such guar-
antees, where only consolidated financial statements are presented, such
information shall relate solely to guarantees of securities of companies no-
included in the consolidation.*

Dart's last footnote, "Commitments and Contingencies" (page 316) disclose-
the minimum annual lease commitments for noncancelable leases in effect as o-
December 31, 1977 for the next five years and the total commitment for all year-
after 1982. The company also is committed to the payment of property taxes
insurance and maintenance related to the leases. Apparently there are no firm-
commitments related to the acquisition of long-lived assets by means other than-
lease.

As with most corporations Dart's contingent liabilities lie in the disposition o-
civil suits that it is defending. None is deemed by management and its counsel to-
have a potentially material and adverse effect on the company's financial position-
or its operations.[1]

BONUS, PROFIT SHARING, AND OTHER SIMILAR PLANS [RULE 3-16 (j)]

*Describe the essential provisions of any such plans in which only directors
officers or key employees may participate, and state, for each of the fisca-
periods for which income statements are required to be filed, the aggregate
amount provided for all plans by charges to expense.*

Dart Industries' profit sharing plan that is limited to directors, officers, or key-
employees is called "Incentive Compensation" (page 314). The essential provisions of the plan are that: (1) the annual awards made to participants are calculated according to a formula approved by the stockholders in 1962; (2) any-
amounts available but not awarded are not available for distribution in the future-
and (3) no outside director participates. One hundred and two officers and-
employees participated in 1977. The compensation expense for both 1976 and-
1977 is disclosed as required.

SIGNIFICANT CHANGES IN BONDS, MORTGAGES, AND SIMILAR DEBT [RULE 3-16(k)]

*Any significant changes in the authorized or issued amounts of bonds, mort-
gages and similar debt since the date of the latest balance sheet being filed for
a particular person or group shall be stated.*

Because Dart Industries discloses no such changes, we can assume that the-
board of directors has authorized no additional debt during the year. The footnote, "Details of Balance Sheet" (page 310), that details the long-term debt outstanding, provides supplemental evidence that there have been no significant-
changes in the company's debt structure during the year.

BASES OF REVENUE RECOGNITION [RULE 3-16(l)]

If sales are made on a deferred basis, such as installment sales or sales of equipment long in process of manufacture, or if sales or revenues are otherwise subject to alternativemethods of revenue recognition, the basis of taking profits into income shall be stated.

The reader of financial statements can assume, unless otherwise informed, that revenue is recognized at the time the sale is made or the service is performed. If the registrant uses an alternative method of revenue recognition, this fact will be disclosed, usually in the summary of accounting principles and practices. Dart's use of the installment method of recognizing sales of resort property is described under "Resort Development Summary of Accounting Policies", (page 311)

DEPRECIATION, DEPLETION, OBSOLESCENCE AND AMORTIZATION.[RULE 3-16(m)]

State the policy followed with respect to—

(1) The provision for depreciation, depletion, obsolescence and amortization of physical properties and capitalized leases, including the methods and, if practicable, the rates used in computing the annual amounts;

(2) The provision for depreciation and amortization of intangible assets or the lack of such provision, including the methods and, if practicable, the rates used in computing the annual amounts;

(3) The accounting treatment for maintenance, repairs, renewals and betterments; and

(4) The adjustment of accumulated depreciation, depletion, obsolescence and amortization at the time the properties are retired or otherwise disposed of, including the disposition of any gain or loss on sale of such properties.

Dart's description of accounting policies relating to the provisions for depreciation, depletion, obsolescence and amortization appear in "Properties and Depreciation" and in "Intangibles (Summary of Accounting Policies)" (page 302). The amount of depreciation and amortization expense is disclosed as a separate line item in the comparative "Statement of Earnings and Retained Earnings" (page 305) and the "Statement of Changes in Financial Position" (page 307). Notice that the disclosure of the methods and rates used in computing the provisions for depreciation and amortization is expressed in quite general terms, and that even though Dart's methods of accounting for repairs, maintenance and disposals conform to the textbook description of generally accepted accounting principles, they are set out in the footnote.

CAPITAL STOCK OPTIONED, SOLD OR OFFERED FOR SALE TO DIRECTORS, OFFICERS AND KEY EMPLOYEES [RULE 3-16(n)]

(1) A brief description of the terms of each option arrangement shall be given, including (i) *the title and amount of securities subject to option;* (ii) *the year or*

years during which the options were granted; and (iii) *the year or years during which the optionees became, or will become, entitled to exercise the options.*

(2) State (i) *the number of shares under option at the balance sheet date, and the option price and the fair value thereof, per share and in total, at the dates the options were granted;* (ii) *the number of shares with respect to which options became exercisable during each period presented, and the option price and the fair value thereof, per share and in total, at the dates the options became exercisable;* (iii) *the number of shares with respect to which options were exercised during each period, and the option price and the fair value thereof, per share and in total, at the dates the options were exercised; and* (iv) *the number of unoptioned shares available, at the beginning and at the close of the latest period presented, for the granting of options under an option plan.*

(3) A brief description of the terms of each other arrangement covering shares sold or offered for sale to only directors, officers and key employees shall be given, including the number of shares, and the offered price and the fair value thereof per share and in total, at the dates of sale or offer to sell, as appropriate.

(4) The required information should be summarized and tabulated, as appropriate, with respect to all option plans as a group and other plans for shares sold or offered for sale as a group.

(5) State the basis of accounting for such arrangements and the amount of charges, if any, reflected in income with respect thereto.

Dart describes its stockholder approved noncompensatory stock option plan in the footnote, "Stock Options," page (313). From it we can determine the following:

1 (i) *Stock subject to option:*

Options outstanding	577,200
Available for grant	+ 679,600
Total Common Stock	1,256,800

(ii) *Years options granted:*

1977	None
Prior to 1977-Exercised	1,364,200
Outstanding at 1/1/77	+ 643,400
Total prior to 1977	2,007,600

(iii) *Years optionees are entitled to exercise options:*
The period beginning one year after grant date and ending five or ten years thereafter.

2 (i) *Number and value of shares under option at 12/31/77:*
577,200 at option price and fair market value per share of $21.21 to $46.69, or $20,659,000 in total.

(ii) *Number and value of shares becoming exercisable:*
Cannot be determined for 1976 or 1977. If no shares were granted in 1976, none would have become exercisable in 1977.

(iii) *Number and value of optioned shares exercised:*
16,000 at $21.21–$33.61 per share, or $428,000 in total.

(iv) *Unoptioned shares available at 12/31/77:* 679,600.

3 *Terms of other exclusive offerings to directors, officers and key employees:* None.

4 *Disclosure:* As required in tabulated form.

5 *Basis of accounting:* Proceeds are credited to the capital accounts (see the Statements of Capital Stock and Capital in Excess of Par Value). No charge against revenues appears in the Statement of Earnings and Retained Earnings indicating that the plan is non-compensatory in nature.

INCOME TAX EXPENSE [RULE 3-16(o)]

(1) Disclosure shall be made, in the income statement or a note thereto, of the components of income tax expense, including (i) *taxes currently payable;* (ii) *the net effects, as applicable, of* (a) *timing differences (Indicate separately the amount of the estimated tax effect of each of the various types of timing differences, such as depreciation, warranty costs, etc., where the amount of each such tax effect exceeds five percent of the amount computed by multiplying the income before tax by the applicable statutory Federal income tax rate; other differences may be combined) and* (b) *operating losses; and* (iii) *the net deferred investment tax credits. Amounts applicable to United States Federal income taxes, to foreign income taxes and to other income taxes shall be stated separately for each major component. Amounts applicable to foreign or other income taxes each of which are less than five percent of the total of the major component need not be separately disclosed.*

(2) If it is expected that the cash outlay for income taxes with respect to any of the succeeding three years will substantially exceed income tax expense for such year, that fact should be disclosed together with the approximate amount of the excess, the year (or years) of occurrence and the reasons therefor.

(3) Provide a reconciliation between the amount of reported total income tax expense (benefit) and the amount computed by multiplying the income (loss) before tax by the applicable statutory Federal income tax rate, showing the estimated dollar amount of each of the underlying causes for the difference. If no individual reconciling item amounts to more than five percent of the amount computed by multiplying the income before tax by the applicable statutory Federal income tax rate, and the total difference to be reconciled is less than five percent of such computed amount, no reconciliation need be provided unless it would be significant in appraising the trend of earnings. Reconciling items that are individually less than five percent of the computed amount may be aggregated in the reconciliation. The reconciliation may be presented in percentages rather than in dollar amounts. Where the reporting person is a foreign entity, the income tax rate in that person's country of domicile should normally be used in making the above computation, but different rates should not be used for subsid-

iaries or other segments of a reporting entity. When the rate used by a reporting foreign person is other than the United States Federal corporate income tax rate, the rate used and the basis for using such rate shall be disclosed.

Dart Industries' footnote, "Income Taxes" (page 312) properly discloses components of income tax expense, broken down into federal, foreign, and state portions.

1	(i)	*Taxes currently payable:*	$93,300,000
	(ii)	*Net effects of:*	
		(a) Timing differences	(1,800,000)
		(b) Operating losses	0
		Income tax expense	91,500,000

(iii) *Net deferred investment tax credit:* None. Investment tax credits are applied to reduce federal income tax expense in the year the credit arises. (See "Income Taxes" ("Summary of Accounting Policies").)

2 *Excess cash outlay for income taxes over provision in the next three years:* None is reported, therefore we can conclude that there will be none.

3 *Reconciliation between total income tax expense and the amount computed by multiplying income by the statutory rate of 48%:*
The reconciliation appears as the last table in the footnote. Reconciling items are state and foreign income taxes, the investment tax credit, and miscellaneous.

WARRANTS OR RIGHTS OUTSTANDING [RULE 3-16(p)]

Information with respect to warrants or rights outstanding at the date of the related balance sheet shall be set forth as follows:

(1) Title of issue of securities called for by warrants or rights.

(2) Aggregate amount of securities called for by warrants or rights outstanding.

(3) Date from which warrants or rights are exercisable and expiration date.

(4) Price at which warrant or right is exercisable.

Dart Industries had no stock warrants or rights outstanding as of December 31, 1977. If it had, there would be footnote disclosure of the above four items.

LEASED ASSETS AND LEASE COMMITMENTS [RULE 3-16(q)]

Any contractual arrangement which has the economic characteristics of a lease such as a "heat supply contract" for nuclear fuel, shall be considered a lease for purposes of this rule. Leases covering oil and gas production rights and min eral and timber rights are not to be considered leases for purposes of this rule. For purposes of this rule, a financing lease is defined as a lease which, during the noncancelable lease period, either (i) covers 75 percent or more of the economic life of the property or (ii) has terms which assure the lessor a full recovery of the fair market value (which would normally be represented by his investment) of the property at the inception of the lease plus a reasonable return on the use of the assets invested subject only to limited risk in the realization of the residual interest in the property and the credit risks generally associated with secured loans. The disclosures set forth under sections (1) and (2) below are only required if gross rental expense in the most recent fiscal year exceeds one percent of consolidated revenues.

(1)   Total rental expense (reduced by rentals from subleases, with disclosure of such amounts) entering into the determination of results of operations for each period for which an income statement is required shall be disclosed. Rental payments under short-term leases for a month or less which are not expected to be renewed need not be included. Contingent rentals, such as those based upon usage or sales, shall be reported separately from the basic or minimum rentals. Rentals on noncapitalized financing leases shall be shown separately for both categories of rentals reported.

(2)   The minimum rental commitments under all noncancelable leases shall be disclosed, as of the date of the latest balance sheet required in the aggregate (with disclosure of the amounts applicable to noncapitalized financing leases) for (i) each of the five succeeding fiscal years; (ii) each of the next three five year periods; and (iii) the remainder as a single amount. The amounts so determined should be reduced by rentals to be received from existing noncancelable subleases (with disclosure of the amounts of such rentals). For purposes of this rule, a noncancelable lease is defined as one that has an initial or remaining term of more than one year and is noncancelable, or is cancelable only upon the occurrence of some remote contingency or upon the payment of a substantial penalty.

(3)   Additional disclosures shall be made to report in general terms: (i) the basis for calculating rental payments if dependent upon factors other than the lapse of time; (ii) existence and terms of renewal or purchase options, escalation clauses, etc.; (iii) the nature and amount of related guarantees made or obligations assumed; (iv) restrictions on paying dividends, incurring additional debt, further leasing, etc.; and (v) any other information necessary to assess the effect of lease commitments upon the financial position, results of operations, and changes in financial position of the lessee.

(4)   For all noncapitalized financing leases there shall be disclosed: (i) The present values of the minimum lease commitments in the aggregate and by major categories of properties, such as real estate, aircraft, truck fleets and other equipment. Present values shall be computed by discounting net lease payments (after subtracting, if practicable, estimated, or actual amounts, if any, applicable to taxes, insurance, maintenance and other operating expenses) at the interest rate implicit in the terms of each lease at the time of entering into the lease. Such disclosure shall be made as of the date of any balance sheet required. If

the present value of the minimum lease commitments is less than five percent of the sum of long-term debt, stockholders' equity and the present value of the minimum lease commitments, and if the impact on net income required to be disclosed under (iv) below is less than three percent of the average net income for the most recent three years, this disclosure is not required; (ii) either the weighted average interest rate (based on present value) and range of rates or specific interest rates for all lease commitments included in the amount disclosed under (i) above; (iii) the present value of rentals to be received from existing noncancelable usbleases of property included under (i) above based on the interest rates implicit in the terms of the subleases at the times of entering into the subleases; (iv) the impact upon net income for each period for which an income statement is required if all noncapitalized financing leases were capitalized, related assets were amortized on a straight-line basis and interest cost was accrued on the basis of the outstanding lease liability. The amounts of amortization and interest included in the computation shall be separately identified. If the impact on net income is less than three percent of the average net income for the most recent three years, that fact may be stated in lieu of this disclosure. In calculating average net income, loss years should be excluded. If losses were incurred in each of the most recent three years, the average loss shall be used for purposes of this test.

The problem of accounting for and reporting lease arrangements has been with us for a long time. The SEC, in *ASR No. 132,* refers to the problem of measurement in lease accounting to the FASB. It later found that professional pronouncements *(APS Opinions No. 5, 7, 27, and 31)* had not established adequate standards of disclosure. *ASR No. 147* specifically cites the lack of a requirement for lessees to disclose the present value of their financing lease obligations and the impact on net income of capitalizing such leases.

In the absence of definitive action by the FASB the SEC issued *ASR No. 184* in November, 1975, substantially amending Rule 3-16(q) and upgrading its standards of accounting and reporting leases. The accounting profession then upgraded its standards with the publication of *FASB Statement No. 13* in November, 1976, and in response the SEC issued *ASR No. 225* conforming its lease accounting and disclosure requirements to those of the FASB.

Statement 13 affects all leases entered into after January 1, 1977. But, while it encourages early retroactive reporting of leases with prior inception dates, it offers a moratorium that delays until January 1, 1981 the requirement to report all outstanding leases in conformance with its provisions. The SEC viewed this delay as unwarranted for publicly held companies and tentatively proposed, subject to further evaluation, that financial statements for fiscal years ending after December 24, 1977, be restated unless a "problem" existed.

A problem was defined as a situation wherein capitalization of capital leases, as defined in Statement 13, "would result in the violation or probable future violation . . . of a restrictive clause in an existing loan indenture or other agreement." After evaluating comments on the proposal, the SEC issued *ASR No.*

235 in which the accelerated date for reporting all leases under the provisions of Statement 13 was permitted to stand. Furthermore, if Rule 3-16 disclosure is not made because of an unresolved problem related to restrictive clauses in loan indentures or other agreements, the problem and its impact must be disclosed in the footnotes.

Finally, lessors, who have not in the past been subject to Rule 3-16(a), are now, beginning in the fiscal years ending after December 24, 1978, governed by 3-16(q) (2). The additional year's delay was granted in order to permit lessors to gather the information necessary to conform with the extended provisions of Rule 3-16.

Dart's gross rental expense in 1977 exceeds the Rule 3-16(q) materiality level of one percent of consolidated revenues and, therefore, it makes all necessary disclosures. The company conforms to the accounting disclosure requirements of *FASB Statement No. 13* for all leases outstanding during the reporting period, that is, it capitalizes all leases under which the company has assumed the benefits and risks of ownership of the leased property. Rule 3-16(q) (4) is, therefore, inapplicable, as is the requirement in Rule 3-16(q) (1) to show separately rental expense on noncapitalized leases.

Note that although Statement 13 requires disclosure of future minimum lease payments for the five succeeding years, Rule 3-16(q) (2) also requires the future minimum rental commitment related to noncancelable leases for each of the next three five-year periods and for the remainder as a single amount. Dart apparently presents as a single amount all minimum rental commitments remaining beyond the first five years and does not break them out into five-year groups. This and all other disclosure of lease information is located in the balance sheet, and in the footnotes "Obligations Under Capital Leases" and "Commitments and Contingencies" (pages 315 and 316).

INTEREST CAPITALIZED [RULE 3-16(r)]

(1)   The amount of interest cost capitalized in each period for which an income statement is presented shall be shown within the income statement. Companies other than electric, gas, water and telephone utilities which follow a policy of capitalizing interest cost shall make the following additional disclosures required by items (2) and (3) below.

(2)   The reason for the policy of interest capitalization and the way in which the amount to be capitalized is determined.

(3)   The effect on net income for each period for which an income statement is presented of following a policy of capitalizing interest as compared to a policy of charging interest to expense as incurred.

Companies that had instituted a policy of capitalizing interest prior to June 21, 1974 may continue to do so on a consistent basis *(ASR No. 163)* but no registrant can extend the practice to new types of assets. Dart reports no capitalized interest.

DISAGREEMENTS ON ACCOUNTING AND FINANCIAL DISCLOSURE MATTERS [*RULE 3-16(s)*]

Disagreements on accounting and financial disclosure matters.—If, (1) within the twenty-four months prior to the date of the most recent financial statements, a Form 8-K has been filed reporting a change of accountants, (2) included in the Form 8-K there was a reported disagreement on any matter of accounting principles or practices or financial statement disclosure, (3) during the fiscal year in which the change of accountants took place or during the subsequent fiscal year there have been any transactions or events similar to those which involved the reported disagreement, and (4) such transactions or events were material and were accounted for or disclosed in a manner different from that which the former accountants apparently would have concluded was required, state the existence and nature of the disagreement and also state the effect on the financial statements if the method had been followed which the former accountants apparently would have concluded was required. These disclosures need not be made if the method asserted by the former accountants ceases to be generally accepted because of authoritative standards or interpretations subsequently issued.

Because Form 8-K is not distributed to stockholders, this provision serves to inform the company's investors of the occurrence of disagreements between management and the independent accountants over accounting principles, practices, or disclosure matters. Dart disclosed no such disagreements with its independent accountants, Price Waterhouse & Co.

Rule 3-16(s) was adopted via *ASR No. 165* to require the disclosure of the *fact* that a disagreement had occurred between management and the independent accountant and the *effect* that changing accountants had on the financial statements.

Rule 3-16(s) was amended by *ASR No. 194* in 1974, to require the disclosure of the fact of disagreement (and concomitant effect) *only* when a change in accountants occurred that resulted in the registrant's continuing to pursue an accounting practice or principle that was not acceptable to the former accountant.

DISCLOSURE OF SELECTED QUARTERLY FINANCIAL DATA IN NOTES TO FINANCIAL STATEMENTS [*RULE 3-16(t)*]

(1)   Exemption. This rule shall not apply to any registrant that does not meet both of the following two tests:

   (i)   First test. The registrant:

     (A)   has securities registered pursuant to Section 12(b) of the Securities Exchange Act of 1934 (other than mutual life insurance companies); or

     (B)   is an insurance company that is subject to the reporting requirements of Section 15(d) of that Act and has securities which also meet the tests set forth in C(1) and C(2) below; or

     (C)   has securities registered pursuant to Section 12(g) of that Act which also

(1)   Are quoted on the National Association of Securities Dealers Automated Quotation System; and

(2)   Meet the following criteria:

   (i)   Three or more dealers stand willing to, and do in fact, make a market in such stock including making regularly published bona fide bids and offers for such stock for their own accounts; or the stock is registered on a securities exchange that is exempted by the Commission from registration as a national securities exchange pursuant to Section 5 of the Securities Exchange Act of 1934.

      (a)   For purposes of this subsection, the insertion of quotations into the National Association of Securities Dealers Automated Quotation System by three or more dealers on at least 10 business days during the six month period immediately preceding the fiscal year for which the financial statements are required shall satisfy the requirement that three dealers be making a market.

   (ii)   There continue to be 800 or more holders of record, as defined in Rule 12g5-1[§240.12g5-1] under the Exchange Act, of the stock who are not officers, directors, or beneficial owners of 10 percent or more of the stock.

   (iii)   The issuer continues to be a U.S. corporation.

   (iv)   There are 300,000 or more shares of stock outstanding in addition to shares held beneficially by officers, directors, or beneficial owners of more than 10 percent of the stock.

   (v)   In addition, the issuer shall meet two of the three following requirements:

      (a)   The shares described in subsection (d) continue to have a market value of at least $2.5 million.

      (b)   The minimum representative bid price of such stock is at least $5 per share.

      (c)   The issuer continues to have at least $2.5 million of capital, surplus, and undivided profits.

Instructions. *1. The computations acquired by* (v)(a) *and* (v)(b) *shall be based on the average of the closing representative bid prices as reported by NASDAQ for the 20 business days immediately preceding the fiscal year for which the financial statements are required.*

   2.   The computation required by *(v)(c)* **shall be as at the last business day of the fiscal year immediately preceding the fiscal year for which the financial statements are required.**

   (ii)   Second test. The registrant and its consolidated subsidiaries (A) have had a net income after taxes but before extraordinary items and the cumulative effect of a change in accounting, of at least $250,000 for each of the last three fiscal years; or (B) had total assets of at least $200,000,000 for the last fiscal year end.

(2)   Disclosure shall be made in a note to financial statements of net sales, gross profit (net sales less costs and expenses associated directly with or allocated to products sold or services rendered), income before extraordinary item and

cumulative effect of a change in accounting, per share data based upon such income, and net income for each full quarter within the two most recent fiscal years and any subsequent interim period for which income statements are presented.

(3) When the data supplied in paragraph (t)(2) of this section varies from the amounts previously reported on the Form 10-Q filed for any quarter, such as would be the case when a pooling of interests occurs or where an error is corrected, reconcile the amounts given with those previously reported describing the reason for the difference.

(4) Describe the effect of any disposals of segments of a business, and extraordinary, unusual or infrequently occurring items recognized in each full quarter within the two most recent fiscal years and any subsequent interim period for which income statements are presented, as well as the aggregate effect and the nature of year-end or other adjustments which are material to the results of that quarter.

(5) Where this note is part of financial statements which are presented as audited, it may be designated "unaudited."

(6) Paragraphs (t)(1) through (t)(4) of this section shall not apply to a foreign private issuer not required to report quarterly financial information on Form 10-Q, provided, however, that a foreign registrant which reports or is required to report interim financial information on Form 6-K shall disclose such data in the manner provided in paragraphs (t)(1) through (t)(4) with respect to the financial information reported on Form 6-K.

ASR No. 177 announces the imposition of Rule 3-16(t), requiring publicly traded corporations to present unaudited interim financial information in filings with the SEC and in their annual reports to stockholders.

Dart's securities are traded principally on the New York Stock Exchange and therefore are registered under Section 12(b) of the Securities Exchange Act of 1934. Dart and its consolidated subsidiaries had both: (1) net income after tax but before extraordinary items and the cumulative effect of a change in accounting of at least $250,000 in each of the past three years; and (2) total assets of at least $200 million as of December 31, 1977. The company, therefore, meets both tests for the application of Rule 3-16(t) and it must present footnote disclosure of interim financial data. The decision diagram in Exhibit 6-2 simplifies the determination of Rule 3-16(t) applicability. As is permitted, Dart's footnote is unaudited (page 315); but the auditors must nonetheless perform review procedures as prescribed by the *AICPA Statement on Auditing Standards No. 24.*

Rule 3-16(t) requires summarized financial information for the most recent two fiscal years and for any subsequent stub period presented including: (1) net sales, (2) gross profit, (3) income before extraordinary items and the cumulative effect of a change in accounting principles, (4) net income, and (5) per share amounts (primary and fully diluted) of (3) above.

Dart reports net sales, income before extraordinary items, etc., and net income [(1), (3) and (4) above] and the sum of cost of goods sold and operating expenses

Exhibit 6-2   Decision Diagram—Exemptions Under Rule 3-16(t) of Regulation S-X

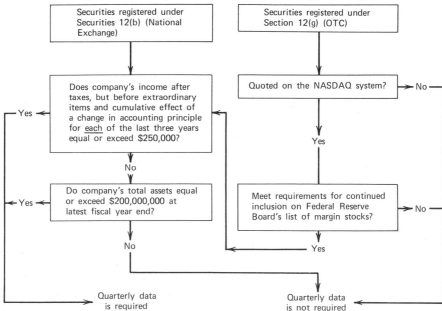

SOURCE. *SEC Rules on Interim Financial Information,* Ernst and Whinney, Financial Reporting Developments, Retrieval Number 38385, December 1975, p. 11.

It does not show gross profit (2) and its earnings per share figures are calculated on net income, not on income before extraordinary items and the cumulative effect of a change in accounting principles.

Had any of the following been material, Dart would have made additional disclosure of:

1.   The effect of any disposals of a segment of a business.
2.   Extraordinary, unusual or infrequently occurring items.
3.   The aggregate effect and nature of year-end or other adjustments.

CHANGES IN ACCOUNTING PRINCIPLES AND PRACTICES AND RETROACTIVE ADJUSTMENTS OF ACCOUNTS (RULE 3-07)

(a)   Any change in accounting principles or practice, or in the method of applying any accounting principles or practice, made during any period for which financial statements are being filed which materially affects comparability of such financial statements with those of prior periods, and the effect thereof upon the net income of the period in which such change is made and, if practicable, of the prior periods for which financial statements are being filed, shall be disclosed in an appropriate manner.

(b)   Any material retroactive adjustment made in income statements during any period for which financial statements are being filed, and the effect thereof upon

net income of prior periods shall be disclosed in a note to the appropriate finan-cial statement; provided, however, that such disclosures need not be made (1) if they have been made in filings with the Commission in prior years or (2) the financial statements which are being retroactively adjusted have not previously been filed with the Commission or otherwise made public.

The use of financial statements is predicated on the assumption that account-ing principles and practices remain consistent from one period to the next. For several reasons this ideal situation cannot always be enjoyed. Professional accounting pronouncements change as do regulatory requirements. Internal changes occur within the registrant: estimates upon which the financial state-ments are based change, segments are discontinued, subsidiaries are added, to name just a few.

The question of fair disclosure is rarely as difficult as when a registrant change from one accounting principle to another. Not only is the principle of consistency violated, but there also exists a need to evaluate whether the change is for the better. That is, in light of current conditions, is the new way *preferable* to the old?

The nature of such changes in principles and their attendant effects on the financial statements must be disclosed in the footnotes and discussed by manage-ment in its analysis of operations. A change that is not preferable is unacceptable in an SEC filing under the Securities Act since it results in a qualified accoun-tant's opinion (as regards consistency). A change in accounting practice requires disclosure and qualification but not an evaluation of preferability by the auditor (Refer to *Staff Accounting Bulletin No. 32.*)

The SEC views preferability in terms of the individual firm's circumstances. A change is justified if management's judgment and plans are not unreasonable and the auditor may use this criterion in evaluating the change. An accountant therefore, may prefer one change for one client and a completely opposite change for a second client if, in the clients' circumstances the basis for the change is not unreasonable.[5]

Form 10-Q contains specific requirements for reporting when a change in accounting has occurred. The registrant must include as an exhibit a letter from its independent accountants in the first Form 10-Q filed after the date of the change stating "whether or not the change is to an alternative principle which in [the accountant's] judgment is preferable under the circumstances . . . ." The primary burden of proof in justifying the change, however, falls upon manage-ment. No letter is required when an accounting change is made in response to a pronouncement by the FASB.[6]

Disclosure of Unusual Risks and Uncertainties in Financial Reporting (Accounting Series Release No. 166)

A number of situations developed during the 1973-74 recession in which signifi-cant and increasing business uncertainties were not fully reflected in the financia reporting of registrants. These included cases in which unique or special circumstances arose that affected an enterprise's ability to measure current results, cases in which changing economic circumstances substantially changed the risk characteristics of certain assets, and cases in which the assumptions that underlie the use of certain accounting principles in certain situations became subject to substantial uncertainty.

Although a large number of estimates is required in the preparation of financial statements, for example, management's estimates of the economic lives of assets, it ordinarily is not necessary for management to point out that they have been made and that some uncertainty exists as a result. Investors generally are aware of the need for such estimates.

On the other hand, when unusual circumstances arise or where there are significant changes in the degree of business uncertainty existing in a reporting entity, a registrant has the responsibility for communicating these items in its financial statements. It is not sufficient to assume that the numbers shown in conventional fashion on the face of the financial statements necessarily will inform investors adequately. The basic accounting model is by its very nature a single valued one in which a single best estimate is reflected in the face of the statements. While in most cases, this presentation effectively communicates a corporation's financial position and results of operations, under some conditions of major uncertainty it may not adequately inform investors of the realities of the business being reported. In such cases, registrants must consider the need for substantial and specific disclosure of such uncertainties and, in extreme cases, the need for deviation from the conventional reporting model. In addition, independent public accountants must consider the need for disclosure of such uncertainties in their reports.

Therefore, the SEC identified the following examples of uncertainties for which disclosure might be appropriate:

1. Expansion of information by financial institutions regarding loan loss reserves to include adequacy of security, level of delinquencies, concentration of portfolio, etc.
2. Displaying declines in the value's of marketable securities on the face of the financial statements.
3. Disclosure of the uncertainty as to recovery of deferral of fuel costs by public utilities.
4. Disclosure of significant dependence upon a small number of projects.
5. Disclosure of the cost of raw materials where the price is still under negotiation.

This list is not intended to be all-inclusive and could not be because changing conditions produce new uncertainties and resolve old ones on a continuing basis.

The information, when material, should be given for all periods covered by the financial statements. Income statement amounts are considered material if they are material in relation to either investment income or net income; balance sheet amounts are considered material if they are material in relation to stockholders' equity. The form these disclosures may take include footnote, statement caption, and range estimates, as determined to be appropriate by management.

Oil and Gas Reserves (Rule) 3-18.

The most recent addition to disclosure of financial information requirements occured in August, 1978. Congress charged the SEC with developing uniform accounting standards for crude oil and natural gas producers via the Energy Policy and Conservation Act of 1975. The act provided that the SEC could rely on the accounting profession's standard-setting process long as the SEC was assured that FASB pronouncements would result in a degree of compliance equal to that of standards set by the SEC itself. The FASB issued its statement establishing the successful efforts method of accounting for reserves which was met immediately by opposition from small oil companies. The SEC, responding to pressure from certain members of Congress, issued Rule 3-18. Rule 3-18 proposes the development of an alternative accounting standard called the "reserve recognition" method and permits registrants to use either full cost or successful efforts methods until the reserve recognition method is worked out.

The provisions and implications of the rule are very complex. Because it applies to specialized industrial accounting standards, a full discussion is beyond the scope of this text. Briefly, the rule requires that producers of natural gas and crude oil disclose the value of estimated future net revenue from the production of proven reserves. The value of the future net revenue is expressed in terms of current market prices. The method goes beyond the disclosure of financial information in footnotes or schedules. It means that companies must treat their reserves as assets, capitalized at current market value of the estimated reserves, and they must expense all exploration costs in the period they are incurred.

Accounting Series Releases No. 257 and 258 amend Rule 3-18. The SEC has proposed that information concerning proven oil and gas reserves can be presented in a section of the financial statements identified as unaudited for fiscal years ending before December 26, 1980 in order that the profession has an opportunity to develop the necessary auditing standards.

Segments of a Business Enterprise, International Operations

Dart Industries' disclosures under the captions, "Segment Operating Data," "Geographic Operating Data," and "International Operations" comply with *Statement of Financial Accounting Standards No. 14,* "Financial Reporting for Segments of a Business Enterprise." The SEC announced in *ASR No. 236* the issuance of a new uniform disclosure regulation, S-K. S-K does not affect footnote disclosure; it conforms reporting required in filings with the SEC and in reports to stockholders with that of *Statement No. 14.* We will examine the provisions of *Statement No. 14* in Chapter 7. Dart's footnotes entitled "Supplementary Earnings Statement Information" remain to be discussed in Chapter 7.

SCHEDULES

The SEC has designed a series of nineteen formats, known as schedules, by means of which the registrant can communicate detailed financial information. The majority of the schedules itemize the component amounts of certain balance sheet accounts. Other schedules pertain to various information needs ranging from warrants or rights to supplementary income statement information. Although the schedules are not part of the financial statements, the independent accountant is associated with them. Therefore, the opinion letter must be modified accordingly. Dart Industries, for example, filed Schedules I, II, V, VI and XII (pages 345–349) in its Form 10-K. Price Waterhouse & Co. extends the scope of its opinion letter to such additional financial data by referencing the data in its consent letter on page 338. A more usual method of bring the schedules under the opinion letter is discussed in Chapter 8.

Dependent upon the materiality of the schedule total, Rule 5-04 determines which schedules are to be filed by commercial and industrial registrants. These requirements are summarized in Exhibit 6-3.

Registrants may show information required by any schedule in the financial statements or footnotes and omit the schedule if the alternative presentation is clear and not confusing. Dart chose to do so with Schedule XVI, "Supplementary Income Statement Information (page 366)." This is a common method of disclosing Schedule XVI data. For the reader's convenience detailed instructions for schedule presentation appear in Appendix D. The schedules filed by Dart in its Form 10-K are those commonly filed and comparison with the schedule requirements in Appendix D is encouraged. A detailed discussion of filing instructions lies beyond the scope of this text.

SUMMARY   We have discussed the two means by which registrants can convey additional financial information needs—footnotes and schedules. Footnotes are a part of the financial statements and as such are filed with the SEC and incorporated in the company's annual report to stockholders. Schedules are separate from the financial statements, although they provide highly detailed financial information. They are required by Rule 5-04 in forms (e.g., Form S-1 or 10-K) filed with the SEC.

Although the scope of the auditor's report usually is limited to the financial statements and footnotes, Rule 5-04 requires the independent accountant to examine the schedules also. As a result, the auditor's report must be amended in some way to include the schedules within the scope of the opinion filed with the SEC.

Wherever possible, the SEC has endeavored to conform its requirements to those of the FASB and the AICPA. In the case of establishing principles of accounting measurement and auditing standards (other than standards of independence), this has resulted in the agency's observing a virtual hands-off policy. In the case of disclosure, however, it becomes apparent that the SEC and professional standards interface, with the SEC being perhaps the more dominant force.

Exhibit 6-3 Schedules to be Filed by Commercial and Industrial Registrants

Schedule as of the Date of the Most Recent Balance Sheet		Omit If All Conditions Are Met
I	Marketable Securities—Other Security Investments (rule 12-02)	—
IX	Bonds, Mortgages and Similar Debt (Rule 12-10)	a + b
XI	Guarantees of Securities of Other Issuers (Rule 12-12)	a + b
XIII	Capital Shares (Rule 12-14)	a + b + c
XIV	Warrants or Rights (Rule 12-15)	a + b
XV	Other Securities—(Form following Schedules IX, XI, XIII, or XIV, as appropriate)	a + b
XVII	Real Estate and Accumulated Depreciation (Rule 12-42)	—
XVIII	Mortgage Loans on Real Estate (Rule 12-43)	—
XIX	Other Investments—(form following Schedules I or III, as appropriate)	—

For each period for which an income statement is filed:

II	Amounts Receivable from Underwriters, Promoters, Directors, Officers, Employees, and Principal Holders (other than Affiliates) of Equity Securities of the Person and its Affiliates (Rule 12-03)	—
III	Investments in, Equity in Earnings of, and Dividends Received from Affiliates and Other Persons (Rule 12-04)	—
IV	Indebtedness of Affiliates and Other Persons— Not Current (Rule 12-05)	—
V	Property, Plant and Equipment (Rule 12-06)	—
VI	Accumulated Depreciation, Depletion and Amortization of Property, Plant and Equipment (Rule 12-07)	—
VII	Intangible Assets, Preoperating Expenses and Similar Deferrals (Rule 12-08)	—
VIII	Accumulated Depreciation and Amortization of Intangible Assets (Rule 12-09)	—

Exhibit 6-3   (*Continued*)

Schedule as of the Date of the Most Recent Balance Sheet		Omit If All Conditions Are Met
X	Indebtedness to Affiliates and Other Persons— Not Current (Rule 12-11)	—
XII	Valuation and Qualifying Accounts and Reserves (Rules 12-12)	—
XVI	Supplementary Income Statement Information (Rule 12-16)	—

KEY: a   Financial statements are being filed as part of an annual report or other periodic report.
     b   The information that would be shown in the respective columns of such schedule would reflect no changes in any issue of securities of the registrant or any significant subsidiary in excess of five percent of the outstanding securities of such issue as shown in the most recently filed annual report containing the schedule.
     c   Any information required by column G of Schedule XIII, Capital Shares, is shown in the related balance sheet or in a note thereto.

FOOTNOTES FOR CHAPTER 6

[1] The reporting of loss contingencies is presently under study by the AICPA. However, the following footnote accompanying McDonnell Douglas Corporation's 1975 financial statements illustrates the nature of disclosure required when the potential effect of legal action on the registrant's financial position is significant:

"*Note K: Litigation.* MDC is a defendant in 16 lawsuits, including five determined to be class actions and two brought derivatively on behalf of MDC, arising out of sales of common stock and debentures of Douglas Aircraft Company, Inc. in 1966 before its merger into MDC. MDC and lead counsel for plaintiffs have submitted an agreement to the trial judge in New York City to terminated the litigation by MDC's paying $5,000,000 into a fund to settle all claims including plaintiffs' attorneys fees and other expenses. Other defendants and an insurance company have agreed to reimburse MDC for $1,550,000 of the settlement payment. Counsel for MDC are of the opinion that the proposed settlement will be approved by the judge and consummated. The amount of the settlement has been provided in prior years' financial statements.

"MDC and Eastern Air Lines, Inc. have both appealed a $24,500,000 judgment against MDC for alleged inexcusable delays in the delivery of DC-8s and DC-9s ordered prior to the April 1967 merger of Douglas into McDonnell. Provisions have been made in the financial statements for the potential liability.

"MDC is also a defendant in a number of product liability cases, including actions alleging substantial compensatory and punitive damages as a result of the crash of a DC-10 aircraft operated by Turkish Airlines on 3 March 1974. Insurance coverage is believed to be adequate to cover such damages as may reasonably be assessed in all of these actions.

"MDC is also defendant in other civil actions, some of which are covered by insurance. These actions are considered either without merit or the potential liability would not materially affect the financial condition of MDC, although the aggregate amount of damages alleged is substantial."

[2] General Host Corporation's financial statements for 1975 include the following footnote:

"*Note 8: Shareholders' Equity.* At December 27, 1975 a total of 6,866,016 shares of the Company's common stock was reserved for issuance upon the exercise of outstanding common stock purchase warrants at an aggregate exercise price of $270,680,000. Of this total, 6,635,753 warrants are exercisable at $40 per share and expire on January 31, 1979, and 230,263 are exercisable at $22.80 per share and expire on August 5, 1978. Under the terms of the $40 warrants the Company may reduce their exercise price for limited periods an amount not in excess of $33\frac{1}{3}\%$ of the exercise price then in effect and the Company's 7% subordinated debentures may be used at par in payment of the exercise price. In addition, 1,270,613 shares are reserved for issuance upon conversion of the Company's 11% debentures at the rate of $16 per share and 149,407 shares are reserved for conversion of the Company's 5% debentures at the rate of $27 per share."

[3] *Accounting Series Release No. 151,* Disclosure of Inventory Profits Reflected in Income in Periods of Rising Prices, January 3, 1974.

[4] Land is included but noncapitalized financing leases are not included in the size determination test, however, once the size test is met, land is not ordinarily considered part of productive capacity but noncapitalized financing leases are.

[5] See *Staff Accounting Bulletin No. 14* for the interpretation of this concept.

[6] *Accounting Series Release No. 195* eliminated the requirement for auditors to comment in their letter accompanying the 10-Q financial statements.

GLOSSARY

Consolidated Statements Include the operating results of a corporation's subsidary (ies) with inter-company transactions eliminated.

Footnote Appended to financial statements as supplemental information for specific items in a statement.

Foreign Currency Any currency other than the currency used by the enterprise in its financial statements.

Option The contractual privilege of purchasing an asset (shares or stock) for a specified price.

Pension Plan An arrangement whereby a company undertakes to provide its retired employees with benefits that can be determined or estimated in advance.

Replacement Cost The lowest amount that would have to be paid in the normal course of business to obtain a *new* asset of equivalent operating or productive capability.

Right Provides current security holders the privilege of participating on a pro rata basis in a new offering of securities.

Schedule. Detailed financia l information presented in a form prescribed by the SEC in Regulation S-X, Article 12.

Warrant A security that grants the holder the right to purchase a specific number of shares of the security to which the warrant is attached at a specified price and usually within a stated period of time.

QUESTIONS

1. What is the distinction between footnotes and schedules? Which must be filed with the SEC? Which contains the more detailed information?

2. Where is a statement of the accounting principles and practices in the preparation of the financial statements found?
3. What is the rule with respect to disclosure of the principles used in consolidating or combining financial statements?
4. Discuss *ASR No.3*.
5. Must unrealized gains or losses in foreign currencies be disclosed?
6. Discuss the rule governing revenue recognition.
7. Discuss the rule governing depreciation, depletion, obsolescence, and amortization.
8. Discuss the rule governing income tax expense.
9. What is the relationship between *ASR No. 225* and *FASB Statement No.13?*
10. Discuss Rule 3-16(s) and *ASR No.194*.
11. Must interim financial statements be audited? What is the auditor's responsibility with respect to interim financial statements as set forth in *AICPA Statement on Auditing Standards No.24?*
12. Review Appendix D. Under what circumstances may a registrant omit filing a schedule?
13. What is the independent auditor's responsibility with respect to the information in a schedule?

Appendix

D

Regulation S–X Schedules

Rule 5-04 requires industrial and commercial registrants to submit specified schedules containing financial information in addition to financial statements and footnotes. These schedules must be presented in a standardized format as set forth in Article 12 of Reg S-X. This appendix matches the Rule 5-04 filing requirement with the standard form of each schedule.*

*The captions referred to in the Rule 5-04 filing requirements excerpted in this appendix relate to Regulation S-X, Rule 5-02, the Balance Sheet standards, numbered consecutively from 1-40. That is, most the Article 12 schedules explain the components of balance sheet captions.

Schedule I   Marketable Securities—Other Security Investments

The schedule prescribed by 12-02 shall be filed—

(1) In support of caption 2 of a balance sheet, if the greater of the aggregate cost or the aggregate market value of other security investments as of the balance sheet date constitutes 10 percent or more of total assets.

(2) In support of caption 12 of a balance sheet, if the greater of the aggregate cost or the aggregate market value of other security investments as of the balance sheet date constitutes 10 percent or more of total assets.

(3) In support of captions 2 and 12 of a balance sheet, if the greater of the aggregate cost or aggregate market value of marketable securities as of the balance sheet date constitutes 15 percent or more of total assets.

(4) In support of captions 2 and 12 of a balance sheet, if the greater of the aggregate cost or aggregate market value of the securities as of the balance sheet date of any issuer reported under either caption 2 or caption 12 constitutes two percent or more of total assets.

Column A	Column B	Column C	Column D	Column E[4]
Name of issuer[1] and title of each issue[2]	Number of shares or units—principal amount of bonds and notes	Cost of each issue	Market value[3] of each issue at balance sheet date	Amount at which each portfolio of equity security issues and each other security issue carried in the balance sheet

[1]For the purpose of this schedule, each of the following groups of entities shall be considered as one issuer: (a) the United States Government and its agencies; (b) any state of the United States and its agencies; (c) a political subdivision of the United States and its agencies; (d) a foreign government and its agencies and political subdivisions; and (e) a corporation and its majority owned subsidiaries. If a security listed herein is guaranteed by or considered a moral obligation of another issuer named herein, provide, in a note keyed to each issuer, a brief description of the terms of such guarantee or obligation.

[2](a) Each issue shall be stated separately, except that reasonable groupings, without enumeration, may be made of securities of any issuer for which the greater of the aggregate cost or aggregate market value is less than two percent of total assets.

(b) In the case of bank holding companies group separately (1) securities of banks and (2) other securities, and in column C show totals for each group.

[3]Market value shall be based on market quotations at the balance sheet date or, if such quotations are not available, on determinations of fair value made in good faith by the board of directors.

[4]Column E shall be totaled to correspond to the respective balance sheet captions.

SCHEDULE II AMOUNTS RECEIVABLE FROM UNDERWRITERS, PROMOTERS, DIRECTORS, OFFICERS, EMPLOYEES, AND PRINCIPAL HOLDERS (OTHER THAN AFFILIATES) OF EQUITY SECURITIES OF THE PERSON AND ITS AFFILIATES

The schedule prescribed by Rule 12-03 shall be filed with respect to each person among the underwriters, promoters, directors, officers, employees, and principal holders (other than affiliates) of equity securities of the person and its affiliates, from whom an aggregate indebtedness of more than $20,000 or one percent of total assets, whichever is less, is owed, or at any time during the period for which related income statements are required to be filed was owed. For the purposes of this schedule, exclude in the determination of the amount of indebtedness all amounts receivable from such persons for purchases subject to usual trade terms, for ordinary travel and expense advances and for other such items arising in the ordinary course of business.

Column A	Column B	Column C	Column D		Column E	
			Deductions		Balance at end of period	
Name of debtor[1]	Balance at beginning of period	Additions	(1) Amounts collected[2]	(2) Amounts written off	(1) Current	(2) Not current

[1]Include in this schedule both accounts receivable and notes receivable and provide in a note hereto pertinent information, such as the due date, interest rate, terms of repayment and collateral, if any, for the amounts receivable from each person named in column A as of the date of the most recent balance sheet being filed.

[2]If collection was other than in cash, explain.

SCHEDULE III **INVESTMENT IN, EQUITY IN EARNINGS OF, AND DIVIDENDS RECEIVED FROM AFFILIATES AND PERSONS**

The schedule prescribed by Rule 12-04 shall be filed in support of caption 10 of each balance sheet. This schedule may be omitted if (1) neither the sum of captions 10 and 11 in the related balance sheet nor the amount of caption 31 in such balance sheet exceeds five percent of total assets as shown by the related balance sheet at either the beginning or end of the period or (2) there have been no material changes in the information required to be filed from that last previously reported.

Column A	Column B		Column C		Column D		Column E		Column F
	Balance at beginning of period		Additions		Deductions		Balance at end of period		Dividends received during the period from investments not accounted for by the equity method[5]
	(1)	(2)	(1)	(2)	(1)	(2)	(1)	(2)	
Name of issuer and description of investment[1]	Number of shares or units.[2] Principal amount of bonds and notes	Amount in dollars	Equity taken up in earnings (losses) of affiliates and other persons for the period[3]	Other[4]	Distribution of earnings by persons in which earnings (losses) were taken up[5]	Other[6]	Number of shares or units.[2] Principal amount of bonds and notes	Amount in dollars[7]	

[1](a) Group separately securities of (1) subsidiaries consolidated; (2) subsidiaries not consolidated; (3) other affiliates; and (4) other persons, the investments in which are accounted for by the equity method, showing shares and bonds separately in each case. Investments in individual affiliates which, when considered with related advances, exceed two percent of total assets shall be stated separately. Dividends from (1) marketable securities and (2) other security investments shall also be included and may be shown in separate aggregate amounts.

(b) Those foreign investments, the enumeration of which would be detrimental to the registrant, may be grouped.

[2]Disclose, in the column or in a note hereto, the percentage of ownership interest represented by the shares or units, if material.

[3]The total of column C(1) shall be reconciled with the amount of the related income statement caption.

[4]Briefly describe each item in column C(2); if the cost thereof represents other than a cash expenditure, explain. If acquired from an affiliate (and not an original issue of that affiliate) at other than cost to the affiliate, show such cost, provided the acquisition by the affiliate was within two years prior to the acquisition by the person for which the statement is filed.

[5]As to any dividends other than cash, state the basis on which they have been taken up in the accounts, and the justification for such action. If any such dividends received from affiliates have been credited in the accounts in an amount differing from that charged to retained earnings by the disbursing company, state the amount of such difference and explain.

[6]Briefly describe each item in column D(2) and state: (a) Cost of items sold and how determined; (b) amount received (if other than cash, explain); and (c) disposition of resulting profit or loss.

[7]The total (or a sub-total) of column E(2) shall be reconciled with the amount reported under caption 10 of the related balance sheet.

SCHEDULE IV INDEBTEDNESS OF AFFILIATES AND OTHER PERSONS —NOT CUR RENT

The schedule prescribed by Rule 12-05 shall be used in support of caption 11 o each balance sheet, however, the required information may be presented sepa rately on Schedule III or Schedule X. This schedule may be omitted if (1) neithe the sum of captions 10 and 11 in the related balance sheet nor the amount o caption 31 in such balance sheet exceeds five percent of total assets as shown b the related balance sheet at either the beginning or end of the period or (2) ther have been no material changes in the information required to be filed from tha previously reported.

Column A	Column B	Column C
Name of person[1]	Balance at beginning of period	Balance at end of period[2]

[1]The persons named shall be grouped as in the related schedule required for investments in affiliates and other persons. The information called for shall be shown separately for any persons whose investments were shown separately in such related schedule.

[2]For each person named in column A, explain in a note hereto the nature and purpose of any increase during the period that is in excess of 10 percent of the related balance at either the beginning or end of the period.

SCHEDULE V PROPERTY, PLANT AND EQUIPMENT

The schedule prescribed by Rule 12-06 shall be filed in support of caption 14 of each balance sheet, provided that this schedule may be omitted if the total shown by caption 14 does not exceed five percent of total assets as shown by the related balance sheet at both the beginning and end of the period exceeded five percent of total assets as shown by the related balance sheet at either the beginning or end of the period.

Column A	Column B	Column C	Column D	Column E	Column F
Classification[2]	Balance at beginning of period[3]	Additions at cost[4]	Retirements[5]	Other changes— add (deduct)— describe[6]	Balance at end of period

[1]Comment briefly on any significant and unusual additions, abandonments, or retirements, or any significant and unusual changes in the general character and location, of principal plants and other important units, which may have occurred within the period.

[2](a) Show by major classifications, such as land, buildings, machinery and equipment, leaseholds, or functional grouping. If such classification is not present or practicable, this may be stated in one amount. The additions included in column C shall, however, be segregated in accordance with an appropriate classification. If property, plant and equipment abandoned is carried at other than a nominal amount indicate, if practicable, the amount thereof and state the reasons for such treatment. Items of minor importance may be included under a miscellaneous caption.

(b) **Public utility companies.** — A public utility company shall, to the extent practicable, classify utility plant by the type of service rendered (such as electric, gas, transportation and water) and shall state separately under each of such service classifications the major subclassifications of utility plant accounts.

[3]If neither the total additions nor total deductions during any of the periods covered by the schedules amount to more than 10 percent of the ending balance of that period and a statement to that effect is made, the information required by columns B, C, D and E may be omitted for that period, provided that the totals of columns C and D are given in a note hereto and provided further that any information required by instructions 4, 5 and 6 shall be given and may be in summary form.

[4]For each change in accounts in column C that represents anything other than an addition from acquisition, and for each change in that column that is in excess of two percent of total assets, at either the beginning or end of the period, state clearly the nature of the change and the other accounts affected. If cost of property additions represents other than cash expenditures, explain. If acquired from an affiliate at other than cost to the affiliate, show such cost, provided the acquisition by the affiliate was within two years prior to the acquisition by the person for which the statement is filed.

[5]If changes in column D are stated at other than cost, explain if practicable.

[6]State clearly the nature of the changes and the other accounts affected. If provision for depreciation, depletion and amortization of property, plant and equipment is credited in the books directly to the asset accounts, the amounts shall be stated in column E with explanations, including the accounts to which charged.

SCHEDULE VI ACCUMULATED DEPRECIATION, DEPLETION AND AMORTIZATION OF PROPERTY, PLANT AND EQUIPMENT

The schedule prescribed by Rule 12-07 shall be filed in support of caption 15 of each balance sheet. This schedule may be omitted if Schedule V is omitted.

Column A	Column B	Column C	Column D	Column E	Column F
Description[2]	Balance at beginning of period	Additions charged to costs and expenses	Retirements	Other changes— add (deduct)— describe	Balance at end of period

[1]Insofar as amounts for depreciation, depletion and amortization are credited to the property accounts, such amounts shall be shown in the schedule of property, plant and equipment, as there required.

[2]If practicable, accumulated depreciation shall be shown to correspond with the classifications of property set forth in the related schedule of property, plant and equipment, separating especially depreciation, depletion, amortization and provision for retirement.

SCHEDULE VII INTANGIBLE ASSETS, PREOPERATING EXPENSES AND SIMILAR DEFERRALS

Part A of the schedule prescribed by Rule 12-08 shall be filed in support of caption 16 and Part B shall be filed in support of caption 20 of each balance sheet, provided that either part may be omitted if the total shown by the related blance sheet caption does not exceed five percent of total assets as shown in the related balance sheet at both the beginning and end of the period and if neither the additions nor the deductions during the period exceeded five percent of total assets as shown by the related balance sheet at the beginning or end of the period.

Column A	Column B	Column C	Column D		Column E	Column F
			Deductions[6]			
Description[3]	Balance at beginning of period[4]	Additions at cost— describe[5]	(1) Charged to costs and expenses	(2) Charged to other accounts— describe	Other changes— add (deduct)— describe	Balance at close of period

[1]The information required shall be presented in two parts: Part A—Intangible assets. Part B—Preoperating expenses and similar deferrals.

[2]If in the accounts it is not practicable to separate intangible assets from property, plant and equipment, the information here required may be included in the schedule for property, plant and equipment. In such event state in the balance sheet any known amount of intangibles so included with an indication that a further unknown amount of intangibles is also so included.

[3]Show by major classifications in each part, such as franchises, goodwill, etc. If such classification is not present or practicable, each part may be stated in one amount. The additions included in column C shall, however, be segregated in accordance with an appropriate classification. Items of minor importance may be included under a miscellaneous caption in each part.

[4]If neither the total additions nor total deductions of a part during any of the periods covered by the schedules amount to more than 10 percent of the closing balance of the part for that period and a statement to that effect is made, the information required by columns B, C, D and E may be omitted for that part for that period by any company other than a public utility company. Any information required by instruction 5 or 6 shall, however, be given and may be in summary form.

[5]For each change in intangible asset accounts in column C that represents anything other than an addition from acquisition, and for each change in that column in either Part A or B that is in excess of two percent of total assets at either the beginning or end of the period, state clearly the nature of the change and the other accounts affected. If cost of additions represents other than cash expenditures, explain. If acquired from an affiliate at other than cost to the affiliate, show such cost, provided the acquisition by the affiliate was within two years prior to the acquisition by the person for which the statement is filed.

[6]If provision for depreciation and amortization of intangible assets is credited in the books directly to the intangible asset account, the amounts shall be stated in column D with explanations, including the accounts to which charged. If the changes in column D represent anything other than regular amortization in either Part A or B, state clearly the nature of the changes.

[7]If an account for accumulated depreciation or amortization is maintained for any item of preoperating expenses and similar deferrals, Rule 12-09 shall apply to such accounts and that schedule shall be divided into Parts A and B as shown above.

SCHEDULE VIII ACCUMULATED DEPRECIATION AND AMORTIZATION OF INTANGIBL ASSETS

The schedule prescribed by Rule 12-09 shall be filed in support of caption 17 c each balance sheet. This schedule may be omitted if Schedule VII is omitted.

Column A	Column B	Column C		Column D	Column E
		Additions			
Description[2]	Balance at beginning of period	(1) Charged to costs and expenses	(2) Charged to other accounts— describe	Deductions— describe	Balance at end of period

[1]Insofar as amounts for depreciation and amortization are credited to the intangible asset accounts, such amounts shall be shown in the schedule of intangible assets, as there required.

[2]If practicable, accumulated depreciation and amortization shall be shown to correspond with the classifications set forth in the related schedule of intangible assets.

[3]See Instruction 7 of Rule 12-08.

SCHEDULE IX   BONDS, MORTGAGES AND SIMILAR DEBT

The schedule prescribed by Rule 12-10 shall be filed in support of caption 29 of a balance sheet.

Column A	Column B	Column C	Column D		Column E	Column F	Column G	Column H	
			Amount included in column C, which is		Amount included in sum extended under caption "bonds, mortgages and similar debt" in related balance sheet[2]	Amount in sinking and other special funds of issuer thereof[3]		Amount held by affiliates for which statements are filed herewith[4]	
Name of issuer and title of each issue[1]	Amount authorized by indenture	Amount issued and not retired or cancelled	(1) Held by or for account of issuer thereof	(2) Not held by or for account of issuer thereof			Amount pledged by issuer thereof[3]	(1) Persons included in con-solidated statement[5]	(2) Others

[1]Include in this column each issue authorized, whether issued or not and whether eliminated in consolidation or not. For each issue listed give the information called for by columns B to H, inclusive.

[2]This column is to be totaled to correspond to the related balance sheet caption. If amounts shown in this column differ from face amounts shown in column C or D, explain.

[3]Indicate by means of an appropriate symbol any amounts not included in subcolumn D(1).

[4]Affiliates for which statements are filed herewith shall include affiliates for which separate financial statements are filed and those included in consolidated or combined statements, other than the issuer of the particular security.

[5]Include in this subcolumn only amounts held by persons included in the consolidated statement in support of which this schedule is being filed. If not eliminated in the consolidation, explain in a note.

SCHEDULE X   INDEBTEDNESS TO AFFILIATES AND OTHER PERSONS — NOT CURRENT

The schedule prescribed by Rule 12-11 shall be filed in support of caption 31 of each balance sheet; however, the required information may be presented separately on Schedule III or Schedule IV. This schedule may be omitted if (1) neither the sum of captions 10 and 11 in the related balance sheet nor the amount of caption 31 in such balance sheet exceeds five percent of total assets as shown by the related balance sheet at either the beginning or end of the period, or (2) there have been no material changes in the information required to be filed from that last previously reported.

Column A	Column B	Column C
Name of person[1]	Balance at beginning of period	Balance at end of period[2]

[1]The persons named shall be grouped as in the related schedule required for investments in affiliates and other persons. The information called for shall be shown separately for any persons whose investments were shown separately in such related schedule.

[2]For each person named in column A, explain in a note hereto the nature and purpose of any increase during the period that is in excess of 10 percent of the related balance at either the beginning or end of the period.

SCHEDULE XI GUARANTEES OF SECURITIES OF OTHER ISSUERS

The schedule prescribed by Rule 12-12 shall be filed with respect to any guarantees of securities of other issuers by the person for which the statement is filed.

Column A	Column B	Column C	Column D	Column E	Column F	Column G
Name of issuer of securities guaranteed by person for which statement is filed	Title of issue of each class of securities guaranteed	Total amount guaranteed and outstanding[2]	Amount owned by person or persons for which statement is filed	Amount in treasury of issuer of securities guaranteed	Nature of guarantee[3]	Nature of any default by issuer of securities guaranteed in principal, interest, sinking fund or redemption provisions, or payment of dividends[4]

[1]Indicate in a note to the most recent schedule being filed for a particular person or group any significant changes since the date of the related balance sheet. If this schedule is filed in support of consolidated statements or combined statements, there shall be set forth guarantees by any person included in the consolidation or combination, except that such guarantees of securities which are included in the consolidated or combined balance sheet need not be set forth.

[2]Indicate any amounts included in column C which are included also in column D or E.

[3]There need be made only a brief statement of the nature of the guarantee, such as "Guarantee of principal and interest," "Guarantee of interest" or "Guarantee of dividends." If the guarantee is of interest or dividends, state the annual aggregate amount of interest or dividends so guaranteed.

[4]Only a brief statement as to any such defaults need be made.

SCHEDULE XII   VALUATION AND QUALIFYING ACCOUNTS AND RESERVES

The schedule prescribed by Rule 12-13 shall be filed in support of valuation a⸱ qualifying accounts and reserves included in each balance sheet but not includ⸱ in Schedule VI or VIII. (See Rule 3-02.)

Column A	Column B	Column C		Column D	Column E
		Additions			
Description[1]	Balance at beginning of period	(1) Charged to costs and expenses	(2) Charged to other accounts— describe	Deductions— describe	Balance at end of period

[1]List, by major classes, all valuation and qualifying accounts and reserves not included in specific schedules. Identify each such class of valuation and qualifying accounts and reserves by descriptive title. Group *(a)* those valuations and qualifying accounts which are deducted in the balance sheet from the assets to which they apply and *(b)* those reserves which support the balance sheet caption, *Reserve*. Valuation and qualifying account⸱ and reserves as to which the additions, deductions and balance⸱ were not individually significant may be grouped in one tota⸱ and in such case the information called for under columns ⸱ and D need not be given.

SCHEDULE XIII CAPITAL SHARES

The schedule prescribed by Rule 12-14 shall be filed in support of caption 35 of a balance sheet.

Column A	Column B	Column C	Column D		Column E		Column F		Column G	
			Number of shares included in column C which are		Shares issued or outstanding as shown on or included in related balance sheet under caption "capital shares"		Number of shares held by affiliates for which statements are filed herewith[4]		Number of shares reserved for options, warrants, conversions and other rights	
Name of issuer and title of issue[2]	Number of shares authorized by charter	Number of shares issued and not retired or cancelled	(1) Held by or for account of issuer thereof	(2) Not held by or for account of issuer thereof	(1) Number	(2) Amount at which shown[3]	(1) Persons included in consolidated statements[5]	(2) Others	(1) Directors, officers and employees	(2) Others

[1]Indicate in a note to the most recent schedule being filed for a particular person or group any significant changes since the date of the related balance sheet.

[2]Include in this column each issue authorized, whether issued or not and whether eliminated in consolidation or not, provided that when this schedule is filed in support of a consolidated statement the information required by columns A to G, inclusive, need not be given as to any consolidated subsidiary if substantially all of the outstanding shares of each issue of capital shares (other than directors' qualifying shares) of such subsidiary are held by one or more of the persons included in such consolidated statement; if the answer to columns G(1) and (2) would be none; and if a note indicating such omission is given. For each issue or group listed give the information called for by columns B to G, inclusive.

[3]This column is to be totaled to correspond to the related balance sheet caption. In the case of consolidated subsidiaries only the minority interest need be set forth.

[4]Affiliates for which statements are filed herewith shall include affiliates for which separate financial statements are filed and those included in consolidated or combined statements, other than the issuer of the particular security.

[5]Include in this subcolumn only amounts held by persons included in the consolidated statement in support of which this schedule is being filed. If not eliminated in the consolidation, explain in a note.

SCHEDULE XIV   WARRANTS OR RIGHTS

The schedule prescribed by Rule 12-15 shall be filed with respect to warrants rights granted by the person for which the statement is filed to subscribe for purchase securities to be issued by such person.

Column A	Column B	Column C	Column D	Column E	Column F	Column G
Title of issue of securities called for by warrants or rights	Amount of securities called for by each warrant or right	Number of warrants or rights outstanding[2]	Aggregate amount of securities called for by warrants or rights outstanding	Date from which warrants or rights are exercisable	Expiration date of warrants or rights	Price at which warrant or right exercisable

[1]Indicate in a note to the most recent schedule filed for a particular person or group any significant changes since the date of the related balance sheet.

[2]State separately amounts held by persons for which separat financial statements are filed or which are included in consoli dated or combined statements, other than the issuer of the par ticular security.

SCHEDULE XV   OTHER SECURITIES

If there are any classes of securities not included in Schedules IX, XI, XIII c XIV, set forth in this schedule information concerning such securities corre sponding to that required for the securities included in such schedules. Informa tion need not be set forth, however, as to notes, drafts, bills of exchange, c bankers' acceptances having a maturity at the time of issuance of not exceedin one year.

No format has been established for reporting other securities. Registrant needing to disclose information required by Rule 5-04 (below) should prepare special schedule following along the lines of Schedules IX, XI, XIII and XIV, a appropriate in the individual circumstances.

CHEDULE XVI   SUPPLEMENTARY INCOME STATEMENT INFORMATION

The schedule prescribed by Rule 12-16 may be omitted for each income statement in which sales or operating revenues were not of significant amount. This schedule may also be omitted if the information required by column B and instructions 3 and 4 thereof is furnished in the income statement or in a note thereto.

Column A	Column B[2]
Item	Charged to costs and expenses
1. Maintenance and repairs	
2. Depreciation, depletion and amortization of property, plant and equipment	
3. Depreciation and amortization of intangible assets, preoperating costs and similar deferrals[6]	
4. Taxes, other than income taxes[3]	
5. Rents[4]	
6. Royalties	
7. Advertising costs[5]	

[1]State, for each of the items noted in column A which exceeds one percent of total sales and revenues as reported in the related income statement, the amount called for in column B.

[2]Totals may be stated in column B without further designation of the accounts to which charged.

[3]State separately each category of tax which exceeds one percent of total sales and revenues.

[4]Include rents applicable to leased personal property.

[5]This item shall include all costs related to advertising the company's name, products or services in newspapers, periodicals or other advertising media.

[6]State separately each category of costs amortized.

SCHEDULE XVII   REAL ESTATE AND ACCUMULATED DEPRECIATION

The schedule prescribed by Rule 12-42 shall be filed for real estate (and t
related accumulated depreciation) held by persons a substantial portion of who
business is that of acquiring and holding for investment real estate or interests
real estate or interests in other persons a substantial portion of whose business
that of acquiring and holding real estate or interests in real estate for investme
Real estate used in the business shall be excluded from the schedule.

				(For Certain Real Estate Companies)					
Column A	Column B	Column C	Column D	Column E		Column F	Column G	Column H	Column I
Description[2]	Encumbrances	Initial cost to company	Cost capitalized subsequent to acquisition	Gross amount at which carried at close of period[3 4 5 6 7]		Accumulated depreciation	Date of con-struction	Date Acquired	Life on which depreciatio in latest income statements is compute
		Land / Buildings and im-provements	Improve-ments / Carrying costs	Land / Buildings and im-provements / Total					

[1]All money columns shall be totaled.

[2]The description for each property should include type of property (e.g., unimproved land, shopping center, garden apartments, etc.) and the geographical location.

[3]The required information is to be given as to each individual investment included in column E except that an amount not exceeding five percent of the total of column E may be listed in one amount as "miscellaneous investments".

[4]In a note to this schedule, furnish a reconciliation, in the following form, of the total amount at which real estate was carried at the beginning of each period for which income statements are required, with the total amount shown in column E:

Balance at beginning of period . . . . $ . . . .
  Additions during period:
    Acquisition through foreclosure $ . . . .
    Other acquisitions . . . .
    Improvements, etc. . . . .
    Other (describe) . . . .
                                         $ . . . .

Deductions during period:
  Cost of real estate sold . . . . $ . . . .
  Other (describe) . . . .
Balance at close of period . . . . $ . . . .

If additions, except acquisitions through foreclosure, represent other than cash expenditures, explain. If any of the changes during the period result from transactions, directly or indirectly with affiliates, explain the bases of such transactions and state the amounts involved.

A similar reconciliation shall be furnished for the accumulated depreciation.

[5]If any item of real estate investments has been written down or reserved against, describe the item and explain the basis for the write-down or reserve.

[6]State in a note to column E the aggregate cost for Federal income tax purposes.

[7]The amount of all intercompany profits included in the total of column E shall be stated if material.

SCHEDULE XVIII   MORTGAGE LOANS ON REAL ESTATE

The schedule prescribed by Rule 12-43 shall be filed by persons specified under Schedule XVII for investments in mortgage loans on real estate.

(For Certain Real Estate Companies)

Column A	Column B	Column C	Column D	Column E	Column F	Column G	Column H
Description[2][3][4]	Interest rate	Final maturity date	Periodic payment terms[5]	Prior liens	Face amount of mortgages	Carrying amount of mortgages[3][6][7][8][9]	Principal amount of loans subject to delinquent principal or interest[10]

[1]All money columns shall be totaled.

[2]The required information is to be given for each individual mortgage loan which exceeds three percent of the total of column G.

[3]If the portfolio includes large numbers of mortgages most of which are less than three percent of column G, the mortgages not required to be reported separately should be grouped by classifications that will indicate the dispersion of the portfolio, i.e., for a portfolio of mortgages on single family residential housing. The description should also include number of loans by original loan amounts (e.g., over $100,000, $50,000-$99,999, $20,000-$49,000, under $20,000) and type loan (e.g., VA, FHA, Conventional). Interest rates and maturity dates may be stated in terms of ranges. Data required by columns D, E and F may be omitted for mortgages not required to be reported individually.

[4]Loans should be grouped by categories, e.g., first mortgage, second mortgage, construction loans, etc., and for each loan the type of property, e.g., shopping center, high rise apartments, etc., and its geographic location should be stated.

[5]State whether principal and interest is payable at level amount over life to maturity or at varying amounts over life to maturity. State amount of balloon payment at maturity, if any. Also state prepayment penalty terms, if any.

[6]In a note to this schedule, furnish a reconciliation, in the following form, of the carrying amount of mortgage loans at the beginning of each period for which income statements are required, with the total amount shown in column G:

Balance at beginning of period . . . . $. . . . .
  Additions during period:
    New mortgage loans . . . . $. . . . .
    Other (describe) . . . .
                                 $. . . . .
Deductions during period:
  Collections of principal . . . . . . $. . . . .
  Foreclosures . . . .
  Cost of mortgages sold . . . .
  Amortization of premium . . . .
  Other (describe) . . . .
Balance at close of period . . . . $. . . . .

If additions represent other than cash expenditures, explain. If any of the changes during the period result from transactions, directly or indirectly with affiliates, explain the bases of such transactions, and state the amounts involved. State the aggregate mortgages (a) renewed and (b) extended. If the carrying amount of new mortgages is in excess of the unpaid amount of the extended mortgages, explain.

[7]If any item of mortgage loans on real estate investments has been written down or reserved against, describe the item and explain the basis for the write-down or reserve.

[8]State in a note to column G the aggregate cost for Federal income tax purposes.

[9]The amount of all intercompany profits in the total of column G shall be stated, if material.

[10](a) Interest in arrears for less than three months may be disregarded in computing the total amount of principal subject to delinquent interest.

(b) Of the total principal amount, state the amount acquired from controlled and other affiliates.

SCHEDULE XIX   OTHER INVESTMENTS

If there are any other investments, under caption 5-02-13 or elsewhere in a ba
ance sheet, not required to be included in Schedule I or III, there shall be se
forth in a separate schedule information concerning such investments corre
sponding to that prescribed by Schedule I. This schedule may be omitted if th
total amount of such other investments does not exceed five percent of tota
assets as shown by such balance sheet.

No format has been established for reporting other investments. Registrant
needing to disclose information required by Rule 5-04 (below) should prepare ;
special schedule following along the lines of Schedules I or III, as appropriate ii
the individual circumstances.

7 Reporting to Shareholders and the SEC

It does not matter whether financial statments are prepared for use in a 1933 Act registration or in a periodic report required under the 1934 Act. The standards of disclosure that they must meet are perfectly uniform. The blance sheet incorporated in a Form S-1 meets the same criteria as one transmitted in the annual report to stockholders. This uniformity gives us the option of using the same financial statements in a number of different reports.

The financial statements and their footnotes also complement other financial information required in both reports to stockholders and to the SEC. It is not surprising, therefore, that the consistency in standards from one report to another goes beyond the financial statements. For example, the summary of operations and management's discussion and analysis present information that supports information presented in the financial statements; companies also describe their business operations by industry and geographic segment in conformance with the provisions of FASB *Statement of Financial Accounting Standards No. 14*, that means that the description of business interfaces with footnotes to the financial statments.

The SEC has recognized the growing need for a method of establishing uniform standards for financial information other than that contained in the financial statements. Standards for the summary of earnings and management's analysis are located in the individual reporting forms and in Regulation 14A, so that a change in the standard would necessitate an amendment to each individual SEC form.[1] Therefore, when the SEC issued its standards for reporting the description of business by industry segment, it created a new document, Regulation S-K. The standards of S-K apply to a number of reports; a change in a standard can be made once and for all by revising one regulation.

The purpose of this chapter is to provide some perspective, to illustrate the role that the financial statements (and, by extension, the independent accountant) play in the various reports, namely the: (1) Form S-1; (2) annual report to stockholders; (3) Form 10-K; (4) quarterly report to stockholders; and (5) Form 10-Q.

INCORPORATION AND INTEGRATION

Considerable time and accounting costs often can be saved by using the same financial information for multiple purposes, and companies economize by incorporating or integrating financial information into their reports. That is, they can refer to financial statments, or portions thereof, from prior reports when responding to a request for information in a current report, or they can make one entire report do the work of two.

Incorporation

Reports distributed to the public cannot contain references by incorporation because they must be complete in and of themselves. Therefore, the annual report to stockholders, quarterly report to stockholders and the prospectus (Part I of Form S-1) cannot contain referenced information. Reports filed with the SEC, however, can contain references from reports to the public; that is, information from the annual report to stockholders can be referenced in the 10-K, but not vice versa.[2]

When the prior and current reports come under the provisions of the same law, for example, the Securities Exchange Act of 1934, incorporation can be accomplished freely by referencing a specific item filed in a prior report to the request for information in the current report and including a copy of the referenced document. If the prior report is filed under the provisions of a different statute, however, it is necessary that the independent accountant be informed of the fact because this changes his legal liability. If the entire set of financial statements is incorporated, a manually signed opinion letter must be included in the filing. If portions of the financial statements are referenced and included in the filing, an accountant's consent letter must be placed in the exhibit section of the filing. Chapter 8 discusses this matter further.

It has been possible to incorporate information by reference into Form 10-K since 1942 (*ASR No. 41*). Of all the forms the 10-K is most suited to incorporating data and therefore the SEC has issued Rule 12b-23 to establish the following standards:

1. Information referenced must be clearly identified by page, paragraph, caption, and the like.
2. When a document is partially incorporated, it must be identified clearly in the reference.
3. An express statement incorporating the information must be made at the particular place in the report where the information is required.
4. No information can be incorporated if doing so would render the report incomplete, unclear or confusing.

When financial statements appearing in the annual report to stockholders are incorporated in the 10-K, it is critical to name the statements specifically in order to avoid the implication that the entire annual report is being referenced. Remember that whatever is referenced is "filed" and brings legal liability under the same statute as the filing.[3]

Integration

It has become increasingly desirable, as the 10-K and annual report to stockholders disclosures become more alike, to integrate the two reports. Individual corporations have taken a step in this direction by voluntarily filing financial statements in one report that meets the extended disclosure requirements of another. On June 17, 1977, the SEC took the intermediate step toward establishing a combined Form 10-K and annual report to stockholders. It issued Guide 4[4] setting guidelines for the preparation of integrated reports to shareholders. The guide permits the filing of an integrated report in lieu of the Form 10-Q, and also in satisfaction of Rule 14a-3 proxy statement requirements.

Integrated reports should meet the following standards: They should include:

1. Full and complete answers to all items required by the form (10-K or 10-Q), cross referenced in the report if the response to a certain item of required disclosure is separated within the report.
2. If Part II of the 10-K is omitted, a definitive proxy or information statement.
3. Any additional information or exhibit necessary to prevent the filing from being misleading.
4. For the purposes of Form 10-K, a cover page, answer to Item 10 and required signatures. For Form 10-Q, a cover page, response to Part II and required signatures.
5. A cross reference sheet indicating the location of information required by item of the form.
6. A disclaimer of any action on the part of the SEC to approve or disapprove the report or to pass upon its accuracy or adequacy.

SUMMARY OF OPERATIONS AND MANAGEMENT'S DISCUSSION AND ANALYSIS

The summary of operations (also called the summary of earnings) is:[5]

> . . . a highly condensed form of profit and loss statement designed to apprise the investor, in a convenient fashion, of the financial results of the operation of the business for a reasonable period. (ASR No. 62)

Management must discuss a change in any item of revenue or expense that appears in the summary of operations or in Schedule XVI, the Supplementary Income Statement Information if: (1) the account increased or decreased from the prior period amount by more than 10 percent and (2) changed by more than 2 percent of average net income (loss) for the most recent three years presented. For example, Dart's net sales increased by 8 percent from 1976 to 1977. This change does not meet the first criterion for disclosure, but does meet the second because net sales increased by $124,748,000, or approximately 130 percent of average net income. Therefore, Dart's management discusses the change on page 372 of its analysis. (This detail is not required in the annual report to shareholders, but because the "Summary of Operations" and "Managements Discussion and Analysis" are incorporated into the 10-K from the annual report the company has conformed voluntarily). The summary is required for a minimum period of the most recent five years unless the nature of the issuer is such that a longer period is necessary to show trends clearly. Management's discussion and analysis is required for the most recent two years comparing each year's operations with that of the prior year.

Although the contents of the summary of operations vary slightly depending upon the report with which it is associated, Form 10-K requirements are typical and include:

1. Net sales or operating or other revenues.
2. Cost of goods sold or operating or other expenses (or gross profit).
3. Interest expense.
4. Income tax expense.
5. Income from continuing operations.
6. Discontinued operations, less applicable tax.
7. Income or loss before extraordinary items.
8. Extraordinary items, less applicable tax.
9. Cumulative effects of changes in accounting principles.
10. Net income or loss.
11. Earnings per share (primary and fully diluted).
12. Dividends per share.
13. Any other information appropriate in the light of the issuer's individual circumstances.

Material changes in earning-per-share amounts that result from other than changes in net income, such as an issuer's trading in its own securities, should be included in the discussion (SAB No. 29). Notice that Dart Industries "Summary of Operations" also reports depreciation and amortization expense in addition to the above categories, and it omits any disclosures that would not be material. Dart also presents its data in the recommended order, with the most recent year in the left column.

The registrant must determine the most appropriate means of conveying necessary information—either by presenting additional years' data, by footnote, or both. Conditions that might necessitate additional disclosure include:

1. Changes in the nature of the registrant's business operations (entering a new industry, etc.).
2. Operations of a predecessor corporation included in the financial data.
3. Atypical earnings (loss) in the report period. (For example, low cost of

goods sold caused by the purchase of another company at a substantial discount from book value.)
4. Declining net income/sales ratio.
5. Declining absolute net income coincident with increasing sales.
6. Recent or prospective cost increases. (For example, new compensation arrangements with officers.)
7. Recent reductions in selling prices or rates.
8. Unusual relationship of taxes to pre-tax income.
9. Seasonality of business.
10. Effects of casualties.

Form S-1 lists the following information requirements that must be disclosed in the summary of operations, usually in the form of a footnote:

1. In the case of a restatement (e.g., resulting from a business combination), a reconciliation of sales or revenues and net income with amounts previously reported is required in the year of restatement.
2. The number of shares used in the earnings per share calculation and the basis for determining same may require presentation in the form of an exhibit.
3. Any changes in accounting principles or practices or methods of applying same must be described.
4. Differences between actual and estimated amounts of material, unusual charges or credits to income must be explained.
5. A warning that the summary should be read in conjunction with the financial statements.

Some companies prefer to present five-year comparative income statements in lieu of the summary of operations. By doing so they can eliminate the two-year comparative income statements in response to Item 13 but must make certain minor adaptations to the data, such as rewording the title.

The purpose of management's discussion and analysis is to explain any effects on the data presented in the summary of operations that would make the data not indicative of current or future operations. It highlights the registrant's financial trends. Placed as it is near the front of the prospectus, its importance to readers in most cases exceeds that of the other financial statements, and this status is reflected by the emphasis that the SEC places on its review. It is usually presented on a consolidated basis only and the types of matters discussed normally include:

1. Material (as defined in Chapter 5) changes in revenues and expenses from prior amounts.
2. Changes in accounting principles or practices or in the method of their application that have a material effect on net income. (This integrates with the footnote disclosure.).
3. Any other matters that would make the data misleading.

Staff Accounting Bulletin No. 3 offers guidelines for the preparation of this information. In general, the discussion of material periodic changes should be limited to: (1) the latest interim period presented and the comparable interim period in the immediately preceding fiscal year; (2) the most recent fiscal year presented and the fiscal year immediatly preceding it; and (3) the second most recent fiscal year presented and the fiscal year immediatly preceding it. There may be circumstances, however, under which an explanation of revenue or expense item changes between two or more of the earlier periods of the five-year summary may be material to an understanding of the summary. Further, to better explain revenue and expense item changes for interim periods, it may be necessary to give an analysis of changes between consecutive fiscal quarters.

Although it is not feasible to specify all of the subjects that should be covered in the discussion and analysis of the summary, the following are examples that registrants should consider in making disclosure:

1. Material changes in product mix or in the relative profitability of lines of business.
2. Material changes in advertising, research, development, product introduction or other discretionary costs.
3. The acquistion or disposition of a material asset other than in the ordinary course of business.
4. Material and unusual charges or gains, including credits or charges associated with discontinuation of business.
5. Material changes in assumptions underlying deferred costs and the plan for amortization of such costs.
6. Material changes in assumed investment return and in actuarial assumptions used to calculate contributions to pension funds.
7. The closing of a material facility or material interruption of business or completion of a material contract.
8. Disclosure of unusual risks and uncertainties.

The textual analysis should be presented in a manner that will best communicate the significant elements necessary to a clear understanding by the investor of the financial results. Favorable as well as unfavorable trends and changes should be discussed. Tables and charts may be used where appropriate, but a mechanistic approach to this analysis that uses boiler plate or compliance jargon should be avoided.[6]

Because of the nature of quarterly data Instruction 5 of 10-Q also requires a narrative analysis of the results of operations as follows:

The registrant shall provide a narrative analysis of results of operations explaining the reasons for material changes in the amount of revenue and expense items between the most recent quarter and the quarter immediately preceding it, between the most recent quarter and the same calendar quarter in the preceding year, and, if applicable, between the current year to date and the same calendar period in the preceding year. Explanations of material changes should include, but not be limited to, changes in the various elements which determine revenue and expense levels such as unit sales volume, prices charged and paid, production levels, production cost variances, labor costs and discretionary spending programs. In addition, the analysis should include an explanation of the effect of any changes in accounting principles and practices or in the method of their application that have a material effect on net income as reported.

DESCRIPTION OF BUSINESS—INDUSTRY SEGMENTS

A description of business, a narrative describing the business operations of the registrant and its subsidiaries, is required by Form S-1 (Item 9) and Form 10-K (Item 1). The matters that should be discussed in the two forms differ slightly and Exhibit 7-1 compares them. Rules 14a3 and 14c3 also require (in the annual report to stockholders) a "brief description of the business done by the issuer and its subsidiaries during the most recent fiscal year which . . ., in the opinion of management, indicates the general nature and scope of the business of the issuer and its subsidiaries." (Dart Industries' "Business" appears on page 326 by way of illustration.)

As Exhibit 7-1 indicates, some of the topics in the S-1 and 10-K require information to be reported by industry segment. Regulation S-K defines the standards of reporting this information.[7] The regulation was issued in order to conform reporting to the SEC with *Statement of Financial Accounting Standards No. 14*, "Financial Reporting for Segments of a Business Enterprise."

Developments Leading to Regulation S-K

Registrants have reported financial information regarding segments of their operations since 1969 when the SEC began line-of-business reporting in the Description of Business item of Form S-1. The requirement was extended to Form 10-K in 1970, and in 1974 line-of-business information was also made mandatory in the narrative section of the annual report to stockholders. (Dart Industries' "Segment and Geographic Operating Information" is shown on page 326, and its "Description of Business Operations" begins on page 329.)

The SEC did not define the term, line-of-business. Rather, the responsibility of determining meaningful segments that reflect the particular company's operations and organizational concepts was placed on management. Lines-of-business could be combined into one class when there were material intersegment transfers of goods or services. A class was reported upon if it contributed 10 percent or more to total sales and revenues in either of the most recent two fiscal years (15 percent for small companies). No more than ten classes of business were required to be reported.

Statement No. 14 defines the basic industry segment as being the profit center. Profit centers can be aggregated into groups until they cross industry lines, as defined by the U.S Office of Mangement and Budget's *Standard Industrial Classification Manual*, at which point an industry segment is defined. Because the 10 percent materiality standard holds true for industry segments as well as for lines-

Exhibit 7-1   Description of Business Comparison of Forms S-1 and 10-K

Topic	Required by: S-1	Required by: 10-K
General development of the business	x	x
Competitive conditions in the industry(ies)	x	c
Principal products and services, markets and methods of distribution	x	–
Material backlogs	x	c
Sources and availability of essential raw materials	x	c
Importance of patents, trade marks, licenses, franchises and concessions held	x	c
Extent to which business is seasonal	x	c
If company proposes to enter or has recently entered a new line of business or introduced a new product, a copy of any feasibility study conducted	x	–
Registrant's and industry practices regarding working capital	x	–
Material contracts subject to renegotiation or termination	x	–
Nature and results of any bankruptcy, etc.	x	–
°Estimated expenditures for research and development, public announcements of new products or lines of business requiring a material investment, approximate number of fulltime employees engaged in the research	x	c
°Material effects of complying with environmental regulations	x	c
°Number of employees	x	c
Industry segment data for: (1) total sales and revenues, (2) income (or loss) before income taxes and extraordinary items, (3) identifiable assets	x	x
Geographic area data for: (1) total sales and revenues, (2) income (or loss) before income taxes and extraordinary items, (3) identifiable assets, (4) export sales	x	x
Class of products or services: (2) amount or percentage of total sales and revenues	x	x
Importance of operations in foreign countries—risks, volume and relative profitability	x	x
Name(s) of major customers	x	c

KEY: x = Describe the status of the matter as of the date of the financial statements.
      c = Describe significant changes occurring since the date of the last financial statements.
     – = No disclosure required.
     ° = Disclose significant industry data.

of-business and the limit of ten reportable segments remains in effect, the definition of "industry" varies depending upon the registrant's operations. The industry segments of a highly diversified conglomerate are defined more broadly than a machinery manufacturer's, for example. In many cases, then, industry segments are identical to the registrant's lines-of-business because this is the approach that management had used originally to define lines-of-business.[8]

Regulation S-K

Regulation S-K is effective for fiscal years ending after March 15, 1978, however at that time data were to have been reported retroactively for all fiscal years ending after December 15, 1976. Therefore, Dart Industries' future annual reports will disclose industry segment data meeting the standards of Regulation S-K.

For registrants whose industry segments and lines-of-business are not the same: (1) if the company has previously filed line-of-business data, its five-year summary can, during the transition period, consist of lines-of-business data for all fiscal years ending up to December 15, 1976 and industry segment data for all years thereafter; (2) if the company has not previously filed line-of-business data, it must report industry segment data for all five years on a retroactive basis. Any material lack of comparability between line-of-business and industry segment groupings must be explained; that is, the issuer should "state, to the extent possible, which segments are equivalent or substantially similar to each of the lines of business, the approximate percentage of the line of business included in each industry segment and the basis for the new classification." By December 15, 1981, all data reported in the description of business will be industry segment data.

Form 10-Q does not solicit industry segment data unless a segment's performance indicates that the data presented "may not be indicative of current or future operations of the segment."

Industry segment data must be presented in Forms S-1, 10, and 10-K and in the narrative sections of the annual report to the stockholders.[9] Regulation S-K requires industry segment data for the company's holdings of property as described in Form S-1, "Description of Property," (Item 10) and Form 10-K, "Properties," (Item 3). Refer to Exhibit 7-2 for a summary of the regulation or form to which the amended disclosure provisions of Regualtion S-K apply.

Regulation S-K also requires the inclusion of a remuneration table that discloses the remuneration of the five most highly compensated executive officers or directors of the registrant whose total cash and cash-equivalent remuneration exceeds $50,000. The form of the table prescribed in Regulation S-K requires: (1) the name of the individual; (2) the capacities in which served; (3) salaries, fees, directors' fees, commissions, and bonuses; (4) securities or property, insurance benefits or reimbursement, personal benefits; and (5) aggregate of contingent forms of remuneration. The valuation of noncash items is determined by the actual incremental cost to the registrant unless such costs are significantly less than that the recipient would have to pay to obtain the benefits, in which case the aggregate value to the recipient should be disclosed in a footnote to the table.

Exhibit 7-2 Schedule of Amendments (Regulation or Form to Which Amended Disclosure Provisions Apply)

	Regulation S-K	Form S-1	Form S-7	Form S-8	Form 10	Form 10-K	Annual Report to Shareholders	Certain Proxy and Information Statements
1. Amendments to disclosure items—Disclosure of:								
(a) Five-year historical financial information relating to industry segments	X	X	X	X	X	X	X	X
(b) Five-year historical financial information relating to foreign and domestic operations	X	X	X	X	X	X	X	X
(c) Amount of export sales for each of the last five years	X	X	X	X	X	X	X	X
(d) Information about the business focusing on industry segments	X	X			X	X		
(e) Identification of industry segments using material properties	X	X			X	X		
2. Form amendments to exhibits—filing as exhibits contracts material to registrant or which are specifically referred to in the business description	X	X			X	X		

SOURCE: Securities and Exchange Commision, Regulation S-K.

THE ANNUAL REPORT TO STOCKHOLDERS

We showed, in Chapter 4,[10] that the SEC has obtained jurisdiction over the contents of the annual report to stockholders because the report contain information required in the proxy and information statements regularly distributed to stockholders. Regulation 14A, "Solicitation of Proxies Under the Securities Exchange Act of 1934," is the authoritative source of disclosure requirements for proxy solicitations and Rule 14a-3 of that regulation sets the standards for the annual report. (Regulation 14C provides the same function for information statements required in conjunction with meetings in which proxies are not solicited but members are being elected to the board of directors.) Through Rules 14a-3 and 14c-3 the requirements of other SEC pronouncements come to bear upon the annual report. Indeed, we used Dart Industries' annual report to illustrate the requirements originating in Regulations S-X and S-K, and in Forms S-1 and 10-K. Exhibit 7-3 illustrates the complexity of these relationships.

The amount of financial information required by Regulation 14A varies depending upon several factors; whether: (1) proxies are being solicited, (2) the meeting for which the proxies are being solicited is an annual meeting, (3) members are being elected to the board of directors, and (4) the subject of the vote itself. Exhibit 7-4 presents a decision diagram of Regulation 14A requirements for financial information; and Exhibit 7-5 cross references Rule 14a-3 requirements to our example, Dart Industries' annual report to stockholders, for the purpose of illustrating the fact that virtually every feature of an annual report is specified by regulation.

Exhibit 7-3   The Organization of Documents Affecting the Annual Report to Stockholders

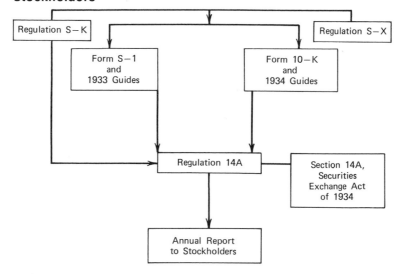

Exhibit 7-4   Regulation 14A Requirements for Financial Information—A Decision Diagram

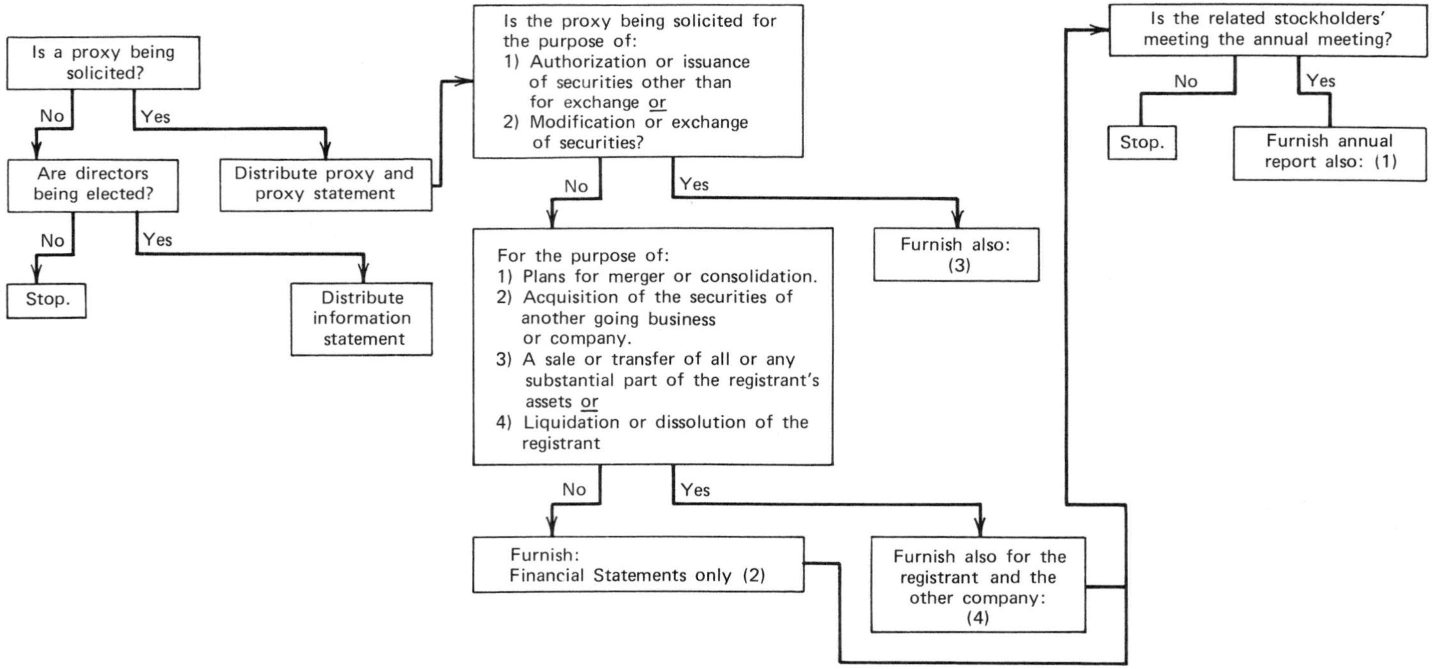

Is a proxy being solicited?

No → Are directors being elected?

No → Stop.

Yes → Distribute proxy and proxy statement

Are directors being elected? Yes → Distribute information statement

Is the proxy being solicited for the purpose of:
1) Authorization or issuance of securities other than for exchange or
2) Modification or exchange of securities?

Yes → Furnish also: (3)

No → For the purpose of:
1) Plans for merger or consolidation.
2) Acquisition of the securities of another going business or company.
3) A sale or transfer of all or any substantial part of the registrant's assets or
4) Liquidation or dissolution of the registrant

Yes → Furnish also for the registrant and the other company: (4)

No → Furnish: Financial Statements only (2)

Is the related stockholders' meeting the annual meeting?

Yes → Furnish annual report also: (1)

No → Stop.

Rule 14a-3 Requirement

	Caption	(Page)

Rule 14a-3 Requirement

1. *Annual Report*
Summary of operations and management's discussion and analysis
Description of business

Identity of directors and executive officers

Identity of principal market where voting securities are traded, and high/low sales prices and dividends paid for past eight quarters
Undertaking to provide, without charge, Form 10-K
2. *Financial Statements*
Balance sheet
Income Statement
Statement of securityholder's equity

Statement of changes in financial position
(Footnote dislosure as required by Regulation S-X)

Reconcilation of differences between 10-K and statements
Schedule XVI, Supplementary Earnings Statement Information
Opinion letter
3. *Additional information*
4. *Additional information*
Voluntarily disclosed information

Caption (Page)

Five-Year Summary of Operations (___)
Management's Discussion and Analysis (___)
Company Description (___)
Sales and Pre-tax Earnings by Operating Segments (___)

Operations Review—Direct Selling (___)
• Consumer Products (___)
• Chemical-Plastics (___)
• Glass Containers (___)
• Dart Resorts (___)

Companies, Products and Group Management (___)
Board of Directors (___)
Officers and Committees (___)
Investor Information (___)

Investor Information (___)

Balance Sheet (___)
Statement of Earnings and Retained Earnings (___)
Statement of Capital Stock (___)
Statement of Capital and Excess of Par Value (___)
Statement of Changes in Financial Position (___)
Summary of Accounting Policies (___)
Notes to Financial Statements (___)
None needed—no differences
Supplementary Earnings Statement Information (___)

Report of Independent Accountants (___)
Not required
Not required
Year in Brief (___)
Letter to Stockholders (___)
Ten Years at a Glance
Announcement of annual meeting (___)

FORM 10-K

Public companies prepare their annual report to the SEC following the organization and specifications of Form 10-K. As with the annual report to stockholders, the interrelationships between authoritative sources that affect the 10-K are complex; Exhibit 7-6 diagrams them. Form 10-K is due 90 days after the end of the fiscal year; but the Article 12 schedules can be filed in an amendment up to 120 days after fiscal year-end.

Exhibit 7-7 lists the items of information required by Form 10-K. Registrants provide the information in the prescribed order, and include even those items that are inapplicable. [See Dart Industries' 10-K, Items 7,8 and 10 (page 335.)] Items 14-18 (Part II) duplicate information required in the proxy (information) statement sent to stockholders; therefore, if a definitive statement is filed not later than 120 days after the fiscal year-end, these items can be omitted from the 10-K. Notice that this is what Dart has done (page 337).

Dart's Item I ("Business") narrative beginning on page 326 provides essen the same information as in its annual report. Notice that certain subheadings ("Foreign Operations," "Trademarks and Patents," "Environmental Protection," and "Employees") correspond directly with the topics identified in Exhibit 7-1. Item 2, "Summary of Operations," information has been incorporated by reference from the annual report to stockholders. Item 3, "Properties," is segmented into domestic and foreign groupings in accordance with Regulation S-K. Item 4, "Parents and Subsidiaries" (page 333) identifies all companies affiliated with Dart and the ways in which they are accounted for. Item 5, "Legal Proceedings," reports on the same matters as the footnote entitled "Commitments and Contingencies," but is considerably more specific as to the legal actions it faces. Item 6, "Increases and Decreases in Outstanding Securities and

Exhibit 7-6   The Organization of Documents Affecting Forms 10-K and 10-Q

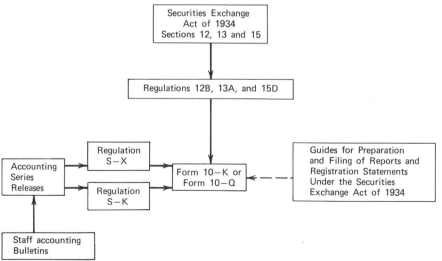

Exhibit 7-7 Form 10-K Table of Contents

Item	Caption
	Part I
1	Business
2	Summary of Operations
3	Properties
4	Parents and subsidiaries
5	Legal proceedings
6	Increases and decreases in outstanding securities and indebtedness
7	Changes in securities and changes in security for registered securities
8	Defaults on senior securities
9	Approximate number of equity security holders
10	Submission of matters to a vote of security
11	Executive officers of registrant
12	Indemnification of directors and officers
13	Financial statements, exhibits filed, and reports on Form 8-K
	Part II
14	Security ownership of certain beneficial owners and management
15	Directors of the registrant
16	Remuneration of directors and officers
17	Options granted to management to purchase securities
18	Interest of management and others in certain securities

Indebtedness,'' brings together information provided in the financial statements and footnotes.

The occurrence of an event covered by Item 7, 8, or 10 (Changes in securities and changes in security for registered securities, defaults upon senior securities, or the submission of certain matters to a vote of security holders) precipitated the need to file a Form 8-K report prior to *ASR No. 206*. In an effort to simplify reporting, the SEC has made these events reportable in the Form 10-Q or 10-K for the quarter in which they occur.

Item 11 information regarding executive officers goes beyond that provided in the annual report to stockholders in that it gives their ages and a brief past history. Dart's Item 12, ''Imdemnification of Directors and Officers'' (page 336) illustrates that information can be incorporated from past years' filings.

Item 13a contains the financial statements, footnotes, and additional information (Article 12, schedules and sundry exhibits). Notice that Dart has incorporated the financial statments in their entirety and has incorporated specific portions of the remainder of the annual report. Item 13b requires the inclusion of any Form 8-K filed in the fourth quarter; Dart filed none. Finally, one of the exhibits that must be filed with the 10-K is a manually signed opinion letter from the independent accountants. A manually signed opinion letter is also included with the Form 10-K that is sent to the stock exchange(s) on which the company's stock is traded.

Financial Statements

The "Instructions as to Financial Statements" specify that a balance sheet, income statement, and statement of changes in financial position be filed as part of Forms 10-K. Statements for the current fiscal year and prior year must be presented in comparative columnar form and be audited. The entities for which financial statements are required are:

1. The consolidated entity—the parent and more than 50 percent owned affiliates.
2. The "registrant," that is, the parent company. (Under the conditions discussed below, these statments can be eliminated and the basis for the elimination stated in the list of financial statements filed with the 10-K.).
3. Each majority-owned subsidiary not consolidated and each 50-percent-or-less-owned-person for which the investment is accounted for by the equity method by the registrant or a consolidated subsidiary of the registrant. (This requirement does not apply to holdings which represent ten percent or less of the registrant's total assets, sales and revenues, or income before income taxes and extraordinary items.).
4. Each affiliate whose securities constitute a substantial portion of the collateral securing any class of registered securities.

The financial statements of the parent company can be eliminated if: (1) it is primarily an operating company and the total minority interest of all consolidated subsidiaries does not exceed 5 percent of the total consolidated assets; or (2) the registrant's total assets, exclusive of investments in and advances to its consolidated subsidiaries, constitute 75 percent or more of total consolidated assets and the registrant's share of sales and revenues (exclusive of interest and dividends from the subsidiaries) and equity in subsidiary income is 75 percent or more of the total consolidated amounts for sales, revenues and income.

Statements for subsidiaries required by (3) above can be filed as amendments to the 10-K when their fiscal years end during the time period 90 days before to 90 days after that of the parent.

Because Form 10-K must be filed at the end of every fiscal year;[11] companies that change their fiscal year usually must file "short period" financial statements in an "interim" Form 10-K. The decision diagram in Exhibit 7-8 shows under what conditions the 10-K must be filed and whether the financial statements must be audited.

Exhibit 7-8   Decision Diagram Short Period Financial Statements

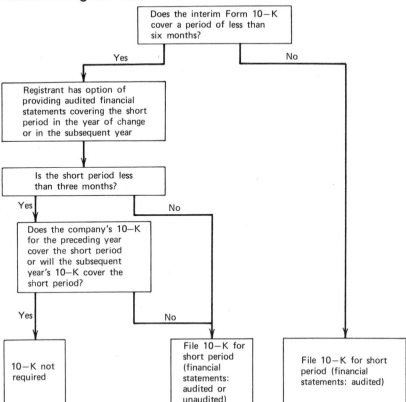

SOURCE.   SEC Reporting Form 10-K, Ernst and Whinney, 1975.

FORM 10-Q AND THE QUARTERLY REPORT TO STOCKHOLDERS

All registrants who file Form 10-K with the SEC also file a Form 10-Q for each of the first three fiscal quarters within 45 days of each quarter's end. The diagram in Exhibit 7-6 shows that the flow of authority affecting the 10-Q is the same as that for the 10-K. Any differences between quarterly and annual reports is due to the requirements of the forms themselves.

Exhibit 7-9 lists the items required by Form 10-Q. The quarterly report to stockholders is not required by the SEC, but rather by the exchange(s) on which the registrant's securities are sold (and some companies voluntarily distribute quarterly reports to their stockholders). The quarterly report to stockholders therefore need not meet the requirements of Part I of Form 10-Q. Dart Industries, for example, has elected to report on its 1978 annual meeting in its first quarter report (pages 375–390) and has, accordingly, eliminated management's analysis and other items called for in Part I. Therefore, Dart cannot incorporate its quarterly report to stockholders in compliance with Part I requirements. And, accord-

Exhibit 7-9 Form 10-Q Table of Contents

Item	Caption
	Part I
	A quarterly report to stockholders can be submitted in compliance with Part I if it meets the following requirements:
1	Financial statements
2	Management's analysis of quarterly income statements
3	Other financial information
4	Review by independent public accountant
5	Exhibits
	Part II
1	Legal proceedings
2	Changes in securities
3	Changes in security for registered securities
4	Defaults on senior securities
5	Increase in amount outstanding of securities or indebtedness
6	Decrease in amount outstanding of securities or indebtedness
7	Submission of matters to a vote of security holders
8	Other materially important events
9	Exhibits and reports on Form 8-K

ing to its disclosure on page 400 of its 10-Q, Dart has nothing to report for any item in Part II. Notice that Part II items 2 to 9 are those that *ASR No. 206* removed from Form 8-K.

The financial statements incorporated in Form 10-Q are condensed and reported on a consolidated basis. A condensed income statment only is required for any subsidiary that is not consolidated or any 50 percent or less owned person for which the investment is accounted for the equity method and who files a separate annual income statement. The criteria used in condensing the financial statements for Form 10-Q are presented in Exhibit 7-10.

The quarterly financial statements cover a variety of fiscal periods. The balance sheets presented in Form 10-Q are dated as of the end of the most recent quarter and the comparative prior year's quarter. The income statement periods reported on, however, are:

1. The most recent fiscal quarter and the corresponding period of the preceding fiscal year.
2. The period between the end of the last fiscal year and the end of the most recent fiscal quarter and corresponding period of the preceding fiscal year.

3. (Optional) The cumulative 12-month period ended during the most recent fiscal quarter and the corresponding fiscal year.

The statement of changes in financial position covers Period (2) above and, optionally, Period (3). Dart Industries does not make the optional disclosure; and because the income statement on page 395 reports the first fiscal quarter, cumulative statements are inapplicable.

The financial statements need not be audited, but because interim data are required in the annual reports, these data are usually subject to a limited review. If the review has been conducted, the registrant may so state, but must then indicate whether all adjustments and disclosures proposed by the accountants have been reflected, and include as an exhibit a letter from the accountants commenting on the representations. (Refer to Dart's footnote on page 399 and Price Waterhouse & Co.'s confirming letter on page 402.)

10-Q Additional Disclosures

In addition to the financial statements discussed above, certain other financial information must be disclosed. Some information is required of all registrants; some arises as the result of specific financial events. Information provided by all registrants includes:[12]

Exhibit 7-10   10-Q Financial Statement Condensation Criteria

Financial Statements	Criteria
Balance sheet	• Account detail limited to Regulation S-X major (numbered) captions except for 5-02.6, inventories, where raw materials, work-in-process, and finished goods should be disclosed separately. • If the amount in a caption has not changed by 25 percent since the previous balance sheet and it is less than 10 percent of total assets, it may be combined with others.
Income statement	• Account detail limited to Regulation S-X major (numbered) captions. • If the amount in a caption has not changed by more than 20 percent compared with the next preceding comparable income statement and it is less than 15 percent of *average* net income for the most recent three years, it may be combined with others.
Statement of sources and applications of funds	• Disclosure may be limited to funds provided by operations and • Other sources and applications of funds that exceed 10 percent of the average of funds provided by operations for the most recent three years.

1. *Management's analysis of quarterly income statements* Requires comparisons to be made between three sets of periods: (Dart, page 398).
   a. The most recent quarter and the comparable quarter or the preceding year.
   b. The current year-to-date and the comparable period of the preceding year.
   c. The most recent quarter and the quarter immediately preceding it. Material changes in such amounts as:
      1. Unit sales volume.
      2. Prices charges and paid
      3. Production levels.
      4. Production cost variances
      5. Labor costs, and
      6. Discretionary spending programs are specifically cited in *ASR No. 177* as being relevant to this analysis.

2. *All adjustments necessary to a fair statement of the results of the interim period (Dart, page 396)* Accompanied by management's statement to that effect. (For example, adjustments should be made for appropriate estimates to provide for bonus and profit sharing arrangements normally determined or settled at year-end.).

3. *Additional information* Includes any disclosures of information related to the periodic report that is of significance to investors (For example, cyclical or seasonal business patterns, major uncertainties, significant accounting changes under consideration, or dollar amounts of backlog.).

4. *Changes in accounting principles* (other than those required by FASB pronouncements) disclose the:
   1. Date of change.
   2. Reasons for making the change.
   3. In a letter from the auditors, their judgment of whether the change is to an alternative principle that is preferable under the circumstances.

Circumstances that require additional information include:

1. MATERIAL PRIOR PERIOD ADJUSTMENTS. Disclose their nature and effect on net income, total and per share, on any prior period and on any retained earnings. If results of operations for any period reported herein have been adjusted retroactively by such an item subsequent to the intital reporting of such period, similar disclosure of the effect of the change shall be made.

2. FORM 8-K. Disclose if the form is required to be filed because of:
   a. Material unusual charges or credits to income, or
   b. A change in independent accountants.

3. POOLING OF INTERESTS DURING THE CURRENT PERIOD. The interim financial statements for both the current year and the preceding year shall reflect the combined results of the pooled businesses. Supplemental disclosure of

the separate results of the combined entities for periods prior to the combination shall be given with appropriate explanations.

4. PURCHASES OF MATERIAL BUSINESS INTERESTS DURING THE CURRENT YEAR. Disclose pro forma results of operations for the current year to the end of the most recent fiscal quarter (and the comparable period) as if the companies were combined since the beginning of the reporting period. Minimum pro forma information, on a total and per share basis is:
   a. Income before extraordinary items.
   b. Cumulative effect of accounting changes.

5. DISPOSAL OF SIGNIFICANT PORTION OF THE BUSINESS DURING THE CURRENT YEAR. Disclose its effect on revenues and net income, total and per share, for all periods.

THE REGISTRATION STATEMENT—FORM S-1

Most companies issuing securities to the public file a registration statement on Form S-1, the general purpose form; however, three other, abbreviated, registration forms are common. Form S-7 can be used by issuers who are already registered under the 1933 Act and who, for the previous three years, have been punctual in the filing of required reports with the SEC; Form S-16 is for large, stable companies and registrants making secondary security offerings; and Form S-18 is for issues wherein the proceeds from the sale of securities do not exceed $3 million. The flow of authority governing the registration statements is diagrammed in Exhibit 7-11. Notice that the registration statement is, unlike reports

Exhibit 7-11   Organization of Documents Affecting Form S-1

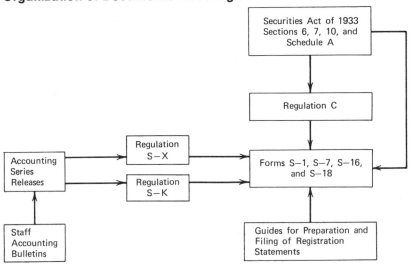

Exhibit 7-12   Comparison of Forms S-1 and 10

Topic	Item Number Form S-1	Item Number Form 10	Schedule A Reference
Cover page:	X	X	1,3,23
Prospectus:			
Distribution Spread	1	—	15,16,17,19
Plan of Distribution	2	—	5,17
Use of Proceeds to Registrant	3	—	13,21
Sales Otherwise Than for Cash	4	—	15
Capital Structure	5	—	9
Summary of Operations	6	—	—
Organization of Registrant	7	1	2
Parents of Registrant	8	2	1
Description of Business	9	3	8
Description of Property	10	4	—
Organization within 5 Years	11	5	20
Legal Proceedings	12	6	—
Capital Stock Being Registered	13	14	11
Long-Term Debt Being Registered	14	15	12
Other Securities Being Registered	15	16	10
Directions and Executive Officers	16	7	4
Remuneration of Directors and Officers	17	9	14
Options to Purchase Securities	18	10	10
Principal Holders of Securities	19	11	6,7
Interest of Management and Others in Certain Transactions	20	13	22,24
Financial Statements	21	18	25,26.27
Part II:			
Marketing arrangements	22	—	—
Other Expenses of Issuance and Distribution	23	—	18
Relationship with Registrant of Experts Named in Registration Statement	24	—	—
Sales to Special Parties	25	—	16
Recent Sales of Unregistered Securities	26	17	—
Subsidiaries of Registrant	27	—	—
Franchises and Concessions	28	—	—
Indemnification of Directors and Officers	29	8	—
Treatment of Proceeds from Stock Being Registered	30	—	—
Financial Statements and Exhibits	31	—	28,29,30,31
Number of Equity Security Holders	—	12	—

filed under the Securities Exchange Act of 1934, impacted directly by the statutory provisions of the Securities Act of 1933; more specifically, Section 7 and Schedule A of the act set certain standards for the financial statements and auditor's consent and report that have been incorporated in Form S-1.

As we observed in Chapter 3, the S-1 is subdivided into two parts, the Prospectus and Part II. Exhibit 7-12 lists the items required by Form S-1. Companies applying for a position on- a stock exchange also must file Form 10 with the SEC. Since Form 10 and the S-1 are quite similar in content, we will not specifically reference a Form 10.[13] Rather, Exhibit 7-12 compares the requirements for the two forms and references the statutory provisions of Schedule A of the Securities Act.

We present the Form S-1 registration statement of Global Marine, Inc. filed in connection with an offering of approximately \$30 million in $12\frac{3}{8}$ percent debentures for purposes of illustration and urge that it be compared with the disclosure items listed in Exhibit 7-12. Although disclosure of business risk is necessary to make the financial information not misleading in annual reports, the requirements for the disclosure of risk are quite a bit more stringent in the S-1. Each filing presents unique problems of its own. For example, S-1 registrations occasionally are filed by companies with negative retained earnings whose only hope for survival hinges on a successful issue of new securities. This information would be clearly spelled out in the S-1. Global Marine's disclosure of risk however, is limited to operating risk, described in "Business" (page 414), although the \$30 million bond offering represents an amount also 60 percent that of stockholders' equity and the financing plan includes additional debt from other sources. Notice, too, the warnings on page 403 that the securities have not been approved or disapproved by the SEC and on page 404 (in conformance with the requirements of Item 22), that the underwriters will engage in market stabilization activities.

Finally, the report of the independent public accountants appears of page 437. In conformance with S-1 requirements, Coopers & Lybrand also give their written consent to be named as experts in the S-1 filing. The consent letter will be discussed in Chapter 8.

Financial Statements

Financial information is allocated between the Prospectus and Part II of the S-1.The Prospectus (Part I) includes:

1. An audited balance sheet.
2. Audited three-year comparative income statements.
3. Audited three-year comparative statements of changes in financial position.
4. The Summary of Operations and Management's Analysis and Discussion.
5. Article 12 Schedule XVI, Supplementary Income Statement Information.
6. Where applicable, Article 12 Schedules 27, 42, and 43 (Summary of Investments in Securities—Other Than Securities of Affiliates, Real Estate and Accumulated Depreciation, and Mortgage Loans on Real Estate, respectively).

7. Supplementary disclosure of special provisions such as:
   a. A reorganization of the registrant during the periods for which income statements are presented, or a plan for future reorganization.
   b. A purchase or pooling of interests during the periods for which income statements are presented for the succession to other businesses and that meet certain criteria.
   c. Pro forma information for intended purchases or poolings for acquistions not reported by the equity method.

Whereas Part II includes the following:

1. Article 12 Schedules (other than 5 and 6 above).
2. Historical financial information (if not filed previously pursuant ot the Securities Act of 1933 or the Securities Exchange Act of 1934) such as:
   a. Any material restatements of capital shares resulting in the transfer from the capital accounts to other stockholders' equity or reserve accounts.
   b. Any material revaluations of property.
   c. Material amounts of debt discount and expense on long-term debt still outstanding that have been written off earlier than as required.
   d. Material amounts of long-term debt or preferred shares retired.
   e. Any other material changes in other stockholders' equity with the exception of the closing of the income account and dividend payments
   f. Information regarding any significant predecessor of the registrant from the beginning of the period to the date of succession.

Financial statements are required for the parent registrant and on a consolidated basis. If the parent meets certain conditions and if both its investment i its subsidiaries and the subsidiaries' sale and revenues are less than 25 percent of total assets, sales or revenues respectively, only consolidated statements need be presented. Financial statements also are required for subsidiaries not consolidated and 50-percent-or-less-owned persons accounted for by the equity method that meet the criteria for inclusion under Rule 4-03 of Regulation S-X.

The criteria for determining the fiscal periods for which financial statement must be presented are rather complex; the decision process is diagrammed in Exhibit 7-13 for the balance sheet and in Exhibit 7-14 for the income statement and statements of changes in financial position. Global Marine (page 439) filed an audited balance sheet for the registrant and for the entity on a consolidated basis as of the end of its 1977 fiscal year. Because the filing date of the registration statement is July 25, 1978, interim balance sheets must be presented as well Global Marine meets the three criteria for filing unaudited interim period balance sheets dated within six months of the filing date, but the company has elected fil statements dated as of its second quarter's end.

Audited income statements and statements of changes in financial position are presented for the most recent three fiscal years and unaudited statements for the period from the date of the last audited balance sheet to the date of the interim balance sheet (the "stub period") complete the presentation on page 441.

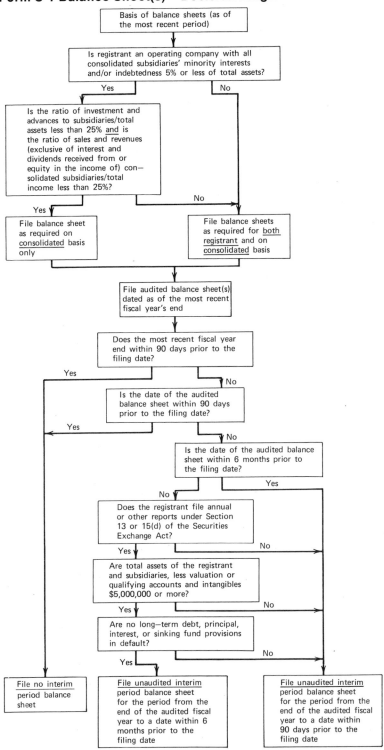

Exhibit 7-14   Form S-1 Income Statements—Decision Diagram

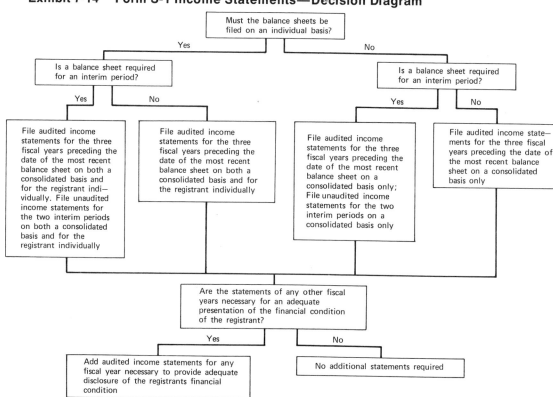

SUMMARY   The SEC requries considerably more financial information than that ordinaril contained in the financial statements, footnotes and Article 12 schedules. Tw principal sources of such financial information are the summary of operation (and management's discussion and analysis) and the description of business While most requirements for financial information come from the individua forms themselves, or from Regulations 14A and C, the SEC has issued Regula tion S-K whose purpose it is to bring uniformity to the requirements of the var ious reports. The first topic of S-K is industry segment reporting intended t bring SEC requirements in line with industry segment reporting standards o *FASB Statement NO. 14*; but other pronouncements are being added to the reg ulation.

Because of this uniformity of requirements financial information can be incor porated from one report to another and it is possible to integrate two entir reports if the integrated report meets the requirements of both; for example combined Form 10-K and an annual report to stockholders.

Notwithstanding uniformity requirements for financial information disclosure each form has different requirements for the financial information that must b included in the filing and whether or not it must be audited. Exhibit 7-15 sum marizes these requirements.

Exhibit 7-15   Summary of Statements Requiring the Auditor's Opinion

| Form | Balance Sheet | | Income Statement and Funds Statement | | | Article 12 Schedules Audited | Summary of Operations (May be required to be audited) |
	Audited at latest Fiscal Year-End	Unaudited Interim	Audited	Unaudited Interim			
S-1	Yes	May be required	3 years	Yes		Yes	5 years and 2 years interim
10-K (and annual report to stockholders	Yes, plus audited comparative prior year	No	2 years	No		Yes	5 years
10-Q	No[14]	Condensed	No[14]	Condensed		No	No

[1] For example, *Guide No. 22* of the *Guides for the Preparation and Filing of Registration Statements Under the Securities Act of 1933* and *Guide No. 4* of the *Guides for the Preparation and Filing of Reports and Registration Statements under the Securities Exchange Act of 1934*.

[2] Specifically, information from the following sources can be referenced in response any 10-K item:

a. Definitive proxy statement or information statement,
b. Report to security holders, or
c. Prospectus filed pursuant to Rule 424(b) or (c) under the Securities Act of 1933. Refer also to Rule 12b-32.

[3] The 10-Q has similar provisions for incorporating the quarterly report to stockholders Part I of the form. Rule 411 of Regulation C permits limited incorporation by reference Part II of Form S-1. And Item 15(d) of Regulation 14A allows the annual report to stockholders to be incorporated by reference in the proxy statement.

[4] In the *Guides for Preparation and Filing of Reports and Registration Statements Under the Securities Exchange Act of 1934*.

[5] The summary and analysis are required by provisions of Item 6 of Form S-1 (and *Guide 22*), Item 2 of Form 10-K (and *Guide 1*), and Rule 14a-3 of Regulation 14A.

[6] *Accounting Series Release No. 159*.

[7] Notice the difference in function between Regulation S-X and Regulation S-K. Regulation S-X establishes standards for the disclosure in the financial statements, footnotes and schedules of information with which the independent accountant is directly involved. This information is identified in the scope of paragraph of the opinion letter. Regulation S-K, on the other hand, establishes disclosure standards for those parts of the reports for which the independent accountant has only indirect involvement. That is, the auditor reviews the remainder of the report in order to ascertain that the financial statements and footnotes are fairly stated. A description of business, for example, that contradicts the financial statements or that reveals a matter heretofore unknown to him would necessitate an extension of the investigation.

[8] *Accounting Series Release No. 244* offers guidelines for classifying the operations of an issuer by industry segment.

[9] If it is applicable and significant, the following information is required:

- Description of business operatons by segment.

- Five-year industry segment data
  - Revenues
    - Sales to unaffiliated customers
    - Sales or transfers to other segments
  - Operating porfit or loss
  - Identifiable assets

- Five-year geographic area data
  - Revenues
    - Sales to unaffiliated customers
    - Sales or transfers to other segments
  - Operating profit or loss
  - Identifiable assets

- Five-year product class data

- Revenues for "any class of similar products or services" that represent 10 percent or more of consolidated revenue in either of the past two years (15 percent for small companies)

- Foreign operations
  - Significant foreign operations if reported in the past and expected to be reported in the future.
  - Risks attendant to foreign operations and any dependence on one or more of the registrant's industry segments upon such foreign operations.

- Intersegment and intrasegment sales when made at prices substantially different from market and segment operating results are affected materially.

- Names of major customers representing 10 percent or more of consolidated sales.

- Restatement of prior segment data when
  - The financial statements as a whole have been restated and
  - There is a change in the way the registrant's products or services have been grouped from other than a change in the nature of operations or the result of a segment losing or gaining in significance.

[10] The reader who is unfamiliar with the general processes involved in reporting under the 1933 and 1934 Acts should review Chapters 3 and 4 before proceeding with the remainder of this chapter.

[11] See Dart Industries' Form 10-K on page 339 that discloses the reasons for not including the subsidiaries' statements or the parent's individual financial statements.

[12] See Regulations 13A and 15D.

[13] The financial statements required to be filed with Form 10, however, differ in several ways from those of Form S-1. Form 10 requirements are not as stringent as regards the balance sheet dates. The (audited) balance sheet date may, for a Form 10 filing, be of the most recent fiscal year unless the fiscal year has ended within 90 days of the filing date. If it has ended within 90 days of the filing date, the balance sheet date may be as of the close of the preceding year except that then an amendment must be filed within 90 days of the close of the year supplying an audited balance sheet as of the end of the latest fiscal year. The income statement must also be audited and cover the three-year period preceding the date of the most recent balance sheet. No interim ("stub period") financial statements are required.

[14] *Accounting Series Release No.* 274 exempts accountants from "experts liability" under the Securities Act for alleged false and misleading interim financial statements.

QUESTIONS
1. What is Form 10-K?
2. How often and when must 10-K be filed?
3. What regulation determines the form and content of Form 10-K?
4. Distinguish between Parts I and II of 10-K.
5. Should 10-K be thought of simply as a form to be filled out and turned in to the SEC?
6. If all the items in the 10-K are carefully completed by the registrant, can the reporting corporation be absolutely assured that it has complied with adequate disclosure requirements?
7. What is meant by line-of-business or "segment" reporting?
8. Would you say that the fairness and accuracy of information disclosed in financial statements is the primary responsibility of the management of the registrant and only a secondary responsibility of the independent accountant?

9. If a registrant changes its certifying accountant, must it so report on an 8-K, in the company's proxy statement, or both?

10. Discuss a few of the 10-K disclosure requirements that must also be included in the registrant's annual report to the shareholders.

11. Does the SEC have any restrictions on the registrant making profit projections and other forecasts?

12. Must the information required by Form 10-Q be audited? What is the Regulation S-X requirement with respect to independent auditors regarding interim financial reports?

13. Can a footnote explanation in a financial statement render acceptable what would otherwise be an unacceptable accounting principle?

14. Must Form 10-Q include a management analysis of the corporation's affairs?

15. Must management comment upon any known material factors that might influence future trends and results, favorably or unfavorably?

8 The Auditor's Professional Standards

The professional standards of certified public accountants, who "practice before the SEC" must conform with both the AICPA Code of Professional Ethics and SEC requirements. An accountant is considered to be practicing before the SEC if he: (1) prepares any statement, opinion or other paper that is filed with the SEC as part of a registration statement, application, or report, and (2) consents to the association of his name with the filing. Where the SEC finds an accountant has not conformed to the applicable standards, it may take any of several administrative actions that are provided for in its *Rules of Practice*.

Of all the professional standards enumerated in the AICPA's Code of Professional Ethics, the SEC places greatest emphasis upon the accountant's independence. We will review briefly the provisions of the Code pertaining to independence, and then will examine the SEC's standards of independence as stated in Rule 2-01(b) of Regulation S-X. The many Accounting Series Releases summarized in Appendix E at the end of this chapter announce SEC disciplinary administrative action against accountants. The cause of action in most cases is lack of independence. Therefore, the accounting series releases illustrate by example the SEC's concept of independence.

This chapter also discusses the standards for auditors' representations, (opinions, letters of consent, comfort letters). With the Code of Professional Ethics and Regulation S-X as a basis, the many situations in which the auditor must commit to writing his position regarding an SEC matter will be considered.

RULES OF PRACTICE—ADMINISTRATIVE ACTIONS

The enforcement powers of the SEC summarized in Exhibit 2-10 include powers that enable the agency to enforce high professional standards for those permitted to practice before it. Although the SEC can go through the federal courts to obtain criminal judgments against accountants, it has a far more direct and efficient means of dealing with substandard professional practices—suspension and disbarment. Suspension is a temporary cessation of the right to practice. Disbarment is permanent. Before imposing either sanction, the SEC must grant the accountant the opportunity to be heard.

Suspension from practice means that the accountant: (1) may not sign an opinion contained in any registration statement, report, application or amendment filed with the SEC during the period of suspension, (nor may a registration statement that includes his signature become effective), and (2) may not represent a client or discuss any problem related thereto with the SEC.

The Rules of Practice [Rules 2(e) and (f)] define the conditions under which an accountant can be suspended or disbarred, as follows:

1. Where the Commission determines that the professional does not "possess the requisite qualifications to represent others."
2. If the professional is "lacking in character or integrity or (found) to have engaged in unethical or improper professional conduct."
3. If he has "willfully aided and abetted the violation of any provision of the Federal securities laws . . . or the rules and regulations thereunder."
4. If his license to practice as an accountant has been "revoked or suspended in any State, Territory, District, Commonwealth, or Possession."
5. If he "has been convicted of a felony, or of a misdemeanor involving moral turpitude."
6. If he has been found guilty of "contemptuous conduct at any hearing before the Commission or a hearing officer."

Further, the SEC may dispense with the preliminary hearing and temporarily suspend from practice an accountant:

1. Who has been "permanently enjoined by a court of competent jurisdiction by reason of his misconduct in an action brought by the Commission from violation or aiding and abetting the violation of any provision of the Federal securities laws . . . or of the rules and regulations thereunder."
2. "Found by any court of competent jurisdiction in an action brought by the Commission to which he is a party or found by (the) Commission in any administrative proceeding to which he is a party to have violated or aided and abetted the violation of any provision of the Federal securities laws . . . or of the rules and regulations thereunder (unless the violation was found not to have been willful)."

Provision 1 above makes such a course of action highly risky, for without favorably disposing of the accusation, an accountant could be suspended by the SEC at any time in an unrelated action. Since provisions of suspension affect *all* the accountant's clients, hundreds of registrants having no involvement in the matter giving rise to the accusation could be severely punished for the sins of their auditors. The consequences of disbarring one of the Big 8 accounting firms would be horrendous. With this in mind corporations increasingly evaluate their auditors in terms of their exposure to such action and the SEC has been very sparing in the exercise of its power. Indeed, the policy of the SEC has been to suspend or disbar small firms (usually having only one or two partners, few employees and few, if any, SEC registrants as clients) but individual partners of the larger firms. The disciplinary actions taken against the larger firms as a whole include evaluation by outside experts of the firm's audit procedures (the "peer review"); suspension of the firm's right to accept audit engagements from new clients for a stated period of time; and other provisions intended to improve the quality of audit services performed by the firm (*ASR No. 186*).

PROFESSIONAL STANDARDS

The accountant's standards of professional practice have become more and more stringent in the past 40 years. The impetus for greater rigor has come both from the profession and from the SEC—it is a reciprocal relationship. An example of this reciprocity is this: The accounting profession has long taken the position that financial statements are the representations of management. This position is reiterated most recently in *Statement on Auditing Standards No. 1*. The SEC placed its imprimatur in 1947 with *Accounting Series Release No. 62* saying:

> *The fundamental and primary responsibility for the accuracy of information filed with the Commission and disseminated among the investors rests upon management. Management does not discharge its obligations in this respect by the employment of independent public accountants, however reputable.*

Conversely, as a result of its investigation of the McKesson-Robbins fraud (*ASR No. 19*, Appendix E) the SEC amended Regulation S-X to require the auditor's opinion to state whether "the audit was made in accordance with generally accepted auditing standards applicable under the circumstances." Having, up to that point, concerned itself only with audit procedures, the profession was obliged to both revise the form of the auditor's opinion and for the first time to define appropriate audit standards for observing the physical count of inventories.

INDEPENDENCE—AICPA

> *A certified public accountant should maintain his integrity and objectivity and, when engaged in the practice of public accounting, be independent of those he serves.*[1]

The accounting profession has devoted considerable attention to the condition of independence. The Code of Professional Ethics defines the state of independence in the negative, that is, independence is compromised if:

1. During the period of his professional engagement, or at the time of expressing his opinion, he or his firm:
   a. Had or was committed to acquire any direct or material indirect financial interest in the enterprise (this standard applies to all partners and professional employees participating in the audit or located in an office of the firm participating in a significant portion of the audit).
   b. Had any joint closely held business investment with the enterprise or any officer, director or principal stockholder thereof which was material in relation to his personal or his firm's net worth.
   c. Had any loan to or from the enterprise or any officer, director or principal stockholder thereof . . .

2. During the period covered by the financial statements, during the period of the professional engagement or at the time of expressing an opinion, he or his firm
   a. Was connected with the enterprise as a promoter, underwriter or voting trustee, a director or officer or in any capacity equivalent to that of a member of management or of an employee.
   b. Was a trustee of any trust or executor or administrator of any estate if such trust or estate had a direct or material indirect financial interest in the enterprise; or was a trustee for any pension or profit-sharing trust of the enterprise.

Further, an accountant who provides bookkeeping services, computer rental, systems design, and other services imperils his independence. The Code provides that:

1. The CPA must not have any relationship or combination of relationships with the client or any conflict of interest which would impair his integrity and objectivity.
2. The client must accept the responsibility for the financial statements as his own.
3. The CPA must not assume the role of employee or of management conducting the operations of an enterprise.
4. The CPA, in making an examination of financial statements prepared from books and records which he has maintained completely or in part, must conform to generally accepted auditing standards. The fact that he has processed or maintained certain records does not eliminate the need to make sufficient audit tests.

The Code cites other factors that might compromise an accountant's independence:

1. Knowingly misrepresenting facts.
2. Incompetence.
3. Associating his name with financial statements where the examination of

records does not comply with generally accepted auditing standards. A recent interpretation of the AICPA Rules of Conduct makes litigation or the expressed intention to commence litigation reason to consider the auditor's opinion to be impaired.[2]

4. Performing services for contingent fees.
5. Discreditable acts.
6. Engaging in incompatible occupations.

INDEPENDENCE—SEC

Independence is a statutory requirement. The Securities Act requires that the financial statements filed with a registration statement bear the opinion of an independent accountant. The SEC has implemented the requirement for independence through its:

Regulation S-X, (Rule 2-01).
Reporting and filing forms, (e.g., Form S-1).
Accounting Series Releases.
Securities Releases.
Decisions and reports.

To be recognized by the SEC as being an independent accountant, a practitioner must meet two qualifications:

1. The accountant must be "duly registered and in good standing under the laws of the place of his residence or principal office," and
2. He must, in fact, be independent.

Regulation S-X states two conditions, the existence of either of which will cause the accountant to be considered not independent:

1. Where, "during the period of his professional engagement to examine the financial statements being reported on or at the date of his report, he or his firm or a member thereof had, or was committed to acquire, any direct financial interest or any material indirect financial interest. . . ."
2. Where, "during the period of his professional engagement to examine the financial statements being reported on, at the date of his report or during the period covered by the financial statements, he or his firm or a member thereof was connected as a promoter, underwriter, voting trustee, director, officer, or employee. . . ."

The SEC does not confine itself to the relationships existing in connection with the filing of reports, but, rather, "gives appropriate consideration to all relevant circumstances. . . ." That is, the SEC judges the cumulative effect of all of the auditor's relationships with his client. Although one factor might not indicate a lack of independence, two or more factors, when considered together, could present an undeniable presumption of flawed independence. Where the accountant is in doubt as to his independence, the SEC staff is available to help resolve the question.

Form S-1 makes the registrant (hence, his accountant) responsible for disclosing conditions that jeopardize the accountant's independence, requiring that:

> *If any expert named in the registration statement as having prepared or certified any part thereof was employed for such purpose on a contingent basis or, at the time of such preparation or certification or at any time thereafter, had a substantial interest in the registrant or any of its parents or subsidiaries or was connected with the registrant or any of its subsidiaries as a promoter, underwriter, voting trustee, director, officer or employee, he must furnish a brief statement of the nature of such contingent basis, interest or connection.*

Failure to disclose a prohibited relationship can be construed as a deliberate attempt to conceal. The conditions which require disclosure are, of course, prescribed by the Code of Professional Ethics.

Another test of independence is the degree to which the accountant's behavior has been adversely affected, that is, the conscious falsification of facts is contrary to a presumption of his independence. *Accounting Series Release No. 37* states that:

> *Perhaps the most critical test of the actuality of an accountant's independence is the strength of his insistence upon full disclosure of transactions between the company and members of its management as individuals; accession to the wishes of the management in such cases must inevitably raise a serious question as to whether the accountant is in fact independent. Moreover, in considering whether an accountant is in fact independent, such accession to the wishes of the management is no less significant when it occurs with respect to the financial statements included in an annual report to security holders or otherwise made public than when it occurs with respect to statements required to be filed with the Commission.*

The SEC, in *ASR No. 264*, rejected the need to proscribe accountant-provided management advisory services entirely, but identified steps an accounting firm should consider in determining whether the firm's management advisory services jeopardize its independence. The firm should:

1. Evaluate the financial dependence of the firm on MAS revenues.
2. Take care to ensure the firm serves only in an advisory capacity and avoids making management decisions.
3. Avoid situations where the firm reviews its own work.
4. Considers the possible ways in which providing MAS would enhance the quality of audit services.

From time to time the SEC publishes decisions in which it has found accountants to be not independent. *Accounting Series Release Nos. 2, 22, 47, 81, 112, 126 and 234* serve this purpose describing dozens of independence-related decisions. The cases can be classified into:

1. Timing of the independent state.
2. Relationships of interested parties.
   a. Family.
   b. Partners of the accountant.
   c. Affiliated companies.

3. Financial dependence.
   a. Family.
   b. Indemnification of accountant.
   c. Substantial financial interest.
   d. Foreign auditors.

4. Operational dependence.
   a. Audit committee.
   b. Auditors as officers, promoters, etc.
   c. Auditors as managerial decision makers, stewards of assets.
   d. Bookkeeping services.
   e. Incompatible businesses.

Timing of the Independent State

Relationships between auditors and their clients constantly are in a state of flux, and therefore independence must be evaluated constantly, For example, it is possible for an auditor to be independent as to his opinion contained in the Form S-1 registration and not be independent with regard to the "bring-up" prospectus filed six months later. It is possible for an accountant who has performed write-up services for a client in the past to gain independence by taking appropriate action when the firm goes public.

> **ASR No. 81:** *Financial statements for the first two years of the three-year period required to be included in a registration statement had been "certified" by an individual practitioner who gave up his practice to become an executive of the registrant. Independence: not independent for the two-year period.*

Relationships of Interested Parties

Independence of the accountant depends on the relationships between the accountant, members of his family, partners and employees of his firm, and the affiliation of related firms and the accountant's client. The relationship that a retired partner has, whether direct or indirect, impairs the independent accounting firm as a whole if the partner's current income is affected in any way by the amount of the firm's earnings.

FAMILY

ASR No. 47: *The assistant treasurer and chief accountant of the registrant was the son of a partner in the accounting firm that audited the financial statements of the registrant. The son was living with his father at the time but was under the supervision of the company's treasurer. Independence: the son's employment compromised the father's independence, and therefore, the firm's.*

PARTNERS AND EMPLOYEES

ASR No. 81: *A partner in an accounting firm acted as controller and supervised some aspects of the registrant's accounting procedures. A partner must be independent as to all audits performed by the firm of which he is a partner. Independence: the partner's employment compromised the independence of all partners in the firm.*

AFFILIATED COMPANIES

ASR No. 126: *Four partners of an accounting firm were among the six founders of a company which was engaged in the same type of business and was directly competitive with an audit client. In addition to owning stock, the accountants also served as directors and officers. The president of the client company was informed of their investment and did not object to the business venture. He continued their tenure as auditors. Independence: not independent.*

Financial Dependence

Where the personal fortune of the accountant or of a person closely related to him stands to affect his independent judgment, he is not independent.

CONTINGENT FEES

ASR No. 81: *Shares of stock in a registrant, held by an accountant's wife, had originally been received by him in settlement of his audit fee. Independence: the accountant was not independent.*

INDEMNIFICATION OF ACCOUNTANT

ASR No. 22: *The president of a registrant had used the accountant's name for a period of years as a false caption on the books of account of an affiliate not audited by the accountant. When the accountant learned of the fact, he protested and obtained a letter of indemnification in connection with the use of his name but permitted the continued use of his name after his protest. Independence: the apparent overriding authority over the accountant* *assumed by the company's president constituted evidence of lack of independence.*

FOREIGN AUDITORS

ASR No. 112: *Where the financial statements of a division or subsidiary which represents a non-material segment of an international business are examined by another accounting firm or its affiliated firm, the accountant would be not independent only if securities of the parent company or the subsidiary are owned by any of the partners of the other accounting firm or its affiliated firm who are: (1) located in the office which makes the examination of the division or subsidiary or (2) otherwise engaged in such examination.*

PARTICIPATION IN CLIENT'S VENTURES

ASR No. 144: *Partners or employees of the accounting firm accepted payments from the client's general partners purportedly representing profits from participation in the purchase and sale of "hot issues." Independence: not independent.*

Operational Dependence

Where the functions performed by an auditor may cause the subordination of professional judgment, the auditor is not independent. *ASRs Nos. 2* and *22* make an accountant who has been, during the period under review, an officer, director, promoter, underwriter, employee, or voting trustee, not independent. *ASR No. 126* declares that managerial and decision-making functions are the responsibility of the client and not of the independent accountant. Independence is jeopardized where advice ends and managerial responsibility begins. And managerial responsibility begins when the accountant becomes, or appears to become so identified with the client's management that he or she is indistinguishable from it.

Audit Committee

The existence of an audit committee strengthens the accountant's apparent independence. *ASR No. 126* states that:

> *An important consideration in determining whether an accountant is independent is the relationship between the company, its stockholders and the accountants. Ratification of accountants by stockholder vote and attendance of accountants at the company's annual meeting to answer stockholder questions are desirable actions to strengthen the accountant's independent position. The existence of an audit committee of the board of directors,* particularly if composed of outside directors, *should also strengthen such independence: and the SEC urges registrants to establish audit committees composed of outside directors again in ASR No. 123 (Authors' emphasis).*

As a result of its investigation into the McKesson and Robbins fraud, the SEC proposed the following recommendations in 1940 (*Accounting Series Release No. 19*). The following recommendations have been widely adopted:

1. The election of auditors at the annual stockholders' meeting.
2. The creation of a committee comprised of outside directors for the purpose of nominating the auditors.
3. Mandatory attendance of the auditors at the annual stockholders' meeting.
4. Addressing of the auditor's report to the stockholders or board of directors rather than to management.
5. A separate report stating the amount of audit work performed and any reasons for not completing an audit engagement, addressed to the board of directors.

AUDITORS AS OFFICERS, PROMOTERS, ETC.

ASR No. 47:   *A partner in an accounting firm served as a member of the board of directors of a registrant, having been appointed to that position by a Federal court following a reorganization. Independence: the firm was not independent.*

AUDITORS AS MANAGERIAL DECISION MAKERS, STEWARDS OF ASSETS

ASR No. 81:   *An accounting firm which certified the financial statements of a registered investment company had exclusive custody of the key to the company's safe deposit box. Under these conditions, the accountants were acting as custodian of the securities portfolio and were in the position of auditing their own work. Independence: not independent.*

BOOKKEEPING SERVICES

ASR No. 47:   *The accounting firm that certified the financial statements of a registrant had in the past followed the practice of drawing up the monthly journal records of the company from underlying documents that had been prepared by the registrant's staff. These journal records were posted to the appropriate ledgers by the certifying accountants. At the end of the year the audit engagement was undertaken by personnel of the certifying accountant who were not connected with the original recording of the accounting data. Independence: Although the* Code of Professional Ethics *would permit this relationship, SEC standards prohibit a finding of independence where the firm which has prepared the books, or has participated in their preparation, also audits the records.*

ASR No. 126:   *The client's employees prepared printed tapes from books of original entry to be read on an optical scanner and transmitted to the accountant's office. The accountants did not edit the tapes' input but forwarded them to a service bureau, and received the print-outs of financial statements and* *general ledgers for relay to the client. Independence: An accountant providing computer services of any kind for a client is not independent with respect to that client.*

INCOMPATIBLE BUSINESSES[3]

ASR No. 81: *Two partners in an accounting firm certifying the financial statements of a registrant were also partners of a law firm engaged by the registrant to pass upon the legality of the securities which were being offered. Independence: Not independent.*

Litigation and Unpaid Professional Fees

Finally, the SEC has proposed rules defining the circumstances in which an accountant involved in litigation against a client will be considered not independent. The proposed rule limits a finding of "not independent" to cases where the litigation is related to audit work. An exception to this rule would be where the controversy is material in relation to the audit fee. Closely associated with litigation is the problem of unpaid professional fees. Unless the client has made a firm commitment to pay all overdue amounts for prior years' audit services and all other professional services, the accountant is not independent.

In both cases the necessary candor and full communication between the accountant and the client is presumed not to exist. Also, there is a strong possibility that the auditor's professional judgment is biased.

Certain other legal actions also jeopardize the accountant's independence. For example, when both the accountant and management are defendants in a civil action initiated by a third party, their common legal interest in defending the case makes it doubtful that the accountant can continue to exercise impartial professional judgment. The naming of accountant and client as codefendants in a civil suit, however, does not, in and of itself, prove the lack of independence. Each case must be evaluated on its own merits.

AUDITOR'S REPRESENTATIONS—THE OPINION

Generally accepted auditing standards pertaining to the audit opinion are stated in the Code of Professional Ethics as follows:[1]

1. The report shall state whether the financial statements are presented in accordance with generally accepted principles of accounting.
2. The report shall state whether such principles have been consistently observed in the current period in relation to the preceding period.
3. Informative disclosures in the financial statements are to be regarded as reasonably adequate unless otherwise stated in the report.
4. The report shall either contain an expression of opinion regarding the financial statements, taken as a whole or an assertion to the effect that an opinion cannot be expressed. When an over-all opinion cannot be expressed,

the reasons therefor should be stated. In all cases where an auditor's name is associated with financial statements, the report should contain a clear-cut indication of the character of the auditor's examination, if any, and the degree of responsibility he is taking.

Regulation S-X, Rule 2-02, provides that:

(a). . . The accountant's report (1) shall be dated, (2) shall be signed man-ually, (3) shall indicate the city and state where issued; and (4) shall identify without detailed enumeration the financial statements covered by the report.

(b). . . The accountant's report (1) shall state whether the audit was made in accordance with generally accepted auditing standards; and (2) shall des-ignate any auditing procedures deemed necessary by the accountant under the circumstances of the particular case which have been omitted, and the reasons for their omission.

(c). . . The accountant's report shall state clearly: (1) the opinion of the accountant in respect of the financial statements covered by the report and the accounting principles and practices reflected therein; and (2) the opinion of the accountant as to the consistency of the application of the accounting principles, or as to any changes in such principles which have a material effect on the financial statements. . . .

(d). . . Any matters to which the accountant takes exception shall be clearly identified, the exception thereto specifically and clearly stated, and, to the extent practicable, the effect of each such exception on the related financial statements given.

The unqualified, or "clean" opinion, therefore, is the opinion sought by the SEC, and in many cases the registration statement cannot become effective until changes have been made in the financial statements to permit the auditor's issu-ing an "unqualified" opinion.

(e). . . If the financial statements covered by the accountant's report desig-nate as "unaudited" the note [detailing quarterly financial data], it shall be presumed that appropriate professional standards and procedures with respect to the data in the note have been followed by the independent accountant who is associated with the unaudited footnote by virtue of reporting on the financial statements in which it is included. . . .

Thus, the short form opinion, with which we are all familiar, (refer to the exam-ple on page 437), reflects the influence of both the Code of Professional Ethics and Regulation S-X, whereas the opinion on page 316 combines the scope and opinion paragraphs.

The SEC has interpreted Rule 2-02 in such a way that disclaimers, adverse and piecemeal opinions are unacceptable for use in SEC filings. The qualified opinion is unacceptable when it is required because of:[5]

1. A scope limitation (e.g., "Except as noted in the succeeding paragraph, our examination was made in accordance with generally accepted auditing standards. . . . "); or
2. Negative assurances (e.g., "On the basis of the examinations and tests made by us, we have no reason to believe that the inventories as set forth in the accompanying statements are unfairly stated.").

The accountant's ability to issue a qualified opinion in situations where there are material unresolved matters (uncertainties) or going concern problems is also severely restricted.

Professional standards regarding the qualified opinion have recently been scrutinized by the profession's AICPA Commission on Auditors' Responsibilities (the Cohen Commission), the SEC, and Congress. Should the recommendations made by the Commission on Auditors' Responsibilities be implemented, the profession would not allow qualified opinions "subject to" material uncertainties or going concern problems.

Opinions with other qualifications are accepted by the SEC but only if their effect on investor welfare is favorable.

Scope Limitation

Many corporations find no need for an audit until they "go public," and while the managements of some companies are foresighted enough to engage an independent accountant a year or more in advance of filing the first registration statement, some are not. A company going public, but that has never been audited previously, presents many problems, especially those concerned with verifying the beginning balances in the receivables and inventory accounts. *Accounting Series Release No. 90* requires that alternative audit procedures for confirming accounts receivable and observing inventory count be taken to support an unqualified opinion. Where records are inadequate to permit this, an unqualified opinion is inappropriate:

> *It is recognized that some auditing procedures commonly applicable in the examination of financial statements for the latest year for which a certified profit and loss statement is filed, such as the independent confirmation of accounts receivable or the observation of inventory-taking, are either impracticable or impossible to perform with respect to the financial statements of the earlier years and, hence, would not be considered applicable in the circumstances. . . .*
>
> *However, the independent accountant must satisfy himself by appropriate methods. . . .*

The auditor can express an opinion upon completion of a first audit, but lost and inadequate records may give rise to questions as to the reliability of the results shown in the financial statements and may make it impracticable to apply alternative audit procedures. Alternative procedures must be adequate to sup-

port an unqualified opinion as to the fairness of presentation of the income state
ment by year. If the accountant is not satisfied with the results of his examina
tion, he should not issue an affirmative opinion. If the accountant is not in a
position to express an affirmative opinion as to the fairness of the presentation
of earnings year by year, the registration statement is defective is defective
because the certificate does not meet the requirements of Rule 2-02.

First-Time Audits

A corollary requirement in expressing an opinion upon the completion of a first
time audit is that the middle paragraph, while proving useful to describe the
alternative procedures applied in a first-time audit, may not contain phrases such
as "we have found nothing that might serve to confuse the reader as to the
position the auditor is taking." The opinion must either be unqualified based on
a favorable examination of the records, or the opinion must make clear that the
results of the examination were not acceptable. The reader must be able to determine the outcome of the examination with confidence.

Material Uncertainties

The auditor's role in expressing an opinion where there are material uncertainties
is to evaluate the adequacy of disclosure of the "business risk," that is, the
uncertainty of alternative events. Disclosure conforming to *ASR No. 166* should
be adequate to permit financial statement users to evaluate for themselves the
probable outcome of the uncertainties. Adequate disclosure minimizes the potential for "information risk" inherent in communications of this sort; that is, the
error caused by transmitting data is minimized. If the auditor believes the disclosure to be adequate, usually no qualification would be necessary because the
financial statements meet generally accepted accounting standards. This reason-
ing, expressed in the Cohen Commission report, has not as yet been adopted by
the SEC or the AICPA. Therefore, *ASR No. 90* remains in effect permitting a
"subject to" qualification regarding the disclosure of matters that cannot be
resolved at the time of the opinion.

Going Concern Problems

The auditor faces a similar issue of adequate disclosure when the registrant has
going concern problems. The Cohen Commission recommends elimination of the
qualified opinion in favor of expanded disclosure; however, the SEC still accepts
qualified opinions under certain circumstances. Ordinarily the question of going
concern arises in a 1933 Act registration.

Many corporations "going public" are in dire financial straits, so much so that
a significant portion of any funds received from the sale of securities would be
used to pay off creditors. The SEC prefers that a corporation, finding itself in
such a position, put its affairs in order prior to a public offering rather than by
means of one. However, where the registrant adequately discloses the use to
which the proceeds of the offering and any additional financing will be put and

where they are sufficient to pay off the identified liabilities and proposed expenditures, a qualified opinion is acceptable.

In other circumstances when financial statements are prepared on a going concern basis and there is serious doubt as to whether or not the preparation of the statements on that basis is warranted, a question arises as to whether the financial statements have in fact been certified. An opinion qualified as to the appropriateness of the going concern assumption in that case would cause the registrant's statements to be considered defective in that the accountant's opinion would not meet the requirements of Rule 2-02.

ASR No. 115 illustrates several opinions describing circumstances under which reporting on the going concern basis is not warranted. For example:

> *Substantial losses have been experienced during the past four years and nine months and continuation of the business is dependent upon the Company's attaining sufficiently profitable operations and/or additional capital to satisfy all its liabilities as they become due. . . . In our opinion, subject to the Company's ability to attain profitable operations and/or to successfully obtain additional capital, the accompanying financial statements. . . .*

In summary, then, *ASR No. 90* requires that any time:

> *. . . the accountant is not in a position to express an affirmative opinion as to the fairness of the presentation of earnings year by year, the registration statement is defective because the certificate does not meet the requirements of Rule 2-02 of Regulation S-X. If the accountant is not satisfied with the results of his examination he should not issue an affirmative opinion. If he is satisfied, any reference from the opinion paragraph to an explanatory paragraph devoted solely to the scope of the audit is inconsistent and unnecessary . . . A "subject to" or "except for" opinion paragraph in which these phrases refer to the scope of audit, indicating that the accountant has not been able to satisfy himself on some significant element in the financial statements, is not acceptable in certificates filed with the Commission in connection with the public offering of securities. The "subject to" qualification is appropriate when the reference is to a middle paragraph or to footnotes explaining the status of matters which cannot be resolved at statement date.*

Consistency

Since the issuance of *ASR No. 195*, SEC requirements for the disclosure of accounting changes and the auditor's opinion regarding them are the same as professional standards. *ASR No. 195* removes the requirement to comment in the opinion letter on accounting changes due to altered conditions (accounting estimates) because the effects of such changes must be disclosed via a footnote and in management's analysis.

Changes in accounting principles do require comment in the opinion letter in that they violate the condition of consistency. Disclosure requirements have been discussed in Chapter 5.

Form 10-Q as revised by *ASR No. 177*, requires that changes in accounting principles be reported by the registrant in the quarter in which they occur and that the filing include an exhibit letter from the independent accountant stating " . . . whether or not the change is to an alternative principle which in his judgment is preferable under the circumstances. . . ." This letter is discussed in this chapter.

Other Opinions

The auditor's opinion usually refers to the balance sheet, income statement, changes in retained earnings statement, and changes in financial position statement. The other opinions occasionally required in an SEC filing pertain to:

1. The summary of earnings statement.
2. Pro forma statements.
3. Amendments to prior filings.
4. Article 12 Schedules.

Summary of Earnings Statement (ASR No. 62) Although the SEC does not, occasionally the underwriter in an S-1 filing insists that the summary of earnings statement be audited. In other filings, too, the auditor's name inadvertently can be "associated" with the statement because of the relationship of its data to information contained in the audited statements. Association of the auditor's name with a financial statement lends credibility to the statement and the summary of earnings statement is considered to be the most influential financial statement in SEC filings. Therefore, the SEC holds that it is generally improper and misleading for an accountant to permit his name to be used in connection with data regarding any period covered by a summary of earnings statement or to undertake to express his professional opinion as to the fairness of the representations made for such period in the summary of earnings statement unless he has made an examination for such period in accordance with generally accepted auditing standards applicable in the circumstances.

Where, during the period covered by the statement, there is a change of auditors, each auditor assumes responsibility for the period that he has audited. Occasionally, the entire period (e.g., five years in the case of the summary of earnings statement) is not covered by the auditor's opinion. Where audit procedures have been performed to verify the period covered by the income statement (usually three years), it is often acceptable to the underwriters that the opinion cover only those years' data in the summary of earnings statement. In any case, if the registrant represents that the independent accountant has "examined" or "reviewed" the data, *Accounting Series Release No. 62* requires that the accountant's opinion letter also must be furnished. Our example in Chapters 6 and 7, Dart Industries, Inc., does not refer to the summary of earnings statement. If the opinion is to cover the summary of earnings statement in addition to the usual statements, the scope paragraph can simply be extended to include the title of the summary and the period for which the auditor is assuming responsibility.

Pro Forma Statements   There are conditions under which pro forma statements disclose a fairer picture of the registrant's finances than statements prepared on an historical basis. For example where:

1. A company offers to exchange its stock for the stock of a second company (a pooling).
2. The predecessor company is a partnership or proprietorship (e.g., a partnership acquisition accounted for as a pooling of interests).
3. The predecessor was operated as part of a going business (e.g., a public offering of securities is made to purchase a division of an operating company).

Discontinued operations and accounting changes present a need for pro forma type disclosures; however, these matters are not at issue here.

Where an auditor's opinion is required for pro forma financial statements, usually in a prospectus:

1. The underlying financial statements must have been examined by the auditor.
2. All professional pronouncements must have been complied with to permit an unqualified opinion related to the principles used in combination.
3. SEC rules have been complied with.

If all three conditions are met, the scope paragraph of the standard short-form opinion can simply be modified to indicate that the financial statements are prepared on a pro forma rather than on an historical basis. For example, the scope paragraph can be modified by the statement: "The financial statements give retroactive effect to the acquisition of Company B on a 'pooling of interests' basis."

It is often the case that the auditors of the acquiring corporation did not examine the records of the acquiree and the scope paragraph would reflect this. For example: "We did not examine the financial statements of Company B which statements were examined by other public accountants whose reports thereon have been furnished to us and are included in this prospectus. Our opinion expressed herein, insofar as it relates to the amounts included for Company B is based solely upon such reports."[6]

Rule 170, under the Securities Act, prohibits the use of pro forma statements that:

> . . . *purport to give effect to the receipt and application of any part of the proceeds from the sale of securities for cash shall not be used unless such securities are to be offered through underwriters and the underwriting arrangements are such that the underwriters are or will be committed to take and pay for all of the securities, if any are taken, prior to or within a reasonable time after commencement of public offering, or if the securities are not so taken to refund to all subscribers the full amount of all subscription payments made for the securities. The caption of any such financial statement*

shall clearly set forth the assumptions upon which such statement is based. The caption shall be in type at least as large as that used generally in the body of the statement.

The independent accountant must issue his opinion before the S-1 registration statement is filed, hence before the acquisition has transpired. If the terms of the registration do not meet the conditions of Rule 170, a short-form opinion is improper. The accountant can avoid this problem by issuing a "preliminary" opinion for inclusion with the initial filing based on information received from the parties to the acquisition as to the terms of the offering. The preliminary opinion is prefaced by the statement:

> . . . *The statements give effect retroactively on a pro forma basis to the acquisition of Company B on a "pooling of interests" basis, which transaction is expected to be consummated on _____. When that transaction has been consummated, we would expect to be in a position to issue the following report:*
>
> *(The short-form opinion disclosing the pro forma basis of the financial statements would follow.)*

Rule 15cl-9 (Securities Exchange Act) also requires disclosure of the assumptions used to prepare the pro forma statements in cases where the proceeds derive from a sale or exchange of securities, as follows:

> *The term "manipulative . . . device . . . is hereby defined to include the use of financial statements purporting to give effect to the receipt and application of any part of the proceeds from the sale or exchange of securities, unless the assumptions upon which each such financial statement is based are clearly set forth as part of the caption to each such statement in type at least as large as that used generally in the body of the statement.*

Amendments Where the SEC's deficiency letter causes the financial statements to be revised, the accountant's opinion, also, must reflect responsibility for the revised statements. An amended report might be worded as follows:

> *Our report dated___ covering the financial statements of Company A, filed as a part of the annual report to Form 10-K for the year ended___ is hereby extended to relate to such financial statements as have been amended as of _____.*

Schedules Article 12 schedules also must bear the opinion of the independent accountant. Because the financial statements (and the auditor's opinion relating thereto) appear in the Prospectus of Form S-1 whereas the schedules are required by Item 31, most accountants issue a separate opinion covering the schedules

Examination of Financial Statements by More Than One Accountant

Company A is issuing stock, the proceeds from which will be used to purchase Company B. The auditors of the two companies are not the same firm. The auditors of a publicly held U.S. company with a foreign subsidiary have no office in the foreign country and the subsidiary's books are audited by a local firm abroad. When more than one accounting firm is involved in an SEC filing, responsibility must be distributed.

Regulation S-X, Rule 2-05, provides that if no mention is made in the principal accountant's opinion of the audit performed by another accountant, the principal accountant assumes responsibility for the work of all acountants. If other accountants are to bear responsibility for their own work: (1) the principal accountant's report must be limited in scope and refer to the other accountant's audit; and (2) the opinion(s) of the other accountant(s), meeting the provisions of Rules 2-01 and 2-02, must also be filed.

AUDITOR'S REPRESENTATIONS—LETTERS

Many parties cooperate to assist the public corporation in issuing securities and reporting to the SEC. Each depends on the others to perform their duties honestly and competently and this interdependence must be documented. For example, in all engagements the auditor obtains a representation from management stating, among other things, that all known liabilities are recorded in the books of account. Because of the impracticality of performing an extensive search for unrecorded liabilities, a step that would be prohibitively expensive, the auditor obtains management's assurances and places the burden of truth on another party. He does likewise with representations from counsel. On the other hand, the accountant is also called upon to assume responsibility for his participation in the filing. This responsibility is, in certain cases, more extensive than that required by professional standards. The representations will be discussed in four categories:

1. *Assurances.* To succeeded auditors and to the underwriters.
2. *Consents.* Permitting the auditor's name to be "associated" with the financial statements and schedules of a filing.
3. *SEC correspondence.* Responses to notification of cursory review and deficiency letters, and proxy-related approval.
4. *Form-related letters.* 10-Q quarterly data review and preferability comments; and 8-K response from the succeeded auditors.

Allocation of Responsibility Among Auditors   Quite commonly the registrant will have had more than one auditor for the time period covered by the SEC filing. This is especially so when a company makes its first public offering of securities. Although each auditor is responsible for only the period of time that he has audited, the succeeded auditor depends upon the new auditor to disclose to him any information that would impair the fairness of the financial statements on which he had issued his original opinion. The need for a reexamination of facts arises because the former auditor's potential legal liability has increased. The auditor of a privately held company is liable under common law for gross negligence to parties expected to use the financial statements. The accountant performs his audit and issues his opinion on that basis. If the company goes public, his opinion will probably be used by persons he could not have anticipated would use his opinion. His legal liability is now statutorily (and enormously) expanded.

The current accountant customarily provides the succeeded accountant with a "negative assurance" letter similar to the one illustrated in Exhibit 8-1.

Assurances to the Underwriters—the Comfort Letter Any party considered to be an "underwriter" in the offering can request a comfort letter from the auditor. Because the underwriter must be able to prove that he has exercised due diligence in offering securities for sale to the public, the terms of the underwriting agreement with the issuer usually require that the auditor make certain specific representations to the underwriter. AICPA *Statement on Auditing Standards No. 1, Section 630*, establishes professional requirements for a comfort letter and the terms of the underwriting agreement determine the letter's specific contents.[7]

EXHIBIT 8-1 LETTER TO SUCCEEDED FIRM

Former Accountant:

With respect to the consent to the inclusion of your opinion dated _____ in the registration statement on Form S-1 of *The Company* to be filed _____, with the Securities and Exchange Commission under the Securities Act of 1933, as amended, relating to your examination of the balance short and income statement for *The Company* for the year _____, we advise you as follows:

We have made an examination of the financial statements . . . Our examination was made in accordance with generally accepted auditing standards . . . In connection with that examination nothing has come to our attention which in our judgment would indicate that there have been any events, etc., which would have a material effect on the statements identified in Paragraph 1 of this letter.

If anything comes to our attention prior to the effective date of the registration statement which, in our judgment could have a material effect on the financial statements of *The Company* examined by you, we will notify you promptly.

Signed_____
Present Accountant

Exhibit 8-2 contains a sample letter to the underwriters. Notice that it is addressed to the representative of the underwriter, with a copy to the registrant. The letter is dated on or just prior to the closing date. Our sample letter contains assurances that the financial statements do comply with the published rules and regulations of the SEC. Other assurances that the underwriters may request relate to the auditor's independence, certain unaudited financial data, and changes in financial statement items during the period subsequent to the date of the financial statements contained in the registrant's filing. *Statement on Auditing Standards No. 1* includes several other examples of letters to the underwriters.

EXHIBIT 8-2   COMFORT LETTER TO THE UNDERWRITERS

Underwriters' Representative
(Address)

Dear Sirs:

This letter is written at the request of (Company) to comply with Section _____, of an underwriting agreement dated _____ between (Company) and *Underwriters' Representative* as representatives of the several underwriters.

We have examined the balance sheet of the Company as of December 31, 1976, the related income statement for the three years then ended, the related statement of changes in retained earnings and statement of changes in financial position, and our opinion with respect to the foregoing is included in the Registration Statement (File No. _____) filed by the Company under the Securities Act of 1933.

In our opinion, the above-mentioned financial statements examined by us and included in the Registration Statement and the related Prospectus, as amended at the time such Registration Statement became effective, comply as to form in all material respects with the applicable accounting requirements of the Securities Act of 1933 and of the published rules and regulations of the Securities and Exchange Commission thereunder with respect to Registration Statements on Form S-1.

This letter is solely for the information of the Company and the Underwriters and not to be referred to in whole or in part in the Registration Statement or Prospectus or in any similar document, or quoted by excerpt or reference outside the underwriting group in connection with the registration under the Act or the sale of securities, except for any reference to it in the underwriting agreement or in any list of closing documents.

Yours very truly,

cc. The Company

Consents

The registrant cannot associate the accountant's name with the financial statements filed under either the Securities Act or Securities Exchange Act unless a written consent to be named as an expert is included as an exhibit in the registration statement and/or the accountant's report is signed manually. Exhibit 8-3 illustrates the simplest form of consent letter.

EXHIBIT 8-3 **ACCOUNTANT'S CONSENT**

We consent to the use in the Registration Statement and Prospectus of Company A relating to the sale of common stock of our reports dated ——— accompanying the financial statements and schedules of Company A contained in such Registration Statement, and to the use of our name in the Prospectus.

(City)
(Date)

The auditor's consent is necessary under the following conditions:

1. When his name is associated with the financial statements in a filing under the Securities Act.
2. When the auditor's opinion letter regarding financial statements, that were prepared for filing to meet other statutory requirements, is incorporated by reference in a current filing. (For example, an opinion covering audited financial schedules prepared for use in a 10-K filing may be incorporated.)
3. When the summary of earnings statement has been reviewed by the auditor and the registrant associates the auditor's name with the statement.
4. When financial statements are amended. The accountant must consent to the use of his name for the changes made and, if necessary, must perform appropriate audit procedures to assure himself of the accuracy of the changes.
5. When financial information in the "bring-up" prospectus differs from or is in addition to that presented in the original prospectus. The completion of appropriate review procedures is necessary here too.

The contents of consent letters vary according to the reason for the consent and the scope of responsibility that the accountant wishes to assume. All consent letters, however, must be signed manually and dated.

Once the accountant's opinion letter and consent have been filed with the SEC it may become necessary to withdraw them. This situation would occur, for example, if the accountant discovered information regarding the registrant that indicated the opinion and financial statements could not be relied upon. In this case it is necessary for the accountant to see that the SEC is notified in writing of the need to withdraw the opinion and consent.

SEC Correspondence

When comments in the SEC's deficiency letter relate to accounting matters, the accountant occasionally deals directly with the agency in resolving the problem. If the accountant supports the client's method of accounting that has been questioned by the SEC, he can prepare a letter defending the client's position. He serves, in this instance, as the client's advocate, but the SEC, in considering the representations contained in the letter, will hold him to the standards of independence discussed previously.

Another form of correspondence with the SEC is a response from the accountant acknowledging notification by the SEC that a filing will receive a cursory or summary review in lieu of the customary review. The form of the sample letter in Exhibit 8-4 indicates the implications of such limited reviews.

EXHIBIT 8-4   RESPONSE TO NOTIFICATION OF LIMITED SEC REVIEW

Dear Sirs:

We have received a copy of your letter dated————relating to registration statement (SEC File No.————) filed with the Commission by Company A. Accordingly, we are aware that "the staff has made only a cursory (summary) and not a customary review of the registration statement, which may not be relied upon in any degree to indicate that the registration statement is true, complete, or accurate."

In connection with our reports on financial statements filed pursuant to the Securities Act of 1933, we are aware of our statutory responsibilities under the act.

(Signed)

A third type of correspondence with the SEC involves preliminary proxy material. Preliminary proxy material is not required to include a written consent and the opinion may be unsigned. Since this can leave doubt as to whether the preliminary material has been reviewed by the accountant and whether he is aware of its having been filed, the SEC now requires a letter from the accountant stating that the material has been reviewed and he is willing to permit the use of his opinion in the financial statements to be filed later with the definitive proxy material.

Form-Related Letters

Form 10-Q   Item K of Form 10-Q provides:

The financial information included in this form need not be reviewed prior to filing by an independent public accountant. If, however, a review of the data is made in accordance with established professional standards and procedures for such a review, the registrant may state that the independent accountant has performed such a review.

Professional standards for a limited review of interim financial information have been defined in *Statement on Auditing Standards No. 24.* The purpose of the review is to ascertain that the information is presented in conformity with *APB Opinion No. 28* and *FASB Statement No. 3.* The accountant issues a report (not an opinion letter) regarding the interim financial information and:

If [*the registrant indicates that the interim financial information has been reviewed*], *the registrant shall indicate whether all adjustments or additional disclosures proposed by the independent accountant have been reflected in the data presented, and, if not why not. In addition, a letter from the registrant's independent accountant confirming or otherwise commenting upon the registrant's representations and making such other comments as the independent accountant deems appropriate may be included as an exhibit to the form.*

The Form 10-Q requirement for management to report the nature, effect, and justification for any change in accounting principle in the quarter in which the change occurs reflects the disclosure requirements of *APB Opinion No. 20:* "The justification for the change should explain clearly why the newly adopted accounting principle is preferable." The form also requires disclosure of the date of the accounting change, and the reasons for making it. The SEC turns the tables on the accountant, however, requiring that the registrant file an exhibit in the first Form 10-Q filed subsequent to the change. The exhibit consists of a letter from the independent accountant " . . . indicating whether or not the change is to an alternative principle which in his judgment is preferable under the circumstances. . . . No letter need be filed when the change is made in response to a standard adopted by the Financial Accounting Standards Board which requires such change."

The question of what determined a "preferable" alternative principle perplexed the accountants who were responsible for issuing the letter. In response, the SEC acknowledged that the same change is not necessarily preferable for all of the accountant's clients. For example, Client A could conceivably change from FIFO to LIFO for inventory valuation purposes while Client B changed from LIFO to FIFO. Depending on the justification for the change, both clients could be deemed to have made a change to a preferable alternative (*Staff Accounting Bulletin No. 6, Topic 6*).

Form 8-K   Finally, when there is a change in the registrant's "certifying" accountant, the registrant must file a current report (Form 8-K). Requirements for disclosing the event and the accountant's responsibility for responding to the representations of management are detailed in Item 4 of Form 8-K, Changes in Registrant's Certifying Accountant:

If an independent accountant who was previously engaged as the principal accountant to audit the registrant's financial statements resigned (or indicates he declines to stand for re-election after the completion of the current audit) or is dismissed as the registrant's principal accountant, or another independent accountant is engaged as principal accountant, or if an independent accountant on whom the principal accountant expressed reliance in his report regarding a significant subsidiary resigns (or formally indicates he declines to stand for re-election after the completion of the current audit) or is dismissed or another independent accountant is engaged to audit that subsidiary:

(a) State the date of such resignation (or declination to stand for re-election) dismissal or engagement.

(b) State whether in connection with the audits of the two most recent fiscal years and any subsequent interim period preceding such resignation, dismissal or engagement there were any disagreements with the former accountant on any matter of accounting principles or practices, financial statement disclosure, or auditing scope or procedure, which, disagreements if not resolved to the satisfaction of the former accountant would have caused him to make reference in connection with his report to the subject matter of the disagreement(s); also, describe each such disagreement. The disagreements required to be reported in response to the preceding sentence include both those resolved to the former accountant's satisfaction. Disagreements contemplated by this rule are those which occur at the decision-making level; i.e., between personnel of the registrant responsible for presentation of its financial statements and personnel of the accounting firm responsible for rendering its report.

(c) State whether the principal accountant's report on the financial statements for any of the past two years contained an adverse opinion or a disclaimer of opinion or was qualified as to uncertainty, audit scope, or accounting principles; also describe the nature of each such adverse opinion, disclaimer or opinion, or qualification.

(d) The registrant shall request the former accountant to furnish the registrant with a letter addressed to the Commission stating whether he agrees with the statements made by the registrant in response to this item and, if not, stating the respects in which he does not agree. The registrant shall file a copy of the former accountant's letter as an exhibit with all copies of the Form 8-K required to be filed pursuant to. . . .

(e) State whether the decision to change accountants was recommended or approved by: (1) any audit or similar committee of the Board of Directors, if the issuer has such a committee; or (2) the Board of Directors, if the issuer has no such committee.

The SEC, in *ASR No. 247*, encourages the disclosure of the reasons for all changes in independent accountants, although to do so is purely voluntary.

SUMMARY   The professional standards of any accountant practicing before the SEC must conform to the Code of Professional Ethics and SEC requirements set forth in Regulation S-X, Article 2, and the accounting series releases. To practice before the SEC the accountant must be licensed and in good standing in his state of residence and be, in fact, independent. The authority by which the SEC disciplines accountants who violate its standards are delineated in the Rules of Practice.

The standard of independence has been imposed statutorily by the Securities Act and as a result, the SEC has devoted diligent efforts to defining and enforcing that standard. The concept of independence, while defined by both the profession and the SEC in negative terms, narrows down to whether or not the accountant's position is one in which his opinion appears to be possibly influenced by his relationships. This is determined not by relationships taken in isolation of each other, but rather by reference to the cumulative effect of all relationships.

Rule 2-02 establishes standards for the audit opinion. The forms of opinions accepted by the SEC are limited to unqualified and some qualified opinions. Qualifications are unacceptable that are based on:

A scope limitation.

Negative assurances.

Inconsistency regarding application of accounting principles where the change is not to a "preferred" method, or

Some going concern problems.

In addition to opinions required for the basic financial statements, the auditor may be called on to provide an opinion for:

The summary of earnings statement.

Pro forma statements.

Amendments, and

Article 12 schedules.

The opinion also is affected when more than one accountant assumes responsibility for financial statements contained in a filing—Rule 2-05 applies.

The accountant must make other representations in connection with SEC filings by means of letters. The purpose of the letters is to communicate the extent of responsibility the accountant assumes and to give assurance to other liable parties. The letters take the form of:

Assurances (to other accountants or to the underwriters).

Consents (to permit association of his name with filed financial statements and schedules).

SEC correspondence, and

Form-related letters.

FOOTNOTES [1]American Institute of Certified Public Accountants, Code of Professional Ethics, Effective March 15, 1973.

[2]*Journal of Accountancy*, (January, 1978), pp. 86–7.

[3]*ASR No. 126* describes occupations with conflicting interest implications as being: (1) accountant-attorney, (2) accountant-broker-dealer, and (3) accountant-commercial competitor. The Metcalf Report (*Improving the Accountability of Publicly Owned Corporations and Their Auditors—Report of the Subcommittee on Reports, Accounting and Management of the Committee on Governmental Affairs,* U.S. Senate, 11, 1966) identifies the following services as being detrimental to a presumption of independence: (1) executive search, (2) market analysis, (3) plant layout, (4) product analysis, and (5) actuarial services.

[4]See D. R. Carmichael, *Risk and Uncertainty in Financial Reporting and the Auditor's Role,* 1976, 47 pp.

[5]See *APB Nos. 20, 28* and *FASB Statement No. 3.*

[6]*AICPA Statement on Auditing Standards No. 1* provides further standards for the auditor's opinion.

[7]Examples throughout this chapter have been modified from illustrations in Louis H. Rappaport, *SEC Accounting Practice and Procedure,* (Third Edition), New York: The Ronald Press Company, (1972).

QUESTIONS
1. Define "practicing before the Commission."
2. What is the application of the AICPA Code of Professional Ethics?
3. What is the significance of Rule 2(e)?
4. Discuss the concept "auditor independence" with respect to its statutory meaning.
5. What is the substance of Regulation S-X Rule 2-02?
6. Discuss the conditions under which an accountant can become subject to SEC disciplinary action.
7. What is the SEC's position toward qualified opinions?
8. What is meant by "a questionable going concern basis" and the concept's relationship to SEC reporting requirements?
9. Under what circumstances can the auditor write a "subject to" qualification?
10. What is the SEC's position with respect to negative assurances in an auditor's opinion?
11. Discuss fully the auditor's responsibility with respect to a summary of earnings statement.
12. Under what circumstances is an accountant's consent letter required?
13. Why is it imperative that the auditor maintain "an independence in mental attitude?"
14. Can an auditor be sued by the purchaser of newly issued securities?
15. What is the distinction between the responsibility of the auditor and of the registrant's management?
16. What is the distinction between auditing standards and auditing procedures?
17. What do standards deal with specifically? Procedures?

Appendix

E

Disciplinary Actions Taken Against Accountants

ASR NO.	Facts	SEC Findings
19	• Four brothers with previous criminal records, under assumed names, organized and operated McKesson and Robbins, Inc., a publicly-traded corporation in the pharmaceutical industry. • By the use of fictitious transactions supported by phony source documents and nonexistent companies management carried out its deception: (1) Inventory was overstated by fictitious purchases from a Canadian vendor purportedly holding the goods for the account of McKesson-Robbins. The inventory was not observed by the auditors. (2) Fictitious sales (and accounts receivable) were reported. Accounts receivable were not confirmed. • The auditors followed generally accepted auditing standards. • The accounting profession established two new standards: (1) The requirement to confirm receivables. (2) The requirement to observe physical inventory count.	• GAAS had been observed and the profession had taken appropriate action to correct the deficiencies disclosed. • An important responsibility of the CPA firm (and the profession) is to train staff. • It is the responsiblity of the CPA firm to supervise properly its staff. The excessive use of temporary staff during busy season defeats this goal. • Checking the reputation of the management of a new client is well warranted. • Gross overstatements in accounts should be found. • Audit should include activities of management. • Stockholders should elect and nonofficer directors should nominate auditors.
28	• Accountant owned securities of registrant amounting to an estimated 8 percent of his net worth. • Accountant allowed his name to be used and helped conceal the existence of a trading account in the registrant's securities.	• Accountant was not independent and had engaged in improper professional conduct. • Accountant suspended for 60 days.
84	• Accountant had made no audit of registrant's affairs, had not examined registrant's books, accepted without question the financial statements prepared by registrant's own employee, split fee with said employee, and certified other statements without audit or examination.	• Accountant engaged in unethical and improper conduct.
51	• Accountant certified statements of insolvent corporation.	• Accountant resigned. Resignation accepted.

ASR NO.	Facts	SEC Findings
59	• Accountant failed to make a physical examination and comparison with the books and records of all securities on hand or otherwise in the possession of registrant. • Registrant's position in all securities was not balanced. • Written confirmation of customer's accountants were not obtained. • Bank balances were not reconciled at a date subsequent to the date of the audit. • Examination of accounting records was not made according to generally accepted auditing standards. • Audit omitted certain of the Commission's audit requirements.	• Accountant suspended for one year.
64	• The Registration statement contained misstatements and omissions of material facts. • The Prospectus did not disclose that prior to marketing the new product, the company had no field experience as to its usefulness; that mechanical defects had resulted in dealer dissatisfaction with the product that caused dealers to cancel their orders and exclusive selling agreements with the company. • Financial statements overstated net worth and inventories; failed to disclose unrecoverable costs of grarantees; understated the amortization rate of deferred expenses. • System and the controls were deficient and there was a necessity for the revision of the cost system in general.	• Registration statement was deficient in its description of the product and that the financial statements were inaccurate and misleading. No action against accountants. This is a report on an SEC interpretation.
67	• Balance sheets in the registration statement were materially misleading. • Work-in-process inventory and profit and loss statement were overstated.	• Accountants have been "sufficiently impressed with the inadequacy of their former policies and have materially revised them." • Proceedings were dismissed.
68	• Accountants overstated the value of a leasehold appearing in the balance sheet.	• One of the accountants was suspended for 30 days; the second accountant (partner) was suspended for 1 year.
73	• Accountants grossly overstated intangible assets in the financial statements.	• Accountants engaged in improper professional conduct. • Accountants were suspended for 10 days.
77	• Accountant qualified his opinion with the statement that the examination of the branch office of a broker-dealer was "limited to a verification of reported assets and liabilities." • Partner in charge of the branch office had reported fictitious purchases and sales of commodities and fictitious profits to the principal office. • Bank confirmed certain liabilities and an account of the firm, but not an account of the branch partner, carried in his own name but used for company transactions.	• Accountant did not receive the information about the branch partner's account. • Proceedings dismissed.

ASR NO.	Facts	SEC Findings
78	• Accountants filed financial statements which understated reserves for uncollectible accounts, overstated current assets, listed as due from customers material amounts which represented advances to subsidiaries. • Income statement made insufficient provision for losses on uncollectible accounts.	• Accounting firm improperly relied upon unsupported representations of management with respect to these matters.
82	• Accountant's partner was promoter, principal officer, and controlling stockholder of registrant. • Partners attempted to conceal the fact.	• Accounting firm disbarred pending Commission's approval of reinstatement. • Partner suspended for 30 days.
87	• (See ASR No. 82.)	• Accountant reinstated.
88	• Accountants certified statements that were false and misleading in their presentation of assets, liabilities, and capital. • Stated that an audit had been made, when it had not. • Accountant in 1958 gave false testimony under oath in prior Commission proceedings.	• Because of the gravity of the misconduct accountants were disbarred.
91	• Accountant certified materially false and misleading statements; had not seen the company's books and records but relied entirely on statements prepared by another accountant; and was under influence or direction of company officers.	• Accountant guilty of unethical and improper professional conduct and was disbarred.
92	• Accountant, a junior partner in the firm, prepared a balance sheet for a proposed corporation on the basis solely of information supplied on the telephone which was materially false and misleading. • Junior partner not authorized by the firm to sign statements, did so against firm's rules while senior partner was absent. • Junior partner was disciplined by his firm. • There was no other improper professional practice by a member or employee of the firm.	• Accountant disbarred pending Commission's approval of reinstatement; period for at least one year. • Disciplinary action against the firm as such is not warranted. • Proceedings dismissed.
94	• Accountant charged with engaging in conduct which would bring disciplinary action, applied for a discontinuance of further proceedings on the ground that his health will be seriously impaired and would continue to be so for several years.	• Accountant tendered a formal, written resignation agreeing that he will not practice before the Commission in any way in the future; that his resignation is permanent. • Resignation accepted.
97	• Accountant failed to obtain confirmations of customers' accountants; did not properly balance securities positions or verify securities in transfer; certified financial statements of a mutual fund for periods when company of which he was principal stockholder and co-manager made loans collateralized by securities to salesmen and customers of broker-dealer which was principal under-	• Accountant suspended for 60 days.

ASR NO.	Facts	SEC Findings
	writer and a broker for the fund and, through an affiliate, its investment.	
101	• (See ASR No. 92)	• Accountant reinstated.
104	• Accusation: The accountant did not adhere to generally accepted auditing standards.	• Accountant resigned from practice without admitting guilt. • Resignation accepted.
105	• Accusations: Financial statements and schedules prepared or certified by the accounting firm were materially false and misleading and did not present fairly the financial position and results of the company; merchandise inventories were substantially overstated; and accounts payable were substantially understated. • An audit properly conducted would have detected the inaccuracy and falsity of the inventory and accounts payable figures. • Accountants knew or should have known that the financial statements and related schedules were false; that the examinations were not made in accordance with generally accepted auditing standards; and that they engaged in unethical and improper professional conduct. • Senior partner died. • Partnership had been dissolved.	• The remaining accountant, without admitting the allegations against him, voluntarily resigned. • Resignation accepted.
108	• Accusation: There may have been a lack of adherence to generally accepted auditing standards and its minimum audit requirements, as follows: (1) Failure to obtain written confirmation of bank balances and obtain bank balances at the audit date. (2) Failure to obtain bank statements and cancelled checks from the depositories and reconcile the balances. (3) Failure to obtain written confirmations of customers' accounts, open contractual commitments, etc. (4) Failure to review and on a test basis obtain written confirmation of customers' accounts closed.	• Accountant, without admitting guilt, submitted resignation. • Resignation accepted.
109	• Accusation: There may have been a lack of adherence to generally accepted auditing standards.	• Accountant submitted resignation. • Resignation accepted.
110	• Accountant's audits were deficient as follows: (1) Did not maintain a general ledger and therefore did not compare the "ledger accounts" with a trial balance obtained from the general ledger and did not compare the aggregates of subsidiary ledgers with their respective control accounts. (2) Did not balance securities positions as at the audit date. (3) Did not balance and confirm customers' money balances and securities positions.	• Accountant, without admitting guilt, submitted resignation. • Resignation accepted.

ASR NO.	Facts	SEC Findings
	(4) Loans to clients totaling about $525,496; including about $34,000 payable to banks, were omitted from the statement of financial condition thereby improperly showed a capital position of $38,311. (5) Failed to check the proceeds of such loans into bank accounts and to verify expenditures therefrom. (6) Accountant was not independent.	
127	• Under Rules of Practice Rule 2(e)(2) was disbarred, by examiner. • Time for filing petition requesting review had passed.	• Examiner's order declared effective.
129	• Accusation: Accountant violated antifraud provisions of the Securities Exchange Act of 1934 by recommending to his clients and others the purchase of investment contracts without disclosing that he was paid a substantial fee for each sale consummated.	• Accountant resigned, no guilt admission. • If he subsequently applies for readmission to practice, the allegations in the injunctive action shall, for the purposes of any such application only, be deemed proven.
139	• Following the entry of an injunction permanently enjoining an accountant from violating the antifraud provisions of Section 10(b) of the Securities Exchange Act of 1934 and Rule 10b-5 thereunder, he submitted an offer to resign. • Accountant represented that he had never practiced before the Commission, and he agreed that, should he apply for reinstatement of the privilege of practicing or appearing before the Commission pursuant to the Commission's Rules of Practice, the allegations in the injunctive action may be deemed proven only for purposes of such application.	• Resignation accepted.
143	• Accountant, an employee of a public accounting firm, participated, under the supervision of a partner in the firm, in the audit of records of a registered broker-dealer; failed to comply with generally accepted auditing standards and the Commission's instructions for the Form; failed to evaluate the effectiveness of the broker-dealer's existing internal controls to determine the need for extending the scope of the examination; failed to inquire into material poststatement events and to obtain sufficient evidence to afford a reasonable basis for the unqualified opinion given to the broker-dealer.	• Accountant censured.
144	• Allegations: Accountants were not independent and were not qualified to certify the financial statements of their client because partners or employees of accounting branch office, during the period of time when they were working on the preparation of such financial statements, received payment from the general partners of their client company totalling approximately $17,000 in the guise of profits from participation in the purchase and sale of "hot issues."	• Accountants consented to the entry of the permanent injunction.

ASR NO.	Facts	SEC Findings
53	• Allegations: Company and certain of its directors, officers and associates intentionally deceived the accountant by making untrue representations and by furnishing false information in connection with its audit. • Conduct of the audits did not meet professional standards: (1) Failed to obtain sufficient independent evidentiary material to support its professional opinion. (2) Failed fully to appraise the significance of information known to it and to extend sufficiently its auditing procedures under conditions which called for great professional skepticism.	• Deception does not relieve accountant of responsiblity to perform audit in conformity with generally accepted auditing standards. • Accountants consented to the entry of an order containing certain findings, conclusions and remedial sanctions: (1) Censure by the Commission (2) Required to adopt, maintain, and comply with procedures which shall be submitted to the Commission for its review and approval within thirty (30) days after the date hereof, to prevent future violations of the federal securities laws, which procedures shall provide: (A) Specific review designed to determine involvement of management in material transactions. (B) Qualitiative periodic review at least once every two years of all accountants' offices under the control and supervision of accountants' national staff to evaluate and ensure the quality of the audit engagements of such offices. (3) Investigation at the expense of the accountants conducted by the Commission. (4) For a period of twelve (12) months accountants' branch office will not accept or undertake any new SEC engagement. (5) For twelve (12) months accountant will not accept or undertake any new professional engagement of any client whose business, revenues and net profit (loss) is materially derived from real estate development or sales. (6) Commission retains jurisdiction of this matter pending final receipt of a report of its investigation.
157	• Settlement between client corporations and its auditors arising out of an audit performed by accountant of the inventory of a subsidiary of the corporation was not properly disclosed.	• Accountant consented to the entry of an order censuring the firm and to the publication of certain findings and conclusions by the Commission.
158	• Accountant prepared and disseminated false certified financial statements.	• Commission accepted accountant's sworn statement not to practice before the Commission.
160	• Accountants failed to comply with generally accepted auditing standards.	• Accountant suspended from appearing or practicing before the Commission for 18 months.

ASR NO.	Facts	SEC Findings
161	• Accountant prepared and certified materially false and misleading financial statements.	• Permanently suspended from appearing or practicing before the Commission.
167	• Accusation: Accountants reported transactions as bona-fide and arms length when they were not.	• Accountants consented to a judgement of permanent injunction.
168	• Accusation: Accountants certified consolidated statement of operations which materially overstated net sales and net earnings because the sales transactions had not been substantially completed as of the end of the accounting year. • In addition, the revenues reported as a result of such sales were substantially uncertain of collectibility.	• Accountants consented to a judgement of permanent injunction.
170	• Accusation: Accountant knew or should have known the financial statements were false and misleading in that they failed to disclose that principal assets were grossly overstated. • Accountant failed to review sufficient competent evidentiary material to afford a reasonable basis for the expression of his opinion on the certified financial statement of his client.	• Accountant disbarred; can in approximately 18 months apply for reinstatement.
173	• Accountant's audits were inadequate in a number of problem areas.	• Commission ordered accountants not to accept any new SEC clients for a six month period.
172	• Accusation: Company overstated sales; was subsequently declared bankrupt.	• Accountant did not perform the auditing engagement in accordance with generally accepted auditing standards. • Accountant appears to have been a victim of a deliberate scheme to defraud, including the misrepresentation and concealment of certain material facts, perpetrated by certain management and supervisory personnel of the client company. • Accountant censored.
176	• Accusation: Accountant certified statements where the allowance for doubtful accounts was inadequate under the circumstances since a significant portion of the leases were uncollectable; the leases were seriously delinquent and the value of the underlying collateral was insufficient. • Company continued to recognize revenues on these leases. • Net loss was understated; statements were false and misleading.	• A more diligent audit might have uncovered these problems. • Accountant cannot accept any new public clients until after a report had been submitted to the Commission for review evidencing accountant's evaluation of his auditing procedures and professional practice.
179	• Accountants certified statements which recorded "Marketable Securities" at their face value when there was no	• Accountant disbarred; can apply for reinstatement in approximately two years if:

ASR NO.	Facts	SEC Findings
	market for the bonds and their historical cost was less; "appraisal surplus" was falsely recorded on the books to reflect the difference between the cost of the bonds and the valuation placed on them; interest on the bonds was recorded as an asset despite the fact that interest on the bonds had been in default for almost two years; treasury stock was improperly recorded on the books as an asset.	(1) He enrolls in and attends a total of 100 or more hours of professional seminars or college courses dealing with the registration and disclosure requirements of the federal securities laws and generally accepted accounting principles and auditing standards during the period of his suspension. (2) Nothing has occurred during the suspension period that would be a basis for adverse action against accountant.
186	• Accountant involved in a kickback scheme.	• Accountant disbarred; after 22 months, may apply for reinstatement provided he has attended courses or seminars to the extent of at least 40 hours for the 12 months immediately preceding his application for readmission.
187	• SEC alleged that accountant violated the antifraud provisions of the Securities Act.	• Accountant consented to resign his privilege to appear before the Commission.
191	• Accountant knew that the purpose of his client's bank borrowings was to increase the amount of cash of the client at the end of three fiscal quarters to qualify for the favorable tax treatment afforded investment companies under Subchapter M of the Internal Revenue Code. Accountant knew or should have known that the investment company did not intend otherwise to use the proceeds of the loans in the operations of the company. Company repaid the notes to the bank on the first banking day following the day of the end of the fiscal quarters concerned.	• One accountant was suspended for 60 days. The other accountant was censored.
192	• Accountant violated Rule 10b-5 of the 1934 Act by certifying financial statements when the accountant did not, in fact, audit the company.	• Accountant permanently disbarred.
196	• Client companies engaged in fraudulent conduct which deceived the auditors, but the auditors failed to take reasonable steps to ensure the maintenance of a professional audit review. Auditors certified client's financial statements in which bogus assets and earnings were reported. Accountant also did not review prior firm's audit.	• Accounting firm agreed not to accept audit engagements for new SEC clients for a period of 6 months, and agreed to a review of its audit practices by a committee acceptable to the SEC and the firm.
198	• Accountant permitted his name and status to be used on financial statements transcribed on his letterhead stationary without auditing the company.	• Commission accepted accountant's resignation.
99	• Accountant violated certain provisions of the securities laws in connection with the offer and sale of common stock.	• Accountant permanently disbarred.

ASR NO.	Facts	SEC Findings
200	• Accountant had direct and indirect interest in the securities of client firm during the audit engagement.	• Accountant not independent. Suspended for 30 days.
201	• Accountant violated Section 17a of 1934 Act by willfully certifying a materially false and misleading statement of financial condition.	• Commission accepted accountant's resignation.
202	• Accountant violated Rule 10b-5 of the 1934 Act selling unregistered securities by means of false and misleading statements.	• Accountant permanently disbarred.
204	• Accountant violated Rule 10b-5 of 1934 Act certifying false and misleading financial statements in which the values of the receivables and investments were materially overstated.	• Accountant permanently disbarred.
207	• Accountant engaged in various fraudulent reporting and proxy violations in connection with the issuance of financial statements.	• Accountant permanently disbarred.
208	• Accountant violated the antifraud provisions of the federal securities laws by failing to review diligently client's (an issuer) offering circular which included inaccurate financial and other information.	• Commission accepted accountant's resignation.
209	• Accountants certified statements that reported wholly fictitious income and also failed to examine closely the working papers of predecessor auditors.	• Firm agreed not to accept new SEC clients for a period of 60 days, and agreed to a review of its audit practices by a committee acceptable to the SEC and the firm.
210	• Accountants certified statements which included fraudulent overstatement of inventory by reason of the inclusion of material amounts of nonexistent inventory.	• Firm agreed not to accept new SEC clients for a period of 60 days and will participate in the AICPA's program of voluntary quality control review of the firm's general audit practice.
212	• Accountant certified massive overstatements of assets and sales during each of the years 1968 through 1971.	• Accountant permanently disbarred.
213	• Accountant certified financial statements without in fact performing any substantial auditing procedures.	•Accountant permanently disbarred.
214	• Accountant accepted kickbacks from client.	• Accountant permanently disbarred.
215	• Accountant had direct and material indirect interests in the clients of two firms in which he was a partner, thereby compromising the independence of the firm.	• Commission accepted accountant's resignation.
216	• Accountant violated Rule 10b-5 of 1934 Act by aiding and abetting violations of the antifraud provisions of the secu-	• Commission accepted accountant's resignation.

ASR NO.	Facts	SEC Findings
	rities laws in connection with the preparation of client's annual audited financial statements.	
217	• Same as ASR No. 216.	Same as ASR No. 216.
221	• A prior temporary suspension ruled permanent.	
222	• A prior temporary suspension ruled permanent	
223	• Accountant certified financial statements in which the tax reports were false and misleading.	• Accountant agreed not to accept new SEC clients for a period of 30 days and will participate in the AICPA's program of voluntary quality control review of the firm's general audit practice.
224	• A prior temporary suspension ruled permanent.	
227	• Accountants' client company concealed illegal kickback schemes and filed misleading financial statements with the Commission. Accounting firm failed to implement generally accepted auditing standards which would have enabled discovery of the fraud.	• Accounting firm agreed to an assessment of its auditing procedures, policies and practices in the conduct of its SEC audit practice by a committee acceptable to the staff of the Commission. Firm agreed not to accept new SEC clients for a period of 60 days.
230	• Accountant willfully participated in client's scheme to falsify closing inventory figures.	• Commission accepted accountant's resignation.
231	• Accountant knowingly participated in client's scheme to falsify closing inventory values resulting in falsely increasing earnings.	• Commission accepted accountant's resignation.
232	• Same as ASR 231.	• Same as ASR 231.
233	• Accountant certified statements of a broker/dealer who was in violation of the Commission's net capital rule.	• Accountant agreed to a program of continuing education and his firm agreed to the AICPA's quality review program.
238	• Clients certified statements filed with the Commission materially overstated earnings and assets using fraudulent and improper accounting procedures.	• Accountants agreed to return the audit fees to the Chapter X Receiver and to a review of the firm's audit practices by an independent committee.
239	• Accountant certified statements that concealed known losses on various loans. Accountant also agreed to client's use of questionable accounting procedures.	• Accountant suspended for 60 days and agreed to submit subsequent work performed to an independent auditor for review.
240	• An accountant is reinstated after a temporary suspension.	
241	• Accountant certified statements in a 10-K filing in which	• Various accountants of the firm sus-

ASR NO.	Facts	SEC Findings
	the loss reserves (automobile insurance company) were materially understated and in which unacceptable accounting procedures were used for revenue recognition.	pended 60 to 90 days. The firm agreed to an examination of its audit practice by an independent commission. Firm also agreed that the branch office involved will not accept any new SEC audit engagements in that branch office's geographic service area for four months.
243	• Client certified statements in which the opinion did not state (1) the accounting principles reflected in the financials; (2) the consistency of the application of the accounting principles; (3) the changes in accounting principles which had a material effect on the financial statements and rendered them misleading.	• Commission accepted accountant's resignation.
246	• Accountant facilitated a manipulation in the trading market of the common stock of client company, as well as an illegal distribution of unregistered shares by creating through purchases the false appearance of an active trading market in the stock. Accountant also prepared financial statements improperly treating receivables and income, thereby reflecting an inflated net worth.	• Commission accepted accountant's resignation.
248	• Accountant certified financial statements that included the earnings of companies acquired by issuer under pooling-of-interest accounting even though pooling requirements were not made. Auditors also relied on management's unsupported and questionable representations, thus failing to comply with generally accepted auditing standards.	• Accountant suspended for 15 months and the firm censored.
249	• An accountant is reinstated after a temporary suspension.	

Epilogue

Our text begins by showing how congressional investigations into the securities market practices of the 1920s and early 1930s led to the SEC and the modern accounting profession. It is perhaps ironic that we now end on the same note; for, if the primary impetus of change in the accounting profession in the 1960s and early 1970s was litigation, investigations and the enactment of federal laws characterize the late 1970s.

INVESTIGATIONS

Congressman John Moss' Subcommittee on Oversight and Investigations (the Moss Committee) issued the first of the final reports on investigations into the practices of the accounting profession in 1976. Senator Lee Metcalf's Subcommittee on Reports, Accounting, and Management (the Metcalf Committee) issued the results of its investigation, ''Improving the Accountability of Publicly Owned Corporations and Their Auditors,'' a year later in November 1977.[1] In the same month the SEC's Advisory Committee on Corporate Disclosure (the Sommer Committee, named for A. A. Sommer, Jr., the SEC Commissioner who directed the study) also issued its report. During the same period that public investigations were under way, the Financial Accounting Foundation was reexamining the organization and methods of the FASB and the American Institute of Certified Public Accountants was engaged in a radical restructuring that culminated, in September 1977, in the subdivision of the Institute into two parts: The SEC Practice Section and a Private Companies Practice Section.[2] The accounting profession, meanwhile, was performing a comprehensive reexamination of the audit function. The Commission on Auditors' Responsibilities (the Cohen Commission),[3] an independent commission, was established by the American Institute of Certified Public Accountants in 1974 to:

> . . . develop conclusions and recommendations regarding the appropriate
> responsibilities of independent auditors . . . (to) consider whether a gap may
> exist between what the public expects or needs and what auditors can and

should reasonably expect to accomplish. If such a gap does exist, . . . to determine how the disparity can be resolved.

The final report of the Commission was released in early 1978.

The central issue in all of these investigations was whether the accounting profession should continue to be primarily self-disciplined and self-regulated or whether the federal government should assume a more direct role in the setting of accounting and auditing standards. The accounting profession, the SEC and the Metcalf Committee generally favored the retention of these powers in the private sector, subject to definitive action by the accounting profession to come to grips with the deficiencies identified by the investigations. The Metcalf investigation, however, found a need to enhance public confidence in the following areas that the committee found to be deficient and/or perceived by the public to be in need of change:

1. Accountant's independence.
2. The profession's resolve and ability to develop and maintain a viable system of self-regulation and self-discipline.
3. The processes by which accounting and auditing standards are promulgated.
4. The auditing and financial reporting of publicly held companies.

And the Committee delegated the responsibility of overseeing the profession's self-regulatory activities to the SEC. The Moss Committee took the opposite stand in favor of direct public regulation.

In this context SEC Chairman Harold M. Williams made a commitment, while testifying before the Metcalf Committee, to monitor the efforts being made by the profession to correct the deficiencies in the self-regulation process that had been identified by the various investigations. The first of its reports, "The Accounting Profession and the Commission's Oversight Role," was issued in June 1978. It concluded that "the potentially best approach to developing governance mechanisms to enable the profession to meet the challenges facing accountants today and in the future is for the profession to remain under essentially private direction, but with active oversight from the Commission." Nonetheless, the influence of the Moss position is evident in recent bills before Congress, and the accounting profession remains under the gun to protect its powers of self-regulation.

FEDERAL LAWS

The Energy Policy Conservation Act of 1975 gives the SEC the responsibility of establishing accounting practices for all persons engaged in the production of crude oil and natural gas. It provides that the SEC may rely on standards promulgated by the Financial Accounting Standards Board if it is assured that the FASB requirements will be observed by the oil and gas producers to the same extent as if prescribed by the SEC itself. It also set December 22, 1977, as a deadline for the issuance of new standards. This provision placed the SEC in the position of having to impose its standards, in lieu of the FASB's, in the event that the FASB did not meet the legal deadline. If the FASB did promulgate such standards, the SEC was obligated to ascertain that there was sufficient support for the FASB's position within the business community to assure that the requirements would be observed. Therefore, although the FASB was able to meet the deadline with its *Statement No. 19* supporting the successful efforts method of accounting for development costs, it was still necessary for the SEC to hold hearings for the purpose of evaluating the likelihood of adoption by the industry. The hearings were without precedent and the SEC was careful to emphasize that they also set none,[4] that the hearings were mandated by law and in no way affected the long-standing relationship of the two organizations.

The Foreign Corrupt Practices Act of 1977 went even further in the direction of establishing accounting practices by the public sector. Following the discovery by concurrent investigations in 1973 that illegal payments were being made surreptitiously from the same corporate funds as foreign bribes, the act proscribes inaccurate records, off-the-book accounts, and the like, and the bribing of foreign persons by any employee or agent of reporting companies. It requires reporting companies to make and keep books, records and accounts that, in reasonable detail, accurately and fairly reflect the transactions and dispositions of the assets of the issuer. And it requires the companies to devise and maintain a system of internal accounting controls sufficient to provide reasonable assurances that:

1. Transactions are executed in accordance with management's specific authorization.
2. Transactions are recorded as necessary: (a) to permit preparation of financial statements in conformity with generally accepted accounting principles or other applicable criteria; and (b) to maintain accountability for its assets.
3. Access to assets is permitted only in accordance with management authorization.
4. The recorded accountability for assets is compared with existing assets at reasonable intervals and appropriate action is taken with respect to any differences.[5]

All companies that report under the Securities Exchange Act of 1934 are subject to the provisions of this law even if they do not engage in foreign operations. Stated simply, in addition to making illegal certain payments to foreign parties, the Foreign Corrupt Practices Act amends the Securities Exchange Act to make inaccurate accounting records and inadequate internal controls a federal crime. This recent public attention to internal controls has altered the independent auditor's responsibility to review and report on internal controls. Some recommendations of the Cohen Committee deal with this problem. The act, for example, has accelerated the likelihood that independent audit committees, as a crucial element of internal controls, will be mandated by the action of some standard-setting body.[6] It has also made the need for corporate codes of conduct a desir able feature of internal controls and as a result the law has extended the need fo the auditor to check and report on compliance with such codes.

In order to implement the new law, the SEC has codified rules relating to th maintenance of records and preparation of reports in Regulation 13B-2. This new regulation provides that "no person shall directly or indirectly, falsify or caus to be falsified, any book, record or account subject to . . . The Securitie Exchange Act" and prohibits officers and directors of the issuer from makin materially false, misleading or incomplete statements to an accountant in con nection with any audit or examination of the financial statements of the issuer o the filing of required reports.

Disclosure standards, too, are affected because any activity in violation of th act is, by definition, material and must be disclosed. Certain other activities however, although not in violation of the law, may also be material and thei disclosure may be necessary to prevent other disclosures from being misleading. Defining which acts are or are not legal has traditionally been beyond the audi tor's area of expertise; however, the Corrupt Foreign Practices Act has placed the auditor in the middle of this decision. The act, then, created an interdepen dence between attorney and accountant that had not existed before.

Enactment of the Foreign Corrupt Practices Act is having its most profoun effect on the accounting profession in the area of internal control. The SEC ha proposed for comment rules that would require a management statement on internal accounting control in Form 10-K and annual reports to stockholders Included is a provision requiring that the statement be examined and reported on by an independent accountant. If enacted, this provision would require the profession to establish professional standards for reviewing and reporting on internal control.

COMMISSION ON AUDITORS' RESPONSIBILITIES

Many of the recommendations in the "Commission on Auditors' Responsibili ties' Report" deal with the burdens placed on the profession through the force of law (court actions, congressional investigations, and laws). The Commission identified weaknesses and specified remedies in such areas as:

1. The gaps between public expectations and professional standards regarding the affirmative duty to seek out corporate wrong-doing (e.g., illegal pay ments and detection of fraud) and independence.
2. The division of responsibility among management, counsel and the audito for financial statements, internal controls, and corporate adherence to the law.
3. The differing needs of large and small business.
4. Communicating with users of financial statements (via a reworded opinion letter and management's representations to the public).

Its recommendations for changes in the methods of self-regulation were aimed at strengthening self-discipline from within the profession by such means as:

1. Voluntary disclosure by accounting firms of financial and operations information.
2. Rotation of audit personnel (rather than rotation of the entire firm) at regular intervals.
3. A system of peer review including "long form" reports with limited public dissemination.
4. Groups within audit firms to oversee the review process in a manner similar to corporate audit committees.
5. Improved disciplinary methods (public disclosure of disciplinary actions and more timely investigations of matters that are also being examined in the courts or by the SEC).

On the other hand, the Commission requested a limitation on auditors' legal liability and a safe harbor provision for all new areas of auditor involvement.

THE METCALF COMMITTEE

The Metcalf Committee, however, was bolder in its recommendations to develop a financial reporting system responsive to the needs of its constituents, a system that would provide evidence of its fairness to all groups. It, too, observed gaps between what was and should be true regarding auditors' independence and in meeting the needs of small business. But it found that many communication problems between the profession and the public could be diminished by "daylight":

1. Applied to the accounting and audit standards-setting process.
2. In the public disclosure of audit firms' financial operating data.
3. Through disclosure in the proxy statement of all services provided by the company's audit firm.
4. By regular reviews of audit firms and public reports to the SEC of the results of the reviews.
5. By ending artificial restrictions against advertising.
6. By devoting more attention and resources to provide corporate financial information for average people.

The Committee would enhance independence and responsibility for audit representations through:

1. The use of independent corporate audit committees.
2. A study of the problems of rotating auditors.

3. The requirement that the partner in charge of an audit personally sign the opinion letter.

It supported the establishment of professional schools of accounting and improved research in audit methodology. It specifically mentioned the need to improve the standards of disclosure relating to illegal activities. And it found that the Cohen Committee did not address the problem of incompatible management advisory services adequately. Services such as executive recruiting, actuarial and other non-accounting services, it found, put the auditor in the situation of auditing his own work and were obtained by means of an unfair competitive advantage; appropriate services would more likely be accounting related in nature like computer and systems studies.

The Metcalf Committee made many other observations, but we will return now to the subject of self-regulation of the accounting profession. The committee found that accounting firms wanting to audit public companies needed an organization by which to set and enforce standards of auditing, that membership in the organization should be mandatory and that the SEC should provide an oversight function, reporting regularly to Congress on the progress of self-regulation. The primary feature of the organization's quality control mechanism was a mandatory external quality review performed by broad based audit teams of independent members from outside the public accounting field. Reports of the reviews were to be filed with the SEC and made available to the public. It is in this view of self-regulation that the Metcalf Committee report differs most strikingly from the Cohen Commission recommendations and serves as the impetus for the creation of the SEC Practice Section of firms within the AICPA.

THE SEC PRACTICE DIVISION

In creating the SEC Practice Section, the AICPA Council made membership voluntary, but by one year after its inception firms representing approximately 95 percent of all SEC audits had enrolled. Because of this willingness to participate in the section, the SEC, in its first annual report to Congress ("The Accounting Profession and the Commission's Oversight Role") saw the lack of mandatory membership to be no serious impediment to the profession's self-regulation.

The objectives of the section are to achieve the following:

1. Improve the quality of practice by CPA firms before the SEC through the establishment of practice requirements for member firms.
2. Establish and maintain an effective system of self-regulation of member firms by means of mandatory peer reviews, required maintenance of appropriate quality controls and the imposition of sanctions for failure to meet membership requirements.
3. Enhance the effectiveness of the section's regulatory system through the

monitoring and evaluation activities of an independent oversight board composed of public members.

4. Provide a forum for development of technical information relating to SEC practice.

The stated objectives, then, acknowledged many of the recommendations of the Metcalf Committee.

The section's activities are supervised by an Executive Committee appointed by the AICPA. Its peer review activities are directed by the Peer Review Committee, and, in response to the Metcalf recommendation for independent oversight by outsiders, a Public Oversight Board comprised of five distinguished members from outside the profession. The board:

1. Monitors and evaluates the regulatory and sanction activities of the Peer Review and Executive Committees to assure their effectiveness.
2. Determines that the Peer Review Committee is ascertaining that firms are taking appropriate action as a result of peer reviews.
3. Conducts continuing oversight of all other activities of the section.

To assure greater independence from the Executive Committee, the board members nominate their own successors. The board, however, has no direct authority over the section and the SEC is certain to monitor the extent of its influence with care. The AICPA, too, is presently examining ways in which to give the board clearer authority than it currently has to review sanctions and participate in peer reviews and is studying a provision that board members cannot be fired by the Executive Committee, but only by the board itself.[8]

Although the section's peer review procedure remains to prove its worth as a disciplinary and quality control device, some initial SEC staff objections to it have been answered already. For example:

1. When a proposed peer review concerns a litigated audit, an alternative peer review in the same industry can be substituted.
2. Firm-on-firm peer reviews (one independent accounting firm auditing another rather than a broad-based independent review body as recommended by the Metcalf Committee) will be taken and reviewed by another level in the review process.
3. Disciplinary action will be taken where necessary even when the court proceedings are unresolved.
4. An in-depth study of the means by which the peer review process can be extended to foreign affiliates of accounting firms is under way.

Another issue currently under study is whether the peer review reports should be made public.

The disciplinary structure is untested in many respects, then. The SEC report to Congress indicates that a successful self-regulatory system must:

1. Include people from outside the profession.
2. Have sufficient powers and resources to resolve changing problems.
3. Be firm, timely, even-handed and fair.

The peer review element is perhaps the most important one in the section's self regulation program; and it must include:

1. The establishment of reviewer standards.
2. Meaningful quality control standards.
3. A structure that instills public acceptance and confidence.
4. Candor with respect to the Public Oversight Board and the SEC.

SEC ADVISORY COMMITTEE ON CORPORATE DISCLOSURE

The operations of the SEC have been scrutinized by the Metcalf Committee as well as by the SEC's own Advisory Committee on Corporate Disclosure. The Metcalf Committee emphasized the need for the SEC to provide an oversight function over the SEC Practice Section of the AICPA and it specifically recommended that all independent accounting firms that audit publicly held companies report to the SEC on a regular basis.

The Advisory Committee offered many suggestions that the SEC has already implemented. You will recognize those that we have already discussed. The SEC has revised its rule making procedures to spell out a statement of concepts underlying an issue before it proposes a new rule for public comment. It has backed the Financial Accounting Standards Board on its pronouncement concerning industry segment reporting and other professional pronouncements. It has expanded the use of Form S-16, encouraged registrants to integrate Form 10-K and the annual report to stockholders and has strengthened requirements for management's discussion and analysis.

Many of the projects currently under way stem from the committee's recommendations. The SEC is monitoring the impact of its rules, developing guidelines for industry accounting standards, and studying the reporting burdens of small businesses. It is currently developing a single form to meet the reporting requirements of both the 1933 and 1934 Acts. It is defining the conditions under which disclosure of social accounting information is desirable and has encouraged the reporting by public companies of unaudited "soft" data such as earnings projections policies.[9] Finally, numerous changes in the proxy disclosure requirements have either already been implemented or are proposed.

In June 1978 the SEC amended its rules requiring disclosure in a registrant's proxy statement of the following:

For the fiscal year most recently completed, describe each professional service provided by the principal accountant and state the percentage relationship which the aggregate of the fees for all non-audit services bear to the audit fees, and, except as provided below, state the percentage relationship which the fee for each non-audit service bears to the audit fees, indicate whether, before each professional service provided by the principal accountant was rendered, it was approved by, and the possible effect on the independence of the accountant was considered by, (1) any audit or similar committee of the Board of Directors and (2) for any service not approved by an audit or similar committee, the Board of Directors.

This provision is intended to provide stockholders with sufficient information to judge for themselves the independence of the company's auditors.

The proposed changes are primarily intended to improve methods of corporate governance, and they reflect the SEC's philosophy that this must be accomplished through the efforts of three interdependent parties: the auditor, the legal counsel, and the company's management and directors. In the face of recent professional efforts to restructure the accounting profession, the focus has turned to the responsibilities of registrants' legal counsel, management and directors. (A proposal to require registrant's attorneys to blow the whistle on clients engaging in illegal activities was recently shelved, for example.)

By far, however, the burden of improving corporate governance falls on management and directors; and the SEC has used proxy disclosure as a means of doing so. Specific rule changes presently under consideration include the following. Nominees to the board of directors must be identified as to their independence from management. Directors are classified into one of three groups; management, directors affiliated with management (investment brokers, legal counsel, and the like), and independent directors.[10] Only the third category would be eligible for membership on committees requiring independence in their members (that is, the audit committee, those committees that approve executive and director compensation, or oversee corporate ethics). An interesting feature of the independent audit committee issue is that the SEC, in the above proposal, has defined the functions of a committee generally known as an "audit committee." Should a company disclose that it has an audit committee, but the committee does not, in fact, perform all the specified functions, the company could be guilty of issuing a misleading proxy statement.

Another proposal designed to improve the performance of directors is one that requires the disclosure of how often the board of directors, or any of its committees, meets and the names of any directors who have attended fewer than 75 percent of the meetings. Disclosure of the fact that incumbent directors are being renominated is under consideration as is the requirement to disclose the terms of any settlement of proxy contests for election to the board of directors. Another proposal strengthens the hand of individual directors in that companies would be required to report the nature of any disagreements with directors who resign over a difference of opinion. Finally, stockholders initiating proposals to be placed on the agenda of stockholders' meetings would receive a copy of management's response to their proposal and be given the opportunity to object to those representations.

The Advisory Committee recommended, also, that the SEC establish a statement of objectives for its rule making function, but that it should avoid disclosure rules whose primary purpose it was to regulate corporate conduct. Because such a statement of objectives could be used as a standard in challenges of future rules, the SEC rejected the recommendation.

Whether or not the primary purpose of a given disclosure rule is to regulate corporate conduct is a difficult question. Two recent SEC actions serve to illustrate the tenuous relationship between disclosure and influencing corporate behavior. The SEC amended forms filed under the 1933 and 1934 Acts to require the disclosure of the remuneration of certain directors, executive officers, and officers of the registrant. The remuneration that must be disclosed includes the constructive receipt of salaries, securities or other property, life or health insurance and medical reimbursement plans, and personal benefits such as contributions to pension plans and free rides on the corporate jet. Is this information needed by stockholders to make informed financial decisions, or is it an effort by the SEC to moderate the willingness of management to confer economic benefits upon itself?

Increasingly, takeover bids have been directed at the holders of preferred shares that must be redeemed. The SEC has proposed to require registrants to disclose three stock categories: preferred shares that must be redeemed; preferred shares that cannot be redeemed or that may be redeemed only at the company's option; and common shares. Because preferred shares that must be redeemed usually are held in larger blocks than outstanding common shares it is easier to obtain a percentage interest in a company by purchasing and redeeming preferred shares than by purchasing small holdings of common shares. Will this proposal result in useful information for stockholders, or is this proposal intended to hinder the efforts of takeover bidders?

WHAT PORTENDS FOR THE FUTURE?

The SEC has expressed its intention to oversee the operations of the SEC Practice Section as recommended by the Metcalf Committee and it has indicated that it has sufficient authority to:

1. Oversee the setting of auditing and accounting standards.
2. Effect registration and financial disclosure by accounting firms that audit publicly held corporations (although it presently does not support the publication of annual reports by independent accountants, as recommended by the Metcalf Committee).
3. Review the work of independent accountants and discipline those who do not meet minimum standards.
4. Subpoena information.
5. Effect divestiture of management advisory services by independent auditors.
6. Promulgate standards of independence for auditors.
7. Require the use by publicly owned corporations of independent audit committees.

8. Assure that the auditor's report clearly inform the public of deficiencies and uncertainties.
9. Require the disclosure of the effects of alternative accounting standards on corporate financial statements.

In conclusion, there has been a long standing relationship between the SEC and the accounting profession. It began in 1938 with the issuance of *ASR No. 4* wherein the SEC delegated the authority to set accounting principles to the accounting profession. The relationship was broadened in 1942 to include the promulgation of auditing standards by the accounting profession. At that time the SEC said, in *ASR No. 19*:

We have carefully considered the desirability of specific rules and regulations governing the auditing steps to be performed by accountants in certifying financial statements to be filed with us. Action has already been taken by the accounting profession adopting certain of the auditing procedures considered in this case. We have no reason to believe at this time that these extensions will not be maintained or that further extensions of auditing procedures along the lines suggested in this report will not be made. Further, the adoption of the specific recommendations made in this report as to the type of disclosure to be made in the accountant's certificate and as to the election of accountants by stockholders should insure that acceptable standards of auditing procedure will be observed, that specific deviations therefrom may be considered in the particular instances in which they arise, and that accountants will be more independent of management. Until experience should prove the contrary, we feel that this program is preferable to its alternative—the detailed prescription of the scope of and procedures to be followed in the audit for the various types of issuers of securities who file statements with us—and will allow for further consideration of varying audit procedures and for the development of different treatment for specific types of issuers.

That basic relationship exists today and, given the blessings of Congress, its future is promising.

FOOTNOTES FOR EPILOGUE

[1]Since the death of Senator Metcalf, Senator Thomas Eagleton has assumed the leadership of the investigation and continues the effort to develop " . . . sound public policies for improving the accountability of publicly-owned corporations and their auditors."

[2]A lawsuit challenging this action was dismissed by a New York State court in August 1978.

[3]Named in honor of Manuel F. Cohen, its chairman, also now deceased.

[4]Commissioner Philip A. Loomis in a letter to the editor of *The Wall Street Journal*, August 7, 1978, stated that: "Regardless of whether the commission agrees or disagrees with the FASB in this stance, its decision will not result in a change in its policy of supporting the FASB and must not be regarded as undermining either the FASB or self-regulation in the accounting profession. This situation is unique in that the direct respon-

sibility for the development of accounting practices for oil and gas producers was placed on the commission. . . ."

[5]The Foreign Corrupt Practices Act amends the Securities Exchange Act to include these provisions. See also *ASR No. 242* and Securities Exchange Act Release 34-15772.

[6]See *The Wall Street Journal,* July 28, 1978, page 30, in which the SEC's general counsel, Harvey L. Pitts, is quoted as suggesting that the law in conjunction with the SEC's power of general rule-making "could provide the basis for a commission rule requiring issuers . . . to utilize an independent audit committee."

[7]The *SEC Report on Questionable and Illegal Corporate Payments and Practices* submitted to the Senate Committee on Banking, Housing and Urban Development on May 12, 1976 offers guidelines for determining whether or not a specific fact is material.

[8]Membership rules of the section follow:

1. Ensure that all partners, shareholders and proprietors resident in the United States who are qualified for AICPA membership are members of the AICPA.
2. Adhere to quality control standards established by the AICPA Quality Control Standards Committee.
3. Submit to peer reviews of the firm's accounting and audit practice every three years or at such additional times as designated by the Executive Committee, the reviews to be conducted in accordance with review standards established by the section's Peer Review Committee.
4. Ensure that all professionals in the firm resident in the United States, including CPAs and non-CPAs, participate in at least 40 hours of continuing professional education annually.
5. Assign a new audit partner to be in charge of each SEC engagement which has had another audit partner in charge for a period of five consecutive years and prohibit such incumbent partner from returning to in charge status on the engagement for a minimum of two years except as follows:

   a. This requirement shall not become effective until two years after becoming a member.
   b. In unusual circumstances the chief executive partner of a firm or his designee may grant no more than one two-year extension so long as there is an in-depth supplemental review by another partner, or
   c. An application for relief is granted by the Peer Review Committee on the basis of unusual hardships.

6. Ensure that a concurring review of the audit report by a partner other than the audit partner in charge of an SEC engagement is required before issuance of an audit report on the financial statements of an SEC registrant. The Peer Review Committee may authorize alternative procedures where this requirement cannot be met because of the size of the member firm.
7. File with the section for each fiscal year of the United States firm (covering offices maintained in the United States and its territories) the following information to be open to public inspection:

   a. Form of business entity (e.g., partnership or corporation) and identification of domestic affiliates rendering services to clients.
   b. Description or chart of internal organizational structure and international organization (including the nature of relationships maintained in each geographic region).

c. Number and location of offices.

d. Total number of partners and non-CPAs with parallel status within the firm's organizational structure.

e. Total number of CPAs (including partners).

f. Total number of professional staff (including partners).

g. Total number of personnel (including No. 6).

h. Number and names of SEC clients for which the firm is principal auditor of record and any changes of such clients.

i. Number of SEC audit clients each of whose total domestic fees exceed 5 percent of total domestic firm fees and the percentage which each of these clients' fees represent to total domestic firm fees.

j. A statement indicating that the firm has complied with AICPA and SEC independence requirements.

k. Disclosure regarding pending litigation as required under generally accepted accounting principles and indicating whether such pending litigation is expected to have a material effect on the firm's financial condition or its ability to serve clients.

l. Gross fees for accounting and auditing, tax and MAS expressed as a percentage of total gross fees.

8. Maintain such minimum amounts and types of accountants' liability insurance as shall be prescribed from time to time by the Executive Committee.

9. When determining its scope of management advisory services place primary emphasis on accounting and financial related areas (see footnote for explanation) and refrain from performing management advisory services engagements for audit clients whose securities are registered with the SEC that

a. Would create a loss of the firm's independence for the purpose of expressing opinions on financial statements of such clients.

b. Are predominantly commercial in character and inconsistent with the firm's professional status as certified public accountants.

c. Are inconsistent with the firm's responsibilities to the public.

d. Consist of the following types of services:

(1) Psychological testing.

(2) Public opinion polls.

(3) Merger and acquisition assistance for a finders' fee.

e. Will be proscribed by the Executive Committee after further study and which comprise portions of what is included under the broad classifications of marketing consulting and plant layout as tentively outlined . . .

f. May be proscribed by the Executive Committee from time to time after further study based on the concepts described above in . . .

10. Report annually to the Audit Committee or Board of Directors (or its equivalent in a partnership) of each SEC audit client of the total fees received from the client for management advisory services during the year under audit and a description of the type of such services rendered.

11. Report to the Audit Committee or Board of Directors (or its equivalent in a partnership) of each SEC audit client on the nature of disagreements with the management of the client on financial accounting and reporting matters and auditing procedures which, if not satisfactorily resolved, would have caused the issuance of a qualified opinion on the client's financial statements.

12. Pay dues as established by the Executive Committee and comply with the rules and regulations of the section as established from time to time by the Executive Committee and with the decisions of the Executive Committee in respect of matters within its competence, to cooperate with the Peer Review Committee in connection with its duties, including disciplinary proceedings, and to comply with any sanction which may be imposed by the Executive Committee.

[9]In November 1978 the SEC issued *Guides 62* and *5* of the *Guides for Preparation and Filing of Registration Statements under the Securities Acts of 1933* and *1934* respectively. The guides pertain to voluntary disclosure of projections of a company's future economic performance. (*Securities Act Releases 33-5992 and 5993*). In June 1979 the SEC adopted a rule (Securities Act Release 33-6084) providing a "safe harbor from applicable liability provisions of the federal securities laws for statements made in filings with the Commission or in annual reports to shareholders that contain or relate to projections." The safe harbor is limited to: (1) a statement containing a projection of revenues, income (loss), earnings (loss) per share, capital expenditures, dividends, capital structure or other financial items; (2) a statement of management's plans and objectives for future operations; (3) a statement of future economic performance contained in management's discussion and analysis of the summary of earnings; and (4) disclosed statements of the assumptions underlying or relating to any of the statements described above.

[10]In reponse to strong public opposition this proposal has been shelved. Chairman Harold Williams, however, in January 1978 proposed informally that all directors eventually be independent of management, so it cannot be assumed that this issue is dead.

QUESTIONS

1. What is the central issue in all of the recent investigations of the accounting profession?
2. Discuss the four areas in which the Metcalf Committee believes the accounting profession to be deficient.
3. Which investigation recommended direct public regulation of the accounting profession?
4. What is the SEC's current position with respect to regulation of the accounting profession?
5. What is the SEC's responsibility with respect to the Energy Policy Conservation Act of 1975?
6. Discuss the substance of the Foreign Corrupt Practices Act of 1977 and the SEC's responsibility with respect to this act.
7. Do inadequate internal controls and inaccurate accounting constitute a federal crime?
8. What are the purposes of the proposed bill to establish a National Organization of Securities and Exchange Commission Accountancy?
9. Discuss the weaknesses identified by the Commission on Auditor's responsibilities.
10. What is the SEC Practice Section?
11. What is the SEC's position with respect to improvement in the methods of corporate governance?
12. What is an audit committee?

Appendix

F Bibliography

ABBREVIATIONS

AJ	Accountants' Journal
AR	Accounting Review
BL	Business Lawyer
CPAJ	CPA Journal
FAJ	Financial Analysts Journal
FE	Financial Executive
GWLR	George Washington Law Review
HBR	Harvard Business Review
JA	Journal of Accountancy
JBF	Journal of Business Finance
LCP	Law and Contemporary Problems
LJP	The Law Journal Press
MA	Management Accounting
NYULR	New York University Law Review
VLR	Vanderbilt Law Review
WCPA	Woman CPA
WMLR	William and Mary Law Review

This textbook should be used in conjunction with the principles, practices, standards and procedures set forth by the authoritative bodies. The instructor can recommend to students the opinions, statements, and so forth that he thinks should be reviewed in conjunction with a specific SEC rule or accounting series release. Intermediate and advanced accounting students will be familiar with the principles of the private rule-making bodies whose principles the SEC rules parallel. Accordingly, it is not an oversight that the FASB Statements and AICPA pronouncements are omitted from this bibliography, and their omission by no means is intended to minimize the importance of the authoritative principles and practices.

There has been a steady growth in the number of seminars, special programs, meetings, and the like concerning SEC matters. The AICPA, State Boards of

Accountancy, the American Law Institute/American Bar Association Joint Committee on Education; and the Practicing Law Institute are a few of the organizations sponsoring periodic programs featuring securities laws and accounting regulations. Usually, transcriptions of the proceedings can be purchased by interested persons unable to attend the meetings.

For those who wish to learn more about the securities markets and stock exchanges, the trading rules of the New York Stock Exchange are found in the Exchange's *Constitution,* and the rules covering over-the-counter transactions are in the National Association of Securities Dealers *Constitution.* (The rules of the various regional exchanges are, in substance, patterned after NYSE rules.) Historical perspective can be gained from Robert Sobel's *The Great Bull Market. Wall Street in the 1920's,* (W. W. Norton & Company); Hillel Black's, *The Watchdogs of Wall Street* (William Morrow and Company); James M. Landis' "The Legislative History of the Securities Act of 1933," *George Washington Law Review* 28 (10-59) 44–5; and T. A. Wise and the Editors of *Fortune, The Insiders: a Stockholder's Guide to Wall Street* (Doubleday & Company). Books of a pedagogical nature are Loll and Buckley's *The Over-the-Counter Securities Markets: A Review Guide* (Prentice-Hall); Leffler and Farwell's *The Stock Market* (The Ronald Press Company); and Eiteman and Dice *The Stock Market.*

Finally, probably the best source of information is current articles that constitute the substance of this bibliography. Accounting technology is in the same state of constant and rapid change as other professions, business management, and the sciences in the American economy. Any information needed for problems of current interest usually can be found in any of the various accounting journals. The authors have found the cumulative indexes of the journals very helpful for research. An excellent starting point for researching legal questions is the *Index of Legal Periodicals* under the "Securities" classification. This bibliography concludes with a reference list of leading cases by accounting topic.

ARTICLES

Anton, H. "Objectives of Financial Accounting: Review and Analysis." JA, January 1976, p. 40.

Armstrong, M. "The Politics of Establishing Accounting Standards." JA, February 1977, p. 76.

Arnett, H. "The Concept of Fairness." AR, April 1967, p. 291.

Asebrook, R. and Carmichael, D. "Reporting on Forecasts: A Survey of Attitudes." JA, August 1973, p. 38.

Axelson, K. "A Businessmen's Views on Disclosure." JA, July, 1975, p. 42.

Barnes, J. "More Efficient Auditing Through an Understanding of the Materiality Concept." JA, May 1973, p. 78.

Baron, C., Johnson, D., Searfoss, D., and Smith, C. "Uncovering Corporate Irregularities: Are We Closing the Expectation Gap?" JA, October 1977, p 56.

Backman, J. "Economist Looks at Accounting for Business Combinations." FAJ, July-August 1970, p. 39.

Bastable, C. "Is SEC Replacement Cost Data Worth the Effort?" JA, October 1977, p. 68.

Bastable, C. and Merriwether, J. "Fifo in an Inflationary Environment." JA, March 1975, p. 49.

Beaver, W. "Current Trends in Corporate Disclosure." JA, January 1978, p. 44.

Bedingfield, J. "The Effect of Recent Litigation on Audit Practice." JA, May 1974, p. 55.

Bedingfield, J. and Loeb, S. "Auditor Changes—An Examination. SEC Form 8-K." JA, March 1974, p. 66.

Bell, P. and Johnson, L. "Current Replacement Costs: A Qualified Opinion." JA, November 1976, p. 63.

Bencivenga, J. and Carmichael, D. "Reporting on Lack of Independence." JA, March 1970, p. 68.

Benson, B. "Lawyers' Responses to Audit Inquiries—A Continuing Controversy." JA, July 1977, p. 72.

Benston, G. "Evaluation of the Securities Exchange Act of 1934." FE, May 1974, p. 28.

Berton, L. "Accounting in the 1980s: Peering into the Future." JA, May 1976, p. 74.

Bierman, H. and Cyckman, T. "New Look at Deferred Taxes." FE, January 1974, p. 40.

Bierman, H. and Dukes, R. "Accounting for Research and Development Costs." JA, April 1975, p. 48.

Black, S. and Koch, A. "Replacement Cost—Charting the Uncharted Sea." JA, November 1976, p. 72.

Block, M. "Extent of Disclosure in Audited vs. Unaudited Statements." JA, January 1977, p. 86.

Boxer, D. "Business Combinations: Reporting to the SEC." JA, April 1973, p. 67.

Brasfield, K. "The CPA and Federal Government—Opportunities and Responsibilities." JA, July 1971, p. 71.

Bullard, R. "Pooling of Interest vs. Purchase: Effects on EPS." WCPA, October 1974, p. 6.

Burton, J. "Disclosure and Professional Competence." JA, August 1972, p. 24.

Burton, J. "Financial Reporting in an Age of Inflation." JA, February 1975, p. 68.

Burton, J. "SEC Enforcement and Professional Accountants: Philosophy, Objectives and Approach." VLR, January 1975, p. 19.

Burton, J. "Some General and Specific Thoughts on the Accounting Environment." JA, October 1973, p. 40.

Burton, J. "The Changing Face of Financial Reporting." JA, February 1976, p. 60.

Burton, J. "The Profession's Institutional Structure in the 1980s." JA, April 1978, p. 63.

Burton, J. "The SEC and the World of Accounting in 1974." JA, July 1974, p. 59.

Buzby, S. "The Nature of Adequate Disclosure." JA, April 1974, p. 38.

Buzby, S. and Falk, H. "A New Approach to the Funds Statement." JA, January 1974, p. 55.

Carmichael, D. "Corporate Accountability and Illegal Acts." JA, January 1977, p. 77.

Carmichael, D. "Cumulative Aspects of Materiality." JA, December 1969, p. 61.

Carmichael, D. "Financial Forecasts—The Potential Role of Independent CPAs." JA, September 1974, p. 84.

Carmichael, D. "SEC's ASR No. 115, Certification of Financial Statements." JA, May 1970, p. 78.

Carmichael, D. "The Auditor's Role and Responsibilities." JA, August 1977, p. 55.

Carmichael, D. "What is the Independent Auditor's Responsibility for the Detection of Fraud?" JA, November 1975, p. 76.

Carmichael, D. and Bencivenga, J. "SAP No. 42. Lack of Independence—Some Reporting Problems." JA, August 1972, p. 79.

Casey, W. "Disclosure and Form 10-K." JA, October 1972, p. 73.

Chalmers, G. "Over-Accountable Accountants? A Proposal for Clarification of the Legal Responsibilities Stemming from the Audit Function." WMLR (Fall 1974) p. 71.

Champagne, J., Matoney, J. Jr. and Vangermeersch, R. "Big Eight Influence Over State Boards: Debunking the Metcalf Report." JA, November 1977, p. 100.

Chang, D. and Liao, S. "Measuring and Disclosing Forecast Reliability." JA, May 1977, p. 76.

Chazen, C. and Solomon, K. "The Art of Defensive Auditing." JA, October 1975, p. 66.

Chazen, C. and Solomon, K. "Use of Legal Opinions in the Audit Process." JA, November 1973, p. 46.

Chilton, C. "Use of Controls in an Accounting Firm." JA, January 1977, p. 36.

Clay, R. Jr. and Holder, W. "A Practitioner's Guide to Accounting for Leases." JA, August 1977, p. 61.

Coakley, W. "Accountants' Legal Liability." JA, July 1968, p. 58.

Cohen, M. "Some Problems of Disclosure." JA, May 1968, p. 61.

Copeland, R., Strawser, R., and Binns, J. "Accounting for Investments in Common Stock." FE, February 1972, p. 36.

Copeland, R., Wojdak, J., and Shank, J. "Use Lifo to Offset Inflation." HBR, May-June 1971, p. 91.

Corless, J. and Norgaard, C. "User Reactions to CPA Reports on Forecasts." JA, August 1974, p. 46.

Cottle, D. "Short-form Report." JA, August 1972, p. 22.

Davidson, S. and Weil, R. "Comments on 'Are You Ready for Inflation Accounting.'" JA, September 1975, p. 109.

Davis, E. and Kelley, J. "The Engagement Letter and Current Legal Developments." JA, December 1972, p. 54.

Deaton, W. and Weygandt, J. "Disclosures Related to Pension Plans." JA, January 1975, p. 44.

DeFliese, P. "Accounting for Leases: A Broader Perspective." FE, July 1974, p. 14.

Ditkoff, J. "Financial Tax Accounting at the Crossroads." JA, August 1977, p. 69.

Duncan, R. "Professional Responsibility." AJ, July 1974, p. 451.

Earle, V. "Accountants on Trial in a Theatre of the Absurd." *Fortune,* May 1972, p. 227.

Earle, V. "Litigation Explosion." JA, March 1970, p. 65.

Earle, V. "The Fairness Myth." VLR, January 1975, p. 147.

Ehrenberg, A. "Annual Reports Don't Have to be Obscure." JA, August 1976, p. 88.

Fiflis, T. "Views on Legal and Ethical Responsibilities of Accountants." BL, March 1975, p. 186.

Foster, W. "Illogic of Pooling." FE, December 1974, p. 21.

Giese, J. and Klammer, T. "Achieving the Objectives of APB Opinion No. 19." JA, March 1974, p. 54.

Gleim, I. "Standards of Disclosure for Supplementary Data." JA, April 1973, p. 50.

Godick, N. and Miller, R. "Applying APB Opinions Nos. 23 and 24." JA, November 1973, p. 55.

Grauer, J. and Estes, T. "The Law-Abiding Accountant: Ethics, Standards, Principles." JA, May 1974, p. 90.

Gridley, F. "Accounting for R&D Costs." FE, April 1974, p. 18.

Hampson, J. "Accountants' Liability—The Significance of Hochfelder." JA, December 1976, p. 69.

Hanson, W. "Focus on Peer Review, Illegal Payments and Lawyers' Letters." JA, May 1976, p. 90.

Hawkins, D. "Controversial Accounting Changes." HBR, March-April 1968, p. 20.

Henry, E. "A New Funds Statement Format for Greater Disclosure." JA, April 1975, p. 56.

Hershey, D. "Accountants' Liability—A Lawyer's View." JA, June 1976, p. 94.

Hill, H. "Reporting on Uncertainties by Independent Auditors." JA, January 1973, p. 55.

Hill, H. "Responsibilities and Liabilities of Auditors and Accountants—An Accountant's View." BL, March 1975, p. 169.

Holmes, W. "Toward Standards for Materiality." (Response by Sam M. Woolsey) JA, June 1976, p. 62.

Hoyle, J. "Mandatory Auditor Rotation: The Arguments and an Alternative." JA, May 1978, p. 69.

Isbell, D. "Rules for Being Sued." JA, April 1972, p. 84.

Isbell, D. and Carmichael, D. "Disclaimers and Liability—The Rhode Island Trust Case." JA, April 1973, p. 37.

Jaenicke, H. and Rascoff, J. "Segment Disposition: Implementing APB Opinion No. 30." JA, April 1974, p. 63.

Johnson, L. and Bell, P. "Current Replacement Costs: A Qualified Opinion." JA, November 1976, p. 63.

Kanaga, W. "Inflation, Instability and Accounting." JA, September 1977, p. 104.

Kapnick, H. "Accounting Principles—Concern or Crisis?" FE, October 1974, p. 23.

Kay, R. "Disagreements Under Accounting Series Release No. 165." JA, October 1976, p. 75.

Kelley, J. "More on Engagement Letters." JA, August 1974, p. 24.

King, A. "Fair Value Reporting." MA, March 1975, p. 25.

King, A. "More on Depreciation in an Inflationary Economy." JA, February 1977, p. 46.

Konrath, L. "The CPA's Risk in Evaluating Internal Control." JA, October 1971, p. 53.

Kramer, A. "The Significance of the Hochfelder Decision." CPAJ, August 1976, p. 11.

Krauss, F. "The Legislative Year in Review." JA, October 1977, p. 22.

Kripke, H. "Rule 10(b)-5 Liability and 'Material Facts'." 46 NYULR, 1061 (1971).

Kripke, H. "Summary of Accountant's Liability Since Hochfelder." LJP, *Changing SEC Financial Disclosure and Accounting Rules*, 1977, p. 492.

Kripke, H. "The SEC, the Accountants, Some Myths and Some Realities." 45 NYULR, 1151 (1970).

Landis, J. "The Legislative History of the Securities Act of 1933." GWLR 28 (10-59) p. 445.

Landman, A. "Engagement Letters." JA, December 1973, p. 40.

Lee, T. "A Case for Cash Flow Reporting." JBF, Summer 1972, p. 27.

Lewis S. "Needed: A More Definitive Funds Statement." JA, September 1976, p. 48.

Lorensen, L. "Interim Financial Information—A Legal View." JA, December 1973, p. 74.

Lowe, H. "The Classification of Corporate Stock Equities." AR, July 1961, p. 425.

Lynch, T. "Accounting for Investments in Equity Securities by the Equity and Market Value Methods." FAJ, January-February 1975, p. 62.

Lytle, R. "Accounting Interpretations." JA, November 1973, p. 82.

Lytle, R. "Accounting Interpretation. Disclosure of 'Leveraged Lease' Transactions by Lessors." JA, November 1973, p. 84.

McGill, B. "CPA's v. the SEC." JA, August 1973, p. 88.

McRae, T. "Representation Letters from a Company's Legal Counsel—Auditing and Reporting Considerations." JA, November 1973, p. 76.

Mancuso, S. "Even More on Lifo." JA, July 1972, p. 36.

Mandel, J. and Altschul, D. "Financial Forecasts and Projections: A Pitfall for the Uninitiated Accountant." JA, May 1977, p. 46.

Marvin, M. "Small Firms and SEC Registration." JA, May 1977, p. 80.

Mautz, R. "A Few Words for Historical Cost." FE, January 1973, p. 23.

Maxfield, T. "Disclosure and Professional Competence." JA, August 1972, p. 23.

Miller, S. and Subak, J. "Impact of Federal Securities Laws: Liabilities of Officers, Directors, and Accountants." BL, January 1975, p. 387.

Most, K. and Winters, A. "Focus on Standard Setting: From Trueblood to the FASB." JA, February 1977, p. 67.

Needham, J. "Independence" JA, May 1971, p. 9.

Olson, E. "Accountants' Liability: Hochfelder and Beyond." LJP, *Changing SEC Financial Disclosure and Accounting,* 1977, p. 486.

Olson, W. "A Look at the Responsibility Gap." JA, January 1975, p. 52.

Olson, W. "The Search for Fairness in Financial Reporting." JA, May 1976, p. 82.

Pacter, P. "Line-of-Business Earnings Disclosures in Recent SEC Filings." JA, October 1970, p. 52.

Pacter, P. "Reports to the SEC." JA, September 1971, p. 78.

Parrish, M. *Securities Regulation and the New Deal* (New Haven, Conn: Yale University Press, 1970).

Parson, J. "What Makes a Managing Partner?" JA, September 1977, p. 64.

Pines, J. "The Securities and Exchange Commission and Accounting Principles." LCP, Autumn 1965, p. 727.

Pointer, L. "Disclosing Corporate Tax Policy." JA, July 1973, p. 56.

Rappaport, A. "Economic Impact of Accounting Standards—Implications for the FASB." JA, May 1977, p. 89.

Rayburn, F. "Pooling of Interests: The Status of Enforcement." JA, October 1975, p. 82.

Reiling, H. and Taussig, R. "Recent Liability Cases—Implications for Accountants." JA, September 1970, p. 39.

Revsine, L. and Thies, J. "Price Level Adjusted Replacement Cost Data." JA, May 1977, p. 71.

Revsine, L. and Weygandt, J. "Accounting for Inflation: The Controversy." JA, October 1974, p. 72.

Richard, D. "An Analysis of Early Investment Credits." JA, September 1968, p. 51.

Roberts, A. and Gabhart, D. "Statement of Funds: A Glimpse of the Future?" JA, April 1972, p. 54.

Rosenfield, P. "Confusion Between General Price-Level Restatement and Current Value Accounting." JA, October 1972, p. 63.

Rosenfield, P. "Current Replacement Value Accounting—A Dead End." JA, September 1975, p. 63.

Schaeler, C. Jr. "Lifo—Tax Conformity and Report Disclosure Problems." JA, January 1976, p. 52.

Schorr, B., "Overhauling the Securities Laws," *Wall Street Journal,* December 21, 1978.

Schuchart, J. and Sanders, W. "Pension Fund Considerations." MA, March 1972, p. 49.

Seidler, L. "Accountant: Account for Thyself." JA, June 1973, p. 38.

Seidler, L. "Chaos in Accounting: Will It Continue?" FAJ, March-April 1972, p. 88.

Sharp, R., Tolman, R. and Skousen, K. "Corporate Disclosure of Budgetary Data." JA, May 1972, p. 50.

Shefsky, L. and Schwartz, E. "Disclosures and Reporting Under SEC's ASR No. 115." JA, September 1973, p. 53.

Shwayder, K. "Accounting for Exchange Rate Fluctuation." AR, October 1972, p. 747.

Skousen, K. "Standards for Reporting by Lines of Business." JA, February 1970, p. 39.

Smith, J. "Computation of Lessor's Impact Interest Rate Under FASB Statement No. 13." JA, January 1978, p. 34.

Smith, R. and Haried, A. "Accounting for Marketable Equity Securities." JA, February 1977, p. 54.

Solomon, K., Chazen, C. and Augenbraun, B. "Who Judges the Auditor, and How?" JA, August 1976, p. 67.

Solomon, K. and Muller, H. "Illegal Payments: Where the Auditor Stands." JA, January 1977, p. 51.

Sommer, A. Jr. "Accountant's Counsel—Advice to My Client." BL, January 1969, p. 593.

Sommer, A. Jr. "Differential Disclosure: To Each His Own." JA, August 1974, p. 55.

Sommer, A. Jr. "Financial Reporting and the Stock Market—The Other Side." FE, May 1974, p. 36.

Sommer, A. Jr. "The Lion and the Lamb: Can the Profession Live with 'Cooperative Regulation'?" JA, April 1978, p. 70.

Sprouse, R. "Accounting for What-You-May-Call-Its." JA, October 1966, p. 45.

Stamp, E. and Mason, A. "Current Cost Accounting: British Panacea or Quagmire?" JA, April 1977, p. 66.

Stone, R. "Some Security and Integrity Controls in Small Computer Systems." JA, February 1976, p. 36.

Stoppelman, J. "Accountants and Rule 10(b)-5: After Hochfelder." JA, August 1977, p. 49.

Taper, E. "Independence—Our Public Image." JA, August 1968, p. 65.

Tierney, C. "General Puchasing Power Myths." JA, September 1977, p. 90.

Titard, P. "Independence and MAS—Opinions of Financial Statement Users." JA, July 1971, p. 47.

Van Arsdell, S. "Criteria for Determining Materiality." JA, October 1975, p. 72.

Weygandt, J. and Deaton, W. "Disclosures Related to Pension Plans." JA, January 1975, p. 44.

Wheat, F. "Toward a More Rational Disclosure Policy." JA, September 1968 p. 56.

Wiesen, J. "The Cohen Commission Report: A Perspective on Disclosure Regulation." JA, August 1977, p. 90.

Williams, H. "Audit Committees—The Public Sector's View." JA, September 1977, p. 71.

Williams, H. "The Profession's Future: New SEC Chairman Harold Williams Speaks Out." JA, September 1977, p. 42.

Woolsey, S. "Approach to Solving the Materiality Problem." JA, March 1973, p. 47.

Wyatt, A. "Competence and Independence in Auditing." JA, April 1972, p. 71.

Wyatt, A. "Leases Should be Capitalized." CPAJ, September 1974, p. 35.

Wyatt, A. "The Economic Impact of Financial Accounting Standards." JA, October 1977, p. 92.

BOOKS AND PUBLICATIONS

Accounting Series Releases and Staff Accounting Bulletins, (Chicago: Commerce Clearing House, Inc., September 1977).

Annual Report of the SEC (Washington, D.C.: U.S. Government Printing Office).

Berman, S., *GOING PUBLIC: A Practical Handbook of Procedures and Forms* (Englewood Cliffs, N.J.: Prentice-Hall, Inc., 1974).

Black, H., *The Watchdogs of Wall Street,* (New York: William Morrow and Company, 1962).

Business Lawyer (Chicago: American Bar Association, published five times yearly).

Carmichael, D. and Makela, B., ed., *Corporate Financial Reporting: The Benefits and Problems of Disclosure* (New York: American Institute of Certified Public Accountants, 1976).

Choka, A. *An Introduction to Securities Regulation* (Chicago: Twentieth Century Press, Inc., 1958).

Ellenberger, J. and Mahar, E., *Legislative History of the Securities Act of 1933 and Securities Exchange Act of 1934* (South Hackensack, N.J.: Fred B. Rothman and Co., 1973).

Evans, J. "The Accounting Profession and the SEC: A Partnership Under Attack." LJP, *Changing SEC Financial Disclosure and Accounting Rules,* 1977, p. 65.

Federal Securities Act Handbook (Philadelphia: Joint Committee on Continuing Legal Education of the American Law Institute and the American Bar Association, 1959).

Federal Securities Law Manual (New York: Sorg Printing Company, 1963).

Federal Securities Law Reporter (Chicago: Commerce Clearing House, 1964).

Hawkins, D. *Corporate Financial Reporting* (Homewood, Ill.: Richard D. Irwin, Inc., 1977).

Jennings, R., and Marsh, H., *Securities Regulation,* 3rd Ed. (Mineola, N.Y.: The Foundation Press, Inc., 1972).

Loss, L. *Securities Regulation* (Boston: Little, Brown and Company, 1961).

Parrish, M., *Securities Regulation and the New Deal* (New Haven, Conn.: Yale University Press, 1970).

Pecora, F., *Wall Street Under Oath,* (New York: Simon and Schuster, 1939).

Rappaport, L. *SEC Accounting Practice and Procedure* (New York: The Ronald Press Company, 1972).

Sobel, R. *The Great Bull Market. Wall Street in the 1920's* (New York: W. W. Norton and Company, Inc., 1968).

Wise, T., *The Insiders: A Stockholder's Guide to Wall Street* (New York: Doubleday & Company, Inc., 1962).

Wiesen, J. Research Stdy No. 2, *The Securities Acts and Independent Auditors: What Did Congress Intend?,Work of the Securities and Exchange Commission* (Washington, D.C.: U.S. Government Printing Office).Commission on Auditors' Responsibilities, 1978.

BIBLIOGRAPHY OF CASES BY ACCOUNTING TOPIC

Deferred Charges

Cox **v.** *Leahy,*Supreme Court of New York, Appellate Division, Third Department, 1924, 209 App. Div. 313, 204, N.Y.S. 741.

L. P. Larson, Jr., Co. **v.** *William Wrigley, Jr., Co.,*United States Court of Appeals, Seventh Circuit, 20 F. 2d 830.

Bowe **v.** *Provident Loan Corporation,*Supreme Court of Washington, 1922. 120 Wash. 574, 208 P. 22.

Ebbert **v.** *Plymouth Oil Co.,*Supreme Court of Pennsylvania, 1940. 338 Pa. 13 A. 2d. 42.

Contingencies/Probable Losses

*Edwards v. International Pavement Co.,*Supreme Judicial Court of Massachusetts, 1917, 227 Mass. 206, 116 N.E. 266.

*Brown v. Helvering,*Supreme Court of the United States, 1933. 291 U.S. 193, 54 S. Ct. 356.

*In Brown & Williamson Tobacco Corp.,*16 T.C. 432 (1951), appeal dismissed 194 F. 2d 537 (6th Cir. 1952).

*United States v. S. S. White Dental Mfg. Co.,*Supreme Court of the United States, 1927. 274 U.S. 398, 47 S. Ct. 598.

Continental Tie & Lumber Co. **v.** *United States,*Supreme Court of the United States, 1932. 286 U.S. 290, 52 S. Ct. 529.

Taxes

Lucas v. *American Code Co.,*Supreme Court of the United States, 1930. 28 U.S. 445,50, S. Ct. 202.

Pierce Estates, Inc. v. *Commissioner,*195 F. 2d 475 (3rd Cir. 1952).

Whitaker v. *Commissioner,*259 F. 2d 379 (5th Cir. 1958).

United States v. *Consolidated Edison Co.,* Supreme Court of the United States, 1961. 366 U.S. 380, 81 S. Ct. 1326.

United States v. *Anderson,* 269 U.S. 422, 46 S. Ct. 131.

Dixie Pine Products Co. v. *Commissioner,* 320 U.S. 516, 64 S. Ct. 364.

Gaul v. *Kiel & Arthe Co.* Court of Appeals of New York, 1910. 199 N.Y. 472, 92 N.E. 1069.

Lucas v. *Ox Fibre Brush Co.,* 281 U.S. 115, 119, 50 S. Ct. 273 (1930).

Long-Term Liabilities

Commissioner v. *Schmoll Fils Associated, Inc.,* United States Court of Appeals, Second Circuit, 1940. 110 F. 2d 611.

Jewel Tea Co. v. *United States,* 2 Cir., 90 F. 2d 451, 452.

Commissioner v. *O.P.P. Holding Corp.,* 2 Cir., 76 F. 2d 11.

Gooding Amusement Co. v. *Commissioner,* 236 F. 2d 159 (6th Cir. 1956), cert. denied 352 U.S. 1031, 77 S. Ct. 595 (1957).

Gilbert v. *Commissioner,* 248 F. 2d 399 (2d Cir. 1957).

Helvering v. *Union Pacific R. Co.* Supreme Court of the United States, 1934, 293 U.S. 282, 55 S. Ct. 165.

Great Western Power v. *Commissioner,* Supreme Court of the United States, 1936. 297 U.S. 543, 56 S. Ct. 576.

Retained Earnings

Willcuts v. *Milton Dairy Co.,* Supreme Court of the United States, 1927. 285 U.S. 215, 48 S. Ct. 71.

Edwards v. *Douglas,* Supreme Court of the United States, 269 U.S. 204, 214, 46 S. Ct. 85.

LaBelle Iron Works v. *United States,* 256 U.S. 377, 388, 41 S. Ct. 528.

Hutchinson v. *Curtiss,* 45 Misc. 484, 92 N.Y.S. 70 (Sup. Ct. 1904).

Wittenberg v. *Federal Mining and Smelting Co.* 15 Del. Ch. 147, 133 A. 48, aff'd 15 Del. Ch. 409, 138 A. 347 (1927).

Hayman v. *Morris,* 36 N.Y.S. 2d 756, 768 (Sup. Ct. 1942).

Robinson v. *Wangemann,* 75 F. 2d 756, 757, 758 (5th Cir. 1935).

Treasury Stock

Glenn L. Martin Co. v. *United States,* District Court, D. Maryland, 1937. F. Supp. 562.

Vanderlip v. *Los Molinos Land,* 56 Cal. App. 2d 747, 133 P. 2d 467 (1943).

Income Realization

United States v. *Schillinger,* United States Supreme Court, S.D.N.Y., 1976. 27 Fed. Cas. 973.

Jennery v. *Olmstead,* New York Supreme Court, Third Dept., 1995. 36 Hun 536.

Stein v. *Strathmore Worsted Mills,* Supreme Judicial Court of Massachusetts 1915. 221 Mass. 86, 108 N.E. 1029.

Eisner v. *Macomber,* Supreme Court of the United States, 1920. 252 U.S. 189, 4 S. Ct. 189, 64 L.Ed. 521.

Tooey v. *C. L. Percival Co.,* Supreme Court of Iowa, 1921. 192 Iowa 267, 18 N.W. 403.

Hill v. *International Products Co.,* 129 Misc. 25, 46, 220 N.Y.S. 711, 731 (1925)

Artnell Company v. *Commissioner of Internal Revenue,* United States Court c Appeals, Seventh Circuit, 1968. 400 F. 2d 981.

Hagen Advertising Displays, Inc. v. *Commissioner of Internal Revenue,* Unite States Court of Appeals, Sixth Circuit, 1969. 407 F. 2d 1105.

Schuessler v. *Commissioner of Internal Revenue,* 230 F. 2d 722 (5thhCir. 1956).

Harrold v. *Commissioner of Internal Revenue,* 192 F. 2d 1002 (4th Cir. 1951).

Hilinski v. *Commissioner of Internal Revenue,* 237 F. 2d 703 (6thhCir. 1956).

Intangibles

Richmond Television Corporation v. *United States* United States Court o Appeals, Fourth Circuit, 1965. 354 F. 2d 410.

United States v. *Hilton Hotzls Corporation* 397 U.S. 580, 90 S. Ct. 1307, 25 L Ed. 2d 585 (1970).

Woodward v. *Commissioner of Internal Revenue,* 397 U.S. 572, 90 S. Ct. 1302 25 L. Ed. 2d 577 (1970).

L. P. Larson Jr. Co. v. *William Wrigley Jr., Co.,* 20 F. 2d 830 (7th Cir. 1927).

Seaboard Finance Co. v. *Commissioner,* 367 F. 2d 646 (9th Cir., 1966).

Super Food Services Inc. v. *United States,* 416 F. 2d 1236 (7th Cir., 1969).

R. M. Boe v. *Commissioner,* 307 F. 2d 339 (9th Cir., 1962).

Depreciation

Kansas City Southern Ry. Co. v. *U.S., v.* U.S., 112 F. Supp. 164 (Ct. Cl., 1953)

Denver & Rio Grande Western R. Co. v. *C.I.R.,* 279 F. 2d 368 (10th Cir. 1960)

Hertz Corporation v. *United States,* 364 U.S. 122, 80 S. Ct. 1420, 4 L. Ed. 2 1603 (1960).

United States v. *New York Telephone Company,* Supreme Court of the Unite States, 1946. 326 U.S. 638 66 S. Ct. 393 90 L. Ed. 371.

Massey Motors, Inc. v. *United States,* Supreme Court of the United States, 1960 364 U.S. 92 80 S. Ct. 1911, 4 L. Ed. 2d 592.

Parkersburg Iron & Steel Co. v. *Burnet,* United States Court of Appeals Fourt Circuit 1931. 48 F. 2d 163.

Buckland v. *United States,* United States District Court, D. Connecticut 1946.

Crocker Bank v. *Commissioner,* 59 F. 2d 37 (1932).

Phillips & Eaton v. *Commissioner,* 20 Tax Ct. 455 (1953).

Connally Realty Co. v. *Commissioner,* 81 F. 2d 221 (5th Cir. 1936).

Collingwood v. *Commissioner,* 20 T.C. 937 (195)).

New York Edison v. *Maltbie,* 244 App. Div. 685, 281 N.Y.S. 223 (1935).

U.S. v. *Ludey,* 274 U.S. 295 (1926).

American Telephone & Telegraph v. *U.S.,* 299 U.S. 232, 57 S. Ct. 170 (1936).

Inventories/Cost of Goods Sold

Finance & Guaranty Co. v. *Commissioner,* 50 F. 2d 1061 (4th Cir. 1931).

Pierce Arrow Motor Car Co. v. *United States,* 9 F. Supp. 577 (Ct. Cl. 1935).

Empire Laboratories Inc. v. *Golden Distributing Corp.,* 266hMass. 418, 164 N.E. 772 (1929).

Francisco Sugar Co. v. *Commissioner,* 47 F. 2d 555 (2d Cir. 1931).

Spiegel May, Stern & Co. v. *U.S.,* 37 F. 2d 988 (Ct. Cl. 1930).

Commissioner v. *Bullock's,* 81 F. 2d 1002 (9th Cir. 1936).

Herring v. *Gage, Fed. Cas. No. 6-422* (C.C.N.D.N.Y. 1878).

Barde Steel Products Corporation v. *Commissioner,* United States Circuit Court of Appeals, Second Circuit, 1930. 40 F. 2d 412.

Lucas, Commissioner, v. *North Texas Lumber Co.,* 281 U.S. 11, 50 S. Ct. 184, 74 L. Ed. 668.

Mandelbaum v. *Goodyear Tire & Rubber Co.,* United States Circuit Court of Appeals, Eighth Circuit, 1925. 6 F. 2d 818.

Lucas v. *Kansas City Structural Steel Co.,* 281 U.S. 264, 50 S. Ct. 263.

Hutzler Brothers Co. v. *Commissioner,* United States Tax Court, 1947. 8 T.C. 14.

Green Sales Co., Inc. v. *United Cigar-Whelan Stores Corporation,* New York County Index No. 9559-1951.

Bedford Mills, Inc. v. *United States,* 59 F. 2d 263 (Ct. Cl. 1932).

Bibb Mfg. Co. v. *Rose,* 81 F. 2d 228 (5th Cir. 1936).

Branch v. *Kaiser,* 291 Pa. 543, 140A. 498 (1928).

Hill v. *International Products Co.,* Supreme Court of New York, New York County, 1925 129 Misc. 25 220 N.Y.S. 711.

Bowman & Bordon, Inc. v. *Rohr,* United States District Court, D. Massachusetts, 1969. 296 F. Supp. 847, aff'd per curiam 417 F. 2d 780 (1st Cir. 1969).

Vitex Mfg. Co. v. *Caribtex Corp.,* 377 F. 2d 795 (3rd Cir. 1967).

E. W. Bliss Company v. *United States,* United States District Court, N.D. Ohio, 1963. 224 F. Supp. 374.

Speed v. *Transamerica Corp.,* 99 F. Supp. 808 (D. Del. 1951), 135 F. Supp. 176 (D. Del. 1955) modified 235 F. 2d 369 (3rd Cir. 1956).

Leases

Atwater Kent Mfg. v. *Commissioner,* 43 F. 2d 441 (3rd Cir. 1930).

Frank & Seder Co. v. *Commissioner,* 44 F. 2d 147 (3rd Cir. 1930).

W. P. Brown Co. v. *Commissioner,* 26 B.T.A. 1192 (1932).

Pension Costs

New England Telephone & Telegraph Company, 53 F. Supp. 400 (D. Mass. 1943).

Stockholder Equity

Cox v. *Leahy,* Supreme Court of New York, Appellate Division, Third Department, 1924. 209 App. Div. 313, 204 N.Y.S. 741.

Equitable Life Assurance Society of United States v. *Union Pacific R.R. Co.,* 16 App. Div. 81, 147 N.Y. Supp. 382, affirmed 212 N.Y. 360, 106 N.E. 92, L.R.A 1915D, 1052.

Shaw v. *Ansaldi Co., Inc.,* 178 App. Div. 589, 599, 165 N.Y. Supp. 872.

Gilbert Paper Co. v. *Prankard,* 204 App. Div. 83, 198 N.Y. Supp. 25.

Randall v. *Bailey,* Supreme Court of New York, New York County, 1940. 2 N.Y.S. 2d 173. Aff'd 288 N.Y. 280, 43 N.E. 2d 43 (1942).

Mountain State Steel Foundries, Inc. v. *Commissioner of Interna Revenue,* United States Court of Appeals, Fourth Circuit, 1960. 284 F. 2d 737.

Goldberg v. *Peltier,* 75 R.I. 314, 66 A. 2d 107.

Bolmer Bros. Inc. v. *Bolmer Const. Co., Inc.,* Sup., 114 N.Y.S. 2d 530.

Randall v. *Bailey,* 288 N.Y. 280, 43 N.E. 2d 43.

Morris v. *Standard Gas & Electric Co.,* 31 Del Ch. 20, 63 A. 2d 577.

Acker v. *Girard Trust Co.,* 3 Cir., 42 F. 2d 37.

Friedman v. *Video Television, Inc.,* 281 App. Div. 815, 118 N.Y.S. 2d 844.

Berks Broadcasting v. *Craumer,* 356 Pa. 620, 52 A. 2d 571 (1947).

George E. Warren Co. v. *United States* 76 F. Supp. 587 (D. Mass. 1948).

Titus v. *Piggly Wiggly Corp.,* 2 Tenn. App. 184 (1925).

Kingston v. *Home Life Insurance Company,* 11 Del. Ch. 258, 101 A. 898 (Ch 1917).

Business Combinations

Cintas v. *American Car & Foundry Co.,* Court of Chancery of New Jersey, 1942 131 N.J. Eq. 419, 25 A. 2d 418.

Ray Consolidated Copper Co. v. *United States,* 268 U.S. 373 (1925).

Meyers v. *Cowdin,* 47 N.Y.S. 2d 471 (Sup. Ct. 1944).

United States v. *New York Tel. Co.,* 326 U.S. 638 66 S. Ct. 393 (1946).

National Carbide Corp. v. *Commissioner,* 336 U.S. 422, 69 S. Ct. 726 (1949).

Cash on Hand and in Banks

People v. *Dilliard,* Court of Appeals of New York, 1936. 271 N.Y. 403, 3 N.E 2d 572.

Sturgis v. *Meade County Bank,* 38 S.D. 317, 320, 161 N.W. 327, 328 (1917).

United States v. *Peters,* 87 F. 984 (C.C.D. Wash. 1898).

Hegeman v. *Corrigan,* 195 N.Y. 1, 87 N.E. 792 (1909).

Receivables

Hutchinson v. *Curtiss,* 45 Misc. 484, 92 N.Y.S. 70 (1904).

Lucas v. *North Texas Lumber Co.,* 281 U.S. 11, 50 S. Ct. 184 (1930).

Evergreen Cemetery Ass'n v. *Burnet,* 59 App. D.C. 397, 45 F. 2d 667 (1930).

Standard Lumber Co., 28 B.T.A. 352 (1933).

Frost Lumber Indus. v. *Commissioner,* 128 F. 2d 693 (5th Cir. 1942).

Commissioner v. *Segall,* 114 F. 2d 706 (6th Cir. 1940).

Inland Seed Co. v. *Washington-Idaho Seed Co.,* 160 Wash. 244, 294 Pac. 991 (1931).

Spring City Foundry Co. v. *Commissioner,* 292 U.S. 182, 54 S. Ct. 644 (1934).

People v. *Grout,* Supreme Court of New York, Appellate Division, Second Department, 1916. 174 App. Div. 608, 161 N.Y.S. 718.

O'Conner v. *Ludlan,* 92 F. 2d 50 (2d Cir. 1937).

South Texas Lumber Co. v. *Commissioner,* 333 U.S. 496, 68 S. Ct. 695 (1948).

Daley v. *United States,* United States Court of Appeals, Ninth Circuit, 1957. 243 F. 2d 466. Cert. denied 355 U.S. 832, 78 S. Ct. 46.

Maloney v. *Hammond,* 9 Cir., 1949, 176 F. 2d 780.

Deferred Tax Liability/Interperiod Tax Allocation

Appalachian Power Co. v. *AICPA,* 177 F. Supp. 345 (S.D.N.Y. 1959).

City of Alton v. *Commerce Commission,* Supreme Court of Illinois, 1960. 19 Ill. 2d 76, 165 N.E. 2d 513.

City of Chicago v. *Illinois Commerce Comm.,* 4 Ill. 2d 554, 123 N.E. 2d 500.

City of Pittsburgh v. *Pennsylvania Public Utility Comm.,* 1957, 182 Pa. Super. 551, 573 /74, 128 A. 2d 372.

Central Maine Power Co. v. *Public Utilities Comm.,* 153 Me. 228, 136 A. 2d 726.

City of Pittsburgh v. *Pennsylvania Public Utilities Comm.,* 182 Pa. Super. 551, 128 A. 2d 372.

Alabama-Tennessee Natural Gas Company v. *Federal Power Commission,* United States Court of Appeals, Fifth Circuit, 1966. 395 F. 2d 318. Certiorari denied, 385 U.S. 847, 87 S. Ct. 69, 17 L.Ed. 2d 78.

United States v. *Klinger,* 2 Cir., 1952, 199 E. 2d 645.

Midwestern Gas Transmission Co. v. *Federal Power Commission,* 388 F. 2d 444 (7th Cir. 1968), cert. denied 392 U.S. 928, 88 S. Ct. 2286, 20 L.Ed. 2d 1386 (1968).

Pittsburgh v. *Pennsylvania, P.U.C.,* 187 Pa. Super. 341, 144 A. 2d 648, 25 P.U.R. 3d 273 (1958).

Pacific Telephone & Telegraph Company, 77 P.U.R. 3d 1 (1968).

Cost Accounting

Vitex Mfg. Co. v. *Caribtex Corp.,* 377 F. 2d 795 (3rd Cir. 1967).

Standard Oil Company, 41 F.T.C. 263, aff'd 173 F. 2d 210 (7th Cir. 1949), rev'd on other grounds, 340 U.S. 231, 71 S. Ct. 240 (1950).

Piggly Wiggly Corporation v. *United States,* United States Court of Claims, 1949. 81 F. Supp. 819.

Re Washington Gas Light Co., District of Columbia Public Utilities Commission, 1949. 83 P.U.R. (N.S.) 4.

Chelrob v. *Barrett,* Court of Appeals of New York, 1944. 293 N.Y. 442, 57 N.E. 2d 825.

Butler Bros. v. *McColgan,* Supreme Court of the United States, 1942. 315 U.S. 501, 62 S. Ct. 701, 86 L. Ed. 991.

Great Atlantic & Pacific Tea Co. v. *Grosjean,* 301 U.S. 412, 57 S. Ct. 772, 8
    L.Ed. 1193, 112 A.L.R. 293.
American Can Co. v. *Russellville Canning Co.,* United States Court of Appeals
    Eighth Circuit, 1951. 191 F. 2d 38.
Bruce's Juices, Inc., v. *American Can Co.,* 330 U.S. 743, 67 S. Ct. 1015, 91 L.Ed.
    1219.
Armour & Co. v. *Bowles,* United States Emergency Court of Appeals, 1945. 14
    F. 2d 529.

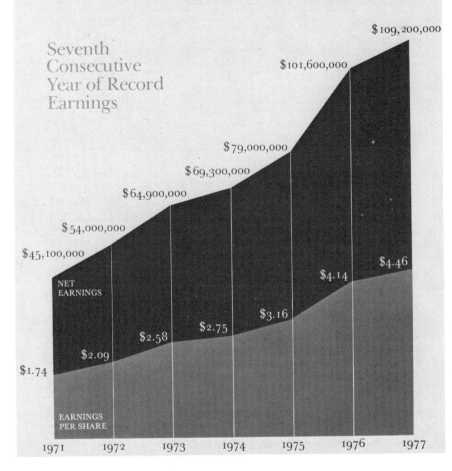

Dart Industries Inc.
1977 Annual Report

Seventh
Consecutive
Year of Record
Earnings

$109,200,000

$101,600,000

$79,000,000

$69,300,000

$64,900,000

$54,000,000

$45,100,000

NET
EARNINGS

$4.14

$4.46

$3.16

$2.75

$2.58

$2.09

$1.74

EARNINGS
PER SHARE

1971   1972   1973   1974   1975   1976   1977

Table of Contents

Annual Meeting

Company Description 1

The Year in Brief 2

Sales and Pre-tax Earnings by
Operating Segments 2

Letter to Stockholders 3

Operations Review 7

Companies, Products and
Group Management 15

Financial Statements 17

Summary of Accounting Policies 18

Five-Year Summary of Operations
and Management's Discussion 33

Ten Years at a Glance 35

Board of Directors 37

Officers and Committees 38

Investor Information 39

The Annual Meeting of Stockholders of Dart Industries Inc. will be held at 9 a.m. on Thursday May 4, 1978, at Corporate Headquarters, 8480 Beverly Boulevard, Los Angeles, California.

NOTE: Product names printed in *italics* on all pages indicate trademarks.

Company Description

Dart Industries Inc. is a diversified company with emphasis on the manufacturing and marketing of consumer products, chemicals, plastics and packaging.

Its products are marketed directly to consumers in the home or through retail outlets, or indirectly through intermediate manufacturers and converters whose products are used by consumers.

An enterprise of more than 40 operating divisions and approximately 31,000 employees, Dart Industries is divided into four primary operating segments—Direct Selling, Consumer Products, Chemical-Plastics and Glass Containers.

Among Dart Industries' better known products are *Tupperware* plastic containers for preparing, storing and serving food, *West Bend* cookware and electric housewares, *Syroco* home decorative accessories, *Coppercraft Guild* giftware and *Wilsonart* decorative laminates.

Other products include *El Rexene* plastic resins used in the manufacture of packaging materials and a variety of consumer products, and *Thatcher* glass containers and bottles for the packaging of foods and beverages.

Still other products include chemical and plastic specialties, pollution control equipment and services, and plastic cups, tubes and containers.

Of the Company's total operations, approximately 25 percent of sales and 39 percent of after-tax earnings come from activities outside the United States. These activities include *Tupperware* plastic containers, plastic packaging and chemical specialties.

Corporate headquarters for Dart Industries is in Los Angeles, California. The mailing address is P.O. Box 3157, Terminal Annex, Los Angeles, California 90051.

The Year in Brief

		1977	1976
Operations	Net sales	$1,600,988,000	$1,476,240,000
	Earnings before taxes	200,696,000	190,613,000
	Net earnings	109,196,000	101,613,000
	Earnings per share of Common Stock		
	Primary	4.46	4.14*
	Fully diluted	4.18	3.88*
	Return on average		
	Stockholders' equity	13.6%	14.0%
	Return on net sales	6.8%	6.9%
At Yearend	Current assets	$ 795,037,000	$ 708,883,000
	Current liabilities	274,486,000	243,283,000
	Working capital	520,551,000	465,600,000
	Long term debt	238,716,000	241,188,000
	Stockholders' equity	846,013,000	765,077,000
	Shares of Common Stock outstanding	23,132,600	23,111,200*
	Shares of Preferred Stock outstanding	2,948,500	2,953,500

*Adjusted for 3% Common Stock dividend paid in May 1977.

Sales and Pre-tax Earnings by Operating Segments

(Dollar amounts in millions)	1977		1976		1975		1974		1973	
	SALES	EARNINGS	SALES	EARNINGS	SALES	EARNINGS	SALES	EARNINGS	SALES	EARNINGS
Direct Selling	$ 575	$146.3	$ 512	$133.1	$ 459	$108.5	$ 394	$ 98.0	$305	$ 77.1
Consumer Products	206	25.5	244	27.8	237	19.8	241	20.4	208	16.4
Chemical and Plastics	253	18.3	232	33.8	170	31.6	205	65.4	135	23.8
	315	28.5	279	17.1	228	11.6	227	23.7	203	23.2
Glass Containers	260	21.7	229	29.8	199	30.1	163	18.8	142	13.4
Resort Development	16	(1.9)	10	(15.3)	10	(17.5)	9	(34.9)	10	(7.2)
Adjustments and eliminations	(24)	(6.0)	(30)	(7.9)	(23)	(6.4)	(21)	(8.4)	(10)	(2.9)
Corporate items		(31.7)		(27.8)		(21.2)		(42.3)		(21.3)
Totals	$1,601	$200.7	$1,476	$190.6	$1,280	$156.5	$1,218	$140.7	$993	$122.5

Direct Selling includes Tupperware sales as follows: 1977—$509; 1976—$442; 1975—$382; 1974—$312; 1973—$232. For additional segment operating detail see page 24.

Letter to Stockholders

During 1977, Dart Industries achieved a number of its major objectives for the year, which were outlined at the Annual Meeting of Stockholders in May, and moved substantially forward on others. These achievements included the following:

1. Net earnings, earnings per share and sales reached record highs;

2. The program for correction or elimination of problem areas was advanced significantly, providing the base for an improved return on investment;

3. Studies defining the overall growth strategy of the Company as a whole and long-term growth plans for its divisions are underway;

4. A study of dividend policy was undertaken and although not completed, indicates your Company's current and anticipated ability to support an all-cash dividend at a substantially higher level than heretofore. Initial implementing steps were taken early in 1978;

5. The Company's organizational capabilities, including its depth of management, were strengthened with the infusion of new management talents and the realignment of responsibilities to better utilize the capabilities of present senior management.

Another Record Year

Net earnings, earnings per share and sales increased in 1977 for the seventh consecutive year. Net earnings and earnings per share were at record levels of $109.2 million and $4.46 respectively, compared with $101.6 million and $4.14 in 1976. Sales reached $1.6 billion, up from $1.5 billion in 1976.

The improved results came principally from an excellent increase in Tupperware division sales, a substantial gain in profitability from the plastics segment of the Chemical-Plastics Group and a significant reduction in the loss in resort operations.

These positives overcame sizable declines in chemical and glass container operations. Chemical operations were depressed by lower than expected prices in the polyolefins area and slow attainment of efficient production levels at the new polypro-

pylene plant in Bayport, Texas. Glass container results were lowered by a combination of higher costs that could not be offset by price increases and a four-week industry-wide strike of mold makers.

Operations outside the United States contributed $42.3 million in after-tax earnings, 39 percent of the total, compared with $33.3 million, 33 percent of the total in 1976. Sales from these operations were $400 million compared with $364 million in 1976.

Losses on foreign currency translation in 1977 and 1976 were not material.

Business Reassessment

In line with management's policy of continually reassessing Dart Industries' businesses, the decision was made to close down or sell direct selling cosmetics operations in Australia and Mexico and to change the operating methods, including reductions in product lines and personnel and other streamlining actions, for the direct selling cosmetics divisions in Europe and for a consumer products operation. In addition, provision has been made for phasing out or selling certain chemical operations. Divisions involved in these actions accounted for net sales of $67 million in 1977.

Provision for the costs of these actions, which include writedowns of properties, goodwill and other assets as well as accruals for termination benefits and other costs, aggregated $11.7 million after related tax benefits, or approximately 51 cents per share. Such provision was charged to earnings in December 1977.

Cash Dividend Increased

Following a review of overall dividend policy, the Board of Directors at its meeting of January 30, 1978, raised the cash dividend 60 percent from 25 cents to 40 cents quarterly, or from an annual rate of $1.00 to $1.60 per share of Common Stock. This was the sixth consecutive year that the cash dividend was increased. At the same time, the decision was made to eliminate the three percent stock dividend.

The Board's intention to consider both increases in the cash dividend and possible stock dividends was announced at its February 1977 meeting. At that time, the Board also increased the cash dividend to 25 cents and declared a three percent stock dividend on the Common Stock.

The change to an all-cash dividend reflects the Board's and management's confidence in the future earnings growth of the Company. It is believed this growth will generate sufficient funds for identified needs and continued expansion of current businesses and the addition of attractive new investment opportunities as they arise, as well as payment of appropriate dividends.

Management believes the three percent stock dividend, which had been paid annually since 1959, had served its purpose of conserving cash to finance the growth of Company operations overall and particularly the expansion of the Tupperware division during the '60's and early '70's. The Company would not have been able to grow, relying principally on internal financing, without the stock dividend policy.

In view of the present and substantially higher base of earnings, your Company now can replace the Common Stock dividend with a higher cash dividend than it formerly paid without impeding continued growth.

Financial Condition

An important basis for the dividend action is the Company's exceptionally strong balance sheet. At year-end 1977, current ratio (current assets compared with current liabilities) was 2.9:1. Cash and marketable securities were $246 million and total assets increased to $1.4 billion. Common Stockholders' equity was $699 million, the equivalent of $30.20 per share of Common Stock. Debt was reduced to a ratio of 28 cents to $1.00 of equity.

Return on total capital, which has averaged 10.1 percent over the five-year period ending in 1977, was 11.0 percent at year-end 1977 and 10.9 percent in 1976.

Return on average Stockholders' equity was 13.6 percent in 1977 compared with 14.0 percent in 1976. Return on equity over the five years ending in 1977 averaged 12.7 percent.

Capital Expenditures

In 1977, capital expenditures totaled $94.6 million; $115 million has been budgeted for 1978.

These expenditures continue to be heavily weighted in those divisions that are providing returns on investment approaching, equalling or exceeding 15 percent after-tax.

Depreciation and amortization was $59 million in 1977, up from $52 million in 1976.

The investment tax credit in 1977 applied to reduce United States income taxes was $5.5 mil-

lion. In 1976 this figure was $6.9 million. For 1978, the investment tax credit is currently expected to be $3.9 million.

Management Changes

A number of important actions were taken in 1977 to provide for an orderly transition and to further strengthen and increase the depth of Dart Industries' top management team in the areas of day-to-day operations and forward planning. All group operations continue to report to the Company president, as does the Corporate Staff.

Phillip D. Matthews, Executive Vice President, Finance and Administration.

In August, Phillip D. Matthews, 39, joined the Company as executive vice president, Finance and Administration, and chief financial officer, with responsibility for Corporate Staff administration. He also was elected to the Board of Directors. Mr. Matthews formerly was a senior vice president with Frito-Lay, Inc., a division of Pepsico, Inc. Previously, he had held a series of increasingly responsible financial and operating positions with Pepsico.

He succeeded Donald H. Brewer, 65, who retired from active employment on December 31, 1977, but continues as a member of the Board's Audit and Executive Committees. We are extremely fortunate to have Mr. Brewer's continued advice and participation as an outside director and as a member of two important committees of the Board.

Also in August, the merger of the Chemical and Plastics Groups was effected into one operating group, with John P. Del Favero, 49, as president. Mr. Del Favero has been with Dart Industries since April 1976, when he was appointed president of the Plastics Group. He was elected a vice president of the Company in May of that year and a member of the Board of Directors last August.

In order to strengthen Consumer Products marketing activities, F. William Graham, 40, became a vice president of the Company and president of the Consumer Products Group on December 1. Mr. Graham formerly was group vice president and general manager of the Fashion Group of companies of General Mills, Inc. While with that firm, he developed and implemented its expansion into a major new growth area, then supervised the companies he was instrumental in acquiring.

Ralph M. Knight, 62, former chairman of the Chemical Group, has joined the office of the Chairman of the Board, where he has a lead role in exploring and nurturing technological opportunities as part of Dart Industries' search for new growth areas. He also is providing technical advice on chemical operating matters and continues to serve as an executive vice president and a member of the Board of Directors.

Robert T. Beattie, 66, former president of the Consumer Products Group, also has joined the office of the Chairman and continues as an executive vice president and member of the Board of Directors. He is focusing his attention on acquisitions and divestitures, as well as the forward planning of the Company's various consumer-oriented businesses.

New Outside Directors

Dwayne O. Andreas, 59, was elected to the Board of Directors in November 1977. Mr. Andreas is chairman and chief executive of Archer-Daniels-Midland Company, of Decatur, Illinois, a firm that purchases, processes and markets agricultural crops and the resulting products. He also is a member of the Board of Directors of the National City Bank of Minneapolis, Lone Star Industries and White Motor Corporation, and is active in numerous civic and charitable organizations.

At the Board's January 1978 meeting, William E. Simon, 50, former Secretary of the Treasury, was elected a director. Mr. Simon, well known for his financial expertise, is presently senior consultant with Blyth Eastman Dillon & Co., Inc., an investment banking firm, and senior advisor at Booz Allen & Hamilton, Inc., a management consulting firm. He also is on the Board of Directors of Citibank and Citicorp, INA Corporation, and Xerox Corporation. An active supporter of public service and educational organizations, Mr. Simon serves as president of the John M. Olin Foundation, chairman of the National Energy Foundation and a trustee of Lafayette College and Georgetown University. In late 1973, Mr. Simon was named administrator of the Federal Energy Office and in 1974 was appointed the 63rd Secretary of the Treasury in the administration of President Ford.

Outlook for 1978

Our primary objective for 1978 is that Dart Industries achieve another record year, which would be its eighth consecutive year of improved earnings. Barring the unforeseen, we currently anticipate that it will.

Justin Dart, Chairman, left,
Thomas P. Mullaney, President.

JUSTIN DART
Chairman

THOMAS P. MULLANEY
President

February 27, 1978

Operations Review

Direct Selling*

All ages enjoy preparing and serving food with the assistance of colorful *Tupperware* plastic containers and the multi-use *West Bend Slo-Cooker Plus* electric cooker. Other consumer products shown on opposite page include *Thermo-Serv* insulated serving ware; *Coppercraft Guild* serving accessories and jewelry; *Syroco Decorette* wall plaques; and *West Bend Silverstone* and stainless steel cookware, electric appliances and *Quik-Drip* coffeemaker. The table and counter top are *Wilson-art* decorated laminate in the Butcher Block pattern.

The Tupperware division in 1977 started its second quarter century by once again setting new sales records in North and South America, the Pacific and European areas.

All the indices important to the continued success of Tupperware were up from 1976 levels— retail sales, home parties held, attendance at these parties and sales per party. In addition, and keeping pace with the increased Tupperware division's sales from $442 million in 1976 to $509 million in 1977, were the continued growth to record highs in the size of its worldwide network of independent distributors, managers and dealers.

Operations outside the United States continued to contribute more than 50 percent of the total sales and earnings of the division. However, the United States market, the oldest of its operations, contributed a larger percentage increase over 1976 sales and earnings than did the total of operations outside the United States, once again demonstrating the ongoing growth potential for the Tupperware division.

The accomplishment of Tupperware Brazil has been particularly outstanding. Sales began in mid-1976 and growth has been so rapid that 25 new injection molding machines to manufacture *Tupperware* products had to be added to the original 10-machine plant near Rio de Janeiro starting in mid-1977. Prospects for continued growth are excellent, and accordingly, a second manufacturing plant has been purchased near Sao Paulo and is expected to be in production in 1978.

Other expansions during 1977 included the move to a larger plant in Venezuela and initiation of construction on a new, larger plant near Auckland, New Zealand. In Japan, a new 200,000 square-foot warehouse and distribution center was formally opened during the first quarter. Plans for a new production facility in Portugal have been presented to authorities in that country.

Financial data for Miracle Maid and Coppercraft Guild are included in Direct Selling in the operating segment table on pages 2 and 24; operations of these two divisions are reported under Consumer Products.

Production capacity was added during the year in Mexico, Greece and Canada. The growth prospects in Canada, indicated by an increase of 20 percent in the number of independent distributors serving that country, warranted the opening of new office facilities in Toronto and the preparation of plans for a second manufacturing plant to be located in Western Canada.

New Products

In each of the over 30 countries served by the division, an average of six new *Tupperware* products were introduced in 1977, adding to the interest and excitement of holding and attending parties. Development currently underway includes new *Tupperware* products for food preparation, serving and storing that will provide for product introductions into the 1980's, while long-

New *Tuppercraft* Planting System will be introduced at Tupperware home parties during 1978. The system includes a planter and well with an easy-view watering indicator, planting medium and decorative stones, liquid nutrient, and instructional brochure. This indoor planting system will be available in various sizes and colors. The large size is pictured below.

range market and technical research is involved in planning for 1985 and beyond.

Late in 1977, the beginning of a new series of non-food oriented, in-home use products, the *Tuppercraft* Planting System, was introduced to independent dealers, managers and distributors in the United States. Included is an attractive planter and well to hold the planting medium and water. The well has an easy-viewing indicator to show the proper water level. The reaction to this new line has been enthusiastic and it is expected to be introduced at Tupperware home parties in the United States during the first half of 1978.

New Markets
New countries for the division are under constant evaluation. The reception of *Tupperware* products in Brazil has encouraged the Company to enter Argentina and Chile. Plans are currently underway and in this connection land has been purchased in Argentina near Buenos Aires for construction of a manufacturing plant. In 1977 sales were initiated in Morocco. The division is in the process of entering Iran.

Vanda Beauty Counselor
A number of actions have been taken relating to the Vanda Beauty Counselor division in line with the Company's policy of correcting or eliminating divisions operating at a loss. Direct selling cosmetics operations in Italy were phased out during 1977, with losses associated with the closing provided for at year-end 1976.

As stated in the Letter to Stockholders, the decision was made to close down or sell Vanda Beauty Counselor operations in Australia and Mexico. These operations now have been sold. Also, provision was made to change the operating methods, including reductions of product lines and personnel and other streamlining actions, in European operations. Provision for the cost of these actions is reflected in 1977 earnings.

Of the remaining direct selling cosmetics operations, Canada and South Africa continued to operate profitably in 1977. Sales in the United States, potentially the largest single market for *Vanda Beauty Counselor* cosmetics and toiletries, were about the same as in 1976.

Consumer Products

Results for the Consumer Products Group were lower than 1976 levels because of charges to earnings relating to the decision to consolidate certain product lines and streamline operations within the Home Furnishings and Giftware division.

Housewares Division
West Bend is a leading, quality producer of aluminum and stainless steel cookware, small electric appliances and home humidifiers. Earnings in 1977 improved over 1976 and a number of *West Bend* brand products strengthened their market position. The division manufactured its two millionth humidifier since starting production of these products in 1965, and now is the largest humidifier manufacturer in the country.

In addition, the *West Bend Slo-Cooker Plus* electric cooker and the *West Bend* Wok, respectively introduced in 1976 and 1974, presently are the number one selling brands in their retail markets. The success of these products reflects consumer interest in preparing simple, low-cost meals at home.

West Bend's position as the number one pro-

West Bend introduced *Stir Crazy,* the electric corn popper with its own built-in stirring rod, in late 1977. The popper decreases popping time while increasing the volume of popped corn received from the same amount of kernels. It pops from two to six quarts at one time.

ducer of electric corn poppers was strengthened further in 1977 with introduction of the *Stir Crazy* popper. Other new products introduced in 1977 include an automatic egg cooker, a bag maker-sealer, and the *Slim Line* automatic grill.

The Specialty Steel division of West Bend, which supplies stainless steel cookware to independent direct selling distributors, realized a strong growth in sales and earnings.

*Miracle Maid,** a premium line of quality cookware that is sold directly to the consumer in the United States and Canada through demonstrations in the home, experienced customer price resistance to an improved product line introduced early in 1977. This factor, along with dealer inexperience in demonstrating the new line, resulted in decreased sales and earnings in 1977. Although the improved line is more expensive than the former *Miracle Maid* product line, its

Financial data on Miracle Maid and Coppercraft Guild, whose products are sold directly in the home, are included in Direct Selling in the operating segment table on pages 2 and 24.

superior appearance and durability, plus ease of cleaning, are expected to result in improved sales in 1978.

The extensive realignment begun in 1976 of the Housewares division's manufacturing facilities to improve productivity has been completed and provides important cost-saving efficiencies, which should give West Bend a more competitive position in 1978.

Home Furnishings and Giftware Division
Coppercraft Guild,* which manufactures copper giftware and sells its products directly to the consumer, recorded an excellent increase in earnings. Improved recruiting of independent dealers, an upgraded product line and the record number of parties held were contributing factors.

Syroco had moderate gains in earnings and sales of decorative home accessories. The new *Decorette* line of wall decorations, designed for retail stores and mass merchandisers, has been well received. Gains also were recorded in sales to direct selling companies.

Thermo-Serv, a manufacturer of insulated serving accessories, and Nappe-Smith, manufacturer of insulated bags and specialty carrying cases, had higher earnings on sales that compared favorably with 1976. Plans are underway to combine Nappe-Smith and Babcock-Phillips, manufacturer of hassocks and casual furniture, in order to provide additional production capacity for Nappe-Smith and streamline the operations of both divisions.

Chemical-Plastics

The combining of the former Chemical and
Plastics Groups was effected in 1977, with the
new group comprising over one-third of Company
sales. Technical, marketing and economic benefits
are expected to result from the combination. The
divisions in the new group are related principally
through their applications of chemical and plastics
technology to diversified products and markets.
Plastic raw materials and a variety of chemical
and plastic-based specialties and other end
products are manufactured and sold to industrial,
consumer, construction, automotive and
appliance markets.

CHEMICAL OPERATIONS
Chemical operations achieved record sales in
1977. However, lower operating earnings in the
plastic raw materials sector, as well as provisions
for selling or closing certain operations, resulted in
substantially lower earnings than the prior year,
despite improvements in both the Chemical Specialties and Environment and Services sectors.

Plastic Raw Materials Sector
The Plastic Raw Materials sector's earnings
were lower than the year before because of the
inability to fully pass on increased costs. In
addition, performance was hampered by delayed
attainment of efficient production levels at the new
polypropylene plant* in Bayport, Texas. Prime
product yield at the new plant improved during
the year and operations neared design capacity of
150 million pounds annually by year-end.

Margin pressures were responsible for lower
earnings from low-density polyethylene sales even
though shipments were 90 percent of total capacity of 400 million pounds annually. The new low-
density polyethylene plant* at Bayport is in start-
up. When in full production it will add 150 million
pounds per year to capacity and will enable the
sector to keep pace with the anticipated long-
range growth in market demand for this product.

Competitive pressures kept earnings at
Consolidated Thermoplastics Company* essen-

Jointly owned with El Paso Products Company

tially unchanged from 1976 despite increased
sales of packaging film.

Styrenics operations reduced their losses from
the prior year on the strength of higher sales of
polystyrene and more favorable prices for acrylo-
nitrile-butadiene-styrene (ABS). Current management projections are that for the next several
years, this industry will continue to experience
over-capacity in relation to demand.

Operations of the Southwest Latex division,
manufacturer of styrene latices for carpet and
paper applications, have been terminated.

Chemical Specialties Sector
The Chemical Specialties sector attained
record sales and earnings with the improvement
registered almost across the board.

Wilson Products, particularly in Europe, benefited from high sales of colorants to the wire and
cable industry. The Synthetic Products division
also showed a good increase in earnings on
stronger sales of stearates and stabilizers used in
the manufacture of plastic and rubber products.

The Catalyst division experienced strong
growth during 1977 and began construction on a
new perester plant at its Bayport location so the
division can participate further in the rapidly
growing market for these products, which are used
in the manufacture of plastic resins.

Results for Fiberfil, a manufacturer of fiberglass-reinforced thermoplastics, were off from a
year ago. Its automotive-application sales were
affected principally by intensified competition,
which kept price increases at a level insufficient to
recover cost increases.

The Chemical Specialties sector is receiving
special attention and emphasis in the Company's
future growth plans because of the balance it can
provide in relation to the more cyclical Plastic
Raw Materials sector.

Environment and Services Sector
The Environment and Services sector, led by
continuing excellent results of its Capital Controls
division (chlorinators and water purification

Wilson Products produces color concentrates used in the manufacture of plastic parts for automobiles, appliances and other products. One of the largest uses is in color coating of wire and cable such as telephone cable, shown above left, which contains more than 100 color-coded wires.

Chem-Surf decorative laminate and *Soli-Core* matching edging, manufactured by the Wilsonart division, have helped put an end to drab laboratories. The chemical and stain-resistant laminate and solid color edgings are available in 12 colors, including Tangerine shown above right in installation at Scottsdale Memorial Hospital, Scottsdale, Arizona.

control systems) and the receipt of orders for Fluid-Ionic Systems' wet electrostatic precipitators, showed good improvement in 1977 from depressed levels of the prior year.

Demand for Capital Controls' products has required an expansion of the division's existing production facilities at Colmar, Pennsylvania.

Fluid-Ionic Systems' *Hydro-Precipitrol* wet electrostatic precipitators, used to remove airborne pollutants in industrial plants, successfully completed product testing at a number of industrial locations in 1976 and early 1977.

The newly formed Fiberglass Equipment division, combining two of the divisions producing pollution control equipment and components, was negatively impacted by less than expected demand as well as the development costs for system components.

Development and Engineering Sector

In view of the increasing emphasis on strengthening the Company's technology base, construction began in 1977 on expanded research and development facilities in Paramus, New Jersey. The expanded facilities will support on-going and new process and product development programs for the combined Chemical-Plastics Group operations.

Programs conducted during 1977 assisted in improving cost effectiveness of manufacturing processes and reducing the group's energy consumption by approximately nine percent. Development and commercial scale testing was completed on a second generation catalyst used in the manufacture of polypropylene. Use of the new product provided more efficient and less costly conversion of propylene into polypropylene in initial plant-scale trials.

PLASTICS OPERATIONS

Plastics operations recorded a substantial earnings improvement in 1977 on a 13 percent sales increase. Equally important was the progress made in improving the return on investment of these operations and the sale or elimination of a number of marginal businesses. These latter actions

included selling surgical instrument operations in Europe and a counter top manufacturing division in the United States and reorganizing the hospital disposable products operations in the United States along with several packaging operations in Europe.

Decorative Building Products Sector

The Decorative Building Products sector, producer of *Wilsonart* laminates for interior surfacing in homes and commercial buildings, recorded new highs in sales and earnings aided equally by its emphasis upon service to consumers and the continued strength of housing, remodeling and commercial construction markets.

The long-term outlook for the sector's products led to the decision to expand capacity. Construction will begin in 1978 on a second manufacturing plant for high pressure laminates to be located near Asheville, North Carolina. The plant is expected to start producing in 1979 to serve *Wilsonart* customers in the eastern United States more efficiently, and initially will add 20 percent capacity to the sector's existing facility at Temple, Texas.

Specialties Sector

The Specialties sector's results continued to improve substantially.

Colorite Plastics is now the largest producer of plastic garden hose in the United States and one of the largest compounders of non-toxic plastics used to manufacture food packaging and medical and hospital products.

The operations of divisions manufacturing tubing for ball point pens, sealing specialties, and a variety of other end products have experienced excellent growth in recent years. These operations have been combined to form a new division— Action Technology. The combining of these operations is expected to provide administrative efficiencies and expedite their entrance into new markets such as hose and tubing for medical applications and consumer products.

The Seamco sporting goods operation in its first full year at its new La Grange, Georgia, plant returned to profitable operations.

Thompson Industries is introducing Decorator Designed *Styrocup* containers and Deluxe and Party Styroware utensils into retail outlets. The containers are available in three designs—swirly brown and tan, yellow and green sunflower, and yellow and orange fern—while the new tray-packed plastic utensils may be purchased in gold, orange and white.

Packaging Sector

Packaging operations, which include plastic bottles, tubes and closures, also showed improvement in 1977 despite the negative impact of a 10-week strike at Thatcher Plastic Packaging's Muscatine, Iowa, plant. Improvement in plastic bottle operations overseas from depressed 1976 levels was the primary contributor to the overall improvement in operations.

Styro Products Sector

Styro Products sector earnings were behind 1976 levels principally due to pricing pressures in plastic foam drinking cup markets in the United States.

Rexcel, aided by record sales and the success of its new process-print technology used in the manufacture of plastic dairy containers, achieved an excellent improvement over 1976 levels. The new technology, which Rexcel pioneered in the United States, makes it possible to print colored pictorial scenes on the exterior sidewalls of tapered plastic food containers.

While operations in Canada achieved satisfactory results in 1977, the decline in value of the Canadian dollar in relation to the U.S. dollar resulted in lower reported earnings.

Current indications are for margin improvement during 1978 for Thompson Industries' plastic foam drinking cups. The division is in an excellent position to further capitalize on its already strong mid-America market penetration through the addition in 1977 of a new plant in Higginsville, Missouri. In addition, the division has introduced a decorated plastic foam cup line into the retail market, which is expected to add to growth.

Health Care Sector

The Health Care sector, which showed favorable sales and earnings improvement in 1977, is expected to benefit further from extensive attention by new management in the development of business strategies, including emphasis on products for the growing hospital disposable products market.

Glass Containers

Thatcher Glass Manufacturing Company is the fourth largest United States producer of glass containers. The company operates six manufacturing plants, plus two mold-making facilities. Glass containers for beer account for the largest part of Thatcher's product mix, while containers for wine, liquor and food combined represent the next largest percentage. Containers for soft drinks are the smallest percentage.

While Thatcher's sales increased in 1977, earnings were down from the prior year. Severe weather conditions during the first quarter, rising costs that could not be passed on to customers through price increases, and a month-long strike of mold makers—which impacted operations in the third and fourth quarters—were the factors affecting earnings. The industry-wide strike reduced Company earnings by $4.5 million pre-tax, or nine cents per share. Thatcher's labor contracts now extend into 1980.

Capital expenditures for glass container operations, which have averaged $18 million annually over the past five years, have been principally for the purpose of keeping Thatcher's manufacturing plants thoroughly up-to-date, improving return on investment through greater production efficiency, and making incremental expansions in production capacity where market conditions warrant. In addition, provisions have been made for converting furnaces so they can use oil as well as natural gas for fuel, for installing pollution control equipment, and for modifying bottle-making machinery for the faster production of lighter weight containers.

As a result of the latter program, Thatcher now has the ability to produce lightweight beer containers at most of its plants. These containers weigh approximately seven percent less than conventional beer bottles and make it possible for bottlers to achieve faster filling speeds. Being able to produce the new containers at a majority of its plants is expected to help Thatcher achieve a larger share of the beer packaging market.

The activity of introducing and attempting to implement legislation designed to reduce litter continues at all levels of government. When such legislation appears discriminatory toward the packaging industry in general and glass containers in particular, Thatcher and other members of the glass container industry continue to oppose it. Thatcher believes that legislation such as the state of Washington broad-based tax on all products producing litter is far more desirable than legislation that singles out the packaging industry.

Dart Resorts

Dart Resorts had a 63 percent increase in sales in 1977, highlighted by outstanding sales at the Bear Valley Springs resort community, which is located in Southern California north of Los Angeles. Operating losses were very sharply reduced from 1976.

More than 1,000 homesite sales were recorded at Bear Valley Springs during 1977, over twice the number sold in 1976. Approximately 78 percent of the total inventory of 3,860 homesites in this project had been sold by year-end.

The 18-month ban on homesite sales at Tahoe Donner, the Company's other resort community, was lifted following an appeal by Dart Resorts and five days of public hearings. The ban had been issued by the California Department of Real Estate for the area north of Lake Tahoe—including Tahoe Donner—pending assurance of adequate sewage disposal facilities in the area. Sales of homesites were resumed late in December after obtaining the necessary state and federal public reports on the property. Approximately 1,900 homesites, 32 percent of the total inventory at Tahoe Donner, had been sold prior to the ban.

Building by property owners continued at a very brisk pace at both resort communities with over 100 new homes constructed during the year. There are now approximately 630 private-owner homes and over 200 condominiums completed at the two projects.

The year also saw the sale of remaining homesite inventories at the Alta Sierra, Prosser Lakeview Estates and Valley Hi resort developments in three separate transactions. The Company had only a minority interest in the first two projects.

Dart Industries Inc.

Companies, Products & Group Management

Direct Selling Group

HAMER F. WILSON, *Executive Vice President of the Company; Chairman of the Direct Selling Group.*

HEADQUARTERS: *Orlando, Florida*

TUPPERWARE DIVISION: *food preparation, storage and serving containers; toys*
VANDA BEAUTY COUNSELOR DIVISION: *cosmetics and toiletries*

Consumer Products Group

F. WILLIAM GRAHAM, *Vice President of the Company; President of the Consumer Products Group.*

HEADQUARTERS: *Los Angeles, California*

BABCOCK-PHILLIPS: *furniture, cushions, pillows, hassocks*
COPPERCRAFT GUILD—COPPERCRAFT GUILD CANADA: *copper giftware, jewelry and decorative items*
NAPPE-SMITH COMPANY: *insulated bags, specialty carrying cases*

SYROCO-SYROCO CANADA: *home decorative accessories, casual furniture*
THERMO-SERV: *insulated and non-insulated serving ware*
THE WEST BEND COMPANY—WEST BEND OF CANADA: *cookware, electric housewares, humidifiers*

Chemical-Plastics Group

JOHN P. DEL FAVERO, *Vice President of the Company; President of the Chemical-Plastics Group.*

HEADQUARTERS: *Los Angeles, California*

CHEMICAL OPERATIONS

PLASTIC RAW MATERIALS SECTOR

CONSOLIDATED THERMOPLASTICS: *packaging film (jointly owned with El Paso Products Company)*
REXENE POLYOLEFINS COMPANY: *polyethylene, polypropylene and olefins (joint venture with El Paso Products Company, olefins by El Paso)*
REXENE STYRENICS: *polystyrene, ABS, oriented polystyrene sheeting*

CHEMICAL SPECIALTIES SECTOR

CATALYST DIVISION-AZTEC/PURECHEM: *organic peroxides and peresters, titanium trichloride*
ELECTROCHEMICALS: *chemicals for electroplating*
FIBERFIL: *fiberglass-reinforced and filled thermoplastics*
SYNTHETIC PRODUCTS: *metallic stearates, vinyl stabilizers*
WILSON PRODUCTS: *color concentrates and dispersions*

ENVIRONMENT AND SERVICES SECTOR

CAPITAL CONTROLS: *chlorinators and control systems for water purification and waste treatment*
ENVIRONMENTAL RESEARCH COMPANY: *air and water pollution control systems*
FIBERGLASS EQUIPMENT DIVISION: *Century fiberglass-reinforced plastic tanks, pipe, and air scrubbers; Heil pollution control and chemical processing equipment*
FLUID-IONIC SYSTEMS: *wet electrostatic precipitators for industrial air pollution control*
LANCY LABORATORIES: *waste treatment engineering and services*

DEVELOPMENT AND ENGINEERING SECTOR

Research and development, facilities construction

PLASTICS OPERATIONS

DECORATIVE BUILDING PRODUCTS SECTOR

WILSONART: *decorative laminates, laminated art*

PACKAGING SECTOR

THATCHER PLASTIC PACKAGING: *tubes, closures, seals*
IMCO COMPANIES (BELGIUM, HOLLAND, ENGLAND, SPAIN, AUSTRALIA): *plastic bottles*

STYRO PRODUCTS SECTOR

THOMPSON INDUSTRIES, REXCEL, CANADA CUP, INSULPAK, LTD., CAMIRA, N.V.: *plastic cups, food containers and dinnerware*

SPECIALTIES SECTOR

(1)ACTION PLASTICS: *extruded specialties*
AMERICAN GASKET AND RUBBER: *aerosol gaskets, rubber products*
ACTION PLASTICS AND RUBBER COMPANY (BELGIUM): *extruded specialties and aerosol gaskets*
COLORITE PLASTICS: *garden hose, compounding*
SEAMCO: *sporting goods and recreational products*

HEALTH CARE SECTOR

SEAMLESS HOSPITAL PRODUCTS: *medical and surgical products*

Glass Containers Group

WILLIAM H. GREENBERG, *Vice President of the Company; President of the Glass Containers Group.*

HEADQUARTERS: *Greenwich, Connecticut*

THATCHER GLASS: *convenience packaging*

Dart Resorts

SIDNEY M. KARSH, *President of Dart Resorts.*

HEADQUARTERS: *Los Angeles, California*

DART RESORTS: *marketing of resort community homesites*

(1) In January 1978, operations of Action Plastics, American Gasket and Rubber and Action Plastics and Rubber were combined into Action Technology and, along with Colorite Plastics, were made part of the Chemical Specialties sector. Financial data on these operations for 1977 and 1976 are included in the Plastics operating segment.

Financial Statements

Dart Industries Inc.
and Consolidated Subsidiaries

Years Ended December 31,
1977 and 1976

Dart Industries Inc. and Consolidated Subsidiaries

Summary of Accounting Policies

Basis of consolidation The consolidated financial statements include the accounts of Dart and its subsidiaries except for its wholly-owned insurance subsidiary, whose operations are not significant, and two less than 50% owned foreign corporations, all of which are accounted for on the equity method. Significant intercompany accounts and transactions are eliminated.

Dart is a party to a joint operating agreement whereby it has an undivided 50% interest in plant and other assets relating to the production and marketing of certain petrochemicals, and is also a 50% owner of a plastics processing corporation with the same other party. The accompanying statements include 50% of the assets, liabilities, income and costs and expenses of these jointly owned activities.

Translation of foreign currencies Foreign subsidiary balance sheet accounts for inventories, prepaid expenses, deferred income taxes, properties, investments and other assets are translated into United States dollar equivalents at historical exchange rates; cash, receivables and all liability accounts are translated at yearend exchange rates. Income and expense accounts are translated at the average rate of exchange in effect during the year except for cost of goods sold, depreciation and amortization which are translated at historical rates. Exchange gains and losses are included in the determination of current year earnings.

Inventories Inventories are valued at the lower of cost or market. In general, cost as applied to inventory valuation represents purchase or manufacturing cost applied on the first-in, first-out method. Obsolete and damaged merchandise is excluded.

Properties and depreciation Expenditures for additions, improvements, replacements, betterments and major renewals are added to the properties accounts. Properties retired, or otherwise disposed of, are eliminated from the asset accounts and the related amounts of accumulated depreciation are eliminated from the accumulated depreciation accounts. Gains and losses from disposals are included in earnings. Expenditures for maintenance, repairs and minor renewals are charged to earnings as incurred.

Depreciation of properties is provided chiefly on a straight line basis over the estimated average useful lives of the various assets. Lives used for calculating depreciation rates for the principal asset classifications are as follows: buildings and improvements—10 to 50 years; machinery and equipment—3 to 20 years.

Intangibles Intangibles having limited lives are amortized over their estimated useful lives. Certain intangibles acquired prior to October 31, 1970 are considered to have an unlimited life and are not being amortized.

Research and development Expenditures for research and development are charged to earnings as incurred.

Income taxes Provision is made for deferred income taxes and future income tax benefits applicable to timing differences between book and tax income. Declining balance and guideline depreciation and the instalment method of income recognition generally are used in the determination of income for tax purposes where applicable.

Investment tax credits are applied to reduce federal income tax expense in the year the credit arises.

Dart and its domestic subsidiaries file a consolidated federal income tax return. Provision is made for United States income taxes on earnings of foreign subsidiaries except for those which are expected to be invested indefinitely.

Resort development Resort lot sales are accounted for on the instalment method until actual collection experience for a project indicates that collectibility of receivable balances is reasonably predictable, after which the accrual method will be used. Under the instalment method, the gross profit less direct selling expenses related to the portion of the sales price which is not received in cash is deferred at the time of sale and recognized as cash is collected. In the opinion of management, at December 31, 1977 none of Dart's projects qualifies for the accrual method.

Interest and property taxes relating to land held for sale or improvement are charged to earnings as incurred. Land and improvements are valued at the lower of cost or estimated net realizable value.

Dart Industries Inc. and Consolidated Subsidiaries

Balance Sheet
December 31, 1977 and 1976

Assets	1977	1976
Current assets:		
Cash, including time deposits of $27,696,000 in 1977 and $18,428,000 in 1976	$ 63,033,000	$ 49,106,000
Marketable securities, at cost which approximates market	183,069,000	140,271,000
Total cash and marketable securities	246,102,000	189,377,000
Accounts and notes receivable, less allowance for doubtful accounts of $11,969,000 in 1977 and $12,495,000 in 1976	191,191,000	181,901,000
Inventories	310,262,000	296,240,000
Prepaid expenses	14,782,000	14,765,000
Deferred future income tax benefits	32,700,000	26,600,000
Total current assets	795,037,000	708,883,000
Resort development assets	53,657,000	57,144,000
Properties:		
Properties owned	832,003,000	770,463,000
Properties leased under capital leases	23,678,000	23,363,000
	855,681,000	793,826,000
Less accumulated depreciation	350,996,000	317,480,000
Total properties	504,685,000	476,346,000
Investments and other assets:		
3M Company common stock held in escrow for exchange by holders of 4¼% and 4¾% debentures, at cost (market value: 1977—$41,080,000; 1976—$47,961,000)	35,162,000	35,162,000
Other assets, receivables and investments	40,270,000	34,499,000
Intangibles relating to businesses purchased, less amortization	11,425,000	14,445,000
Total investments and other assets	86,857,000	84,106,000
Total Assets	**$1,440,236,000**	**$1,326,479,000**

SEE ACCOMPANYING NOTES TO FINANCIAL STATEMENTS AND SUMMARY OF ACCOUNTING POLICIES.

Liabilities and Stockholders' Equity	1977	1976
Current liabilities:		
Accounts payable	$ 73,378,000	$ 68,737,000
Accrued compensation	42,151,000	39,742,000
Other accrued expenses	97,455,000	77,987,000
Short term loans, foreign	13,471,000	16,350,000
Current instalments of obligations under capital leases	981,000	1,260,000
Current instalments of long term debt	8,450,000	6,407,000
Income taxes	38,600,000	32,800,000
Total current liabilities	274,486,000	243,283,000
Resort development liabilities	9,324,000	8,909,000
Obligations under capital leases, less current instalments	12,897,000	13,522,000
Long term debt, less current instalments	238,716,000	241,188,000
Deferred income taxes	58,800,000	54,500,000
Stockholders' equity:		
Preferred Stock, $5.00 par value		
Authorized, 3,000,000 shares		
Series A $2 Cumulative Convertible (aggregate liquidating preference in 1977—$149,050,000)		
Issued, 2,981,000 shares in 1977 and 2,986,000 shares in 1976	14,905,000	14,930,000
Common Stock, $1.25 par value		
Authorized, 35,000,000 shares		
Issued, 23,133,300 shares in 1977 and 22,438,800 shares in 1976	28,917,000	28,048,000
Capital in excess of par value	299,828,000	279,029,000
Retained earnings	503,910,000	444,617,000
	847,560,000	766,624,000
Less cost of reacquired shares of capital stock— Preferred—32,500; Common—700	1,547,000	1,547,000
Total stockholders' equity	846,013,000	765,077,000
Total Liabilities and Stockholders' Equity	$1,440,236,000	$1,326,479,000

Dart Industries Inc. and Consolidated Subsidiaries

Statement of Earnings and Retained Earnings
For the years ended December 31, 1977 and 1976

	1977	1976
Income:		
Net sales	$1,600,988,000	$1,476,240,000
Other income	21,804,000	18,552,000
	1,622,792,000	1,494,792,000
Costs and Expenses:		
Cost of goods sold and operating expenses	951,062,000	876,401,000
Selling, distribution and administrative expenses	391,099,000	358,588,000
Depreciation and amortization	59,423,000	52,422,000
Interest expense	20,512,000	16,768,000
	1,422,096,000	1,304,179,000
Earnings Before Income Taxes	200,696,000	190,613,000
Provision for income taxes	91,500,000	89,000,000
Net Earnings	109,196,000	101,613,000
Retained earnings at beginning of year	444,617,000	386,013,000
	553,813,000	487,626,000
Dividends:		
Cash—		
Preferred—$2 per share	5,902,000	5,908,000
Common—$1.00 and $.66 per share	22,787,000	15,045,000
Common Stock, 3%, 673,500 shares at $31.50 per share		
paid in May 1977 and 653,500 shares at $33.75 per share		
paid in May 1976	21,214,000	22,056,000
	49,903,000	43,009,000
Retained Earnings at End of Year	$ 503,910,000	$ 444,617,000
Net Earnings Per Share of Common Stock:		
Primary	$4.46	$4.14
Fully diluted	$4.18	$3.88

SEE ACCOMPANYING NOTES TO FINANCIAL STATEMENTS AND SUMMARY OF ACCOUNTING POLICIES.

Dart Industries Inc. and Consolidated Subsidiaries

Statement of Capital Stock

For the years ended December 31, 1977 and 1976

	1977		1976	
	SHARES ISSUED	AMOUNT	SHARES ISSUED	AMOUNT
Preferred Stock				
At Beginning of Year	2,986,000	$14,930,000	2,986,400	$14,932,000
Upon conversion into Common Stock	(5,000)	(25,000)	(400)	(2,000)
At End of Year, Including Reacquired Shares	2,981,000	$14,905,000	2,986,000	$14,930,000
Common Stock				
At Beginning of Year	22,438,800	$28,048,000	21,766,800	$27,209,000
For stock dividend	673,500	842,000	653,500	817,000
Upon exercise of options	16,000	20,000	18,100	22,000
Upon conversion of Preferred Stock	5,000	7,000	400	
At End of Year, Including Reacquired Shares	23,133,300	$28,917,000	22,438,800	$28,048,000

Statement of Capital in Excess of Par Value

For the years ended December 31, 1977 and 1976

	1977	1976
At Beginning of Year	$279,029,000	$257,169,000
Excess of fair value over par value of Common Stock issued as stock dividend	20,373,000	21,239,000
Excess of option prices over par value of Common Stock issued upon exercise of options	408,000	619,000
Upon conversion of Preferred Stock	18,000	2,000
At End of Year	$299,828,000	$279,029,000

Dart Industries Inc. and Consolidated Subsidiaries

Statement of Changes in Financial Position

For the years ended December 31, 1977 and 1976

	1977	1976
Working Capital Provided by:		
Net earnings	$109,196,000	$101,613,000
Items not affecting working capital—		
Depreciation and amortization	59,423,000	52,422,000
Deferred income taxes	4,300,000	5,100,000
Provided by operations	172,919,000	159,135,000
Increase in long term debt and capital lease obligations	7,848,000	35,530,000
Reduction of investment in resort development	3,902,000	12,010,000
Dispositions of properties, investments and other assets	7,261,000	13,246,000
Other	3,676,000	7,568,000
Total Working Capital Provided	195,606,000	227,489,000
Working Capital Used for:		
Properties acquired	94,571,000	120,604,000
Cash dividends paid—		
Preferred Stock	5,902,000	5,908,000
Common Stock	22,787,000	15,045,000
Decrease in long term debt and capital lease obligations	10,945,000	10,869,000
Other	6,450,000	3,540,000
Total Working Capital Used	140,655,000	155,966,000
Working Capital Increase	$ 54,951,000	$ 71,523,000
Changes in Components of Working Capital:		
Cash and marketable securities	$ 56,725,000	$ 32,573,000
Accounts and notes receivable	9,290,000	19,540,000
Inventories	14,022,000	36,424,000
Other current assets	6,117,000	11,108,000
Accounts payable	(4,641,000)	(10,336,000)
Accrued expenses	(21,877,000)	(9,456,000)
Short term loans, foreign	2,879,000	(7,198,000)
Income taxes	(5,800,000)	(1,400,000)
Other current liabilities	(1,764,000)	268,000
Working Capital Increase	$ 54,951,000	$ 71,523,000

SEE ACCOMPANYING NOTES TO FINANCIAL STATEMENTS AND SUMMARY OF ACCOUNTING POLICIES.

Dart Industries Inc. and Consolidated Subsidiaries

Notes to Financial Statements

		NET SALES		OPERATING PROFIT	
		1977	1976	1977	1976
Segment operating data	Direct Selling	$ 575,417,000	$ 512,344,000	$146,349,000	$133,100,000
	Consumer Products	206,113,000	244,275,000	25,519,000	27,837,000
	Chemical and	252,714,000	232,312,000	18,272,000	33,783,000
	Plastics	315,298,000	278,542,000	28,522,000	17,105,000
	Glass Containers	260,067,000	228,886,000	21,714,000	29,808,000
	Resort Development	16,204,000	9,956,000	(1,869,000)	(15,325,000)
	Adjustments and eliminations	(24,825,000)	(30,075,000)	(6,063,000)	(7,915,000)
	Corporate items			(31,748,000)	(27,780,000)
	Consolidated	$1,600,988,000	$1,476,240,000	$200,696,000	$190,613,000

Geographic operating data

United States

Western Hemisphere (outside United States)

Europe and Africa

Pacific Area

Adjustments and eliminations

Corporate items

Consolidated

The various segments of Dart comprise principally the following products and services: **Direct Selling**—Tupperware brand plastic food preparation, storage and serving containers; Vanda Beauty Counselor cosmetics and toiletries; Miracle Maid cookware and Coppercraft Guild giftware; **Consumer Products**—West Bend electric housewares and cookware; Syroco home decorative accessories and giftware; **Chemical**—plastic raw materials, chemical specialties and environmental equipment and services; **Plastics**—decorative building products, styro and specialty products and packaging; **Glass Containers**—glass bottles for sale to brewers, distillers, soft-drink manufacturers and food processors; **Resort Development**—marketing of resort community homesites.

Net sales by segment and by geographic area include both sales to outsiders, as reported in Dart's statement of earnings, and sales from one segment to another or from one geographic area

	IDENTIFIABLE ASSETS		CAPITAL EXPENDITURES		DEPRECIATION AND AMORTIZATION	
	1977	1976	1977	1976	1977	1976
	$ 389,150,000	$ 355,885,000	$31,937,000	$ 46,985,000	$17,396,000	$13,964,000
	111,603,000	126,664,000	4,129,000	4,289,000	4,553,000	5,250,000
	200,842,000	173,879,000	23,570,000	25,174,000	9,471,000	8,677,000
	179,865,000	177,059,000	11,460,000	13,924,000	9,273,000	8,951,000
	178,711,000	174,457,000	18,192,000	26,620,000	17,791,000	14,949,000
	53,556,000	57,150,000	20,000	152,000	185,000	234,000
	(4,556,000)	(3,966,000)				
	331,065,000	265,351,000	5,283,000	3,612,000	754,000	397,000
	$1,440,236,000	$1,326,479,000	$94,591,000	$120,756,000	$59,423,000	$52,422,000

	NET SALES		OPERATING PROFIT		IDENTIFIABLE ASSETS	
	1977	1976	1977	1976	1977	1976
	$1,211,179,000	$1,122,148,000	$144,368,000	$139,687,000	$ 835,406,000	$ 815,516,000
	96,434,000	85,302,000	21,866,000	14,372,000	71,085,000	53,333,000
	225,650,000	208,072,000	43,422,000	42,179,000	136,764,000	135,111,000
	82,342,000	75,087,000	25,418,000	24,767,000	67,309,000	58,542,000
	(14,617,000)	(14,369,000)	(2,630,000)	(2,612,000)	(1,393,000)	(1,374,000)
			(31,748,000)	(27,780,000)	331,065,000	265,351,000
	$1,600,988,000	$1,476,240,000	$200,696,000	$190,613,000	$1,440,236,000	$1,326,479,000

to another. Sales between segments and between geographic areas generally are recorded on the same basis as sales to outsiders. Sales between segments aggregated $24,825,000 in 1977 and $30,075,000 in 1976 with the major portion thereof representing sales from the Consumer Products and Chemical segments to the Direct Selling segment. Intercompany sales between geographic areas aggregated $14,617,000 in 1977 and $14,369,000 in 1976 with the major portion thereof representing sales from the United States to other areas. Export sales from the United States to outside customers are not significant.

Operating profit by segment and by geographic area represents revenues less operating expenses under the control of operating management. Corporate items include the cost of corporate staff functions, interest expense, foreign exchange gains and losses, and other expenses of the Company as a whole reduced by certain other income, mainly investment earnings.

Dart Industries Inc. and Consolidated Subsidiaries

Notes to Financial Statements (continued)

		1977	1976
Details of Balance Sheet	ACCOUNTS AND NOTES RECEIVABLE:		
	Trade	$189,656,000	$178,878,000
	Other	13,504,000	15,518,000
		203,160,000	194,396,000
	Less allowance for doubtful accounts	11,969,000	12,495,000
		$191,191,000	$181,901,000
	INVENTORIES:		
	Raw materials and supplies	$ 97,908,000	$ 95,476,000
	Work in process	42,068,000	33,320,000
	Finished goods	170,286,000	167,444,000
		$310,262,000	$296,240,000
	PROPERTIES, AT COST		
	(excluding resort development assets):		
	Land	$ 16,802,000	$ 16,253,000
	Buildings and improvements	229,373,000	212,414,000
	Machinery and equipment	592,650,000	539,135,000
	Construction in progress	16,856,000	26,024,000
		855,681,000	793,826,000
	Less accumulated depreciation	350,996,000	317,480,000
		$504,685,000	$476,346,000
	LONG TERM DEBT, LESS CURRENT INSTALMENTS:		
	7½% Sinking Fund Debentures, due April 1, 1996, $60,000,000, less unamortized discount	$ 59,812,000	$ 59,796,000
	4¼% Subordinated Debentures, due July 15, 1997 (exchangeable for 10.75 shares of 3M Company common stock per $1,000 debenture)	60,000,000	60,000,000
	4¾% Subordinated Debentures, due August 15, 1987 (exchangeable for 10.1 shares of 3M Company common stock per $1,000 debenture)	20,000,000	20,000,000
	Unsecured notes— 4.042% to 5.75%, due in annual instalments to 1987	33,433,000	38,557,000
	9⅞%, due in annual instalments from 1978 to 1995	47,200,000	50,000,000
	Other	18,271,000	12,835,000
		$238,716,000	$241,188,000

Business combinations and dispositions

In 1977 and 1976, Dart acquired certain businesses for cash and accounted for such acquisitions as purchases. The operating results of these businesses have been included in Dart's financial statements from the dates of acquisition and were not significant.

In January 1977, Dart sold its United States Rexall Drug Company operations for approximately $16,000,000 in cash. The impact of this sale, after provisions made in years prior to 1976 and related tax benefits, was not material to net earnings. Rexall had net sales of $45,000,000 in 1976 and nominal pre-tax operating earnings.

In December 1977, the decision was made to close down or sell direct selling cosmetics operations in Australia and Mexico and to change the operating methods, including reductions in product lines and personnel and other streamlining actions, for the direct selling cosmetics divisions in Europe and for a consumer products

operation. In addition, provision has been made for phasing out or selling certain chemical operations. Provision for the costs of these actions, which include writedowns of properties, goodwill and other assets as well as accruals for termination benefits and other costs, aggregates $11,733,000 after related tax benefits, which approximates 51 cents per share. Divisions involved in these actions accounted for net sales of $67,000,000 and $70,000,000, in 1977 and 1976, respectively, with pre-tax operating losses which were not material in either year. Decisions were made in 1977 and 1976 to sell or otherwise terminate certain other businesses; their operations were not significant.

International operations

A summary of accounts relating to foreign subsidiaries at December 31 (excluding intercompany accounts) follows:

	1977	1976
ASSETS:		
Current assets	$199,885,000	$171,103,000
Properties	114,520,000	101,445,000
Investments and other assets	11,501,000	6,990,000
Total assets	325,906,000	279,538,000
LIABILITIES:		
Current liabilities	91,540,000	85,892,000
Long term debt and deferred income taxes	29,050,000	21,500,000
Total liabilities	120,590,000	107,392,000
Net assets of foreign subsidiaries in consolidation	$205,316,000	$172,146,000

Net sales from operations outside the United States were $399,786,000 in 1977 and $364,090,000 in 1976. Exchange losses were not material in either year. Undistributed earnings of foreign subsidiaries included in consolidation were $27,667,000 for 1977 and $9,522,000 for 1976 and aggregated $133,674,000 at December 31, 1977. Dart has not considered it necessary to provide for deferred United States income taxes in excess of available foreign tax credits on this total because it has been or is expected to be reinvested outside the United States for an indefinite period of time. Dividends of $14,636,000 in 1977 and $23,817,000 in 1976 were received from foreign subsidiaries.

Resort development operations

A summary of accounts relating to resort development operations at December 31 (excluding intercompany accounts) follows:

	1977	1976
ASSETS:		
Cash, prepaid expenses, etc.	$ 2,260,000	$ 791,000
Notes receivable, 6% to 9%	29,950,000	27,480,000
Deferred profit on land sales	(10,606,000)	(9,327,000)
Land and improvements	28,568,000	33,706,000
Properties and other assets	3,485,000	4,494,000
Total assets	$53,657,000	$57,144,000
LIABILITIES:		
Accounts payable, accrued costs and expenses, etc.	$ 9,324,000	$ 8,909,000
Total liabilities	$ 9,324,000	$ 8,909,000

Principal collections on notes receivable are due in the five years subsequent to December 31, 1977 as follows: 1978—$3,801,000; 1979—$3,882,000; 1980—$4,011,000; 1981—$2,997,000; 1982—$1,892,000.

Dart Industries Inc. and Consolidated Subsidiaries

Notes to Financial Statements (continued)

Total estimated costs to complete improvements relating to active projects, based on management estimates and engineering studies, amount to $5,000,000 and anticipated expenditures relating to such improvements are expected to be incurred as follows: 1978—$2,200,000; 1979—$1,200,000; after 1979—$1,600,000.

"Cost of goods sold and operating expenses" includes deferred profit on resort lot sales of $4,811,000 for 1977 and $2,255,000 for 1976. Profit, previously deferred, taken into earnings aggregated $2,616,000 for 1977 and $1,899,000 for 1976.

Income taxes

Income taxes charged to earnings consist of the following:

	1977	1976
PAYABLE CURRENTLY:		
Federal	$50,100,000	$52,900,000
Foreign	35,200,000	31,000,000
State	8,000,000	7,600,000
	93,300,000	91,500,000
TAX EFFECT OF TIMING DIFFERENCES:		
Federal	200,000	(5,100,000)
Foreign	(2,100,000)	2,600,000
State	100,000	
	(1,800,000)	(2,500,000)
Provision for income taxes	$91,500,000	$89,000,000

The tax effect of timing differences, resulting from variances between accounting for financial statement purposes and accounting for tax purposes, is as follows:

	1977	1976
Depreciation	$ 3,900,000	$ 9,560,000
Instalment sales	(1,600,000)	(2,340,000)
Accrued taxes and other expenses not deductible until paid	200,000	(6,600,000)
Provision for elimination, change or sale of certain operations	(4,300,000)	(3,120,000)
Tax effect of timing differences	$ (1,800,000)	$ (2,500,000)

Income taxes charged to earnings differ from an amount computed using the United States federal income tax rate of 48%. A reconciliation between an amount computed using the 48% rate and the provision for income taxes is as follows:

	1977	1976
Amount computed using the 48% rate	$96,300,000	$91,500,000
Increases (reductions) in taxes result from:		
State income taxes	4,200,000	4,000,000
Foreign income taxes	(3,700,000)	1,500,000
Investment tax credit	(5,500,000)	(6,900,000)
Other	200,000	(1,100,000)
Provision for income taxes	$91,500,000	$89,000,000

Short term loans and borrowing arrangements

Short term loans, foreign, are unsecured and aggregated a maximum of $23,636,000 and $19,318,000 at any monthend in 1977 and 1976, respectively. Weighted average borrowings and interest rates during the year, based on amounts outstanding at each monthend, were $19,559,000 and 11.1% in 1977 and $11,723,000 and 11.3% in 1976.

At December 31, 1977 and 1976, the weighted average interest rates were 11.0% and 11.8%, respectively.

Unused lines of short term credit, primarily with United States banks, totaled $44,200,000 at December 31, 1977 and provide for unsecured ninety day loans generally at the banks' prime rates. Compensating balance requirements under these credit lines are not material.

Long term debt

Total principal payments due on long term debt in the five years subsequent to December 31, 1977 are as follows: 1978—$8,450,000; 1979—$8,605,000; 1980—$8,400,000; 1981—$8,404,000; 1982—$12,061,000.

The 7½% Debentures are due April 1, 1996. Through the operation of a mandatory sinking fund, Dart is obligated to redeem $4,000,000 aggregate principal amount of these Debentures on April 1 in each of the years 1982 through 1995. Dart has the option to redeem through the sinking fund an additional $4,000,000 aggregate principal amount in each such year. All sinking fund redemptions, mandatory or optional, are to be made at 100% of the principal amount of the debentures redeemed. Debentures acquired or redeemed otherwise than through the operation of the sinking fund may be credited against the sinking fund requirements.

Under loan agreements with certain insurance companies, approximately $300,000,000 of the consolidated retained earnings at December 31, 1977 is not restricted as to payment of cash dividends. The agreements impose no restrictions on payment of stock dividends.

Stock options

1,256,800 shares of Dart Common Stock are reserved for options granted or available for grant to officers and employees under stockholder approved stock option plans. Options for 1,364,200 shares were exercised prior to 1977.

Under the plans, the option purchase price for all options granted is 100% of the fair market value of the shares on the date of grant. Options granted are exercisable in instalments after one year and before the end of five years or ten years depending on the nature of the option. Proceeds received from exercise of options are credited to the capital accounts. No options were granted in 1977.

A summary of changes during 1977 follows:

	SHARES	OPTIONS OUTSTANDING PRICE RANGE	AMOUNT
At beginning of year	643,400	$21.21 to $48.85	$23,790,000
Adjustment for stock dividend	17,900		
Options exercised	(16,000)	$21.21 to $33.61	(428,000)
Options canceled	(68,100)	$30.65 to $48.85	(2,703,000)
At end of year	577,200	$21.21 to $46.69	$20,659,000

At December 31, 1977, options for 499,600 shares of Common Stock were exercisable at prices ranging from $21.21 to $46.69 and 679,600 shares were available for grant.

Preferred Stock

Holders of the Series A $2 Cumulative Convertible Preferred Stock are entitled to receive $2 per share annual cash dividends, to one vote per share and, upon any voluntary liquidation, dissolution or winding up, to receive $50 per share plus accrued unpaid dividends. Each share of the Preferred Stock is convertible by the holder into Common Stock on a share for share basis adjusted for stock dividends in excess of 3% in any one year or for recapitalization. The Preferred Stock may be called for redemption at $55 per share plus accrued unpaid dividends.

Retirement plans

Dart and certain of its United States subsidiaries continued the contributory profit sharing retirement plan, established in 1955, and the non-contributory pension plan, established in 1975, which together constitute the principal retirement program covering all employees who have one or more years of employment with Dart, and who are not covered by a collective bargaining agreement or by another Company-sponsored retirement plan. Dart and its subsidiaries also have several

Notes to Financial Statements (continued)

pension plans covering substantially all of their employees not covered by the principal retirement program, including certain employees in foreign countries.

The contribution to be made under the Dart profit sharing plan amounted to $8,114,000 for 1977 and was $8,243,000 for 1976. The total pension expense was $11,619,000 for 1977 and $10,216,000 for 1976 which includes, as applicable, amortization of prior service cost principally over a period of 30 years.

The aggregate Dart contribution to the profit sharing plan in any year is based upon consolidated earnings before federal income taxes, as defined, is limited to 6% of such earnings and cannot exceed the amount deductible for federal income tax purposes. The computations include net earnings of certain divisions whose employees do not participate in the Dart plan, but who participate in previously existing retirement plans which have been continued in effect.

With respect to pension plans, Dart's policy is, generally, to contribute pension cost accrued. The actuarially computed value of vested benefits for all plans exceeded, as of December 31, 1977, the total of pension fund assets and accruals by about $26,800,000. The total estimated unfunded prior service cost relative to all pension plans in effect was approximately $55,700,000 at December 31, 1977.

Incentive compensation

Under the formula incorporated in Dart's 1962 stockholder approved Incentive Compensation Plan for principal officers and key employees, the Incentive Compensation Committee and the Executive Committee of the Board of Directors awarded to 102 principal officers and key employees $2,531,000 ($1,956,000 for 1976) of the total of $8,403,000 available for 1977. No outside director participates in this plan.

Pursuant to stockholder authority granted in 1962, various other approved plans are in effect for divisions and subsidiaries of Dart. No principal officer or director participates in these plans. The above named committees awarded $6,268,000 ($6,509,000 for 1976) to 427 persons in these categories. The total amount available under the plans was $12,652,000.

Amounts available but not awarded under such plans are not available for future awards.

Capital expenditures

It is estimated that capital expenditures for 1978 will be about $115,000,000.

Earnings per share of Common Stock

Primary earnings per share are based on the weighted average number of shares of Common Stock outstanding during each period increased by the effect of dilutive stock options. Such increased average shares were 23,160,200 for 1977 and 23,124,500 for 1976. Net earnings attributable to Common Stock are after deducting Preferred dividend requirements.

Fully diluted earnings per share are based on the weighted average number of shares of Common Stock outstanding during each period, assumption of conversion of Series A $2 Cumulative Convertible Preferred Stock and assumption of exercise of all dilutive stock options. Such increased average shares were 26,126,700 for 1977 and 26,167,900 for 1976.

All per share amounts give retroactive effect to stock dividends paid.

Supplementary earnings statement information

Charges to costs and expenses for the years ended December 31 include the following:

	1977	1976
Maintenance and repairs	$51,091,000	$44,120,000
Taxes, except income taxes:		
Payroll	26,606,000	24,240,000
Property, business and other	11,803,000	11,727,000
Advertising	10,298,000	10,922,000
Research and development	9,347,000	7,239,000

Unaudited general description of the impact of inflation

Dart's diverse lines of business have generally experienced inflationary pressures on production and other costs to varying degrees based upon changes in price levels of the basic raw materials and other goods and services used by each business in its operations. The magnitude of the changes fluctuates from business to business and within businesses by geographic area. The ability of each business to compensate for increases in the prices of specific goods and services by increasing sales prices is affected by competitive conditions in the markets in which the businesses operate. The diversity of Dart's businesses has tended to minimize overall any adverse effects on earnings from uncompensated inflation in any one of its operations.

Replacing items of plant and equipment with assets having equivalent productive capacity has usually required a greater capital investment than was required to purchase the assets being replaced. The additional capital investment principally reflects the cumulative impact of inflation on the long-lived nature of these assets.

Dart's annual report on Form 10-K (a copy of which is available upon request) contains specific information with respect to yearend 1977 and 1976 estimated replacement cost of inventories and productive capacity and the approximate effect which estimated replacement cost would have had on the computation of cost of goods sold and depreciation expense for each year.

Unaudited interim financial information

	1977			
	FIRST QUARTER	SECOND QUARTER	THIRD QUARTER	FOURTH QUARTER
Net sales	$369,916,000	$412,834,000	$393,401,000	$424,837,000
Cost of goods sold and operating expenses	220,877,000	240,441,000	247,690,000	242,054,000
Earnings before taxes	43,871,000	63,712,000	41,804,000	51,309,000
Net earnings	23,171,000	33,912,000	24,404,000	27,709,000
Earnings per share of Common Stock:				
Primary	.94	1.40	.99	1.13
Fully diluted	.89	1.29	.94	1.06

	1976			
	FIRST QUARTER	SECOND QUARTER	THIRD QUARTER	FOURTH QUARTER
Net sales	$358,884,000	$370,905,000	$362,453,000	$383,998,000
Cost of goods sold and operating expenses	209,574,000	214,564,000	220,998,000	231,265,000
Earnings before taxes	52,324,000	52,698,000	39,499,000	46,092,000
Net earnings	27,674,000	26,798,000	21,799,000	25,342,000
Earnings per share of Common Stock:				
Primary	1.13	1.10	.88	1.03
Fully diluted	1.06	1.02	.83	.97

Obligations under capital leases

Dart has recorded as assets certain properties and property rights acquired by the Company under capital leases. The related discounted lease obligations are set forth separately in the accompanying balance sheet. Dart has no legal responsibility for payments under the terms of any of these leases except for rent, insurance, taxes and maintenance.

The current and long term portions of obligations under capital leases aggregating $13,878,000 represent future minimum lease payments under capital leases reduced

Notes to Financial Statements (continued)

to present value by deducting $12,753,000 as the amount representing interest. Future minimum lease payments, including amounts representing interest, are payable as follows: 1978—$1,875,000; 1979—$1,880,000; 1980—$1,844,000; 1981—$1,810,000; 1982—$1,789,000; after 1982—$17,433,000.

Commitments and contingencies

Dart leases real estate, transportation equipment and other machinery and equipment under short and long term, cancelable and noncancelable lease agreements which generally provide for fixed monthly payments over the terms of the leases. Many leases require additional payments for property taxes, insurance and maintenance.

Rental expense (reduced by sublease income of $2,797,000 in 1977 and $2,612,000 in 1976) totaled $31,935,000 in 1977 and $30,632,000 in 1976.

Minimum rental commitments under noncancelable leases in effect at December 31, 1977, are payable as follows: 1978—$28,149,000; 1979—$16,201,000; 1980—$9,488,000; 1981—$6,955,000; 1982—$5,320,000; after 1982—$15,921,000. Future sublease rentals receivable total $7,241,000.

Dart is a defendant in certain purported class action suits, in which substantial damages are claimed, involving its Tahoe Donner resort development project and its former Rexall Drug operations. In addition, certain other law suits have been filed against Dart relative to its present and former operations. In the opinion of management and legal counsel, the ultimate disposition of the suits would not have a materially adverse effect on Dart's financial position or results of operations.

Report of Independent Accountants

606 South Olive Street
Los Angeles 90014

February 26, 1978

To the Board of Directors and
Stockholders of Dart Industries Inc.

In our opinion, the accompanying consolidated financial statements on pages 18 to 32 present fairly the financial position of Dart Industries Inc. and consolidated subsidiaries at December 31, 1977 and 1976, and the results of their operations and the changes in their financial position for the years then ended, in conformity with generally accepted accounting principles consistently applied. Our examinations of these statements were made in accordance with generally accepted auditing standards and accordingly included such tests of the accounting records and such other auditing procedures as we considered necessary in the circumstances.

Price Waterhouse & Co.

Dart Industries Inc. and Consolidated Subsidiaries

Management's Discussion and Analysis

Dart Industries' net sales and net earnings have increased in each of the past five years. Certain trends during the recent past are discussed below.

1977 Compared with 1976

Net sales in 1977 increased $125 million (8%) compared with 1976. All operating segments, except Consumer Products, realized sales gains with Direct Selling accounting for approximately half of the total increase. Consumer Products sales in 1976 included $45 million from the United States Rexall Drug Company operations which were sold in January 1977. Net sales from operations outside the United States were $400 million, an increase of $36 million (10%) over 1976 and accounted for 25% of total 1977 net sales.

Cost of goods sold and operating expenses increased $75 million (9%) compared with 1976. Margins in the Chemical and Glass Containers segments were depressed by the inability to increase prices sufficiently to compensate for higher raw material, labor and operating costs and, in Glass Containers, by a four-week industry-wide strike of mold makers. Improved margins in the remaining segments offset these declines with the result that the relationship of cost of goods sold and operating expenses to net sales remained constant at 59% in both years.

Depreciation and amortization increased $7 million (13%) compared with 1976 and results from continuing plant expansions.

Interest expense increased $4 million (22%) compared with 1976 as a result of $25 million of long term borrowing in December 1976 and higher levels of foreign short term loans.

Provision for income taxes increased $3

million (3%) compared with 1976 as a result of increased earnings. The effective tax rate declined from 47% to 46%, principally as a result of lower effective foreign tax rates.

1976 Compared with 1975

Net sales in 1976 increased $196 million (15%) over the 1975 level. Sales improvements were most significant in the Direct Selling, Chemical and Plastics lines of business where combined volume increases exceeded $120 million. The remaining portion of the sales increase was generally attributed to increases in selling prices throughout all lines of business. Net sales from operations outside the United States were $364 million, an increase of $24 million (7%) over 1975, and accounted for 25% of total 1976 net sales.

Cost of goods sold and operating expenses increased $89 million (11%) over the 1975 level and was a lesser percentage of net sales in 1976 (59%) than in 1975 (62%). Increased sales volume and sales prices more than offset increased costs of raw materials, labor and overhead except in the Chemical line of business which came under increased pressure on margins.

Depreciation and amortization increased $6 million (13%) over 1975 as a result of large expenditures on properties in the past two years.

Interest expense increased $2 million (16%) over 1975 principally as a result of $25 million of long term borrowing in December 1975.

Provision for income taxes increased $12 million (15%) over 1975 reflecting the improvement in earnings, while the effective tax rate declined from 50% to 47%, principally as a result of investment tax credits aggregating $7 million in 1976.

Dart Industries Inc. and Consolidated Subsidiaries

Five Year Summary of Operations

(Dollar amounts in thousands except per share data)	1977	1976	1975	1974	1973
For the Year					
Net sales	$ 1,600,988	$ 1,476,240	$ 1,280,407	$ 1,218,042	$ 993,322
Cost of goods sold and operating expenses	951,062	876,401	787,474	724,204	600,878
Depreciation and amortization	59,423	52,422	46,228	44,105	38,703
Interest expense	20,512	16,768	14,484	14,648	13,915
Earnings before taxes	200,696	190,613	156,488	140,690	122,522
Provision for income taxes	91,500	89,000	77,500	71,393	57,600
Net earnings	109,196	101,613	78,988	69,297	64,922
Earnings per share of Common Stock					
Primary	4.46	4.14	3.16	2.75	2.58
Fully diluted	4.18	3.88	3.01	2.63	2.47
Cash dividends per share of Common Stock	1.00	.66	.57	.42	.29
Cash dividends paid					
Common Stock	22,787	15,045	13,041	9,334	6,538
Preferred Stock	5,902	5,908	5,910	5,913	5,913
Common Stock dividends	3%	3%	3%	3%	3%
Net earnings applicable to Common Stock after Preferred dividend requirements	103,294	95,705	73,078	63,384	59,009
Properties acquired	94,571	120,604	93,351	70,730	67,176
At Yearend					
Current assets	$ 795,037	$ 708,883	$ 609,238	$ 556,309	$ 417,311
Current liabilities	274,486	243,283	215,161	215,036	171,529
Working capital	520,551	465,600	394,077	341,273	245,782
Properties (net)	504,685	476,346	414,719	370,039	342,319
Total assets	1,440,236	1,326,479	1,190,687	1,114,858	1,035,722
Long term debt	238,716	241,188	214,133	193,380	197,878
Deferred income taxes	58,800	54,500	49,400	51,900	54,400
Stockholders' equity	846,013	765,077	683,776	623,738	568,560
Shares of stock outstanding					
Common	23,132,600	23,111,200	23,091,700	23,088,600	22,890,300
Preferred	2,948,500	2,953,500	2,953,900	2,956,300	2,956,400
Stockholders					
Common	28,789	30,231	31,141	32,088	32,110
Preferred	5,204	5,696	5,929	6,028	5,476
Employees	31,201	29,801	28,612	29,566	28,483

The shares of Common Stock outstanding, cash dividends per share and earnings per share for 1976 and prior years have been adjusted retroactively to give effect to subsequent stock dividends.

Dart Industries Inc. and Consolidated Subsidiaries

Ten Years at a Glance

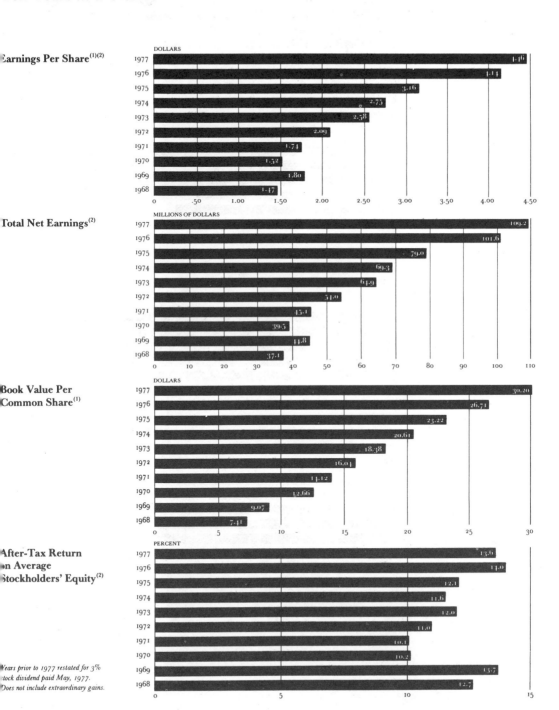

Earnings Per Share[1][2]

DOLLARS

Year	Value
1977	4.46
1976	4.14
1975	3.46
1974	2.75
1973	2.58
1972	2.09
1971	1.74
1970	1.52
1969	1.80
1968	1.47

Total Net Earnings[2]

MILLIONS OF DOLLARS

Year	Value
1977	109.2
1976	101.6
1975	79.0
1974	69.3
1973	64.9
1972	54.9
1971	45.1
1970	39.5
1969	44.8
1968	37.1

Book Value Per Common Share[1]

DOLLARS

Year	Value
1977	30.20
1976	26.71
1975	23.22
1974	20.61
1973	18.38
1972	16.04
1971	14.12
1970	12.66
1969	9.07
1968	7.41

After-Tax Return on Average Stockholders' Equity[2]

PERCENT

Year	Value
1977	13.6
1976	14.0
1975	12.1
1974	11.6
1973	12.0
1972	11.0
1971	10.1
1970	10.2
1969	13.7
1968	12.7

Years prior to 1977 restated for 3%
stock dividend paid May, 1977.
Does not include extraordinary gains.

320

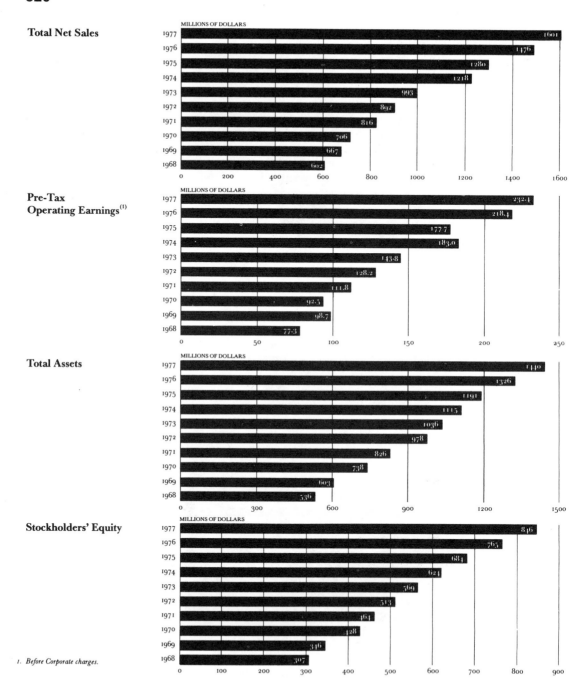

Total Net Sales

Pre-Tax Operating Earnings[1]

Total Assets

Stockholders' Equity

1. *Before Corporate charges.*

Board of Directors

Officers and Committees

Officers

Justin Dart, *Chairman of the Board of Directors and Chief Executive Officer*

Thomas P. Mullaney, *President and Chief Operating Officer*

Robert T. Beattie, *Executive Vice President*

Ralph M. Knight, *Executive Vice President*

Phillip D. Matthews, *Executive Vice President, Finance and Administration, and Chief Financial Officer*

Hamer F. Wilson, *Executive Vice President; Chairman, Direct Selling Group*

Russell K. Bolton, *Vice President and General Counsel*

*Walter Bond, *Vice President; Executive Vice President, Tupperware International*

Vincent R. Cucina, *Vice President, Financial Planning*

Elmer M. Davis, *Vice President; President, Housewares division, Consumer Products Group*

John P. Del Favero, *Vice President; President, Chemical-Plastics Group*

F. William Graham, *Vice President; President, Consumer Products Group*

William H. Greenberg, *Vice President; President, Glass Containers Group*

*Joseph Hara, *Vice President; President, Tupperware U.S. and Executive Vice President, Tupperware International*

Thomas M. Mullen, *Vice President and Treasurer*

William R. Palmer, *Vice President and Controller*

John C. Phifer, *Vice President; President, Chemical Specialties sector, Chemical-Plastics Group*

Herschel A. Phillips, *Vice President, Labor Relations*

James P. Schwartz, *Vice President; President, Styro Products sector, Chemical-Plastics Group*

Norman Wicks, *Vice President, Corporate Relations*

Edgar Thedens, *Secretary*

Executive Committee

Justin Dart, *Chairman*

Curtis Barkes

Donald H. Brewer

Edward E. Carlson

William T. Gossett

Thomas P. Mullaney

Holmes Tuttle

Dale Reis, *Secretary*

Audit Committee

Curtis Barkes, *Chairman*

Donald H. Brewer

Edward E. Carlson

William T. Gossett

Holmes Tuttle

R. D. Ziegler

Stock Option and Incentive Compensation Committee

Holmes Tuttle, *Chairman*

Edward E. Carlson

William T. Gossett

Retirement Plans Committee

Russell K. Bolton, *Chairman*

Robert T. Beattie

Phillip D. Matthews

Ralph Wilson, Jr.

R. D. Ziegler

Robert MacPhail, *Secretary*

Nominating Committee

Justin Dart, *Chairman*

Curtis Barkes

Holmes Tuttle

*Elected Company vice president February 27, 1978.

Investor Information

1977	FIRST QUARTER	SECOND QUARTER	THIRD QUARTER	FOURTH QUARTER	FULL YEAR
Stock price range—high/low[1]					
Common	34½/29⅜	39/30⅝	38½/34½	37⅜/32	39/29⅜
Preferred	39/33¼	41⅜/35	40¾/37	40/34¼	41⅜/33¼
Cash dividends paid					
Common	.25	.25	.25	.25	1.00
Preferred		1.00		1.00	2.00

1976	FIRST QUARTER	SECOND QUARTER	THIRD QUARTER	FOURTH QUARTER	FULL YEAR
Stock price range—high/low[1]					
Common[2]	38⅝/25⅞	34¾/30⅞	36¾/31¼	35⅜/28½	38⅝/25⅞
Preferred	41½/32¼	40¼/34	40⅜/35½	40/32½	41½/32¼
Cash dividends paid					
Common	.16	.16	.16	.20	.66[2]
Preferred		1.00		1.00	2.00

1. Dart Industries' Common and Preferred Stocks are traded principally on the New York Stock Exchange under the symbols "D" and "DPr," respectively. Prices noted are based on NYSE market prices.

2. Adjusted for 3% Common Stock dividend paid in May 1977.

Transfer Agents and Registrars
Morgan Guaranty Trust Company of New York
New York, N. Y.

State Street Bank and Trust Company
Boston, Mass.

Bank of America National Trust and Savings Association
San Francisco, Calif.

Additional copies of this Annual Report, or copies of the Company's Form 10-K, will be furnished upon request free of charge.

Write to:

Corporate Secretary
Dart Industries Inc.
P.O. Box 3157, Terminal Annex
Los Angeles, California 90051

Another Way to Look at Company Revenues

Dart Industries' revenues for 1977 totaled $1.6 billion compared with $1.5 billion in 1976

Approximately 26 percent of total revenues in 1977 and 1976 were paid to employees in wages and benefits

Net profit in 1977 was 6.7 percent of revenues compared with 6.8 percent in 1976

Approximately 5 percent of revenues in 1977 and 1976 were retained in the Company for investment in new plant and equipment and the creation of new jobs

Approximately 1.8 percent of revenues were paid to stockholders in cash dividends in 1977 — 1.4 percent were paid in 1976

SECURITIES AND EXCHANGE COMMISSION

WASHINGTON, D.C. 20549

Form 10-K

Annual Report Pursuant to Section 13 or 15(d) of the
Securities Exchange Act of 1934

For the fiscal year ended December 31, 1977   Commission File No. 1-3894

DART INDUSTRIES INC.

(Exact name of registrant as specified in its charter)

Delaware
(State of
Incorporation)

95-1455570
(I.R.S. Employer
Identification Number)

8480 Beverly Boulevard, Los Angeles, California
(Address of Principal Executive Offices)

90048
(Zip Code)

Registrant's telephone number (213) 658-2000

Securities registered pursuant to Section 12(b) of the Act:

Title of Each Class	Name of Each Exchange on Which Registered
Common Stock, par value $1.25 per share	New York Stock Exchange Boston Stock Exchange Pacific Stock Exchange
Series A $2 Cumulative Convertible Preferred Stock	New York Stock Exchange Pacific Stock Exchange
7½% Sinking Fund Debentures due April 1, 1996	New York Stock Exchange
4¼% Subordinated Debentures due July 15, 1997	New York Stock Exchange

Securities registered pursuant to Section 12(g) of the Act:

None

Indicate by check mark whether the registrant (1) has filed all reports required to be filed by Section 13 or 15(d) of the Securities Exchange Act of 1934 during the preceding 12 months (or for such shorter period that the registrant was required to file such reports), and (2) has been subject to such filing requirements for the past 90 days. Yes _X_   No ___ .

The number of shares of the registrant's Common Stock outstanding on December 31, 1977 was 23,132,579.

Item 1. BUSINESS

Dart Industries Inc. is a diversified company engaged in the manufacturing and marketing of consumer products, chemicals, plastics and packaging. Its products are marketed directly to consumers in the home or through retail outlets, or indirectly through intermediate manufacturers and converters whose products are sold to consumers. Dart Industries Inc. also owns resort communities in California which include homesites, condominiums and recreational housing.

Dart was organized under the laws of the State of Delaware in 1928 as the successor to a business originally established in 1902. In 1969 its name was changed from Rexall Drug and Chemical Company. As used herein, the term "Dart" includes Dart Industries Inc. and its subsidiaries, unless the context otherwise indicates. Dart's principal executive offices are located at 8480 Beverly Boulevard, Los Angeles, California 90048, and its telephone number is 213-658-2000.

Segment and Geographic Operating Information

The operating segments of Dart are (i) Direct Selling, (ii) Consumer Products, (iii) Chemical, (iv) Plastics, (v) Glass Containers and (vi) Resort Development. Set forth below is certain information relating to the operating segments and geographic operating data.

SEGMENT OPERATING DATA
(Thousands of Dollars)

	Net Sales				
	1973	1974	1975	1976	1977
Direct Selling	$ 305,026	$ 393,877	$ 459,345	$ 512,344	$ 575,417
Consumer Products	208,548	241,214	236,802	244,275	206,113
Chemical-Plastics Group					
Chemical	135,100	204,703	170,150	232,312	252,714
Plastics	202,874	227,173	227,506	278,542	315,298
Glass Containers	142,090	162,519	199,449	228,886	260,067
Resort Development	9,639	9,465	10,423	9,956	16,204
Adjustments and eliminations	(9,955)	(20,909)	(23,268)	(30,075)	(24,825)
Consolidated	$ 993,322	$1,218,042	$1,280,407	$1,476,240	$1,600,988

	Operating Profit				
	1973	1974	1975	1976	1977
Direct Selling	$ 77,108	$ 98,003	$ 108,485	$ 133,100	$ 146,349
Consumer Products	16,433	20,448	19,767	27,837	25,519
Chemical-Plastics Group					
Chemical	23,838	65,385	31,638	33,783	18,272
Plastics	23,239	23,663	11,644	17,105	28,522
Glass Containers	13,430	18,752	30,091	29,808	21,714
Resort Development	(7,186)	(34,923)	(17,545)	(15,325)	(1,869)
Adjustments and eliminations	(2,912)	(8,437)	(6,443)	(7,915)	(6,063)
Corporate items	(21,428)	(42,201)	(21,149)	(27,780)	(31,748)
Consolidated	$ 122,522	$ 140,690	$ 156,488	$ 190,613	$ 200,696

SEGMENT OPERATING DATA (Continued)

(Thousands of Dollars)

	Identifiable Assets				
	1973	1974	1975	1976	1977
Direct Selling	$ 198,500	$ 252,678	$ 283,282	$ 355,885	$ 389,150
Consumer Products	142,572	154,967	138,872	126,664	111,603
Chemical-Plastics Group					
Chemical	95,363	124,467	150,529	173,879	200,842
Plastics	149,035	171,162	167,158	177,059	179,865
Glass Containers	126,339	138,602	152,624	174,457	178,711
Resort Development	113,367	87,866	72,542	57,150	53,556
Adjustments and eliminations	(3,406)	(4,819)	(3,632)	(3,966)	(4,556)
Corporate items	213,952	189,935	229,312	265,351	331,065
Consolidated	$1,035,722	$1,114,858	$1,190,687	$1,326,479	$1,440,236

	Capital Expenditures				
	1973	1974	1975	1976	1977
Direct Selling	$ 25,588	$ 23,132	$ 35,653	$ 46,985	$ 31,937
Consumer Products	9,704	5,346	3,645	4,289	4,129
Chemical-Plastics Group					
Chemical	5,245	12,880	20,221	25,174	23,570
Plastics	16,231	14,748	13,571	13,924	11,460
Glass Containers	10,249	14,456	20,143	26,620	18,192
Resort Development	2,282	1,057	254	152	20
Corporate items	159	168	118	3,612	5,283
Consolidated	$ 69,458	$ 71,787	$ 93,605	$ 120,756	$ 94,591

	Depreciation and Amortization				
	1973	1974	1975	1976	1977
Direct Selling	$ 8,766	$ 10,592	$ 11,312	$ 13,964	$ 17,396
Consumer Products	5,176	5,490	5,600	5,250	4,553
Chemical-Plastics Group					
Chemical	6,699	7,108	7,538	8,677	9,471
Plastics	6,669	8,092	8,329	8,951	9,273
Glass Containers	10,557	12,039	12,694	14,949	17,791
Resort Development	335	243	263	234	185
Corporate items	501	541	492	397	754
Consolidated	$ 38,703	$ 44,105	$ 46,228	$ 52,422	$ 59,423

GEOGRAPHIC OPERATING DATA

(Thousands of Dollars)

	Net Sales				
	1973	1974	1975	1976	1977
United States	$ 786,632	$ 935,372	$ 951,981	$1,122,148	$1,211,179
Western Hemisphere (outside United States)	55,068	76,262	84,877	85,302	96,434
Europe and Africa	125,964	166,119	192,886	208,072	225,650
Pacific Area	33,895	55,399	67,827	75,087	82,342
Adjustments and eliminations	(8,237)	(15,110)	(17,164)	(14,369)	(14,617)
Consolidated	$ 993,322	$1,218,042	$1,280,407	$1,476,240	$1,600,988

	Operating Profit				
	1973	1974	1975	1976	1977
United States	$ 101,671	$ 124,268	$ 110,851	$ 139,687	$ 144,368
Western Hemisphere (outside United States)	6,253	11,079	11,782	14,372	21,866
Europe and Africa	26,584	31,712	35,665	42,179	43,422
Pacific Area	10,814	18,477	22,280	24,767	25,418
Adjustments and eliminations	(1,372)	(2,645)	(2,941)	(2,612)	(2,630)
Corporate items	(21,428)	(42,201)	(21,149)	(27,780)	(31,748)
Consolidated	$ 122,522	$ 140,690	$ 156,488	$ 190,613	$ 200,696

	Identifiable Assets				
	1973	1974	1975	1976	1977
United States	$ 679,238	$ 727,224	$ 744,861	$ 815,516	$ 835,406
Western Hemisphere (outside United States)	36,534	49,179	53,214	53,333	71,085
Europe and Africa	83,721	109,310	115,883	135,111	136,764
Pacific Area	23,942	41,538	49,526	58,542	67,309
Adjustments and eliminations	(1,665)	(2,328)	(2,109)	(1,374)	(1,393)
Corporate items	213,952	189,935	229,312	265,351	331,065
Consolidated	$1,035,722	$1,114,858	$1,190,687	$1,326,479	$1,440,236

Net sales by segment and by geographic area include both sales to outsiders, as reported in Dart's statement of earnings, and sales from one segment to another or from one geographic area to another. Sales between segments and between geographic areas generally are recorded on the same basis as sales to outsiders. Sales between segments aggregated $9,955,000 in 1973, $20,909,000 in 1974, $23,268,000 in 1975, $30,075,000 in 1976 and $24,825,000 in 1977 with the major portion thereof representing sales from the Consumer Products and Chemical segments to the Direct Selling segment. Intercompany sales between geographic areas aggregated $8,237,000 in 1973, $15,110,000 in 1974, $17,164,000 in 1975, $14,369,000 in 1976 and $14,617,000 in 1977 with the major portion thereof representing sales from the United States to other areas. Export sales from the United States to outside customers are not significant.

Operating profit by segment and by geographic area represents revenues less operating expenses under the control of operating management. Corporate items include the cost of corporate staff functions, interest expense, foreign exchange gains and losses, and other expenses of the company as a whole reduced by certain other income, mainly investment earnings. In 1974, corporate items included a loss on marketable securities of $16,145,000.

The "Consumer Products" operating segment includes the United States operations of Rexall Drug Company which were sold early in January 1977.

Description of Operations of Dart
Direct Selling

Dart's direct selling business is comprised of Tupperware, Vanda Beauty Counselor, Miracle Maid and Coppercraft Guild.

Tupperware sells a broad line of high-quality plastic food preparation, storage and serving containers. Sales were $232 million in 1973, $312 million in 1974, $382 million in 1975, $442 million in 1976 and $509 million in 1977. These high-style quality items are sold in more than 30 countries directly in the home through a network of authorized independent distributors and independent managers and dealers through the "home party" plan. The party-plan method of sales is designed to enable the purchaser to appreciate through demonstration the proper use of TUPPERWARE® products. Distributor and dealer sales efforts are supported through a program of sales promotions, sales and training aids, and motivational conferences.

Manufacturing plants are located in Rhode Island, Tennessee, Idaho, South Carolina and fourteen foreign countries (Australia, Belgium, Brazil, Canada, France, Greece, Japan, Mexico, New Zealand, the Philippines, the Republic of South Africa, Spain, the United Kingdom and Venezuela). Construction of a new manufacturing facility in New Zealand which was begun in 1977 to replace the existing facility is scheduled for completion in 1978. Construction of a second manufacturing plant in Brazil and a new plant in Argentina is scheduled to begin in 1978. Plans for a new production facility in Portugal have been submitted to authorities for review in that country.

The Tupperware division has a continuing program of new product development. Development currently underway includes new TUPPERWARE® products for food preparation, serving and storage that will provide for future product introduction. During 1978, the TUPPERCRAFT® Planting System, which is comprised of a container with a well and indicator to show the proper water level, planting medium and nutrient, will be introduced for sale at Tupperware home parties.

TUPPERWARE® products compete with a broad range of food storage, serving and packaging items which are primarily sold through retail outlets. Tupperware competes with other companies by providing quality products for which it makes its own molds, as well as by providing product demonstrations to consumers, by its full lifetime warranty policy and through the development of new products. In addition, Tupperware and the other direct selling operations of Dart are subject to competition for party datings from other direct selling organizations both for similar and for unrelated products.

Vanda sells VANDA® cosmetics and toiletries directly to consumers in Canada, France, the Republic of South Africa, the United Kingdom and the United States. Manufacturing is done by Vanda or by outside manufacturers. Sales operations in Italy were terminated in 1977, sales operations in Belgium are being terminated in 1978, and operations in Australia and Mexico were sold early in 1978. During 1978, Vanda plans to change its operating methods in Europe including reducing product lines and personnel.

Dart manufactures cookware and giftware which it sells directly to consumers principally in the United States and Canada under the trademarks MIRACLE MAID® and COPPERCRAFT GUILD®.

Consumer Products

Dart's consumer products operations include the manufacture and sale to distributors or retailers of housewares and giftwares.

Dart manufactures and sells cookware, small electric housewares, humidifiers, serving ware and thermal food containers. In addition, it manufactures and sells various home furnishing items including decorative accessories, tables, casual furniture, hassocks, cushions and pillows. Products are sold through department stores, variety stores, mail order, premium users and independent direct selling businesses. Trademarks include WEST BEND®, THERMO-SERV®, SYROCO® and BABCOCK-PHILLIPS®. Manufacturing plants are located in West Bend, Wisconsin and seven other locations in the United States and three in Canada. Dart is continuously engaged in developing new consumer products and restyling existing lines.

Products made by Dart's Consumer Products group compete with products made by numerous other companies in highly competitive markets primarily in the United States and Canada. Important competitive factors include price, product performance, warranties and service, and the development of new products. In 1977 West Bend was the largest portable humidifier manufacturer in the United States. In addition, a WEST BEND® electric cooker and a WEST BEND® electric wok were among the leading brands in their retail markets at the end of 1977. West Bend is also a leading producer of electric corn poppers.

In January 1977, Dart sold the manufacturing facility, franchise drug operations and private label division of the United States Rexall Drug Company. Dart's Rexall Drug Division continues to produce drug and drug-related products in the Republic of South Africa.

Chemical — Plastics

During 1977, Dart's Chemical and Plastics groups were combined into one group. The divisions in the new group apply chemical and plastics technology to diversified products and markets.

Chemicals

Dart's operations in chemicals are comprised of the manufacture and sale of plastic raw materials, chemical specialties and processing and environmental equipment.

Dart is engaged in manufacturing plastic raw materials such as polyethylene and polypropylene at facilities in Bayport, Texas and Odessa, Texas, and in manufacturing petrochemical feedstocks such as olefins at the Odessa facility, through a 50%-owned joint venture with El Paso Products Company. Under the joint venture, a new polypropylene plant in Bayport, Texas became operational in late 1976 and by the end of 1977 was operating near design capacity of 150,000,000 pounds of resin per year. The joint venture's new low density polyethylene plant in Bayport with a rated capacity of 150,000,000 pounds of resin per year became operational in late 1977.

Marketing of plastic raw materials is by Dart's Rexene Styrenics Company and Rexene Polyolefins Company which manufacture and sell styrenic resins and polyolefin resins, respectively. Although Rexene Polyolefins operates subject to the policy guidance of the joint venture, Rexene Styrenics operates independently of the joint venture. Plastic film is made and sold at three plants in California, Wisconsin and Delaware by a company 50%-owned by Dart and 50%-owned by El Paso Products Company.

Dart also manufactures and sells chemical specialties including reinforced thermoplastics for various applications including automotive parts, brighteners and strippers for electroplating, color concentrates and coatings, organic peroxides and peresters, titanium trichloride, stearates and stabilizers. Dart provides pollution control services and manufactures and sells products to purify water, treat industrial waste and control air pollution. The products include chlorinators and control systems, air scrubbers, wet electrostatic precipitators, reinforced plastic tanks, and related equipment.

A research staff in Paramus, New Jersey has made commercially significant advancements in chemical research for the joint venture and Dart's own operations. Technology has been licensed to others both domestically and abroad. Construction began in 1977 on expanded research and development facilities in Paramus. The expanded facilities will support increased research and development programs for the combined Chemical-Plastics group operations.

Plastics

Dart manufactures and sells through its Styro Products sector foamed plastic cups, plastic cutlery and food containers. Foamed plastic cups are manufactured in various parts of the United States and Canada, the United Kingdom and The Netherlands, and also in Japan through a joint venture.

Through its Specialties sector Dart manufactures and sells extrusions, garden hose, athletic equipment, sealing specialties and tubes for ball point pens. Garden hose is sold under the trademarks COLORITE® and GERING®, athletic equipment is sold under the trademark SEAMCO® and surgical products are sold under the trademark SEAMLESS®. Dart is the largest producer of plastic garden hose in the United States and one of the largest compounders of non-toxic plastics used to manufacture food packaging and medical and hospital products.

Dart's Decorative Building Products sector manufactures and sells high pressure decorative laminates for interior surfacing under the WILSONART® trademark. Such products are manufactured in Temple, Texas and distributed throughout the United States. Construction will begin in 1978 on a second manufacturing facility in North Carolina.

The Packaging sector manufactures tubes, closures and seals in the United States and plastic bottles overseas.

The Health Care sector manufactures and markets prepackaged medical kits. Its surgical instrument manufacturing facility in Germany was sold during 1977.

Products made by Dart's Chemical-Plastics group are sold in highly competitive markets in the United States and in many foreign countries. Important competitive factors include price, product performance and dependability, and the development of new products and processes.

Glass Containers

The Thatcher division manufactures a line of glass bottles at its owned plants in California, Florida, Illinois, Indiana, New Jersey and New York for sale to distillers, brewers, soft-drink manufacturers, food processors and certain other users. Thatcher is the fourth largest United States producer of glass containers. Approximately 67% of Thatcher's total production is in glass containers for beer and beverages. Approximately 95% of beer and soft drink container production is in non-returnable bottles.

Thatcher research has led to advancement in improving high-speed production and inspection of bottles, increasing melting speed of glass and eliminating air pollutants from furnaces. In addition, Thatcher developed and manufactures a beer bottle weighing less than the conventional 12-ounce container through improved glass distribution.

Because of the anticipated continued shortage of natural gas, Thatcher has converted several furnaces in order to utilize either natural gas or alternative fuels. Thatcher also promotes the recycling of used bottles to conserve fuel because less fuel is required for firing furnaces when recycled glass is used.

During 1977, additional legislation designed to reduce litter and discourage the use of non-returnable containers of all kinds was proposed at the Federal, state and local levels. It is too early to predict what effect such legislation will have on glass container sales.

Resort Development

Dart entered the resort development business in 1969. It purchased properties in California which are suitable for resort homes within reasonable driving time of metropolitan centers. Dart's resort developments are located at Bear Valley Springs, comprised of 24,950 acres 120 miles north of Los Angeles and at Tahoe Donner, comprised of 4,000 acres 16 miles north of Lake Tahoe. Sales efforts at Tahoe Donner were resumed in late 1977 after having been suspended pending assurance to governmental authorities on the availability of adequate sewage disposal facilities.

Foreign Operations

Several segments of Dart's business have significant operations outside the United States. Approximately 25 percent of Dart's total sales in 1977 were attributable to foreign operations. Dart believes that foreign operations in the aggregate do not present substantial risks.

Trademarks and Patents

Dart owns a substantial number of trademarks and patents registered in the United States and in other countries. A number of the trademarks are of significant importance to Dart's operations, among them TUPPERWARE®, WEST BEND®, SYROCO®, MIRACLE MAID®, COPPER-CRAFT GUILD®, WILSONART®, THERMO-SERV®, REXENE® and EL REXENE®. Dart also grants licenses under patents and know-how developed by Dart, primarily in chemical operations, where a significant income is derived from such licensing.

Environmental Protection

Compliance with laws and regulations protecting the environment by Dart or its customers and suppliers is not anticipated to materially affect Dart's operations.

Employees

Dart on December 31, 1977 had approximately 31,200 employees, of whom approximately 7,900 were located outside the United States. Present litigation based upon alleged violations of federal, state or local civil rights statutes is not material.

Item 2. SUMMARY OF OPERATIONS

The Summary of Operations for the five years ended December 31, 1977 appearing on page 34 (except for that portion denominated "At Yearend") and Management's Discussion and Analysis appearing on page 33 of Dart's 1977 Annual Report to stockholders are incorporated herein by reference and are attached hereto as Exhibit 2.

Item 3. PROPERTIES

Dart's net investment at December 31, 1977 within and outside the United States in (i) land, (ii) buildings and improvements, (iii) machinery and equipment and (iv) construction in progress is as follows:

	United States	Foreign	Total
	(Thousands of Dollars)		
Land	$ 10,515	$ 6,287	$ 16,802
Buildings and improvements	121,889	42,400	164,289
Machinery and equipment	243,092	63,646	306,738
Construction in progress	14,669	2,187	16,856
	$390,165	$114,520	$504,685

For further information on material properties of Dart, see "Business" in response to Item 1.

Item 4. PARENTS AND SUBSIDIARIES

DART INDUSTRIES INC. (Registrant)	Percentage of Voting Securities Owned by Immediate Parent
Botellas y Envases Plasticos, S.A. (Spain)	100%
Camira Europe B.V. (The Netherlands)	100%
Consolidated Thermoplastics Company (Delaware)	50%
Dart Argentina S.A. (Argentina)	100%
Dart Chemical Services GmbH (W. Germany)	100%
Dart Chemical Specialties, S.A. (Belgium)	100%
Dart de Venezuela C.A. (Venezuela)	100%
Dart do Brasil Industria e Comercio Limitada (Brazil)	100%
Adota Artigos Domesticos Ltda. (Brazil)	100%
Dart Environment and Services Company (Delaware)	100%
Dart Europe S.A. (France)	100%
Dart Export Corporation (Delaware)	100%
Dart Hellas S.A.I. (Greece)	100%
Dart Iberica, S.A. (Spain)	100%
Dart (Philippines), Inc. (the Philippines)	100%
Dart Industries Belgium S.A. (Belgium)	100%
Societe d'Expansion des Matieres Plastiques S.A. (Belgium)	100%
Dart Industries Canada Limited (Canada)	100%
Dart Industries Deutschland GmbH (W. Germany)	100%
Dart Industries GmbH (Austria)	100%
Dart Industries Hong Kong Limited (Hong Kong)	100%
Dart Industries Limited (the United Kingdom)	100%
Insulpak Limited U.K. (the United Kingdom)	100%
Dart Industries Mortgage Company (Delaware)	100%
Dart Industries Nederland B.V. (The Netherlands)	100%
Dart Industries (New Zealand) Limited (New Zealand)	100%
Dart Insurance Company Limited (the United Kingdom)	100%
Dart Products National Limited (Canada)	100%

Dart is presently complying with several compliance schedules with respect to the discharge of materials into the environment. Dart is also involved in certain administrative proceedings relating to the discharge of substances into the environment, none of which is material.

Item 6. INCREASES AND DECREASES IN OUTSTANDING SECURITIES AND INDEBTEDNESS

1. Common Stock

    (A) (1) December 31, 1976

Shares issued	22,438,793
Treasury shares	742
Shares outstanding	22,438,051

    (2) December 31, 1977

Shares issued	23,133,321
Treasury shares	742
Shares outstanding	23,132,579
Increase in shares outstanding	694,528

    (B) The increase in the number of shares outstanding set forth above resulted from the following transactions:

    (1) The issuance on May 26, 1977 of 673,475 shares of Dart's Common Stock as a 3% stock dividend. Such issuance did not involve a "sale" as such term is defined in Section 2(3) of the Act.

    (2) The issuance and delivery during 1977 of 5,071 shares of Common Stock of Dart as the result of the conversion of 5,071 shares of Preferred Stock of Dart. The issuance of such shares was exempt from registration under Section 3(a) (9) of the Act.

    (3) The issuance and delivery during 1977 of 15,982 shares of Common Stock of registrant under registrant's stock option plan. Such shares were issued pursuant to a prospectus included in registration statements on Form S-8 filed with the Securities and Exchange Commission.

2. Series A $2 Cumulative Convertible Preferred Stock

    (A) (1) December 31, 1976

Shares issued	2,986,016
Treasury shares	32,500
Shares outstanding	2,953,516

    (2) December 31, 1977

Shares issued	2,980,945
Treasury shares	32,500
Shares outstanding	2,948,445
Decrease in shares outstanding	5,071

    (B) The decrease in the number of shares outstanding set forth above resulted from the conversion in 1977 by stockholders of 5,071 shares of Series A $2 Cumulative Convertible Preferred Stock of Dart into Common Stock of Dart.

Item 7. CHANGES IN SECURITIES AND CHANGES IN SECURITY FOR

REGISTERED SECURITIES

No response to this item is required.

Item 8. DEFAULTS UPON SENIOR SECURITIES

No response to this item is required.

Item 9. APPROXIMATE NUMBER OF EQUITY SECURITY HOLDERS

(A) Title of Class	(B) Number of holders of record as of December 31, 1977
Common Stock	28,789
Series A $2 Cumulative Convertible Preferred Stock	5,204

Item 10. SUBMISSION OF MATTERS TO A VOTE OF SECURITY HOLDERS

No response to this item is required.

Item 11. EXECUTIVE OFFICERS OF REGISTRANT

The following are the executive officers of Dart, their ages, their present positions with Dart, the period during which they have held such positions and a brief account of their previous positions during the past five years if they first became an executive officer during such period. Officers are elected annually to serve one year terms or until their successors are elected.

Justin Dart, 70, Chairman of the Board of Directors since 1966, Director since 1943 and Chief Executive Officer since 1946.

Thomas P. Mullaney, 45, President, Chief Operating Officer and Director since November 1976. During the past five years prior to joining Dart, Mr. Mullaney was president and chief executive officer of Wilson Sporting Goods, a division of PepsiCo, Inc.

Phillip D. Matthews, 39, Executive Vice President, Finance and Administration, Chief Financial Officer, and Director since August 1977. During the past five years prior to joining Dart, Mr. Matthews was senior vice president of Frito-Lay, Inc. and vice president of Wilson Sporting Goods, divisions of PepsiCo, Inc.

Robert T. Beattie, 66, Director since 1968 and Executive Vice President since October 1975, formerly President of the Consumer Products Group from August 1975 until December 1977. During the past five years Mr. Beattie previously served as Vice President.

Ralph M. Knight, 62, Director since 1962, Executive Vice President since September 1974, and formerly President and Chief Executive Officer of Dart's former Chemical Group from 1960 until August 1977. Mr. Knight first became an executive officer of Dart in 1960.

Hamer F. Wilson, 64, Director since 1961 and Executive Vice President since 1969. Mr. Wilson has served as Chairman and Chief Executive Officer of Dart's Direct Selling Group since 1966.

Russell K. Bolton, 57, Director since 1969, Vice President since 1966 and General Counsel since 1964.

Walter Bond, 48, Vice President since February 1978, and Executive Vice President, Tupperware International since January 1974. During the past five years, Mr. Bond previously served as President of Tupperware Europe, Africa, and the Middle East.

Vincent R. Cucina, 42, Vice President, Financial Planning, since July 1974. During the past five years, Mr. Cucina previously served as Vice President in Dart's Corporate Group and Director and Assistant Director of Financial Analysis and Review.

Elmer M. Davis, 55, Vice President since October 1975 and President of the Housewares division of the Consumer Products Group since September 1975. During the past five years, Mr. Davis previously served as Executive Vice President of Dart's former Plastics Group and President of Dart's Plastics Specialties division.

John P. Del Favero, 49, Director since August 1977, Vice President since 1976 and President of Dart's Chemical-Plastics Group since August 1977. Mr. Del Favero was President of Dart's former Plastics Group from April 1976 to August 1977. During the past five years prior to joining Dart, Mr. Del Favero was president and chief executive officer of U.S. Natural Resources Inc.

F. William Graham, 40, Vice President and President of Dart's Consumer Products Group since December 1977. During the past five years prior to joining Dart, Mr. Graham was group vice president and general manager of the Fashion Group of General Mills, Inc. and vice president of General Mills, Inc.

William H. Greenberg, 55, Vice President since October 1975 and President of Dart's Glass Containers Group since June 1975. During the past five years, Mr. Greenberg previously served as Senior Vice President, Sales and Marketing of Dart's Glass Containers Group.

Joseph Hara, 53, Vice President since February 1978, Director since July 1969, Executive Vice President of Tupperware International since January 1974 and President of Tupperware U.S. since 1966.

Thomas M. Mullen, 52, Vice President since 1972 and Treasurer since 1970.

William R. Palmer, 53, Vice President since 1972 and Controller since 1970.

John C. Phifer, 48, Vice President since May 1976 and President, Chemical Specialties sector, Chemical-Plastics Group since January 1978. During the past five years, Mr. Phifer previously served as Executive Vice President, Finance and Administration and Executive Vice President, Planning and Controls, both for Dart's former Chemical Group.

Herschel A. Phillips, 55, Vice President, Labor Relations, since 1968.

James P. Schwartz, 45, Vice President since February 1976 and President of Dart's Styro Products sector, Chemical-Plastics Group since February 1971. During the past five years Mr. Schwartz previously served as President of Dart's former Styro and Specialty Products sector.

Norman Wicks, 61, Vice President since 1972, most recently responsible for Corporate Relations.

Edgar Thedens, 53, Secretary since 1967.

Item 12. INDEMNIFICATION OF DIRECTORS AND OFFICERS

The information requested is unchanged from the information set forth in Registrant's 1970 Annual Report on Form 10-K as filed with the Securities and Exchange Commission.

Item 13. FINANCIAL STATEMENTS, EXHIBITS FILED, AND REPORTS ON FORM 8-K

(a) 1. Financial Statements. The financial statements included on pages 18 through 32 in Dart's 1977 Annual Report to stockholders are set forth in full as Exhibit 1 hereto and hereby incorporated by reference. The additional financial data listed in the index on page 15 is to be read in conjunction with such financial statements.

2. Exhibits:

1   Pages 18 through 32 from the 1977 Annual Report to stockholders of Dart Industries Inc.

2   Pages 33 and 34 from the 1977 Annual Report to stockholders of Dart Industries Inc.

3   Basis of Computation of Per Share Earnings.

4   By-Laws of Dart as amended January 30, 1978.

(b) No reports on Form 8-K were filed during the three months ended December 31, 1977.

Items 14 - 18

Omitted. Dart has filed a definitive proxy statement, which involved the election of directors, pursuant to Regulation 14A since the close of its fiscal year.

SIGNATURE

Pursuant to the requirements of Section 13 or 15(d) of the Securities Exchange Act of 1934, the registrant has duly caused this annual report to be signed on its behalf by the undersigned thereunto duly authorized.

DART INDUSTRIES INC.

EDGAR THEDENS

Edgar Thedens
Secretary

March 27, 1978

CONSENT OF INDEPENDENT ACCOUNTANTS

To the Board of Directors and
   Stockholders of Dart Industries Inc.

   We hereby consent to the application of our report, which appears on page 32 of the 1977 Annual Report to stockholders of Dart Industries Inc., to the additional financial data listed in the following index when this data is read in conjunction with the financial statements in such 1977 Annual Report to stockholders; our report and the financial statements have been incorporated in this Annual Report on Form 10-K. The examinations referred to in our report included examinations of the additional financial data.

                              PRICE WATERHOUSE & CO.

Los Angeles, California
February 26, 1978

DART INDUSTRIES INC.
AND CONSOLIDATED SUBSIDIARIES

INDEX TO ITEM 13(a)

December 31, 1977

The 1976 and 1977 financial statements, together with the report thereon of Price Water-house & Co. dated February 26, 1978, appearing on pages 18 to 32 of the 1977 Annual Report to stockholders are incorporated in this Form 10-K Annual Report. With the exception of the aforementioned information and the information incorporated in Item 2, the 1977 Annual Report to stockholders is not to be deemed filed as part of this report. The following additional financial data should be read in conjunction with the financial statements in such 1977 Annual Report to stockholders. Schedules not included with this additional financial data have been omitted because they are not applicable or the required information is shown in the financial statements or notes thereto. Separate financial statements of subsidiaries not consolidated and 50% or less owned persons accounted for by the equity method which are not shown herein have been omitted because, if considered in the aggregate, they would not constitute a significant subsidiary.

ADDITIONAL FINANCIAL DATA

1976 and 1977

	Page
Additional financial information	16-20
Schedules —	
I — Marketable securities — other security investments	21
II — Amounts receivable from underwriters, promoters, directors, officers, employees and principal holders of equity securities other than affiliates	22
V — Property, plant and equipment	23
VI — Accumulated depreciation and amortization of property, plant and equipment	24
XII — Reserves	25

The individual financial statements of the registrant have been omitted since the registrant is primarily an operating company and all subsidiaries included in the consolidated financial statements, in the aggregate, do not have minority equity interests and/or indebtedness to any person other than the registrant or its consolidated subsidiaries in amounts which together exceed 5 percent of total consolidated assets at December 31, 1977, excepting indebtedness incurred in the ordinary course of business which is not overdue and which matures within one year from the date of its creation.

DART INDUSTRIES INC.
AND CONSOLIDATED SUBSIDIARIES

ADDITIONAL FINANCIAL INFORMATION
For the Years Ended December 31, 1976 and 1977

Inventories

The amounts of inventories used in computation of cost of goods sold are as follows:

December 31, 1975	$259,816,000
December 31, 1976	296,240,000
December 31, 1977	310,262,000

Stock option plan

A summary of changes in the stockholder approved stock option plan from January 1, 1976 through December 31, 1977 follows:

	Year ended December 31,	
	1976	1977
Options which became exercisable:		
Number of shares	102,500	80,400
Option prices —		
Per share range	$21.21 to $48.85	$21.21 to $44.91
Total	$3,536,000	$2,748,000
Fair value at date exercisable —		
Per share range	$31.07 to $35.92	$32.06 to $37.69
Total	$3,380,000	$2,792,000
Options exercised during the period:		
Number of shares	18,600	16,000
Option prices —		
Per share range	$22.73 to $34.62	$21.21 to $33.61
Total	$ 641,000	$ 428,000
Fair value at date exercised —		
Per share range	$33.38 to $36.35	$30.50 to $38.69
Total	$ 659,000	$ 547,000
Options canceled:		
Number of shares	85,500	68,100
Option prices —		
Per share range	$21.80 to $46.25	$30.65 to $48.85
Total	$2,907,000	$2,703,000

At December 31, 1977 there were 577,200 shares under option at prices ranging from $21.21 to $46.69 per share totaling $20,659,000 (including 499,600 shares which currently were exercisable at prices ranging from $21.21 to $46.69 per share and totaling $18,350,000). There were 610,400 shares available for granting at December 31, 1976 and 679,600 shares at December 31, 1977.

Option shares and prices have been adjusted to reflect applicable stock dividends paid subsequent to dates of grant.

DART INDUSTRIES INC.
AND CONSOLIDATED SUBSIDIARIES

ADDITIONAL FINANCIAL INFORMATION (Continued)
For the Years Ended December 31, 1976 and 1977

Replacement Cost Information (Unaudited)

In compliance with rules of the Securities and Exchange Commission, Dart has estimated certain replacement cost information for inventories, properties, cost of goods sold, and depreciation and amortization. The amounts reported are the result of the calculations described below and are not necessarily indicative of the amounts for which the assets could be sold or management's intentions for replacement of such assets, nor are they necessarily representative of costs that might be incurred in a future period. The data in the following table should be read in conjunction with the explanations and comments below.

	1976		1977	
	Estimated Replacement Cost	Comparable Historical Cost	Estimated Replacement Cost	Comparable Historical Cost
At Year end:				
Inventories	$ 290,000,000	$279,041,000	$ 305,000,000	$296,698,000
Properties —				
Gross	$1,155,000,000	$731,822,000	$1,264,000,000	$780,259,000
Net of accumulated depreciation	$ 630,000,000	$425,910,000	$ 676,000,000	$447,933,000
For the year:				
Cost of goods sold and operating expenses	$ 869,000,000	$826,080,000	$ 914,000,000	$883,095,000
Depreciation and amortization	$ 73,000,000	$ 50,982,000	$ 80,000,000	$ 56,273,000

DART INDUSTRIES INC.
AND CONSOLIDATED SUBSIDIARIES

ADDITIONAL FINANCIAL INFORMATION (Continued)

For the Years Ended December 31, 1976 and 1977

The following table reconciles the historical cost amounts as reflected in the financial statements to the related totals for which replacement cost data are provided.

| For 1976 | Inventories | Properties | | Cost of Goods Sold | Depreciation and Amortization |
		Gross	Net		
Totals as reflected in financial statements	$296,240,000	$793,826,000	$476,346,000	$876,401,000	$52,422,000
Less amounts for which replacement cost data have not been provided —					
Certain assets which management does not intend to replace	17,199,000	20,120,000	8,552,000	50,321,000	941,000
Land and construction in progress		41,884,000	41,884,000		
Amortization of intangibles					499,000
Historical cost amounts for which replacement cost data are provided	$279,041,000	$731,822,000	$425,910,000	$826,080,000	$50,982,000

DART INDUSTRIES INC.
AND CONSOLIDATED SUBSIDIARIES

ADDITIONAL FINANCIAL INFORMATION (Continued)
For the Years Ended December 31, 1976 and 1977

For 1977	Inventories	Properties Gross	Properties Net	Cost of Goods Sold	Depreciation and Amortization
Totals as reflected in financial statements	$310,262,000	$855,681,000	$504,685,000	$951,062,000	$ 59,423,000
Less amounts for which replacement cost data have not been provided —					
Certain assets which management does not intend to replace	13,564,000	41,764,000	23,094,000	67,967,000	2,698,000
Land and construction in progress		33,658,000	33,658,000		
Amortization of intangibles					452,000
Historical cost amounts for which replacement cost data are provided	$296,698,000	$780,259,000	$447,933,000	$883,095,000	$ 56,273,000

The estimated replacement cost of inventories generally was calculated by using revised standard costs reflecting current purchase prices and production costs and including estimated replacement cost depreciation. No allowance was made for improved efficiency or reduced operating costs which might occur if manufacturing facilities were replaced. Replacement cost of goods sold was estimated through adjustment of historical costs for average cost changes during the period.

The methods used in estimating replacement cost of properties were established after a comprehensive review of productive capacity by operating segments in 1976. Such methods included the utilization of engineering estimates, vendor quotations or published prices, Dart's current cost of plant construction, and indexing of historical cost data, as appropriate. Depreciated replacement cost and replacement cost depreciation were estimated by relating accumulated depreciation expense to the cost of various groups of assets, excluding fully depreciated assets, and applying the resultant ratios to the computed replacement cost.

The replacement cost data presented herein does not reflect the overall impact of inflation on Dart's financial position or results of operations. Dart has not attempted to quantify the impact of inflation on assets and liabilities other than inventories and properties and there are unresolved conceptual problems in doing so. Further, although the replacement cost data disclosed herein have, in Dart's view, been reasonably estimated, the estimating procedures require that certain assumptions and subjective decisions be made which render the results inherently imprecise.

**DART INDUSTRIES INC.
AND CONSOLIDATED SUBSIDIARIES**

ADDITIONAL FINANCIAL INFORMATION (Continued)

For the Years Ended December 31, 1976 and 1977

It would be a misuse of these data to attempt to derive an inflation adjusted statement of earnings or financial position. Management fully expects that whenever it replaces plant or equipment in any of its business operations such replacements would be based on studies of expected rates of return and would normally only be approved if target rates of return could be equalled or exceeded.

DART INDUSTRIES INC. AND CONSOLIDATED SUBSIDIARIES

SCHEDULE I — MARKETABLE SECURITIES — OTHER SECURITY INVESTMENTS

Column A	Column B	Column C	Column D	Column E
Name of issuer	Principal amount or maturity value	Cost	Market value	Per balance sheet (at cost)
Short term securities:				
United States Treasury Bills and Notes	$ 43,555,000	$ 42,463,000	$ 42,248,000	
Bankers Trust	6,000,000	6,000,000	6,000,000	
Bank of America	9,000,000	8,997,000	8,999,000	
Bank of Montreal	6,065,000	6,001,000	6,001,000	
Bank of Nova Scotia	8,520,000	8,500,000	8,500,000	
Bear Stearns & Co.*	2,040,000	2,040,000	2,040,000	
A. G. Becker*	5,000,000	5,000,000	5,000,000	
Chase Manhattan Bank	10,002,000	9,960,000	9,963,000	
Chemical Bank	3,000,000	2,998,000	2,998,000	
Citibank Nassau	6,000,000	6,000,000	6,000,000	
Continental Bank Nassau	6,000,000	6,000,000	6,000,000	
Continental Ill. Nat'l Bk. & Tr.	3,000,000	3,000,000	3,000,000	
Credit Lyonnaise	6,037,000	6,000,000	6,000,000	
Donaldson Lufkin*	1,500,000	1,500,000	1,500,000	
Electricite De France	2,000,000	1,997,000	1,997,000	
FNB Chicago Grand Cayman	6,000,000	6,000,000	6,000,000	
First Pennsylvania	2,013,000	2,010,000	2,010,000	
Fuji Bank	4,004,000	4,000,000	4,000,000	
Ford Motor Company	1,000,000	1,017,000	1,000,000	
General Motors Accept. Corp.	7,014,000	7,002,000	7,002,000	
Harris Trust Co.	4,000,000	4,000,000	4,000,000	
Huntoon Paige*	408,000	408,000	408,000	
E. F. Hutton*	260,000	260,000	260,000	
Inland Steel	500,000	449,000	443,000	
Int'l Bk. for Rec. & Dev.	3,000,000	3,052,000	2,987,000	
Manufacturers Hanover	5,000,000	4,968,000	4,989,000	
Mitsubishi Bank	5,005,000	5,000,000	5,000,000	
Mitsui Bank	5,016,000	5,000,000	5,000,000	
Morgan Guaranty Tr. Co.	7,000,000	7,001,000	7,000,000	
Ontario Hydro Electric	2,757,000	2,740,000	2,740,000	
Pacific Tel. & Tel.	1,000,000	957,000	944,000	
R. N. B. Dallas	1,000,000	985,000	985,000	
Sears Roebuck & Co.	2,025,000	2,013,000	2,013,000	
Second District SEC*	9,673,000	9,673,000	9,673,000	
Other miscellaneous		78,000	78,000	
Total short term securities	$184,394,000	$183,069,000	$182,778,000	$183,069,000
3M Company Common Stock	847,000 shares	$ 35,162,000	$ 41,080,000	$ 35,162,000

* Resale agreements secured primarily by U.S. government securities.

DART INDUSTRIES INC. AND CONSOLIDATED SUBSIDIARIES

SCHEDULE II — AMOUNTS RECEIVABLE FROM UNDERWRITERS, PROMOTERS, DIRECTORS, OFFICERS, EMPLOYEES AND PRINCIPAL HOLDERS OF EQUITY SECURITIES OTHER THAN AFFILIATES

Column A	Column B	Column C	Column D		Column E	
			Deductions		Balance at end of year	
Name of debtor	Balance at beginning of year	Additions	Amounts collected	Other	Current	Not current
(For the year ended December 31, 1976)						
A. C. Papadakis	$103,986	$115,674	$ 51,954		$167,706	
(For the year ended December 31, 1977)						
A. C. Papadakis	$167,706	$ 28,687	$ 53,159		$143,234	

A. C. Papadakis is manager of the Greek branch of Dart Industries Belgium S.A. and managing director of Dart Hellas S.A.I. Mr. Papadakis is neither an officer nor a director of Dart Industries Inc. The loan from Dart Industries Belgium S.A. is evidenced by a promissory note, which bears interest at the rate of 8½% per annum. It is expected that the loan will be repaid by 1980.

DART INDUSTRIES INC. AND CONSOLIDATED SUBSIDIARIES

SCHEDULE V — PROPERTY, PLANT AND EQUIPMENT

Column A Classification	Column B Balance at beginning of year	Column C Additions at cost	Other (b)	Column D Retirements or sales	Column E Transfers	Column F Balance at end of year
(For the year ended December 31, 1976)						
Land	$ 14,309,000	$ 2,860,000	$ —	$ 1,257,000	$ 341,000	$ 16,253,000
Buildings and improvements	192,514,000	28,177,000	96,000	7,904,000	(469,000)	212,414,000
Machinery and equipment	446,937,000	111,623,000	1,280,000	20,833,000	128,000	539,135,000
Construction in progress	48,080,000	(22,056,000) (a)	—	—	—	26,024,000
	$701,840,000	$120,604,000 (c)	$1,376,000	$29,994,000		$793,826,000
(For the year ended December 31, 1977)						
Land	$ 16,253,000	$ 1,094,000	—	$ 565,000	$ 20,000	$ 16,802,000
Buildings and improvements	212,414,000	21,061,000	—	7,108,000	3,006,000	229,373,000
Machinery and equipment	539,135,000	81,584,000	—	25,043,000	(3,026,000)	592,650,000
Construction in progress	26,024,000	(9,168,000) (a)	—	—	—	16,856,000
	$793,826,000	$ 94,571,000		$32,716,000		$855,681,000

Notes:

(a) Net change during the year.

(b) Fair value of property, plant and equipment of businesses acquired in transactions accounted for as purchases.

(c) Includes deposits on machinery and equipment transferred from other assets.

DART INDUSTRIES INC. AND CONSOLIDATED SUBSIDIARIES

SCHEDULE VI — ACCUMULATED DEPRECIATION AND AMORTIZATION OF PROPERTY, PLANT AND EQUIPMENT

Column A	Column B	Column C	Column D	Column E	Column F
Description	Balance at beginning of year	Additions charged to costs and expenses	Retirements or sales	Transfers	Balance at end of year
(For the year ended December 31, 1976)					
Buildings and improvements	$ 57,733,000	$ 7,458,000	$ 4,338,000	$ (620,000)	$ 60,233,000
Machinery and equipment	229,388,000	44,465,000	17,226,000	620,000	257,247,000
	$287,121,000	$51,923,000	$21,564,000	—	$317,480,000
(For the year ended December 31, 1977)					
Buildings and improvements	$ 60,233,000	$ 8,205,000	$ 3,547,000	$ 193,000	$ 65,084,000
Machinery and equipment	257,247,000	50,581,000	21,723,000	(193,000)	285,912,000
	$317,480,000	$58,786,000	$25,270,000	—	$350,996,000

DART INDUSTRIES INC. AND CONSOLIDATED SUBSIDIARIES

SCHEDULE XII — RESERVES

Column A	Column B	Column C	Column D	Column E
Description	Balance at beginning of year	Additions charged to costs and expenses	Deductions	Balance at end of year
(For the year ended December 31, 1976)				
Reserves deducted from assets to which they apply:				
Doubtful accounts and notes, discounts, etc. classified under current assets	$12,764,000	$ 5,126,000	$ 5,395,000	$12,495,000
Marketable securities, classified under current assets	1,087,000	—	192,000	895,000
Deferred profit on resort development receivables	7,463,000	4,886,000	3,022,000	9,327,000
Other assets, receivables and investments	2,915,000	494,000	555,000	2,854,000
	$24,229,000	$10,506,000	$ 9,164,000	$25,571,000
(For the year ended December 31, 1977)				
Reserves deducted from assets to which they apply:				
Doubtful accounts and notes, discounts, etc. classified under current assets	$12,495,000	$ 4,640,000	$ 5,166,000	$11,969,000
Marketable securities, classified under current assets	895,000	—	895,000	—
Deferred profit on resort development receivables	9,327,000	4,811,000	3,532,000	10,606,000
Other assets, receivables and investments	2,854,000	1,934,000	376,000	4,412,000
	$25,571,000	$11,385,000	$ 9,969,000	$26,987,000

EXHIBIT *I*

DART INDUSTRIES INC. AND CONSOLIDATED SUBSIDIARIES

FINANCIAL STATEMENTS

This exhibit is a photocopy of the summary of accounting policies, the financial statements and the related notes thereto, and the Report of Independent Accountants included in the 1977 Annual Report to stockholders of Dart Industries Inc.

Dart Industries Inc. and Consolidated Subsidiaries

Summary of Accounting Policies

Basis of consolidation The consolidated financial statements include the accounts of Dart and its subsidiaries except for its wholly-owned insurance subsidiary, whose operations are not significant, and two less than 50% owned foreign corporations, all of which are accounted for on the equity method. Significant intercompany accounts and transactions are eliminated.

Dart is a party to a joint operating agreement whereby it has an undivided 50% interest in plant and other assets relating to the production and marketing of certain petrochemicals, and is also a 50% owner of a plastics processing corporation with the same other party. The accompanying statements include 50% of the assets, liabilities, income and costs and expenses of these jointly owned activities.

Translation of foreign currencies Foreign subsidiary balance sheet accounts for inventories, prepaid expenses, deferred income taxes, properties, investments and other assets are translated into United States dollar equivalents at historical exchange rates; cash, receivables and all liability accounts are translated at yearend exchange rates. Income and expense accounts are translated at the average rate of exchange in effect during the year except for cost of goods sold, depreciation and amortization which are translated at historical rates. Exchange gains and losses are included in the determination of current year earnings.

Inventories Inventories are valued at the lower of cost or market. In general, cost as applied to inventory valuation represents purchase or manufacturing cost applied on the first-in, first-out method. Obsolete and damaged merchandise is excluded.

Properties and depreciation Expenditures for additions, improvements, replacements, betterments and major renewals are added to the properties accounts. Properties retired, or otherwise disposed of, are eliminated from the asset accounts and the related amounts of accumulated depreciation are eliminated from the accumulated depreciation accounts. Gains and losses from disposals are included in earnings. Expenditures for maintenance, repairs and minor renewals are charged to earnings as incurred.

Depreciation of properties is provided chiefly on a straight line basis over the estimated average useful lives of the various assets. Lives used for calculating depreciation rates for the principal asset classifications are as follows: buildings and improvements—10 to 50 years; machinery and equipment—3 to 20 years.

Intangibles Intangibles having limited lives are amortized over their estimated useful lives. Certain intangibles acquired prior to October 31, 1970 are considered to have an unlimited life and are not being amortized.

Research and development Expenditures for research and development are charged to earnings as incurred.

Income taxes Provision is made for deferred income taxes and future income tax benefits applicable to timing differences between book and tax income. Declining balance and guideline depreciation and the instalment method of income recognition generally are used in the determination of income for tax purposes where applicable.

Investment tax credits are applied to reduce federal income tax expense in the year the credit arises.

Dart and its domestic subsidiaries file a consolidated federal income tax return. Provision is made for United States income taxes on earnings of foreign subsidiaries except for those which are expected to be invested indefinitely.

Resort development Resort lot sales are accounted for on the instalment method until actual collection experience for a project indicates that collectibility of receivable balances is reasonably predictable, after which the accrual method will be used. Under the instalment method, the gross profit less direct selling expenses related to the portion of the sales price which is not received in cash is deferred at the time of sale and recognized as cash is collected. In the opinion of management, at December 31, 1977 none of Dart's projects qualifies for the accrual method.

Interest and property taxes relating to land held for sale or improvement are charged to earnings as incurred. Land and improvements are valued at the lower of cost or estimated net realizable value.

Dart Industries Inc. and Consolidated Subsidiaries

Statement of Earnings and Retained Earnings

For the years ended December 31, 1977 and 1976

	1977	1976
Income:		
Net sales	$1,600,988,000	$1,476,240,000
Other income	21,804,000	18,552,000
	1,622,792,000	1,494,792,000
Costs and Expenses:		
Cost of goods sold and operating expenses	951,062,000	876,401,000
Selling, distribution and administrative expenses	391,099,000	358,588,000
Depreciation and amortization	59,423,000	52,422,000
Interest expense	20,512,000	16,768,000
	1,422,096,000	1,304,179,000
Earnings Before Income Taxes	200,696,000	190,613,000
Provision for income taxes	91,500,000	89,000,000
Net Earnings	109,196,000	101,613,000
Retained earnings at beginning of year	444,617,000	386,013,000
	553,813,000	487,626,000
Dividends:		
Cash—		
Preferred—$2 per share	5,902,000	5,908,000
Common—$1.00 and $.66 per share	22,787,000	15,045,000
Common Stock, 3%, 673,500 shares at $31.50 per share		
paid in May 1977 and 653,500 shares at $33.75 per share		
paid in May 1976	21,214,000	22,056,000
	49,903,000	43,009,000
Retained Earnings at End of Year	$ 503,910,000	$ 444,617,000
Net Earnings Per Share of Common Stock:		
Primary	$4.46	$4.14
Fully diluted	$4.18	$3.88

SEE ACCOMPANYING NOTES TO FINANCIAL STATEMENTS AND SUMMARY OF ACCOUNTING POLICIES.

Dart Industries Inc. and Consolidated Subsidiaries

Balance Sheet
December 31, 1977 and 1976

Assets	1977	1976
Current assets:		
Cash, including time deposits of $27,696,000 in 1977 and $18,428,000 in 1976	$ 63,033,000	$ 49,106,000
Marketable securities, at cost which approximates market	183,069,000	140,271,000
Total cash and marketable securities	246,102,000	189,377,000
Accounts and notes receivable, less allowance for doubtful accounts of $11,969,000 in 1977 and $12,495,000 in 1976	191,191,000	181,901,000
Inventories	310,262,000	296,240,000
Prepaid expenses	14,782,000	14,765,000
Deferred future income tax benefits	32,700,000	26,600,000
Total current assets	795,037,000	708,883,000
Resort development assets	53,657,000	57,144,000
Properties:		
Properties owned	832,003,000	770,463,000
Properties leased under capital leases	23,678,000	23,363,000
	855,681,000	793,826,000
Less accumulated depreciation	350,996,000	317,480,000
Total properties	504,685,000	476,346,000
Investments and other assets:		
3M Company common stock held in escrow for exchange by holders of 4¼% and 4¾% debentures, at cost (market value: 1977—$41,080,000; 1976—$47,961,000)	35,162,000	35,162,000
Other assets, receivables and investments	40,270,000	34,499,000
Intangibles relating to businesses purchased, less amortization	11,425,000	14,445,000
Total investments and other assets	86,857,000	84,106,000
Total Assets	**$1,440,236,000**	**$1,326,479,000**

SEE ACCOMPANYING NOTES TO FINANCIAL STATEMENTS AND SUMMARY OF ACCOUNTING POLICIES.

Liabilities and Stockholders' Equity	1977	1976
Current liabilities:		
Accounts payable	$ 73,378,000	$ 68,737,000
Accrued compensation	42,151,000	39,742,000
Other accrued expenses	97,455,000	77,987,000
Short term loans, foreign	13,471,000	16,350,000
Current instalments of obligations under capital leases	981,000	1,260,000
Current instalments of long term debt	8,450,000	6,407,000
Income taxes	38,600,000	32,800,000
Total current liabilities	274,486,000	243,283,000
Resort development liabilities	9,324,000	8,909,000
Obligations under capital leases, less current instalments	12,897,000	13,522,000
Long term debt, less current instalments	238,716,000	241,188,000
Deferred income taxes	58,800,000	54,500,000
Stockholders' equity:		
Preferred Stock, $5.00 par value		
Authorized, 3,000,000 shares		
Series A $2 Cumulative Convertible (aggregate liquidating preference in 1977—$149,050,000)		
Issued, 2,981,000 shares in 1977 and 2,986,000 shares in 1976	14,905,000	14,930,000
Common Stock, $1.25 par value		
Authorized, 35,000,000 shares		
Issued, 23,133,300 shares in 1977 and 22,438,800 shares in 1976	28,917,000	28,048,000
Capital in excess of par value	299,828,000	279,029,000
Retained earnings	503,910,000	444,617,000
	847,560,000	766,624,000
Less cost of reacquired shares of capital stock— Preferred—32,500; Common—700	1,547,000	1,547,000
Total stockholders' equity	846,013,000	765,077,000
Total Liabilities and Stockholders' Equity	**$1,440,236,000**	**$1,326,479,000**

Dart Industries Inc. and Consolidated Subsidiaries

Statement of Capital Stock
For the years ended December 31, 1977 and 1976

	1977		1976	
	SHARES ISSUED	AMOUNT	SHARES ISSUED	AMOUNT
Preferred Stock				
At Beginning of Year	2,986,000	$14,930,000	2,986,400	$14,932,000
Upon conversion into Common Stock	(5,000)	(25,000)	(400)	(2,000)
At End of Year, Including Reacquired Shares	2,981,000	$14,905,000	2,986,000	$14,930,000
Common Stock				
At Beginning of Year	22,438,800	$28,048,000	21,766,800	$27,209,000
For stock dividend	673,500	842,000	653,500	817,000
Upon exercise of options	16,000	20,000	18,100	22,000
Upon conversion of Preferred Stock	5,000	7,000	400	
At End of Year, Including Reacquired Shares	23,133,300	$28,917,000	22,438,800	$28,048,000

Statement of Capital in Excess of Par Value
For the years ended December 31, 1977 and 1976

	1977	1976
At Beginning of Year	$279,029,000	$257,169,000
Excess of fair value over par value of Common Stock issued as stock dividend	20,373,000	21,239,000
Excess of option prices over par value of Common Stock issued upon exercise of options	408,000	619,000
Upon conversion of Preferred Stock	18,000	2,000
At End of Year	$299,828,000	$279,029,000

SEE ACCOMPANYING NOTES TO FINANCIAL STATEMENTS AND SUMMARY OF ACCOUNTING POLICIES.

Dart Industries Inc. and Consolidated Subsidiaries

Statement of Changes in Financial Position
For the years ended December 31, 1977 and 1976

	1977	1976
Working Capital Provided by:		
Net earnings	$109,196,000	$101,613,000
Items not affecting working capital—		
Depreciation and amortization	59,423,000	52,422,000
Deferred income taxes	4,300,000	5,100,000
Provided by operations	172,919,000	159,135,000
Increase in long term debt and capital lease obligations	7,848,000	35,530,000
Reduction of investment in resort development	3,902,000	12,010,000
Dispositions of properties, investments and other assets	7,261,000	13,246,000
Other	3,676,000	7,568,000
Total Working Capital Provided	195,606,000	227,489,000
Working Capital Used for:		
Properties acquired	94,571,000	120,604,000
Cash dividends paid—		
Preferred Stock	5,902,000	5,908,000
Common Stock	22,787,000	15,045,000
Decrease in long term debt and capital lease obligations	10,945,000	10,869,000
Other	6,450,000	3,540,000
Total Working Capital Used	140,655,000	155,966,000
Working Capital Increase	$ 54,951,000	$ 71,523,000
Changes in Components of Working Capital:		
Cash and marketable securities	$ 56,725,000	$ 32,573,000
Accounts and notes receivable	9,290,000	19,540,000
Inventories	14,022,000	36,424,000
Other current assets	6,117,000	11,108,000
Accounts payable	(4,641,000)	(10,336,000)
Accrued expenses	(21,877,000)	(9,456,000)
Short term loans, foreign	2,879,000	(7,198,000)
Income taxes	(5,800,000)	(1,400,000)
Other current liabilities	(1,764,000)	268,000
Working Capital Increase	$ 54,951,000	$ 71,523,000

SEE ACCOMPANYING NOTES TO FINANCIAL STATEMENTS AND SUMMARY OF ACCOUNTING POLICIES.

Dart Industries Inc. and Consolidated Subsidiaries

Notes to Financial Statements

		NET SALES		OPERATING PROFIT	
		1977	1976	1977	1976
Segment operating data	Direct Selling	$ 575,417,000	$ 512,344,000	$146,349,000	$133,100,000
	Consumer Products	206,113,000	244,275,000	25,519,000	27,837,000
	Chemical and	252,714,000	232,312,000	18,272,000	33,783,000
	Plastics	315,298,000	278,542,000	28,522,000	17,105,000
	Glass Containers	260,067,000	228,886,000	21,714,000	29,808,000
	Resort Development	16,204,000	9,956,000	(1,869,000)	(15,325,000)
	Adjustments and eliminations	(24,825,000)	(30,075,000)	(6,063,000)	(7,915,000)
	Corporate items			(31,748,000)	(27,780,000)
	Consolidated	$1,600,988,000	$1,476,240,000	$200,696,000	$190,613,000

Geographic operating data	United States
	Western Hemisphere (outside United States)
	Europe and Africa
	Pacific Area
	Adjustments and eliminations
	Corporate items
	Consolidated

The various segments of Dart comprise principally the following products and services: **Direct Selling**—Tupperware brand plastic food preparation, storage and serving containers; Vanda Beauty Counselor cosmetics and toiletries; Miracle Maid cookware and Coppercraft Guild giftware; **Consumer Products**—West Bend electric housewares and cookware; Syroco home decorative accessories and giftware; **Chemical**—plastic raw materials, chemical specialties and environmental equipment and services; **Plastics**—decorative building products, styro and specialty products and packaging; **Glass Containers**—glass bottles for sale to brewers, distillers, soft-drink manufacturers and food processors; **Resort Development**—marketing of resort community homesites.

Net sales by segment and by geographic area include both sales to outsiders, as reported in Dart's statement of earnings, and sales from one segment to another or from one geographic area

	IDENTIFIABLE ASSETS		CAPITAL EXPENDITURES		DEPRECIATION AND AMORTIZATION	
	1977	1976	1977	1976	1977	1976
	$ 389,150,000	$ 355,885,000	$31,937,000	$ 46,985,000	$17,396,000	$13,964,000
	111,603,000	126,664,000	4,129,000	4,289,000	4,553,000	5,250,000
	200,842,000	173,879,000	23,570,000	25,174,000	9,471,000	8,677,000
	179,865,000	177,059,000	11,460,000	13,924,000	9,273,000	8,951,000
	178,711,000	174,457,000	18,192,000	26,620,000	17,791,000	14,949,000
	53,556,000	57,150,000	20,000	152,000	185,000	234,000
	(4,556,000)	(3,966,000)				
	331,065,000	265,351,000	5,283,000	3,612,000	754,000	397,000
	$1,440,236,000	$1,326,479,000	$94,591,000	$120,756,000	$59,423,000	$52,422,000

	NET SALES		OPERATING PROFIT		IDENTIFIABLE ASSETS	
	1977	1976	1977	1976	1977	1976
	$1,211,179,000	$1,122,148,000	$144,368,000	$139,687,000	$ 835,406,000	$ 815,516,000
	96,434,000	85,302,000	21,866,000	14,372,000	71,085,000	53,333,000
	225,650,000	208,072,000	43,422,000	42,179,000	136,764,000	135,111,000
	82,342,000	75,087,000	25,418,000	24,767,000	67,309,000	58,542,000
	(14,617,000)	(14,369,000)	(2,630,000)	(2,612,000)	(1,393,000)	(1,374,000)
			(31,748,000)	(27,780,000)	331,065,000	265,351,000
	$1,600,988,000	$1,476,240,000	$200,696,000	$190,613,000	$1,440,236,000	$1,326,479,000

to another. Sales between segments and between geographic areas generally are recorded on the same basis as sales to outsiders. Sales between segments aggregated $24,825,000 in 1977 and $30,075,000 in 1976 with the major portion thereof representing sales from the Consumer Products and Chemical segments to the Direct Selling segment. Intercompany sales between geographic areas aggregated $14,617,000 in 1977 and $14,369,000 in 1976 with the major portion thereof representing sales from the United States to other areas. Export sales from the United States to outside customers are not significant.

Operating profit by segment and by geographic area represents revenues less operating expenses under the control of operating management. Corporate items include the cost of corporate staff functions, interest expense, foreign exchange gains and losses, and other expenses of the Company as a whole reduced by certain other income, mainly investment earnings.

Dart Industries Inc. and Consolidated Subsidiaries

Notes to Financial Statements (continued)

		1977	1976
Details of Balance Sheet	ACCOUNTS AND NOTES RECEIVABLE:		
	Trade	$189,656,000	$178,878,000
	Other	13,504,000	15,518,000
		203,160,000	194,396,000
	Less allowance for doubtful accounts	11,969,000	12,495,000
		$191,191,000	$181,901,000
	INVENTORIES:		
	Raw materials and supplies	$ 97,908,000	$ 95,476,000
	Work in process	42,068,000	33,320,000
	Finished goods	170,286,000	167,444,000
		$310,262,000	$296,240,000
	PROPERTIES, AT COST		
	(excluding resort development assets):		
	Land	$ 16,802,000	$ 16,253,000
	Buildings and improvements	229,373,000	212,414,000
	Machinery and equipment	592,650,000	539,135,000
	Construction in progress	16,856,000	26,024,000
		855,681,000	793,826,000
	Less accumulated depreciation	350,996,000	317,480,000
		$504,685,000	$476,346,000
	LONG TERM DEBT, LESS CURRENT INSTALMENTS:		
	7½% Sinking Fund Debentures, due April 1, 1996, $60,000,000, less unamortized discount	$ 59,812,000	$ 59,796,000
	4¼% Subordinated Debentures, due July 15, 1997 (exchangeable for 10.75 shares of 3M Company common stock per $1,000 debenture)	60,000,000	60,000,000
	4¾% Subordinated Debentures, due August 15, 1987 (exchangeable for 10.1 shares of 3M Company common stock per $1,000 debenture)	20,000,000	20,000,000
	Unsecured notes—		
	4.042% to 5.75%, due in annual instalments to 1987	33,433,000	38,557,000
	9⅞%, due in annual instalments from 1978 to 1995	47,200,000	50,000,000
	Other	18,271,000	12,835,000
		$238,716,000	$241,188,000

Business combinations and dispositions

In 1977 and 1976, Dart acquired certain businesses for cash and accounted for such acquisitions as purchases. The operating results of these businesses have been included in Dart's financial statements from the dates of acquisition and were not significant.

In January 1977, Dart sold its United States Rexall Drug Company operations for approximately $16,000,000 in cash. The impact of this sale, after provisions made in years prior to 1976 and related tax benefits, was not material to net earnings. Rexall had net sales of $45,000,000 in 1976 and nominal pre-tax operating earnings.

In December 1977, the decision was made to close down or sell direct selling cosmetics operations in Australia and Mexico and to change the operating methods, including reductions in product lines and personnel and other streamlining actions, for the direct selling cosmetics divisions in Europe and for a consumer products

operation. In addition, provision has been made for phasing out or selling certain chemical operations. Provision for the costs of these actions, which include writedowns of properties, goodwill and other assets as well as accruals for termination benefits and other costs, aggregates $11,733,000 after related tax benefits, which approximates 51 cents per share. Divisions involved in these actions accounted for net sales of $67,000,000 and $70,000,000, in 1977 and 1976, respectively, with pre-tax operating losses which were not material in either year. Decisions were made in 1977 and 1976 to sell or otherwise terminate certain other businesses; their operations were not significant.

International operations

A summary of accounts relating to foreign subsidiaries at December 31 (excluding intercompany accounts) follows:

	1977	1976
ASSETS:		
Current assets	$199,885,000	$171,103,000
Properties	114,520,000	101,445,000
Investments and other assets	11,501,000	6,990,000
Total assets	325,906,000	279,538,000
LIABILITIES:		
Current liabilities	91,540,000	85,892,000
Long term debt and deferred income taxes	29,050,000	21,500,000
Total liabilities	120,590,000	107,392,000
Net assets of foreign subsidiaries in consolidation	$205,316,000	$172,146,000

Net sales from operations outside the United States were $399,786,000 in 1977 and $364,090,000 in 1976. Exchange losses were not material in either year. Undistributed earnings of foreign subsidiaries included in consolidation were $27,667,000 for 1977 and $9,522,000 for 1976 and aggregated $133,674,000 at December 31, 1977. Dart has not considered it necessary to provide for deferred United States income taxes in excess of available foreign tax credits on this total because it has been or is expected to be reinvested outside the United States for an indefinite period of time. Dividends of $14,636,000 in 1977 and $23,817,000 in 1976 were received from foreign subsidiaries.

Resort development operations

A summary of accounts relating to resort development operations at December 31 (excluding intercompany accounts) follows:

	1977	1976
ASSETS:		
Cash, prepaid expenses, etc.	$ 2,260,000	$ 791,000
Notes receivable, 6% to 9%	29,950,000	27,480,000
Deferred profit on land sales	(10,606,000)	(9,327,000)
Land and improvements	28,568,000	33,706,000
Properties and other assets	3,485,000	4,494,000
Total assets	$53,657,000	$57,144,000
LIABILITIES:		
Accounts payable, accrued costs and expenses, etc.	$ 9,324,000	$ 8,909,000
Total liabilities	$ 9,324,000	$ 8,909,000

Principal collections on notes receivable are due in the five years subsequent to December 31, 1977 as follows: 1978—$3,801,000; 1979—$3,882,000; 1980—$4,011,000; 1981—$2,997,000; 1982—$1,892,000.

Dart Industries Inc. and Consolidated Subsidiaries

Five Year Summary of Operations

(Dollar amounts in thousands except per share data)	1977	1976	1975	1974	1973
For the Year					
Net sales	$ 1,600,988	$ 1,476,240	$ 1,280,407	$ 1,218,042	$ 993,322
Cost of goods sold and operating expenses	951,062	876,401	787,474	724,204	600,878
Depreciation and amortization	59,423	52,422	46,228	44,105	38,703
Interest expense	20,512	16,768	14,484	14,648	13,915
Earnings before taxes	200,696	190,613	156,488	140,690	122,522
Provision for income taxes	91,500	89,000	77,500	71,393	57,600
Net earnings	109,196	101,613	78,988	69,297	64,922
Earnings per share of Common Stock					
Primary	4.46	4.14	3.16	2.75	2.58
Fully diluted	4.18	3.88	3.01	2.63	2.47
Cash dividends per share of Common Stock	1.00	.66	.57	.42	.29
Cash dividends paid					
Common Stock	22,787	15,045	13,041	9,334	6,538
Preferred Stock	5,902	5,908	5,910	5,913	5,913
Common Stock dividends	3%	3%	3%	3%	3%
Net earnings applicable to Common Stock after Preferred dividend requirements	103,294	95,705	73,078	63,384	59,009
Properties acquired	94,571	120,604	93,351	70,730	67,176
At Yearend					
Current assets	$ 795,037	$ 708,883	$ 609,238	$ 556,309	$ 417,311
Current liabilities	274,486	243,283	215,161	215,036	171,529
Working capital	520,551	465,600	394,077	341,273	245,782
Properties (net)	504,685	476,346	414,719	370,039	342,319
Total assets	1,440,236	1,326,479	1,190,687	1,114,858	1,035,722
Long term debt	238,716	241,188	214,133	193,380	197,878
Deferred income taxes	58,800	54,500	49,400	51,900	54,400
Stockholders' equity	846,013	765,077	683,776	623,738	568,560
Shares of stock outstanding					
Common	23,132,600	23,111,200	23,091,700	23,088,600	22,890,300
Preferred	2,948,500	2,953,500	2,953,900	2,956,300	2,956,400
Stockholders					
Common	28,789	30,231	31,141	32,088	32,110
Preferred	5,204	5,696	5,929	6,028	5,476
Employees	31,201	29,801	28,612	29,566	28,483

The shares of Common Stock outstanding, cash dividends per share and earnings per share for 1976 and prior years have been adjusted retroactively to give effect to subsequent stock dividends.

Dart Industries Inc. and Consolidated Subsidiaries

Five Year Summary of Operations

(Dollar amounts in thousands except per share data)	1977	1976	1975	1974	1973
For the Year					
Net sales	$ 1,600,988	$ 1,476,240	$ 1,280,407	$ 1,218,042	$ 993,322
Cost of goods sold and operating expenses	951,062	876,401	787,474	724,204	600,878
Depreciation and amortization	59,423	52,422	46,228	44,105	38,703
Interest expense	20,512	16,768	14,484	14,648	13,915
Earnings before taxes	200,696	190,613	156,488	140,690	122,522
Provision for income taxes	91,500	89,000	77,500	71,393	57,600
Net earnings	109,196	101,613	78,988	69,297	64,922
Earnings per share of Common Stock					
Primary	4.46	4.14	3.16	2.75	2.58
Fully diluted	4.18	3.88	3.01	2.63	2.47
Cash dividends per share of Common Stock	1.00	.66	.57	.42	.29
Cash dividends paid					
Common Stock	22,787	15,045	13,041	9,334	6,538
Preferred Stock	5,902	5,908	5,910	5,913	5,913
Common Stock dividends	3%	3%	3%	3%	3%
Net earnings applicable to Common Stock after Preferred dividend requirements	103,294	95,705	73,078	63,384	59,009
Properties acquired	94,571	120,604	93,351	70,730	67,176
At Yearend					
Current assets	$ 795,037	$ 708,883	$ 609,238	$ 556,309	$ 417,311
Current liabilities	274,486	243,283	215,161	215,036	171,529
Working capital	520,551	465,600	394,077	341,273	245,782
Properties (net)	504,685	476,346	414,719	370,039	342,319
Total assets	1,440,236	1,326,479	1,190,687	1,114,858	1,035,722
Long term debt	238,716	241,188	214,133	193,380	197,878
Deferred income taxes	58,800	54,500	49,400	51,900	54,400
Stockholders' equity	846,013	765,077	683,776	623,738	568,560
Shares of stock outstanding					
Common	23,132,600	23,111,200	23,091,700	23,088,600	22,890,300
Preferred	2,948,500	2,953,500	2,953,900	2,956,300	2,956,400
Stockholders					
Common	28,789	30,231	31,141	32,088	32,110
Preferred	5,204	5,696	5,929	6,028	5,476
Employees	31,201	29,801	28,612	29,566	28,483

The shares of Common Stock outstanding, cash dividends per share and earnings per share for 1976 and prior years have been adjusted retroactively to give effect to subsequent stock dividends.

Dart Industries Inc. and Consolidated Subsidiaries

Notes to Financial Statements (continued)

Total estimated costs to complete improvements relating to active projects, based on management estimates and engineering studies, amount to $5,000,000 and anticipated expenditures relating to such improvements are expected to be incurred as follows: 1978—$2,200,000; 1979—$1,200,000; after 1979—$1,600,000.

"Cost of goods sold and operating expenses" includes deferred profit on resort lot sales of $4,811,000 for 1977 and $2,255,000 for 1976. Profit, previously deferred, taken into earnings aggregated $2,616,000 for 1977 and $1,899,000 for 1976.

Income taxes

Income taxes charged to earnings consist of the following:

	1977	1976
PAYABLE CURRENTLY:		
Federal	$50,100,000	$52,900,000
Foreign	35,200,000	31,000,000
State	8,000,000	7,600,000
	93,300,000	91,500,000
TAX EFFECT OF TIMING DIFFERENCES:		
Federal	200,000	(5,100,000)
Foreign	(2,100,000)	2,600,000
State	100,000	
	(1,800,000)	(2,500,000)
Provision for income taxes	$91,500,000	$89,000,000

The tax effect of timing differences, resulting from variances between accounting for financial statement purposes and accounting for tax purposes, is as follows:

	1977	1976
Depreciation	$ 3,900,000	$ 9,560,000
Instalment sales	(1,600,000)	(2,340,000)
Accrued taxes and other expenses not deductible until paid	200,000	(6,600,000)
Provision for elimination, change or sale of certain operations	(4,300,000)	(3,120,000)
Tax effect of timing differences	$ (1,800,000)	$ (2,500,000)

Income taxes charged to earnings differ from an amount computed using the United States federal income tax rate of 48%. A reconciliation between an amount computed using the 48% rate and the provision for income taxes is as follows:

	1977	1976
Amount computed using the 48% rate	$96,300,000	$91,500,000
Increases (reductions) in taxes result from:		
State income taxes	4,200,000	4,000,000
Foreign income taxes	(3,700,000)	1,500,000
Investment tax credit	(5,500,000)	(6,900,000)
Other	200,000	(1,100,000)
Provision for income taxes	$91,500,000	$89,000,000

Short term loans and borrowing arrangements

Short term loans, foreign, are unsecured and aggregated a maximum of $23,636,000 and $19,318,000 at any monthend in 1977 and 1976, respectively. Weighted average borrowings and interest rates during the year, based on amounts outstanding at each monthend, were $19,559,000 and 11.1% in 1977 and $11,723,000 and 11.3% in 1976.

operation. In addition, provision has been made for phasing out or selling certain chemical operations. Provision for the costs of these actions, which include writedowns of properties, goodwill and other assets as well as accruals for termination benefits and other costs, aggregates $11,733,000 after related tax benefits, which approximates 51 cents per share. Divisions involved in these actions accounted for net sales of $67,000,000 and $70,000,000, in 1977 and 1976, respectively, with pre-tax operating losses which were not material in either year. Decisions were made in 1977 and 1976 to sell or otherwise terminate certain other businesses; their operations were not significant.

International operations

A summary of accounts relating to foreign subsidiaries at December 31 (excluding intercompany accounts) follows:

	1977	1976
ASSETS:		
Current assets	$199,885,000	$171,103,000
Properties	114,520,000	101,445,000
Investments and other assets	11,501,000	6,990,000
Total assets	325,906,000	279,538,000
LIABILITIES:		
Current liabilities	91,540,000	85,892,000
Long term debt and deferred income taxes	29,050,000	21,500,000
Total liabilities	120,590,000	107,392,000
Net assets of foreign subsidiaries in consolidation	$205,316,000	$172,146,000

Net sales from operations outside the United States were $399,786,000 in 1977 and $364,090,000 in 1976. Exchange losses were not material in either year. Undistributed earnings of foreign subsidiaries included in consolidation were $27,667,000 for 1977 and $9,522,000 for 1976 and aggregated $133,674,000 at December 31, 1977. Dart has not considered it necessary to provide for deferred United States income taxes in excess of available foreign tax credits on this total because it has been or is expected to be reinvested outside the United States for an indefinite period of time. Dividends of $14,636,000 in 1977 and $23,817,000 in 1976 were received from foreign subsidiaries.

Resort development operations

A summary of accounts relating to resort development operations at December 31 (excluding intercompany accounts) follows:

	1977	1976
ASSETS:		
Cash, prepaid expenses, etc.	$ 2,260,000	$ 791,000
Notes receivable, 6% to 9%	29,950,000	27,480,000
Deferred profit on land sales	(10,606,000)	(9,327,000)
Land and improvements	28,568,000	33,706,000
Properties and other assets	3,485,000	4,494,000
Total assets	$53,657,000	$57,144,000
LIABILITIES:		
Accounts payable, accrued costs and expenses, etc.	$ 9,324,000	$ 8,909,000
Total liabilities	$ 9,324,000	$ 8,909,000

Principal collections on notes receivable are due in the five years subsequent to December 31, 1977 as follows: 1978—$3,801,000; 1979—$3,882,000; 1980—$4,011,000; 1981—$2,997,000; 1982—$1,892,000.

At December 31, 1977 and 1976, the weighted average interest rates were 11.0% and 11.8%, respectively.

Unused lines of short term credit, primarily with United States banks, totaled $44,200,000 at December 31, 1977 and provide for unsecured ninety day loans generally at the banks' prime rates. Compensating balance requirements under these credit lines are not material.

Long term debt

Total principal payments due on long term debt in the five years subsequent to December 31, 1977 are as follows: 1978—$8,450,000; 1979—$8,605,000; 1980—$8,400,000; 1981—$8,404,000; 1982—$12,061,000.

The 7½% Debentures are due April 1, 1996. Through the operation of a mandatory sinking fund, Dart is obligated to redeem $4,000,000 aggregate principal amount of these Debentures on April 1 in each of the years 1982 through 1995. Dart has the option to redeem through the sinking fund an additional $4,000,000 aggregate principal amount in each such year. All sinking fund redemptions, mandatory or optional, are to be made at 100% of the principal amount of the debentures redeemed. Debentures acquired or redeemed otherwise than through the operation of the sinking fund may be credited against the sinking fund requirements.

Under loan agreements with certain insurance companies, approximately $300,000,000 of the consolidated retained earnings at December 31, 1977 is not restricted as to payment of cash dividends. The agreements impose no restrictions on payment of stock dividends.

Stock options

1,256,800 shares of Dart Common Stock are reserved for options granted or available for grant to officers and employees under stockholder approved stock option plans. Options for 1,364,200 shares were exercised prior to 1977.

Under the plans, the option purchase price for all options granted is 100% of the fair market value of the shares on the date of grant. Options granted are exercisable in instalments after one year and before the end of five years or ten years depending on the nature of the option. Proceeds received from exercise of options are credited to the capital accounts. No options were granted in 1977.

A summary of changes during 1977 follows:

	SHARES	OPTIONS OUTSTANDING PRICE RANGE	AMOUNT
At beginning of year	643,400	$21.21 to $48.85	$23,790,000
Adjustment for stock dividend	17,900		
Options exercised	(16,000)	$21.21 to $33.61	(428,000)
Options canceled	(68,100)	$30.65 to $48.85	(2,703,000)
At end of year	577,200	$21.21 to $46.69	$20,659,000

At December 31, 1977, options for 499,600 shares of Common Stock were exercisable at prices ranging from $21.21 to $46.69 and 679,600 shares were available for grant.

Preferred Stock

Holders of the Series A $2 Cumulative Convertible Preferred Stock are entitled to receive $2 per share annual cash dividends, to one vote per share and, upon any voluntary liquidation, dissolution or winding up, to receive $50 per share plus accrued unpaid dividends. Each share of the Preferred Stock is convertible by the holder into Common Stock on a share for share basis adjusted for stock dividends in excess of 3% in any one year or for recapitalization. The Preferred Stock may be called for redemption at $55 per share plus accrued unpaid dividends.

Retirement plans

Dart and certain of its United States subsidiaries continued the contributory profit sharing retirement plan, established in 1955, and the non-contributory pension plan, established in 1975, which together constitute the principal retirement program covering all employees who have one or more years of employment with Dart, and who are not covered by a collective bargaining agreement or by another Company-sponsored retirement plan. Dart and its subsidiaries also have several

Dart Industries Inc. and Consolidated Subsidiaries

Notes to Financial Statements (continued)

pension plans covering substantially all of their employees not covered by the principal retirement program, including certain employees in foreign countries.

The contribution to be made under the Dart profit sharing plan amounted to $8,114,000 for 1977 and was $8,243,000 for 1976. The total pension expense was $11,619,000 for 1977 and $10,216,000 for 1976 which includes, as applicable, amortization of prior service cost principally over a period of 30 years.

The aggregate Dart contribution to the profit sharing plan in any year is based upon consolidated earnings before federal income taxes, as defined, is limited to 6% of such earnings and cannot exceed the amount deductible for federal income tax purposes. The computations include net earnings of certain divisions whose employees do not participate in the Dart plan, but who participate in previously existing retirement plans which have been continued in effect.

With respect to pension plans, Dart's policy is, generally, to contribute pension cost accrued. The actuarially computed value of vested benefits for all plans exceeded, as of December 31, 1977, the total of pension fund assets and accruals by about $26,800,000. The total estimated unfunded prior service cost relative to all pension plans in effect was approximately $55,700,000 at December 31, 1977.

Incentive compensation

Under the formula incorporated in Dart's 1962 stockholder approved Incentive Compensation Plan for principal officers and key employees, the Incentive Compensation Committee and the Executive Committee of the Board of Directors awarded to 102 principal officers and key employees $2,531,000 ($1,956,000 for 1976) of the total of $8,403,000 available for 1977. No outside director participates in this plan.

Pursuant to stockholder authority granted in 1962, various other approved plans are in effect for divisions and subsidiaries of Dart. No principal officer or director participates in these plans. The above named committees awarded $6,268,000 ($6,509,000 for 1976) to 427 persons in these categories. The total amount available under the plans was $12,652,000.

Amounts available but not awarded under such plans are not available for future awards.

Capital expenditures

It is estimated that capital expenditures for 1978 will be about $115,000,000.

Earnings per share of Common Stock

Primary earnings per share are based on the weighted average number of shares of Common Stock outstanding during each period increased by the effect of dilutive stock options. Such increased average shares were 23,160,200 for 1977 and 23,124,500 for 1976. Net earnings attributable to Common Stock are after deducting Preferred dividend requirements.

Fully diluted earnings per share are based on the weighted average number of shares of Common Stock outstanding during each period, assumption of conversion of Series A $2 Cumulative Convertible Preferred Stock and assumption of exercise of all dilutive stock options. Such increased average shares were 26,126,700 for 1977 and 26,167,900 for 1976.

All per share amounts give retroactive effect to stock dividends paid.

Supplementary earnings statement information

Charges to costs and expenses for the years ended December 31 include the following:

	1977	1976
Maintenance and repairs	$51,091,000	$44,120,000
Taxes, except income taxes:		
Payroll	26,606,000	24,240,000
Property, business and other	11,803,000	11,727,000
Advertising	10,298,000	10,922,000
Research and development	9,347,000	7,239,000

Dart Industries Inc. and Consolidated Subsidiaries

Notes to Financial Statements (continued)

pension plans covering substantially all of their employees not covered by the principal retirement program, including certain employees in foreign countries.

The contribution to be made under the Dart profit sharing plan amounted to $8,114,000 for 1977 and was $8,243,000 for 1976. The total pension expense was $11,619,000 for 1977 and $10,216,000 for 1976 which includes, as applicable, amortization of prior service cost principally over a period of 30 years.

The aggregate Dart contribution to the profit sharing plan in any year is based upon consolidated earnings before federal income taxes, as defined, is limited to 6% of such earnings and cannot exceed the amount deductible for federal income tax purposes. The computations include net earnings of certain divisions whose employees do not participate in the Dart plan, but who participate in previously existing retirement plans which have been continued in effect.

With respect to pension plans, Dart's policy is, generally, to contribute pension cost accrued. The actuarially computed value of vested benefits for all plans exceeded, as of December 31, 1977, the total of pension fund assets and accruals by about $26,800,000. The total estimated unfunded prior service cost relative to all pension plans in effect was approximately $55,700,000 at December 31, 1977.

Incentive compensation

Under the formula incorporated in Dart's 1962 stockholder approved Incentive Compensation Plan for principal officers and key employees, the Incentive Compensation Committee and the Executive Committee of the Board of Directors awarded to 102 principal officers and key employees $2,531,000 ($1,956,000 for 1976) of the total of $8,403,000 available for 1977. No outside director participates in this plan.

Pursuant to stockholder authority granted in 1962, various other approved plans are in effect for divisions and subsidiaries of Dart. No principal officer or director participates in these plans. The above named committees awarded $6,268,000 ($6,509,000 for 1976) to 427 persons in these categories. The total amount available under the plans was $12,652,000.

Amounts available but not awarded under such plans are not available for future awards.

Capital expenditures

It is estimated that capital expenditures for 1978 will be about $115,000,000.

Earnings per share of Common Stock

Primary earnings per share are based on the weighted average number of shares of Common Stock outstanding during each period increased by the effect of dilutive stock options. Such increased average shares were 23,160,200 for 1977 and 23,124,500 for 1976. Net earnings attributable to Common Stock are after deducting Preferred dividend requirements.

Fully diluted earnings per share are based on the weighted average number of shares of Common Stock outstanding during each period, assumption of conversion of Series A $2 Cumulative Convertible Preferred Stock and assumption of exercise of all dilutive stock options. Such increased average shares were 26,126,700 for 1977 and 26,167,900 for 1976.

All per share amounts give retroactive effect to stock dividends paid.

Supplementary earnings statement information

Charges to costs and expenses for the years ended December 31 include the following:

	1977	1976
Maintenance and repairs	$51,091,000	$44,120,000
Taxes, except income taxes:		
Payroll	26,606,000	24,240,000
Property, business and other	11,803,000	11,727,000
Advertising	10,298,000	10,922,000
Research and development	9,347,000	7,239,000

At December 31, 1977 and 1976, the weighted average interest rates were 11.0% and 11.8%, respectively.

Unused lines of short term credit, primarily with United States banks, totaled $44,200,000 at December 31, 1977 and provide for unsecured ninety day loans generally at the banks' prime rates. Compensating balance requirements under these credit lines are not material.

Long term debt

Total principal payments due on long term debt in the five years subsequent to December 31, 1977 are as follows: 1978—$8,450,000; 1979—$8,605,000; 1980—$8,400,000; 1981—$8,404,000; 1982—$12,061,000.

The 7½% Debentures are due April 1, 1996. Through the operation of a mandatory sinking fund, Dart is obligated to redeem $4,000,000 aggregate principal amount of these Debentures on April 1 in each of the years 1982 through 1995. Dart has the option to redeem through the sinking fund an additional $4,000,000 aggregate principal amount in each such year. All sinking fund redemptions, mandatory or optional, are to be made at 100% of the principal amount of the debentures redeemed. Debentures acquired or redeemed otherwise than through the operation of the sinking fund may be credited against the sinking fund requirements.

Under loan agreements with certain insurance companies, approximately $300,000,000 of the consolidated retained earnings at December 31, 1977 is not restricted as to payment of cash dividends. The agreements impose no restrictions on payment of stock dividends.

Stock options

1,256,800 shares of Dart Common Stock are reserved for options granted or available for grant to officers and employees under stockholder approved stock option plans. Options for 1,364,200 shares were exercised prior to 1977.

Under the plans, the option purchase price for all options granted is 100% of the fair market value of the shares on the date of grant. Options granted are exercisable in instalments after one year and before the end of five years or ten years depending on the nature of the option. Proceeds received from exercise of options are credited to the capital accounts. No options were granted in 1977.

A summary of changes during 1977 follows:

| | OPTIONS OUTSTANDING | | |
	SHARES	PRICE RANGE	AMOUNT
At beginning of year	643,400	$21.21 to $48.85	$23,790,000
Adjustment for stock dividend	17,900		
Options exercised	(16,000)	$21.21 to $33.61	(428,000)
Options canceled	(68,100)	$30.65 to $48.85	(2,703,000)
At end of year	577,200	$21.21 to $46.69	$20,659,000

At December 31, 1977, options for 499,600 shares of Common Stock were exercisable at prices ranging from $21.21 to $46.69 and 679,600 shares were available for grant.

Preferred Stock

Holders of the Series A $2 Cumulative Convertible Preferred Stock are entitled to receive $2 per share annual cash dividends, to one vote per share and, upon any voluntary liquidation, dissolution or winding up, to receive $50 per share plus accrued unpaid dividends. Each share of the Preferred Stock is convertible by the holder into Common Stock on a share for share basis adjusted for stock dividends in excess of 3% in any one year or for recapitalization. The Preferred Stock may be called for redemption at $55 per share plus accrued unpaid dividends.

Retirement plans

Dart and certain of its United States subsidiaries continued the contributory profit sharing retirement plan, established in 1955, and the non-contributory pension plan, established in 1975, which together constitute the principal retirement program covering all employees who have one or more years of employment with Dart, and who are not covered by a collective bargaining agreement or by another Company-sponsored retirement plan. Dart and its subsidiaries also have several

Unaudited general description of the impact of inflation

Dart's diverse lines of business have generally experienced inflationary pressures on production and other costs to varying degrees based upon changes in price levels of the basic raw materials and other goods and services used by each business in its operations. The magnitude of the changes fluctuates from business to business and within businesses by geographic area. The ability of each business to compensate for increases in the prices of specific goods and services by increasing sales prices is affected by competitive conditions in the markets in which the businesses operate. The diversity of Dart's businesses has tended to minimize overall any adverse effects on earnings from uncompensated inflation in any one of its operations.

Replacing items of plant and equipment with assets having equivalent productive capacity has usually required a greater capital investment than was required to purchase the assets being replaced. The additional capital investment principally reflects the cumulative impact of inflation on the long-lived nature of these assets.

Dart's annual report on Form 10-K (a copy of which is available upon request) contains specific information with respect to yearend 1977 and 1976 estimated replacement cost of inventories and productive capacity and the approximate effect which estimated replacement cost would have had on the computation of cost of goods sold and depreciation expense for each year.

Unaudited interim financial information

	1977			
	FIRST QUARTER	SECOND QUARTER	THIRD QUARTER	FOURTH QUARTER
Net sales	$369,916,000	$412,834,000	$393,401,000	$424,837,000
Cost of goods sold and operating expenses	220,877,000	240,441,000	247,690,000	242,054,000
Earnings before taxes	43,871,000	63,712,000	41,804,000	51,309,000
Net earnings	23,171,000	33,912,000	24,404,000	27,709,000
Earnings per share of Common Stock:				
Primary	.94	1.40	.99	1.13
Fully diluted	.89	1.29	.94	1.06

	1976			
	FIRST QUARTER	SECOND QUARTER	THIRD QUARTER	FOURTH QUARTER
Net sales	$358,884,000	$370,905,000	$362,453,000	$383,998,000
Cost of goods sold and operating expenses	209,574,000	214,564,000	220,998,000	231,265,000
Earnings before taxes	52,324,000	52,698,000	39,499,000	46,092,000
Net earnings	27,674,000	26,798,000	21,799,000	25,342,000
Earnings per share of Common Stock:				
Primary	1.13	1.10	.88	1.03
Fully diluted	1.06	1.02	.83	.97

Obligations under capital leases

Dart has recorded as assets certain properties and property rights acquired by the Company under capital leases. The related discounted lease obligations are set forth separately in the accompanying balance sheet. Dart has no legal responsibility for payments under the terms of any of these leases except for rent, insurance, taxes and maintenance.

The current and long term portions of obligations under capital leases aggregating $13,878,000 represent future minimum lease payments under capital leases reduced

Dart Industries Inc. and Consolidated Subsidiaries

Notes to Financial Statements (continued)

to present value by deducting $12,753,000 as the amount representing interest. Future minimum lease payments, including amounts representing interest, are payable as follows: 1978—$1,875,000; 1979—$1,880,000; 1980—$1,844,000; 1981—$1,810,000; 1982—$1,789,000; after 1982—$17,433,000.

Commitments and contingencies

Dart leases real estate, transportation equipment and other machinery and equipment under short and long term, cancelable and noncancelable lease agreements which generally provide for fixed monthly payments over the terms of the leases. Many leases require additional payments for property taxes, insurance and maintenance.

Rental expense (reduced by sublease income of $2,797,000 in 1977 and $2,612,000 in 1976) totaled $31,935,000 in 1977 and $30,632,000 in 1976.

Minimum rental commitments under noncancelable leases in effect at December 31, 1977, are payable as follows: 1978—$28,149,000; 1979—$16,201,000; 1980—$9,488,000; 1981—$6,955,000; 1982—$5,320,000; after 1982—$15,921,000. Future sublease rentals receivable total $7,241,000.

Dart is a defendant in certain purported class action suits, in which substantial damages are claimed, involving its Tahoe Donner resort development project and its former Rexall Drug operations. In addition, certain other law suits have been filed against Dart relative to its present and former operations. In the opinion of management and legal counsel, the ultimate disposition of the suits would not have a materially adverse effect on Dart's financial position or results of operations.

Report of Independent Accountants

606 South Olive Street
Los Angeles 90014

February 26, 1978

To the Board of Directors and
Stockholders of Dart Industries Inc.

In our opinion, the accompanying consolidated financial statements on pages 18 to 32 present fairly the financial position of Dart Industries Inc. and consolidated subsidiaries at December 31, 1977 and 1976, and the results of their operations and the changes in their financial position for the years then ended, in conformity with generally accepted accounting principles consistently applied. Our examinations of these statements were made in accordance with generally accepted auditing standards and accordingly included such tests of the accounting records and such other auditing procedures as we considered necessary in the circumstances.

Price Waterhouse & Co.

EXHIBIT 2

DART INDUSTRIES INC. AND CONSOLIDATED SUBSIDIARIES

**FIVE YEAR SUMMARY OF OPERATIONS
AND MANAGEMENT'S DISCUSSION AND ANALYSIS**

This exhibit is a photocopy of the five year summary of operations and management's discussion and analysis included in the 1977 Annual Report to stockholders of Dart Industries Inc.

Dart Industries Inc. and Consolidated Subsidiaries

Management's Discussion and Analysis

Dart Industries' net sales and net earnings have increased in each of the past five years. Certain trends during the recent past are discussed below.

1977 Compared with 1976

Net sales in 1977 increased $125 million (8%) compared with 1976. All operating segments, except Consumer Products, realized sales gains with Direct Selling accounting for approximately half of the total increase. Consumer Products sales in 1976 included $45 million from the United States Rexall Drug Company operations which were sold in January 1977. Net sales from operations outside the United States were $400 million, an increase of $36 million (10%) over 1976 and accounted for 25% of total 1977 net sales.

Cost of goods sold and operating expenses increased $75 million (9%) compared with 1976. Margins in the Chemical and Glass Containers segments were depressed by the inability to increase prices sufficiently to compensate for higher raw material, labor and operating costs and, in Glass Containers, by a four-week industry-wide strike of mold makers. Improved margins in the remaining segments offset these declines with the result that the relationship of cost of goods sold and operating expenses to net sales remained constant at 59% in both years.

Depreciation and amortization increased $7 million (13%) compared with 1976 and results from continuing plant expansions.

Interest expense increased $4 million (22%) compared with 1976 as a result of $25 million of long term borrowing in December 1976 and higher levels of foreign short term loans.

Provision for income taxes increased $3 million (3%) compared with 1976 as a result of increased earnings. The effective tax rate declined from 47% to 46%, principally as a result of lower effective foreign tax rates.

1976 Compared with 1975

Net sales in 1976 increased $196 million (15%) over the 1975 level. Sales improvements were most significant in the Direct Selling, Chemical and Plastics lines of business where combined volume increases exceeded $120 million. The remaining portion of the sales increase was generally attributed to increases in selling prices throughout all lines of business. Net sales from operations outside the United States were $364 million, an increase of $24 million (7%) over 1975, and accounted for 25% of total 1976 net sales.

Cost of goods sold and operating expenses increased $89 million (11%) over the 1975 level and was a lesser percentage of net sales in 1976 (59%) than in 1975 (62%). Increased sales volume and sales prices more than offset increased costs of raw materials, labor and overhead except in the Chemical line of business which came under increased pressure on margins.

Depreciation and amortization increased $6 million (13%) over 1975 as a result of large expenditures on properties in the past two years.

Interest expense increased $2 million (16%) over 1975 principally as a result of $25 million of long term borrowing in December 1975.

Provision for income taxes increased $12 million (15%) over 1975 reflecting the improvement in earnings, while the effective tax rate declined from 50% to 47%, principally as a result of investment tax credits aggregating $7 million in 1976.

Dart Industries Inc. and Consolidated Subsidiaries

Management's Discussion and Analysis

Dart Industries' net sales and net earnings have increased in each of the past five years. Certain trends during the recent past are discussed below.

1977 Compared with 1976

Net sales in 1977 increased $125 million (8%) compared with 1976. All operating segments, except Consumer Products, realized sales gains with Direct Selling accounting for approximately half of the total increase. Consumer Products sales in 1976 included $45 million from the United States Rexall Drug Company operations which were sold in January 1977. Net sales from operations outside the United States were $400 million, an increase of $36 million (10%) over 1976 and accounted for 25% of total 1977 net sales.

Cost of goods sold and operating expenses increased $75 million (9%) compared with 1976. Margins in the Chemical and Glass Containers segments were depressed by the inability to increase prices sufficiently to compensate for higher raw material, labor and operating costs and, in Glass Containers, by a four-week industry-wide strike of mold makers. Improved margins in the remaining segments offset these declines with the result that the relationship of cost of goods sold and operating expenses to net sales remained constant at 59% in both years.

Depreciation and amortization increased $7 million (13%) compared with 1976 and results from continuing plant expansions.

Interest expense increased $4 million (22%) compared with 1976 as a result of $25 million of long term borrowing in December 1976 and higher levels of foreign short term loans.

Provision for income taxes increased $3 million (3%) compared with 1976 as a result of increased earnings. The effective tax rate declined from 47% to 46%, principally as a result of lower effective foreign tax rates.

1976 Compared with 1975

Net sales in 1976 increased $196 million (15%) over the 1975 level. Sales improvements were most significant in the Direct Selling, Chemical and Plastics lines of business where combined volume increases exceeded $120 million. The remaining portion of the sales increase was generally attributed to increases in selling prices throughout all lines of business. Net sales from operations outside the United States were $364 million, an increase of $24 million (7%) over 1975, and accounted for 25% of total 1976 net sales.

Cost of goods sold and operating expenses increased $89 million (11%) over the 1975 level and was a lesser percentage of net sales in 1976 (59%) than in 1975 (62%). Increased sales volume and sales prices more than offset increased costs of raw materials, labor and overhead except in the Chemical line of business which came under increased pressure on margins.

Depreciation and amortization increased $6 million (13%) over 1975 as a result of large expenditures on properties in the past two years.

Interest expense increased $2 million (16%) over 1975 principally as a result of $25 million of long term borrowing in December 1975.

Provision for income taxes increased $12 million (15%) over 1975 reflecting the improvement in earnings, while the effective tax rate declined from 50% to 47%, principally as a result of investment tax credits aggregating $7 million in 1976.

EXHIBIT 2

DART INDUSTRIES INC. AND CONSOLIDATED SUBSIDIARIES

**FIVE YEAR SUMMARY OF OPERATIONS
AND MANAGEMENT'S DISCUSSION AND ANALYSIS**

This exhibit is a photocopy of the five year summary of operations and management's discussion and analysis included in the 1977 Annual Report to stockholders of Dart Industries Inc.

Dart Industries Inc.
Report of 1978 Annual Meeting & First Quarter Report

Eighth Consecutive Year of Increased Earnings Forecast

Improvement Anticipated in all Operating Segments for 1978

Quarterly Cash Dividend of 40 Cents Declared

Results for 3 Months Ended March 31:

	1978	1977
Earnings per Share	$1.11	$.94
Net Earnings in Millions	$27.3	$23.2
Net Sales in Millions	$408	$370

DART INDUSTRIES INC.
CORPORATE HEADQUARTERS
8480 Beverly Boulevard
Los Angeles, California 90048

Table of Contents

Balance Sheet 2

Statement of Earnings 6

Statement of Changes in Financial Position 8

Appointment of Inspectors of Election 9

Election of Directors 9

Approval of Accountants 9

Mr. Dart's Remarks 10

Mr. Mullaney's Remarks 12

Questions and Answers 23

Dividends Declared 24

Investor Information 25

Directors Present at the Meeting 26

**TO THE OWNERS OF
DART INDUSTRIES INC.**

The Annual Meeting of Stockholders of Dart Industries Inc. was held at corporate headquarters, 8480 Beverly Boulevard, Los Angeles, California on May 4, 1978. More than seventy-two percent of the outstanding stock of the Company was represented at this meeting.

Following is a summary of actions taken and remarks made at the meeting.

Report of First Quarter Operations

DART INDUSTRIES INC. AND CONSOLIDATED SUBSIDIARIES

Balance Sheet
(UNAUDITED)
(dollars in thousands)

| | March 31, | |
Assets	1978	1977
Current assets:		
Cash	$ 65,686	$ 51,853
Marketable securities, at cost which approximates market	163,426	136,313
Total cash and marketable securities	229,112	188,166
Accounts and notes receivable, less allowance for doubtful accounts of $12,804 in 1978 and $12,709 in 1977	226,844	211,396
Inventories	323,782	297,535
Prepaid expenses	15,693	15,989
Deferred future income tax benefits	31,114	26,747
Total current assets	826,545	739,833
Resort development assets	51,908	56,468
Properties:		
Properties owned	845,333	775,731
Properties leased under capital leases	23,697	24,417
	869,030	800,148
Less accumulated depreciation	363,154	320,256
Total properties	505,876	479,892
Investments and other assets:		
3M Company common stock held in escrow for exchange by holders of $4\frac{1}{4}\%$ and $4\frac{3}{4}\%$ debentures, at cost (market value: 1978–$37,056; 1977–$42,456)	35,162	35,162
Other assets, receivables and investments	46,385	36,836
Intangibles relating to businesses purchased, less amortization	11,133	14,332
Total investments and other assets	92,680	86,330
Total assets	$1,477,009	$1,362,523

Liabilities and Stockholders' Equity	March 31,	
	1978	1977
Current liabilities:		
Accounts payable	$ 73,805	$ 69,234
Accrued compensation	40,329	38,345
Other accrued expenses	105,846	82,284
Short term loans, foreign	16,771	23,636
Current instalments of obligations under capital leases	836	1,441
Current instalments of long term debt	9,109	6,067
Income taxes	47,295	41,837
Total current liabilities	293,991	262,844
Resort development liabilities	7,841	8,612
Obligations under capital leases, less current instalments	12,757	13,853
Long term debt, less current instalments	238,688	240,858
Deferred income taxes	59,590	53,436
Stockholders' equity:		
Preferred Stock	14,901	14,928
Common Stock	28,921	28,062
Capital in excess of par value	299,917	279,299
Retained earnings	521,950	462,178
	865,689	784,467
Less cost of reacquired shares of capital stock— Preferred—32,500; Common—700	1,547	1,547
Total stockholders' equity	864,142	782,920
Total liabilities and stockholders' equity	$1,477,009	$1,362,523

DART INDUSTRIES INC. AND CONSOLIDATED SUBSIDIARIES

Statement of Earnings

Note to Statement of Earnings

(UNAUDITED)

(dollars in thousands except per share amounts)

	For the Three Months Ended March 31,	
	1978	1977
Income:		
Net sales	$408,190	$369,916
Other income	6,288	5,053
	414,478	374,969
Costs and expenses:		
Cost of goods sold and operating expenses	245,500	220,877
Selling, distribution and administrative expenses	95,243	90,656
Depreciation and amortization	15,936	14,400
Interest expense	5,505	5,165
	362,184	331,098
Earnings before income taxes	52,294	43,871
Provision for income taxes	25,000	20,700
Net earnings	$ 27,294	$ 23,171
Net earnings per share of Common Stock*:		
Primary	$ 1.11	$ .94
Fully diluted	$ 1.04	$ .89
Cash dividends per share of Common Stock	$ .40	$ .25
Shares of Common Stock outstanding	23,136,000	23,122,300

*Earnings per share have been computed as follows: primary—after providing for Preferred dividend requirements and based on the weighted average number of shares of Common Stock outstanding increased by the effect of dilutive stock options; fully diluted—based on the weighted average number of shares of Common Stock outstanding and assumption of exercise of all dilutive stock options retroactive to the beginning of each year or later dates of grant and assumption of conversion of all shares of Preferred Stock to Common Stock retroactive to January 1, 1977.

DART INDUSTRIES INC. AND CONSOLIDATED SUBSIDIARIES

Statement of Changes in Financial Position
(UNAUDITED)

(dollars in thousands)

	For the Three Months Ended March 31,	
	1978	1977
Working capital provided by:		
Net earnings	$27,294	$23,171
Items not affecting working capital—		
Depreciation and amortization	15,936	14,400
Deferred income taxes	790	(1,064)
Provided by operations	44,020	36,507
Other sources of working capital	3,668	5,558
Total working capital provided	47,688	42,065
Working capital used for:		
Properties acquired	17,708	21,935
Cash dividends paid— Common Stock	9,254	5,610
Other uses of working capital	8,723	3,131
Total working capital used	35,685	30,676
Working capital increase	$12,003	$11,389

The foregoing unaudited figures include, in the opinion of management, all adjustments (consisting only of normal recurring adjustments) necessary to a fair presentation of such figures. The results for the three months ended March 31, 1978 are not necessarily indicative of operations for the full year.

WILLIAM R. PALMER, Vice President and Controller

JUSTIN DART
Chairman

Justin Dart Forecasts Record Year

Now, you all know that we had a record year last year, and improved first quarter results, which we announced last week.

Earnings per share on the Common Stock for the first quarter were $1.11, 18 percent ahead of last year's 94 cents. Net earnings in the first quarter were $27.3 million compared with $23.2 million a year ago, and sales were 10 percent ahead at $408 million compared with $370 million.

Earnings improvement in the first quarter was especially satisfactory because it was a dismal winter. The weather was terrible, and we were wondering whether or not we were going to be ahead in the first quarter. Fortunately, we landed on our feet.

First quarter results strengthened our conviction in the forecast made earlier this year that 1978 results will be a record and Dart Industries' eighth consecutive year of improved earnings.

Tom Mullaney will give you a report on the state of the Company, but first, I would like to tell you how Tom and I work together. It sounds a little improbable, but we're partners. If you'll look at the Annual Report, you'll find under my name, "Chairman," and under Tom's name, "President." There's no further designation, because we didn't quite know how to say that we were partners.

Tom is the professional manager and I guess I'm kind of the "seat-of-the-pants" entrepreneur. We make an awfully good combination. I loosen him up a little, and he tightens me up a little. The balance is just great.

Tom is responsible for day-to-day operations. We confer on matters of policy—financial matters, personnel developments, and so on. And, we get along just fine.

Now, my job is to help get rid of the mistakes that I have committed in the past and also to look for new opportunities on the outside. I'm joined in what is called "the Office of the Chairman" by Ralph Knight, who we all know is a very highly technical, competent guy, and by Bob Beattie, who we know has served this Company as sort of a utility player with great distinction for a long time. So, I'll be very disappointed if Ralph and Bob and I are not able to come up with some new, interesting and exciting opportunities for the future.

Now, here's our president, my partner, Tom Mullaney.

THOMAS P. MULLANEY
President

President Reviews Objectives and Performance

Thank you, Jus....partner. Good morning! I'm delighted to have this opportunity to bring Stockholders up-to-date on the health of the Company.

Briefly stated, it is very, very good.

As you know, we came out of 1977 with our seventh consecutive year of increased earnings; our strongest balance sheet ever; put several problems behind us; strengthened our management team; and I think, are enjoying improved external attitudes towards the Company.

And, we entered 1978 with good momentum. Jus commented on our excellent first quarter and that simply reinforces his confidence and mine that 1978 will be our eighth straight year of improved earnings.

Now, against this brief overview, I'd like to do three things this morning. First, bring you up-to-date on the progress we made against the objectives we set forth at this meeting last year with you; then briefly review how 1978 is unfolding; and then I'd like to make a few comments about the future of Dart Industries.

Management Team Strengthened

With regard to the objectives we set last year, as you know, Dart Industries has had a long, consistent record of growth based on diversification, and everything that we have been doing is aimed at enhancing that track record. In addition to having a record year last year, we wanted to do three other things. The first was to be sure we strengthened our management team. I'm delighted to say that I think we made substantial progress on that scene.

And, I would like to introduce to you the group executives that does deliver all of those profits...a therefore, that group that rates highest in the hea of both Justin and myself. Some familiar faces a some new faces....And, at the risk of embarrassi some of those who've already been introduced, I going to ask our wonderful operating group stand again. We'll start with the mother, fath grandfather and uncle of Tupperware, Hamer W son. It's obvious that Hamer is the dean of group and an inspiration to anyone who has chance to work with him. Next, Bill Greenbe who is responsible for guiding Thatcher to new r ords. Seated next to Bill is a fellow who has all o sudden converted Dart Resorts from a big proble to no problem at all, and in fact, a wonderful o portunity for us, Sid Karsh.

Here on my left, the new head of our combin Chemical-Plastics Group, and an old hand arou here now...he's been here all of two years...Jo Del Favero. The newest member of the team, a indeed a new face, joined us just last December head up our consumer products business—Bill G ham. And finally, even though Jus introduced h earlier as our Chief Financial Officer, I'd like y to meet one more time a fellow who's very impo tant in the overall conduct of our affairs includi helping me think about a variety of problems this Company, Phil Matthews.

We have in these gentlemen a "first team" t can't be beat. And importantly, each one of the is busy with his own group, making certain that have a management team both in depth and in the functions. They should be very proud.*

Justin commented on the advancements we ha made in our forward planning with Bob Beat and Ralph Knight, and I just think we are in ve good shape in terms of the depth of our mana ment team. That does not mean we are resting our laurels. All through 1978 we're going to working further on the development of our ma agement team, and I would predict that proc will go on for several years because we are de cated to having the best possible manageme group.

Executive photos on following page.

PHILLIP D. MATTHEWS
Executive Vice President,
Finance and Administration,
and Chief Financial Officer

HAMER F. WILSON
Executive Vice President;
Chairman, Direct Selling Group

JOHN P. DEL FAVERO
Vice President; President,
Chemical-Plastics Group

F. WILLIAM GRAHAM
Vice President; President,
Consumer Products Group

WILLIAM H. GREENBERG
Vice President; President,
Glass Containers Group

SIDNEY M. KARSH
President of Dart Resorts

Quality of Earnings Improving

Our second objective of 1977 was aimed at improving the quality of our earnings by either fixing, selling or maximizing the cash flow from operations that either did not meet our performance standards or did not fit with our long term directions. The actions that we took at year-end 1977 were detailed to you in the Shareholder report mailed in January, and again in our Annual Report in March. I think you can see that we are continuing on this program, as indicated by the recent sale of our styrenics division, and also of Rexall-South Africa.

This program of analyzing, upgrading and, where necessary, purifying our businesses is one we're going to stay with because of our conviction that one of our most important goals in the company is to improve the return on capital of this enterprise. We're committed to doing that and to continuing the program of upgrading our businesses.

Strategic Direction Being Reexamined

Our other 1977 objective involved the reexamining of our strategic direction and of our financial policies to be certain continued growth and profitability were in our future. We are very pleased to say that we like the possibilities we see. Simply stated, our diversified operating philosophy, and our formidable financial resources, provide us with an excellent opportunity to forge continued growth.

As evidence of our confidence in our financial position and prospects, in January your directors increased substantially the cash dividend of the Common Stock. This was the sixth consecutive year of increase in the dividend, which is now at what we think is a quite attractive rate of 30 percent of earnings. We are very, very pleased at the reaction to this dividend move. Our Shareholders and the financial community are almost unanimous in their enthusiasm for this action. I should state that a few Stockholders did write to us with contrary opinions about eliminating the stock dividend, and Jus is going to comment on this a little later in the meeting.

In short, I think in 1977 we did a pretty good job of developing Dart's people, upgrading Dart's businesses, and updating our philosophy and strategies for the future.

So much for the past. How is 1978 unfolding? Our basic objective for this year, not surprisingly, is to make certain we have the eighth consecutive year of increased earnings, and at the same time to improve our return on Stockholders' equity. Barring the unforeseen, we are confident that we will attain this objective.

Let me review the outlook group by group, and, I'll start with direct selling.

Review of Operations: Direct Selling

We believe our direct selling businesses, which in 1977 accounted for about 60 percent of our pre-tax operating earnings, will have another record year in 1978. Both Tupperware and Coppercraft Guild are having fine years. Long standing problems we've had at Vanda Beauty Counselor I think are behind us, and we look forward to substantial reduction of losses there, moving toward break-even.

Given the importance of Tupperware to our overall activities, I'd like to elaborate a little bit further on Tupperware division plans for 1978.

Most of you will remember how wet and cold it was in January and February, and would recognize there would not be too many home parties held in that kind of weather. But the resiliency of our direct selling business and the fantastic recovery skills of our Tupperware management were best exhibited by the fact that Tupperware U.S. had a fine first quarter...well ahead of a year ago. And, I think it's this ability to bounce back, whether the problem be climate or economic, that makes this wonderful Tupperware business even more attractive.

Tupperware Division Expansion Continues

As witness to its continued vitality, in 1978, including the carry-over funds from 1977, Tupperware will be investing approximately $50 million in additional capital. This will be for molds for new, exciting products; molds for expansion of our existing product line; molding machines for Brazil a[nd] Venezuela; a second Canadian plant to be locat[ed] in Manitoba, West Canada; and a new plant a[nd] sales office to be located in Argentina...all parts [of] the puzzle of this wonderfully expanding busine[ss].

In this connection, our Annual Report noted si[g]nificant growth of our business operations in t[he] Western Hemisphere outside the United State[s]. That refers to our Tupperware growth in Sou[th] America. I just came back from a 10-day review [of] our sales organization and manufacturing faciliti[es] there, and I'm delighted to say we are all very e[n]thused about our prospects in South America. T[he] potential of both Venezuela and Brazil continues [to] unfold, and we're looking forward with enthusias[m] to being in both the Argentina and Chile marke[ts].

I've commented here a little bit on South Ame[r]ica. I wouldn't want you to think we have any less[er] expectations for the rest of the world. In Nor[th] America, Europe and the Pacific, Tupperware co[n]tinues to perform exceedingly well. Worldwide la[st] year Tupperware grew at over 15 percent per yea[r]. That momentum continues.

All in all, the Tupperware future has never bee[n] clearer or more promising.

Now, let me turn to our chemical-plasti[c] business.

Wilsonart, Chemical Specialties Performance Strong

This combined group represents a company [of] nearly $600 million in sales and almost $44 milli[on] in pre-tax earnings. For the past two years, Joh[n] Del Favero and his team have been working [to] streamline and improve the quality of earnings i[n] that group. While they still have some work left [to] do in terms of improving our return on investme[nt] and ensuring the long term growth strategy for th[e] business, the management of that group is we[ll] suited to do the job, and we're confident of our fu[ture there.

For 1978 we expect good improvement over 197[7] results. Our first quarter was ahead of a year ag[o] despite the cost of our new polyethylene plant star[t] up. As we look ahead, improved second quart[er]

...nds in polyethylene sales, more normalized plant operations and firming up of prices in the market ...l lead us to believe that the outlook there is more ...omising. At the same time, our business at Wilmart and Chemical Specialties remains very ...ong, and all of this adds to our optimism that ...78 will indeed be a good year for us in that part ...our business.

Turning to Consumer Products...as we reported, ...e weather gave us fits and induced some produc...n and sales problems which resulted in a flat first ...arter for this segment of our business, with the ...ousewares division, and particularly the West ...nd Company, hard hit. However, our Home Fur...shings division, led by improved results at Syroco, ...ished well ahead of a year ago. With the weather ...hind us, and hopefully a more optimistic con...mer in the latter part of the year, we expect to ...ish nicely ahead of a year ago in that segment. For the longer term, we are dedicated to building ...stronger, larger consumer products business, and ...e think Bill Graham's background ably lends it...lf to that task, and we're delighted to have him ...th us on that.

...ass Container Operations Brightening

Now looking toward our glass container busi...ss...Thatcher Glass, in the first quarter of this ...ar had operating earnings running 20 percent ...ead of a year ago, and operated near its practical ...pacity. The outlook for the balance of the year is ...do more of the same...to indeed be at capacity. That, along with a modest price increase, which ...e desperately need to cover the rising costs of la...r, materials and energy, and which is planned for ...id-year implementation, should all add up to a ...e year for Thatcher, both in terms of its return ...investment and its overall level of profitability. Lastly, a word about Dart Resorts. The sales ...ce at our two remaining developments is excel...nt. Bear Valley Springs is 85 percent sold out, and ...omentum in the first quarter of this year just ...uldn't be better.

At Tahoe Donner, where we are back selling after ...18-month ban, sales in the first quarter totaled

$1.6 million. This project's 6,000 sites are now one-third sold out. In fact, our current trends support our expectations that our resort operations will break-even this year, and into the black in 1979.

In short, I think our strengths, as evidenced by our people and our business, should make 1978 another good year for our Shareholders.

Two Key Challenges Ahead

Now if I may, I would like to conclude with just a few comments about the future of Dart Industries.

In planning the long term growth of our Company, I see two key challenges ahead of us.

The first is for us to grow our existing businesses faster and further than heretofore, both through increased internal development, and through logical add-on acquisitions. When I talk about growing our existing businesses faster, naturally I am excluding Tupperware because I'm not sure how you grow that any faster than Hamer has done.

The second key challenge we have is to identify and invest in quality new business areas. Dart Industries is, as we have said in our annual report to Shareholders and in all meetings with investors, a diversified company. And we believe the future will continue to favor the diversified company which can adapt more easily to a rapidly changing world. Thus, we are dedicated to building Dart Industries into an ever greater enterprise, characterized by having diversified businesses of sustained earnings potential.

To implement this growth philosophy, on the one hand we are actively searching, as Jus indicated, for quality companies of established size that can make a direct immediate impact on our earnings. At the same time, we are searching for the longer term emerging markets and new technologies that can be important to our long term growth. And obviously we hope to invest prudently in the most promising of these new areas.

Thanks to the many years of dedicated leadership by Justin and his peers, in my opinion Dart Industries is well positioned to grow in the future. There is no doubt in my mind that this company, finely tuned, is up to the challenges of the next few years. We're already at work charting some of the responses to what we see are the long term challenges to us...including the problems of inflation and ever bigger government.

I think the fuel for our future is a young, aggressive group of professionally trained managers, working in tandem with the seasoned entrepreneurs and operating people who have built this Company. We think this combination is unbeatable, and we do pledge to all of you our untiring efforts to reward you for your confidence in the Company.

Thanks so much for being with us.

Mr. Dart: Thank you, partner. I've done a lot of things for this Company...some good, some bad. But, I never did a better job in my life than in recruiting my partner, Tom Mullaney.

Mr. Dart's Appeal to Stockholders

Mr. Dart: Before proceeding, I would like to make as impassioned an appeal to our Shareholders as I know how to make.

No business, including Dart Industries, can function any better or do any better than the political and economic climate in which it operates.

In my opinion, there is no question that an organized, motivated business community, together with Shareholders, can successfully win the fight for private enterprise.

We are not asking that you do this necessarily to help the Company, but by helping the Company you are going to help yourself.

Let me point out to you that if you were British citizens and you owned Dart stock, Great Britain would collect up to 97 percent of your dividends in taxes. That is not a very lovely situation to be in. And if citizens are apathetic, the same tax rates could happen here.

Now, let me read you a quote from the Labor Prime Minister of England, Callaghan: (This you won't believe coming from the Labor Prime Minister.)

"We used to think that you could just spend your way out of a recession and increase employment by cutting taxes and boosting government spending tell you in all candor that that option no long exists and that insofar as it ever did exist, it o worked by injecting a bigger dose of inflation i the economy followed by a higher level unemployment."

Then do we assume that everything is now goi to go right for England? Not at all. The labor uni structure the Labor government helped to create now in charge and will not respond to the Prir Minister.

The Japanese economy is an example whe proper balance exists...where labor, governme and business work in harmony for the good of t overall. This cooperation and balance has creat one of the most productive, strongest and rapic growing economies in the world today. I believe t United States can learn from that country as we

Inflation is the deadliest enemy of us all. Inf tion affects mostly those with low incomes in o society. Many of us really maybe couldn't care t much what our groceries cost, but the person at t lower end of the spectrum cares and is getting hu

Inflation is caused by big Government, Fede deficits, and wage increases in excess of product ity. In 1950 the cost of Government per family w $1,600. Now it is $9,600.

This administration is offering inflationary leg lation, and the Congress, God bless them, is knoc ing it down. They beat back common situs, th knocked off the consumer agencies, they knock off limitation of corporate political action comm tee contributions to election campaigns. Th knocked off the funding from the public purse political campaigns, and that has come about b cause the shareholders of America, the corporatio of America, the associations of America have ma themselves felt with their letters and their pho calls. The Congressmen and the Senators are n responding to the will of the people.

We have coming up on the 15th of May the L bor Reform Bill. Please write your Senators, b cause this bill has passed the House. It can stopped in the Senate with a filibuster.

I urge every one of you to support the defeat of this bill.

ination of Stock Dividend Discussed

would like to turn to questions we faced this
. One of the major ones was the stock dividend.
ve been selling the merits of stock dividends for
ears and rather successfully, I thought. Some
kholders agreed with me, judging from a few of
etters we received.

ow, let me tell you why we decided to eliminate
stock dividend and increase the cash dividend.
market has switched from a personal market to
institutional market, and the financial commu-
now gives no credit at all to a stock dividend.
y say it is just a piece of paper and therefore
were recording our yield on a very, very low
s. Because of the institutional market, in addi-
to other factors, we changed our policy.

e eliminated the stock dividend and increased
cash dividend from $1.00 to $1.60 per year, and
carefully monitored the stock market reaction.
call your attention to the graph over the dais.
chart below.) The day we changed the divi-

Dart Industries Inc. 1978 Stock Performance

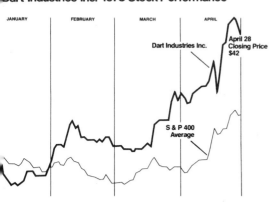

d policy the two lines crossed, and you can read
stock averages on the lower line and the price
art on the upper line. Up to now it says that
did the right thing, painful as it may have been
ose of us who didn't want to pay ordinary taxes
ividends. We used to be able to cash our shares
n a capital gains basis. I hope the results are
sing to you. They are pleasing to Tom and me
Phil, and your Directors.

Now, I would throw the floor open for other
questions.

Question: Do you expect to increase the stock dividend sometime this year to get it up to where it
matches the combined stock dividend as well as
cash dividend?

Mr. Mullaney: As a matter of policy, we are not
going to continue the stock dividend. So, I think
your question would be, "Would there be an increase in the cash dividend." That's something that
obviously your directors keep under continuous
study, and we have indicated that each February,
and more often if necessary, we will review our dividend policy to see that it is consistent with earnings. We expect to continue to pay out the cash that
on balance represents the best blend of both our
Shareholder interests and the needs of the Company, but I would not want to predict any future
dividend move at the moment.

Mr. Dart: Are there other questions?

The Secretary: No. We have one motion.

Voice: I move that the first meeting of the newly
elected Board of Directors be held in the offices of
the Company immediately following the termination of this meeting and that the meeting be
adjourned.

The motion was seconded and carried.

Mr. Dart: The meeting is adjourned. Thank you all
for coming.

The meeting was adjourned at 9:40 a.m.

Dividends Declared

Following the Annual Meeting, the Board of Directors declared a quarterly cash dividend of 40 cents per share on the Common Stock of the Company. The dividend is payable June 9, 1978, to Common Stockholders of record May 18, 1978. The Board also declared a first half dividend of $1 per share on the Series A $2 Cumulative Convertible Preferred Stock payable June 30, 1978, to Preferred Stockholders of record June 7, 1978.

Respectfully submitted,

JUSTIN DART
Chairman

THOMAS P. MULLANEY
President

May 4, 1978

INVESTOR INFORMATION

(Based on New York Stock Exchange Data)

Closing Market Price—Common Stock—39
(At March 31, 1978)

High/Low Price Range:

	1978		1977	
	High	Low	High	L
First Quarter	39¾	34	34½	2

Dart Industries NYSE Trading Volume:

First Quarter 1978	1,285

Last Quarterly Dividend Payment:

Amount	
Paid On	March 21,

388

389

Outside Directors Present

WAYNE O. ANDREAS

CURTIS BARKES

R. D. ZIEGLER

* WILLIAM E. SIMON

ONALD H. BREWER

EDWARD E. CARLSON

† JOHN C. CORNELIUS

† GENERAL ALFRED M. GRUENTHER

ILLIAM T. GOSSETT

FRANKLIN B. POLLOCK

* *Not present*
† *Director Emeritus*

WOOD R. QUESADA

STANLEY M. RUMBOUGH, JR.

COB W. STUTZMAN, M.D.

HOLMES TUTTLE

Other Inside Directors Present

ROBERT T. BEATTIE

RUSSELL K. BOLTON

JOSEPH HARA

RALPH M. KNIGHT

RALPH WILSON, JR., D.D.S.

Additional copies of this
Quarterly Report will be
furnished upon request free
of charge. Copies of the
Company's Form 10Q will also
be furnished upon request
free of charge.
Write to:

Corporate Secretary
Dart Industries Inc.
P.O. Box 3157, Terminal Annex
Los Angeles, California 90051

FORM 10-Q

SECURITIES AND EXCHANGE COMMISSION

WASHINGTON, D.C. 20549

Quarterly report under Section 13 or 15(d)
of the Securities Exchange Act of 1934

———————

For Quarter Ended March 31, 1978
Commission File Number 1-3894

DART INDUSTRIES INC.

Incorporated in Delaware   I.R.S. Employer Identification
                                 No. 95-1455570

8480 Beverly Boulevard
Los Angeles, California 90048
Telephone number (213) 658-2000

Indicate by check mark whether the registrant (1) has filed all reports
required to be filed by Section 13 or 15(d) of the Securities Exchange
Act of 1934 during the preceding 12 months (or for such shorter period
that the registrant was required to file such reports), and (2) has
been subject to such filing requirements for the past 90 days.
Yes__X__.   No_____.

The number of shares of Common Stock, par value $1.25 per share
outstanding at March 31, 1978 was 23,136,000.

Part 1.   Financial Information

DART INDUSTRIES INC. AND CONSOLIDATED SUBSIDIARIES

STATEMENT OF EARNINGS
(unaudited)

	For the Three Months Ended March 31,	
	1978	1977
Income:		
Net sales	$408 190 000	$369 916 000
Other income	6 288 000	5 053 000
	414 478 000	374 969 000
Costs and expenses:		
Cost of goods sold and operating expenses	245 500 000	220 877 000
Selling, distribution and administrative expenses	95 243 000	90 656 000
Depreciation and amortization	15 936 000	14 400 000
Interest expense	5 505 000	5 165 000
	362 184 000	331 098 000
Earnings before income taxes	52 294 000	43 871 000
Provision for income taxes	25 000 000	20 700 000
Net earnings	$ 27 294 000	$ 23 171 000
Net earnings per share of Common Stock:		
Primary	$1.11	$.94
Fully diluted	$1.04	$.89
Cash dividends per share of Common Stock	$ .40	$.25

DART INDUSTRIES INC. AND CONSOLIDATED SUBSIDIARIES

BALANCE SHEET

(unaudited)

ASSETS	March 31, 1978	March 31, 1977
Current assets:		
Cash	$ 65 686 000	$ 51 853 000
Marketable securities, at cost which approximates market	163 426 000	136 313 000
Total cash and marketable securities	229 112 000	188 166 000
Accounts and notes receivable, less allowance for doubtful accounts of $12,804,000 in 1978 and $12,709,000 in 1977	226 844 000	211 396 000
Inventories	323 782 000	297 535 000
Prepaid expenses	15 693 000	15 989 000
Deferred future income tax benefits	31 114 000	26 747 000
Total current assets	826 545 000	739 833 000
Resort development assets	51 908 000	56 468 000
Properties:		
Properties owned	845 333 000	775 731 000
Properties leased from others	23 697 000	24 417 000
	869 030 000	800 148 000
Less accumulated depreciation	363 154 000	320 256 000
Total properties	505 876 000	479 892 000
Investments and other assets:		
3M Company common stock held in escrow for exchange by holders of 4-1/4% and 4-3/4% debentures, at cost (market value: 1978 - $37,056,000; 1977 - $42,456,000)	35 162 000	35 162 000
Other assets, receivables and investments	46 385 000	36 836 000
Intangibles relating to businesses purchased, less amortization	11 133 000	14 332 000
Total investments and other assets	92 680 000	86 330 000
Total assets	$1 477 009 000	$1 362 523 000

DART INDUSTRIES INC. AND CONSOLIDATED SUBSIDIARIES

BALANCE SHEET

(unaudited)

	March 31,	
LIABILITIES AND STOCKHOLDERS' EQUITY	1978	1977
Current liabilities:		
Accounts payable	$ 73 805 000	$ 69 234 000
Accrued compensation	40 329 000	38 345 000
Other accrued expenses	105 846 000	82 284 000
Short term loans, foreign	16 771 000	23 636 000
Current instalments of obligations under capital leases	836 000	1 441 000
Current instalments of long term debt	9 109 000	6 067 000
Income taxes	47 295 000	41 837 000
Total current liabilities	293 991 000	262 844 000
Resort development liabilities	7 841 000	8 612 000
Obligations under capital leases, less current instalments	12 757 000	13 853 000
Long term debt, less current instalments	238 688 000	240 858 000
Deferred income taxes	59 590 000	53 436 000
Stockholders' equity:		
Preferred Stock	14 901 000	14 928 000
Common Stock	28 921 000	28 062 000
Capital in excess of par value	299 917 000	279 299 000
Retained earnings	521 950 000	462 178 000
	865 689 000	784 467 000
Less cost of reacquired shares of capital stock- Preferred - 32,500; Common - 700	1 547 000	1 547 000
Total stockholders' equity	864 142 000	782 920 000
Total liabilities and stockholders' equity	$1 477 009 000	$1 362 523 000

DART INDUSTRIES INC. AND CONSOLIDATED SUBSIDIARIES

STATEMENT OF CHANGES IN FINANCIAL POSITION
(unaudited)

	For the Three Months Ended March 31,	
	1978	1977
Working capital provided by:		
Net earnings	$27 294 000	$23 171 000
Items not affecting working capital -		
Depreciation and amortization	15 936 000	14 400 000
Deferred income taxes	790 000	(1 064 000)
Provided by operations	44 020 000	36 507 000
Other sources of working capital	3 668 000	5 558 000
Total working capital provided	47 688 000	42 065 000
Working capital used for:		
Properties acquired	17 708 000	21 935 000
Cash dividends paid -		
Common Stock	9 254 000	5 610 000
Other uses of working capital	8 723 000	3 131 000
Total working capital used	35 685 000	30 676 000
Working capital increase	$12 003 000	$11 389 000

DART INDUSTRIES INC. AND CONSOLIDATED SUBSIDIARIES

NOTES TO FINANCIAL STATEMENTS

	March 31,	
Details of Balance Sheet	1978	1977
Accounts and notes receivable:		
Trade	$225 359 000	$208 624 000
Other	14 289 000	15 481 000
	239 648 000	224 105 000
Less allowance for doubtful accounts	12 804 000	12 709 000
	$226 844 000	$211 396 000
Inventories:		
Raw materials and supplies	$ 94 956 000	$ 89 455 000
Work in process	45 835 000	39 342 000
Finished goods	182 991 000	168 738 000
	$323 782 000	$297 535 000

Accounting policies

The financial information included in this report has been prepared in accordance with the accounting policies reflected in the financial statements incorporated by reference in Form 10-K filed with the Securities and Exchange Commission for the year ended December 31, 1977. In the opinion of the Company all adjustments, consisting only of normal recurring adjustments, necessary for a fair statement of the results for the unaudited first three months of 1978 and 1977 have been made.

DART INDUSTRIES INC. AND CONSOLIDATED SUBSIDIARIES
NOTES TO FINANCIAL STATEMENTS
(continued)

Earnings per share of Common Stock

Primary and fully diluted earnings per share of Common Stock have been computed in accordance with provisions of Accounting Principles Board Opinion.15. Accordingly, the following weighted average number of shares have been used in the computations:

	1978	1977
Average number of shares outstanding during the period	23 134 000	23 114 400
Net shares issuable in connection with dilutive stock options based upon use of the treasury stock method	44 600	16 200
Average number of primary shares	23 178 600	23 130 600
Net additional shares issuable in connection with all dilutive stock options based upon use of the treasury stock method	25 300	200
Shares issuable upon conversion of Series A $2 Cumulative Convertible Preferred Stock	2 947 700	2 953 200
Average number of fully diluted shares	26 151 600	26 084 000

Net earnings applicable to Common Stock is after deducting Preferred dividend requirements of $1,474,000 for 1978 and $1,477,000 for 1977.

DART INDUSTRIES INC. AND CONSOLIDATED SUBSIDIARIES

Management's Analysis of Quarterly Statements:

Net sales for the first quarter of 1978 increased $38 million (10%) compared with the first quarter of 1977. Net sales of the Direct Selling and Chemical-Plastics operations were significantly ahead of last year while Consumer Products, Glass Containers and Resort Development sales were slightly ahead of the 1977 first quarter.

Cost of goods sold and operating expenses for the first quarter of 1978 increased $25 million (11%) compared with the first quarter of 1977. Higher operating expenses in the polyolefin sector, principally due to start-up costs of the company's new manufacturing facilities at Bayport, Texas, were offset by improved margins in other operations with the result that cost of goods sold and operating expenses as a percent of net sales remained at 60% for the comparative periods.

Selling, distribution and administrative expenses; depreciation and amortization; and interest expense for the first quarter of 1978 increased a combined $6 million (6%) compared with the first quarter of 1977 reflective of the increased business activity of the company.

Earnings before income taxes for the first quarter of 1978 increased $8 million (19%) compared with the first quarter of 1977 for the reasons commented upon above. Income taxes were provided at a fractionally higher effective rate in 1978 (47.8% compared with 47.2%) in recognition of increased state taxes with the result that net earnings increased $4 million (18%) compared with the 1977 first quarter.

Compared with the fourth quarter of 1977, first quarter 1978 net sales and net earnings were down $17 million (4%) and $.4 million (1%), respectively. The sales decline reflects a minor seasonality of company operations. Fourth quarter 1977 net earnings reflect a net charge of $12 million for the close down, sale or change in operating methods of certain divisions, which was disclosed in the company's 1977 annual report.

DART INDUSTRIES INC.

Review by Independent Public Accountants:

The March 31, 1978 and 1977 financial statements included in this filing on Form 10-Q have been reviewed by Price Waterhouse & Co., independent accountants, in accordance with established professional standards and procedures for such reviews. All adjustments or additional disclosures proposed by Price Waterhouse & Co. have been reflected in the data presented.

The report of Price Waterhouse & Co. commenting upon their reviews is included as Exhibit I.

400

DART INDUSTRIES INC.

<u>Part II.</u>   <u>Other Information</u>

None.

DART INDUSTRIES INC.

S I G N A T U R E

Pursuant to the requirements of the Securities Exchange Act of 1934, the Registrant has duly caused this report to be signed on its behalf by the undersigned, thereunto duly authorized, in the City of Los Angeles, State of California, on May 11, 1978.

DART INDUSTRIES INC.
Registrant

By:
William R. Palmer
Vice President and Controller
(Principal Accounting Officer)

<u>EXHIBIT   I</u>

606 SOUTH OLIVE STREET
LOS ANGELES, CALIFORNIA 90014
213-625-4400

May 11, 1978

To the Board of Directors
of Dart Industries Inc.

We have made limited reviews, in accordance with standards established by the American Institute of Certified
Public Accountants, of the accompanying consolidated financial statements, appearing on pages 1 to 6 of the accompanying Form 10-Q, of Dart Industries Inc. and consolidated subsidiaries as of March 31, 1978 and 1977 and for the three-
month periods then ended. Since we did not make audits of
such periods, we express no opinion on the financial statements referred to above. To comply with the requirements of
the Securities and Exchange Commission, we confirm the Company's representations concerning proposed adjustments and
disclosures included on page 8 of the accompanying Form 10-Q
for the periods ended March 31, 1978 and 1977 in accordance
with the related instruction 7.

PRICE WATERHOUSE & CO.

PROSPECTUS

$25,000,000

Global Marine Inc.

12⅜% Senior Subordinated Debentures due August 1, 1998
(Interest payable February 1 and August 1)

The Debentures will be redeemable at the option of the Company, as a whole at any time or in part from time to time, at 112.375% of their principal amount prior to August 1, 1979, and thereafter at prices declining to 100% on and after August 1, 1988, together in each case with accrued interest, except that no such redemption may be made prior to August 1, 1983, directly or indirectly, using borrowed funds having an interest cost of less than 12.41% per annum.

Sinking fund payments sufficient to retire $1,875,000 principal amount of Debentures annually commencing August 1, 1988 are calculated to retire 75% of the issue prior to maturity. The Company may deliver Debentures in lieu of cash in making sinking fund payments.

The Debentures will be subordinated to all Senior Indebtedness (as defined) of the Company. As of May 31, 1978, the Company's Senior Indebtedness was approximately $6,092,000. However, one of the Company's subsidiaries as of that date had additional indebtedness of $137,650,000 (net of $7,500,000 expected to be redeemed). Restrictions relating to such indebtedness may, until maturity, affect the subsidiary's ability to provide funds to the Company for payment of the Debentures. See **"Secured Debt."** The subsidiary's indebtedness, together with the Senior Indebtedness of the Company, is secured by substantially all of the assets of the Company and its subsidiaries. The Debentures will be senior to the Company's 5% Subordinated Debentures due 1984.

Application will be made to list the Debentures on the New York Stock Exchange, subject to meeting such Exchange's listing requirements.

THESE SECURITIES HAVE NOT BEEN APPROVED OR DISAPPROVED BY THE SECURITIES AND EXCHANGE COMMISSION NOR HAS THE COMMISSION PASSED UPON THE ACCURACY OR ADEQUACY OF THIS PROSPECTUS. ANY REPRESENTATION TO THE CONTRARY IS A CRIMINAL OFFENSE.

	Price to Public (1)	Underwriting Discounts (2)	Proceeds to the Company (1) (3)
Per Debenture	99.75 %	3.4 %	96.35 %
Total	$ 24,937,500	$ 850,000	$ 24,087,500

(1) Plus accrued interest from August 1, 1978 to the date of delivery.

(2) The Company has agreed to indemnify the Underwriters against certain liabilities, including liabilities under the Securities Act of 1933.

(3) Before deducting expenses of the Company estimated at approximately $420,000.

The Debentures are being offered by the Underwriters subject to prior sale and when, as and if delivered to and accepted by the Underwriters, and subject to approval of certain legal matters by counsel. It is expected that delivery of the Debentures will be made against payment therefor on or about August 1, 1978 in New York, New York.

Drexel Burnham Lambert
INCORPORATED

July 25, 1978

IN CONNECTION WITH THIS OFFERING, THE UNDERWRITERS MAY OVER-ALLOT OR EFFECT TRANSACTIONS WHICH STABILIZE OR MAINTAIN THE MARKET PRICE OF THE DEBENTURES OFFERED HEREBY AT A LEVEL ABOVE THAT WHICH MIGHT OTHERWISE PREVAIL IN THE OPEN MARKET. SUCH STABILIZING, IF COMMENCED, MAY BE DISCONTINUED AT ANY TIME.

AVAILABLE INFORMATION

The Company has filed with the Securities and Exchange Commission a registration statement (herein, together with all amendments thereto, called the "Registration Statement") under the Securities Act of 1933 for the registration of the 12⅜% Senior Subordinated Debentures (the "Debentures") offered hereby. This Prospectus omits certain of the information set forth in the Registration Statement. For further information with respect to the Company and such securities, reference is made to the Registration Statement and to the exhibits and schedules filed therewith, copies of which may be obtained from the Commission upon the payment of the charge prescribed by it, or examined without charge at its offices in Washington, D.C. Each statement made in this Prospectus referring to a document filed as an exhibit to the Registration Statement is qualified by reference to the exhibit for a complete statement of its terms and conditions.

As filed with the Securities and Exchange Commission on July 25, 1978

Registration No. 2-61944

SECURITIES AND EXCHANGE COMMISSION

Washington, D.C. 20549

AMENDMENT NO. 2

TO

Form S-1

REGISTRATION STATEMENT

Under

THE SECURITIES ACT OF 1933

GLOBAL MARINE INC.

(Exact name of registrant as specified in its charter)

811 West Seventh Street, Los Angeles, California 90017

(Address of principal executive offices)

WILLIAM R. THOMAS, Senior Vice President,

Finance and Administration

Global Marine Inc.

811 West Seventh Street

Los Angeles, California 90017

(Name and address of agent for service)

213-680-9550

(Registrant's telephone number)

Copies to:

STANLEY F. FARRAR, ESQ.

Lillick McHose & Charles

707 Wilshire Boulevard

Los Angeles, California 90017

LOUIS M. CASTRUCCIO, ESQ.

Irell & Manella

1800 Avenue of the Stars

Los Angeles, California 90067

Approximate date of commencement of proposed sale to the public:

As soon as practicable after the effective date of this Registration Statement

PROSPECTUS SUMMARY

The following summary information is qualified in its entirety by the detailed information and Consolidated Financial Statements and notes thereto appearing elsewhere in this Prospectus.

THE COMPANY

Global Marine Inc. is principally engaged in marine oil and gas drilling in offshore areas of the world pursuant to contracts with major oil companies. Contracts for the Company's two newest drill ships (construction completed on one in June 1977 and anticipated on the second in August 1978) have substantially improved the Company's revenue and earnings outlook.

SUMMARY OF OFFERING

Issue	$25,000,000 12⅜% Senior Subordinated Debentures due August 1, 1998.
Payment of Interest	February 1 and August 1.
Redemption	Redeemable at 112.375% of the principal amount prior to August 1, 1979, and thereafter at prices declining annually to 100% on and after August 1, 1988. Not redeemable prior to August 1, 1983, with borrowed money having an interest cost of less than 12.41% per annum.
Sinking Fund	Annual payments commencing August 1, 1988, to retire 75% of the issue prior to maturity.
Subordination	Subordinated to Senior Indebtedness (as defined) of the Company, which aggregated approximately $6,092,000 as of May 31, 1978 and which does not include approximately $137,650,000 (net of $7,500,000 expected to be redeemed) of indebtedness of one of the Company's subsidiaries. Restrictions relating to the subsidiary's indebtedness may, until maturity, affect the subsidiary's ability to provide funds to the Company for payment of the Debentures. See "Secured Debt."
Use of Proceeds	To provide a portion of the funds required to purchase one jack-up drilling rig, and for other purposes which may include the purchase of an additional jack-up rig and the conversion of existing drill ships to platform tenders.

SELECTED FINANCIAL INFORMATION
(Dollars in thousands except for per share amounts)

Summary of Consolidated Statement of Operations	1973	1974	1975	1976	1977	1977 (Unaudited)	1978
Revenues	$ 67,265	$ 88,927	$104,479	$ 83,863	$ 85,462	$ 29,593	$ 43,741
Income (loss) before provision for income taxes and other items	9,955	10,120	4,523*	(3,998)*	(12,547)*	(4,293)*	4,106*
Provision for income taxes (benefit)	4,679	4,617	1,939	(2,396)	(5,732)	(2,197)	1,221
Extraordinary item	—	—	—	(1,261)	—	—	—
Accounting change	—	—	—	—	274	274	—
Net income (loss)	5,276	5,503	2,584	(2,863)	(6,541)	(1,822)	2,885
Earnings (loss) per share	1.20	1.26	.59	(.66)	(1.50)	(.42)	.65
Funds from operations	$ 16,626	$ 16,348	$ 18,494	$ 13,471	$ 8,318	$ 3,967	$ 7,855
Ratio of earnings to fixed charges Actual	5.67	4.03	1.70	.71	.25	.40	1.69
Pro Forma	—	—	—	—	.21	.34	1.39

Year Ended December 31 (1973–1977); Five Months Ended May 31 (1977 Unaudited, 1978).

* See "Management's Discussion and Analysis of Consolidated Summary of Operations" with respect to the expensing of interest during construction and other items not generally included in the Company's ongoing operations.

Summary of Consolidated Balance Sheet	December 31, 1977	Actual May 31, 1978	Pro Forma May 31, 1978 (Unaudited)
Net working capital	$ 10,574	$ 11,026	$ 34,691
Total assets	252,515	247,606	272,606
Total indebtedness for borrowed money	161,604	157,774	182,774
Stockholders' equity	$ 44,086	$ 47,049	$ 47,049

THE COMPANY

Global Marine Inc. is principally engaged in the operation of marine oil and gas drilling vessels in offshore areas of the world pursuant to contracts with major oil companies of the United States and other countries. The Company's fleet consists of ten self-propelled drill ships currently operating, one drill ship under construction, one drilling platform tender and one drill ship under conversion to a tender.

In June 1977, the Company added to its fleet a new dynamically positioned drill ship, the GLOMAR PACIFIC, and it will add a sister ship, the GLOMAR ATLANTIC, upon delivery expected in August 1978. The GLOMAR PACIFIC is operating under a contract with Exxon Company, U.S.A. to be in effect through mid-1982, and upon delivery the GLOMAR ATLANTIC will begin operating under a three-year contract with Standard Oil Company of California. In the first five months of 1978, the operations of the GLOMAR PACIFIC provided 21% of the Company's operating revenues and 43% of operating profit (operating revenues less operating expenses and depreciation). The GLOMAR ATLANTIC is expected to make a similar contribution when it becomes operational.

In addition to the new drill ship construction program, the Company in late 1977 began upgrading its fleet by either converting its eight oldest vessels to platform tenders or disposing of them, and by installing more modern drilling equipment on other vessels. In this connection, the Company in 1977 wrote down to their estimated net realizable value seven vessels and related equipment and supplies scheduled for sale, conversion or other disposition by a total of $8,643,000. One older drill ship has been converted to a platform tender and the conversion of another drill ship is presently underway. Two additional vessels were sold in March 1978 and a third in May 1978. This reduction of the drill ship fleet, combined with a higher level of offshore drilling activity, has resulted in increased utilization of the Company's vessels; 98% during the first five months of 1978 as compared to 69% during the corresponding prior year period. See "Business — Vessel Utilization." The Company also plans to diversify its drilling fleet by acquiring one, and possibly two, jack-up drilling rigs. See "Use of Proceeds and Capital Expenditures" and "Business — Diversification."

In addition to offshore drilling activities, the Company is engaged in marine-related developmental engineering, marine weather forecasting, and logistic support (consisting of purchasing, crating and forwarding materials and supplies) of worldwide petroleum operations. The Company also has acquired exploratory oil, gas and mineral property rights for its own account.

The Company was incorporated in California in 1955 and reincorporated in Delaware in 1964. Its principal executive offices are located at 811 West Seventh Street, Los Angeles, California 90017, and its telephone number is 213-680-9550. The term "Company" as used herein refers to Global Marine Inc. and, unless the context otherwise requires, to its consolidated subsidiaries and two affiliated companies in which it holds interests of 40% and 50%.

USE OF PROCEEDS AND CAPITAL EXPENDITURES

The net proceeds to the Company from the sale of the Debentures are estimated at $23,665,000. At least $5,000,000 of such proceeds will be applied toward the acquisition of a new jack-up drilling rig. For a description of the rig and its intended operations, see "Business — Diversification."

A contract for the construction of the rig has been entered into with Davie Shipbuilding Limited of Levis, Quebec, Canada, with delivery anticipated in July 1979. The Company estimates that the delivered cost of the rig will be approximately $25,000,000. In addition to its contribution from the proceeds of the sale of Debentures, the Company plans to finance the purchase price with borrowings from an agency of the Canadian government and the Company's private banking group. The Canadian government agency pursuant to its direct loan program has committed to advance $12,000,000 upon delivery of the rig, on condition that the Company have obtained a two-year drilling contract for the rig. The Company anticipates borrowing an additional $8,000,000 from its banking group as a secured term loan upon delivery. If the government agency does not become obligated on its loan commitment, the Company anticipates that the deficiency will be supplied primarily with the proceeds of the present offering, with additional advances by the banks or with funds from other sources.

The Company has written Davie Shipbuilding Limited indicating that, upon concluding satisfactory financing arrangements and obtaining an operating contract for its first jack-up rig, the Company may acquire an additional jack-up rig depending upon market demand, price of the rig, available financing and the extent to which the proceeds of the present offering have been applied toward the purchase of the first rig.

The Company also is considering the sale of certain of its older drill ships or their conversion to platform tenders. It is probable that a portion of the proceeds will be applied to any such conversions. See "Business — Diversification."

Pending utilization, the proceeds of the offering will be added to working capital and may be invested in short-term, interest-bearing obligations.

CAPITALIZATION

The following table reflects the consolidated capitalization of Global Marine Inc. and consolidated subsidiaries as of May 31, 1978, and on a pro forma basis giving effect to the sale of the Debentures.

Title of Class and Amount Authorized	Outstanding	Pro Forma(4)
	(Thousands of Dollars)	
Secured Long-Term Debt(1)		
Senior Indebtedness(2)	$ 6,092	$ 6,092
U.S. Government Guaranteed Bonds(3)	137,650	137,650
	143,742	143,742
Less current maturities	7,927	7,927
Total Secured Long-Term Debt	135,815	135,815
Subordinated Long-Term Debt		
12⅜% Senior Subordinated Debentures due 1998	—	25,000
5% Subordinated Debentures due 1984	6,532	6,532
	6,532	31,532
Less current maturities	700	700
Total Subordinated Long-Term Debt	5,832	30,832
Stockholders' Equity		
Preferred Stock, without par value	—	—
Common Stock, 50¢ par value	2,209	2,209
Additional paid-in capital	10,396	10,396
Retained earnings	35,309	35,309
Less — treasury stock (58,181 shares of Common Stock)	865	865
Total Stockholders' Equity	47,049	47,049
Total Capitalization	$188,696	$213,696

(1) Secured by substantially all of the assets of the Company and its subsidiaries.

(2) For a description of Senior Indebtedness as of May 31, 1978, see **"Secured Debt — Parent Company Debt."** For the definition of Senior Indebtedness, see "Description of Debentures — Subordination of Debentures."

(3) The U.S. Government Guaranteed Bonds are obligations of Global Marine Deepwater Drilling Inc., a wholly-owned subsidiary of Global Marine Inc. See **"Secured Debt."** The $137,650,000 is net of approximately $7,500,000 principal amount of Bonds expected to be redeemed at par following delivery of the GLOMAR ATLANTIC with a portion of certain escrowed funds held by the U.S. Maritime Administration. Release of these funds is expected within three months after the delivery of the GLOMAR ATLANTIC. See Note 6 of Notes to Consolidated and Parent Company Financial Statements.

(4) The pro forma amounts do not take into account borrowings which the Company plans to make upon delivery of the new jack-up drilling rig anticipated in July 1979. See "Use of Proceeds and Capital Expenditures."

CONSOLIDATED SUMMARY OF OPERATIONS

The following Consolidated Summary of Operations of Global Marine Inc. and subsidiaries, except as it relates to the five-month period ended May 31, 1977, has been examined by Coopers & Lybrand, independent certified public accountants, whose report is included elsewhere in this Prospectus. Information contained in the summary for the five-month period ended May 31, 1977, in the opinion of management, reflects all adjustments (all of which were normal recurring accruals) necessary to a fair presentation of the results of operations for the period then ended. The following statement should be read in conjunction with the related notes thereto and the Consolidated Financial Statements and related notes appearing elsewhere in this Prospectus.

	Year Ended December 31,					Five Months Ended May 31,	
	1973	1974	1975	1976	1977	1977	1978
						(Unaudited)	
	(Dollars in thousands except per share data)						
Operating Revenues:							
Marine drilling	$ 52,679	$ 67,232	$ 82,186	$ 75,925	$ 79,780	$ 27,061	$ 40,505
Other	14,586	21,695	22,293	7,938	5,682	2,532	3,236
Total operating revenues	67,265	88,927	104,479	83,863	85,462	29,593	43,741
Expenses:							
Operating	44,403	61,869	76,713	58,029	56,183	21,600	25,253
Depreciation	8,538	9,717	12,223	14,517	15,439	5,557	6,750
General and administrative	2,514	3,259	3,983	4,168	4,678	1,801	2,766
Exploration and development	686	1,043	993	1,678	1,992	136	554
Provision for loss on disposition of vessels and equipment (Note 3)	—	—	—	—	8,643	—	—
Gain on disposition of vessels and equipment	—	—	—	—	—	—	(729)
	56,141	75,888	93,912	78,392	86,935	29,094	34,594
Operating income (loss)	11,124	13,039	10,567	5,471	(1,473)	499	9,147
Other income (expense):							
Interest expense	(2,131)	(3,335)	(6,429)	(13,805)	(16,027)	(6,326)	(5,937)
Interest income	664	207	152	4,250	4,735	1,583	1,144
Miscellaneous	298	209	233	86	218	(49)	(248)
Total other income (expense)	(1,169)	(2,919)	(6,044)	(9,469)	(11,074)	(4,792)	(5,041)
Income (loss) before income taxes (benefit) and other items shown below	9,955	10,120	4,523	(3,998)	(12,547)	(4,293)	4,106
Income taxes (benefit) (Note 11)	4,679	4,617	1,939	(2,396)	(5,732)	(2,197)	1,221
Income (loss) before items shown below	5,276	5,503	2,584	(1,602)	(6,815)	(2,096)	2,885
Extraordinary charge, net of related income tax effect (Note 4)	—	—	—	(1,261)	—	—	—
Cumulative effect on years prior to 1977 of accounting changes, net of related income tax effect (Note 5)	—	—	—	—	274	274	—
Net income (loss)	$ 5,276	$ 5,503	$ 2,584	$ (2,863)	$ (6,541)	$ (1,822)	$ 2,885
Average shares outstanding (000)	4,413	4,370	4,360	4,345	4,371	4,351	4,410
Income (loss) per common and common equivalent shares:							
Income (loss) before items shown below	$1.20	$1.26	$ .59	$ (.37)	$(1.56)	$(.48)	$ .65
Extraordinary charge	—	—	—	(.29)	—	—	—
Cumulative effect of accounting changes	—	—	—	—	.06	.06	—
Net income (loss)	$1.20	$1.26	$ .59	$ (.66)	$(1.50)	$(.42)	$ .65

	Year Ended December 31,					Five Months Ended May 31,	
	1973	1974	1975	1976	1977	1977	1978
						(Unaudited)	
	(Dollars in thousands except per share data)						
Pro forma amounts assuming accounting changes applied retroactively:							
Income (loss) before extraordinary charge	$ 5,168	$ 5,721	$ 3,168	$ (2,024)	$ (6,815)	$ (2,096)	$ 2,885
Income (loss) per share	1.17	1.31	.73	(.47)	(1.56)	(.48)	.65
Net income (loss)	$ 5,168	$ 5,721	$ 3,168	$ (3,285)	$ (6,815)	$ (2,096)	$ 2,885
Net income (loss) per share	1.17	1.31	.73	(.76)	(1.56)	(.48)	.65
Ratio of Earnings to Fixed Charges(c)	5.67	4.03	1.70	.71	.25	.40	1.69

(a) Amounts for years prior to 1977 have been reclassified to conform to 1977 classifications.

(b) No cash dividends have been declared on common stock.

(c) The ratio of earnings to fixed charges has been computed by dividing net income before fixed charges and income taxes by fixed charges. Fixed charges consist of interest expense including amortization of bond discount and payments on capitalized leases. The unaudited ratio of earnings to fixed charges after extraordinary charges in 1976 was .53. The unaudited pro forma ratios for the year ended December 31, 1977 and the five months ended May 31, 1977 and 1978, after giving effect only to the issuance of the Debentures, are .21, .34 and 1.39, respectively. The pro forma ratios were calculated without regard to borrowings which the Company plans to make upon delivery of the new jack-up drilling rig anticipated in July 1979 and to any earnings which could be realized from the proceeds of this offering.

(d) Note references refer to Notes to Consolidated and Parent Company Financial Statements.

(e) The initial annual interest requirement on the Debentures will be $3,093,750.

MANAGEMENT'S DISCUSSION AND ANALYSIS OF CONSOLIDATED SUMMARY OF OPERATIONS

The new drill ship construction program combined with upgrading the Company's fleet through conversion or sale has had a major impact on the Company's recent consolidated summary of operations. The following table shows (i) the net pre-tax interest expense resulting from the Company's policy of expensing interest on borrowings for ship construction and (ii) the pre-tax income or expense, primarily impacting operating results for 1977, resulting from other recent events which occur infrequently in the Company's ongoing operations in the magnitudes indicated below.

	Year Ended December 31,			Five Months Ended May 31,	
	1975	1976	1977	1977	1978
	(Rounded to nearest hundred thousand)				
Construction interest expense net of interest income on related escrow funds	($1,600,000)	($2,300,000)	($3,300,000)	($1,700,000)	($1,200,000)
Other significant income (expense) items which occur infrequently in the Company's ongoing operations:					
Sale of certain property			300,000		900,000
Provision for relocation					(700,000)
GLOMAR ATLANTIC contract amendment (including interest)			5,500,000		
Provision for loss on disposition of vessels and equipment			(8,600,000)		
Provision for doubtful accounts			(1,000,000)		
Reduction in value of certain mineral rights			(1,100,000)		
Total	($1,600,000)	($2,300,000)	($8,200,000)	($1,700,000)	($1,000,000)

Five Month Period Ended May 31, 1978 Compared With Five Month Period Ended May 31, 1977

During the first five months of 1978, the Company had net income of $2.9 million, an improvement of $4.7 million over the prior year comparative period loss. These improved operating results were due primarily to contributions from the new GLOMAR PACIFIC during 1978 (the vessel was under construction during the 1977 period) and higher vessel utilization (98% vs. 69%) attributable to the general increase in activity of the worldwide offshore drilling market and elimination of certain of the older vessels in the Company's fleet. See "Business — Vessel Utilization." During the first five months of 1977, net interest costs on the construction of both the GLOMAR PACIFIC and the GLOMAR ATLANTIC were $1.7 million, while during the same period in 1978 net interest costs on the construction of the GLOMAR ATLANTIC were $1.2 million. During the first five months of 1978, approximately $.9 million was realized on the sale of certain vessels and related equipment and from the conveyance of the Company's 4% interest in the Polyglomar Driller.

The increase in revenues was accounted for primarily by approximately $9 million from the addition of the GLOMAR PACIFIC, with the balance primarily due to increased fleet utilization. The increase in operating expense was due to the addition of the GLOMAR PACIFIC (partially offset by a decrease in the size of the fleet), a general increase in the cost of labor and operating supplies, and costs, estimated at $700,000, of relocating the headquarters of the drilling operations to Houston.

Interest income during both periods was derived from funds held in escrow for construction of the GLOMAR PACIFIC (delivered June 1977) and the GLOMAR ATLANTIC (still under construction). This escrow fund income decreased from the 1977 period to the 1978 period as funds were used for construction, but additional interest income was derived during the 1978 period from funds invested in certificates of deposit since January in connection with the Company's restructuring of its bank credit lines. See Note 6 of Notes to Consolidated and Parent Company Financial Statements.

Other expense increases were due to increased staffing costs and the expense of drilling a dry hole in the Philippines.

1977 Compared With 1976

In 1977, the Company incurred a net after tax loss of $6.5 million, an increase of $3.7 million of losses over 1976. The major factor contributing to the net loss was a provision for loss amounting to $8.6 million before taxes on disposition of older vessels and equipment and related supplies which had become marginal or unprofitable and had limited future prospects in the market. Other important factors contributing to the loss were a $1.0 million provision for a doubtful account with a foreign customer and a $1.1 million charge to expense to recognize that the Company's activity relative to its nickel laterite deposit in the Philippines would not be commercially viable in the foreseeable future due to the severe decline in world market prices; these factors were partially offset by $5.5 million of marine drilling revenue and interest income received from Standard Oil Company of California due to the amendment of the GLOMAR ATLANTIC contract. Marine drilling revenues also increased as a result of significant revenues from the GLOMAR PACIFIC during the second half of the year. These increases were partially offset by a decrease of $2.3 million in other revenues and lower utilization rates and day rates for older vessels.

Net interest costs on the construction of the GLOMAR PACIFIC (prior to its commencement of operation in late June 1977) and the GLOMAR ATLANTIC, which were expensed by the Company, were $3.3 million in 1977 compared to $2.3 million in 1976.

Other operating revenues and other operating expenses decreased $2.3 million and $1.4 million in 1977 from 1976, primarily because of termination of the GLOMAR EXPLORER program as of September 30, 1976. Marine drilling expenses decreased $.4 million in 1977.

Depreciation expense increased $.9 million due to the GLOMAR PACIFIC beginning operations in late June 1977, partially offset by the absence of depreciation charges for the GLOMAR TENDER I (formerly the GLOMAR SIRTE) while it was undergoing conversion to a drilling platform tender in 1977. Net interest expense increased $1.7 million due primarily to increased borrowings to finance construction of new drill ships, offset in part by $1.5 million of interest income earned on funds received in connection with the agreement to reduce the term of the GLOMAR ATLANTIC contract. The provision for income tax benefit, as a percentage of loss before income tax benefit, decreased from the prior year due to losses attributable to foreign operations for which no United States or foreign tax benefits were available and amortization of investment tax credits amounting to $.9 million in 1977 as compared to $.6 million in 1976.

Effective January 1, 1977, the Company changed its methods of accounting for vessel drydock costs and materials and supplies costs. Costs incurred in drydocking vessels in 1977 were deferred and will be amortized over a two year period; materials and supplies below a stated minimum unit price were charged to expense as purchased. In prior periods, drydock costs were charged to expense as incurred, and all materials and supplies were inventoried and charged to expense as used in operations. The new method of accounting for vessel drydock costs was adopted to recognize that operations in future periods would benefit from vessel drydocking, and an improved method of matching expenses with revenues would be achieved. The new method of accounting for materials and supplies was adopted to improve record keeping efficiency. The accounting changes increased the 1977 net loss by $74,000. The cumulative effect of the accounting changes on years prior to 1977 amounted to $274,000 (after deducting income taxes of $253,000). The pro forma amounts shown in the summary of operations give effect to the retroactive application of these accounting changes, including related tax effect.

1976 Compared With 1975

During 1976, operating revenues declined by $20.6 million and the Company sustained a net loss of $2.8 million, a $5.4 million decline in earnings compared with a net income of $2.6 million in 1975. Net interest costs on the construction of vessels, which costs were expensed by the Company, were $2.3 million in 1976 and $1.6 million in 1975. Marine drilling revenues decreased $6.3 million in 1976 due to a decline in vessel utilization, a situation which evidenced itself in the fourth quarter of 1975, continued during 1976 and became particularly severe in the fourth quarter of 1976. The Company's vessel utilization declined from 85% in 1975 to 65% in 1976, partially because of the Company's reluctance at that time to lower its day rates despite unfavorable changes in the supply of and demand for offshore drilling rigs.

The decline in other revenues of $14.4 million was attributable mainly to a reduction and eventual termination, as of September 30, 1976, of the GLOMAR EXPLORER Program. Marine drilling operating expenses declined $7.2 million in 1976 due to the decreased drilling activity. This decline was not proportionate with the decline in revenues due to the continuation of fixed costs and certain maintenance and minimum standby costs incurred on the vessels without contracts. Other operating expenses declined approximately $11.5 million due primarily to the expiration of the GLOMAR EXPLORER Program.

Depreciation expense increased $2.3 million due to a full year's provision for the GLOMAR JAVA SEA. Exploration and development expenses for 1976 increased by approximately $.7 million over 1975 due primarily to an increase in the provision for abandonments of several non-productive oil and gas leases. Net interest expense increased $3.3 million for the year due to the increased debt associated with construction and operation of new vessels. The provision for income tax benefit in 1976 consisted of $1.8 million attributable to the loss before the extraordinary charge and $.6 million amortization of investment tax provision. In 1975, the income tax provision was approximately $2.4 million less the amortization of the investment tax credit of $.4 million.

The Company refinanced a substantial portion of its long-term debt in 1976. Prepayment penalties and other associated expenses aggregating $2,425,000, net of the related income tax benefit of $1,164,000, have been shown as an extraordinary charge of $1,261,000.

BUSINESS

The Company is primarily a contractor engaged in the operation of offshore oil and gas drilling vessels. The Company also provides ocean-oriented engineering, weather and logistics services, and has acquired exploratory oil, gas and mineral rights for its own account. The following table sets forth the percentage contributions to the Company's operating revenues and operating profit (see "Consolidated Summary of Operations" above) of the marine drilling and other operations described above:

	Year Ended December 31,					Five Months Ended May 31,	
	1973	1974	1975	1976	1977	1977	1978
						(Unaudited)	
Operating Revenues:							
Marine Drilling	78.3%	75.6%	78.7%	90.5%	93.4%	91.4%	92.6%
Other Operations	21.7%	24.4%	21.3%	9.5%	6.6%	8.6%	7.4%
Operating Profit (Loss)*:							
Marine Drilling	86.7%	81.0%	82.8%	102.0%	107.4%	110.6%	98.7%
Other Operations	13.3%	19.0%	17.2%	(2.0%)	(7.4%)	(10.6%)	1.3%

* Operating revenues less operating expenses and depreciation.

Marine Drilling

The Company's Fleet. The Company's marine drilling fleet consists of ten self-propelled drill ships currently operating, one drill ship under construction, one platform tender and one drill ship under conversion to a platform tender. The newest and most significant vessels in the fleet are the GLOMAR PACIFIC, which was delivered in June 1977, and the GLOMAR ATLANTIC, which is expected to be delivered in August 1978. For a discussion of the importance of these sister ships to the Company's operations, see "Vessel Utilization" below.

The following table lists, by class, each of the Company's vessels with the year it entered service, its current area of operations, and the contracting party and estimated expiration date of the contract (if any) under which it is currently operating. The length, beam, draft and fully loaded displacement tonnage is set forth for each class together with the water depth in which the drilling vessels are designed to drill. All of the Company's vessels are subject to fleet mortgages. See **"Secured Debt."**

Vessel Description	Location	Contracting Party and Estimated Contract Expiration Date
GLOMAR PACIFIC CLASS (450x72x23.5; 14,750 tons; 2,000 feet; dynamic positioning)		
GLOMAR PACIFIC (1977)	Baltimore Canyon Area offshore New Jersey	Exxon Company, U.S.A.; July 1982
GLOMAR ATLANTIC	(under construction)	Standard Oil Company of California; 3 years from delivery
GLOMAR CORAL SEA CLASS (400x65x21; 11,200 tons; 1,000 feet)		
GLOMAR CORAL SEA (1973)	Offshore California	Exxon Company, U.S.A.; January 1979
GLOMAR JAVA SEA (1975)	Gulf of Mexico	Atlantic Richfield Company; October 1980
GLOMAR GRAND ISLE CLASS (400x65x21; 11,200 tons; 600 feet)		
GLOMAR GRAND ISLE (1967)	Gulf of Mexico	Hamilton Brothers Oil Company; August 1978(a)
GLOMAR CONCEPTION (1967)	Offshore California	Standard Oil Company of California; November 1978(a)
GLOMAR CHALLENGER (1968)(b)	Pacific Ocean	National Science Foundation; September 1979
GLOMAR GRAND BANKS (1972)	Offshore Nova Scotia	Nova Scotia Department of Mines; October 1978(a)
GLOMAR TASMAN CLASS (380x64x20; 9,550 tons; 600 feet)		
GLOMAR NORTH SEA (1965)	Mediterranean Sea offshore Sicily	Montedison S.p.A. (Italian national oil company); November 1978(a)
GLOMAR TASMAN (1965)	En route to Singapore	None(a)
GLOMAR V CLASS (268x58x16; 5,500 tons; 600 feet)		
GLOMAR V (1963)	Mediterranean Sea offshore Spain	Shell España N.V.; September 1978(a)

Vessel Description	Location	Contracting Party and Estimated Contract Expiration Date
PLATFORM TENDERS		
GLOMAR TENDER I (1978) (380x64x20; 9,550 tons)	Gulf of Mexico	Tenneco Inc.; March 1980
GLOMAR TENDER II (1978) (268x58x16; 5,550 tons)	(under conversion to a platform tender)	Gulf Oil Company; 1 year from delivery

(a) These vessels have been operating under short-term contracts due to market conditions. Except for the GLOMAR GRAND ISLE, which has a contract with Esso Exploration, S.A. which will commence at the expiration of the present contract with Hamilton Brothers Oil Company and is expected to run through November 1978, these vessels have no signed contracts for future periods; however, the vessels have been or will be actively bid for drilling projects. If market conditions indicate that profitable work is not available, certain vessels may be converted to platform tenders or sold.

(b) The GLOMAR CHALLENGER's tonnage is 10,500; its dynamic positioning capacity has permitted it to recover core samples in ocean depths of 23,095 feet.

The Company's fleet at present is comprised entirely of hull-shape drilling units. Two of the Company's drill ships, the GLOMAR PACIFIC and the GLOMAR ATLANTIC, which have conventional mooring systems using multiple anchors on the ocean floor to keep the vessels in place during drilling operations, also have dynamic positioning capability which enables them to operate in deep water without using their conventional mooring systems. The GLOMAR CHALLENGER also has dynamic positioning capability, but it is not equipped with a conventional mooring system. Vessels with dynamic positioning capability are equipped with multiple thrusters which serve as a station-keeping device in lieu of conventional equipment. These ships are able to operate in deeper waters than those in which conventionally moored offshore drilling rigs can operate. However, drilling activities in water depths requiring dynamic positioning are limited at the present time. The GLOMAR CHALLENGER is the only Company vessel regularly utilizing its dynamic positioning capability.

In addition to the new drill ship construction program which will be completed with the delivery of the GLOMAR ATLANTIC in August 1978, the Company in late 1977 began upgrading its fleet by either converting its eight oldest drilling vessels to platform tenders or disposing of them, and by installing more modern drilling equipment on other vessels. In this connection the Company in 1977 wrote down to their estimated net realizable value seven vessels and related equipment and supplies scheduled for sale, conversion or other disposition by a total of $8,643,000. One older drill ship has been converted to a platform tender, and the conversion of another drill ship is presently underway. Two other vessels were sold in March 1978 and a third in May 1978. The Company expects to convert or sell three additional vessels in the near future. The Company also plans to diversify its drilling fleet by acquiring one, and possibly two, jack-up drilling rigs. See "Use of Proceeds and Capital Expenditures" and "Business — Diversification."

In addition to converting or selling older vessels, the Company has nearly completed the process of improving the marketability of three drill ships of the GLOMAR GRAND ISLE class by installing more advanced equipment on the vessels. This equipment, the majority of which is financed by seven-year leases, is designed to increase the safety and efficiency of the vessels' operations and will enable one of them to drill in deeper water.

Vessel Utilization. The following table sets forth the utilization rates of the Company's fleet for the five years ended December 31, 1977 and for the five month periods ended May 31, 1977 and 1978.

The utilization percentage for a period is based on the ratio of days in the period during which vessels were earning revenues to the total days in the period during which vessels were available for work.

| | Year Ended December 31, | | | | | Five Months Ended May 31, | |
	1973	1974	1975	1976	1977	1977	1978
Vessels Available	12	13	14	14	12	13	11
Percentage Utilization ..	88%	94%	85%	65%	75%	69%	98%

The Company believes that, with the addition to its fleet of the GLOMAR PACIFIC and the GLOMAR ATLANTIC, a more accurate portrayal of the fleet's operations requires taking into account the significantly greater revenue and profit generating capacities of these new vessels as compared to the Company's other drill ships. The average day rate for the two new ships is approximately three times the average day rate for the Company's other drill ships. Additionally, day rates for the Company's platform tenders are generally lower than those for its drill ships. The impact of the GLOMAR PACIFIC class is further increased by the fact that the GLOMAR PACIFIC is subject to a contract which will be in effect through mid-1982, and that the GLOMAR ATLANTIC is subject to a three-year contract from the date it goes into service (expected in August 1978). The following table shows, for each of the Company's three principal groups of vessels as of July 15, 1978, the number of months under contract compared with the months of availability for the years 1978 through 1980. "Vessel Contract Months Available" includes the GLOMAR ATLANTIC (under construction) and the GLOMAR II (under conversion to and shown as a platform tender) from the dates when each is expected to enter service.

| | 1978 | | 1979 | | 1980 | |
	Vessel Contract Months Available	Vessel Months Under Contract	Vessel Contract Months Available	Vessel Months Under Contract	Vessel Contract Months Available	Vessel Months Under Contract
GLOMAR PACIFIC class ..	16	16	24	24	24	24
Other Drill Ships	112	92	108	21	108	9
Platform Tenders	14	14	24	19	24	3
TOTAL	142	122	156	64	156	36

Apart from vessels of the GLOMAR PACIFIC class, six of the Company's drill ships have contracts which are estimated to expire in 1978 and two ships have contracts estimated to expire in 1979. There is no assurance that new contracts will be available for any of these ships, or if contracts are available, that they will provide revenues adequate to cover all fixed and variable operating costs of the vessels, including mobilization costs.

Recent Oversupply Situation. During approximately the period from late 1975 through late 1977, there existed a surplus of offshore drilling rigs of all types, which resulted in intense competition to secure drilling contracts with consequent lower day rates and reduced vessel utilization. The surplus was caused primarily by a steady increase in the construction of new drilling rigs built in response to an expected higher level of industry-wide exploration and drilling activity. However, this higher level of drilling activity did not occur due to foreign and domestic governmental actions such as increases in taxes and royalties on oil and gas production, delays in opening new areas for exploration and, in some cases, the imposition of restrictions intended to protect the marine and coastal environment.

The industry oversupply of offshore drilling rigs began to abate in late 1977 as a result of increases in the price of petroleum products which made higher levels of exploratory and developmental drilling economically feasible, and as a result of a lower number of new rigs coming onto the market. More active exploration activities also may result from further sales of offshore oil and gas leases by the Department of the Interior along the eastern seaboard of the United States, although litigation continues to slow the rate at which such sales might otherwise be made.

Competition. The Company's marine drilling services historically have been provided by self-propelled drilling vessels. Competition is encountered from other types of offshore drilling rigs, including semi-submersible and jack-up rigs. Floating units such as the Company's hull-shape drilling vessels generally are capable of drilling in waters of greater depth than bottom-supported rigs such as jack-ups, but floating units, and hull-shape vessels in particular, are more subject to surface ocean conditions. Hull-shape vessels also have historically been more expensive to construct than jack-up rigs. However, hull-shape rigs generally have a greater capacity than jack-ups or semi-submersibles for carrying supplies and materials for use at drilling sites; they also have advantages in safety, mobility and speed in proceeding to and from work sites and in moving to safety in the event of severe weather or other dangerous conditions. The Company is the only one among its major competitors whose drilling fleet is comprised entirely of hull-shape vessels. For a description of the Company's plan to diversify its drilling fleet, see "Diversification" below.

Numerous firms are engaged in providing the marine drilling services offered by the Company. A number of these competitors have vessels which compete directly with those of the Company, and many of them have substantially greater financial resources. The Company competes with these companies for drilling contracts primarily through sealed bidding, although competition through open bidding occurs occasionally. The offshore drilling business has been marked by rapid technological advances in drilling equipment and techniques. The ability of the Company to compete successfully depends to a great extent on its ability to employ and retain qualified personnel and its ability, financial and otherwise, to utilize technological developments and new drilling techniques as they become available.

Drilling Contracts and Major Customers. Drilling contracts are negotiated individually and vary in their terms and provisions. The rates specified in each contract are generally on a per day basis, payable in United States dollars, and vary depending upon the equipment and services supplied, the areas involved, the duration of the work, competitive conditions and other variables. There is a basic day rate during drilling operations with lower rates for periods of equipment breakdown, adverse weather, or other conditions which may be beyond the control of the Company. When a vessel mobilizes to or demobilizes from an operating area, a contract may provide for different day rates, specified fixed amounts, or for no payment. The longer term contracts have escalation provisions for certain operating expenses.

A contract may be terminated by the customer in the event the drilling ship is destroyed or lost or if drilling operations are suspended for a specified period of time due to a breakdown of major equipment or, in some cases, due to other events beyond the control of either party. Contracts may be for a specified period of time or they may provide for the drilling of a given number of wells.

The Company's business is subject to the usual risks associated with having a limited number of customers for its services. In 1976, approximately 47% of marine drilling operating revenues was attributable to services performed for Exxon Company, U.S.A., Standard Oil Company of California, Atlantic Richfield Company, or their respective affiliates, and the National Science Foundation. Eleven other customers accounted for the remaining marine drilling revenues. In 1977, approximately 63% of such revenues was derived from services performed for the same four principal customers with the remainder provided by sixteen customers. The same four customers accounted for approximately 73% of such revenues during the first five months of 1978 with the remainder provided by fifteen customers. After delivery of the GLOMAR ATLANTIC (under contract to Standard Oil Company of California), the percentage of revenues attributable to these four customers will increase significantly. The Company anticipates that a majority of its marine drilling operating revenues will continue to be attributable to services performed for major oil companies.

During 1977, the Company executed an amendment shortening its long-term drilling contract with Standard Oil Company of California for the use of the GLOMAR ATLANTIC from five years to three years. As a result of this amendment, Global Marine Inc. received a cash payment of approximately $20 million, $9.4 million of which was received in December 1977 with the balance paid in January 1978. This cash sum included $4 million received as partial consideration for reducing the term of the contract, and the balance representing the discounted time value of the cash flow expected to be derived from the GLOMAR ATLANTIC during the last two years of the original five-year contract, adjusted for other related transactions between the companies. The discounted value component of the payment was made as an advance to apply as partial day rate payment for the use of other vessels in the Company's fleet over a period of up to four years. For a discussion of the income effects of this transaction, see "Management's Discussion and Analysis, of Consolidated Summary of Operations — 1977 Compared with 1976". The Company believes this contract amendment has had a favorable impact on its business prospects since the advance payment enabled the Company to restructure its credit lines on more favorable terms, provided cash for use at the latter stages of the depressed rig market to begin conversion efforts on older vessels in its fleet and to upgrade equipment on others, and effectively guaranteed work for part of the Company's fleet during the succeeding four years. The advance payment of partial day rates will cause cash flows in future periods to be less than the corresponding revenues in such periods depending upon vessel usage by Standard Oil Company of California in future periods. However, the portion of day rates paid in cash will be sufficient to cover the Company's direct operating costs. As of May 31, 1978, $12.7 million of the prepayment remained to be applied to vessel usage over the next three years.

Operating Risks, Insurance and Governmental Regulations. The Company's operations are subject to the usual hazards incident to the drilling of oil and gas wells, such as blowouts and fires, many of which hazards can severely damage or destroy equipment. The Company's activities also are subject to perils peculiar to marine operations, such as collision, grounding or damage from severe weather.

The Company maintains broad insurance coverage against general and marine public liability (not including certain risks such as pollution — see below), subject to a $250,000 deductible per occurrence. The Company's drill ships and related equipment are insured against marine and other perils, and in certain cases loss due to war, but not including expropriation, nuclear explosions, delay, loss of use or business interruption. The Company believes it is adequately covered by insurance, but loss of or severe damage to any of its drilling vessels could materially affect its revenue.

The Company's operations are subject to the impact of governmental regulations, including regulations dealing with protection of the environment, promulgated by the federal government and various of its agencies and by state, local and foreign governments. For example, operators of vessels in navigable United States waters and certain offshore areas are liable to the United States government for the cost of removing oil spills for which they may be held responsible, subject to certain limitations; and they must establish financial responsibility to cover such liabilities. The Company has established such financial responsibility. Most of the Company's drilling contracts provide that the Company will be wholly or substantially indemnified by its customers against liabilities for pollution resulting from drilling pursuant to the contracts. The discharge of certain untreated wastes into such navigable waters also is prohibited by law, and vessels operating in such waters must be appropriately equipped to handle such wastes.

The Company does not anticipate that any material expenditures will be required to enable it to comply with existing laws and regulations. However, it is possible that such regulations in the future may add to the costs of operating offshore drilling equipment or may prevent drilling activity entirely. Moreover, Congress is presently considering various proposals designed to establish a comprehensive energy policy for the United States. The Company's business may be affected in varying degrees by any laws and regulations, such as restrictions on oil or gas production, price controls and tax policies, which may evolve out of such proposals.

Additional risks associated with the Company's operations in foreign areas include expropriation, nationalization, foreign exchange restrictions, foreign taxation, changing political conditions, and foreign and domestic monetary policies. To date the Company has experienced no material losses as a result of any of these risk factors. However, local governmental regulations which may in the future become applicable to the industry served by the Company could reduce demand for the Company's services, or such regulations could directly affect the Company in its ability to compete for customers.

Diversification. The Company is in the process of making significant changes in the composition of its fleet. The most significant of these is the proposed acquisition of one or possibly two jack-up drilling rigs. See "Use of Proceeds and Capital Expenditures." The first new rig will be constructed according to a Marathon Le Tourneau design and will be capable of drilling in up to 250 feet of water. The rig will have a movable cantilevered sub-base which will enable it to perform overplatform developmental drilling as well as exploratory drilling. The Company plans to operate the rig in the Gulf of Mexico, where the current demand for jack-ups is high. The Company believes that this increased demand is largely attributable to recent increases in the price of natural gas, which have made it economically feasible for major and independent companies to search for and exploit small fields in developed shallow-water petroleum provinces such as the Gulf. The Company expects the demand for exploration by jack-up rigs to continue for the next three to five years. However, there is no assurance that this will be the case, particularly if discoveries of small fields in developed areas begin to decline.

The second important change in the composition of the Company's fleet is the conversion of at least two and as many as five of the Company's older drill ships to drilling platform tenders. Functions performed by platform tenders include drilling wells in conjunction with fixed platforms, berthing platform crews, platform repair and logistic support. The Company believes that a majority of its tenders for the next several years will service platforms located in the Gulf of Mexico, providing continuation of the present level of exploration activity in the Gulf.

Platform Operation. The Company operates a platform drilling rig in the Celtic Sea under a two-year contract with the owner of the platform.

Glomar Challenger Program. Since its completion in 1968, the GLOMAR CHALLENGER has been under a contract with the Deep Sea Drilling Project of the National Science Foundation. The specifically equipped vessel drills and recovers core samples from beneath the ocean floor. It is equipped with dynamic positioning capability to eliminate the need for anchoring over a core drilling site. Operations under this program are similar to those under an oil and gas drilling contract, but by reason of the term of the contract and the nature of the work, such operations are less subject to the interruption and to the expenses of starting up and shutting down. The GLOMAR CHALLENGER has operated in all major ocean areas of the world except the Arctic Ocean.

Other Operations

Engineering Services. Following experimental and survey work conducted in 1970, the Company designed, supervised the construction of and through 1976 operated the GLOMAR EXPLORER, which has been owned by the U.S. Government since its construction. The Company in June 1978 chartered the GLOMAR EXPLORER from the U.S. Government, and will activate, modify and operate the vessel to test a prototype deep ocean mining system for a consortium headed by Lockheed Missile and Space Co. Participation in the new project will continue for a minimum period of thirteen months. The vessel will be operated pursuant to a management contract under which the Company will be reimbursed for its costs and paid a management fee.

Pursuant to a joint venture terminated at the end of 1975, the Company participated in the design and construction of a prototype air cushion transporter of 100-ton capacity for use by the oil and gas industry in the Canadian Arctic. The Company retained title to the technology thus developed, subject to an obligation to pay its former joint venturer a limited 5% royalty dependent on commercial exploitation. The Company is currently attempting to apply this technology commercially.

In addition, the Company provides developmental engineering services to the worldwide marine industry, with particular emphasis on the marine extractive and energy related industries.

Logistic Services. Since 1970, a Houston-based subsidiary of the Company has provided logistic, procurement and expediting services to the Company's marine drilling subsidiary and the worldwide petroleum industry.

Technical Services. The Company provides technical services directed towards measurement, analysis, description and prediction of the marine environment, including weather forecasting and ship routing.

Oil, Gas and Mineral Rights. Since the late 1960's the Company has secured interests in prospective oil, gas and mineral properties. The following table lists the Company's offshore oil and gas interests as of July 15, 1978 which are being held for further evaluation or exploratory work.

Location	Gross Acres	Percentage Interest
Baffin Bay/Canada	282,754	7.5%
North Sea/U. K.	25,000	10.0%
Arctic Islands/Canada —		
All permits other than Permit A1985	6,456,000	5.0%
Permit A1985	30,148	25.0%
Adriatic Sea/Italy	243,919	15.0%
Southern California	23,040	10.0%

Exploratory work is generally required by the terms of the various leases and concessions in order to maintain the Company's interests. In addition, significant expenditures would be required in order to determine whether or not commercial deposits of oil, gas or other minerals can be produced. The Company has endeavored to limit its own capital expenditures in exploration by negotiating arrangements for third parties to bear exploration costs in exchange for assignments of interests in the properties, as was the case during 1977 when the Company reduced its interest in the Arctic properties (other than Permit A1985) from 25% to 5%.

Research and Development

A portion of the Company's operating revenues for its last five fiscal years which was derived from developmental engineering services could be deemed to involve customer-sponsored research activities. The same will be true for engineering revenues generated during the current year, particularly revenues derived from the new GLOMAR EXPLORER program. However, the Company does not believe that the cost of such research and development activities can be accurately segregated from its operating revenues generally. The Company during the last two years has not incurred for its own account expenses for research relating to the design or development of new products and services, and the Company does not anticipate incurring such expenses in the near future.

Employees

The Company currently has approximately 1,300 employees, about the same number of employees as at the close of fiscal 1977 and down approximately 100 from the number of employees at the close of fiscal 1976. About 200 of the Company's employees perform administrative support functions.

Questionable Payments

The Company's Proxy Statement dated March 28, 1977, described an internal inquiry which the Company was then conducting with respect to possible questionable payments. Upon conclusion of that inquiry, the Company filed a Form 8-K Report with the Securities and Exchange Commission to report the results of the investigation. Later in 1977, the Company became aware of minor payments of a questionable nature relating to operations offshore a foreign country, and a Form 8-K Report was filed to report those payments. The Company has adopted a Business Conduct Policy which prohibits payments and practices generally considered to be of a questionable nature, and also has established a system of internal controls designed to detect and prevent the occurrence of such practices.

Litigation

On April 14, 1976, the Company and its wholly-owned subsidiary, Intermarine Services Inc., initiated legal proceedings in the United States District Court for the Central District of California by serving complaints on Sperry Rand Corporation, Bendix Corporation and Skagit Corporation, the latter a subsidiary of Bendix Corporation. Relief sought is for damages incurred by the Company, claimed to result from the malfunction and failure of certain equipment designed and manufactured by the defendants and installed by them on a drill ship owned by the Company. Aggregate compensatory and exemplary damages claimed by the Company are approximately $20 million. The Company has settled this litigation as to Bendix Corporation and Skagit Corporation for $250,000 and a counter-claim by Bendix and Skagit against the Company has been dismissed. Legal proceedings against the principal defendant, Sperry Rand Corporation, continue. This case presently is in the discovery stage; no pre-trial conference has been scheduled and trial is not expected in the near future.

The Company is a party to various other legal proceedings. The Company believes that any potential liabilities resulting from these proceedings are adequately covered by insurance or are otherwise immaterial.

MANAGEMENT

The Directors and Officers of the Company are as follows:

R. F. Bauer†	60	Chairman of the Board
C. R. Luigs	45	President, Chief Executive Officer and Director
Taylor Hancock	58	Senior Vice President and Secretary
William R. Thomas	58	Senior Vice President and Director
Richard D. Vermeer	40	Vice President and Controller
Thomas J. Roeck, Jr.	34	Treasurer and Assistant Secretary
Thomas M. Andersen	40	Assistant Treasurer
Roy L. Ash*†‡	59	Director
(*)Benno C. Schmidt*†‡	65	Director
Allan Shivers*	71	Director
Sidney A. Shuman*‡	65	Director

* Member of Audit Committee.

† Member of Executive Committee.

‡ Member of Compensation Committee.

(*)Benno C. Schmidt has announced that he intends to resign as a director prior to the commencement, expected later this year, of the drilling of a well off the California coast in the San Pedro area. Since the Company will be the operator on that well and serve as the drilling contractor, and since Freeport Minerals, of which Mr. Schmidt is Chairman of the Board of Directors, is one of the several non-operating partners, there is a possibility that a conflict of interest may develop. This has caused Mr. Schmidt to advise the Company's Board of his intention to resign.

Mr. Bauer has been Chairman of the Board of the Company since 1966.

Mr. Luigs became the Company's President and Chief Executive Officer and a Director in May 1977. Prior to his employment by the Company, he was associated with U.S. Industries, a major diversified manufacturing and services company, serving as President from 1974 to 1976 and as Executive Vice President from 1971 to 1974.

Mr. Hancock has been employed by the Company as General Counsel since 1963.

Mr. Thomas joined the Company in June 1977 as Senior Vice President, Finance and Administration. He was appointed a Director in February 1978. From 1972 until his employment by the Company, Mr. Thomas was Senior Financial Vice President of Pacific Lighting Corporation, a holding company whose principal subsidiary distributes natural gas in Southern California. From 1968 to 1972, he was a Vice President of that company.

Mr. Vermeer joined the Company in April 1976 as Assistant to the President and was elected Vice President in June 1977. From 1971 until his employment by the Company, Mr. Vermeer held various management positions with Kaufman & Broad, Inc., a home building and insurance concern.

Mr. Roeck, who has been with the Company since October 1966, was elected Assistant Treasurer in August 1973 and Treasurer in April 1978.

Mr. Andersen was employed by the Company as Director of Taxes in January 1978 and elected Assistant Treasurer in February 1978. During 1976 and 1977, he was Director of Taxes with Daylin, Inc., a retailer and provider of health services. From 1973 through 1975, he was a Tax Manager with Arthur Andersen & Co.

Mr. Ash, a director of the Company since 1975, is Chairman of the Board and Chief Executive Officer of Addressograph Multigraph Corporation, the principal business of which is the manufacture of duplicating and other business machines. Prior to his employment by Addressograph Multigraph Corporation in 1976, Mr. Ash served as Director of the U. S. Office of Management and Budget from February 1973 through February 1975.

Mr. Schmidt is Managing Partner of J. H. Whitney & Co., a private investment firm, having served in that capacity since 1960. He was elected a director of the Company in 1963.

Mr. Shivers, a director since 1965, is Chairman of the Board of Austin National Bank, Austin, Texas.

Mr. Shuman presently serves as President of Production Group and Vice President of Baker International Corporation, whose principal business is diversified drilling and production service. He has been a Vice President of Baker International Corporation since 1974. He was also President of its Drilling Services Group from 1974 through 1975 and President of Milchem, Inc., a subsidiary of Baker, from 1971 through 1973. Mr. Shuman was appointed a director of the Company in November 1977.

Members of the Company's Board of Directors are elected by stockholders at annual meetings in May of each year to serve until the next annual meeting and until their successors are elected and qualified. The Company's officers, other than Mr. Luigs, are elected by the Board of Directors without a specific term of office since they are subject to removal by the Board at any time; officers are typically elected at the first meeting of the Board of Directors following each annual meeting of stockholders. Mr. Luigs is employed by the Company as President and Chief Executive Officer under a contract expiring in May, 1980.

Remuneration of Directors and Officers

The information set forth in the table below is furnished for the fiscal year ended December 31, 1977, with respect to the Company's directors and its three highest paid officers whose aggregate remuneration from the Company and its subsidiaries exceeded $40,000, and all directors and officers of the Company as a group:

Name of Individual or Identity of Group	Capacity in Which Remuneration Was Received	Aggregate Direct Remuneration(a)	Estimated Annual Benefit Upon Retirement Under Retirement Plan For Employees(b)
R. F. Bauer	Chairman of the Board of Directors	$147,149	$ 94,532
C. R. Luigs	President, Chief Executive Officer and Director	$ 79,760	$ 37,527
Taylor Hancock	Senior Vice President, General Counsel and Secretary	$ 59,614	$ 20,038
All Officers and Directors as a Group(c)		$750,639	

(a) Does not include the fair market value of shares of Common Stock contributed by the Company under its Stock Purchase and Profit Sharing Plan of 1973. See "Incentive Compensation Practice." Based upon participation during the period ended December 31, 1977, the number of shares contributed by the Company for the accounts of the above persons was: Mr. Bauer, 215; and all officers as a group, 485. Messrs. Luigs and Hancock were not participants in the Plan as of December 31, 1977. The information set forth above also does not include any amount attributable to the expiration of restrictions on shares sold under the Company's Restricted Stock Plan of 1969. The amounts set forth above include remuneration paid to persons only for that portion of the year during which they were officers or directors of the Company; Mr. Luigs' salary covers the period from May 23, 1977 to the end of the year, and the amounts do not include remuneration paid after July 31, 1977, to eight officers of operating subsidiaries who ceased to be officers of the Company on that date due to a reorganization of corporate structure. The remuneration amounts set forth above include directors' fees (see note c). The Company furnished automobiles to Messrs. Bauer, Luigs and Hancock at a cost to the Company of approximately $7,200, $2,600 and $1,400, respectively, and to all officers as a group at a total cost of approximately $40,700. Since the Company did not require officers to report the extent of their personal use of the automobiles, the Company is unable to calculate the amount of the cost attributable to personal use.

(b) Amounts exclude a portion of benefits under the current Social Security Law and are based upon present levels of compensation and normal retirement dates. Under the Company's Retirement Plan for Employees, retirement benefits for participants are based on the average monthly compensation during the five-year period in which an employee's compensation is greatest during the fifteen years prior to such employee's retirement. Annual contributions by the Company to the Retirement Plan are determined by actuarial estimates of amounts necessary to fund the Plan on a current basis. An amendment to the Plan effective January 1, 1974, eliminated mandatory employee contributions and created certain past service liabilities. The amount shown for Mr. Bauer includes $7,344 attributable to his contributions to the Plan.

(c) "All Officers and Directors as a Group" constitutes a total of 25 individuals, including four directors who are not employees of the Company (Messrs. Ash, Schmidt, Shivers and Shuman). Each director received remuneration in the amount of $1,000 per quarter and a fee of $500 plus expenses for each directors' meeting attended.

Management Shareholdings

As of May 31, 1978, the Company's directors and officers as a group beneficially owned, directly or indirectly, 290,125 shares of the Company's Common Stock, which constituted approximately 6.6% of the total shares outstanding on that date. Of these beneficially owned shares, 131,052 were shares owned by J. H. Whitney & Co., of which Mr. Benno C. Schmidt is managing partner, and 26,500 were shares deemed to be beneficially owned by directors or officers because such persons had the right to acquire beneficial ownership of the shares through the exercise of stock options at any time within sixty days of May 31, 1978.

INCENTIVE COMPENSATION PRACTICE

The Board of Directors has authorized incentive compensation in the forms described below.

Bonus Awards

Cash bonuses, if any, are awarded to corporate officers at the discretion of the Compensation Committee of the Board of Directors. The Committee is comprised solely of outside directors, none of whom is eligible to receive cash bonuses or any other type of incentive compensation. Cash bonuses, if any, are awarded to key employees other than corporate officers at the discretion of the Chief Executive Officer. No cash bonuses were awarded during 1977. In 1978 the Board of Directors awarded cash bonuses to Messrs. Bauer, Luigs and Hancock of $50,000, $50,000 and $2,500, respectively.

1971 Stock Option and Incentive Plan

The Board of Directors in 1971 adopted the 1971 Stock Option and Incentive Plan, and the Company's stockholders approved the Plan at the Annual Meeting held on May 5, 1971. The Plan was amended in 1977 by action of the Board of Directors and the stockholders (i) to increase to 500,000 the aggregate number of shares covered by the Plan, (ii) to extend the termination date of the Plan to December 31, 1987, and (iii) to authorize the grant of "stock appreciation rights," described in greater detail below, in relation to options which might be or previously had been granted under the Plan. At May 31, 1978, up to 249,900 shares were reserved for issuance by the Company upon future exercises of options granted or to be granted under the amended Plan.

Options granted under the Plan as originally adopted could be either "qualified" options within the meaning of the Internal Revenue Code or "non-qualified" options. Qualified options were granted under the Plan in conformity with certain limitations imposed by the Internal Revenue Code respecting the exercise price, length of option term, and transferability and exercise of options. Under the Tax Reform Act of 1976, the 250,000 additional shares covered by the Plan after its amendment in 1977 can be subjected to non-qualified options only. The Company anticipates that future grants of options under the Plan will be for 10-year terms at exercise prices not less than the fair market value of the Common Stock on the date of grant and that such options will be non-transferable otherwise than by will or the laws of descent and distribution. Upon the expiration of options, any shares which have not been purchased by the optionees may be subjected to newly issued options. Only officers and key employees of the Company and its subsidiaries are eligible to receive options. The Plan is administered by the Board of Directors or its Compensation Committee, which are empowered to select participants and to determine the number of shares to be optioned to each participant.

The 1977 amendments to the Plan authorize the grant of stock appreciation rights ("SAR's") to participants, either concurrently with the grant of options or in relation to options previously granted. An SAR relates to a particular option and entitles the participant, upon simultaneous exercise of the option and the SAR, to receive a cash amount equal to the differential between the exercise price of the option and the market value of the shares covered thereby. SAR's generally may be exercised only at such times and to the extent the options to which they relate are exercisable. It is anticipated that payment upon exercise of SAR's generally will be made in cash; however, the Plan administrators in their sole discretion may settle the amount payable upon exercise of any SAR in shares of Common Stock or a combination of shares and cash. In addition to SAR's, the amended Plan authorizes the grant of options which entitle the participant upon exercise to receive Common Stock equal to the appreciation in value of the stock underlying the option.

On May 31, 1978, 86 employees (including officers) held options to purchase an aggregate of 247,788 shares of the Company's Common Stock. The expiration dates of the options ranged from May 29, 1984 to May 12, 1988, and the exercise prices from $5.84 to $13.13 per share, with the average exercise price of all such options being $8.59 per share. Approximately 80% of the options had exercise prices equal to 100% of the fair market value of the underlying Common Stock on the date of grant; the balance of the options had exercise prices equal to the 85% of the fair market value of the Common Stock on the date of grant. The last reported sales price of the Company's Common Stock on the New York Stock Exchange on July 14, 1978 was $14⅞. The following table sets forth information with respect to options held by officers of the Company as of May 31, 1978:

Name of Individual or Identity of Group	Number of Options	Exercise Price	Expiration Dates
R. F. Bauer	10,000	$10.20	November 6, 1984
	10,000	7.63	March 1, 1987
C. R. Luigs	20,000	9.50	May 23, 1987
Taylor Hancock	3,000	10.20	November 6, 1984
	7,000	7.63	March 1, 1987
All officers as a group (7 individuals)	73,500	5.84 to 13.13	May 29, 1984 to May 12, 1988

1969 Restricted Stock Purchase Plan

In 1969, the Board of Directors adopted the Restricted Stock Plan of 1969. The Plan was approved by stockholder vote on May 7, 1969. Pursuant to the Plan a total of 35,500 shares of Common Stock were sold at the par value of $0.50 per share. No further shares will be issued under the Plan. Shares were issued under the Plan subject to significant restrictions on transfer, and are repurchasable by the Company at the participant's cost (plus 6% interest thereon) in the event the purchaser does not continue to be employed by the Company (or one of its subsidiaries) during the period the restrictions applicable to such shares remain in effect. As of May 31, 1978, a total of 1,800 shares remained subject to such restrictions.

Stock Purchase and Profit Sharing Plan of 1973

Adopted by the Board of Directors on August 1, 1973, and approved by the stockholders on May 19, 1975, the Stock Purchase and Profit Sharing Plan of 1973 permits eligible employees to purchase the Company's Common Stock through payroll deductions which are supplemented by annual contributions by the Company. Between January 1 and May 31 of each year, the Company makes a contribution to the account of each employee who participated in the Plan during the previous year and is still a participant at the time of the Company's contributions. The Company's aggregate annual contribution is a number of shares of Common Stock which equals 25% of the shares purchased through the Plan by all participants during the preceding year. This contribution is made whether or not the Company earned net profits for such preceding year. In addition, in the event the Company earns "pre-tax profits" (as defined in the Plan), the Company contributes an additional 1% of the total shares acquired by participants during the preceding year for each $400,000 of pre-tax profit in that year. Each participant enjoys all rights and bears all risks of share ownership and is free at any time to withdraw his shares from the Plan.

CERTAIN BENEFICIAL SHAREHOLDINGS

On June 3, 1977, a group of investors filed with the Securities and Exchange Commission a Statement on Schedule 13D under the Securities and Exchange Act of 1934 stating that the group members as of that date were the beneficial owners of a total of 227,400 shares of the Company's Common Stock, constituting 5.05% of the shares of the Company's Common Stock then outstanding. The investing group has since filed amendments to the Statement, the latest of which indicated that the group members as of March 30, 1978 were the beneficial owners of a total of 352,400 shares, constituting approximately 8% of the Company's Common Stock then outstanding. The members of the investing group as of March 30, 1978 included Central National Corporation, Cenro Corporation, Sejak Corporation, the Gottesman-Central National Profit Sharing Plan Trust, Joy Ungerleider-Mayerson, Piter Poel, Edgar Wachenheim, III, Kate B. Wallach and Miriam G. Wallach. All of the corporate members of the group are New York corporations. The Company is advised that as of July 15, 1978, the group had acquired an additional 23,600 shares of the Company's Common Stock, bringing to approximately 8.5% the group's percentage ownership of the Company's outstanding Common Stock. The group's Statement on Schedule 13D as initially filed included a representation that there were presently no plans or proposals on the part of any of the persons filing the Statement to acquire control of the Company, and this representation has not been modified or rescinded by the subsequent amendments.

DESCRIPTION OF DEBENTURES

General

The Debentures are to be issued under an Indenture (the "Indenture") to be dated as of July 19, 1978, between the Company and United States Trust Company of New York, as Trustee. The Debentures will bear interest from August 1, 1978, at the rate shown on the cover page of this Prospectus, payable on February 1 and August 1 in each year to holders of record at the close of business on the fifteenth day of the month preceding the interest payment date, commencing February 1, 1979. (Section 2.02 of the Indenture) The Debentures will be due on August 1, 1998, will be issued only in denominations of $1,000, and in integral multiples of $1,000, and will be unsecured obligations of the Company. The Indenture authorizes an aggregate principal amount of $25,000,000 of the Debentures.

The statements under this caption relating to the Debentures and the Indenture are summaries and do not purport to be complete. Such summaries make use of terms defined in the Indenture and are qualified in their entirety by express reference to the Indenture and the cited provisions thereof, a copy of which is filed as an exhibit to the Registration Statement.

Redemption Provisions

The Debentures are to be redeemable at any time at the option of the Company as a whole or from time to time in part (except that no redemption at the option of the Company may be carried out prior to August 1, 1983, directly or indirectly from the proceeds of, or in anticipation of, the issuance of indebtedness for borrowed money having an interest cost, computed in accordance with generally accepted financial practice, of less than 12.41% per annum), or not less than 30 days' nor more than 60 days' prior notice, mailed by first-class mail to the holders' last addresses as they shall appear on the register, at the following prices (expressed in percentages of the principal amount), if redeemed during the twelve months' period beginning August 1 of the years indicated below in each case together with interest accrued to the redemption date:

1978	112.375%	1984		104.950%
1979	111.138	1985		103.713
1980	109.900	1986		102.475
1981	108.663	1987		101.238
1982	107.425	1988 and thereafter		100.000
1983	106.188			

Selection of Debentures for redemption will be made by the Trustee in such manner as it shall deem appropriate and fair in its discretion. The Indenture provides that if any Debenture is to be redeemed in part only, the notice which relates to such Debenture shall state the portion of the principal amount to be redeemed, and shall state that on and after the redemption date, upon surrender of such Debenture, a new Debenture or Debentures in principal amount equal to the unredeemed portion thereof will be issued.

The Debentures are redeemable on similar notice through the operation of the Sinking Fund described below at the principal amount thereof together with interest accrued to the redemption date.

Sinking Fund

The Indenture will require the Company to provide for the retirement, by redemption, of $1.875 million principal amount of Debentures (excluding Debentures issued pursuant to the transfer, exchange or replacement of other Debentures), commencing on August 1, 1988, and in each of the years thereafter to and including 1997 through the operation of the Sinking Fund. The Company may, at its option, receive credit against Sinking Fund payments for the principal amount of (a) Debentures acquired by the Company and surrendered for cancellation, and (b) Debentures redeemed or called for redemption otherwise than through the operation of the Sinking Fund. All or any part of the cash in the Sinking Fund (not required by the Trustee for the redemption or purchase of Debentures through the operation of the Sinking Fund) shall be retained in the Sinking Fund or, at the request of the Company, shall be applied (i) to the redemption of Debentures at their principal amount or (ii) if the aggregate amount of such cash does not exceed $25,000, to the purchase of Debentures at a price not in excess of the principal amount thereof. (Article 5)

Subordination of Debentures

The payment of the principal of and premium, if any, and interest on the Debentures is subordinated in right of payment, as set forth in the Indenture, to the prior payment in full of all Senior Indebtedness of the Company, as defined in the Indenture, whether outstanding on the date of the Indenture or thereafter created, incurred, assumed or guaranteed. Upon (i) the happening of an event of default with respect to any Senior Indebtedness as such default is defined therein or in the instrument under which it is outstanding or (ii) any distribution of the assets of the Company upon any dissolution, winding up, liquidation or reorganization of the Company, the holders of Senior Indebtedness will be entitled to receive payment in full before the Debentures are entitled to receive any payment. If in any of the situations referred to in clause (ii) above a payment is made to the Trustee or to holders of Debentures before all Senior Indebtedness has been paid in full or provision has been made for such payment, the payment to the Trustee or holders of Debentures must be paid over to the holders of the Senior Indebtedness.

Senior Indebtedness is defined as the principal of, premium, if any, and interest on indebtedness (other than the Debentures and the 5% Subordinated Debentures due 1984), whether outstanding on the date of the Indenture or thereafter created, incurred, assumed or guaranteed for money borrowed from or guaranteed to others (including, for this purpose, all obligations incurred under capitalized leases or purchase money mortgages or guarantees of loans to subsidiaries, whether or not such loans have been disbursed), and all renewals, extensions, and refundings thereof, unless in each case the terms of the instrument creating or evidencing the indebtedness provide that such indebtedness is not superior in right of payment to the Debentures. As of May 31, 1978, the amount of outstanding Senior Indebtedness was approximately $6,092,000. See **"Secured Debt"** for a description of the indebtedness of a subsidiary and the restrictions relating to such indebtedness which may affect the subsidiary's ability to provide funds for the payment of the Debentures. There will be no restrictions in the Indenture upon the creation of Senior Indebtedness.

By reason of such subordination, in the event of insolvency, general creditors of the Company may recover less, ratably, than holders of Senior Indebtedness and may recover more, ratably, than holders of Debentures or other subordinated indebtedness. (Articles 1 and 4)

The Indenture provides that the Debentures will be senior in right of repayment to the Company's 5% Subordinated Debentures due 1984 issued under an Indenture dated as of December 1, 1964, between the Company and Chemical Bank, as Trustee.

Dividend Restriction

The Indenture will provide that the Company will not (i) declare or pay any dividend or make any distribution on its capital stock or to its stockholders (other than dividends or distributions payable in its capital stock) or (ii) purchase, redeem or otherwise acquire or retire for value any of its capital stock or permit any subsidiary to do so, if at the time of such action an Event of Default shall have occurred and be continuing or if upon giving effect thereto the aggregate amount expended for all such purposes subsequent to December 31, 1977 shall exceed the sum of (a) the aggregate consolidated net income of the Company accrued subsequent to December 31, 1977, (b) the aggregate net proceeds received by the Company from the issue or sale after December 31, 1977 of capital stock of the Company other than in connection with the conversion of any indebtedness, (c) the aggregate net proceeds received by the Company from the issue or sale of any indebtedness of the Company which has been converted into capital stock of the Company subsequent to December 31, 1977, and (d) $3,000,000; provided, however, that such provisions will not prevent (i) the payment of any dividend within 60 days after the date of declaration if the payment complied with the foregoing provisions on the date of declaration, (ii) the retirement of any shares of the Company's capital stock by exchange for, or out of the proceeds of the substantially concurrent sale of, other shares of its capital stock, (iii) the call for redemption of any convertible preferred stock of the Company under an agreement with responsible underwriters designed to insure that all such stock is converted rather than redeemed or (iv) the exercise of repurchase rights under the Company's Restricted Stock Plan of 1969.

The Trustee

United States Trust Company of New York will be the Trustee under the Indenture.

The Indenture will contain certain limitations on the right of the Trustee, should it become a creditor of the Company, to obtain payment of claims in certain cases, or to realize on certain property received in respect of any such claim as security or otherwise. (Section 10.08) The Trustee will be permitted to engage in other transactions; however, if it acquires any conflicting interest (as defined) it must eliminate such conflict or resign. (Section 10.05)

The holders of a majority in principal amount of all outstanding Debentures will have the right to direct the time, method and place of conducting any proceeding for exercising any remedy available to the Trustee. (Section 7.07) The Indenture will provide that in case an Event of Default (as defined) shall occur (which shall not be cured), the Trustee will be required to use the degree of care of a prudent man in the conduct of his own affairs in the exercise of its power. (Section 10.02) Subject to such provisions, the Trustee will be under no obligation to exercise any of its rights or powers under the Indenture at the request of any of the Debentureholders, unless they shall have offered to the Trustee security and indemnity satisfactory to it. (Section 7.08)

Events of Default and Notice Thereof

The term "Event of Default" when used in the Indenture shall mean any one of the following: failure to pay (whether or not prohibited by the subordination provisions) interest for thirty days or principal (including premium, if any) or any Sinking Fund installment when due; failure to perform any other covenants for sixty days after notice; and certain events of bankruptcy, insolvency or reorganization. (Section 7.01)

The Indenture will provide that the Trustee shall, within ninety days after the occurrence of a default, give to the Debentureholders notice of all uncured defaults known to it (the term default to include the events specified above without grace or notice), provided that, except in the case of default in the payment of principal of and premium, if any, or interest on any of the Debentures or in making any Sinking Fund payment, the Trustee shall be protected in withholding such notice if it in good faith determines that the withholding of such notice is in the interest of the Debentureholders. (Section 10.03)

In case an Event of Default shall have occurred and be continuing, the Trustee or the holders of at least 25% in aggregate principal amount of the Debentures then outstanding, by notice in writing to the Company (and to the Trustee if given by Debentureholders), may declare the principal of all the Debentures to be due and payable immediately. Such declaration may be annulled and past defaults (except, unless theretofore cured, a default in payment of principal, interest or premium, if any, on the Debentures or failure to make any Sinking Fund payment) may be waived by the holders of a majority in principal amount of the Debentures, upon the conditions provided in the Indenture. (Section 7.02)

The Indenture will include a covenant that the Company will file annually with the Trustee a statement regarding compliance by the Company with the terms thereof and specifying any defaults of which the signers may have knowledge. (Sections 6.05 and 15.04)

Modification of the Indenture

Under the Indenture, the rights and obligations of the Company and the rights of Debentureholders may be modified by the Company and the Trustee only with the consent of the holders of not less than 66⅔% in principal amount of the Debentures then outstanding; but no extension of the maturity of any Debentures, or reduction in the principal, interest rate or premium, if any, or extension of the time of payment of interest, or any change in the Sinking Fund requirements, or any other modification in the terms of payment of the principal of, or premium, if any, or interest on the Debentures or reducing the percentage required for modification will be effective against any Debentureholder without his consent. (Section 14.02)

Satisfaction and Discharge of the Indenture

The Indenture will be discharged and cancelled upon payment or redemption of all the Debentures or upon deposit with the Trustee, within not more than six months prior to the maturity of the Debentures, of funds sufficient for such payment or redemption. (Sections 11.01 and 11.02)

SECURED DEBT

The Company's existing indebtedness for borrowed money, other than the 5% Subordinated Debentures due 1984, is secured by substantially all of the assets of the Company. Though only $6,092,000 of such indebtedness is Senior Indebtedness, covenants and restrictions relating to the remaining $137,650,000 (net of $7,500,000 expected to be redeemed), and the debt service thereon, could affect the ability of the Company to pay principal and interest on the Debentures as described in "GMDDI Debt" below.

Parent Company Debt

As of May 31, 1978, Global Marine Inc. had Senior Indebtedness of approximately $6,092,000, of which $3,400,000 represented borrowings from a group of banks for the conversion of a vessel to a platform tender, now called the GLOMAR TENDER I, and $2,606,000 represented the guaranty of a subsidiary's obligations under capitalized leases.

In addition to the $3,400,000 loan, the Company's commercial banking group has committed to loan up to $22,000,000. See Note 6 of Notes to Consolidated and Parent Company Financial Statements. Of this amount, $8,000,000 is available only for use by Global Marine Deepwater Drilling Inc. ("GMDDI"), a wholly-owned subsidiary of Global Marine Inc., to meet certain financial obligations during the construction of the GLOMAR ATLANTIC. Borrowings pursuant to this commitment are secured by, among other things, (1) a cash escrow of approximately $10,800,000 representing the sum received in January 1978 by Global Marine Inc. from Standard Oil Company of California upon the reduction of the term of the drilling contract for the GLOMAR ATLANTIC, (2) all of the stock of GMDDI and its subordinated debt to Global Marine Inc., and (3) fleet mortgages on the vessels of the GLOMAR TASMAN and GLOMAR V classes and the GLOMAR TENDER I and GLOMAR TENDER II and revenues derived therefrom.

The Company anticipates that, upon delivery of the GLOMAR ATLANTIC, expected in mid-August 1978, the $8,000,000 commitment for use by GMDDI will be terminated. Upon such termination, the Company has been advised that its banks will release the escrowed funds. In addition, following delivery of the GLOMAR ATLANTIC, the Company expects to reduce the $14,000,000 balance of the banks' commitment to $5,000,000 and to continue its availability to December 31, 1978.

GMDDI Debt

GMDDI is the sole obligor with respect to United States Government Guaranteed Merchant Marine Bonds relating to eight drill ships, of which approximately $137,650,000 (net of $7,500,000 expected to be redeemed) were outstanding as of May 31, 1978. See Note 3 of Notes to "Capitalization." Since dividends (or payment of subordinated debt) from GMDDI to Global Marine Inc. initially will constitute the primary source of funds for payment of interest on the Debentures, the nature of GMDDI's obligations on the Bonds and, in particular, certain restrictions on GMDDI's ability to pay dividends to Global Marine Inc. imposed as part of the Bond financing are described below.

In 1976, GMDDI issued Bonds in the principal amount of $152,100,000 to provide partial financing for the construction of the GLOMAR ATLANTIC, the GLOMAR PACIFIC and the GLOMAR JAVA SEA and to refinance five other drill ships: the GLOMAR GRAND ISLE, the GLOMAR GRAND BANKS, the GLOMAR CONCEPTION, the GLOMAR CORAL SEA and the GLOMAR CHALLENGER. These ships are owned by GMDDI, are operated for GMDDI by Global Marine Inc. and certain other wholly-owned subsidiaries, and are the subject of a Fleet Mortgage granted to the United States to secure its guarantee of the Bonds under the Merchant Marine Act.

As long as the guarantees of the United States are in effect, GMDDI must obtain advance permission from the U.S. Maritime Administration ("MarAd") before, among other things, disposing of the vessels, entering into certain types of mergers or consolidations, embarking on new business activities, or paying dividends in excess of 40% of GMDDI's net income (as such net income is measured by accounting rules established by MarAd). In addition, other restrictions are imposed upon GMDDI if certain financial tests based on GMDDI's net worth, working capital and long-term debt are not met. Failure to meet such tests may require GMDDI to deposit income derived from the vessels in a restricted use reserve account and/or may eliminate GMDDI's ability to pay cash dividends or make principal or interest payments on subordinated debt. As of May 31, 1978, GMDDI satisfied these financial tests, but it is prevented from paying cash dividends until the delivery of the GLOMAR ATLANTIC. It is significant that the tests are measured against results derived from a system of accounting required by MarAd which differs from generally accepted accounting principles, primarily because the system utilizes a twenty-five year depreciable life for the vessels as compared to the twelve year depreciable life used in the Company's financial statements for GMDDI's vessels. This difference, together with certain others, results in a substantially greater likelihood that GMDDI will meet the financial tests and will be permitted to pay cash dividends.

GMDDI has also entered into an agreement with a major oil company providing for the borrowing of up to $26,000,000 by GMDDI from November 1982 through October 1984, assuming delivery of the GLOMAR ATLANTIC anticipated in mid-August 1978. GMDDI is obligated to borrow if certain conditions occur, including the failure by GMDDI during such period to meet the financial tests referred to in the preceding paragraph and the absence of a contract (which must be satisfactory to MarAd) for the GLOMAR ATLANTIC at that time. Any borrowings under this commitment are guaranteed by Global Marine Inc., and such guaranty is secured by substantially all of Global Marine Inc.'s assets. Such guaranty will constitute Senior Indebtedness within the meaning of the Indenture.

Source of Funds for Repayment of Debentures

Global Marine Inc. anticipates that dividends on GMDDI's common stock after delivery of the GLOMAR ATLANTIC and, to a much lesser extent, management fees received for the operation of GMDDI's vessels, will initially constitute the principal source of funds for payment of interest on the Debentures, and will also provide funds for payments on the Senior Indebtedness and the 5% Subordinated Debentures due 1984. See Note 6 of Notes to Consolidated and Parent Company Financial Statements.

APPLICABILITY OF USURY LAWS

Certain provisions of California law prohibit the making of loans at any interest rate in excess of 10% per annum by non-exempt lenders. If such law is deemed applicable to the Debentures, a non-exempt purchaser or a non-exempt subsequent transferee of the Debentures might be subject to loss of interest paid and to be paid and other possible civil and criminal penalties, including a penalty of treble the interest paid for one year. However, Lillick McHose & Charles, special counsel to the Company, have rendered their opinion to the Company to the effect that, although there is no controlling judicial precedent with respect to the applicability of California usury law to the issuance of the Debentures and the matter is not free from doubt, the clauses in the Indenture which provide that the Debentures and Indenture shall be governed by and construed in accordance with New York law should be honored by a California court or a federal court applying California law so far as they pertain to the question of whether or not the Debentures are usurious. This opinion is based on, among other things, information contained herein, factual representations by the Company, and published judicial decisions and other authorities. The foregoing is a brief summary of the opinion of Lillick McHose & Charles and is qualified in all respects by reference to the full opinion, which has been filed as an exhibit to the Registration Statement of which this Prospectus is a part.

In the opinion of Carter, Ledyard & Milburn, special New York counsel to the Company, although there is no controlling precedent and the matter is not free from doubt, if the Debentures are challenged in a New York court as being usurious, the court should hold that New York law is applicable to the Debentures to the extent provided therein insofar as such law relates to the question of usury. Under New York law the Company may not assert the defense of usury. This opinion is based on, among other things, information contained herein, factual representations by the Company, and published judicial decisions and other authorities.

The Company has agreed that it will not voluntarily claim, and will actively resist any attempts to claim, the benefit of any usury laws against any holder of Debentures. (Section 6.08 of the Indenture)

UNDERWRITING

Subject to the terms and conditions of the Underwriting Agreement between the Company and the Underwriters named below, the Underwriters have severally agreed to purchase from the Company the principal amounts of Debentures set forth opposite their names below.

Name	Principal Amount of Debentures
Drexel Burnham Lambert Incorporated	$ 5,825,000
Bache Halsey Stuart Shields Incorporated	750,000
Bacon, Whipple & Co.	300,000
Robert W. Baird & Co. Incorporated	300,000
Barclay Douglas & Co., Inc.	125,000
Bateman Eichler, Hill Richards Incorporated	300,000
Bear, Stearns & Co.	750,000
William Blair & Company	300,000
Blunt Ellis & Loewi Incorporated	300,000
Blyth Eastman Dillon & Co. Incorporated	750,000
J. C. Bradford & Co.	300,000
Alex. Brown & Sons	400,000
Butcher & Singer Inc.	300,000
Crowell, Weedon & Co.	300,000

Name	Principal Amount of Debentures
Dain, Kalman & Quail Incorporated	$ 300,000
Davis, Skaggs & Co., Inc.	125,000
A. G. Edwards & Sons, Inc.	400,000
First Mid America Inc.	125,000
Goldman, Sachs & Co.	750,000
E. F. Hutton & Company, Inc.	750,000
Janney Montgomery Scott Inc.	300,000
Johnson, Lane, Space, Smith & Co., Inc.	300,000
Kidder, Peabody & Co. Incorporated	750,000
Legg Mason Wood Walker, Incorporated	300,000
Loeb Rhoades, Hornblower & Co.	750,000
McDonald & Company	300,000
Morgan, Olmstead, Kennedy & Gardner Incorporated	125,000
Moseley, Hallgarten & Estabrook Inc.	400,000
The Ohio Company	300,000
Oppenheimer & Co., Inc.	400,000
Paine, Webber, Jackson & Curtis Incorporated	750,000
Parker/Hunter Incorporated	300,000
Piper, Jaffray & Hopwood Incorporated	300,000
Prescott, Ball & Turben	300,000
Rauscher Pierce Securities Corporation	300,000
The Robinson-Humphrey Company, Inc.	300,000
Rotan Mosle Inc.	300,000
L. F. Rothschild, Unterberg, Towbin	750,000
Schneider, Bernet & Hickman, Inc.	125,000
Shearson Hayden Stone Inc.	750,000
Stifel, Nicolaus & Co. Inc.	300,000
Sutro & Co. Incorporated	300,000
Thomson McKinnon Securities Inc.	400,000
Tucker, Anthony & R. L. Day, Inc.	400,000
Underwood, Neuhaus & Co., Incorporated	125,000
Wertheim & Co., Inc.	750,000
Wheat, First Securities, Inc.	300,000
Dean Witter Reynolds Inc.	750,000
Zuckerman, Smith & Co., Inc.	125,000
Total	$25,000,000

The Underwriting Agreement provides that the obligations of the several Underwriters thereunder are subject to approval of certain legal matters by counsel and to various other conditions. The nature of the Underwriters' obligations is such that they are committed to purchase all of the above Debentures if any are purchased.

The Underwriters, for whom Drexel Burnham Lambert Incorporated is acting as Representative, propose to offer the Debentures directly to the public at the public offering price set forth on the cover page of this Prospectus and to certain dealers at such price less a concession not in excess of 2% of principal amount. The Underwriters may allow and such dealers may reallow a concession not in excess of .75% of principal amount to certain other dealers. After the initial offering, the offering price and the other selling terms may be changed.

The Company has agreed to indemnify the Underwriters against certain liabilities, including liabilities under the Securities Act of 1933.

LEGAL OPINIONS

The validity of the Debentures offered hereby will be passed on for the Company by Lillick McHose & Charles, 707 Wilshire Boulevard, Los Angeles, California 90017, and for the Underwriters by Irell & Manella, 1800 Avenue of the Stars, Los Angeles, California 90067. In giving such opinions, Lillick McHose & Charles and Irell & Manella will rely upon Carter, Ledyard & Milburn, 2 Wall Street, New York, New York 10005 as to all matters of New York Law. Lillick McHose & Charles and Carter, Ledyard & Milburn have also passed on certain questions of usury law. See "Applicability of Usury Laws." Carter, Ledyard & Milburn are counsel to United States Trust Company of New York in its capacity as Trustee under the Indenture.

EXPERTS

The separate and consolidated financial statements included in this Prospectus and the related Notes to Consolidated and Parent Company Financial Statements, except as they relate to the unaudited five-month period ended May 31, 1977, have been so included in reliance on the report of Coopers & Lybrand, independent certified public accountants, and on their authority as experts in auditing and accounting.

REPORT OF INDEPENDENT CERTIFIED PUBLIC ACCOUNTANTS

To the Board of Directors
of Global Marine Inc.
Los Angeles, California

We have examined the separate and consolidated balance sheets of Global Marine Inc. and Global Marine Inc. and its subsidiaries as of May 31, 1978 and December 31, 1977 and the related separate and consolidated statements of operations and retained earnings, stockholders' equity and changes in financial position for the five months ended May 31, 1978 and for each of the three years in the period ended December 31, 1977. We have also examined the consolidated summary of operations of Global Marine Inc. and its subsidiaries for the five months ended May 31, 1978 and for each of the five years in the period ended December 31, 1977 included elsewhere in this registration statement. Our examinations were made in accordance with generally accepted auditing standards and, accordingly, included such tests of the accounting records and such other auditing procedures as we considered necessary in the circumstances.

In our opinion, the aforementioned financial statements present fairly the separate and consolidated financial position of Global Marine Inc. and Global Marine Inc. and its subsidiaries at May 31, 1978 and December 31, 1977 and the separate and consolidated results of their operations and retained earnings, changes in stockholders' equity and changes in financial position for the five months ended May 31, 1978 and each of the three years in the period ended December 31, 1977, and the consolidated summary of operations included elsewhere in this registration statement presents fairly the data shown therein for the five months ended May 31, 1978 and for each of the five years in the period ended December 31, 1977, all in conformity with generally accepted accounting principles applied on a consistent basis, except for the changes in 1977, with which we concur, in the method of accounting for vessel drydock costs and materials and supplies, as described in note 5 of notes to consolidated and parent company financial statements.

COOPERS & LYBRAND

Los Angeles, California
July 10, 1978

INDEX TO FINANCIAL STATEMENTS

	Page
Consolidated Summary of Operations	7
Report of Independent Certified Public Accountants	35
Global Marine Inc. and Subsidiaries:	
Consolidated Balance Sheets — May 31, 1978 and December 31, 1977	36
Consolidated Statements of Operations for the Five Months Ended May 31, 1978 and the Three Years Ended December 31, 1977	38
Consolidated Statements of Stockholders' Equity for the Five Months Ended May 31, 1978 and the Three Years Ended December 31, 1977	39
Consolidated Statements of Changes in Financial Position for the Five Months Ended May 31, 1978 and the Three Years Ended December 31, 1977	40
Global Marine Inc. (Parent Company):	
Balance Sheets — May 31, 1978 and December 31, 1977	42
Statements of Operations and Retained Earnings for the Five Months Ended May 31, 1978 and the Three Years Ended December 31, 1977	44
Statements of Changes in Financial Position for the Five Months Ended May 31, 1978 and the Three Years Ended December 31, 1977	45
Notes to Consolidated and Parent Company Financial Statements	46

GLOBAL MARINE INC. AND SUBSIDIARIES

CONSOLIDATED BALANCE SHEETS

(000 omitted)

A S S E T S

	December 31, 1977	May 31, 1978
Current Assets:		
Cash	$ 4,357	$ 384
Temporary investments, at cost which approximates market	—	1,700
Certificates of deposit held in escrow (Note 15)	—	12,575
Construction funds in escrow (Notes 6 and 8)	4,739	4,256
Receivables, less allowances of $1,374,000 in 1977 and $1,397,000 in 1978 (Note 6)	21,771	12,638
Prepaid expenses	2,985	2,547
Materials and supplies	5,068	5,176
Income tax refund receivable	403	400
Deferred income taxes (Note 11)	1,720	1,098
Vessels and equipment segregated for sale (Note 3)	2,715	34
Total current assets	43,758	40,808
Construction funds in escrow (Notes 6 and 8)	26,657	16,053
Properties, at cost (Note 6):		
Vessels and equipment	244,672	259,763
Land and buildings	4,760	4,893
Other	3,942	3,895
	253,374	268,551
Less accumulated depreciation	73,034	79,383
	180,340	189,168
Other:		
Deferred costs and other assets, less allowances for abandonment of $2,803,000 in 1977 and $2,986,000 in 1978	232	100
Unamortized debt financing cost	1,013	969
Investments in joint ventures and deferred expenses	515	508
	1,760	1,577
	$252,515	$247,606

The accompanying notes are an integral part of these statements.

GLOBAL MARINE INC. AND SUBSIDIARIES

CONSOLIDATED BALANCE SHEETS

(000 omitted)

LIABILITIES AND STOCKHOLDERS' EQUITY

	December 31, 1977	May 31, 1978
Current Liabilities:		
Notes payable to banks (Note 6)	$ 4,200	$ —
Current maturities of long-term debt	6,098	8,627
Accounts payable	10,220	8,502
Accrued liabilities:		
Salaries and wages	5,461	6,037
Claims and allowances	1,820	1,744
Interest	4,885	4,105
Accrued income taxes	500	767
Total current liabilities	33,184	29,782
Long-term debt (Note 6)	151.306	149,147
Deferred income taxes (Note 11)	7,673	8,083
Deferred revenues (Note 7)	15,491	12,690
Other long-term liabilities	775	855
Commitments (Note 8)		
Stockholders' Equity:		
Preferred stock, without par value, 150,000 shares authorized, none outstanding	—	—
Common stock, 50¢ par value, authorized 6,000,000 shares; issued 4,418,165 shares in 1977 and 4,418,977 in 1978 (Note 9)	2,209	2,209
Additional paid-in capital	10,343	10,396
Retained earnings (Note 6)	32,424	35,309
	44,976	47,914
Less treasury stock at cost (64,744 shares in 1977 and 58,181 shares in 1978)	890	865
	44,086	47,049
	$252,515	$247,606

The accompanying notes are an integral part of these statements.

GLOBAL MARINE INC. AND SUBSIDIARIES

CONSOLIDATED STATEMENTS OF OPERATIONS
(Dollars in thousands except per share data)

	Year Ended December 31,			Five Months Ended May 31, 1978
	1975	1976	1977	
Revenues:				
Marine drilling	$ 82,186	$ 75,925	$ 79,780	$ 40,505
Other	22,293	7,938	5,682	3,236
Total operating revenues	104,479	83,863	85,462	43,741
Expenses:				
Operating	76,713	58,029	56,183	25,253
Depreciation	12,223	14,517	15,439	6,750
General and administrative	3,983	4,168	4,678	2,766
Exploration and development	993	1,678	1,992	554
Provision for loss on disposition of vessels and equipment (Note 3)	—	—	8,643	—
Gain on disposition of vessels and equipment	—	—	—	(729)
	93,912	78,392	86,935	34,594
Income (loss) from operations	10,567	5,471	(1,473)	9,147
Other income (expense):				
Interest expense	(6,429)	(13,805)	(16,027)	(5,937)
Interest income	152	4,250	4,735	1,144
Miscellaneous	233	86	218	(248)
Total other income (expense)	(6,044)	(9,469)	(11,074)	(5,041)
Income (loss) before income taxes (benefit) and other items shown below	4,523	(3,998)	(12,547)	4,106
Income taxes (benefit) (Note 11)	1,939	(2,396)	(5,732)	1,221
Income (loss) before items shown below	2,584	(1,602)	(6,815)	2,885
Extraordinary charge, net of related income tax effect (Note 4)	—	(1,261)	—	—
Cumulative effect on years prior to 1977 of accounting changes, net of related income tax effect (Note 5)	—	—	274	—
Net income (loss)	$ 2,584	$ (2,863)	$ (6,541)	$ 2,885
Income (loss) per common and common equivalent shares (Note 2):				
Income (loss) before items shown below	$ .59	$(.37)	$(1.56)	$ .65
Extraordinary charge	—	(.29)	—	—
Cumulative effect of accounting changes	—	—	.06	—
Net income (loss)	$ .59	$(.66)	$(1.50)	$ .65
Pro forma amounts assuming accounting changes applied retroactively:				
Income (loss) before extraordinary charge	$ 3,168	$ (2,024)	$ (6,815)	$ 2,885
Income (loss) per share before extraordinary charge	.73	(.47)	(1.56)	.65
Net income (loss)	$ 3,168	$ (3,285)	$ (6,815)	$ 2,885
Net income (loss) per share	.73	(.76)	(1.56)	.65

The accompanying notes are an integral part of these statements.

GLOBAL MARINE INC. AND SUBSIDIARIES

CONSOLIDATED STATEMENTS OF STOCKHOLDERS' EQUITY

For the Three Years Ended December 31, 1977 and the Five Months Ended May 31, 1978

	Common Stock	Additional Paid-in Capital	Retained Earnings	Treasury Stock	Total
Balance, December 31, 1974	$ 2,208,000	$10,307,000	$39,244,000	$ 1,060,000	$50,699,000
Exercise of stock options (1,000 shares)	1,000	12,000	—	—	13,000
Company contribution to employee stock purchase and profit sharing plan (9,796 shares)	—	41,000	—	(89,000)	130,000
Purchase of common stock (10,780 shares)	—	—	—	83,000	(83,000)
Net income	—	—	2,584,000	—	2,584,000
Balance, December 31, 1975	$ 2,209,000	$10,360,000	$41,828,000	$ 1,054,000	$53,343,000
Company contribution to employee stock purchase and profit sharing plan (9,394 shares)	—	(15,000)	—	(102,000)	87,000
Purchase of common stock (2,240 shares)	—	—	—	2,000	(2,000)
Net loss	—	—	(2,863,000)	—	(2,863,000)
Balance, December 31, 1976	$ 2,209,000	$10,345,000	$38,965,000	$ 954,000	$50,565,000
Company contribution to employee stock purchase and profit sharing plan (8,454 shares)	—	(2,000)	—	(65,000)	63,000
Purchase of common stock (1,150 shares)	—	—	—	1,000	(1,000)
Net loss	—	—	(6,541,000)	—	(6,541,000)
Balance, December 31, 1977	$ 2,209,000	$10,343,000	$32,424,000	$ 890,000	44,086,000
Exercise of stock options (812 shares)	—	6,000	—	—	6,000
Company contribution to employee stock purchase and profit sharing plan (6,563 shares)	—	47,000	—	(25,000)	72,000
Net income	—	—	2,885,000	—	2,885,000
Balance, May 31, 1978	$ 2,209,000	$10,396,000	$35,309,000	$ 865,000	$47,049,000

The accompanying notes are an integral part of these statements.

GLOBAL MARINE INC. AND SUBSIDIARIES
CONSOLIDATED STATEMENTS OF CHANGES IN FINANCIAL POSITION
(000 omitted)

	Years Ended December 31,			Five Months Ended May 31,
	1975	1976	1977	1978
SOURCE OF FUNDS:				
Income (loss) before items shown below	$ 2,584	$ (1,602)	$ (6,815)	$ 2,885
Extraordinary charge, net of related income tax effect	—	(1,261)	—	—
Cumulative effect on years prior to 1977 of accounting changes, net of related income tax effect	—	—	274	—
Net income (loss) for the year	2,584	(2,863)	(6,541)	2,885
Add (deduct) items not requiring (providing) funds:				
Depreciation	12,223	14,517	15,439	6,750
Deferred revenues	—	—	(1,709)	(2,801)
Provision for deferred exploration costs	1,166	1,309	1,619	398
Provision for loss on disposition of vessels	—	—	6,057	—
Deferred taxes and investment credits	2,272	290	(6,791)	689
Gain on sale of assets	—	—	—	(101)
Other	249	218	244	35
Funds provided from operations	18,494	13,471	8,318	7,855
Proceeds from sale of U.S. Government Guaranteed Ship Financing Bonds	—	152,100	—	—
Utilization of escrow funds under U.S. Government Guaranteed Ship Financing	—	—	35,477	10,604
Long-term borrowing	29,400	13,834	—	3,484
Advance payments in connection with drilling contract amendment	—	—	17,200	—
Proceeds from sale of property	—	—	—	480
Proceeds from sale of subsidiary	2,464	—	—	—
Other, net, principally book value of assets retired or sold	1,272	2,079	4,902	(108)
	$ 51,630	$181,484	$ 65,897	$ 22,315
USE OF FUNDS:				
Capital expenditures	$ 44,388	$ 43,626	$ 48,464	$ 15,957
Long-term debt repayments	560	77,682	17,531	5,627
Deposits in construction escrow funds under U.S. Government Guaranteed Ship Financing	—	62,134	—	—
Bond issue costs	—	1,125	—	—
Deferred exploration expenditures	1,767	343	273	—
Purchase of common stock	83	2	—	—
Investment in joint ventures	128	—	—	—
(Increase) decrease in deferred income taxes and investment credits	(40)	2,033	(267)	279
Increase (decrease) in working capital	4,744	(5,461)	(104)	452
	$ 51,630	$181,484	$ 65,897	$ 22,315
INCREASE (DECREASE) IN WORKING CAPITAL:				
Cash	$ 341	$ 630	$ 3,016	$ (3,973)
Temporary investments	—	—	—	1,700
Certificates of deposit	—	—	—	12,575
Marketable securities and certificates of deposit	(81)	828	(1,030)	—
Receivables	1,459	(9,935)	5,998	(9,133)
Materials and supplies	301	(917)	(2,621)	108
Prepaid expenses	(65)	784	1,483	(438)
Income tax refund receivable	—	1,547	(1,144)	(3)
Deferred income taxes	430	(4)	(198)	(622)
Vessels and equipment segregated for sale	—	—	2,715	(2,681)
Construction funds in escrow	—	1,956	2,783	(483)
Notes payable to banks	—	—	(4,200)	4,200
Current maturities of long-term debt	3,217	(1,601)	(3,036)	(2,529)
Accounts payable	1,169	2,480	(1,516)	1,718
Accrued liabilities	(2,985)	(2,348)	(1,854)	280
Accrued income taxes	958	1,119	(500)	(267)
Increase (decrease) in working capital	$ 4,744	$ (5,461)	$ (104)	$ 452

The accompanying notes are an integral part of these statements.

GLOBAL MARINE INC.

PARENT COMPANY BALANCE SHEETS

(000 omitted)

ASSETS

	December 31, 1977	May 31, 1978
Current Assets:		
Cash	$ 1,394	$ —
Certificates of deposit held in escrow (Note 15)	—	12,575
Receivables, less allowances of $2,000 in 1977 and 1978 (Note 6)	11,662	1,124
Prepaid expenses	428	247
Materials and supplies	1,047	1,199
Income tax refund receivable	403	400
Deferred income taxes (Note 11)	1,718	1,098
Vessels and equipment segregated for sale (Note 3)	2,106	—
Total current assets	18,758	16,643
Investments in subsidiaries (Note 6):		
Cost plus equity in undistributed earnings	34,232	42,571
Indebtedness from subsidiaries	10,442	5,496
	44,674	48,067
Properties, at cost (Note 6):		
Vessels and equipment	45,104	48,348
Land and buildings	3,959	3,972
Other	2,334	2,150
	51,397	54,470
Less accumulated depreciation	35,088	36,198
	16,309	18,272
Other:		
Unamortized debt financing cost	111	104
Investments in joint ventures and deferred expenses	20	—
	131	104
	$79,872	$83,086

The accompanying notes are an integral part of these statements.

·GLOBAL MARINE INC.

PARENT COMPANY BALANCE SHEETS

(000 omitted)

LIABILITIES AND STOCKHOLDERS' EQUITY

	December 31, 1977	May 31, 1978
Current Liabilities:		
Notes payable to banks (Note 6)	$ 4,200	$ —
Current maturities of long-term debt	363	1,636
Accounts payable, including bank overdraft of $3,209,000 in 1978	977	4,376
Accrued liabilities:		
Salaries and wages	684	830
Claims and allowances	1,797	1,730
Interest	839	1,082
Accrued income taxes	—	528
Total current liabilities	8,860	10,182
Long-term debt (Note 6)	6,599	8,382
Deferred income taxes (Note 11)	4,836	4,783
Deferred revenues (Note 7)	15,491	12,690
Stockholders' Equity:		
Preferred stock, without par value, 150,000 shares authorized, none outstanding	—	—
Common stock, 50¢ par value, authorized 6,000,000 shares; issued 4,418,165 shares in 1977 and 4,418,977 shares in 1978 (Note 9)	2,209	2,209
Additional paid-in capital	10,343	10,396
Retained earnings (Note 6)	32,424	35,309
	44,976	47,914
Less treasury stock at cost (64,744 shares in 1977 and 58,181 shares in 1978)	890	865
	44,086	47,049
	$79,872	$83,086

The accompanying notes are an integral part of these statements.

GLOBAL MARINE INC.

PARENT COMPANY STATEMENTS OF OPERATIONS AND RETAINED EARNINGS

(000 omitted)

	For the Years Ended December 31,			Five Months Ended May 31, 1978
	1975*	1976*	1977	
Marine drilling revenues	$44,442	$23,230	$20,803	$ 5,938
Expenses:				
Operating	27,102	8,964	10,665	3,946
Depreciation	11,869	7,432	4,945	1,406
General and administrative	2,185	2,370	2,239	699
Exploration and development	—	—	1,085	238
Provision for loss on disposition of vessels	—	—	8,643	—
Gain on disposition of vessels and equipment	—	—	—	(528)
	41,156	18,766	27,577	5,761
Income (loss) from operations	3,286	4,464	(6,774)	177
Other income (expense):				
Interest expense	(6,265)	(3,152)	(3,021)	(493)
Interest income	125	1,169	2,671	753
Miscellaneous	145	(147)	(11)	399
Total other income (expense)	(5,995)	(2,130)	(361)	659
Income (loss) before income taxes (benefit) and other items shown below	(2,709)	2,334	(7,135)	836
Income taxes (benefit) (Note 11)	(1,273)	505	(4,408)	(138)
Income (loss) before items shown below	(1,436)	1,829	(2,727)	974
Extraordinary charge, net of related income tax effect (Note 4)	—	(1,261)	—	—
Cumulative effect on years prior to 1977 of accounting changes, net of related income tax effect (Note 5)	—	—	(444)	—
Income (loss) before equity in net income (loss) of subsidiaries	(1,436)	568	(3,171)	974
Equity in net income (loss) of subsidiaries	4,020	(3,431)	(3,370)	1,911
Net income (loss)	2,584	(2,863)	(6,541)	2,885
Retained earnings, at beginning of year	39,244	41,828	38,965	32,424
Retained earnings, at end of year	$41,828	$38,965	$32,424	$35,309

* 1975 and 1976 have been reclassified to conform to 1977 classifications.

The accompanying notes are an integral part of these statements.

GLOBAL MARINE INC.

PARENT COMPANY STATEMENTS OF CHANGES IN FINANCIAL POSITION
(000 omitted)

	Years Ended December 31,			Five Months Ended May 31, 1978
	1975	1976	1977	
SOURCE OF FUNDS:				
Income (loss) before items shown below	$ 2,584	$ (1,602)	$ (6,097)	$ 2,885
Extraordinary charge, net of related income tax effect	—	(1,261)		
Cumulative effect on years prior to 1977 of accounting changes, net of related income tax effect	—	—	(444)	—
Net income (loss) for the year	2,584	(2,863)	(6,541)	2,885
Add (deduct) items not requiring (providing) funds:				
Equity in net (income) loss of subsidiaries	(4,020)	3,431	3,370	(1,911)
Depreciation	11,869	7,432	4,945	1,406
Deferred revenues	—	—	(1,709)	(2,801)
Provision for deferred exploration costs	—	—	1,085	—
Provision for loss on disposition of vessels	—	—	6,057	—
Deferred taxes and investment credits	994	290	(4,416)	295
Other	250	72	164	93
Funds provided from operations	11,677	8,362	2,955	(33)
Long-term borrowing	29,400	13,586	—	3,400
Dividends from subsidiaries	—	—	7,800	—
Advance payments in connection with drilling contract amendment	—	—	17,200	—
Properties transferred to subsidiary	2,464	97,815	848	—
Other, net, principally book value of assets retired or sold	13	109	4,137	356
	$ 43,554	$119,872	$ 32,940	$ 3,723
USE OF FUNDS:				
Capital expenditures	$ 43,757	$ 4,032	$ 5,507	$ 3,696
Long-term debt repayments	560	73,332	14,052	1,634
Purchase of common stock	83	2	—	—
Investments in subsidiaries	—	33,304	1,005	6,428
Net advances to (from) subsidiaries	(13,431)	17,175	2,434	(4,946)
(Increase) decrease in deferred income taxes and investment credits	(1,201)	5	3,010	348
Increase (decrease) in working capital	13,786	(7,978)	6,932	(3,437)
	$ 43,554	$119,872	$ 32,940	$ 3,723
INCREASE (DECREASE) IN WORKING CAPITAL:				
Cash	$ 2,664	$ 339	$ 923	$ (1,394)
Marketable securities and certificates of deposit	—	700	(700)	12,575
Receivables	7,804	(10,855)	10,767	(10,538)
Materials and supplies	871	(4,770)	832	152
Prepaid expenses	453	(121)	96	(181)
Income tax refund receivable	1,075	808	(1,480)	(3)
Deferred income taxes	430	(4)	(200)	(620)
Vessels and equipment segregated for sale	—	—	2,106	(2,106)
Notes payable to banks	—	—	(4,200)	4,200
Current maturities of long-term debt	3,217	1,374	(276)	(1,273)
Accounts payable	(884)	2,676	(624)	(3,399)
Accrued income taxes	(235)	—	—	(528)
Accrued liabilities	(1,609)	1,875	(312)	(322)
Increase (decrease) in working capital	$ 13,786	$ (7,978)	$ 6,932	$ (3,437)

The accompanying notes are an integral part of these statements.

GLOBAL MARINE INC. AND SUBSIDIARIES

NOTES TO CONSOLIDATED AND PARENT COMPANY FINANCIAL STATEMENTS

Note 1 — Summary of Significant Accounting Policies

Principles of Consolidation. The consolidated financial statements include the accounts of the Company and all majority-owned subsidiaries. Investments in unconsolidated subsidiaries and joint ventures are carried at cost plus equity in undistributed earnings since the date of acquisition. All material intercompany accounts and transactions have been eliminated.

Foreign Exchange. Items in foreign currency are not material and gains or losses resulting from translations are credited or charged to income.

Materials and Supplies. Materials and supplies are stated at weighted average cost and principally represent items aboard drilling units with a unit cost over $20 which are expensed as used.

Depreciation and Amortization. Properties and equipment are depreciated on a straight-line method for financial reporting purposes and on an accelerated method for income tax purposes. Estimated useful lives are 5 to 12 years for vessels and equipment, 20 years for buildings and 3 to 20 years for automotive and other. Maintenance and repairs are charged against income as incurred; major replacements and betterments are capitalized. Drydock costs are deferred and amortized over a two year period. Identifiable cost and accumulated depreciation of property sold or retired are removed from the accounts, and resulting gains or losses are included in income.

Deferred Exploration Costs. Acquisition, geological and geophysical and other direct costs relating to offshore mineral, oil and gas concessions and licenses have been capitalized as incurred. Any estimated diminution in value has been charged against income. Future costs will be accounted for in accordance with Statement of Financial Accounting Standards No. 19 but will have no material effect on these financial statements.

Interest Expense. Financing costs relating to construction of drilling vessels are expensed as incurred.

Income Taxes. Provision for income taxes includes federal, state and foreign income taxes. Deferred income taxes are provided for timing differences in the recognition of income and expense and undistributed earnings of foreign subsidiaries. Investment tax credits are deferred and amortized over the estimated useful lives of the related assets. The Company files certain tax returns and computes tax provisions for financial reporting purposes on a consolidated basis. Deferred income taxes are recorded on the Parent Company accounting records. Allocation of income taxes among members of the consolidated group is made on the basis of amounts payable or refundable for each subsidiary on a separate Company basis. Any difference between the amounts allocated and the consolidated amount of tax is retained by the Parent Company.

Note 2 — Net Income (Loss) per Share

Net income (loss) per share is based on the weighted average number of shares of common stock and common stock equivalents outstanding during each period (4,360,149 in 1975, 4,345,323 in 1976, 4,371,298 in 1977 and 4,409,514 in 1978), including all dilutive common stock options.

GLOBAL MARINE INC. AND SUBSIDIARIES

NOTES TO CONSOLIDATED AND PARENT COMPANY FINANCIAL STATEMENTS (Continued)

Note 3 — Vessels and Equipment Segregated for Sale and Provision for Loss on Disposition of Vessels and Equipment

In 1977, the Company reviewed its fleet of vessels in terms of current and future prospects and developed a plan to eliminate marginal or unprofitable vessels and their related materials and supplies via sale, conversion, or other disposition. The provision for loss on disposition of vessels and equipment totalling $8,643,000 in 1977 represents $6,057,000 for reduction to estimated net realizable value of vessels and equipment scheduled for sale, conversion or other disposition and $2,586,000 for reductions in carrying value of materials and supplies applicable to the vessels. The provision has been reduced by estimated amounts (primarily depreciation computed at the pre-writedown cost basis) to be charged to operations in 1978 under existing operating contracts. In May 1978, the Company sold certain primary components of a vessel held for sale to businesses unrelated to the offshore drilling industry and realized a gain of approximately $300,000 net of related income taxes ($.07 per share). The vessel was written down to estimated net scrap value in 1977 since it was no longer considered suitable for offshore drilling operations.

Note 4 — Extraordinary Charge

The Company refinanced a substantial portion of its long-term debt in 1976. Prepayment penalties and other associated expenses aggregating $2,425,000, less related income tax benefit of $1,164,000, have been shown as an extraordinary charge.

Note 5 — Accounting Changes

The Company changed its methods of accounting for vessel drydock costs and materials and supplies costs effective January 1, 1977. Costs incurred in drydocking vessels in 1977 have been deferred and are being amortized over a two year period; materials and supplies below a stated minimum unit price were charged to expense as purchased. In prior periods, drydock costs were charged to expense as incurred, and all materials and supplies were inventoried and charged to expense as used in operations. The new method of accounting for vessel drydock costs was adopted to recognize that operations in future periods would benefit from vessel drydocking, and an improved method of matching expenses with revenues would be achieved. The new method of accounting for materials and supplies was adopted to improve record keeping efficiency. The accounting changes increased the 1977 consolidated net loss by $74,000 ($.02 per share) and 1977 Parent Company net loss by $876,000. The cumulative effect of the accounting changes on years prior to 1977 amounted to a gain of $274,000 (after deducting income taxes of $253,000) on a consolidated basis and a loss of $444,000 (after deducting income tax benefits of $409,000) on a Parent Company only basis. The pro forma amounts shown on the statements of operations give effect to the retroactive application of these accounting changes, including the related tax effect.

Note 6 — Short-Term Bank Borrowings and Long-Term Debt

Short-Term Bank Borrowings

Credit agreements (Title XI Commitment and 1977 Credit Facility) with a commercial banking group led by Bank of America N.T. & S.A. permit the Company to borrow a maximum of $22,000,000.

GLOBAL MARINE INC. AND SUBSIDIARIES

NOTES TO CONSOLIDATED AND PARENT COMPANY
FINANCIAL STATEMENTS (Continued)

Note 6 — Short-Term Bank Borrowings and Long-Term Debt (continued)

At May 31, 1978, there were no short-term borrowings under the 1977 Credit Facility or the Title XI Commitment. The Title XI Commitment funds are available only for the use of Global Marine Deepwater Drilling Inc. ("GMDDI") to enable this subsidiary to meet certain financial requirements during construction of the GLOMAR ATLANTIC currently in progress; 1977 Credit Facility funds are available to satisfy working capital requirements of Global Marine Inc. The Title XI Commitment expires December 31, 1978 or upon delivery of the vessel under construction if sooner; the 1977 Credit Facility expires December 31, 1978. Interest rates under both credit agreements are 120% of the prime interest rate (8½% at May 31, 1978) plus ¾% applicable only to 1977 Credit Facility and commitment fees of ½%, plus 10% of the prime interest rate. The 1977 Credit Facility notes payable outstanding during the twelve months ended December 31, 1977 and for the five months ended May 31, 1978, had a weighted average interest rate of 10.0% and 10.3%, respectively, which was calculated by using the weighted outstanding borrowings and interest rates in effect during the periods. During the twelve months ended December 31, 1977 and the five months ended May 31, 1978, the maximum amount outstanding was $13,146,000 and $8,400,000, respectively, while the average amount outstanding was $11,747,000 and $3,356,000, respectively. As of May 31, 1978, certain properties (net book value of $13,703,000), receivables ($7,790,000), Parent Company investment in outstanding common stock of GMDDI ($37,541,000) and Parent Company note receivable from GMDDI ($3,553,000) were pledged as collateral under both credit agreements.

In connection with the conversion of the GLOMAR SIRTE to a platform tender, the Company and its lenders amended the 1977 Credit Facility to provide $3,400,000 of long-term financing.

Long-Term Debt
Long-term debt was as follows (000 omitted):

	December 31, 1977		May 31, 1978	
	Con- solidated	Parent Company	Con- solidated	Parent Company
Serial Bonds, 6.8% to 8%, due 1978 to 1984	$ 47,750	$ —	$ 45,150	$ —
Sinking Fund Bonds, 8½%, due 1984 to 1998	100,000	—	100,000	—
Subordinated Debentures, 5%, due 1984, $700,000 payable annually (net of unamortized discount of $287,000 in 1977 and $268,000 in 1978)	6,790	6,790	6,532	6,532
Tender conversion financing (long-term portion of 1977 Credit Facility), at variable interest rates of 120% of prime plus ¾% due 1978 to 1980	—	—	3,400	3,400
Obligations under capital leases	2,692	—	2,606	—
Other, due in various installments to 1979	172	172	86	86
	157,404	6,962	157,774	10,018
Less current maturities	6,098	363	8,627	1,636
	$151,306	$ 6,599	$149,147	$ 8,382

GLOBAL MARINE INC. AND SUBSIDIARIES

NOTES TO CONSOLIDATED AND PARENT COMPANY
FINANCIAL STATEMENTS (Continued)

Note 6 — Short-Term Bank Borrowings and Long-Term Debt (continued)

Consolidated long-term debt, excluding obligations under capital leases, is payable $3,438,000 in the remainder of 1978, $9,336,000 in 1979, $10,312,000 in 1980, $8,400,000 in 1981, 1982 and 1983, net of long-term debt repurchased to meet sinking fund requirements. The Parent Company portion of consolidated long-term debt is payable $638,000 in the remainder of 1978, $1,636,000 in 1979, $2,612,000 in 1980, and $700,000 in 1981, 1982 and 1983.

Serial Bonds and Sinking Fund Bonds are guaranteed as to principal and interest by the U.S. Government pursuant to Title XI of the Merchant Marine Act of 1936, as amended. As of May 31, 1978, drilling vessels with a net book value of $113,528,000 and a drilling vessel under construction ($50,130,000) are mortgaged to the U.S. Government as collateral. Serial Bonds are payable $2,800,000 in the remainder of 1978, $7,700,000 annually from 1979 to 1983 and $3,850,000 in 1984. Sinking Fund Bonds are payable $3,850,000 in 1984, $7,700,000 annually from 1985 to 1995, $6,350,000 in 1996, $3,800,000 in 1997 and $1,300,000 in 1998. Construction funds in escrow of $20,310,000 are restricted for use for the GLOMAR ATLANTIC. A final determination of construction costs for the GLOMAR PACIFIC and the GLOMAR ATLANTIC will be made shortly after delivery of the GLO-MAR ATLANTIC. Based upon present construction cost estimates the Company expects approximately $10,000,000 to remain in the escrow fund, $7,500,000 of which will be used to redeem outstanding Sinking Fund Bonds and $2,500,000 of which will be returned to GMDDI. Under the U.S. government's guarantees of the Serial Bonds and Sinking Fund Bonds, GMDDI is restricted from paying dividends until after the delivery of the GLOMAR ATLANTIC, and then may not pay dividends in excess of 40% of GMDDI's net income as such income is measured by accounting policies established by the U.S. Maritime Administration. In addition, other restrictions are imposed upon GMDDI if certain financial tests based on GMDDI's net worth, working capital and long-term debt are not met. As of May 31, 1978, GMDDI satisfied these financial tests.

Capitalized Leases

The Company entered into several capital leases at the end of 1977 for equipment to be installed aboard drilling vessels. The leases have terms of seven years and may be renewed at the Company's option. Leased property under these capital leases aggregated $2,834,000 at December 31, 1977 and May 31, 1978. Depreciation expense for 1977 and 1978 includes $14,000 and $163,000 for amortization of assets recorded under capital leases. Future minimum lease payments under capital leases together with the present value of the net minimum lease payments as of May 31, 1978 were:

Year Ending December 31:	
1978 (remaining at May 31, 1978)	$ 397,000
1979	537,000
1980	512,000
1981	501,000
1982	501,000
1983	501,000
Later years	376,000
Total minimum lease payments	3,325,000
Less amount representing interest	719,000
Present value of net minimum lease payments	$2,606,000

GLOBAL MARINE INC. AND SUBSIDIARIES

NOTES TO CONSOLIDATED AND PARENT COMPANY
FINANCIAL STATEMENTS (Continued)

Note 6 — Short-Term Bank Borrowings and Long-Term Debt (continued)

Under the various borrowing agreements, the Company has agreed to maintain minimum amounts of working capital and net worth, and has agreed to certain restrictions with respect to borrowing, purchase and sale of assets and payment of cash dividends. The Company was in compliance with these provisions at December 31, 1977 and May 31, 1978.

Note 7 — Deferred Revenues

As a result of reducing the term of the GLOMAR ATLANTIC drilling contract from five years to three years in 1977, Standard Oil Company of California has made an advance payment which will be applied to the operating income portion of the day rate relating to such Company's utilization of other drilling vessels over a period ending in 1981. The agreement establishes an annual limitation upon unused amounts which can be carried forward through 1981.

Note 8 — Commitments

At December 31, 1977 and May 31, 1978, there were firm commitments for the completion or construction of new drilling vessels of $16,600,000 and $14,000,000, respectively. In addition, during 1978 a contract has been signed with a shipyard for the construction of a jack-up rig. The Company estimates that the delivered cost of the rig will be $25,000,000.

Note 9 — Common Stock Options

At May 31, 1978, 247,788 common shares were reserved for the exercise of options presently held under the employee stock option plan. Common shares reserved for future option grants were 277,650 and 249,900 at December 31, 1977 and May 31, 1978, respectively. The options outstanding are at prices ranging from $6 to $13. Of these, options for 197,288 and 50,500 shares were granted at 100% and 85% of market at date of grant, respectively, and are exercisable in five equal cumulative installments within ten years thereafter. Options become exercisable in full if more than 50% of the Company's outstanding common stock is acquired by a single group of persons. During 1977, options were granted for 199,850 shares and terminated for 116,850 shares. Options were granted for 29,000 shares and terminated for 1,250 shares during the five months ended May 31, 1978. The Company made no charge to income during 1975, 1976, 1977, or the first five months of 1978 in connection with the options.

The Company may grant stock appreciation rights in tandem with options previously granted or to be granted. These rights entitle the employees to payment, either in cash or common stock, for the increase in market value over the exercise price at the date of exercise. The exercise of either the rights or the options serves to cancel the other. There were no stock appreciation rights outstanding as of December 31, 1977 or May 31, 1978.

Under a restricted stock plan approved by the shareholders in 1969, 35,500 shares of common stock were sold at the par value of $.50 per share. The shares are subject to certain restrictions as to their sale and may be repurchased by the Company under certain conditions. The compensatory value of these shares was deferred ($92,000 at December 31, 1977 and $52,000 at May 31, 1978) and is being ratably charged to expense over the period of restrictions ($96,000 in each of 1975, 1976 and 1977 and $40,000 for the first five months of 1978).

GLOBAL MARINE INC. AND SUBSIDIARIES

NOTES TO CONSOLIDATED AND PARENT COMPANY
FINANCIAL STATEMENTS (Continued)

Note 9 — Common Stock Options (continued)

The following is a summary of shares of common stock under option at May 31, 1978 and options which became exercisable or were exercised since January 1, 1975:

	Number of Shares	Option Price		Market Value at Date of Grant or Exercise or When Exercisable	
		Per Share	Total	Per Share	Total
Shares under option at May 31, 1978 and granted during:					
1974	46,500	$ 9 to $10	$ 465,800	$11 to $12	$ 548,000
1976	4,000	6	23,375	7	27,500
1977	168,288	8 to 11	1,333,509	8 to 11	1,338,509
Five months ended May 31, 1978	29,000	10 to 13	301,125	10 to 13	301,125
	247,788				
Options which became exercisable during:					
1975	60,668	$ 9 to $21	$ 794,823	$ 9 to $15	$ 758,043
1976	40,891	9 to 21	500,648	7 to 10	335,271
1977	14,750	6 to 16	145,463	8 to 9	119,703
Five months ended May 31, 1978	43,211	8 to 10	342,587	10 to 13	467,926
Options exercised during:					
1975 Non-qualified	1,000	$9	$ 9,137	$15	$ 15,937
1976	None	—	—	—	—
1977	None	—	—	—	—
Five months ended May 31, 1978	812	8	6,192	12	9,943

Note 10 — Pension Plans

The Company and its subsidiaries have pension plans covering substantially all of their employees. The Plan applicable to employees covered under the Social Security laws of the United States meets the requirements of the Pension Reform Act of 1974 and is funded on a current basis with related past service cost being amortized over approximately 30 years. The Plan for employees not so covered, primarily non-resident aliens, is being provided for on a similar basis by accrual in the financial statements and the current year cost including similar amortization of past service costs is included in other long-term liabilities. The actuarially computed value of vested benefits for both groups of employees as of December 31, 1977 was less than the total of the pension fund assets and balance sheet accruals.

GLOBAL MARINE INC. AND SUBSIDIARIES

NOTES TO CONSOLIDATED AND PARENT COMPANY
FINANCIAL STATEMENTS (Continued)

Note 10 — Pension Plans (continued)

Pension expense was $161,000 in 1973 ($161,000 for the funded plan), $500,000 in 1974 ($372,000 for the funded plan), $908,000 in 1975 ($706,000 for the funded plan), $1,288,000 in 1976 ($1,024,000 for the funded plan), $1,347,000 in 1977 ($1,157,000 for the funded plan) and $589,000 in 1978 ($531,000 for the funded plan). The Parent Company portion of the consolidated pension expense in 1975, 1976, 1977 and 1978 was $294,000, $276,000, $169,000 and $126,000, respectively, all of which applied to the funded plan.

Note 11 — Income Taxes

The provision for income taxes (benefit) was as follows (000 omitted):

| | Year Ended December 31, | | | | | | | | Five Months Ended May 31, 1978 | |
| | 1973 | 1974 | 1975 | | 1976 | | 1977 | | | |
	Con- solidated	Con- solidated	Con- solidated	Parent Company	Con- solidated	Parent Company	Con- solidated	Parent Company	Con- solidated	Parent Company
Federal:										
Current	$ 738	$ 1,420	$(1,716)	$(2,871)	$(1,574)	$ 341	$ (476)	$ (501)	$ —	$ —
Deferred	2,130	655	1,759	1,759	791	791	(5,915)	(3,554)	1,294	310
Investment tax credit	(167)	(332)	(418)	(418)	(629)	(629)	(877)	(877)	(525)	(525)
	2,701	1,743	(375)	(1,530)	(1,412)	503	(7,268)	(4,932)	769	(215)
State:										
Current	(42)	174	6	(38)	(126)	(126)	(18)	(22)	172	94
Deferred	213	9	83	83	128	128	1	15	(80)	(80)
	171	183	89	45	2	2	(17)	(7)	92	14
Foreign:										
Current	1,807	1,942	2,184	212	1,614	—	400	531	19	186
Long-term	—	749	41	—	(2,600)	—	1,153	—	341	(123)
	1,807	2,691	2,225	212	(986)	—	1,553	531	360	63
Total taxes (benefit) on income	$ 4,679	$ 4,617	$ 1,939	$(1,273)	$(2,396)	$ 505	$(5,732)	$(4,408)	$ 1,221	$ (138)

GLOBAL MARINE INC. AND SUBSIDIARIES

NOTES TO CONSOLIDATED AND PARENT COMPANY
FINANCIAL STATEMENTS (Continued)

Note 11 — Income Taxes (continued)

The deferred income tax provision consisted of the following (000 omitted):

| | Year Ended December 31, | | | | | | Five Months Ended May 31, 1978 | |
	1973 Con-solidated	1974 Con-solidated	1975 Con-solidated and Parent Company	1976 Con-solidated and Parent Company	1977 Con-solidated	1977 Parent Company	Con-solidated	Parent Company
Depreciation for tax purposes in excess of book	$ 2,105	$ 517	$ 2,914	$ 2,015	$ 5,193	$ 5,193	$ 1,181	$ 1,181
Investment tax credit used for tax purposes	529	416	(135)	(968)	—	—	—	—
Exploration costs expensed for tax (books) in excess of book (tax)	(112)	(534)	(344)	519	(489)	(489)	(91)	(91)
Claim payments for tax (book) in excess of book (tax)	(77)	(167)	(273)	200	262	262	34	(34)
Pension plan accrued for tax (book) in excess of book (tax)	(71)	(79)	(179)	(408)	529	529	—	—
Interest income recognized for book (tax) purposes not for tax (book) purposes	—	—	—	(241)	(120)	(120)	8	8
Loan fees expensed for tax (book) in excess of book (tax)	—	—	—	(439)	62	62	11	11
Cash advances recognized for tax purposes not for book purposes	—	—	—	—	(2,410)	(2,410)	(3,321)	(3,321)
Provision for estimated losses on sale of vessels and equipment not deducted for taxes until realized in subsequent periods	—	—	—	—	(3,028)	(3,028)	673	673
Inventory reserve reduction for book and not for tax	—	—	—	—	254	254	17	17
Net operating loss benefit and related utilization — expiring 1984	—	—	—	—	(5,510)	(3,135)	3,273	2,357
Other, net	(31)	511	(141)	241	(657)	(657)	(571)	(571)
	$ 2,343	$ 664	$ 1,842	$ 919	$(5,914)	$(3,539)	$ 1,214	$ 230

GLOBAL MARINE INC. AND SUBSIDIARIES

NOTES TO CONSOLIDATED AND PARENT COMPANY
FINANCIAL STATEMENTS (Continued)

Note 11 — Income Taxes (continued)

Reconciliation of the total provision for income taxes to the current Federal rate of 48% was as follows:

			Year Ended December 31,					Five Months Ended May 31, 1978	
			1975 Consolidated and Parent Company	1976		1977			
	1973 Consolidated	1974 Consolidated		Consolidated	Parent Company	Consolidated	Parent Company	Consolidated	Parent Company
U.S. federal income tax rate	48.0 %	48.0 %	48.0 %	(48.0)%	48.0 %	(48.0)%	(48.0)%	48.0 %	48.0 %
Amortization of investment tax credits	(1.0)	(3.3)	(9.2)	(15.7)	(27.0)	(7.0)	(12.3)	(12.8)	(62.8)
Foreign	—	—	—	—	—	9.1	2.5	(6.6)	—
Other, net	—	.9	4.1	3.7	0.6	0.2	(4.0)	1.1	(1.7)
Effective tax rate	47.0 %	45.6 %	42.9 %	(60.0)%	21.6 %	(45.7)%	(61.8)%	29.7 %	(16.5)%

Unamortized investment tax credits for financial purposes were $10,200,000 and $16,180,000 at December 31, 1977 and May 31, 1978, respectively. Investment tax credits, which can be used to reduce income taxes payable in future years, amounted to $18,290,000 at May 31, 1978 and expire principally in 1981 through 1984.

The Internal Revenue Service has completed an audit of the Company's consolidated tax returns for 1971 through 1974. The IRS has proposed adjustments in the amount of approximately $2,600,000 plus interest relative to the taxation of foreign source income which the Company has not agreed to and is in the process of protesting. The Company has provided for income taxes including federal income taxes on the undistributed earnings of foreign subsidiaries (net of foreign taxes accrued) and, accordingly, if the Company were unsuccessful in its protest, any additional liability would be adequately covered.

GLOBAL MARINE INC. AND SUBSIDIARIES

NOTES TO CONSOLIDATED AND PARENT COMPANY FINANCIAL STATEMENTS (Continued)

Note 12 — Selected Quarterly Financial Data (Unaudited)

	1976 Quarter Ended				1977 Quarter Ended				1978 Quarter Ended
	March 31	June 30	September 30	December 31	March 31	June 30	September 30	December 31	March 31
Consolidated Revenue	$22,533,000	$23,334,000	$21,661,000	$16,335,000	$17,747,000	$17,320,000	$22,604,000	$27,791,000	$25,417,000
Consolidated operating profit (loss)	$ 2,847,000	$ 1,975,000	$ 1,782,000	$(1,133,000)	$ 939,000	$(1,530,000)	$(1,114,000)	$ 232,000	$ 4,556,000
Income (loss) before items shown below, net of related income tax effect	$ 631,000	$ (179,000)	$ (132,000)	$(1,922,000)	$ (699,000)	$(2,496,000)	$(2,698,000)	$ (922,000)	$ 1,111,000
Extraordinary charge	(1,261,000)	—	—	—	—	—	—	—	—
Cumulative effect of accounting changes	—	—	—	—	274,000	—	—	—	—
Net income (loss)	$ (630,000)	$ (179,000)	$ (132,000)	$(1,922,000)	$ (425,000)	$(2,496,000)	$(2,698,000)	$ (922,000)	$ 1,111,000
Average shares outstanding	4,341,988	4,347,157	4,344,825	4,346,817	4,351,114	4,365,581	4,368,584	4,379,440	4,393,062
Income (loss) per common and common equivalent shares:									
Income (loss) before items shown below	$ .14	$(.04)	$(.03)	$(.44)	$(.16)	$(.57)	$(.62)	$(.21)	$ .25
Extraordinary charge	(.29)	—	—	—	—	—	—	—	—
Cumulative effect of accounting changes	—	—	—	—	.06	—	—	—	—
Net income (loss)	$(.15)	$(.04)	$(.03)	$(.44)	$(.10)	$(.57)	$(.62)	$(.21)	$ .25
Pro forma amounts assuming new accounting methods applied retroactively:									
Income (loss) before extraordinary charge	$ 752,000	$ (72,000)	$ (683,000)	$(2,021,000)	$ (699,000)	$(2,496,000)	$(2,698,000)	$ (922,000)	$ 1,111,000
Income (loss) per share	$ .17	$(.02)	$(.16)	$(.46)	$(.16)	$(.57)	$(.62)	$(.21)	$ .25
Net income (loss)	$ (509,000)	$ (72,000)	$ (683,000)	$(2,021,000)	$ (699,000)	$(2,496,000)	$(2,698,000)	$ (922,000)	$ 1,111,000
Net income (loss) per share	$(.12)	$(.02)	$(.16)	$(.46)	$(.16)	$(.57)	$(.62)	$(.21)	$ .25

GLOBAL MARINE INC. AND SUBSIDIARIES

NOTES TO CONSOLIDATED AND PARENT COMPANY
FINANCIAL STATEMENTS (Continued)

Note 12 — Selected Quarterly Financial Data (Unaudited) (continued)

Net income (loss) for the first three quarters of 1977 was restated in the aggregate amount of $596,000 due to accounting changes adopted in the fourth quarter as described in Note 5 to the financial statements. The restatement decreased net loss per share $.04, $.05 and $.05 in the first, second and third quarters, respectively. First quarter net income (loss) was also restated for the cumulative effect of the accounting changes on years prior to 1977, which amounted to $274,000 ($.06 per share) after deducting income taxes of $253,000.

For the quarter ended December 31, 1977, the Company received $4,000,000 consideration for reducing the term of the GLOMAR ATLANTIC drilling contract described in Note 7 to the financial statements plus $1,497,000 of interest income accrued from the date the agreement was signed to the date the agreement was approved by the Maritime Administration of the United States Department of Commerce. These gains were offset, however, by the provision for loss on disposition of vessels and equipment of $8,643,000 as described in Note 3 to the financial statements. The net effect of these items was to increase fourth quarter net loss by $1,636,000 ($.37 per share).

Note 13 — Segment Information

Marine drilling operations constitute a dominant industry segment of the Company and the Parent Company in relation to its other operations. Consolidated marine drilling revenues for 1977 include $17,186,000, $14,201,000 and $10,009,000 from three separate customers and $8,710,000 from a domestic government agency for the year ended December 31, 1977 and $13,330,000, $7,968,000 and $4,743,000 from three separate customers for the five months ended May 31, 1978. Parent Company marine drilling revenues for 1977 include $12,643,000, $3,469,000 and $2,216,000 from three separate customers for the year ended December 31, 1977 and $1,087,000, $876,000, $814,000 and $652,000 from four separate customers for the five months ended May 31, 1978. Geographic segment information for the year ended December 31, 1977 and the five months ended May 31, 1978 is presented below (000 omitted):

GLOBAL MARINE INC. AND SUBSIDIARIES

**NOTES TO CONSOLIDATED AND PARENT COMPANY
FINANCIAL STATEMENTS** (Continued)

Note 13 — Segment Information (continued)

	Year Ended December 31, 1977			Five Months Ended May 31, 1978		
	Assets	Revenues	Operating Income (Loss)	Assets	Revenues	Operating Income (Loss)
CONSOLIDATED:						
United States	$220,583	$ 64,864	$ 8,113	$218,261	$ 34,098	$ 8,875
Foreign	22,545	20,598	(3,442)	14,795	9,643	2,675
Total segments	243,128	85,462	4,671	233,056	43,741	11,550
Interest expense — net	—	—	(11,292)	—	—	(4,793)
Corporate	9,387	—	(5,926)	14,550	—	(2,651)
Consolidated totals	$252,515	$ 85,462	$(12,547)	$247,606	$ 43,741	$ 4,106
PARENT COMPANY:						
United States	$ 23,856	$ 16,784	$ (3,275)	$ 11,719	$ 3,483	$ 576
Foreign	1,955	4,019	(376)	4,984	2,455	896
Total segments	25,811	20,803	(3,651)	16,703	5,938	1,472
Interest expense — net	—	—	(350)	—	—	260
Corporate	54,061	—	(3,134)	66,383	—	(896)
Company totals	$ 79,872	$ 20,803	$ (7,135)	$ 83,086	$ 5,938	$ 836

Revenues consist of services provided to unaffiliated customers; intersegment revenues are not material. Operating income (loss) consists of revenues less direct operating expenses and allocated common expenses benefiting more than one segment. Parent company corporate assets include investments in subsidiaries of $44,674,000 at December 31, 1977 and $48,067,000 at May 31, 1978, which are eliminated on a consolidated basis.

Note 14 — Estimated Replacement Cost Data (Unaudited)

Estimated replacement cost data is provided for certain assets of the Company (excluding vessels not anticipated to be replaced, vessels under construction, and land) in accordance with requirements of the Securities and Exchange Commission. Vessel and equipment replacement cost data was based on a trade association study which included materials and supplies in vessel replacement costs. Data for buildings was estimated by using construction costs per square foot of similar buildings; data for other properties was estimated using recent purchase prices and vendor published prices where possible.

GLOBAL MARINE INC. AND SUBSIDIARIES

NOTES TO CONSOLIDATED AND PARENT COMPANY FINANCIAL STATEMENTS (Continued)

Note 14 — Estimated Replacement Cost Data (Unaudited) (continued)

Although management believes the replacement cost data is reasonably presented in accordance with guidelines established by the Securities and Exchange Commission, readers should be aware of the following:

1. The data is based on the hypothetical assumption that production capacity would be replaced at year end without regard as to whether such replacement was economically desirable or physically possible, or whether required financing would be available. Decisions on replacement will be made in the normal course of business considering economic, regulatory and competitive conditions at the time, and actual costs of replacement may differ significantly from those presented.

2. The data is not intended to represent current value of the assets to the Company or amounts realizable upon sale.

3. The data does not consider other aspects of the impact of inflation on other items in the financial statements or changes in cost relationships based upon the hypothetical replacement of productive capacity at year end.

4. The data should not be used in a simplistic manner to develop the worth of the Company or a revised net income figure.

GLOBAL MARINE INC. AND SUBSIDIARIES

NOTES TO CONSOLIDATED AND PARENT COMPANY FINANCIAL STATEMENTS (Continued)

Note 14 — Estimated Replacement Cost Data (Unaudited) (continued)

(000 omitted)

	1976			1977			May 31, 1978		
	Historical Amounts		Estimated Replacement Cost	Historical Amounts		Estimated Replacement Cost	Historical Amounts		Estimated Replacement Cost
	Reported in Financial Statements	Subject to Replacement Cost		Reported in Financial Statements	Subject to Replacement Cost		Reported in Financial Statements	Subject to Replacement Cost	
Properties at year end:									
Vessels and equipment	$215,060	$102,182	$213,770	$244,672	$161,633	$284,486	$259,763	$178,333	$307,473
Land and buildings	4,703	2,751	5,563	4,760	2,808	5,955	4,893	2,941	6,238
Other	6,123	6,123	6,624	3,942	3,942	4,647	3,895	3,895	4,662
Gross Properties	225,886	111,056	225,957	253,374	168,383	295,088	268,551	185,169	318,373
Accumulated depreciation	67,503	29,204	71,528	73,034	39,352	90,836	79,383	52,099	112,009
Net Properties	$158,383	$ 81,852	$154,429	$180,340	$129,031	$204,252	$189,168	$133,070	$206,364
Depreciation expense for the year ended	$ 14,517	$ 8,271	$ 16,577	$ 15,439	$ 10,396	$ 20,119	$ 6,750	$ 5,870	$ 10,249

GLOBAL MARINE INC. AND SUBSIDIARIES

NOTES TO CONSOLIDATED AND PARENT COMPANY
FINANCIAL STATEMENTS (Continued)

Note 15 — Certificates of Deposit Held in Escrow

The majority of this cash was received from Standard Oil of California in January 1978 as a result of amending the long-term drilling contract for use of the GLOMAR ATLANTIC and was placed in escrow as collateral for potential borrowings under the Company's credit agreements with its commercial banking group. Upon delivery of the GLOMAR ATLANTIC the Company has been advised that its banks will release the escrowed funds.

A small portion of this cash was received relative to the sale of an asset held for sale and such funds have been placed in escrow to be used for approved capital expenditures.

The certificates of deposit generally have a thirty day term. The rate of interest received on such certificates of deposit as of May 31, 1978 was approximately 6.8 percent.

Note 16 — Supplementary Income Statement Information

The following amounts were charged directly to income:

	Year Ended December 31,			Five Months Ended May 31,
	1975	1976	1977	1978
Consolidated:				
Maintenance and repairs	$9,662,000	$9,313,000	$9,286,000	$3,795,000
Taxes, other than income taxes:				
Payroll taxes	$1,574,000	$2,030,000	$1,676,000	$1,159,000
Other	200,000	250,000	364,000	137,000
	$1,774,000	$2,280,000	$2,040,000	$1,296,000
Rents	$2,418,000	$2,778,000	$2,863,000	$1,714,000
Parent Company:				
Maintenance and repairs	$ 641,000	$ 904,000	$1,485,000	$ 588,000
Taxes, other than income taxes:				
Payroll taxes	$ 608,000	$ 629,000	$ 516,000	$ 289,000
Other	166,000	194,000	199,000	97,000
	$ 774,000	$ 823,000	$ 715,000	$ 386,000
Rents	$ 714,000	$ 509,000	$ 831,000	$ 469,000

$25,000,000

Global Marine Inc.

12⅜% Senior Subordinated Debentures
due August 1, 1998

TABLE OF CONTENTS

	Page
Available Information	2
Prospectus Summary	3
The Company	4
Use of Proceeds and Capital Expenditures	5
Capitalization	6
Consolidated Summary of Operations	7
Management's Discussion and Analysis of Consolidated Summary of Operations	8
Business	11
Management	20
Incentive Compensation Practice	23
Certain Beneficial Shareholdings	25
Description of Debentures	25
Secured Debt	29
Applicability of Usury Laws	30
Underwriting	31
Legal Opinions	33
Experts	33
Index to Consolidated Financial Statements	34

PROSPECTUS

Drexel Burnham Lambert
INCORPORATED

July 25, 1978

PART II

INFORMATION NOT REQUIRED IN PROSPECTUS

Item 23. Other Expenses of Issuance and Distribution.

	Amount
Registration fee — Securities and Exchange Commission	$ 5,000
Printing and engraving expenses	$ 88,000
Listing fee — New York Stock Exchange	$ 3,200
Fees and expenses of Trustee	$ 21,000
Legal fees and expenses	$ 85,000
Accounting fees and expenses	$ 200,000
Blue Sky qualification and legal investment survey	$ 8,000
Rating Agency fees	$ 6,750
Miscellaneous	$ 3,050
Total	$ 420,000

Item 31. Financial Statements and Exhibits.

(b) Exhibits

1.1 Form of Underwriting Agreements.

4.1 Form of Debenture (not filed because Debenture will be in standard printer's form).

4.2 Form of Indenture dated as of July 19, 1978 between the registrant and United States Trust Company of New York, Trustee.

6.1 Opinion of Lillick McHose & Charles as to certain legal matters in connection with the offering of the securities being registered.

6.2 Opinion of Carter, Ledyard & Milburn as to matters of New York law in connection with the offering of the securities being registered.

6.3 Opinion of Lillick McHose & Charles as to matters of California law in connection with the offering of the securities being registered.

14.2 Computation of ratio of earnings to fixed charges.

15.1 Power of Attorney.

(d) Consents

The consent and report of the independent certified public accountants is set forth at page II-3 hereof. The consents of counsel are included in the respective opinions filed herewith as Exhibits 6.1 and 6.2 to the Registration Statement.

SIGNATURES

Pursuant to the requirements of the Securities Act of 1933, the Registrant has duly caused this Amendment to Registration Statement to be signed on its behalf by the undersigned, thereunto duly authorized in the City of Los Angeles, and State of California on the 24th day of July, 1978.

GLOBAL MARINE INC.

By _____WILLIAM R. THOMAS_____
                    William R. Thomas
                    Senior Vice President

Pursuant to the requirements of the Securities Act of 1933, this Amendment to Registration Statement has been signed below by the following persons in the capacities and on the dates indicated.

Signature	Title	Date
* _____ (R. F. Bauer)	Chairman of the Board and Director	July 24, 1978
* _____ (C. R. Luigs)	President, Chief Executive Officer and Director	July 24, 1978
* _____ (William R. Thomas)	Director and Senior Vice President (Principal Financial Officer)	July 24, 1978
* _____ (Richard D. Vermeer)	Vice President and Controller (Principal Accounting Officer)	July 24, 1978
* _____ (Roy L. Ash)	Director	July 24, 1978
* _____ (Benno C. Schmidt)	Director	July 24, 1978
* _____ (Allan Shivers)	Director	July 24, 1978
* _____ (Sidney A. Shuman)	Director	July 24, 1978

*By _____WILLIAM R. THOMAS_____   July 24, 1978
              Attorney-in-fact

CONSENT OF ACCOUNTANTS

We consent to the inclusion of the following reports to be used in registering, under the Securities Act of 1933, $25,000,000 of 12⅜% Senior Subordinated Debentures due 1998: (1) our report dated July 10, 1978 accompanying the separate and consolidated financial statements of Global Marine Inc. and Global Marine Inc. and its subsidiaries and, (2) our report dated July 10, 1978 accompanying the supporting schedules listed in Item 31(a) of the Registration Statement.

We also consent to the references to our firm under the captions "Consolidated Summary of Operations" and "Experts" in the prospectus.

COOPERS & LYBRAND

Los Angeles, California
July 24, 1978

REPORT OF INDEPENDENT PUBLIC ACCOUNTANTS

To the Board of Directors of
Global Marine Inc.
Los Angeles, California

We have examined the separate and consolidated balance sheets of Global Marine Inc. and Global Marine Inc. and its subsidiaries as of May 31, 1978 and December 31, 1977 and the related separate and consolidated statements of operations and retained earnings, stockholders' equity and changes in financial position for the five months ended May 31, 1978 and for each of the three years in the period ended December 31, 1977 and the supporting schedules. Our examinations were made in accordance with generally accepted auditing standards and, accordingly, include such tests of the accounting records and such other auditing procedures as we considered necessary in the circumstances.

In our opinion, the supporting schedules listed in Item 31(a) of the Registration Statement present fairly the information required to be set forth therein, in conformity with generally accepted accounting principles applied on a consistent basis except for the changes in 1977, with which we concur, in the methods of accounting for vessel drydock costs and materials and supplies, as described in note 5 of notes to consolidated and parent company financial statements.

COOPERS & LYBRAND

Los Angeles, California
July 10, 1978

CONSENTS OF COUNSEL

The consents of Lillick McHose & Charles, counsel to the registrant, and Carter, Ledyard & Milburn, special New York counsel to the registrant, are included in the respective opinions filed herewith as Exhibits 6.1 and 6.2 to the Registration Statement.

GLOBAL MARINE INC.

SCHEDULE III — INVESTMENTS IN, EQUITY IN EARNINGS OF, AND DIVIDENDS RECEIVED FROM AFFILIATES AND OTHER PERSONS

Issuer (a)	Number of Shares (b)	Balance at Beginning of Year	Equity in Earnings (Losses)	Other Changes Add (Deduct) (c)	Balance at End of Year
Year Ended December 31, 1975:					
Intermarine Services Inc.	1	$ 1,536,000	$ 1,030,000	$ —	$ 2,566,000
Global Marine Drilling Company	1,000	1,759,000	8,000	—	1,767,000
Global Marine Europa Limited	10,000	5,914,000	2,338,000	—	8,252,000
Other	—	2,001,000	644,000	(1,568,000)	1,077,000
		$11,210,000	$ 4,020,000	$(1,568,000)	$13,662,000
Year Ended December 31, 1976:					
Intermarine Services Inc.	1	$ 2,566,000	$ 362,000	$ —	$ 2,928,000
Global Marine Drilling Company	1,000	1,767,000	(1,404,000)	—	363,000
Global Marine Europa Limited	10,000	8,252,000	(1,313,000)	—	6,939,000
Global Marine Caribbean, Inc.	25	(1,768,000)	(93,000)	—	(1,861,000)
Global Marine Deepwater Drilling, Inc.	1,000	—	311,000	33,599,000	33,910,000
Other	—	2,845,000	(1,294,000)	567,000	2,118,000
		$13,662,000	$(3,431,000)	$34,166,000	$44,397,000
Year Ended December 31, 1977:					
Intermarine Services Inc.	1	$ 2,928,000	$ 315,000	$(1,900,000)	$ 1,343,000
Global Marine Drilling Company	1,000	363,000	(2,007,000)	—	(1,644,000)
Global Marine Europa Limited	10,000	6,939,000	(1,552,000)	—	5,387,000
Global Marine Caribbean, Inc.	25	(1,861,000)	(639,000)	—	(2,500,000)
Global Marine Deepwater Drilling, Inc.	1,000	33,910,000	1,451,000	851,000	36,212,000
Other	—	2,118,000	(938,000)	(5,746,000)	(4,566,000)
		$44,397,000	$(3,370,000)	$(6,795,000)	$34,232,000
Five Months Ended May 31, 1978:					
Intermarine Services Inc.	1	$ 1,343,000	$ (83,000)	$ —	$ 1,260,000
Global Marine Drilling Company	1,000	(1,644,000)	727,000	—	(917,000)
Global Marine Europa Limited	10,000	5,387,000	461,000	—	5,848,000
Challenger Minerals, Inc.	100	(2,476,000)	(171,000)	4,500,000	1,853,000
Global Marine Deepwater Drilling, Inc.	1,000	36,212,000	966,000	363,000	37,541,000
Other	—	(4,590,000)	11,000	1,565,000	(3,014,000)
		$34,232,000	$ 1,911,000	$ 6,428,000	$42,571,000

Notes:

(a) Represents investments in common stock of wholly-owned subsidiaries stated at cost plus equity in undistributed earnings. The amounts are eliminated from the consolidated balance sheets.

(b) No changes during the years for subsidiaries listed except for the formation of Global Marine Deepwater Drilling Inc. during 1976.

	1975	1976	1977	1978
(c) Initial investment in new subsidiary	$ —	$33,304,000	$ 42,000	$ —
Additional capital contribution	—	295,000	963,000	4,863,000
	—	33,599,000	1,005,000	4,863,000
Liquidation of subsidiaries	(1,164,000)	567,000	—	—
Dividend to Parent Company	(404,000)	—	(7,800,000)	—
Prior year reclassification from indebtedness to affiliates	—	—	—	1,565,000
	$(1,568,000)	$34,166,000	$(6,795,000)	$ 6,428,000

GLOBAL MARINE INC.

SCHEDULE IV — INDEBTEDNESS OF (TO) AFFILIATES AND OTHER PERSONS — NOT CURRENT

Wholly Owned Subsidiaries(a)	Year Ended December 31,		
	1975(c)	1976(c)	1977(c)
Intermarine Services Inc.	$ 15,431,000	$ 21,452,000	$ (1,619,000)
Global Marine Drilling Company	(7,981,000)	(5,365,000)	(946,000)
Global Marine Europa Limited	(15,402,000)	(15,645,000)	(6,746,000)
Global Marine Caribbean, Inc.	(871,000)	(1,660,000)	2,612,000
Global Marine Deepwater Drilling Inc.	—	9,694,000 (b)	11,029,000
Other	(344,000)	(468,000)	6,112,000
	$ (9,167,000)	$ 8,008,000	$ 10,442,000

	Five months ended May 31, 1978(c)
Intermarine Services Inc.	$ 1,196,000
Global Marine Drilling Company	4,220,000
Global Marine Europa Limited	(8,029,000)
Challenger Minerals, Inc.	375,000
Global Marine Deepwater Drilling Inc.	5,574,000
Other	2,160,000
	$ 5,496,000

Notes:

(a) The amounts are eliminated from the consolidated balance sheets.

(b) Subsidiary formed in 1976.

(c) Fluctuations in year-end balances were due to transfers of working capital excesses or deficiencies between Parent Company and subsidiaries.

GLOBAL MARINE INC. AND SUBSIDIARIES

SCHEDULE V — PROPERTY, PLANT AND EQUIPMENT

Description	Balance at Beginning of Year	Additions at Cost	Retirements or Sales	Other Changes Add (Deduct)	Balance at End of Year
CONSOLIDATED:					
Year ended December 31, 1975:					
Land	$ 1,952,000	$ —	$ —	$ —	$ 1,952,000
Buildings	2,463,000	332,000	3,000	—	2,792,000
Vessels and equipment	141,900,000	34,898,000(a)	1,344,000	—	175,454,000
Other	1,887,000	2,125,000	154,000	1,887,000(b)	5,745,000
	$148,202,000	$ 37,355,000	$ 1,501,000	$ 1,887,000	$185,943,000
Year ended December 31, 1976:					
Land	$ 1,952,000	$ —	$ —	$ —	$ 1,952,000
Buildings	2,792,000	—	41,000	—	2,751,000
Vessels and equipment	175,454,000	40,717,000(a)	1,111,000	—	215,060,000
Other	5,745,000	1,902,000	1,524,000	—	6,123,000
	$185,943,000	$ 42,619,000	$ 2,676,000	$ —	$225,886,000
Year ended December 31, 1977:					
Land	$ 1,952,000	$ —	$ —	$ —	$ 1,952,000
Buildings	2,751,000	57,000	—	—	2,808,000
Vessels and equipment	215,060,000	48,282,000(a)	1,002,000	(17,668,000)(c)	244,672,000
Other	6,123,000	125,000	2,306,000	—	3,942,000
	$225,886,000	$ 48,464,000	$ 3,308,000	$ (17,668,000)	$253,374,000
Five months ended May 31, 1978:					
Land	$ 1,952,000	$ —	$ —	$ —	$ 1,952,000
Buildings	2,808,000	133,000	—	—	2,941,000
Vessels and equipment	244,672,000	15,652,000(a)	561,000	—	259,763,000
Other	3,942,000	172,000	219,000	—	3,895,000
	$253,374,000	$ 15,957,000	$ 780,000	$ —	$268,551,000

Notes:

(a) Includes additions to vessels under construction of $18,458,000 in 1975, $39,346,000 in 1976, $41,683,000 in 1977, and $14,538,000 in 1978.

(b) Reclassification of amount from prior year which represents spare parts, equipment and extra drill pipe capitalized upon issuance to vessels.

(c) Reclassified to vessels and equipment segregated for sale.

GLOBAL MARINE INC. AND SUBSIDIARIES

SCHEDULE V — PROPERTY, PLANT AND EQUIPMENT (Continued)

Description	Balance at Beginning of Year	Additions at Cost	Retirements or Sales	Other Changes Add (Deduct)	Balance at End of Year
PARENT COMPANY:					
Year ended December 31, 1975:					
Land	$ 1,594,000	$ —	$ —	$ —	$ 1,594,000
Buildings	2,035,000	255,000	—	—	2,290,000
Vessels and equipment	140,862,000	34,570,000(a)	1,344,000	—	174,088,000
Other	1,044,000	1,898,000	101,000	1,887,000(b)	4,728,000
	$145,535,000	$ 36,723,000	$ 1,445,000	$ 1,887,000	$182,700,000
Year ended December 31, 1976:					
Land	$ 1,594,000	$ —	$ —	$ —	$ 1,594,000
Buildings	2,290,000	—	43,000	—	2,247,000
Vessels and equipment	174,088,000	2,204,000	566,000	(118,510,000)(c)	57,216,000
Other	4,728,000	772,000	787,000	—	4,713,000
	$182,700,000	$ 2,976,000	$ 1,396,000	$(118,510,000)	$ 65,770,000
Year ended December 31, 1977:					
Land	$ 1,594,000	$ 81,000	$ —	$ —	$ 1,675,000
Buildings	2,247,000	37,000	—	—	2,284,000
Vessels and equipment	57,216,000	4,673,000	768,000	(16,017,000)(d)	45,104,000
Other	4,713,000	716,000	2,247,000	(848,000)(e)	2,334,000
	$ 65,770,000	$ 5,507,000	$ 3,015,000	$ (16,865,000)	$ 51,397,000
Five months ended May 31, 1978:					
Land	$ 1,675,000	$ —	$ —	$ —	$ 1,675,000
Buildings	2,284,000	13,000	—	—	2,297,000
Vessels and equipment	45,104,000	3,666,000	422,000	—	48,348,000
Other	2,334,000	17,000	201,000	—	2,150,000
	$ 51,397,000	$ 3,696,000	$ 623,000	$ —	$ 54,470,000

Notes:

(a) Includes additions to vessels under construction of $18,458,000 in 1975.

(b) Reclassification of amount from prior year which represents spare parts, equipment and extra drill pipe capitalized upon issuance to vessels.

(c) Transfers to wholly-owned subsidiary, Global Marine Deepwater Drilling Inc.

(d) Reclassified to vessels and equipment segregated for sale.

(e) Transfers to wholly-owned subsidiaries.

GLOBAL MARINE INC. AND SUBSIDIARIES

SCHEDULE VI — ACCUMULATED DEPRECIATION OF PROPERTY, PLANT AND EQUIPMENT

Description	Balance at Beginning of Year	Charged to Costs and Expenses	Retirements or Sales	Other Changes Add (Deduct)	Balance at End of Year
CONSOLIDATED:					
Year ended December 31, 1975:					
Buildings	$ 603,000	$ 140,000	$ 1,000	$ —	$ 742,000
Vessels and equipment	46,287,000	11,748,000	144,000	(5,147,000) (a)	52,744,000
Other	834,000	335,000	97,000	—	1,072,000
	$47,724,000	$12,223,000	$ 242,000	$ (5,147,000)	$54,558,000
Year ended December 31, 1976:					
Buildings	$ 742,000	$ 140,000	$ 6,000	$ —	$ 876,000
Vessels and equipment	52,744,000	14,077,000	414,000	(1,007,000) (a)	65,400,000
Other	1,072,000	300,000	145,000	—	1,227,000
	$54,558,000	$14,517,000	$ 565,000	$ (1,007,000)	$67,503,000
Year ended December 31, 1977:					
Buildings	$ 876,000	$ 143,000	$ —	$ —	$ 1,019,000
Vessels and equipment	65,400,000	15,002,000	690,000	(9,100,000) (b)	70,612,000
Other	1,227,000	294,000	118,000	—	1,403,000
	$67,503,000	$15,439,000	$ 808,000	$ (9,100,000)	$73,034,000
Five months ended May 31, 1978:					
Buildings	$ 1,019,000	$ 63,000	$ 3,000	$ —	$ 1,079,000
Vessels and equipment	70,612,000	6,578,000	343,000	—	76,847,000
Other	1,403,000	109,000	55,000	—	1,457,000
	$73,034,000	$ 6,750,000	$ 401,000	$ —	$79,383,000

Notes:

(a) Capital replacements.

(b) Reclassification to vessels and equipment segregated for sale, provision for loss on equipment to be disposed of on vessels scheduled for conversion to tenders, and capital replacements.

GLOBAL MARINE INC. AND SUBSIDIARIES

**SCHEDULE VI — ACCUMULATED DEPRECIATION OF PROPERTY,
PLANT AND EQUIPMENT (Continued)**

Description	Balance at Beginning of Year	Charged to Costs and Expenses	Retirements or Sales	Other Changes Add (Deduct)	Balance at End of Year
PARENT COMPANY:					
Year ended December 31, 1975:					
Buildings	$ 566,000	$ 121,000	$ —	$ —	$ 687,000
Vessels and equipment	46,036,000	11,565,000	121,000	(5,147,000) (a)	52,333,000
Other	484,000	183,000	75,000	—	592,000
	$47,086,000	$11,869,000	$ 196,000	$ (5,147,000)	$53,612,000
Year ended December 31, 1976:					
Buildings	$ 687,000	$ 118,000	$ 5,000	$ —	$ 800,000
Vessels and equipment	52,333,000	7,217,000	196,000	(21,751,000) (b)	37,603,000
Other	592,000	97,000	174,000	—	515,000
	$53,612,000	$ 7,432,000	$ 375,000	$(21,751,000)	$38,918,000
Year ended December 31, 1977:					
Buildings	$ 800,000	$ 122,000	$ —	$ —	$ 922,000
Vessels and equipment	37,603,000	4,744,000	627,000	(8,037,000) (c)	33,683,000
Other	515,000	79,000	111,000	—	483,000
	$38,918,000	$ 4,945,000	$ 738,000	$ (8,037,000)	$35,088,000
Five months ended May 31, 1978:					
Buildings	$ 922,000	$ 52,000	$ 2,000	$ —	$ 972,000
Vessels and equipment	33,683,000	1,333,000	257,000	—	34,759,000
Other	483,000	21,000	37,000	—	467,000
	$35,088,000	$ 1,406,000	$ 296,000	$ —	$36,198,000

Notes:

(a) Capital replacements.

(b) Transfers to wholly-owned subsidiary, Global Marine Deepwater Drilling Inc. $20,695,000
    Capital replacements 1,056,000
    $21,751,000

(c) Reclassification to vessels and equipment segregated for sale, provision for loss on equipment to be disposed of on vessels scheduled for conversion to tenders, and capital replacements.

GLOBAL MARINE INC. AND SUBSIDIARIES

SCHEDULE IX — BONDS, MORTGAGES AND SIMILAR DEBT

	Authorized	Issued and Not Retired	Treasury Bonds	Outstanding
As of December 31, 1977:				
PARENT COMPANY:				
Subordinated Debentures, 5%, due 1984	$ 10,400,000	$ 7,400,000	$323,000	$ 7,077,000
Less unamortized discount				287,000
				6,790,000
Other	—	172,000	—	172,000
	10,400,000	7,572,000	323,000	6,962,000
GLOBAL MARINE DEEPWATER DRILLING INC.				
Serial Bonds, 6.8% to 8%, due 1978 to 1984	52,100,000	47,750,000	—	47,750,000
Sinking Fund Bonds, 8½%, due 1984 to 1998	100,000,000	100,000,000	—	100,000,000
	152,100,000	147,750,000	—	147,750,000
CONSOLIDATED BONDS, MORTGAGES AND SIMILAR DEBT	$162,500,000	$155,322,000	$323,000	154,712,000
Add obligations under capital leases				2,692,000
CONSOLIDATED LONG-TERM DEBT				$157,404,000
As of May 31, 1978:				
PARENT COMPANY:				
Subordinated Debentures, 5%, due 1984	$ 10,400,000	$ 6,800,000	$ —	$ 6,800,000
Less unamortized discount				268,000
				6,532,000
Tender conversion financing at a variable rate of interest of 120% of prime plus ¾% due 1978 to 1980	—	3,400,000	—	3,400,000
Other	—	86,000	—	86,000
	10,400,000	10,286,000	—	10,018,000
GLOBAL MARINE DEEPWATER DRILLING INC.				
Serial Bonds, 6.8% to 8%, due 1978 to 1984	52,100,000	45,150,000	—	45,150,000
Sinking Fund Bonds, 8½%, due 1984 to 1998	100,000,000	100,000,000	—	100,000,000
	152,100,000	145,150,000	—	145,150,000
CONSOLIDATED BONDS, MORTGAGES AND SIMILAR DEBT	$162,500,000	$155,436,000	$ —	155,168,000
Add obligations under capital leases				2,606,000
CONSOLIDATED LONG-TERM DEBT				$157,774,000

GLOBAL MARINE INC. AND SUBSIDIARIES

SCHEDULE XII — VALUATION AND QUALIFYING ACCOUNTS AND RESERVES

Description	Balance at Beginning of Year	Additions Charged to		Deductions (a)	Balance at End of Year
		Expense	Subsidiaries		
Year ended December 31, 1975:					
Allowance for adjustments to accounts receivable:					
Consolidated	$ 220,000	$ 90,000	$ —	$ 20,000	$ 290,000
Parent Company	$ 165,000	$ —	$ —	$ 15,000	$ 150,000
Accrual for claims, allowances and insurance deductibles:					
Consolidated	$2,289,000	$1,866,000	$ —	$1,295,000	$2,860,000
Parent Company	$2,289,000	$ 980,000	$ 886,000	$1,295,000	$2,860,000
Allowance for abandonments:					
Consolidated	$1,504,000	$1,166,000	$ —	$ —	$2,670,000
Parent Company	$1,162,000	$ —	$ —	$ —	$1,162,000
Year ended December 31, 1976:					
Allowance for adjustments to accounts receivable:					
Consolidated	$ 290,000	$ 565,000	$ —	$ 120,000	$ 735,000
Parent Company	$ 150,000	$ 67,000	$ —	$ 197,000	$ 20,000
Accrual for claims, allowances and insurance deductibles:					
Consolidated	$2,860,000	$ 741,000	$ —	$1,234,000	$2,367,000
Parent Company	$2,860,000	$ 188,000	$ 553,000	$1,234,000	$2,367,000
Allowance for abandonments:					
Consolidated	$2,670,000	$1,309,000	$ —	$2,465,000	$1,514,000
Parent Company	$1,162,000	$ —	$ —	$ —	$1,162,000
Year ended December 31, 1977:					
Allowance for adjustments to accounts receivable:					
Consolidated	$ 735,000	$1,029,000	$ —	$ 390,000	$1,374,000
Parent Company	$ 20,000	$ —	$ —	$ 18,000	$ 2,000
Accrual for claims, allowances and insurance deductibles:					
Consolidated	$2,367,000	$1,096,000	$ —	$1,643,000	$1,820,000
Parent Company	$2,367,000	$ 128,000	$ 945,000	$1,643,000	$1,797,000
Allowance for abandonments:					
Consolidated	$1,514,000	$1,619,000	$ —	$ 330,000	$2,803,000
Parent Company	$1,162,000	$1,085,000	$ —	$ —	$2,247,000
Five months ended May 31, 1978:					
Allowance for adjustments to accounts receivable:					
Consolidated	$1,374,000	$ 30,000	$ —	$ 7,000	$1,397,000
Parent Company	$ 2,000	$ —	$ —	$ —	$ 2,000
Accrual for claims, allowances and insurance deductibles:					
Consolidated	$1,820,000	$ 627,000	$ —	$ 703,000	$1,744,000
Parent Company	$1,797,000	$ 231,000	$ 382,000	$ 680,000	$1,730,000
Allowance for abandonments:					
Consolidated	$2,803,000	$ 398,000	$ —	$ 215,000	$2,986,000
Parent Company	$2,247,000	$ 237,000	$ —	$ 215,000	$2,269,000

Note:

(a) Specific items charged to qualifying accounts and reserves.

Index

Accountant's consent, 236
Accountant's responsibility:
  Investment Advisers Act of 1940, 21
  Investment Company Act of 1940, 19
  Proxy process, 94
  Public Utility Holding Company Act of 1935, 17
  Registration Statement, 8
  Securities Act of 1933, 8
  Securities Exchange Act of 1934, 14
  Trust Indenture Act of 1939, 19
Accountant's SEC Manual, 54
Accounting Principles Board:
  Opinions, 13
    No. 5, 152
    No. 7, 152
    No. 20, 238
    No. 27, 152
    No. 28, 88
    No. 31, 152
  Statements, 114
Accounting Profession and the Commission's Oversight Role, 113
Accounting Research Bulletins, 113
  No. 43, 130
Accounting Research Studies, 114
Accounting Series Releases, 51-53, 111-113
  No. 2, 123, 231
  No. 3, 142
  No. 4, 114, 115
  No. 5, 130
  No. 19, 217, 224
  No. 22, 123, 222, 231
  No. 37, 220
  No. 41, 117, 137, 186

  No. 47, 222, 224, 231
  No. 62, 187, 217, 230
  No. 81, 222, 224, 231
  No. 90, 227-229
  No. 102, 122, 128
  No. 112, 123, 231
  No. 113, 130
  No. 115, 229
  No. 118, 129
  No. 119, 133
  No. 122, 133
  No. 123, 123
  No. 124, 129, 130
  No. 126, 123, 222, 224, 231
  No. 132, 152
  No. 142, 133
  No. 144, 123
  No. 147, 152
  No. 148, 120
  No. 151, 164
  No. 159, 212
  No. 163, 153
  No. 165, 154
  No. 166, 228
  No. 177, 156, 230
  No. 184, 152
  No. 186, 217
  No. 188, 129
  No. 194, 154
  No. 195, 164, 229
  No. 206, 199, 202
  No. 234, 231
  No. 235, 153
  No. 236, 160
  No. 244, 212

No. 247, 240
No. 255, 152
No. 257, 160
No. 258, 160
No. 264, 220
Accounting textbooks, articles, 114
Accounting Trends and Techniques, 114
Accounts payable, 126
Accounts receivable, 120-122
   schedule, 168
Advisory Committee on Corporate Disclosure,
   136, 253-254, 260-262
Affiliate, 137
Affiliate companies, 222
Affiliates, schedules, 169-170, 176
AICPA, see American Institute of Certified
   Public Accountants
Aiding and abetting, 71
Allocation of responsibility among auditors,
   233-234
Allowance for doubtful accounts, 121, 131
American Accounting Association, 39
American Institute of Certified Public
   accountants (AICPA), 39, 113, 161, 163,
   253
   Accounting Interpretations, 113
   Code of Professional Ethics, 51, 53, 115, 136,
     215, 217-219, 220, 225, 240
   industry accounting guides, 113
   quality control standards, 264
   Statements of Position (SOP), 114
American Telephone and Telegraph, 10
American Tobacco Company, 10
Amicus Curiae, 46
Amortization, 147
Amount, defined, 137
Annual reports, contents of, 197
Annual report (Form 10-K), 88
APB Opinion, see Accounting Principles Board
Application for listing, 83, 107
Assets subject to lien, 143
Audit committees, 223-224, 261, 265
Auditors, foreign, 223
Auditor's Opinion, 8, 211, 225-230
Auditor's professional standards, 217
   disciplinary actions, 242-252
   auditor's representations, 225-241
   discussion, 215-252
   independence, 217-225
   rules of practice, 215-217
Auditor's representations, 233-240
Authoritative literature, 48-56
Automated quotation system, 155

B. F. Goodrich, 10
Balance sheets, 119
Banking Act of 1933, see Glass Seagall Act of 1933

Bankruptcy, 37, 46
Bear raid, 10
Black Tuesday, 7
Blue Sky laws, 22
Blue Sky reporter, 54
Board of Governors, 13
Bond discounts, premiums, 127
Bonds, 127
Bonds and mortgages, schedule, 175
Bonuses, 146
Bookkeeping services and independence, 224
Book value, 130
Bowne of Los Angeles, Inc., 54, 59
Brain trust, 24
Broker, 24
Brokerage houses, audit of, 13
Broker dealers, 24
Brokers/dealers, 59
Bureau of National Affairs, 56

Capital shares, 123, 128, 179
Capital stock, restrictions on, 147
Cardozo, Judge, 67
Cash and cash items, 119
Caveat emptor, 6
Censure, 46
Ceritorari, Writ of, 46
Chandler Act, 35
Changes in accounting principles, 157-158
Chapter X bankruptcy, 35, 46
Chapter XI bankruptcy, 37, 46
Chicago, 24
Civil action, 46
Civil liability, 68-70, 97-102
Civil litigation, 39
Class of securities, 78
Clean opinion, 226
Closed-end investment company, 24
Closing date, 62, 78
Code of Wartime Practices, 117
Cohen Commission, 253, 256-257
Cohen, Manuel F., 263
Comfort letter, 234-235
Comment letter, 46
Commerce Clearing House, 53, 54
Commission on Auditors' Responsibilities, 253,
   256-257
Commitments, 145
   and contingent liabilities, 128, 145
Compensating balances, 120, 132
Completeness, 118
Congress, 160
Consent action, 46
Consistency, 229
Consolidated financial statements, 135, 164
Consolidation, principles of, 141-142
Conspiracy and false statements, 71

Contingent fees, 222
Contingent liabilities, 145
Cooling-off period, 78
Coopers and Lybrand, 207
Corporate governance/behavior, 261-262
Corporate security issues, volume, 18
Corporation Securities Company of Chicago, 16
Correcting amendment, 65
Cost of tangible goods sold, 131
Court decisions, 56
Criminal action, 46
Criminal code, 71
Criminal liability, 70-71, 102-105
Criminal prosecution, 66
Current assets, 119, 123
Current liabilities, 125
Cursory review, 64
Customary review, 64

Dart Industries, 118ff
Dealer, 25
Debt, changes in, 146
Defaults, 143
Deferred charges, 125
Deferred credits, 128
Deficiency letter, 46, 232
Delaware, 22
Delisting, 11, 46
Democratic convention, 24
Depletion, 147
Depreciation, 147, 172
Dillon Read and Company, 9
Disagreements on accounting disclosures, 154
Disbarment, 46
Disciplinary actions against accountants, 242-252
Disclosure, 11, 114-116, 137
Dividends, 133, 145
Domiciled corporation, 46
Doubtful accounts, allowances for, 121, 131
Douglas Aircraft Company, 163
Due diligence meeting, 62, 78

Eagleton, Senator Thomas, 263
Earnings of subsidiaries, 132
Earnings per share data, 133
Effective date, 78
  of registration, 75
Electric Bond and Share Co., 14
Energy Policy and Conservation Act of 1975,
    160, 254
Equity Funding Corporation of America, 102
Equity in earnings of subsidiaries, 132
Equity method of consolidating, 135
Ernst and Ernst vs. Hochfelder, 102
Escott vs. Barchris Construction Corporation, 82
Ethics, code of, 51, 53, 115, 136, 215, 217-220,
    225, 240

Exchange, 25
Executive order, 10
Exempted securities, 71-72
Exempted transactions, 71-73
Exemptions from registration, 71-73, 76
Exemptions under rule 3-16(t) of Regulation S-X,
    157
Exempt security, 78
Exempt transaction, 78
Experts, 68-69, 78
Extension of time, 89

Fair disclosure, 11, 114-116, 137
Family relationships, 222
Federal Deposit Insurance Corporation (FDIC),
    10
Federal Reserve Board, 12
Federal Reserve System, 13
Federal Securities Law Reporter, 53, 56
FIFO inventory method, 122, 238
Fifty-percent-owned person, 137
Filing, 46
Filing date, 78
Filing fees and expenses, registration, 62
Filing statement, 20
Financial Accounting Standards Board, 39, 113,
    158, 160, 161, 185, 253-254, 263
  Statements and interpretations, 113
    Statement No. 3, 238
    Statement No. 13, 152-153
    Statement No. 19, 255
Financial dependence, 222
Financial Executives Institute, 39
Financial statements, 200
  deficiencies circa 1929, 7
  Regulation S-X, 111-136
First time audits, 228
Fischer vs. Kletz, 80
Fletcher Committee, 24
Flynn, John T., 24
Footnote, defined, 164
Footnote disclosure, required, 140
Footnotes vs. schedules, 139
Foreign auditors, 223
Foreign Corrupt Practices Act of 1977, 255-256
Foreign currency translation, 142-143, 164
Foreign government securities, 48
Forms, 51, 52
  Form S-1, 85, 117, 185-186, 189, 191, 205-211,
    220
    decision diagrams, 209, 210
    vs. Form 10, 206
    and Form 10-K compared, 192
    organization, 205
  Form S-16, 260
  Form 6-K, 156
  Form 8-K, 88-89, 204

Form 10-K, 88-117, 185-187, 188, 191-201
  contents, 199
Form 10-Q, 156, 158, 185, 187, 190, 201-205, 237
  contents, 202-205
Frank vs. Occidental Petroleum Corporation, 102
Fraud laws—States, 22
Full cost method, 160
Funds Statement, 134
Future portends, 262-263

General Electric Company, 14
General Host Corporation, 164
Generally accepted accounting principles, 111, 113-114, 115
George Washington Law Review, 45
Getchell vs. United States, 82
Glass-Seagall Act of 1933, 4, 6, 8-10, 23
Global Marine Inc., 207
Going concern problems, 228
Going public, 83
Gold standard, 24
Great Depression, 2
Green vs. Childree, 109
Greyhound Corporation, 91-92
Guarantees of securities of other issuers, 177
Guides for preparation and filing of registration statements, 212

Heit vs. Weitzen, 109
Herzfelt vs. Laventhol, Krekstein and Co., 110
Hundred-day Congress, 24

Income deductions, 132
Income statement, 130-133
Income tax expense, 132, 149-150
Incompatible businesses, 225
Incorporation and integration, 186
Indebtedness to affiliates, 127
Indemnification of accountants, 222
Indemnification provision, 78
Independence:
  AICPA, 217-219
  SEC, 219-225
Industry accounting practices, 113
Inflation impact, 123
Information statement, 107
Initial margin percentage, 13, 25
Injunctions, 38, 46
Insiders, 13
Installment sales, 121
Insull, Samuel, 15
Insull Utility Investments Inc., 15
Insull Utility System, 16
Insurance:
  and indemnification, 62, 65, 78, 222
  of security accounts, 21

Intangible assets, 124
  schedule, 173-174
Integration, 187
Interest:
  capitalized, 153
  on securities, 131
Interim reports, 88
Internal accounting controls, 255-256
Interstate Commerce Act, 76
Inventories, 122-123
Investment Advisers Act of 1940, 6, 20-21
Investment banker, 25
  defined, 9
  see also Underwriter
Investment Company Act of 1940, 5, 6, 19-20
Investment tax credit, 150
Investments, 124, 184
Issuer, 25
Issuing securities, 57-78

Jeffries and Company Inc., 54, 59
Joint accounts, 10
J. P. Morgan and Company, 9, 15

Kansas, 22
Kellog, Howard L., 54
Kennedy, Joseph P., 10

LaMater, Robert D., 20
Lease commitments, 150-153
Leased assets, 150-153
Legal liability under Securities Exchange Act of 1934, 109-110
Legal liability:
  common law, 80-82
  discussed, 70-71
  Securities Act of 1933, 80-82
Letter of consent, 69, 78
Liabilities under the Securities Act, 14, 66
Liability, 97-105, 128
Libbey-Owens-Ford Glass Company, 10
Licensing laws, states, 22
LIFO inventory method, 122, 238
Listed status, 11, 25, 86
Listing, defined, 11
Litigation and the auditor, 225
Long-term debt, 127
Loomis, Philip A., 263
Los Angeles *Times*, 61

Mail fraud, 39, 71
Maloney Act of 1938, 4, 12-13
Management advisory services, 220, 265
Management's discussion and analysis, 187-191
Managing underwriter, 59
Manipulation, 10-11, 13, 22
Margin call, 13, 25

Marketable securities, 120
   schedule, 167
Maryland, 22
Material, 137
Materiality, 116-117
Material uncertainties, 228
McKesson-Robbins, 217, 224
Metcalf, Senator Lee, 253
Metcalf Committee, 253-258
Minority interests in consolidated subsidiaries,
   128, 132
Moley, Raymond, 24
Mortgage loans on real estate, 183
Mortgages, 127
Moss, Congressman John, 253
Moss Committee, 45, 253-254
Municipal Assistance Corporation (MAC), 120
Mutual Funds:
   closed-end, 20, 25
   open-end, 20, 24

National Association of Accountants, 39
National Association of Securities Dealers
   (NASD), 12, 25, 35, 155
National Banking Act, 9
National City Bank, 9
National City Company, 9
National Security Corp. vs. Lybrand, 81
Negative assurance, 227
New Deal, 1, 24
New York, 11, 22
New York City, 120
New York State, 263
New York Stock Exchange, 7, 10, 25
Newsweek, 61
No-action letters, 36, 46
No-sale rule, 72-73
Notes payable, 126
Notes receivable, 120-122
Notification, 78

Obsolescence, 147
Offering, private, 76-77
Offering date, 78
Officer's stock, 147
Oil and gas accounting, 254-255
Oil and gas reserves, 160
Open-end investment company, 25
Operational dependence, 223
Opinion letter, 8
Option, defined, 164
Options on stock, 147-149
Orrick, Andrew D., 45
Other stockholders' equity, 129-182
Over-the-counter securities, 11, 12, 25, 87

Pandick press, 54
Parent, 137
Participating underwriters, 59
Partners and employees, 222
Pecora, Ferdinand, 1, 24
Peer review, 259
Pension plans, 144-145, 164
Perjury, 71
Person, 137
Poloway, Morton, 54
Pooling, 10
   of interests, 204, 231
Post-effective amendments, 65-66
"Practice before the SEC," 215
Preferability, 158
Preferred shares, 144
Prefiling conferences, 36, 78
Prefiling period, 65-66
Preliminary prospectus, 60
Preoperating expenses, 125
Prepaid expenses, 125
Price amendment, 65
Price Waterhouse & Co., 161
Price-shop, 58
Principles of consolidation, 141-142
Private Companies Practice Section, 253
Private offering, 76-77
Pro forma statements, 231
Professional standards, 217
Profit-sharing plans, 146
Profits on securities, 131
Property, plant and equipment, 124
   schedule, 171
Prospectus, 25
   contents, 207-208
   preliminary, 60
   red herring, 60
   requirements for, 8
Proxies, 25
   discussed, 90-96
   filing, 90
      information statement, 91-96
   notice of annual meeting of shareholders, 91-93
   material, 91-94
   solicitation of, 195
   solicitations, 90
   statement, 90
Proxy materials, 237
Proxy solicitations, 11, 90
Proxy statement, 90, 107
Public Oversight Board, 259-260
Public Utility Holding Company Act of 1935,
   17, 112

Qualified opinion, 226-227
Qualifying accounts and reserves, 178
Quarterly financial data, 154-155
Quarterly reports, 201-205

Radio Corporation of America, 10
Rappaport, Louis H., 54, 106
Reacquired stock, 129
Real estate and accumulated depreciation, 182
Red herring prospectus, 60, 78
Refusal, 46
Registrant, 37, 46
Registration, 25
   laws, states, 22
   record, 58
Registration process:
   amendments, 64
   completing the process, 65
   conditions barring acceleration, 65
   described, 62-65
   effective date, 75
   flowchart, 63
   sales activities allowed, 65
   SEC review, 51-52, 64
Registration statements, 25
   Form S-1, 205
   requirement, 8
Regulated sales activities, 66
Regulations:
   Regulation A, 73-75
      offerings under, 74
      sales activities, 75
      special rules, 74-75
   Regulation S-K, 51, 52-53, 185, 193-197, 212
   Regulation S-X, 49, 51-52, 212, 215, 217-225,
      226
      Accunting Series Releases, 111-113
      balance sheet, 119-130
      consolidated and combined finance
         statements, 135-136
      contents, 112
      discussed, 111-136
      fair disclosure, 114-115
      financial statements, 113-136
      footnotes, 139-160
      generally accepted accounting principles, 111
      income statement, 130-133
      schedules, 161-163, 166-184
      source and application of funds, 134-135
      stockholders' equity, 133-134
      substantial authoritative support, 113
   Regulation T, 12-13
   Regulation U, 12-13
   Regulation 14A, 185
      decision diagram, 196
Relationships of interested parties, 221
Remuneration of officers and directors, 193
Replacement cost, 164
Research and development expenses, 131
Reserve recognition method, 160
Restricted securities, 77-78
Retained earnings, restrictions on, 145

Retirement plans, 144-145
Retroactive adjustments of accounts, 157-158
Revenue, 131
Revenue recognition, bases of, 147
Rhode Island Hospital vs. Swartz, et al., 110
Right, 164
Rights outstanding, 150
Roosevelt, Franklin D., 6, 9, 11, 24
Rule 2-01(b), 215
Rule 10(b)(5), 101-102
Rules of practice, 51, 53, 215-217
Rusch Factors, Inc. vs. Levin, 67, 81

Safeway Stores, 10
Sale, 78
Sales activities, 66
Sales of products, 130
Schedule, 164
Schedules to be filed by commercial and industrial
     registrants, 162
Scienter, 102, 107
Scope limitations, 227-228
Section 11 (a), 68
Section 13, 87
Section 17, 70-71
Section 18, 97-102
Section 24, 70
Section 32 (a), 102
Securities Act:
   accountant's legal liability, 14, 66, 97-105
   amendments, 4, 23
   disclosure, 8
   objectives, 6
   overview, 3
Securities Act of 1933, 3, 4, 6-8, 23, 24, 34,
     48, 53, 111, 115, 185
Securities of affiliates, 123
Securities & Exchange Commission:
   accounting practice and procedure, 54, 106
   administrative offices, 42
   Advisory Committee on Corporate Disclosure,
     136, 253-254, 260-262
   annual report, 32, 40, 44, 51, 55
   authority, 28-29, 48-49
   Broker/Dealer and Investment Adviser
     Directory, 55
   budget, 29
   chairman, 32
   chief accountant, 36-39
   commission, 32
   Congressional oversight, 28-29
   Corporation Index for Active and Inactive
     Companies, 55
   correspondence, 237
   creation, 12
   Digest, 54

Directorate of Economic and Policy
    Research, 40
Directories of Companies Filing Annual
    Reports with the SEC, 55
Division of Corporate Finance, 32, 33, 36-37
Division of Corporate Regulation, 32, 33, 37
Division of Enforcement, 32, 33, 38
Division of Investment Management, 32, 33, 38
Division of Market Regulation, 32, 33, 37-38
Docket, 55
employees, 29, 31
enforcement powers, 42-44
Executive Director, 32
facilities and records, 45
filings with, 8
funding vs. fees collected, 28
Office of Administrative Law Judges, 40
Office of Opinions and Review, 40
Office of the Chief Accountant, 38-39, 53
Office of the Chief Economic Adviser, 40
Office of the General Counsel, 39-40
Official Summary of Securities Transactions
    and Holdings, 55
operating divisions, 32, 33-38
organization and operation, 26-45
Practice Section, 253
regional offices, 40-42
registered stock market participants, 31
registrations with (by year), 30
Report on Questionable and Illegal Payments
    and Practices, 264
Secretary, 32
Securities Violations Bulletins, 55
Staff Services Offices, 38-40
Statistical Bulletin, 55
work of the Securities & Exchange
    Commission, 55
Securities Exchange Act of 1934, 3, 4, 6, 10-14,
    23, 34, 49, 53, 65, 115, 155, 185, 195, 255,
    260
amendments, 89
announcement of stockholders' meeting, 92
annual reports (Form 10-K), 88
annual report to stockholders (Section 14),
    90-94
civil liability, 97-103
criminal liability, 102-104
current report (Form 8-K), 88
exemptions, 104
extension of time, 89-90
filing periodic reports (Section 13), 87
flowchart, 86
independent accountant, 94
information statement, 95
liability, 96-104
obtaining listed status, 83-87
over-the-counter securities, 87

proxies (Section 14), 90-94
proxy statement, 93
quarterly reports, 88
rule 10(b) (5), 101-102
trading securities under, 83-105
Securities Investor Protection Act of 1970,
    5, 6, 21, 23
Securities releases, 53
Securities Speculation: Its Economic Effects, 24
Securities transactions, volume, 84
Security, defined, 25
Segment reporting, 160
Selling short, 13
Selling group, 59, 78
Shonts vs. Hirlimans, 81
Short period financial statements, 201
Short-selling, 10, 25
Solicitation, 78
    of proxies, 195
Sommer, Jr., A. A., 253
Sorg Printing Company, 54
Speculation, 10-11, 22
Spread, 58, 59, 62, 79
Staff Accounting Bulletin:
    No. 1, 120
    No. 3, 190
    No. 6, 238
    No. 14, 164
    No. 29, 188
    No. 32, 158
    No. 33, 106
Standard Industrial Classification Manual, 191
State securities laws, 22-23
Statement of Auditing Standard No. 1, 113,
    217, 235
Statement of Auditing Standard No. 10, 88, 156
Statement of Auditing Standard No. 24, 238
Statement of Changes in Financial Position, 134,
    147
Statement of Financial Accounting Standards
    No. 14, 10, 160, 185, 191
Statement of Other Stockholders' Equity, 133
Statement of Source and Application of Funds,
    134, 147
Stock Market 1929 collapse, 1, 16
Stock market trader, 20
Stock opinions, 147-149
Stockholders meeting, 107
Stop order, 46
Stub period, 208
"Subject to" opinions, 227
Subsidiary, 137
    earnings of, 132
Subsidiary service companies, 17
Substantial authoritative support, 113, 137
Succeeded firm, 234
Successful efforts method, 160

Succinctness, 117-118

Summary of accounting policies, 123, 125, 141, 147

Summary of earnings statements, 230

Summary of operations, 187-191

Summary review, 64

Supplemental information, 65, 181

Supreme Court, 102

Suspension, 46

Syndicates, 10

Tenants 1136 vs. Max Rothenberg & Co., 109

Tender offers, 11

Thompson, Huston, 7

Tombstone advertisement, 60, 79

Touche, Ross & Co., 54

Transfer taxes, 62

Treasury stock, 129

Trust agreement, 17

Trust indenture, 17

Trust Indenture Act of 1939, 3, 5, 6, 18-19, 23, 34, 53

U.S. House of Representatives:
Banking Committee, 7, 24
Interstate and Foreign Commerce Committee, 28
Moss Committee, 45, 253-254
Subcommittee on Oversight and Investigations, 45, 253-254

U.S. Office of Management and Budget, 191

U.S. Senate:
Banking and Currency Committee, 24, 28
Committee on Banking and Currency, 1
Metcalf Committee, 45, 253-258

Subcommittee on Reports, Accounting, and Management, 45, 253-258

U.S. Solicitor-General, 28

U.S. Supreme Court, 28

Ultramares vs. Touche, 67, 76, 80

Unamortized bond discounts and premiums, 127

Undertakings, 66-67, 79

Underwriter, 9, 57
fee, 58

Underwriting agreement, 58-59, 79

Underwriting syndicate, 59

Underwriting team, 59-60

Unearned income, 121

Uniform System of Accounts, 17

United Corporation, 15

United States Code Annotated, 56

United States vs. Benjamin, 82

United States vs. Bruce, 82

United States vs. Natelli, 102, 110

United States vs. Simon, 102, 110

United States vs. White, 82

Unlisted status, 11, 104

Unlisted trading privilege, 108

Unpaid fees to auditors, 225

Unqualified opinion, 226

Unusual risks and uncertainties, 158-159

Waiting period, 76

Wall Street Journal, 20, 24, 61, 263, 264

Wall Street Under Oath, 24

Warrants, 164
outstanding, 150
and rights, schedule, 180

Warren, Gorham and Lamont, 56

Williams, Harold M., 254, 266

Working capital, 134

Part I